DISCARDED

Confrontation, Conflict, and Dissent:

A Bibliography of A Decade of Controversy, 1960-1970

by

ALBERT JAY MILLER

The Scarecrow Press, Inc.
Metuchen, N.J.   1972

Library of Congress Cataloging in Publication Data

Miller, Albert Jay.
 Confrontation, conflict, and dissent.

 1. U. S.--Social conditions--1960- --Bibliography. 2. Dissenters--U. S.--Bibliography. I. Title.
 Z7165.U5M53   016.3091'73'092   78-189440
 ISBN 0-8108-0490-5

Copyright 1972 by Albert Jay Miller

To my students who always demanded alternatives
in points of view regardless of the topic under
discussion, with affectionate thanks

"The Universal and chief cause of revolutionary feeling is the desire of equality, when men think they are equal to others who have more than themselves; or again, the desire of inequality and superiority, when conceiving themselves to be superior, they think they have more but the same or less than their inferiors; pretensions which may or may not be just."

ARISTOTLE

CONTENTS

Preface		vii
Acknowledgments		x
I.	Confrontation, General	
	Books	11
	Editorials	98
	Periodicals	145
II.	Firearms, Control and Regulation	
	Books	263
	Editorials	264
	Periodicals	266
III.	The Gap in Generations, and the Drug Dilemma	
	Books	270
	Editorials	282
	Periodicals	288
IV.	Police-Community Relations	
	Books	297
	Editorials	307
	Periodicals	310
V.	The Pregnant Question--Sex Education	
	Books	322
	Editorials	333
	Periodicals	334
VI.	Student Dissent	
	Books	344
	Editorials	364
	Periodicals	374
VII.	Anti-Ballistic Missile Systems	
	Books	414
	Editorials	418
	Periodicals	421

VIII.	Civil Disobedience, Violence and Non-Violence	
	Books	427
	Editorials	438
	Periodicals	443
IX.	Military Service--Compulsory and Voluntary	
	Books	461
	Editorials	465
	Periodicals	469
X.	List of Alternative Tabloids	476
Index		483

PREFACE

The verb "confront" has recently developed many diverse and complex meanings. According to the dictionary, it is "to stand in front of, to face in hostility, to set in opposition for examination or comparison."

Dramatic confrontations at Berkeley in 1964-1965 originated over political activity and freedom of speech. Then, confrontations between university officials and students became more complex, with specific demands by students dissatisfied with their educational relationship with the establishment. This relationship led to student activism when university rules and regulations resulted in what students believed to be personal indignities. Students objected to everything from housing requirements to grading systems in use, and mostly they objected to the fact that the existing curriculum had no relevance to their needs for living, much less to the careers they wanted to pursue. After Berkeley similar confrontations followed at other major institutions, and now have become a part of a national crisis in efforts to reform the university.

Americans are becoming keenly aware of the place that confrontations play in their lives. Citizens are increasingly involved in issues where certain groups try vociferously to exert their influence for positive social change. Let the reader consider for the moment such conflicts as: sit-ins, marches, demonstrations, crises, and strikes. These disturbances are not temporary. Individuals and groups, locally, nationally and internationally, contend that their ideas can radically alter the prevailing attitudes of the so-called establishment.

Many controversies have begun in idealistic terms, only to have ended in violence and bloodshed. Now, an essential part of America's national characteristics includes such concepts as counter-revolution, militant Pentagonism, revolution, aggression, radical new leftism, repression, racism, dissent, violence, insurrection, civil disobedience, and radical rightism. These terms have not evolved overnight but represent change which has been instigated by vast movements in political, cultural, ideological, social and intellectual life.

In his article, "Gearing U.S. Policy to the World's Great Trends," (Fortune, May 1, 1969, p. 65) Max Ways identifies six world-wide trends which represent movements, and he indicates that, "most of these trends have been gathering strength for twenty years or more. In the last five years they have accelerated." These trends have accelerated because of the pressures exerted upon man by the technological age and they represent "material progress, education, individuality, nationality, internationality, and power," with implications for U.S. foreign policy in the future.

To believe that all our institutions are in a state of revolution is to witness the recent events in Kent State and Jackson State Universities; the sex revolution; the ecological and environmental crisis; the police-community dilemma; the gap in generations--and the great urgency with which these problems beg for resolution. The university has itself come into heavy debate over its function and role in society. Many believe the crisis to be politically motivated.

The dilemma at all levels seems to defy solution and to threaten the very tenets of American democracy. Implicated in this turbulent phenomena are aspects of priorities, values, and beliefs, which each individual must bear upon his own conscience in solving his own unique problems in relationship to all the others. He must be held responsible for his actions.

In this bibliography we shall be concerned with confrontation from a divisional point of view which the word certainly seems to suggest. The compiler has limited himself to an examination of the contemporary phenomena which bear the characteristics of the six world-wide trends previously mentioned, with emphasis on the United States. Many items listed contain genuine radical thought for our time, and deserve to be recorded. The period between 1960 and 1970 is emphasized, although earlier publications are included which give some historical perspective to the bibliography as a whole. Within each controversial area, there are many viewpoints presented. The plan is to present within each area as many alternatives as could be found. A great deal of time and effort went into the search for matching alternatives.

Items include reports, interviews, documents, pamphlets, diaries, letters, journals--intimate areas of human experience, which can be described as our social history. Regardless of how the researcher views the compilation, the legacy of move-

movements, both as rhetoric, and as social history remains significant for us.

Items are listed in alphabetical order within main areas. A sample entry for each includes:

(Book)
1. Ali, Tariq, (ed.) The New revolutionaries. A handbook of the international radical left. N.Y.: Morrow, 1969.

(Editorial)
2. "Confrontation at University of Miami," <u>Daily Planet</u>, 02   28   20   01   70
[month, day, page, col., & year]

(Periodical)
3. Berger, Dan "Why Cambodia? <u>Distant Drummer</u>, 05   07 08   03   70

The bibliography includes as many of the "underground" or "alternative press tabloids" as the compiler could find in his examination of files in major libraries of the country. This includes tabloids related to the military, as well as those in high schools. In the editorial sections the title is used as the entry when no author could be established. Music, art, and sculpture have been deleted unless controversial aspects are covered.

An honest attempt has been made by the compiler to be objective and impartial in gathering, collecting, indexing, and presenting this material for the various disciplines, as well as for the curious layman. The compilation is not intended to shock, or to present the sensational aspects of the areas of controversy, or to present politically motivated viewpoints at the exclusion of others; but rather, to guide the reader to the available literature in the field of his interest, presenting all points of view. In this manner he may determine for himself whether or not the material is relevant to his needs.

ACKNOWLEDGMENTS

Certain colleagues gave to me helpful suggestions in the organization and basic plan of the bibliography. I am grateful to Mr. Robert Bonner, Mr. Jackson Lethbridge, and Mrs. Mary Lou Grendon, all of the Pennsylvania State University Commonwealth Campus System.

I am especially indebted to the many major libraries in all parts of the nation for their permission to have access to files of underground tabloids, as well as microfilmed copies, made available on interlibrary loan.

I am also indebted to Mrs. Antoinette Pisegna, Library para-professional of the New Kensington Campus Library who proofread the manuscript, and in general drew to my attention various aspects of the organization of the bibliography.

Thanks, too, to Reverend Dennis C. Benson, Director of Inter-Church Broadcast Commission of Western Pennsylvania, who gave helpful suggestions concerning the section on "The Gap in Generations."

Carole A. Miller, Librarian of the Wilkinsburg Public Library, Pittsburgh, gave to me the basic collection of alternative tabloids which was collected and displayed at various conferences throughout the state. These formed the nucleus of the project when it first began some three years ago, and I am grateful to Carole for these.

No portion of the bibliography has the sanction of any association, institution, society, or organization. Their approval was never asked for, however; my sins of omission and commission are purely my own, for I alone am responsible for the selection of the items which appear in the bibliography.

I. CONFRONTATION, GENERAL

BOOKS

1   Abernathy, Mabra G. Civil liberties under the constitution. N.Y.: Dodd, 1968.

1a Abraham, H.J. Judicial process: an introductory analysis of the courts of the United States, England, and France. N.Y.: Oxford University Press, 1968.

2   Abraham, Roger D. Positively black. New Jersey: Prentice-Hall, 1970. (Deals with the history of the negroes in the U.S. Includes notes and bibliog.)

3   Abse, Dannie. Medicine on trial. N.Y.: Crown, 1969. (Discusses controversial aspects of medical experimentation using humans as subjects)

4   Ackerman, Nathan, F. Beatman, and S. Sherman. Expanding theory and practice in family therapy. N.Y.: Family Service, 1967.

5   Ackerman, Nathan W. (et al.). Summerhill: for and against. Hart, 1970. (Collected essays covering controversial educational topics.)

6   Adams, A. John, and Joan Martin Burke. Civil rights: a current guide to the people, organizations and events. A CBS news reference book. N.Y.: R.R. Bowker, 1970.

7   Adams, James L. The Growing church lobby in Washington. N.Y.: Eerdmans, 1970. (Contains various approaches concerning participation in the governmental processes in relation to social issues.)

8   Adler, Renata. Toward a radical middle; fourteen pieces of reporting and criticism. N.Y.: Random, 1970. (Description of contemporary events of the 60's which the author terms as "radical middle"; selections originally appeared in the New Yorker.)

9   African Research Group. The CIA in Africa. Boston: ARG, 1969. (Pam.) (The CIA and its dealings in Africa.)

10 Aiken, L. Bertrand Russell's philosophy of morals. N.Y.: Humanities Press, 1963.

11 Aiken, Michael, Louis Ferman, and Harold L. Sheppard. Economic failure, alienation, and extremism. Michigan: University of Michigan Press, 1968. (Impact of unemployment on the jobless when the Packard Motor Company closed in Detroit.)

12 Ali, Tariq (ed.). The New revolutionaries; a handbook of the international radical left. N.Y.: Morrow, 1969.

13 Allen, Jonathan (ed.). March 4: Scientists, students, and society. Mass.: MIT Press, 1970. (A record of an important event with transcripts and panel discussions concerning student and faculty protest.)

14 Alsop, Stewart. The Center. N.Y.: Harper, 1968. (An examination of politics and power in Washington, D.C.)

15 Altizer, Thomas J. J. The Descent into hell: a study of the radical reversal of Christian consciousness. Philadelphia: Lippincott, 1970.

16 _____, and William Hamilton. Radical theology and the death of God. N.Y.: Bobbs-Merrill, 1966. (Radical theology in American Protestantism and controversies during the middle 60's.)

17 Altshuler, Alan A. Community control: the black demand for participation in large American cities. N.Y.: Pegasus, 1970. (Reform proposals in favor of community control.)

18 American Civil Liberties Union. The Trial of Elizabeth Gurley Flynn. Introduction by Corliss Lamont. N.Y.: Horizon Press, 1968.

19 American Friends Service Committee. Anatomy of anticommunism. N.Y.: Hill and Wang, 1969.

20 _____. Peace in Vietnam; a new approach in Southeast Asia. N.Y.: Hill and Wang, 1966.

General

21 _____. Weapons for counterinsurgency--chemical, biological, anti personnel, incendiary, narmic. Philadelphia: AFSC, 1970. (Pam.) (A description of counterinsurgency weapons.)

22 _____. Who shall live? Man's control over birth and death. N.Y.: Hill and Wang, 1970. (Contemporary problems considered in light of preserving human life.)

22a American Jewish Committee. What is extremism? N.Y.: AJC, 1968. (Pam.) (Questions and answers concerning the radical left and right.)

23 Amundson, Robert. The Last word? Denver, Colo.: Loretto Heights College, 1969. (Research Center on women)

24 Anthony, Earl. Picking up the gun. A report on the black panthers. N.Y.: Dial, 1970.

25 Appleman, Philip. The Silent explosion. Boston: Beacon Press, 1967. (The controversial population problem and how to control it.)

26 Aptheker, Herbert. Essays in the history of the American negro. New ed. N.Y.: International Press, 1964.

27 _____. Marxism and alienation. N.Y.: Humanities Press, 1966.

28 _____. The Negro today. N.Y.: Marzani and Munsell, 1962. (Paper)

29 _____. Soul of the republic: the negro today. N.Y.: Marzani and Munsell, 1964. (Paper)

30 Archer, Jules. The Extremists: Gadflies of American society. N.Y.: Hawthorn, 1969.

31 Armbrister, Trevor. The True story of the Pueblo affair. N.Y.: Coward-McCann, 1970.

32 Armstrong, John A. The Soviet Union: toward confrontation or coexistence? Headline Series. June, 1970. Number 201. (Pam.)

33 Ash, William. Marxism and moral concepts. N.Y.: Monthly Review Press, 1964.

34 Ashley, Paul P. Say it safely; legal limits in publishing, radio, and television. 3rd ed. Seattle: University of Washington Press, 1966. (Aspects "legal and otherwise" of the right to privacy.)

35 Ashmore, Harry S. Mission to Hanoi. N.Y.: Putnam, 1968. (Southeast Asia and the Vietnam War.)

36 _____. The Other side of Jordan. N.Y.: Norton, 1960. (The plight of the negro, the race question, and implications for the future.)

37 Atcheson, Richard. What the hell are they trying to prove Martha? N.Y.: John Day, 1970. (Includes sections on communal living, marijuana, and sense therapy.)

38 Aukofer, Frank A. City with a chance. Milwaukee, Wisconsin: Bruce, 1968. (Description of the riots of Milwaukee in 1967.)

39 Aumann, F. The Changing American legal system: selected phases. N.Y.: Da Capo, 1969. (Advocates reform in selected phases of the law.)

40 Baier, Kurt, and Nicholas Reschee (eds.). Values and the future: the impact of technological change on American values. N.Y.: Free Press, 1968. (A study of changing American values from the present to the year 2000 by seventeen scholars. Topics include such controversial subjects as sex, race, and power among others.)

41 Baldwin, James (et al.). Black anti-semitism and Jewish racism. N.Y.: Baron, 1969.

42 _____. The Fire next time. N.Y.: Dial Press, 1963.

43 _____. Nobody knows my name. More notes of a native son. N.Y.: Dial Press, 1961.

44 _____. Malcolm X, and Martin Luther King, Jr. The Negro protest. Boston: Beacon, 1963.

45 Barbour, Floyd B. (ed.). The Black seventies. Boston: Porter Sargent, 1970. (There are three sections:

General   15

   Outward, Inward, and Forward characterize the black
   power revolt.)

46 Barbour, I. Issues in science and religion. New Jersey:
   Prentice-Hall, 1966. (Controversial questions concerning the issues involved between science and religion.)

47 Barbour, Russell B. Black and white together; plain
   talk for white Christians. Boston: United Church
   Press, 1967.

48 Barker, Charles A. Problems of world disarmament.
   Boston: Houghton Mifflin, 1963. (The Arms control
   controversy.)

49 Barker, Lucius Jefferson, and Twiley Wendell Barker
   (comps.). Civil liberties and the constitution; cases
   and commentaries. New Jersey: Prentice-Hall,
   1970. (Also available in paper) (Various interpretations of civil liberties, civil rights, and the constitution.)

50 _____, and Twiley Wendell Barker. Freedoms,
   courts, politics: studies in civil liberties. New
   Jersey: Prentice-Hall, 1965.

51 Barndt, Joseph R. Why black power? N.Y.: Friendship Press, 1968.

52 Barnet, Richard J. The Economy of death. N.Y.:
   Atheneum, 1969. (Issues and questions of economy
   of human lives in the Vietnam struggle.)

53 _____. Intervention and revolution. N.Y.: World,
   1968. (American intervention in the Vietnam War,
   and controversial domestic issues at home.)

54 Baruch, Ruth, Marion Jones, and Pirkle Jones. The
   Vanguard: a photographic essay on the black panthers.
   Boston: Beacon, 1970. (Historical document of our
   times.)

55 Baughman, Emmett E. Negro and white children; a
   psychological study in the rural south. N.Y.: Academic Press, 1968.

56 Baumgartner, J. Stanley. The Lonely warriors. N.Y.: Nash, 1970. (A book arguing for and in favor of the military-industrial-complex.)

57 Bayer, Alan, and Robert F. Baruch. The Black student in American colleges. Washington, D.C.: American Council on Education. Research Reports. v.4, No. 2, 1969.

58 Beal, Christopher, and D.A. D'Amato (eds.). The Realities of Vietnam. N.Y.: Public Affairs Press, 1968.

59 Beals, Carleton. Great guerrilla warriors. New Jersey: Prentice-Hall, 1970.

60 Bedau, Hugo A. (ed.). The Death penalty in America. Chicago: Aldine, 1968.

61 Behrman, S.J. (ed.). Fertility and family planning; a world view, by S.J. Behrman, Leslie Corsa, Jr., and Ronald Freedman, editors. Michigan: University of Michigan Press, 1969. "Papers collected from a conference held Nov. 15-17, 1967 as part of the University of Michigan's sesquicentennial observance."

62 Belfrage, Sally. Freedom summer. N.Y.: Viking, 1965.

63 Bell, Daniel. The End of ideology. Illinois: Free Press, 1960. (Collection of essays covering various forms of ideology and implications for the future.)

64 Bell, Jack. Mr. Conservative: Barry Goldwater. N.Y.: Doubleday, 1962.

65 Belli, Melvin M. The Law revolution. Vol. 1— Criminal law. California: Sherbourne, 1968.

66 Bendiner, Robert. The Politics of schools; a crisis in self-government. N.Y.: Harper and Row, 1969. (Concerned with the politics of confrontation in the governance of American schools and the current crisis in education.)

67 Benello, C. George, and Dimitri Roussopoulos (eds.). The Case for participatory democracy: some prospects for the radical society. N.Y.: Grossman, 1970.

General 17

68 Benne, Kenneth D. Education for tragedy: essays in disenchanted hope for modern man. Lexington: University of Kentucky Press, 1967. (The quest for community.)

69 Bennett, Lerone Jr. Confrontation: black and white; foreword by A. Philip Randolph. Chicago: Johnson Publishing Co., 1965.

70 _____. The Negro mood. Chicago: Johnson Publishing Co., 1964.

71 _____. Pioneers in protest. Chicago: Johnson Publishing Co., 1968. (Early pioneers in the movement. A status report.)

72 Benoit, Emile, and Kenneth E. Boulding. Disarmament and the economy. Michigan: Michigan University Center for research in conflict resolution. N.Y.: Harper, 1964.

73 Benston, Margaret. The Political economy of women's liberation. San Francisco, California: Bay Area Radical Education Project, 1969. (Pam.)

74 Berberding, William P., and Duane E. Smith (eds.). The Radical left: the abuse of discontent. Boston: Houghton, 1970. (Essays by Irving Kristol, Nathan Glazer, John Osborne, and others.)

75 Berg, Ivar. Education and jobs: the great training robbery. Foreword by Eli Ginzberg. Published for the Center for Urban Education. N.Y.: Praeger, 1970. (The relationship between educational credentials and job productivity.)

76 Berger, Morroe. Equality by statute; the revolution in civil rights. Rev. ed. N.Y.: Doubleday, 1967.

77 Berger, Peter L., and Richard John Neuhaus. Movement and revolution. N.Y.: Doubleday, 1970. (A dialogue between conservative Berger and radical Neuhaus.)

78 Bergler, Edmund. One thousand homosexuals. N.Y.: Cooper Square, 1960.

79 Bernard, Jessie. Academic women. Pennsylvania: Pennsylvania State University Press, 1964.

80 Berrigan, Daniel. Night flight to Hanoi; war diary with eleven poems. N.Y.: Macmillan, 1968.

81 _____. The Trial of the Catonsville nine. Boston: Beacon Press, 1970.

82 Berrigan, Philip. Prison journals of a Priest revolutionary. N.Y.: Holt, Rinehart and Winston, 1970. (Berrigan's imprisonment for destroying draft files.)

83 _____. A Punishment for peace. N.Y.: Macmillan, 1969.

84 Berson, Lenora E. Case study of a riot; the Philadelphia story. N.Y.: Institute of Human Relations Press, 1966.

85 Berube, M. R., and M. Gittel (eds.). Confrontation at Ocean Hill-Brownsville. N.Y.: Praeger, 1969.

86 Binzen, Peter. Whitetown, U.S.A. N.Y.: Random, 1970. (Related and focuses on "ethnic groups that differ from the basic white Protestant Anglo-Saxon settlers in religion, language, and culture." A Philadelphia Bulletin book.

87 Bird, Caroline. Born female: the high cost of keeping women down. N.Y.: McKay, 1968.

87a _____, Helen Hacker, and Everett C. Hughes (et al.). The Secondary social status of women: class and caste applied to women's position. Chicago: VWLM, 1969. (Pam.)

88 Bird, O. The Idea of justice. N.Y.: Praeger, 1967. (Presents various approaches to reform in the courts in the U.S.)

89 Birmingham, John (ed.). Our time is now; notes from the high school underground. N.Y.: Praeger, 1970. (A compilation of underground selections by a high school graduate and editor of his own paper.)

General

90   Black, Eugene R. Alternative in Southeast Asia. N.Y.: Praeger, 1969.

91   Black Panther Party. All power to the people: the story of the Black Panther Party. California: Peoples' Press, 1970. (Pam.)

92   Blackschleger, Herb. Revolution à la Blackschleger. Boston: Christopher, 1970. (A proposal is presented for a complete revision of our governmental structure.)

93   Blaustein, Albert P., and Robert L. Zangrando (eds.). Civil rights and the American negro: a documentary history. N.Y.: Simon and Schuster, 1968. (Paper)

94   Bloodworth, Dennis. An Eye for the dragon: Southeast Asia observed, 1954-1970. N.Y.: Farrar, Straus and Giroux, 1970.

95   Bloomstein, Morris J. Verdict: the jury system. N.Y.: Apollo, 1968. (The administration of justice and reform in the courts.)

95a Bloy, Myron B. Jr. (ed.). Multi-media worship: a model and nine viewpoints. N.Y.: Seabury, 1969. ("Worship as Celebration and Confrontation," by Howard Moody. "Worship as Revolution.")

96   Blum, A. Teacher unions and associations: a comparative study. Illinois: University of Illinois Press, 1969.

97   Blumberg, Abraham S. Criminal justice: problems of American society. Chicago: Quadrangle, 1970.

98   Boggs, James. Racism and the class struggle: further pages from a black worker's notebook. N.Y.: Monthly Review Press, 1970. (Includes "The City is the Black Man's Land," by Boggs, as well as other selections concerning the black revolution in the U.S.)

99   Bonachea, Rolando E., and Nelson P. Valdes (eds.). Che: selected writings of Ernesto Guevara. Mass.: MIT Press, 1970. (Also available in paper)

(Letters, writings, speeches and interviews of Guevara's career and his ideology.)

100 Bondurant, Joan V. Conquest of violence: the Gandhian philosophy of conflict. Rev. ed. California: University of California Press, 1965.

101 Bonhoeffer, Dietrich. Letters and papers from prison. N.Y.: Macmillan, 1962. (The viewpoint is radical theology, and the conflict between religion and values.)

102 Boorstein, Daniel J. The Decline of radicalism. N.Y.: Random, 1969.

103 Borgstrom, Georg. The Hungry planet, modern world at the edge of famine. N.Y.: Collier Macmillan, 1970. (Population control and the food shortage in the U.S.)

104 Borne, Etienne. Atheism. N.Y.: Hawthorne, 1961.

105 Bosch, Juan. Pentagonism; a substitute for imperialism. N.Y.: Grove Press, 1969.

106 Bottomore, T. B. Critics of society, radical thought in North America. N.Y.: Pantheon, 1968. (Critical analysis and overview of the problems of American society and some possible causes.)

107 Boulding, Kenneth E. Conflict and defense; a general theory. N.Y.: Harper, 1962. (Addressed to the general theory of international relations.)

108 _____ (ed.). Peace and the war industry. Chicago: Aldine, 1970.

109 Bouma, Donald H. The Dynamics of school integration. Michigan: Eerdmans, 1968.

110 Bowles, Chester. The Conscience of a liberal. Selected writings and speeches. Introduced and edited by Henry Steele Commager. N.Y.: Harper and Row, 1962. (Articles about the U.S. and world revolution, and the crises that face us.)

General   21

111   Boyd, Malcolm. My fellow Americans. N.Y.: Holt,
      1970. (The author probes into the many controver-
      sial aspects of American society.)

112   _____. The Underground Church. Baltimore, Mary-
      land: Penguin, 1969.

113   _____. You can't kill the dream. Reflections by
      Malcolm Boyd. Photos compiled by Bruce Roberts.
      The American dream, by Eric Sevareid. Richmond:
      John Knox Press, 1968.

114   Bracey, John H., Jr., August Meier, and Elliott Rud-
      wick (eds.). Black nationalism in America. N.Y.:
      Bobbs-Merrill, 1970. (Includes historical documents
      concerning this highly serious and controversial top-
      ic.)

115   Braden, William. The Age of aquarius: technology and
      the cultural revolution. Chicago: Quadrangle, 1970.
      (Study of revolt in America.)

116   Brandt, Floyd S. Conflict and cooperation; cases in
      labor-management behavior. Homewood, Illinois:
      R. D. Irwin, 1967.

117   Brazier, Arthur M. Black self-determination: the
      story of the Woodlawn organization. Chicago: Eerd-
      mans, 1969.

118   Breckenridge, Adam C. The Right to privacy. Ne-
      braska: University of Nebraska Press, 1970.
      (Chronology of the place of privacy examining de-
      cisions of the U.S. Supreme Court.)

119   Breines, Paul. Critical interruptions: new-left per-
      spectives on Herbert Marcuse. N.Y.: Herder and
      Herder, 1970.

120   Breitman, George. The Last year of Malcolm X. N.Y.:
      Merit, 1967. ("Evolution of a revolutionary.")

121   Brenton, Myron. Privacy invaders. N.Y.: Coward
      McCann, 1964. (Infiltration of the private lives of
      American citizens.)

122 Brink, William, and Louis Harris. Black and white. N.Y.: Simon and Schuster, 1967. (Second in a series describing the black mood in America. The other two are "Negro Revolution in America, 1963," and "Report from Black America, 1970.")

123 _____. The Negro revolution in America. N.Y.: Simon and Schuster, 1963. (First in a series describing the black mood in America. The other two are "Report from Black America, 1970," and "Black and White, 1967.")

124 Brisbane, Robert Hughes. The Black vanguard; origins of the negro social revolution, 1900-1960. Valley Forge, Penna.: Judson Press, 1970.

125 Broderick, Francis L., and August Meier (eds.). Negro protest thought in the twentieth century. N.Y.: Bobbs-Merrill, 1965.

125a Brodsky, Stanley L., and Norman E. Eggleston. The Military prison: theory, research, and practice. Illinois: Southern Illinois University Press, 1970.

126 Brody, David. Labor in crisis. Philadelphia: Lippincott, 1965.

127 Brogan, D. W. Political patterns in today's world. N.Y.: Harcourt, Brace and World, 1968.

128 Brookes, Edgar Harry. Power, law, right, and love; a study in political values. North Carolina: Duke University Press, 1963.

129 Broom, Leonard. Transformation of the negro American. N.Y.: Harper, 1965.

129a Broomfield, J. H. Elite conflict in a plural society; twentieth century Bengal. California: University of California Press, 1968.

130 Brown, Donald R. The Role and status of women in the Soviet Union. N.Y.: Teachers College Press, 1968. (A comparative study with U.S. women.)

General   23

131 Brown, Frederic. Chemical warfare; a study in restraints. New Jersey: Princeton, 1968.

132 Brown, Judith, and Beverly Jones. Toward a female liberation movement. Chicago: VWLM, 1969. (Pam.)

133 Brown, Robert McAfee. The Ecumenical revolution. Rev. ed. N.Y.: Doubleday, 1969.

134 Brown, Sam, and Len Ackland (eds.). Why are we still in Vietnam? N.Y.: Vintage, 1970. (Paper) (Chronicles Nixon's Vietnam policy with implications for future foreign policy decisions.)

135 Brown, Turner Jr. Black us. N.Y.: Grove, 1969.

136 Broyles, J. A. John Birch Society; anatomy of a protest. Boston: Beacon, 1964.

137 Brzezinski, Zbigniew. Between two ages: America's role in the technetronic era. N.Y.: Viking, 1970. (Description of social and political implications when technology and electronics are combined to produce a new innovative age.)

137a Bube, Richard H. (ed.). The Encounter between Christianity and science. Michigan: Eerdmans, 1968. ("Conflicts of traditional Christian doctrine with the claims of modern scientific research.")

138 Buber, Martin. Two types of faith. N.Y.: Torchbooks, 1961. (Christian conflict and radical theology.)

139 Buchanan, James M., and Nicos E. Devletoglou. Academia in anarchy: an economic diagnosis. N.Y.: Basic Books, 1970. (Economic analysis applied to the problems of the universities.)

140 Buckley, William F. Jr. The Committee and its critics. A calm review of the House Committee on un-American activities, by William Buckley Jr. and the editors of the National Review. N.Y.: Putnam, 1962.

141 Buckley, William F. Jr. The Jeweler's eye. N.Y.: Putnam, 1968. (Collection of articles written since 1962 on the contemporary American scene.)

142 _____. Rumbles, left and right. N.Y.: Putnam, 1963.

143 _____. Up from liberalism. Rev. ed. N.Y.: Arlington House, 1968.

144 Bull, Hedley. The Control of the arms race: disarmament and arms control in the missile age. 2nd ed. N.Y.: Praeger, 1965.

145 Bullock, Paul (ed.). Watts: the aftermath; an inside view of the ghetto, by the people of Watts. N.Y.: Grove, 1969.

146 Burchett, Wilfred G. Vietnam: inside story of the guerrilla war. N.Y.: International Press, 1965.

147 _____. Vietnam North. International Publishing Co., 1967. (Paper)

148 _____. Vietnam will win. N.Y.: Guardian Books, 1968.

149 Butler, Ed. Revolution is my profession. California: Twin Circle (Distributed by Square Center, Los Angeles) 1968. (A controversial plan for dealing with communism by the radical right.)

150 Buttinger, Joseph. Vietnam: a dragon embattled. N.Y.: Praeger, 1968. 2vols. (Vol. 1--From colonialism to the Vietminh; Vo. 2--Vietnam at war.)

151 _____. Vietnam, a political history. N.Y.: Praeger, 1968.

152 Brodey, W. Changing the family. N.Y.: Potter, 1968. (Prospects for changing the family structure.)

153 Cable, George W. The Silent south. Montclair, New Jersey: Smith, 1969.

154 Cahn, Edmond N. Confronting injustice; the Edmund Cahn reader, edited by Lenore L. Cahn; foreword

General   25

           by Hugo L. Black; general introduction and prefatory
           chapter notes by Norman Redlich. Boston: Little,
           1967.

155   _____. The Great rights. N.Y.: Macmillan, 1963.
           (James Madison lecture series.)

156   _____. The Predicament of democratic man. N.Y.:
           Macmillan, 1961.

157   Cain, Arthur H. Young people and revolution. N.Y.:
           Day, 1970.

158   Calder, Nigel. Unless peace comes, scientific forecast
           of new weapons. N.Y.: Viking Press, 1968.

159   Calderwood, Ann (ed.). The Women's movement.
           (Series) N.Y.: Source Book Press, 1970. (Some
           forty titles and fifty-three volumes contain the history of the women's rights movement, including feminist and anti-feminist documents. Provides source
           materials on the women's movement.)

160   Callahan, Daniel. Abortion: law, choice and morality.
           N.Y.: Macmillan, 1970.

161   Camus, Albert. Resistance, rebellion and death.
           Translated by J. O'Brien. N.Y.: Knopf, 1969.
           (Resistance to governments and rebelliousness.)

162   Canning, Jeremiah W. Values in an age of confrontation. A symposium sponsored by the religion in
           education foundation. Ohio: Charles E. Merrill,
           1970.

163   Capaldi, Nicholas (ed.). Clear and present danger:
           the free speech controversy. N.Y.: Pegasus, 1970.
           (Also available in paper) (The "why" and "where"
           of the free speech movement.)

164   Carlin, Jerome E., Jan Howard, and Sheldon L. Messinger. Civil justice and the poor. N.Y.: Russell Sage Foundation, 1968.

165   Carmichael, Stokely, and Charles V. Hamilton. Black
           power: the politics of liberation in America. N.Y.:
           Random House, 1967. (Also available in paper)

166 Carpenter, Edmund. They became what they beheld. N.Y.: Dutton, 1970. (Electronic media and its impact. Photographs by Ken Heyman.)

167 Carson, Josephene. Silent voices: the southern negro woman today. N.Y.: Delacorte, 1970.

168 Carter, Robert L. (et al.). Equality. Foreword by Charles Adams. N.Y.: Pantheon, 1965.

168a Case, Clifford P., Robert F. Kennedy, and Morris B. Abram. Extremism in America today. N.Y.: American Jewish Committee--American Conversation Series, 1966. (Pam.)

169 Cassara, Beverly Benner. American women: the changing image. Boston: Beacon, 1962.

170 Castro, Fidel. Castro speaks on unemployment. N.Y.: Young Socialist Forum, 1961. (Pam.)

171 _____. History will absolve me. N.Y.: Lyle Stuart, 1970. (Paper)

172 Cayton, Horace R., and George S. Mitchell. Black workers and the new unions. College Park, Maryland: McGrath, 1969.

173 Center For The Study of Democratic Institutions. The Establishment and all that: a collection of major articles selected from the Center Magazine since its beginning in the Fall of 1967. California: The Center, 1970. (Collection of social and political issues from 1959 and on.)

174 Chambers, Bradford (ed.). The Black Panthers speak. N.Y.: New American Library, 1970. (Paper) (A selection of articles with contributions by Eldridge Cleaver, Huey Newton, and Bobby Seale.)

175 _____. Chronicles of black protest. N.Y.: New American Library, 1970. (Paper) (Relates to the struggle for racial equality in the U.S. by a selected list of documents past and present.)

176 _____. Chronicles of negro protest; a background book for young people documenting the history of

General   27

         black power. N.Y.: Parents' Magazine Press,
         1968.

177   Chametsky, J., and S. Kaplan. Black and white in
         American culture. Mass.: University of Massa-
         chusetts, 1969.

178   Che Guevara, Ernesto. Che: selected writings of
         Ernesto Guevara. Edited and introduction by Ro-
         lando E. Bonachea and Nelson P. Valdes. Mass.:
         MIT Press, 1969. (A useful analysis of Che's po-
         litical ideology.)

179   _____. Complete Bolivian diaries of Che Guevara.
         N.Y.: Stein and Day, 1969.

180   _____. Guerrilla warfare. N.Y.: Monthly Review
         Press, 1961.

181   _____. Venceremos! The speeches and writing of
         Ernesto Che Guevara. N.Y.: Macmillan, 1968.
         (Edited by John Gerassi)

182   Chicago Commission On Race Relations. The Negro
         in Chicago, a study of race relations and a race
         riot. Chicago: University of Chicago Press, 1922.
         (Useful for comparative historical background.)

183   Chisholm, Shirley. Unbought and unbossed. Boston:
         Houghton, 1970. (Controversial autobiographical ac-
         count of the woman elected to congress from Brook-
         lyn's 12th Congressional district. For a biography
         of Shirley Chisholm, see Current Biography, Octo-
         ber 1969, p. 92.)

184   Chomsky, Noam. American power and the new man-
         darins. N.Y.: Pantheon, 1969. (Essays concern-
         ing controversial aspects of foreign policy and the
         Vietnam war.)

185   _____. At war with Asia. N.Y.: Pantheon, 1970.

186   _____. Why are we in Vietnam? A review of
         American power. N.Y.: Random House, 1969.

187   Christenson, Reo M. Challenge and decision. N.Y.:
         Harper and Row, 1970. (Confrontation politics.)

188 Clark, Kenneth B. Dark ghetto: dilemmas of social power. Foreword by Gunnar Myrdal. N.Y.: Harper and Row, 1965.

189 Clark, Ramsey. Contempt. Chicago: Swallow, 1970. (Attempts at administration of justice and reform in government.)

190 Clarke, John Henrik. (ed.). Harlem, a community in transition. N.Y.: Citadel, 1965.

191 _____. Malcolm X: the man and his times. N.Y.: Macmillan, 1969. (A collection of writings by negro authors whose contributions evaluate Malcolm X as a leader.)

192 Clarke, Robin. The Silent weapons. N.Y.: McKay, 1969.

193 Clavir, Judy, and John Spitzer (eds.). The Conspiracy trial. Introduction by William Kunstler, N.Y.: Bobbs-Merrill, 1970. (Transcript of the trial of the Chicago 8. For a biography of William M. Kunstler, see Current Biography, v. 32, No. 4, April, 1971, p. 17.)

194 Cleaver, Eldridge. Eldridge Cleaver; past prison writings and speeches. Edited and with an appraisal by Robert Scheer. N.Y.: Random House, 1969. (Also available in paper.)

195 _____. Soul on ice. N.Y.: McGraw-Hill, 1968.

195a Cleghorn, R. Radicalism southern style. N.Y.: American Jewish Committee, 1968. (Pam.)

196 Clergy and Laymen Concerned About Vietnam. In the name of America. N.Y.: Turnpike Press, 1968.

197 Clor, H. Obscenity and public morality. Chicago, Illinois: University of Chicago Press, 1969.

198 Coblentz, Stanton A. Ten crises in civilization. Chicago: Follett Publishing Company, 1970.

199 Cohen, Bernard. Conflict and conformity; a probability model and its application. Cambridge, Mass.:

General 29

MIT Press, 1963.

200 Cohen, Bernard C. The Press and foreign policy. New Jersey: Princeton University Press, 1963. (By utilizing interviews the book attempts to determine the relationship between foreign policy and the coverage and evaluation an event receives in the press.)

201 Cohen, Bernard Lande. Law without order. Capital punishment and the liberals. N.Y.: Arlington House, 1970. (Advocates the case for stern punishment of criminals. Discusses the penal and judicial system in the U.S. and Canada.)

202 Cohen, John (ed.). The Essential Lenny Bruce. N.Y.: Ballantine, 1968. (Paper)

203 Cohen, Mitchell, and Dennis Hale (eds.). The New student left; an anthology edited by Mitchell Cohen and Dennis Hale. With a foreword by Carey McWilliams. Boston: Beacon, 1966.

204 Cohn, Norman. Warrant for genocide, myth of the Jewish conspiracy and protocols of the elders of Zion. N.Y.: Harper and Row, 1969.

205 Coles, Robert. Still hungry in America. Photographs by Al Clayton, introduction by Edward Kennedy. N.Y.: World, 1969.

206 Columbia Broadcasting System, Inc. The People of South Vietnam: how they feel about war. New Jersey: Princeton, 1967. (Opinion Research Corporation)

206a Commission On The Status Of Women. American women. Report of the President's Commission on the status of women. Washington, D.C.: G.P.O., 1963.

206b Committee of Returned Volunteers. Gulf oil corporation: a study in exploitation. N.Y.: CRV., 1970. (Pam.) (Alleged exploitations.)

207 Commoner, Barry. Science and survival. N.Y.: Viking, 1966. (Controversial account of the present state of affairs of science and technology.)

207a Conant, James B. Slums and suburbs: a commentary on schools in metropolitan areas. N.Y.: McGraw-Hill, 1961.

208 Cone, James H. A Black theology of liberation. Philadelphia: Lippincott, 1970. (C. Eric Lincoln series in black religion.)

209 Conkin, Paul K. Two paths to utopia: the Hutterites and the Llano Colony. Lincoln: University of Nebraska Press, 1964. (Utopian movement of the oldest communal Christian sect.)

209a Contempt; transcript of the contempt citations, sentences, and responses of the Chicago Conspiracy 10. N.Y.: Swallow, 1970. (Paper) (The contempt power in perspective, as it was applied by Judge Hoffman. Fundamental legal and political issues are involved.)

210 Coogan, Timothy Patrick. The I.R.A. N.Y.: Praeger, 1970. (Irish political and social questions.)

211 _____. Ireland since the rising. N.Y.: Random, 1968.

212 Cookson, John, and Judith Nottingham. A Survey of chemical and biological warfare. N.Y.: Monthly Review Press, 1970. (Includes a section on disarmament proposals.)

213 Coombs, P. The World educational crisis. N.Y.: Oxford, 1968.

214 Coons, A. Crisis in California higher education. California: Ritchie, 1968.

215 Coons, John E. (ed.). Freedom and responsibility in broadcasting. Illinois: Northwestern University Press, 1961.

216 Cooper, Chester L. The Lost crusade. N.Y.: Dodd, 1970. (Controversial description of American involvement in Vietnam.)

217 Cooper, John Charles. The New mentality. Philadelphia: Westminster, 1969. (Paper) (An analysis of human mentality brought about by contemporary social

General

phenomena of our time.)

218 _____. Radical Christianity and its sources. Philadelphia: Westminster, 1969. (A radical theology.)

219 Copps, John A. (ed.). The Cost of conflict. Michigan: Bureau of Business Research, Graduate School of Business Administration: University of Michigan, 1969. (The third of a four part series of lectures given at Western Michigan University under the sponsorship of the department of economics.)

220 Cornell, R. Youth and communism. N.Y.: Walker, 1965.

221 Corson, William R. The Betrayal. N.Y.: Norton, 1968. (Paper)

222 Corwin, Ronald G. Staff conflict in the public schools. N.Y.: Appleton-Century-Crofts, 1969.

223 Coser, Lewis A. Continuities in the study of social conflict. N.Y.: Macmillan, 1967.

224 _____. The Function of social conflict. Illinois: Free Press, 1956. (Provides historical background.)

225 Coser, R. The Family: its structure and functions. N.Y.: Martins, 1964. (Aspects of family life which seemingly tend to pull it apart, rather than keep it together.)

226 Cottam, Richard W. Competitive interference and 20th century diplomacy. Pittsburgh: University of Pittsburgh Press, 1967.

227 Council On Economic Priorities. Efficiency in death: the manufacturers of anti-personnel weapons. N.Y.: Harper, 1970. (Contract details for weapons--flechettes, land mines, and rockets among others. Some details of company involvement.)

228 Cowan, Paul. The Making of an un-American. N.Y.: Dell, 1970. (Political autobiography.)

Cox, Archibald. Civil rights, the Constitution and the courts. Cambridge: Harvard University Press, 1967.

230 Coyle, David C. Breakthrough to the great society. N.Y.: Oceana, 1965.

231 Crain, Robert L. (et al.). The Politics of school desegregation; comparative studies of community structure and policy making. Chicago: Aldine, 1969. (National opinion research center--Monographs in social research.)

232 Cressey, Donald R. Theft of the nation. The structure and operations of organized crime in America. N.Y. Harper and Row, 1969.

233 Crick, Bernard, and William A. Robson. Protest and discontent. Baltimore: Penguin, 1970.

234 Cross, Robert D. The Emergence of liberal Catholicism in America. Chicago: Quadrangle, 1967.

235 Cruse, Harold. The Crisis of the negro intellectual. N.Y.: Morrow, 1967.

236 _____. Rebellion or revolution? N.Y.: Morrow, 1968. (Essays presenting the present racial impasse.)

237 Currie, Gillette B. Selected essays on the conflict of laws. North Carolina: Duke University Press, 1963.

238 Daane, James. The Anatomy of anti-semitism. Michigan: Eerdmans, 1967.

239 Dahrendorf, Ralf. Conflict after class: new perspectives on the theory of social and political conflict. N.Y.: Humanities Press, 1967.

240 Daniels, Roger, and Harry H. L. Kitana. American racism: exploration of the nature of prejudice. New Jersey: Prentice-Hall, 1970. (The ethnic crisis in California and some suggestions for resolvement.)

241 Dansereau, Pierre (ed.). Challenge for survival: land, air, and water for man in megapolis. N.Y Columbia University Press, 1970.

242 Dash, Samuel, Richard F. Schwartz, and Robert F Knowlton. The Eavesdroppers. N.Y.: Da C

General 33

       1970. (The status of wiretapping in this country. A reprint of the 1959 edition.)

243 Dassman, Raymond E. The Destruction of California. N.Y.: Macmillan, 1965. ("Environmental deterioration in California ... a sociology of environment and the identity of ecology and politics.")

244 David, Jay (ed.). Growing up black. N.Y.: Morrow, 1968.

245 Davies, Alan. Anti-semitism and the Christian mind. N.Y.: Herder and Herder, 1969.

246 Davis, David Brion (ed.). The Fear of conspiracy: images of un-American subversion from the revolution to the present. N.Y.: Cornell, 1970. (A collection of some 85 speeches and documents which describe un-American subversion activities.)

247 De Castro, Josue. The Black book of hunger. Boston: Beacon, 1967.

248 De Coy, Robert H. The Nigger Bible. California: Holloway House, 1969. (Paper) (Controversial and religious aspects of the terms "nigger" and "negro.")

249 Degler, Stanley E. Oil pollution: problems and policies. Washington, D.C.: Bureau of National Affairs, 1969.

249a De Koster, Lester. The Christian and the John Birch Society. Michigan: Eerdmans, 1967. (Paper)

250 De Levita, David J. The Concept of identity. N.Y.: Basic Books, 1966. (Traces the history of the concept and presents some ideas of his own.)

251 Deloria, Vine Jr. We talk, you listen. N.Y.: Macmillan, 1970. (Description of a radical change in the organization and structure of the American Indian society.)

252 Demaris, Ovid. Captive city: Chicago in chains. N.Y.: Lyle Stuart, 1970.

253 Deming, Barbara. Prison notes. N.Y.: Grossman, 1966. (The Non-violent struggle written by one who was a member of the integrated peace walk in Atlanta, Georgia.)

254 Dennis, Lawrence E. Education and woman's life. Washington, D.C.: American Council on Education, 1963.

255 Dentler, Robert A. The Urban R's; race relations as the problem in urban education. N.Y.: Praeger, 1967.

255a De Reuck, Anthony V., and Julie Knight (eds.). Conflict in society; edited by Anthony de Reuck and Julie Knight. Boston: Little, Brown, 1966.

256 Deutscher, Irwin, and Elizabeth J. Thompson. Among the people: encounters with the poor. N.Y.: Basic Books, 1968. (Collections of essays written by social scientists who observed encounters and were able to compare by geographic region.)

257 Devereux, G. A Study of abortion in primitive societies. N.Y.: Julian, 1955. (Interesting comparative studies.)

258 Devlin, Bernadette. Price of my soul. N.Y.: Knopf, 1969. (Confrontations--religious and with police, written by a controversial crusader.)

259 Dewart, Leslie. Christianity and revolution: the lesson of Cuba. N.Y.: Herder and Herder, 1963. (Origin and causes of Cuba's communism, the Church and Christian crisis.)

260 Dewey, John. A Common faith. Conn.: Yale University Press, 1964.

260a Dierenfield, R. B. The Impact of the Supreme Court decisions on religion in public schools. N.Y.: American Jewish Committee, 1967. (Pam.) (Reprinted from Religious Education.)

260b Divoky, Diane (ed.). How old will you be in 1984? Expressions of student outrage from the high school free press. N.Y.: Avon-Discus, 1970. (Paper)

272 Duchene, Francois (ed.). The Endless crisis: a confrontation on America in the seventies. N.Y.: Simon and Schuster, 1970.

273 Duffett, John (ed.). Against the crime of silence: proceedings of the international war crimes tribunal. Introduction by Bertrand Russell. Preface by Noam Chomsky. N.Y.: Simon and Schuster, 1970. (Official transcripts of testimony.)

274 Duffy, Clinton T. Sex and crime. N.Y.: Doubleday, 1965. (Controversial accounts of the theory that "sex is the cause of nearly all deviant behavior." Chronicles ethnic crime patterns.)

275 Dulles, F. The Civil rights commission: 1957-1965. Michigan: Michigan State University, 1968.

276 Duncanson, Dennis J. Government and revolution in Vietnam. N.Y.: Oxford University Press, 1968. (Published under the auspices of the Royal Institute of International Affairs.)

277 Duscha, Julius. Arms, money and politics. N.Y.: Ives Washburn, 1965.

278 Eames, Elizabeth R. Bertrand Russell's theory of knowledge. N.Y.: Braziller, 1969.

279 Earisman, Delbert L. Hippies in our midst: the rebellion beyond rebellion. Philadelphia: Fortress Press, 1968.

280 Ebony. The White problem in America, by the editors of Ebony. Chicago: Johnson Publishing Co., 1966. (First published in Ebony in August, 1965.)

281 Eddy, Elizabeth M. Walk the white line; a profile of urban education. N.Y.: Praeger, 1967.

282 Edwards, D. L. Honest to God debate. Philadelphia: Westminster, 1963.

283 Edwards, David W. Arms control in international politics. N.Y.: Holt, Rinehart and Winston, 1969.

General 35

261 Dixon, Marlene. A Position paper on radical women in the professions: or, up from ridicule. Chicago: VWLM, 1968. (Pam.)

262 _____. Why women's liberation? San Francisco, Calif.: Bay Area Radical Education Project, 1969. (Pam.)

263 Dohen, Dorothy. Women in wonderland. N.Y.: Sheed and Ward, 1960. (Role of the American Catholic woman. "Women do have a place in the world.")

264 Doriot, George F. (ed.). The Management of racial integration in business. N.Y.: McGraw-Hill, 1964.

265 Dorsen, Norman. Frontiers of civil liberties. N.Y.: Pantheon, 1968.

266 Dougherty, James E., and J. F. Lehman Jr. (eds.). Arms control for the late sixties. N.Y.: Van Nostrand, 1969.

266a Douglas, Emily Taft. Margaret Sanger: pioneer of the future. N.Y.: Holt, Rinehart, and Winston, 1970.

266b Douglas, Jack D. (ed.). The Technological threat. New Jersey: Prentice-Hall, 1970.

267 Draper, Theodore. Abuse of power. N.Y.: Viking, 1967.

268 _____. Castro's revolution: myths and realities. N.Y.: Praeger, 1962.

269 _____. The Rediscovery of black nationalism. N.Y.: Viking Press, 1970. (Historical approach to black nationalist themes with a chronology to the present.)

270 Drinan, Robert F. Vietnam and Armageddon; peace, war, and the Christian conscience. N.Y.: Sheed and Ward, 1970.

271 Drinnon, Richard. Rebel in paradise: a biography of Emma Goldman. Boston: Beacon, 1970. (Paper) (A biography of a well-known anarchist.)

General 39

306 Fantini, Maris, Marilyn Gittell, and Richard Magot.
Community control and the urban school. N.Y.:
Praeger, 1970. (Focuses on the "maximum feasible
participation" of the urban poor.)

307 Farber, Seymour M., and Roger H. L. Wilson (eds.).
The Challenge to women. N.Y.: Basic Books,
1966. (Essays on the role of women in today's society.)

308 ———. The Potential of woman: a symposium.
N.Y.: McGraw-Hill, 1963. (A record of the 3rd
symposium held at the University of California medical center.)

309 Feigelson, Naomi. The Underground revolution: hippies, yippies, and others. N.Y.: Funk and Wagnalls, 1970.

310 Feinberg, Gerald. The Prometheus project. N.Y.:
Doubleday, 1969. (Implications of technology and
long-range goals for the human race.)

311 Feldman, Herman. Racial factors in American industry. N.Y.: Jerome S. Czer, 1970. (Racial prejudice in industry as it affects the immigrant, black,
and the Indian.)

312 Ferman, Louis. Negroes and jobs; a book of readings.
Ann Arbor, Michigan: University of Michigan Press,
1968.

313 Figes, Eva. Patriarchal attitudes: women in revolt.
N.Y.: Stein and Day, 1970. (Women's new role in
an ever changing society.)

314 Finn, James. A Conflict of loyalties. N.Y.: Pegasus,
1968.

315 ———. Protest, pacifism and politics. N.Y.: Random House, 1967.

316 Firestone, Shulamith. The Dialectic of sex: the case
for feminist revolution. N.Y.: Morrow, 1970.
(Battle of the sexes.)

317 Fishel, Wesley R. Vietnam: anatomy of a conflict. Oakland, California: Peacock, 1968.

318 Fisher, Paul. Race and the news media. N.Y.: Praeger, 1967.

319 Fisher, W. R., and R. D. Burns. Armament and disarmament: the continuing dispute. California: Wadsworth, 1969.

319a Fishman, Katherine D. Bridging the prejudice gap. N.Y.: American Jewish Committee, 1969. (Pam.) (Second printing and reprinted from The New York Times Magazine.)

320 Flexner, Eleanor. Century of struggle: the women's rights movement in the U.S. Boston: Harvard University Press, 1960.

321 Foner, Philip S. (ed.). The Black Panthers speak. Preface by Julian Bond. Philadelphia: Lippincott, 1970. (Paper) (A legal history of the BPP.)

322 Forer, Lois G. No one will listen; how our legal system brutalizes the youthful poor. N.Y.: John Day, 1970. (Problems of youth within our present legal system, and what effect it has upon the young offender.)

323 Forman, James. Sammy Young Jr.: the first black college student to die in the black liberation movement. N.Y.: Grove Press, 1969.

324 Frank, John P. American law; the case for radical reform. N.Y.: Macmillan, 1969. (Radical recommendations for reform in the judicial system.)

325 Franklin, John Hope. Color and race. Boston: Beacon, 1968.

326 _____. The Negro in 20th century America. N.Y.: Random House, 1967.

327 Frazier, Edward F. On race relations; selected writings. Chicago: University of Chicago Press, 1968.

General   41

328   _____. Race and culture contacts in the modern
       world. Boston: Beacon, 1968.

329   Freed, Leonard. Black in white America. N.Y.:
       Grossman, 1969.

330   Freedom Riders Speak for Themselves. A news and
       letters pamphlet. Detroit, Michigan: Freedom
       Press, 1961. (Paper)

331   Freeman, Howard E., and Norman R. Kurtz. Amer-
       ica's troubles: a casebook on social conflict. New
       Jersey: Prentice-Hall, 1969.

332   Fried, Morton (et al.). War: anthropology of armed
       conflict and aggression. N.Y.: Natural History
       Press, 1968. (Symposium held November 30, 1967
       at the 66th annual general meeting of the AAA.)

333   Friedan, Betty. The Feminine mystique. N.Y.: W.
       W. Norton, 1963.

334   Friedenberg, Edgar A. Coming of age in America:
       growth and acquiescence. N.Y.: Random House,
       1965. (Also available in paper.)

335   Friedman, Leon (ed.). The Civil rights reader; basic
       documents of the civil rights movement. N.Y.:
       Walker, 1967.

335a   _____ (ed.). Obscenity; the complete oral arguments
       before the Supreme Court in the major obscenity
       cases. Introduction by Charles Rembar. N.Y.:
       Random House, 1970.

336   Friedman, Murray. Kensington, U.S.A.; a social sci-
       entist's understanding analysis of the causes of white
       "backlash." N.Y.: American Jewish Committee,
       1968.

337   Friendly, Alfred. Crime and publicity. The impact of
       news on the administration of justice. N.Y.: Ran-
       dom House, 1967. (Examines the conflict between
       fair trial and free press.)

338   Fromm, Erich. May man prevail? An inquiry into the
       facts and fictions of foreign policy. N.Y.:

Doubleday, 1961.

339 Fromm, Erich. Revolution of hope: toward a humanized technology. N.Y.: Harper and Row, 1970. (Paper)

340 Fry, John R. Fire and blackstone. Philadelphia: Lippincott, 1969. (A series of sermons by the pastor of the First Presbyterian Church in the Woodlawn section of Chicago.)

341 Fulbright, J. W. The Pentagon propaganda machine. N.Y.: Liveright, 1970. (Military service's alleged mishandling of public monies. The Pentagon's public information system, and propaganda versus information.)

342 Full, Harold (ed.). Controversy in American education: an anthology of crucial issues. N.Y.: Macmillan, 1967.

343 Fusco, Paul, and George D. Horwitz. La Causa: the California grape strike. N.Y.: Macmillan, 1970.

344 Galbraith, John Kenneth. How to control the military. N.Y.: Signet, 1969.

345 Galula, David. Counter-insurgency warfare. N.Y.: Praeger, 1964.

346 Gardner, Fred. The Unlawful concert; an account of the Presidio mutiny case. N.Y.: Viking Press, 1970. (Court martials and courts of inquiry.)

347 Garfinkel, Herbert. When negroes march. N.Y.: Atheneum, 1968.

348 Garrison, Jim. A Heritage of stone. N.Y.: Putnam, 1970. (Garrison's thesis is interesting in light of what has already developed concerning the assassination of John F. Kennedy.)

349 Geltman, Max. The Confrontation: black power, anti-semitism, and the myth of integration. New Jersey: Prentice-Hall, 1970.

General 43

350 George, Wesley. Biology of the race problems. Alabama: Committee of the Governor of Alabama, 1962.

351 Gerber, A. Sex, pornography and justice. N.Y.: Lyle, Stuart, 1965.

352 Gerberding, William P., and Duane E. Smith (eds.). The Radical left: the abuse of discontent. Boston: Houghton, 1970. (Represented are articles by Howe, Shils, Banfield and Halle.)

353 Gettleman, Marvin E., and David Mermelstein (eds.). The Great society reader: the failure of American liberalism. N.Y.: Random House, 1968. (Vintage book paperback.)

354 Gibson, Elsie. When the minister is a woman. N.Y.: Holt, Rinehart and Winston, 1970. (Controversial questions raised in a study of 270 female ministers.)

355 Gillman, Joseph M. Prosperity in crisis. N.Y.: Marzani and Munsell, 1965.

356 Gilmore, Donald H. Sex, censorship and pornography. California: Greenleaf Classics Inc.: Reed Enterprises Inc., 1970. (Paper)

357 Ginger, Ann Fagan (ed.). Minimizing racism in jury trials. National Lawyers Guild, 1970. (Paper) (The problems of black people and the judicial system in the U.S.)

357a Ginsberg, M. On justice in society. N.Y.: Cornell, 1965.

358 Ginzberg, Eli (ed.). Life styles of educated women. N.Y.: Columbia University Press, 1966.

359 _____. The Middle class negro in the white man's world. N.Y.: Columbia University Press, 1969.

360 _____. The Negro potential. N.Y.: Columbia University Press, 1968.

361 Gish, Arthur G. The New left and Christian radicalism. Michigan: Eerdmans, 1970. (Paper) (Analysis of

the New Left philosophy and a theology of revolution.)

362 Gitlin, Todd, and Nanci Hollander. Uptown: poor whites in Chicago. N.Y.: Harper and Row, 1970.

363 Gittler, Joseph B. Understanding minority groups. N.Y.: Wiley, 1956.

364 Glick, Edward Bernard. Peaceful conflict: the nonmilitary use of the military. Harrisburg, Penna.: Stackpole, 1967.

365 Glock, Charles Y., and Ellen Siegelman. Prejudice U.S.A. N.Y.: Praeger, 1969.

366 Gold, Harry. Combatting social problems; techniques of intervention. N.Y.: Holt, Rinehart and Winston, 1967.

367 Goldberg, Harvey (ed.). American radicals: some problems and personalities. 2nd ed. N.Y.: Monthly Review Press, 1969. (Paper)

368 Goldfarb, Ronald. The Contempt power. N.Y.: Columbia University Press, 1963. (Contempt power and the courts, and what power means to individuals who possess it.)

369 _____. Ransom: a critique of the American bail system; foreword by Arthur J. Goldberg. N.Y.: Harper and Row, 1965. (The role of bail as it is used in the courts and suggestions for proposed reforms.)

370 Goldman, Peter. Report from black America. N.Y.: Simon and Schuster, 1970. (The third in a series describing the black mood in America. The other two volumes are, "The Negro Revolution in America, 1963," and "Black and White, 1967.")

371 Goldston, Robert. The Negro revolution. N.Y.: Macmillan, 1968.

372 Goldwin, Robert A. Left, right and center. Chicago: Rand McNally, 1969.

373 Gollwitzer, Helmut. The Existence of God. Philadelphia: Westminster, 1965.

374 Goode, W. World revolution and family patterns. N.Y.: Free Press, 1963. (Marriage, sexual mores and the family.)

375 Goodman, Mitchell. The Movement toward a new America. Philadelphia: Pilgrim Press, 1970. (Paper) (About the beginnings of a long revolution. Highly illustrated with graphics.)

376 Goodman, Paul. Compulsory mis-education; community of scholars. N.Y.: Random House, 1962.

377 _____. Like a conquered province: the moral ambiguity of America. N.Y.: Random, 1967. (The 6th series of the Massey Lectures. Canadian Broadcasting Corporation. The newer technological development and its impact on the individual.)

378 _____. New reformation. N.Y.: Random House, 1970. (An examination of the radical revolt of youth and an explanation of the modern dilemma in which man finds himself.)

379 _____. Utopian essays and practical proposals. N.Y.: Random House, 1962. (Collected essays include art, censorship, literature, pornography and youth work camps.)

380 Goodman, Walter. All honorable men; corruption and compromise in American life. Boston: Little, 1963.

381 Goodwin, Richard N. Triumph or tragedy. Reflections on Vietnam. N.Y.: Random House, 1966.

382 Gordon, Bernard K. Toward disengagement in Asia: a strategy for American foreign policy. New Jersey: Prentice-Hall, 1969.

383 Gossett, Thomas F. Race: the history of an idea in America. Dallas: Southern Methodist University Press, 1964. (Interesting ideas about race in America.)

384 Gottlieb, David (et al.). Emergence of youth societies: a cross cultural approach. N.Y.: Macmillan, 1966. (Includes a theoretical model for the cross cultural study approach to the training and behavior of adolescents.)

385 Gottschalk, H. Bertrand Russell: a life. London: Baker, 1962. (Autobiographical in approach.)

386 Goulart, Ron. The Assault on childhood. Los Angeles, California: Sherbourne Press, 1969.

387 Goulden, Joseph C. Truth is the first casualty; the Gulf of Tonkin affair. N.Y.: Rand McNally, 1969.

388 Grant, Joanne (ed.). Black protest; history, documents and analyses, 1619 to the present. Connecticut: Fawcett, 1968.

389 Gray, Francine du Plessix. Divine disobedience: profiles in Catholic radicalism. N.Y.: Knopf, 1970.

389a Greeley, Andrew M. Why can't they be like us? N.Y.: American Jewish Committee--Institute of Human Relations Press, 1970. (Pam.) ("Facts and fallacies about ethnic differences and group conflicts in America.")

390 Green, T. N. The Guerrilla--and how to fight him. Selections from the Marine Corps Gazette. N.Y.: Praeger, 1962.

391 Greene, Felix. Vietnam Vietnam. San Gabriel, California: Grass Roots Forum, 1967. (Paper)

392 Greep, Roy O. (ed.). Human fertility and population problems. Mass.: Schenkman Publishing Co., 1964.

393 Gregory, Dick. Dick Gregory from the back of the bus, edited by Bob Orben. N.Y.: Dutton, (n.d.)

394 _____. Nigger; an autobiography with Robert Lipsyte. N.Y.: E. P. Dutton, 1964.

395 _____. The Shadow that scares me. N.Y.: Doubleday, 1968. (Personal attitudes towards living in America.)

General 47

396 _____. Write me in! Edited by James R. McGraw. N.Y.: Bantam Books, 1968.

397 Gregory, Susan. Hey, white girl! N.Y.: Norton, 1970. (Autobiographical)

398 Grier, William H., and Price M. Cobbs. Black rage. N.Y.: Basic Books, 1968. (An application of psychiatric methods to an examination of black life in America.)

399 Griffin, John. Black like me. Boston: Houghton, 1961. (Portions first appeared in Sepia Magazine.)

400 Grisez, Germain G. Abortion: the myths, the realities, and the arguments. N.Y.: World, 1970. (All aspects of the question are examined.)

401 Gross, Beatrice, and Ronald Gross (Comp. and eds.). Radical school reform. N.Y.: Simon and Schuster, 1970. (Failure of American schools, and educational reform.)

402 Group For The Advancement of Psychiatry. The Right to abortion: a psychiatric view. N.Y.: Charles Scribner's, 1970. (By the Committee on Psychiatry and Law.)

403 Guardian Newsweekly. U.S. Genocide in Vietnam. N.Y.: Guardian, 1969. (Pam.)

403a Guerin, Daniel. Anarchism; from theory to practice. Introduction by Noam Chomsky. Trans. by Mary Klopper. N.Y.: Monthly Review Press, 1970.

404 Gurtov, Melvin. The First Vietnam crisis. N.Y.: Columbia University Press, 1967.

405 Hacker, Andrew. The End of the American era. N.Y.: Atheneum, 1970.

405a Halberstam, David. The Making of a quagmire. N.Y.: Random House, 1965.

406 _____. The Unfinished odyssey of Robert Kennedy. N.Y.: Random House, 1969.

407 Hall, Robert E. (ed.). Abortion. N.Y.: Columbia University Press, 1970. 2 vols. (A two-volume work dealing with moral, ethical and medical aspects of abortion.)

408 Halsell, Grace. Soul sister. N.Y.: World, 1969. (The author's experience in Harlem and Mississippi and her treatment by everyone when she painted her face black.)

409 Hamalian, Leo, and Frederick R. Karl (eds.). The Radical vision; essays for the seventies. N.Y.: Crowell, 1970. (Paper) (A collection of essays commenting on a variety of New Left thoughts.)

410 Hamilton, Kenneth M. God is dead: the anatomy of a slogan. Michigan: Eerdmans, 1967. (Paper)

411 Hampden-Turner, Charles. Radical man. Mass.: Schenkman, 1970. (An examination of radicalism in psychological terms oriented towards personal experience.)

412 Handlin, Oscar (ed.). Children of the uprooted. N.Y.: Grosset and Dunlap, 1968.

413 _____. Fire-bell in the night: the crisis in civil rights. Boston: Little, and Atlantic Monthly Press, 1964.

414 Hanh, Thich Nhat. Vietnam: lotus in a sea of fire. San Gabriel: Grass Roots Forum, 1967. (Paper)

415 Hare, Nathan. The Black Anglo-Saxons. N.Y.: Collier Books, 1970. (Paper)

416 Harrington, Michael. The Other America; poverty in the U.S. N.Y.: Macmillan, 1969. (A new intro. to the '62 ed. with the same title.)

417 _____. Toward a democratic left: a radical program for a new majority. N.Y.: Macmillan, 1968. (Also available in paper) (Recommends a radical program of action in the U.S.)

418 Harris, E. The 'Un-American' weapon: psychological warfare. Philadelphia: Lads, 1967.

General

419 Harris, Michael R. Five counter-revolutionists in higher education. Oregon: Oregon State University Press, 1970. (Educational philosophies which run counter to the revolution in American higher education. Articles are by: Irving Babbitt, Albert Jay Nock, Abraham Flexner, Robert Hutchins, and Alexander Meiklejohn.)

420 Harris, Richard. Death of a revolutionary. N.Y.: Norton, 1970. (Ernesto Guevara)

421 _____. The Fear of crime. N.Y.: Praeger, 1969. (Intro. by Nicholas de B. Katzenbach. Original title "The Turning Point" which appeared in the New Yorker.)

422 _____. Justice, the crisis of law, order, and freedom in America. N.Y.: Dutton, 1970. (Conflict in the courts, and the administration of justice.)

423 _____. The Real voice. N.Y.: Macmillan, 1964. (Investigation of the drug industry by Senator Estes Kefauver--Subcommittee on Antitrust and Monopoly.)

423a Hart, Jeffrey. The American dissent; a decade of modern conservatism. N.Y.: Doubleday, 1966.

424 Harvey, Frank. Air war--Vietnam. N.Y.: Bantam Books, 1967.

425 Hassler, Alfred. Saigon, U.S.A. Introduction by Senator George McGovern. N.Y.: E. P. Dutton, 1970. (Inside view of the politics and government of Vietnam.)

426 Hastings, Max. Barricades in Belfast: the fight for civil rights in northern Ireland. N.Y.: Taplinger, 1970.

427 _____. The Fire this time: America's year of crisis. N.Y.: Taplinger, 1969.

427a Havinghurst, Clark C. (ed.). Air pollution control. N.Y.: Oceana, 1969. ("Thinking and action in air pollution control.")

428 Hayden, Tom. Rebellion and repression: testimony by

Tom Hayden before the National Commission on the causes and prevention of violence, and the house un-American activities committee. N.Y.: World, 1969.

429 Hayden, Tom. Rebellion in Newark; official violence and ghetto response. N.Y.: Random, 1967.

430 _____. Trial. N.Y.: Holt, Rinehart, and Winston, 1969. (The Chicago conspiracy trial written by a defendant.)

431 Headley, J. C., and N. N. Lewis. The Pesticide problem: an economic approach to public policy. Maryland: Johns Hopkins Press, 1967.

432 Hedgepeth, William. The Alternative: communal life in new America. N.Y.: Macmillan, 1970. Illustrations by Dennis Stock. (A modern social phenomenon investigated in California, New Mexico, Colorado, and Georgia.)

433 Heer, David M. Society and population. New Jersey: Prentice-Hall, 1968.

434 Hefferlin, J. B. Dynamics of academic reform. California: Jossey-Bass, 1970. (Institutional factors in American education which resist reform.)

435 Heifrich, Harold Jr. The Environmental crisis. Conn.: Yale University Press, 1970.

436 Helper, Rose. Racial policies and practices of real estate brokers. Minneapolis: University of Minnesota Press, 1969.

437 Hendin, Herbert. Black suicide. N.Y.: Basic Books, 1969. (A study of blacks who have attempted suicide and how they differ from whites in having suicidal tendencies. Exploration of life in the ghetto.)

438 Hentoff, N. Black anti-semitism and Jewish racism. N.Y.: Baron, 1969.

439 Herbert, Lewis, (pseud.). Bookchin, Murray. Crisis in our cities. New Jersey: Prentice-Hall, 1965.

440 _____. Our synethetic environment. N.Y.: Knopf, 1962.

General 51

441 Herbers, John. The Lost priority: what happened to the civil rights movement in America. N.Y.: Funk and Wagnalls, 1970. (Description of the failure of the Civil Rights movement in the U.S.)

442 Herndon, James. The Way it 'spozed to be; a report on the classroom war behind the crisis in our schools. N.Y.: Simon and Schuster, 1968.

443 Hernton, Calvin C. Sex and racism in America. N.Y.: Doubleday, 1965. (Racial prejudice in light of negro-white relationships.)

444 _____. White papers for white Americans. N.Y.: Doubleday, 1966.

445 Hersh, Seymour M. Chemical and biological warfare: America's hidden arsenal. N.Y.: Bobbs-Merrill, 1969. (Also available in paper)

446 _____. My Lai 4: a report on the massacre and its aftermath. N.Y.: Random House, 1970. (The Massacre of March 16, 1968.)

447 Herskovits, Melville J. The New world negro; selected papers in Afroamerican studies. Bloomington, Indiana: Indiana University Press, 1966.

448 Herzog, Arthur. The War-peace establishment. N.Y.: Harper and Row, 1965.

449 Hicks, John H. Thoreau in our season. Mass.: University of Massachusetts Press, 1966.

449a Hiestand, Dale L. Economic growth and employment opportunities for minorities. N.Y.: Columbia University Press, 1964.

450 Higbee, J. Development and administration in the New York State law against discrimination. Alabama: University of Alabama, 1966.

451 Higgins, Marguerite. Our Vietnam nightmare. N.Y.: Harper and Row, 1965. (Account of the U.S. involvement in the Vietnam tragedy.)

452 Hine, Robert V. California's utopian colonies.

Connecticut: Yale University Press, 1966. (Paper)

453 Hoffman, Abbie. Revolution for the hell of it. N.Y.: Dial, 1968. (Also available in paper)

454 _____. Woodstock nation; a talk-rock album. N.Y.: Random-Vintage, 1970.

455 Hofstadter, Richard. Academic freedom in the age of the college. N.Y.: Columbia University Press, 1969.

456 Hollins, Elizabeth Jay (ed.). Peace is possible; a reader for laymen. N.Y.: Grossman, 1967. (Collection of addresses advocating that peace in Vietnam is possible.)

457 Honey, P.J. Genesis of a tragedy: the historical background of the Vietnam war. N.Y.: International Publications, 1968.

458 Hook, Sidney. Academic freedom and academic anarchy. N.Y.: Cowles, 1970.

459 _____. In defense of academic freedom. N.Y.: Pegasus, 1970.

460 Hoopes, Townsend. The Limits of intervention. N.Y.: McKay, 1970.

460a Hoover, Mary B. Values to live by. N.Y.: American Jewish Committee, 1968. (Pam.) (A reprint from Parents' Magazine.)

461 Hopper, Columbus B. Sex in prison: Mississippi experiment with conjugal visiting. Louisiana: Louisiana State University, 1969.

462 Horowitz, David (ed.). Containment and revolution. Boston: Beacon, 1968. (Bertrand Russell Centre for Social Research, London. Studies in imperialism, and the cold war. A collection of seven research essays on the cold war controversy.)

463 _____. Empire and revolution. N.Y.: Random House, 1969. (An application of the author's revised Marxist philosophy to U.S. foreign policy.)

General 53

464 Horowitz, Irving Louis. Power, politics and people. N.Y.: Oxford University Press, 1963.

465 Hosmer, Stephen T. Viet-Cong repression and its implications for the future. Lexington, Kentucky: Heath, 1970. (Statistical analysis of repression by the Viet-Cong conducted by the Rand Corporation.)

466 Howe, Irving (ed.). Beyond the new left. N.Y.: McCall, 1970.

467 _____ (ed.). Radical imagination; an anthology from Dissent Magazine. Introduction by Marshall Harrington. N.Y.: New American Library, 1967.

468 _____. Steady work; essays in the politics of democratic radicalism, 1953-1966. N.Y.: Harcourt, Brace and World, 1966.

469 Huberman, Leo, and Paul M. Sweezy. Cuba: anatomy of a revolution. N.Y.: Monthly Review Press, 1960.

470 Hudson, Kenneth. Men and women; feminism and anti-feminism today. Great Britain: David and Charles, 1968.

471 Hughes, Douglas A. Perspectives on pornography. N.Y.: St. Martin's Press, 1970.

471a Hughes, Graham. Law, reason and justice; essays in legal philosophy. N.Y.: New York University Press, 1969.

472 Hughes, Larry. You can see a lot standing under a flare in the Republic of Vietnam; my year at war. N.Y.: Morrow, 1970.

473 Huie, William Bradford. He slew the dreamer: my search, with James Earl Ray, for the truth about the murder of Martin Luther King. N.Y.: Delacorte Press, 1970.

474 Hull, Roger H. Law and Vietnam. N.Y.: Dobbs Ferry, 1968. (Questions the legality of the Vietnam war.)

474a Humphrey, Hubert H. Race in a changing world. N.Y.: American Jewish Committee, 1967. (Pam.) (American Conversations Series)

475 Hunt, Morton. Her infinite variety: the American woman as lover, mate and rival. N.Y.: Harper and Row, 1962.

476 International War Crimes Tribunal. Against the crime of silence. New Jersey: O'Hare Books, 1970.

477 Investigator's Information Service. How to avoid electronic eavesdropping and privacy invasions. Los Angeles, California: IIS., 1967.

478 Isaacs, Harold R. The New world of negro Americans. N.Y.: Day, 1963.

479 Isard, Walter (ed.). Vietnam: some basic issues and alternatives. Essays by Peter Archibald and others. N.Y.: Pitman, 1969.

480 Jackson, George. Soledad brother: the prison letters of George Jackson. Intro. by Jean Genet. N.Y.: Bantam, 1970.

481 Jacobs, Harold. Weatherman. N.Y.: Ramparts Press, 1970. (Political and social ideology.)

482 Jacobs, Paul. The State of the unions. N.Y.: Atheneum, 1963. (Hoffa, and the labor unions.)

483 _____, and Saul Landau (eds.). New radicals: a report with documents. N.Y.: Vintage, 1966. (Development of the New Left, ideologies, and factions.)

484 James, Daniel. Che Guevara; a biography. N.Y.: Stein and Day, 1969.

485 James, H. Crisis in the courts. N.Y.: McKay, 1967.

486 Janeway, Eliot. The Economics of crisis: war, politics, and the dollar. N.Y.: Weybright and Talley, 1968.

487 Janowitz, Morris. Political conflict. Chicago:

General 55

Quadrangel, 1970. (Political conflicts in American politics. Racial violence and social mobility are included among others.)

488 ──────. The Professional soldier: a social and political portrait. Illinois: Free Press, 1960. (Explores the concept of the constabulary force and the controversial aspects of both military personnel and society.)

489 Janson, Donald, and Bernard Eismann. The Far right. N.Y.: McGraw-Hill, 1963.

489a Jencks, Christopher. A Reappraisal of the most controversial educational document of our time. N.Y.: American Jewish Committee, 1969. (Pam.) (Interpretations of the "Coleman Report.")

490 Jessup, Josephine L. The Faith of our feminists. N.Y.: Biblo and Tannen, 1965.

491 Joesten, Joachim. Oswald: assassin or fall guy? N.Y.: Marzani and Munsell, 1965. (Paper)

492 Johnson, Charles S. Backgrounds to patterns of negro segregation. N.Y.: Apollo, 1970.

493 Johnson, Haynes (et al.). Bay of pigs; the leaders' story of the Brigade 2506. N.Y.: Norton, 1964. (The 1961 invasion of Cuba by the leaders of the invasion force.)

494 Johnson, J. R. Marxism and the intellectuals. Detroit, Michigan: Facing Reality Publishing Co., 1962. (Pam.)

495 Johnson, Richard M. The Dynamics of compliance: Supreme Court Decision-making from a new perspective. Evanston, Illinois: Northwestern, 1968.

495a Johnston, Norman (et al.). Sociology of punishment and corrections. N.Y.: John Wiley and Sons, Inc., 1970.

496 Jones, Penn Jr. Forgive my grief. Intro. by Maxwell Geismar. Texas: Midlothian Mirror, 1968. 2 vols. (Various viewpoints of the John F. Kennedy

assassination and the author's criticism of the Warren Commission Report.)

497 Joseph, Stephen M. The Me nobody knows: children's voices from the ghetto. N.Y.: Avon, 1969. (Paper)

498 Joyce, Robert E., and Mary R. Joyce. Let us be born; the inhumanity of abortion. N.Y.: Herder--Franciscan Herald Press, 1970. (Paper) (The case against legalized abortion.)

499 Joyce, W. The Propaganda gap. N.Y.: Harper, 1963.

500 Just, Ward S. Military men. N.Y.: Knopf, 1970. (U.S. military justice, the role of the Army, mission and history.)

501 _____. To what end: report from Vietnam. Boston: Houghton, 1968.

502 Kahin, George, and John Lewis. The United States in Vietnam. N.Y.: Dell, 1967.

503 Kahn, Robert L., and Elise Boulding (eds.). Power and conflict in organizations. N.Y.: Basic Books, 1964. (Conflicts within organizations.)

504 Kardiner, Abram. The Mark of oppression: explorations in the personality of the American negro. N.Y.: World, 1969.

505 Karol, K. S. Guerrillas in power: the course of the Cuban revolution. N.Y.: Hill and Wang, 1970.

506 Katz, Irwin, and Patricia Gurin. Race and the social sciences. N.Y.: Basic Books, 1969. (Eight social scientists describe research about racial inequality which crosses disciplinary areas.)

507 Keech, William R. The Impact of negro voting; the role of the vote in the quest for equality. Chicago: Rand McNally, 1968. (Impact of voting in Durham and Tuskegee.)

508 Keeton, Robert E. Venturing to do justice. Mass.:

General

Harvard, 1969.

509 Kefauver, Estes. In a few hands: monopoly power in America. With the assistance of Irene Till. N.Y.: Pantheon, 1965.

510 Kemelman, Harry. Common sense in education. N.Y.: Crown, 1970. (A critical analysis of today's schools with some suggestions on reforms and how to improve the system from beginning to end.)

511 Kendall, Robert. White teacher in a black school. Chicago: Regnery, 1964.

512 Kenkel, W. The Family in perspective. N.Y.: Appleton, 1965.

513 Kennedy, David M. Birth control in America: the career of Margaret Sanger. Conn.: Yale University Press, 1970.

514 Kennedy, Robert F. To seek a newer world. N.Y.: Doubleday, 1967. (Includes six major topics of political concern: youth, urban crisis, Alliance For Progress, nuclear control, and Vietnam.)

515 Kennedy, Ted. Decisions for a decade. N.Y.: New American Library, 1970. (U.S. Social problems.)

516 Kenner, Martin, and James Petras (eds.). Fidel Castro speaks. N.Y.: Grove Press, 1970.

517 Keppel, Francis. The Necessary revolution in American education. N.Y.: Harper and Row, 1966.

518 No entry.

519 King, Donald B. Legal aspects of the civil rights movement. Detroit, Michigan: Wayne State University Press, 1965.

520 King, Martin Luther Jr. Strength to love. N.Y.: Harper, 1963. (Collection of sermons rejecting violence.)

521 King, Martin Luther Jr. The Trumpet of conscience. N.Y.: Harper, 1968. (Lectures delivered in 1967 concerning negro history and the civil rights movement.)

522 Kippley, John F. Covenant, Christ and contraception. N.Y.: Alba House, 1970. (In defense of the Pope's encyclical on birth control.)

523 Kirkpatrick, Lyman B. Jr. The Real CIA. N.Y.: Macmillan, 1968.

524 Knoebl, Kuno. Victor Charlie: the face of war in Vietnam. N.Y.: Praeger, 1967. (Intro. by Bernard B. Fall. Trans. by Abe Farbstein. Political and ideological aspects of the Vietnam war.)

525 Knowles, Louis L., and Kenneth Prewitt (eds.). Institutional racism in America. New Jersey: Prentice-Hall, 1970. (Paper) (Contributors include Owen Blank among others and an appendix by Harold Baron.)

526 Koch, Thilo. Fighters for a new world. N.Y.: Putnam, 1969. ("Impact on society of these three American leaders." The two Kennedys and Martin Luther King, Jr. They were constantly involved with confrontation from many angles.)

527 Koerner, James D. The Parsons College bubble: a tale of higher education in America. N.Y.: Basic Books, 1970. (Attempts to run a college like a business enterprise. Examines traditional aspects of higher education with recommendations for change.)

528 Kohl, Herbert R. Thirty-six children. N.Y.: New American Library, 1967. (Crisis in urban education and ghetto schools.)

529 Kolakowski, Leszak. Toward a Marxist humanism: essays on the left today. N.Y.: Grove Press, 1968.

530 Kolko, Gabriel. The Roots of American foreign policy. Boston: Beacon, 1969.

General   59

531   _____. Three documents of the National Liberation
       Front. Boston: Beacon Press, 1970. (Paper)

532   Konvitz, M. Expanding liberties. N.Y.: Viking
       Press, 1966.

532a   Kostelanetz, Richard (ed.). Beyond left and right:
       radical thought for our times. N.Y.: Morrow--
       Apollo Editions, 1970. (Paper) (Anthologies from
       provocative thinkers of our time.)

533   Kotler, Milton. Neighborhood government: the local
       foundations of political life. N.Y.: Bobbs-Merrill,
       1969.

534   Kovel, Joel. White racism: a psychohistory. N.Y.:
       Pantheon, 1970. (Provides some insight into the
       black man's plight in western civilization.)

535   Kraslow, David, and Stewart M. Loary. The Secret
       search for peace in Vietnam. N.Y.: Random
       House, 1968.

536   Krislov, Samuel. The Negro in federal employment;
       the quest for equal opportunity. Minnesota: University of Minnesota Press, 1967.

537   Kriyanda (Guru). Cooperative communities: how to
       start them and why. 3rd. ed. San Francisco, California: Ananda Publications, 1969.

538   Kroll, Arthur M. (ed.). Issues in American education:
       commentary on the current scene. N.Y.: Oxford
       University Press, 1970. (Essays discussing issues
       presently confronting American education.)

539   Kuh, Richard H. Foolish figleaves? Pornography in
       and out of court. N.Y.: Macmillan, 1967.

540   Kunen, James S. Strawberry statement: notes of a
       college revolutionist. N.Y.: Random House, 1969.

541   Kurland, Philip B. Politics, the constitution, and the
       Warren Court. Chicago: University of Chicago
       Press, 1970. (Warren Commission Report examined
       in light of constitutional history and government.
       Contains five essays.)

542 Lacouture, Jean. Ho Chi Minh. Trans. by P. Wiles, edited by J. C. Seitz. N.Y.: Random House, 1968.

543 Lacroix, Jean Paul. The Meaning of modern atheism. N.Y.: Macmillan, 1965.

544 Lacy, Leslie Alexander. The Rise and fall of a proper negro: an anthology. N.Y.: Macmillan, 1970.

545 Ladd, Bruce. Crisis in credibility. N.Y.: New American Library, 1968. (Three aspects of the credibility gap in the executive branch of government: secrecy, lying, and news management.)

546 Ladd, Everett C. Negro political leadership in the south. N.Y.: Cornell University Press, 1966.

547 Lader, L. Abortion. N.Y.: Bobbs-Merrill, 1966.

548 Laffin, John. The Anatomy of captivity. N.Y.: Abelard-Schuman, 1968. (Reasons for political imprisonment and the underlying treatment resulting from such.)

549 Laidler, Harry Wellington. Boycotts and the labor struggle: economic and legal aspects. N.Y.: Russell and Russell, 1968.

550 Lane, Mark. Conversations with Americans. N.Y.: Simon and Schuster, 1970. (Accounts of interviews with American soldiers and marines who participated in war crimes and atrocities in Vietnam.)

551 _____. Rush to judgment. N.Y.: Holt, Rinehart, and Winston, 1966. (Some more controversy over the Warren Commission Report.)

552 Lang, Daniel. Casualties of war. N.Y.: McGraw-Hill, 1969.

553 Lapp, Ralph E. Arms beyond doubt; the tyranny of weapons technology. N.Y.: Cowles, 1970. (Growing concern over the acquisition and research on strategic weapons.)

554 _____. The New priesthood; the scientific elite and the uses of power. N.Y.: Harper, 1965.

General

555 ———. The Weapons culture. N.Y.: Norton, 1968. (The rift between science, politics, and arms control.)

556 Larson, Bruce. The Emerging Church. Texas: Word, 1970. (Technological innovations and the goals and priorities of the new Church.)

556a Larson, Richard, and James Olson. I have a kind of fear: confessions from the writings of white teachers and black students in city schools. Illinois: Quadrangle, 1969.

557 Lasch, Christopher. Agony of the American Left. N.Y.: Knopf, 1969. (Surveys the American Left since the twenties.)

558 ———. The New radicalism in America, 1889-1963. N.Y.: Knopf, 1965.

559 Laycock, George. The Diligent destroyers. N.Y.: Doubleday, 1970. (The author wages war on various agencies and industries over the current environmental crisis.)

560 Lazo, Mario. Dagger in the heart: American policy failures in Cuba. N.Y.: Funk and Wagnalls, 1969. (U.S. foreign relations with Cuba.)

561 League of Women Voters of the U.S. Education Fund. The Big water fight. Vermont: Greene, 1966. (The water pollution issue.)

561a Lee, Robert, and Russell Galloway. The Schizophrenic Church: conflict over community. Philadelphia: Westminster Press, 1969. (Paper)

562 Leggett, John C. Class, race, and labor; working-class consciousness in Detroit. N.Y.: Oxford University Press, 1969.

563 Leiden, Carl, and Karl M. Schmitt. Politics of violence: revolution in the modern world. New Jersey: Prentice-Hall, 1968.

564 Leinwand, Gerald (ed.). The Negro in the city; a forthright examination of the black American in urban

society. N.Y.: Washington Square Press, 1968.

565 Le May, Curtis E. America is in danger. N.Y.: Funk and Wagnalls, 1968. (Criticism of American military and diplomatic policies.)

566 Lens, Sidney. The Military-industrial complex. Philadelphia: United Church Press--Pilgrim Press Book, 1969. (Paper)

567 _____. Radicalism in America. Rev. ed. N.Y.: Crowell, 1969. (A revised edition of an earlier work first published in 1966.)

568 Leonard, George B. The Man and woman thing, and other provocations. N.Y.: Delacorte Press, 1970.

569 _____. Education and ecstasy. N.Y.: Delacorte, 1968.

570 Lepp, Ignace. Atheism in our time. N.Y.: Macmillan, 1963.

571 Leshan, Eda J. The Conspiracy against childhood. N.Y.: Atheneum, 1967. (Direct confrontation with traditionalists. A new approach to the education and management of children.)

572 Leslie, G. The Family in social context. N.Y.: Oxford University Press, 1967.

573 Lester, Julius. Revolutionary notes. N.Y.: Grove-- Evergreen-Black Cat, 1969. (Essays concerning the revolution with implications directed toward timely and controversial topics.)

574 Levin, Henry M. Community control of schools. N.Y.: Brookings Institute, 1970. (A conference report as an approach to the issue.)

575 Levin, Murray B. The Alienated voter. N.Y.: Holt, Rinehart, and Winston, 1960.

576 Levitas, Mitchel. America in crisis. N.Y.: Holt, Rinehart, and Winston, 1969. (Photographic essay.)

577 Levy, Charles L. Voluntary servitude: white in the

General 63

negro movement. N.Y.: Appleton-Century Crofts, 1968. (Paper) (Separate power between blacks and whites or integrated movement.)

578 Lewis, Howard R. With every breath you take: the poisons of air pollution, how they are injuring our health, and what we must do about them. N.Y.: Crown, 1965.

579 Lewis, John. The Life and teaching of Karl Marx. N.Y.: International Press, 1965. (Also available in paper.)

580 Lewis, Richard Warren. The Scavengers and critics of the Warren Report. Based on an investigation by Lawrence Schiller. N.Y.: Dell, 1967. (Paper)

581 Liberation News Service. A Book for a fighting movement. N.Y.: Liberation News Service, 1969. (Paper) (Alternately known as "The Bust Book.")

582 Liberation Publishing House. South Vietnam: on the road to victory. South Vietnam: Liberation Publishing House, 1966.

583 Lichtheim, George. The Origins of socialism. N.Y.: Praeger, 1969. (Also available in paper)

584 Lifton, Robert J. The Woman in America. Boston: Houghton Mifflin, 1965.

584a Ligon, J. Frank (ed.). Confrontations. Proceedings of the thirty-first annual Pacific Northwest Conference on Higher Education. Oregon: Oregon State University Press, 1970. (Conference held at Oregon State July 9-11, 1969. Keynote of the conference was "involvement" and topics included: Minorites/Majorities; Rights/Responsibilities; Change/Establishment; An Assessment and Projection.)

584b Lillian, Lewis M. The Impossible revolution; black power and the American dream. N.Y.: Random House, 1968.

585 Lincoln, Charles E. Black Muslims in America. Foreword by Gordon Allport. Boston: Beacon, 1961. (History of the black Muslim movement in the U.S.)

586 _____. Sounds of the struggle; persons and perspectives in civil rights. N.Y.: Morrow, 1967.

586a Lipset, Seymour Martin. Revolution and counter revolution: change and persistence in social structures. N.Y.: Basic Books, 1968.

587 _____, and Earl Raab. The Politics of unreason: right wing extremism in America, 1790-1970. N.Y.: Harper and Row, 1970. (A volume in the Patterns of American Prejudice Series.)

587a Littell, Franklin H. The Church and the body politic. N.Y.: Seabury, 1969. (Controversy in the governmental processes of Churches.)

587b Lobenthal, Joseph S. Growing up clean in America. Intro. by Ramsey Clark. N.Y.: World, 1970.

588 Lockwood, Lee. Castro's Cuba, Cuba's Fidel. American journalist's inside look at today's Cuba. N.Y.: Random House, 1969.

589 Lokos, Lionel. House divided; the life and legacy of Martin Luther King. N.Y.: Arlington House, 1968.

590 Lomax, Louis E. The Negro revolt. N.Y.: Harper and Row, 1962.

591 _____. When the word is given: a report on Elijah Muhammad, Malcolm X. and the black Muslim world. Cleveland: World, 1963. (The Black Muslim movement. Included are addresses and an interview with Malcolm X.)

592 Loomis, Mildred J. (et al.). Go ahead and live. N.Y.: Philosophical Library, 1965. (Available from School of Living, Brookville, Ohio.)

593 Lopez-Fresquet, R. My 14 months with Castro. N.Y.: World, 1966.

594 Lorenz, Konrad. On aggression. N.Y.: Harcourt, Brace and World, 1966.

595 Lothstein, Arthur (ed.). All we are saying: the philosophy of the New Left. N.Y.: Putnam, 1970. (Selections compare political movements with some European thinkers.)

General   65

596   Louis, Debbie. And we are not saved. N.Y.: Doubleday, 1970. (History of the civil rights movement from a worker's participation in the movement.)

597   Lubell, Samuel. The Hidden crisis in American politics. N.Y.: W. W. Norton, 1970. (The author describes the hidden crisis as our inability to resolve all those problems which he calls "unresolved neglects.")

598   Luce, John, and John Sommer. Viet Nam: the unheard voices. N.Y.: Random House, 1969.

599   Luce, Phillip A. The New left. N.Y.: D. McKay, 1966.

599a Lui, William T. Family and fertility; proceeds of the fifth Notre Dame conference on population, Dec. 1-3, 1966. Notre Dame, Indiana: University of Notre Dame Press, 1967.

600   Lukas, J. Anthony. The Barnyard epithet and other obscenities. N.Y.: Harper and Row, 1970. (Paper) (A skeptic view of the courts and the judicial system.)

601   Lundberg, Ferdinand. The Rich and the super rich; a study in the power of money today. N.Y.: Lyle Stuart Inc., 1968.

602   Lynn, Conrad J. Monroe, North Carolina: turning point in American history. Detroit: Correspondence Publishing Co., 1962. (Pam.)

603   McAfee, Kathy, and Myrna Wood. Bread and roses. San Francisco, California: Bay Area Radical Education Project, 1969. (Pam.) (Women's lib. issues.)

604   McAlister, John T. Jr. Vietnam: the origins of revolution. N.Y.: Knopf, 1969.

605   _____, and Paul Mus. The Vietnamese and their revolution. Trans. by Guicharnod. N.Y.: Harper and Row, 1970. (Center for International Studies, Princeton.)

606   Macaulay, Neill. A Rebel in Cuba: an American

memoir. Chicago: Quadrangle, 1970.

607 McCarthy, Richard. The Ultimate folly--war by pestilence, asphyxiation and defoliation. N.Y.: Knopf, 1969.

608 McClellan, Grant S. (ed.). Censorship in the U.S. The Reference Shelf (Series) Vol. XXXIX, No. 3. N.Y.: H.W. Wilson Co., 1967.

608a McConnell, Brian. The History of assassination. Tennessee: Aurora, 1970. (The "whys" of political assassinations.)

609 McCord, John H. (ed.). With all deliberate speed; civil rights theory and reality. Illinois: University of Illinois, 1969.

610 McCord, William. The Urban negro. N.Y.: Norton, 1969.

610a McCormick, Arthur. Population problem. N.Y.: Crowell, 1970.

611 McCormick, Rory. Americans against man. N.Y.: World, 1970.

612 McGinniss, Joe. The Selling of the President, 1968. N.Y.: Pocket Books, 1970.

613 McGrady, M. A Dove in Vietnam. N.Y.: Funk and Wagnalls, 1970.

614 McGrath, Earl J. Should students share the power? A study of their role in college and university governance. Philadelphia: Temple University Press, 1970. (Paper)

615 Mack, Raymond W. Transforming America; patterns of social change. N.Y.: Random, 1967. (Social change and the implications of technology on society.)

616 Mackey, J. P. (ed.). Morals, law and authority. Ohio: Pflaum, 1970. (Controversial Catholic issues on morality and authority.)

616a McLeish, John. Theory of social change; four views

considered. N.Y.: Schocken, 1969.

617 McLennan, Barbara N. (ed.). Crime in urban society. Foreword by Ramsey Clark. N.Y.: Dunellen, 1970. (Critical issues in the crime debate and some problems attending urban crime.)

618 McMillen, Wheeler. Bugs or people? A reasoned answer to opponents of pesticides. N.Y.: Appleton, 1965.

619 McNeill, Don. Moving through here. Intro. by Allen Ginsberg. Epilogue by Paul Williams. N.Y.: Knopf, 1970. (Accounts of New York's Lower East Side, and the hippie movement written by a "former writer for the 'Village Voice'.")

620 McPherson, James M. The Negro's civil war. N.Y.: Pantheon, 1965.

621 McQuilkin, Frank. Think black: an introduction to black political power. N.Y.: Bruce, 1970.

622 McWilliams, Wilson Carey (ed.). The California revolution. N.Y.: Grossman, 1969. (Anthology of articles gathered together giving a picture of the rape of the state of California.)

623 Mader, Julius. Who's who in the CIA, published by Julius Mader. Berlin: Mader, 1968. (Includes "selections from the 3,000 listed agents" and a chart with "several cover organizations used by the CIA.")

624 Magdoff, Harry. The Age of imperialism. N.Y.: Monthly Review Press, 1969.

625 _____. Economic aspects of U.S. imperialism. San Francisco, California: Bay Area Radical Education Project, 1966. (Pam.)

626 Magee, Bryan. The New radicalism. N.Y.: St. Martins Press, 1963.

627 Mailer, Norman. Armies of the night: history as a novel--the novel as history. N.Y.: New American Library, 1968. (Pentagon Peace March, October, 1967.)

628 Mailer, Norman. Miami and the siege of Chicago; an informal history of the Republican and Democratic conventions of 1968. N.Y.: World, 1969.

629 Malcolm X. Malcolm X speaks: selected speeches and statements. N.Y.: Merit, 1965.

630 Mallin, Jay. Che Guevara, on revolution. Florida: University of Miami Press, 1969.

631 Mann, Kenneth W. Deadline for survival. N.Y.: Seabury Press, 1970. (Paper) ("Progress in the fields of ecology, space research, computer analysis, organ transplants, etc." Concern is for the quality of life for survival.)

632 Manning, Robert (ed.). Who we are: an Atlantic chronicle of the U.S. and Vietnam. Boston: Little, Brown and Co., 1969.

633 Manso, Peter (Comp. and ed.). Running against the machine; the Mailer-Breslin campaign. N.Y.: Doubleday, 1969. (Paper) (Afterthoughts of the Mayoralty campaign in New York City.)

634 Mao-Tse-Tung. Quotations from chairman Mao-Tse-Tung. N.Y.: Praeger, 1968.

635 Marcuse, Herbert. Essay on liberation. Boston: Beacon Press, 1969.

636 _____. Negations; essays in critical theory; with translations from the German by Jeremy J. Shapiro. Boston: Beacon, 1969. (Controversial areas concerning aggressiveness in industrial societies, and Marcuse's notions of American society.)

637 _____. One dimensional man; studies in the ideology of advanced industrial society. Boston: Beacon, 1964. (Alternatives in one-dimensional society and thought.)

638 Marek, Franz. Philosophy of world revolution; a contribution to an anthology of theories of revolution, trans. by D. Simon. N.Y.: International Publishers, 1969.

General 69

638a Margolis, Joseph B. Education in the seventies. N.Y.: Spartan Books, 1969.

639 Marine, Gene. The Black Panthers. N.Y.: New American Library, 1969. (Paper)

640 Marshall, Gen. S. L. A. Ambush. N.Y.: Cowles, 1969. (Vietnam War.)

640a Martin, George. Causes and conflicts: the centennial history of the association of the bar of the city of New York. Foreword by Francis T. P. Plimpton. Boston: Houghton, 1970.

641 Martinet, Gilles. Marxism of our time. Trans. by Frances Kelly. N.Y.: Monthly Review Press, 1964.

642 Marty, Martin. Varieties of unbelief. N.Y.: Holt, Rinehart, and Winston, 1964. (Radical theology and atheism.)

643 Marx, Gary T. Protest and prejudice: a study of belief in the black community. N.Y.: Harper, 1967.

644 Mason, Alpheus T. The States rights debate: anti-federalism and the constitution. New Jersey: Prentice-Hall, 1964.

645 Masotti, Louis H. (et al.). A Time to burn? An evaluation of the present crisis in race relations. N.Y.: Rand McNally, 1969.

646 Matson, Floyd W. (ed.). Voices of crisis. Vital speeches on contemporary issues. N.Y.: Odyssey Press, 1966. (Paper)

647 Matthews, Herbert L. Fidel Castro. N.Y.: Simon and Schuster, 1969.

648 Mayer, Martin. The Teachers' strike; New York, 1968. N.Y.: Harper and Row, 1969.

649 Meetham, A. Roger. Atmospheric pollution: its origins and prevention. 3rd rev. ed. N.Y.: Pergamon, 1964.

650 Meiman, Seymour. Pentagon Capitalism: the

management of the new imperialism. N.Y.: McGraw, 1970.

650a Melman, Seymour. Our depleted society. N.Y.: Holt, Rinehart and Winston, 1965.

651 Menashe, Louis, and Ronald Radosh. Teach-ins U.S.A. N.Y.: Praeger, 1967. (Paper)

652 Merriam, Eve. After Nora slammed the door; American women in the 1960's: the unfinished revolution. Cleveland and New York: World, 1964.

653 _____. Man and woman: the human condition. Denver, Colorado: Loretto Heights Research Center On Woman. Loretto Heights College, 1968.

654 Metzger, Walter P. Academic freedom in the age of the university. N.Y.: Colorado University Press, 1969.

655 Meyers, Donald W. The Human body and the law: a medico-legal study. Chicago: Aldine, 1970.

656 Milio, Nancy. Ninety-two-twenty-six Kercheval: the storefront that did not burn. Michigan: University of Michigan Press, 1970. (Interracial conflict.)

657 Miller, Abie. The Negro and the great society. N.Y.: Vintage, 1966.

658 Miller, Arthur R. The Assault on privacy. Michigan: University of Michigan Press, 1970.

659 Miller, Kelly. Radicals and conservatives and other essays on the negro in America. N.Y.: Schocken, 1968.

660 Miller, Michael V. Revolution at Berkeley: crisis in American education. N.Y.: Dial, 1965.

661 Miller, Warren. The Siege of Harlem. Rev. ed. N.Y.: World, 1969.

662 Miller, William. Readings in American values, selected and edited from public documents of the American past. New Jersey: Prentice-Hall, 1964.

General 71

663 Millett, Kate. Sexual politics: a manifesto for revolution. N.Y.: Doubleday, 1970. (For a biography of Kate Millett, see Current Biography, v. 32, No. 1, January, 1971.)

664 Mills, C. Wright. Listen Yankee: the revolution in Cuba. N.Y.: Ballantine Books, 1960. (Also available in paper)

665 _____. The Marxists. N.Y.: Dell, 1962.

666 Mitchell, J. Paul. Race riots in black and white. New Jersey: Prentice-Hall, 1970.

667 Mitchell, Juliet. Women: the longest revolution. San Francisco: BAREP., 1966. (Pam.)

668 Mitford, Jessica. The Trial of Dr. Spock. N.Y.: Knopf, 1969.

669 Molnar, Thomas. The Counter-revolution. N.Y.: Funk and Wagnalls, 1969.

670 Momboisse, Raymond M. Blueprint of revolution; the rebel, the party, the techniques of revolt. Mass.: C.C. Thomas, 1970. (Conditions which are descriptive of revolution and the originating and sustaining causes.)

670a Montagu, Ashley. Man's most dangerous myth: the fallacy of race. New York and Cleveland: World, 1964.

671 Morgan, Richard E. The Politics of religious conflict: Church and state in America. N.Y.: Pegasus, 1970.

672 Morgan, Robin. Sisterhood is powerful: an anthology of writings from the women's liberation movement. N.Y.: Vintage, 1970. (Paper)

673 _____. Women in revolt. N.Y.: Random House, 1969. (Original title: "Women's Liberation Reader.")

674 Morgan, Ruth P. The President and civil rights. N.Y.: St. Martins, 1970. (Paper) (St. Martins series in

American Politics.)

675 Morgenthau, Hans J. Truth and power, essays of a decade, 1960-70. N.Y.: Praeger, 1970. (Essays concerning political truths about persons who are in positions of power. Contains an epilog with ideas for the future.)

676 Mowbray, A. Q. The Thumb on the scale, or the supermarket shell game. Philadelphia: Lippincott, 1967. (Alleged abuses in the food industry.)

677 Mumford, Lewis. The Myth of the machine: the Pentagon of power. N.Y.: Harcourt, Brace Jovanovich, 1970.

678 Mungo, Raymond. Famous long ago: my life and hard times with Liberation News Service. Boston: Beacon, 1970. (A memoir of the movement.)

679 Murphy, Raymond J., and Howard Elinson (eds.). Problems and prospects of the negro movement. California: Wadsworth, 1970.

680 Muse, Benjamin. The American negro revolution: from nonviolence to black power, 1963-1967. Indiana: Indiana University Press, 1968.

681 Myerson, Michael. These are the good old days; coming of age as a radical in America's late, late years. N.Y.: Grossman, 1970.

682 Myrdal, Gunnar. An American dilemma: the negro problem and modern democracy. 20th Anniversary ed. 2 vols. N.Y.: Harper and Row, 1962.

683 _____. The Challenge to affluence. N.Y.: Pantheon, 1963. (U.S. foreign policy and economy.)

684 Nabokov, Peter. Tijerina and the courthouse aid. California: Ramparts Press, 1970. (The raid on the courthouse in New Mexico on June 5, 1967.)

684a Nearing, Helen, and Scott Nearing. Living the good life. N.Y.: Schocken, 1970. (Attempts at subsistence farming at a commune in Vermont.)

General 73

684b Neiburg, H. L. In the name of science. Chicago: Quadrangle, 1966. (Controversial aspects of research and development for defense, military technology, and the role science plays in all of this.)

685 Neill, Alexander S. Freedom--not license! N.Y.: Hart, 1966. (New and controversial concept in the education and management of children.)

686 _____. Summerhill; a radical approach to child rearing. With a foreword by Erich Fromm. N.Y.: Hart, 1960.

687 Nelson, Truman. The Right of revolution. Boston: Beacon, 1968.

688 _____. The Torture of Mothers. Boston: Beacon, 1968. (Also available in paper) (Harlem and the Harlem 6.)

689 Newby, Idus A. Challenge to the court; social scientists and the defense of segregation, 1954-1966. Baton Rouge, Louisiana: Louisiana State University Press, 1967.

690 Newfield, Jack. A Prophetic minority. N.Y.: New American Library, 1970. (Paper) (An analysis of the radical movement of the 60's written by the assistant editor of the Village Voice.)

691 Newman, Albert H. The Assassination of John F. Kennedy: the reasons why. N.Y.: Clarkson N. Potter, Inc., 1970.

692 Newman, Bernard. Background to Vietnam. N.Y.: New American Library, 1970. (Paper)

692a Newman, Edwin S. Civil liberty and civil rights. 5th rev. ed. N.Y.: Oceana, 1970. (Legal rights for the layman.)

693 Nicolaus, Martin. Ruling class sociology. San Francisco, California: Bay Area Radical Educational Project, 1969. (Pam.) (Reprint of a speech given at the A.S.A. meeting.)

693a Nimmo, Dan, and Thomas D. Ungs. American political

patterns. Conflict and consensus. 2nd ed. Boston: Little, 1969.

694   Nordhoff, Charles. Communistic societies of the U.S. N.Y.: Schocken, 1965. (Paper)

695   O'Connor, James. Origins of socialism in Cuba. N.Y.: Cornell University Press, 1970.

696   O'Connor, John (ed.). American Catholic exodus, by Philip Berrigan (and others) Washington, D.C.: Corpus Books, 1969. (Contemporary problems confronting the Catholic Church. Contains descriptions of social action on secular issues as well as the Vietnam War and the Church.)

697   _____. The People versus Rome; radical split in the American Church. N.Y.: Random House, 1969.

698   Oglesby, Carl, and Richard Shaull. Containment and change. Intro. by Leon Howell. N.Y.: Macmillan, 1967. (Contents: Part 1 discusses the aims of U.S. foreign policy in Vietnam and Latin America. Part 2 is based on Richard Shaull's visit to Latin America working with Latin American Student Christian movement.)

699   Olsen, Jack. The Black athlete; a shameful story: the myth of integration in American sport. N.Y.: Time-Life Books, 1968.

700   O'Neill, Robert, and Michael Donovan. Children, Church, and God: the case against formal religious education. New York and Cleveland: World, 1970. (A plea for more meaningful programs in religious education.)

700a _____. Free speech; responsible communication under law. N.Y.: Bobbs-Merrill, 1966.

701   O'Neill, William L. Everyone was brave: the rise and fall of feminism in America. Chicago: Quadrangle, 1969.

702   Oppenheimer, Martin. The Urban guerrilla. Chicago: Quadrangle, 1969.

General 75

702a Orrick, William H. Colleges in crisis. Tennessee: Aurora, 1970. (Based on interviews and observations concerning the events at San Francisco State College in 1968-69.)

703 Osborne, William A. The Segregated Covenant; race relations and American Catholics. N.Y.: Herder and Herder, 1967.

703a Overstreet, Harry A. The Gentle people of prejudice. N.Y.: American Jewish Committee, 1970. (Pam.) (Now in the 20th printing and reprinted from Saturday Review.)

704 _____. The Strange tactics of extremism. N.Y.: Norton, 1964.

705 Owens, Jesse, and Paul G. Neimark. Blackthink: my life as black man and white man. N.Y.: Morrow, 1970. (Anecdotal description by the Olympic champion concerning black culture.)

706 Owens, William A. Black mutiny. Boston: Pilgrim Press, 1969.

707 Pachter, Henry M. Collision course: the Cuban missile crisis and co-existence. N.Y.: Praeger, 1963. (New insight into U.S. foreign policy with Cuba.)

708 Pacific Studies Center. Four articles on the U.S. in Southeast Asia. Palo Alto, California: PSC., 1970. (U.S. in Cambodia, U.S. Foreign Policy, American Universities in Thailand, and the teaching of English to the country's elite.)

709 _____. The Integration of education, science, the military, and ideology in post-war America. Palo Alto, California: PSC., 1969. (Pam.)

710 _____. Strike at G.M. Palo Alto, California: Pacific Studies Center, 1970. (Pam.) (Struggle of negro workers in the automobile industry. G.M. investments.)

711 Packard, Vance. The Naked society. N.Y.: McKay, 1964. (Description of devices used by government and businesses which invade privacy.)

712 Paddock, William, and Paul Paddock. Famine--1975! America's decision: who will survive? N.Y.: Little, 1967. ("Potential role of the U.S. during the time of famines." Contains a proposal for the use of American food.)

713 Parenti, Michael. The Anti-Communist impulse. N.Y.: Random House, 1969.

714 Parkes, James. Anti-semitism. Chicago: Quadrangle, 1969.

715 Parks, David. G I diary. N.Y.: Harper and Row, 1968. ("A diary of a young negro draftee's two-year tour in the Army from induction day in September 1965 through eight months of combat in Vietnam in 1967. Blurb.)

716 Peccli, A. The Chasm ahead. N.Y.: Macmillan, 1969. (Technology the author feels is a threat to human existence.)

717 Peck, James. Freedom ride. N.Y.: Grove, 1963.

718 Peck, Merton J., and Frederick M. Scherer. The Weapons acquisition process: an economic analysis. Mass.: Harvard University Press, 1963.

719 Peckham, Morse. Art and pornography. N.Y.: Basic Books, 1969. (The function of pornography in society and meaning as an art.)

720 Peoples' Press. Ecology and power: the earth belongs to the people. San Francisco, California: Peoples' Press, 1970. (Pam.) (The role of corporations and the polluting problem.)

721 _____. Vietnam: a thousand years of struggle. San Francisco, California: Peoples' Press, 1969. (Pam.)

721a Perry, Helen Swick. The Human be-in. N.Y.: Basic Books, 1970. (The "flower-children," their focus, their ideal of love, their use of drugs, and their freer sexual expressions.)

722 Pettee, George Sawyer. The Process of revolution.

General 77

N.Y.: Howard Fertig, 1969. (First published in 1938)

722a Pettigrew, Thomas. School integration in current perspective. N.Y.: American Jewish Committee, 1969. (A reprint from Urban Review.)

723 Phelan, Lana Clarke, and Patricial Magannis. The Abortion handbook. California: Contact Books, 1969. (Of, for, and about abortion.)

724 Pike, Douglas. Viet-Cong; the organization, and techniques of the National Liberation Front of South Vietnam. Mass.: MIT Press, 1970.

725 _____. War, peace, and the Viet-Cong. Mass.: MIT Press, 1970. (Also available in paper.)

726 Plimpton, George (ed.). American journey; the times of Robert Kennedy. Interviews by Jean Stein. N.Y.: Harcourt, Brace, and World, 1970.

727 Pomeroy, William J. Guerrilla and counter-guerrilla warfare. N.Y.: International, 1964. (Paper)

728 Powell, Theodore. The School bus law: a case study in education, religion, and politics. Connecticut: Wesleyan University Press, 1970.

729 Powledge, Fred. Black power, white resistance; notes on the Civil War. Cleveland: World, 1967.

729a _____. Segregation, northern style. N.Y.: American Jewish Committee, 1967. (Pam.) ("De facto school segregation.")

730 Preston, Richard A., Sydney F. Wise, and Herman O. Werner. Men in arms: a history of warfare and its interrelationship with western society. Rev. ed. N.Y.: Praeger, 1962.

731 Proctor, Samuel D. The Young negro in America: 1960-1980. N.Y.: Association Press, 1966.

732 Proxmire, Senator William. America's military-industrial complex. N.Y.: Praeger, 1970.

733 Proxmire, Senator William. Report from wasteland: America's military-industrial complex. N.Y.: Praeger, 1970.

734 Pustay, John S. Counterinsurgency warfare. N.Y.: Macmillan, 1965. (Guerrilla Warfare.)

735 Quinn, Robert P., Joyce M. Tabor, and Laura K. Gordon. The Decision to discriminate: a study of executive selection. Michigan: Institute for Social Research, 1970. (Paper) (Discrimination against Jews.)

736 _____, Robert L. Kahn, and Joyce M. Tabor. The Chosen few: a study of discrimination in executive selection. Michigan: Institute for Social Research, 1970. (Paper) (Deals primarily with discrimination against Jews.)

737 Quinney, Richard. Crime and justice in society. Boston: Little, 1969.

738 Raab, Earl (ed.). American race relations today. N.Y.: Doubleday, 1962.

739 Rader, Dotson. I ain't marchin anymore. N.Y.: McKay, 1969. (An account of the radical underground, and "life among the disaffected ... their violence, politics, and sex.")

740 Radical Feminism of New York. Notes from the second year. N.Y.: Radical Feminism of New York, (n.d.) (Pam.)

741 Rafferty, Max. Classroom countdown: education at the crossroads. N.Y.: Hawthorne, 1970. (History of education and the crisis at hand.)

742 Raines, John C., and Thomas Dean. Marxism and radical religion: essays toward a revolutionary humanism. Pennsylvania: Temple University Press, 1970. (The New radical religion with trends in religious thought.)

743 Rainwater, Lee, and William L. Yancy. The Monihan report and the politics of controversy; a trans-action social science and public policy report; including the

full text of the Negro Family; the case for national action by Daniel Patrick Moynihan. Mass.: MIT., 1967.

744 Ramparts (eds.). Eco-catastrophe. N.Y.: Harper, 1970. (About ecology and the environmental crisis.)

745 Ramsey, Paul. Fabricated man: the ethics of genetic control. Conn.: Yale University Press, 1970. (Also available in paper) (Aspects of genetic control with moral and religious implications.)

746 _____. War and the Christian conscience: how shall modern war be conducted justly? North Carolina: Duke University Press, 1961. (Christian ethics and the "just war" concept treated with both Protestant and Catholic thought.)

747 Randall, Richard S. Censorship of the movies: the social and political control of a mass medium. Wisconsin: University of Wisconsin Press, 1970.

748 Raskin, Marcus G. The Viet-Nam reader; articles and documents on American foreign policy and the Viet Nam crisis. N.Y.: Vintage Books, 1967.

749 Ray, Michele. The Two shores of hell. N.Y.: McKay, 1968. (Personal observation of the Vietnam war by a photographer who was captured.)

750 Record, Wilson. Race and radicalism. Ithaca: Cornell University Press, 1964.

751 Redding, J. Saunders. On being negro in America. N.Y.: Bobbs-Merrill, 1962.

752 Redekop, John H. The American far right. Michigan: Eerdmans, 1968.

752a Redkey, Edwin S. Black exodus: black nationalist and back-to-Africa movements. New Haven, Conn.: Yale University Press, 1969.

752b Reed, Richard Y. Prejudices: effects on children. N.Y.: American Jewish Committee, 1970. (Pam.) (Reprinted from Childhood Education.)

753 Reeves, Thomas C. (ed.). Foundations under fire. N.Y.: Cornell University Press, 1970. (Views of tax-exempt foundations in America written by critics and supporters.)

754 Reich, Charles A. The Greening of America: how the youth revolution is trying to make America livable. N.Y.: Random House, 1970. (Attempts to provide explanations for the counter-culture.)

755 Reimers, David M. White protestantism and the negro. N.Y.: Oxford University Press, 1965.

756 Reischauer, Edwin O. Beyond Vietnam: U.S. and Asia. N.Y.: Random House, 1968.

757 Rejai, Mostafa (ed.). Mao Tse-Tung on revolution and war. N.Y.: Doubleday, 1968.

758 Rembar, Charles. The End of obscenity: the trials of Lady Chatterly, Tropic of Cancer, and Fanny Hill. N.Y.: Simon and Schuster, 1970.

759 Renfield, Richard. If teachers were free: is curriculum obsolete? Washington, D.C.: Acropolis, 1970. (Foreword by Elizabeth Koontz. Presents a revolutionary view of teaching, learning, and freedom in education.)

760 Resek, Carl. The New radicalism in America: 1889-1963. N.Y.: Knopf, 1963.

761 Resnik, Henry S. Turning on the system; war in the Philadelphia public schools. N.Y.: Pantheon, 1970. (Controversy over school management in the Philadelphia Public Schools.)

762 Reston, James B. To Establish justice, to insure domestic tranquility. N.Y.: Bantam, 1970. (The Eisenhower Commission and the administration of justice.)

763 Rexroth, Kenneth. The Alternative society: essays from the other world. N.Y.: Herder and Herder, 1970.

764 Rham, Edith de. The Love fraud. N.Y.: Clarkson

General

H. Potter, 1965.

765 Ridgeway, James. Closed corporation: American universities in crisis. N.Y.: Ballantine, 1969. (Paper) (Documents the 2200 colleges and universities in the U.S. and their role and participation in the industrial-military-government-educational complex.)

766 _____. The Politics of ecology. N.Y.: Dutton, 1970. (Descriptive accounts of pollutants, sewerage, and the total area of ecology.)

767 Riegel, Robert E. American feminists. Kansas: University of Kansas Press, 1964.

768 _____. American women: a story of social change. Fairleigh Dickinson University Press, 1970.

769 Roberts, Charles. The Truth about the assassination. N.Y.: Grosset and Dunlap, 1967. (Foreword by Pierre Salinger.)

770 Roberts, Myron. The Roots of rebellion: a study of existential America. California: William C. Brown Book Company, 1969. (Paper) (Attempts to explain the ideas of the existentialists to the behavior we see happening in America.)

771 Roche, John P. The Quest for the dream; the development of civil rights and human relations in modern America. Chicago: Quadrangle, 1968. (Human rights and liberties of minority groups.)

772 Rodberg, Leonard S., and Derek Shearer (eds.). The Pentagon watchers: students report on the National Security State. N.Y.: Doubleday, 1970. (Also available in paper) (Weapons system controversy.)

773 Root, Robert, and Shirley W. Hall. Struggle of decency; religion and race in modern America. N.Y.: Friendship Press, 1965.

774 Rose, Arnold M. The Negro in America. N.Y.: Harper, 1964. (A condensed edition of Myrdal's "An American Dilemma.")

775 _____, and Caroline B. Rose (eds.). Minority

problems. N.Y.: Harper and Row, 1965.

776 Rose, Peter I. (ed.). The Ghetto and beyond: essays on Jewish life in America. N.Y.: Random House, 1969.

777 Ross, Ishbel. Sons of Adam, daughters of Eve: the role of women in American history. N.Y.: Harper and Row, 1969.

778 Rosset, Barney (ed.). Evergreen review reader. N.Y.: Grove, 1969. (Anthology of a decade of revolutionary politics, sex, psychic revolution, etc.)

779 Rossiter, Clinton L. Marxism: the view from America. N.Y.: Harcourt, Brace and World, 1960.

780 Roszak, Theodore (ed.). The Dissenting academy: essays criticizing the teaching of the humanities in American universities. N.Y.: Pantheon, 1968.

781 _____. The Making of a counter culture; reflections on the technocratic society and its youthful opposition. N.Y.: Doubleday, 1969.

782 Rovere, Richard H. Waist deep in the big muddy: reflections on 1968. N.Y.: Little, 1968. (The title is from a song written by Pete Seeger. Deals with our present predicament in Vietnam and Southeast Asia, plus our highly controversial foreign relations policy.)

782a Rubenstein, Annette T. (ed.). Schools against children: the case for community control. N.Y.: Monthly Review Press, 1970. (Desegregation vs. integration among other controversial issues.)

783 Rubin, Jerry. Do it! Scenarios of the revolution. Intro. by Eldridge Cleaver. N.Y.: Simon and Schuster, 1970. (Also available in paper)

784 _____. Letter to the movement. N.Y.: New York Review of Books, 1969. (Paper)

785 Russell, Bertrand. War crimes in Vietnam. N.Y.: Monthly Review Press, 1967.

General 83

785a Rustin, Bayard. Black power and coalition politics. N.Y.: American Jewish Committee, 1967. (Pam.) (Reprinted from Commentary.)

786 Said, Abdul A. America's world role in the 70's. New Jersey: Prentice-Hall, 1970.

787 Santmire, H. Paul. Brother earth: nature, God, and ecology in time of crisis. New Jersey: Thomas Nelson Inc., 1970. (The crisis of our environment from a religious viewpoint and the role theology plays.)

788 Sartre, Jean-Paul. On genocide; or a summary of the evidence and the judgments of the international war crimes tribunal. Boston: Beacon, 1968.

789 _____. Sartre on Cuba. N.Y.: Ballantine, 1961. (Paper)

790 Sauvage, Leo. The Oswald affair. N.Y.: World, 1966.

791 Schanche, Don A. The Panther paradox: a liberal's dilemma. N.Y.: McKay, 1970. (A chronicle of the history of the party.)

792 Scheer, Robert. How the U.S. got involved in Vietnam. Center for the Study of Democratic Institutions, 1965.

793 Schell, Jonathan. The Military half; an account of destruction in Quang Ngai and Quong Tin. N.Y.: Vintage, 1968.

794 _____. The Village of Ben Suc. N.Y.: Knopf, 1967.

795 Schelling, Thomas C. The Strategy of conflict. Mass.: Harvard University Press, 1961.

796 Schillaci, Anthony. Movies and morals. Indiana: Fides, 1969. (1970 edition published by Dome. The role of movies in moral development as opposed to movies as price entertainment.)

797 Schiller, Herbert I. Mass communications and American

empire. N.Y.: August M. Kelley Publishers, 1969. ("Mass media, ideological images and the emergent imperial society.")

797a Schiller, Herbert I., and Joseph Dexter Phillips (Comps.). Super-state; readings in the military-industrial complex. Illinois: University of Illinois Press, 1970.

798 Schlesinger, Arthur M. Jr. The Bitter heritage: Vietnam and American democracy, 1941-1966. Boston: Houghton, 1967.

799 Schneir, Walter. Telling it like it was: the Chicago riots. N.Y.: New American Library, 1970. (Paper)

800 Schoenberger, Robert A. The American right wing. Readings in political behavior. N.Y.: Holt, Rinehart and Winston, 1969. (Paper)

801 Schoenbrun, David. Vietnam: how we got in; how to get out. N.Y.: Atheneum, 1968.

802 Schrag, Peter. Village school downtown; political and education--A Boston report. Boston: Beacon, 1967.

803 _____. Voices in the classroom; public schools and public attitudes. Boston: Beacon, 1966.

804 Schuchter, Arnold. Reparations: the Black Manifesto and its challenge to white America. Philadelphia: Lippincott, 1970. ("This book represents the first full-scale attempt to deal directly with the issues and hatred reflected in the Black Manifesto. The author projects a program of redress to be carried out by a new coalition of power centers.")--(Blurb)

805 _____. White power/black freedom. Boston: Beacon, 1969.

806 Schulz, David A. Coming up black: patterns of ghetto socialization. New Jersey: Prentice-Hall, 1969. (Negro families in their own words explain their pressing problems.)

807 Schultz, John. No one was killed: documentation and

General

meditation. Convention week, Chicago, August, 1968. Chicago: Follett, 1969.

808 Schurmann, Franz (et al.). The Politics of escalation in Vietnam. Boston: Beacon, 1966.

809 Schuster, Eunice M. Native American anarchism. A study of left-wing American individualism. N.Y.: Da Capo Press, 1969.

810 Schwartz, Barry N., and Robert Disch. White racism; its history, pathology and practice. N.Y.: Dell, 1970. (Collection of articles on prejudiced views of the black-man.)

811 Scott, Anne F. The Southern lady from pedestal to politics. Chicago: University of Chicago Press, 1970. (Women's changing role in working outside the home.)

812 Scott, Jack. Athletics for athletes. California: Other Ways Book Dept., 1969.

812a Scott, Maurice Jr. Panther genesis. Tennessee: Aurora, 1970. (A research of the Panther organization beginning with the inquest in Chicago.)

813 Scott, Robert L. The Rhetoric of black power. N.Y.: Harper, 1969. (Black Liberation Movement.)

814 Seale, Bobby. Right on; story of the Black Panthers. N.Y.: Random House, 1970.

815 _____. Seize the time: the story of the Black Panther Party and Huey P. Newton. N.Y.: Random House, 1970.

816 Seaman, Barbara. The Doctor's case against the pill. N.Y.: Wyden, 1969.

816a Segal, Judith A. Food for the hungry: the reluctant society. Baltimore: Johns Hopkins Press, 1970.

817 Segal, Ronald. The Americans: a conflict of greed and reality. N.Y.: Viking, 1969. (English title: "America's Receding Future.")

817a Seligman, Ben B. Economics of dissent. Chicago: Quadrangle, 1968. (Foreword by Clarence E. Ayres.)

818 Servan-Schreiber, J. J. The American challenge. N.Y.: Atheneum, 1968. (U.S. imperialism and the Common Market.)

819 Sexton, Patricia Cayo. The Feminized male. N.Y.: Random House, 1969. (Theory is that "real boys are alienated by our schools which favor feminine attitudes and capabilities. The author attempts to show that those boys who succeed in school tend to be feminized.")

820 Shade, William G. (ed.). Seven on black: reflections on the negro experience in America. N.Y.: Lippincott, 1969.

821 Shaffer, Helen B. Status of women. Washington, D.C.: Congressional Quarterly Inc., 1970. (Pam.)

822 Shaplen, Robert. The Lost revolution: the U.S. in Vietnam, 1946-1966. N.Y.: Harper and Row, 1960.

823 _____. The Road from war: Vietnam 1965-1970. N.Y.: Harper and Row, 1970.

824 _____. Time out of hand: revolution and reaction in Southeast Asia. N.Y.: Harper and Row, 1969.

825 Shaw, Russell. Abortion on trial. Ohio: Pflaum, Press, 1969. (Critical examination of the current practices of abortion.)

825a Shirts, R. Garry. Underground high school news paper editors conference. Pilot policy research center progress report number 3. La Jolla, California: Western Behavioral Science Institute. November 15, 1967.

826 Shotwell, Louisa R. The Harvesters: the story of the migrant people. N.Y.: Doubleday, 1961.

826a Silberman, Charles E. Beware the day they change their minds. N.Y.: American Jewish Committee, 1965. (Pam.) (American Jewish Committee examines the civil rights movement. Reprinted from **Fortune**

Magazine.)

827 _____. Crisis in black and white. N.Y.: Random, 1964.

828 _____. Crisis in the classroom: the remaking of American education. N.Y.: Random House, 1970. (Some new proposals presented as innovative aspects of education.)

829 Slater, Philip E. The Pursuit of loneliness: American culture at the breaking point. Boston: Beacon Press, 1970.

830 Sleeper, Charles F. Black power and Christian responsibility; some biblical foundations for social ethics. Nashville, Tennessee: Abington Press, 1969.

831 Smith, Page. Daughters of the promised land: women in American history. N.Y.: Little, 1970.

832 Smith, Robert F. The United States and Cuba: business and diplomacy, 1917-1960. N.Y.: Bookman Associates, 1961.

833 Smith, William Gardner. Return to black America. New Jersey: Prentice-Hall, 1970. (Description of the racial situation in the U.S. in '68 by an expatriate. Areas discussed are Detroit, Newark, Watts, and Harlem.)

833a Snyder, Gary. Earth house hold. N.Y.: New Directions, 1968. (Paper) (The ecology of the earth and the environmental crisis.)

834 Sobel, Lester A. (ed.). Civil Rights, 1960-1966. N.Y.: Facts on File, Inc., 1967.

835 Solanas, Valerie. S C U M Manifesto. N.Y.: Olympia Press, 1968. (Paper) (A radical analysis of a "Society For Cutting Up Men.")

836 Sorokin, Pitirim A. The Sociology of revolution. N.Y.: Howard Fertig, 1969. (Originally published in 1925)

837 Southard, Samuel. People need people. Philadelphia: Westminster Press, 1970. (Priorities that individuals

have established, and the emphasis on both human and social values.)

838 Sovern, Michael I. Legal restraints on racial discrimination in employment. N.Y.: Twentieth Century Fund, 1966.

839 Sperber, Manes. The Achilles heel. N.Y.: Doubleday, 1960. (He is worth reading for his "Essay on the Left" as well as other topics which include antisemitism.)

840 Spike, Robert W. The Freedom revolution and the Churches. N.Y.: Association Press, 1965.

841 Spiro, Melford E. Kibbutz: venture in Utopia. N.Y.: Schocken, 1970.

841a Spock, Benjamin. Children and discrimination. N.Y.: American Jewish Committee, 1967. (Pam.) (Now in the fifth printing and for parents and children.)

841b _____. Do parents teach prejudice? N.Y.: American Jewish Committee, 1966. (Pam.) (A reprint from Ladies' Home Journal.)

842 _____, and Michael Zimmerman. Dr. Spock on Vietnam. N.Y.: Dell, 1968.

843 Stalvey, Lois Mark. The Education of a WASP. N.Y.: Morrow, 1970.

844 Stapp, Andy. Up against the brass. N.Y.: Simon and Schuster, 1970. (The author's battle against the U.S. Army in his efforts at unionization.)

845 Steeger, Henry. You can remake America. N.Y.: Doubleday, 1969. (Suggests specific proposals to alleviate the conditions of the American negro.)

846 Stein, David L. Living the revolution; the Yippies in Chicago. N.Y.: Bobbs-Merrill, 1970.

847 Steiner, Gary A. The People look at television. N.Y.: Knopf, 1963. (Impact of television broadcasting and the news.)

General 89

848 Steiner, Stan. The New Indians. N.Y.: Harper and Row, 1968. (Red Power!)

849 Steinnmann, Anne. Male and female: fact and fiction. Denver, Colorado: Loretto Heights College, Research Center on Woman, 1970.

850 Stern, Karl. The Flight from woman. N.Y.: Farrar, Straus, 1965. (Male-female polarity and its many implications.)

850a Stevenson, Ian. People aren't born prejudiced. N.Y.: American Jewish Committee, 1969. ("Prejudices can be unlearned." Now in the 8th printing.)

851 Stone, Chuck. Black political power in America. Indianapolis: Bobbs-Merrill, 1968.

852 Storing, Herbert J. (Comp.). What country have I?: Political writing of black Americans. N.Y.: St. Martin's, 1970. (Also available in paper)

853 Strauss, Frances. Where did the justice go? The story of the Giles-Johnson Case. Boston: Gambit, 1970. (Administration of justice in the courts.)

854 Stringfellow, William. My people is the enemy. N.Y.: Holt, Rinehart, and Winston, 1964. (Harlem--conditions--situations.)

855 Strong, Donald S. Negroes, ballots, and judges; national voting rights legislation in the federal courts. Alabama: University of Alabama Press, 1968.

856 Strouse, Jean. Up against the law: the legal rights of people under twenty-one. N.Y.: Signet: New American Library, 1970. (Paper) (Detailed and a major book on a major subject.)

857 Sullivan, Neil V., and Evelyn S. Stewart. Now is the time: integration in the Berkeley schools. Indiana: Indiana University Press, 1969. (School desegregation involving various interested groups in the school and civic community.)

857a Sully, Francois. Age of the guerrilla. N.Y.: Parents' Magazine Press, 1968.

858 Sutherland, Elizabeth. The Youngest revolution; a personal report on Cuba. N.Y.: Dial, 1969.

859 Sweezy, Paul M., Leo Huberman, and Harry Magdoff. Vietnam: the endless war. N.Y.: Monthly Review Press, 1970. (Collection of essays by the editors from 1954 and on.)

860 Swomley, J. M. Jr. Religion, the state and the schools. N.Y.: Pegasus, 1968. (Also available in paper)

861 Szwed, John F. (ed.). Black America. N.Y.: Basic Books, 1970. (22 contributors survey the role of the black man and his culture.)

862 Tabor, Robert. The War of the flea: guerrilla warfare in theory and practice. N.Y.: Lyle Stuart, 1970.

863 Target, G. W. Unholy smoke. Michigan: Eerdmans, 1970. (Paper) (Catholic and Protestant religious confrontations in Ireland.)

864 Taylor, Gen. Telford. Nuremberg and Vietnam, a challenge to America. Illinois: Quadrangle Press, 1970.

865 Teodori, Massimo. The New left; a documentary history. N.Y.: Bobbs-Merrill, 1970. (History of the movement by a participant.)

866 Terkel, Studs. Division street America. N.Y.: Pantheon, 1966. (People tell their own story about "division street.")

867 Thomlinson, Ralph. Demographic problems: controversy over population control. California: Dickenson, 1970.

868 Thompson, Hunter S. Hell's angels: a strange and terrible saga. N.Y.: Random House, 1967.

869 Thompson, Mary Lou (ed.). Voices of the new feminism. Boston: Beacon, 1970. (Paper) (Anthology of women actively engaged in the feminist movement.)

General

870 Thompson, Robert. No exit from Vietnam. N.Y.: McKay, 1969.

871 Tinker, Jerry M. (et al.). Strategies of revolutionary warfare. Conn.: S. Chand (distributed by Lawrence Verry) 1969.

872 Toffler, Alvin. Future shock. N.Y.: Random House, 1970. (The pressures of living and the impact of technology on society.)

873 Totten, W. Fred. The Power of community education. Michigan: Pendell, 1970.

874 Trager, Frank N. Why Vietnam? N.Y.: Praeger, 1966. (Controversial book allegedly subsidized by the USIA. Propaganda supposedly involved.)

875 The Trial of the U 2: The exclusive authorized account. Chicago: Translation World Publishers, 1960. (Paper)

876 Tuccille, Jerome. Radical libertarianism; a right wing alternative. N.Y.: Bobbs-Merrill, 1970.

877 Tucker, Frank H. White conscience. N.Y.: Ungar, 1969. (Deals with the race question in relationship to repressive tactics and imperialism.)

878 Tucker, Robert W. The Radical left and American foreign policy. Baltimore: Johns Hopkins Press, 1970.

879 Tucker, Sterling. Beyond the burning; life and death of the ghetto. N.Y.: Association Press, 1968.

880 _____. Black reflections on white power. Michigan: Eerdmans, 1969.

881 Turner, William W. Hoover's F.B.I. The men and the myth. California: Sherbourne Press, 1969.

881a Tyrrell, C. Merton. Pentagon partners, the new nobility. N.Y.: Grossman, 1970. (Mismanagement of weapons controversy.)

882 Udall, Stewart L. The Quiet crisis. Intro. by John

F. Kennedy. N.Y.: Holt, Rinehart and Winston, 1963.

883 Ulam, Adam B. The Unfinished revolution: an essay on the sources of influence of Marxism and Communism. N.Y.: Random House, 1960.

884 Urofsky, Melvin (ed.). Why teachers strike: Teachers' rights and community control. N.Y.: Doubleday--Anchor, 1970. (Confrontations in the teaching profession.)

885 U.S. Civil Service Commission. Study of minority group employment in the federal government. Washington, D.C.: GPO, 1967.

886 U.S. Commission on Civil Rights. Racial isolation in the public schools. (A Research report) Washington, D.C.: GPO, 1967.

887 U.S. Department of Labor. Wage and Labor Standards Administration. Negro women ... in the population and the labor force. Washington, D.C.: GPO, 1968.

887a U.S. Office of Education. Equality of educational opportunity. Washington, D.C.: GPO, 1966.

888 Vahanian, Gabriel. The Death of God. N.Y.: G. Braziller, 1961.

888a Van den Berghe, Pierre L. Academic gamesmanship. N.Y.: Abelard-Schuman, 1970. (Rewards and pitfalls of university teaching as a career.)

889 Vaughan, Paul. The Pill on trial. N.Y.: Coward, 1970. (Post and future history of the pill and its significance for society.)

890 Vetter, Craig. Anti-semitism's last hurrah in American business. N.Y.: American Jewish Committee, 1969. (Pam.) ("Executive suite discrimination." A reprint from Careers Today.)

891 Veysey, Laurence. Law and resistance: American attitudes toward authority. N.Y.: Harper and Row, 1970.

General

891a Vigman, Fred K. Beauty's triumph. Boston: Christopher, 1966.

891b Vivian, C. T. Black power and the American myth. Philadelphia: Fortress Press, 1970. (Also available in paper.)

892 Vizzard, Jack. See no evil. N.Y.: Simon and Schuster, 1970. (Obscenity, censorship and the law.)

893 Von Hoffman, Nicholas. Left at the post. Chicago: Quadrangle, 1970. (America's political and social life mostly documented by "The Washington Post" of '69 and '70. Topics include both national and international issues.)

894 _____. We are the people our parents warned us against. Chicago: Quadrangle, 1968. (Hippies-- their history and culture.)

895 Wagner, Stanley P. The End of revolution: a new assessment of today's rebellions. N.Y.: A.S. Barnes, 1970. (Descriptions of three major revolutions which have confronted man and his recognition of a utopian life for the future.)

896 Wagstaff, Thomas. Black power: the radical response to white America. N.Y.: Free Press, 1969. (Paper) (The "Insight Series" studies in contemporary issues.)

897 Wakefield, Dan. Supernation at peace and war. Boston: Little, 1968. (Examines selected segments of American society, including protests and rebellion.)

898 Walker, Daniel. Rights in conflict. N.Y.: Bantam, 1968.

899 Walker, John. New theology for plain Christians. N.J.: Dimension, 1970. (Paper)

899a Walsh, Chad. From utopia to nightmare. N.Y.: Harper, 1962.

900 Walsh, Robert E. Sorry ... no government today: unions vs. city hall. Boston: Beacon, 1969. ("Problems in labor organization of public employees.")

901 Walton, Hanes. The Negro in third party politics.
     Philadelphia: Dorrance, 1969.

902 Warburg, James P. Disarmament: the challenge of
     the nineteen-sixties. N.Y.: Doubleday, 1961.

903 Warner, W. Lloyd, B. H. Junker, and W. A. Adams.
     Color and human nature: Negro personality development in a northern city. N.Y.: Harper and Row, 1969.

904 Warren, Robert Penn. Who speaks for the Negro?
     N.Y.: Random House, 1966. (Black Liberation Movement.)

905 Washburn, Wilcomb E. (ed.). The Indian and the white
     man. N.Y.: Doubleday, 1964.

906 Washington, Joseph R. Jr. Marriage in black and
     white. Boston: Beacon, 1970. (Paper) (Highly controversial topics by the director of black studies at the University of Virginia.)

907 Waskow, Arthur I. From race riot to sit-in. N.Y.:
     Doubleday, 1967.

908 _____. Running riot: a journey through official
     disasters and creative disorder in American society.
     N.Y.: Herder and Herder, 1970.

909 Waxman, C. I. End of ideology debate. N.Y.: Funk
     and Wagnalls, 1970.

910 Weatherby, William J. Love in the shadows. N.Y.:
     Stein and Day, 1966. (First published in 1965 under title: "Breaking the Silence." The racial question and the Black Liberation Movement.)

911 Weaver, Gary R., and James H. Weaver. The University and revolution. N.J.: Prentice-Hall, 1969.
     (Paper) (Speeches by individuals who survey the scene in educational reform, and suggests some proposals for the governance of colleges and universities.)

912 Weeks, Kent M. Adam Clayton Powell and the Supreme
     Court. N.Y.: Dunellen, 1970. (Political conflicts

in the administration of justice in the judicial system.)

913 Weisberg, Harold. Whitewash. Maryland: Weisberg, 1966. (Analysis of the Warren Commission Report.)

914 Weiss, Peter. Notes on the cultural life of the democratic republic of Vietnam. N.Y.: Dell, 1970.

915 Wells, John M., and Maria Wilhelm (eds.). The People vs. presidential war. Foreword by Senator J. William Fullbright. N.Y.: Dunellen, 1970. (A collection of accounts of individuals connected with the controversial Shea Bill in Massachusetts.)

916 West, D. J. The Young defender. Baltimore: Penguin, 1967. (Juvenile crime and various approaches to treatment, causes, etc.)

917 Westin, Alan F. Privacy and freedom. N.Y.: Atheneum, 1967.

918 White, Ralph K. Vietnam and the silent majority. N.Y.: Harper and Row, 1970.

919 Whitherspoon, Joseph P. Administrative implementation of civil rights. Austin, Texas: University of Texas Press, 1968.

920 Widick, B. J. Labor today; the triumphs and failures of unionism in the U.S. Boston: Houghton, 1964. (Probes into the conditions of trade unions in the U.S.)

921 Wiggins, Sam P. The Desegregation era in higher education. Berkeley, California: McCutchan, 1966.

922 Williams, John A. The King God didn't save. N.Y.: Coward-McCann, 1970. (Biographical appraisal of Martin Luther King, Jr.)

923 Williams, William Appleman. The Great evasion: an essay on the contemporary relevance of Karl Marx and on the wisdom of admitting the heretics into the dialogue about America's future. Chicago: Quadrangle, 1964.

924 Winter, Gibson. Love and conflict: new patterns in family life. N.Y.: Doubleday, 1969.

925 Wise, William. Killer smog. Chicago: Rand McNally, 1968. (Pollution, smog, and the environment.)

925a Wittes, Simon. People and power: a study of crisis in secondary schools. Michigan: University of Michigan: Institute For Social Research, 1970.

926 Wittner, Lawrence S. Rebels against war: the American peace movement, 1941-1960. N.Y.: Columbia University Press, 1970. (The pro and con of pacifism over three decades.)

927 Wolfe, Tom. The Electric Kool-aid-acid test. N.Y.: Farrar, Straus and Giroux, 1968. (The psychedelic movement including drugs and drug culture.)

928 _____. The Kandy-kolored tangerine-flake streamline baby. N.Y.: Farrar-Straus, 1965. (Sketches of "Pop Society" in contemporary society.)

929 _____. Pump house gang. N.Y.: Farrar, Straus and Giroux, 1968. (More about the "Psychedelic Movement.")

930 Wolff, Kurt H. (ed.). The Critical spirit; essays in honor of Herbert Marcuse, edited by Kurt H. Wolff and Barrington Moore, Jr. with the assistance of Heinz Lubasz, Maurice R. Stein, and E. V. Walter. Boston: Beacon, 1968.

931 Wolff, Robert P. In defense of anarchism. N.Y.: Harper and Row, 1970.

932 _____. The Ideal of the university. Boston: Beacon, 1969. (The crisis in higher education and the governance of colleges and universities.)

933 _____. The Poverty of liberalism. Boston: Beacon, 1969. (Also available in paper) (Political concerns of liberalism.)

934 Wolterstorff, Nicholas. Religion and the schools. Michigan: Eerdmans, 1967. (Paper)

General

935 Wood, Forrest G. Black scare: the racial response to emancipation and reconstruction. California: University of California Press, 1970. (Highly controversial book about "white backlash," "white supremacy," and class conflict.)

936 Woolf, Cecil, and John Bagguley. Authors take sides on Vietnam. N.Y.: Simon and Schuster, 1968. (Paper)

937 Woolstonecraft, Mary. A Vindication of the rights of women. N.Y.: Norton, 1970.

938 Wright, Nathan. Black power and urban unrest. N.Y.: Hawthorn, 1967. (Paper)

939 _____. Let's face racism. New Jersey: Thomas Nelson Inc., 1970. ("What young people can do to bring about needed changes regarding racism especially in the area of religious faith.")

940 _____. Let's work together. N.Y.: Hawthorn, 1968.

941 Yglesias, Jose. In the midst of the revolution. N.Y.: Pantheon, 1968. (A look at the Cuban Revolution by an astute observer.)

942 Young, Alfred E. Dissent; exploration in the history of American radicalism. Illinois: Northern Illinois University Press, 1969.

943 Young, Louise (Comp.). Population in perspective. N.Y.: Oxford University Press, 1968.

944 Young, Michael. The Rise of the meritocracy. N.Y.: Random House, 1960. ("All men are equal, but some ...")

945 Young, Whitney. Beyond racism. N.Y.: McGraw-Hill, 1969.

946 Zagoria, Donald S. Vietnam triangle: Moscow, Peking, Hanoi. N.Y.: Pegasus, 1970.

947 Zeitlin, Maurice, and Robert Scheer. Cuba: tragedy in our hemisphere. N.Y.: Grove, 1963.

948 Ziegler, Benjamin Munn (ed.). Desegregation and the Supreme Court. Boston: Heath, 1958. (Problems in American Civilization Series) (Some historical background on the desegregation issue. Excellent intro. to the problem as well as the role of the U.S. Supreme Court.)

949 Zitron, Celia. New York city teachers union, 1916-1964. N.Y.: Humanities Press, 1968.

EDITORIALS

950 "Abortion: political abortion, emotional, intellectual, clinical abortion," Distant Drummer, 07 02 11 01 70

951 "Abortion and the changing law," Newsweek, 75:53-56, April 15, 1970.

952 "Abortion and the courts," Scientific American, 222:50, January, 1970.

953 "Abortion counseling in legal trouble: Rabbi Ticktin on conspiracy charges," Christian Century, 87:68, January 21, 1970.

954 "Abortion debate," Commonweal, 92:131-2, April 24, 1970.

955 "Abortion, ethics, and the law," Bio Science, 20:741, July 1, 1970.

956 "Abortion unlimited," Newsweek, 75:46, March 9, 1970.

957 "Abortions," Rising Up Angry, 07 -- 05 01 69

958 "Abortions on demand," Newsweek, 76:60, July 13, 1970.

959 "ACLU vs. LAS," Distant Drummer, 08 14 03 01 69 (American Civil Liberties Union confronts with the Legal Aid Society.)

General 99

960 "An active week for the PPF," Pittsburgh Point, 10
30 01 02 69 (The Tactical Patrol Force, Vietnam Moratorium demonstration and the grape boycott, all in Pittsburgh.)

961 "ADA vs. Duggan," Pittsburgh Point, 06 26 01 01 69 (Confrontation between the ADA chapter and the District Attorney in Pittsburgh.)

962 "Adventures in racism," North Carolin Anvil, 02 07 01 01 70

963 "Alcoa: facts Alcoa wants you to know about Alcoa," Grok, 06 27 04 01 70

964 "All desegregation orders obeyed--then, school chaos in Greenville, S.C.," U.S. News, 69:26-28, December 7, 1970.

965 "All power to the people," Black Panther, 01 03 05 01 70

966 "All power to the people: RPCC," Grok, 09 -- 09 01 70 (An address to the Plenary Session by Huey P. Newton in Philadelphia.)

967 "Allen Ginsberg meets Julius Hoffman," Distant Drummer, 12 25 03 01 70 (Questions and answers concerning the revolution, ideology and procedures.)

968 "AMA doctors sidestep abortion issue," Guardian, 07 04 04 01 70

969 "Amendment I. Freedom of Religion, Speech, Press, Assembly, and Petition," Two-Cents Plain Dealer, 11 10 01 02 69 (Contains the 4 point educational revision program advocated by the editors of the Dealer at Millersville State College.)

970 "American capitalism and race relations," Two-Cents Plain Dealer, 03 08 01 03 70 (Interracial conflicts and capitalism.)

971 "America's black silent majority," Atlas, 19:27-28, June, 1970.

972 "America's dirty war," Studies On The Left, 1:1-4,

Number 4, 1961. (Causes of the Cuban revolution.)

973 "The Angela Davis Case," Newsweek, 76:18-24, October 26, 1970.

974 "Another action at Duquesne Club," Pittsburgh Point, 06 05 03 01 69 (Demonstration at the Duquesne Club with controversy over admittance.)

975 "Another checkup on drug use by G. I's," U.S. News, 69:33, August 31, 1970. (Drugs and drug abuses in military services.)

975a "Another court rules against customs grabs," Advocate, 09 02 02 04 70 (Concerns the importation of pornography for private use.)

976 "Another defeat for the CIA.," East Village Other, 11 05 09 01 69

977 "Another look ...," Two-Cents Plain Dealer, 12 01 01 01 69 (Of and about all revolutionary movements.)

978 "Anti-war high school students meet in city," Fifth Estate, 10 01 11 01 67 (DHSSMC organizes to protest war in Vietnam.)

979 "Anti-war soldier's hearing begins," Fifth Estate, 01 01 07 02 67 ("Pvt. Robert Luftig vs. defense secretary Robert McNamara.")

980 "The Army stockade," Liberation News Service, 05 24 03 01 69 (Conditions allegedly existing in Army stockades in Missouri, Oregon, and California.)

981 "As secret as the mafia," Two-Cents Plain Dealer, 11 10 04 03 69 (Controversy over how student funds are being managed at Millersville State College.)

982 "Atlantis peace shop busted," Northwest Passage, 08 05 02 01 69 (Alleged material judged as obscene.)

983 "Attorney Bill Kunstler speaks at UFAF conference," Black Panther, 07 26 10 01 69 (The United Front Against Fascism.)

General

984 "Austin Burton runs for president," Fifth Estate, 10 01 11 03 67 ("Red Power" movement as "Chief Burning Wood" runs on the Indian ticket.)

985 "The Ban and the law," Dallas Notes, 12 08 02 01 67 ("Freedom of the entire university community," in all aspects.)

986 "The Bard Hall incident," Two-Cents Plain Dealer, 04 24 01 01 69 (Confrontation over men's living quarters at Millersville State College.)

987 "Bastille Day in the People's Park," Pittsburgh Point, 07 24 01 03 69 (People's Park confrontations in Berkeley described by the Liberation News Service.)

988 "Bath house raided," Los Angeles Free Press, 05 29 08 03 70

989 "The Battle of Manchester Bridge," Pittsburgh Point, 08 28 04 01 69 (Illustrated with pictures and text depicting the Black Coalition's campaign at Three Rivers Stadium in Pittsburgh. Includes a footnote on p. 7.)

990 "Benefit for DEVA," Fifth Estate, 09 01 12 04 67 (Organization of the DEVA in Birmingham, Michigan.)

991 "Berkeley GLF opts out," Advocate, 11 25 09 04 70 (A split in GL fronts on the west coast to establish a gay government in Alpine County, California.)

992 "Berkeley--Ronald Reagan creats the Fascist state," Black Panther, 05 31 07 01 69 (People vs. police over People's Park in Berkeley.)

993 "Beyond protest," Studies On The Left, 7:3-21, Number 1, Jan.-Feb., 1967. (Evolving political strategy of the New Left and its interrelationships with other movements.)

994 "The Big K image: the other side of the mirror," Pencil In Title Of Your Own Choice, 03 -- 02 01 69 (Big Kiski image (Pittsburgh Area) and the establishment of the high school underground newspaper

with the above title.)

995 "Boycott Standard Oil," <u>Guardian</u>, 04 12 22 01 69

996 "Birch Society celebrates 10 years of paranoia," <u>Liberation News Service</u>, 12 28 04 01 68 (Welch outlines his new proposals "to eliminate the cancerous disease of collectivism.")

997 "Birch society 10 years old," <u>Dallas Notes</u>, 01 08 06 02 69 (A chronology of the history of the society.)

998 "The Bird in Savannah," <u>Great Speckled Bird</u>, 07 07 06 01 69 (Establishment of the underground newspaper in Savannah, Georgia.)

999 "Black America, 1970," <u>Time</u>, 94:13-35, April 6, 1970. (Special Issue)

1000 "Black coalition seeking white allies," <u>Pittsburgh Point</u>, 08 21 01 02 69 (Plans by the coalition group for the demonstration at the north side stadium on August 25 in Pittsburgh, Pa.)

1001 "Black Monday," <u>Pittsburgh Point</u>, 09 11 01 01 69 (The "Black Coalition" and their plans for a demonstration on Sept. 15 to be called "Black Monday," in Pittsburgh, Pa.)

1002 "Black Monday wasn't so black," <u>Pittsburgh Point</u>, 09 18 01 03 69 (Comment on the demonstration "Black Monday" by the Pittsburgh Coalition.)

1003 "The Black Panther," <u>Rising Up Angry</u>, 07 -- 01 01 69

1004 "Black Panther under attack," <u>Washington Free Press</u>, 07 01 07 01 69

1005 "Black Panthers in Kansas City--harassment by local Police," <u>Reconstruction</u>, 03 03 05 01 69

1006 "Black Panther's 10 point program," <u>Loop Whole</u>, 10 24 02 01 69

1007 "Black Panthers: who killed Alex Rackley?" <u>Newsweek</u>, 75:22-23, March 30, 1970.

General

1008 "Black Pittsburgh," June, 1970. (A special 8 page supplement) Grok, 06 -- 09 01 70

1009 "Black power, brothers," Guardian, 10 26 08 01 68 (Black power salute and the expulsion of John Carlos, and Tommie Smith from Mexico.)

1010 "Bugs bite back," Economist, 221:1029, December 3, 1966. (The wiretapping controversy.)

1011 "Bugs in the open," Economist, 230:50, March 29, 1969. (More wiretapping.)

1012 "CBS schedules debate--HHH vs. high school students: classroom hookup planned--teachers urge discussions," New Patriot, 11 15 01 01 67 (Nationwide hookup with a debate between high school students and HHH on the Vietnam War.)

1013 "The Cuban revolution: the new crisis in cold war ideology," Studies On The Left, 1:1-3, 1960.

1014 "Black salute barred," Spokane Natural--Chief Joseph, 05 09 10 01 69

1015 "Boardwalk and park place: Madison housing," Connections, 04 22 12 01 69 (Discrimination (alleged) and housing problems in Madison, Wisconsin.)

1016 "Bobby Seale: Black Panther with a mission," Black Panther, 02 07 03 01 70

1017 "Bombers and radicals," Christian Century, 87:1055, September 9, 1970. (Radical ideology.)

1018 "Booksellers for peace can no longer remain silent," Grok, 09 -- 28 01 70 (Calls for the immediate withdrawal of U.S. troops and the adoption of the McGovern-Hatfield amendment.)

1019 "Boston Panthers," Old Mole, 07 18 17 01 69

1020 "Boycott California grapes," Abas, 05 -- 01 02 69

1021 "Boycott post mortem," Berkeley Barb, 10 28 05

01   66   (A boycott of the Oakland Public Schools in California.)

1022   "Boycott: Safeway would sell your mother if you'd eat her," Washington Free Press, 05   16   10   02   69

1023   "Boycott Standard Oil," Black Panther, 05   04   12   01   69

1024   "Brass play games with G. I. lives," Fifth Estate, 04   17   17   01   69 ("A former commandant of the marine corps charges that high ranking officers prefer war to peace.")

1025   "Britain's abortion act," Christian Century, 87:984-985, August 19, 1970.

1026   "Burning of the Panther 21 defense office and law papers," Black Panther, 04   18   10   01   70

1027   "A busy month for the revolution," Pittsburgh Point, 04   02   05   01   70

1028   "Cal State schedules homophile course for fall quarter," Advocate, 09   16   20   01   70 (Part of the homophile movement at Long Beach, California.)

1029   "Calls for radical reconstruction: educational proposal," New Left Notes, 04   22   03   01   66 (Ideology concerning the political left and right.)

1030   "Can Burrell teachers educate?" Pencil In Title Of Your Own Choice, 03   --   05   01   69 (Controversy concerning academic freedom at Lower Burrell High School in Lower Burrell, Pa.)

1031   "Caribbean landhunt on," The Atlantis News, 02   21   01   02   69 (Article includes the selection criteria for an "independent sovereign nation, although still far from economically self-sufficient.")

1032   "Carmichael and 'Black Unity'," Independent Socialist, 04   --   06   01   68 (Stokeley calls for "black unity" as one direction in the black power movement.)

1033   "The Case of Wesley Robert Wells, twenty-seven

years a political prisoner," Black Panther, 06 21 02 01 69

1034 "Censorship and obscenity: a panel discussion," Dickinson Law Review, LXVI, Summer, 1962, pp. 421-441.

1035 "Cesar Chavez here," Pittsburgh Point, 10 30 01 02 69 (Cesar Chavez's appearance and his demonstration at the produce yards where boycotts were arrested last week.)

1036 "Chairman Bobby beaten," Black Panther, 11 29 02 01 69

1037 "Chairman Bobby kidnapped by Berkeley pigs," Black Panther, 08 23 01 01 69

1038 "Chaos in public schools--the Mississippi story," U.S. News, LXVII:24-26, December 8, 1969.

1039 "Chemical war in Ala.," Great Speckled Bird, 12 01 10 01 69 (Article is from a Fort McClellan underground newspaper--G.I. Left Face.)

1040 "Chicano-Anglo fight at Mar Vista High School," San Diego Free Press, 11 30 02 04 68

1041 "Church gives Perry vote of confidence," Advocate, 08 19 05 01 70 (The article deals with the "question of to what extent the church should be involved with social struggle.")

1042 "The CIA as an equal opportunity employer," Black Panther, 06 07 04 01 69

1043 "CIA at Wis.," Connections, 11 01 08 01 67 (Controversy over the CIA and its activities on the University of Wisconsin campus.)

1044 "Circuit court affirms long hair wins," Grok, 04 -- 16 01 70 ("Editor's Note: The following article was reprinted in toto from Civil Liberties, a publication of the ACLU, Number 266, February, 1970.")

1045 "Civil rights," (Special Issue) Studies On The Left,

4:116-117, Number 1, 1964.

1046 "Civil rights and the birth of community," Studies On The Left, 1:1-3, Winter, 1960.

1047 "Civil rights and the northern ghetto," Studies On The Left, 4:3-15, Number 3, 1964.

1048 "Class structure--a non-issue," Two-Cents Plain Dealer, 10 27 02 01 69 (Situation regarding class structure and the student senate at Millersville State College.)

1049 "Class vs. race," G. I. Voice, 05 02 02 -- 69

1050 "Classrooms now on wheels," East Village Other, 02 07 05 04 69 (Schools in Philadelphia and Colorado experiment with audiobuses to implement the 40 some odd hours which students spend riding a bus to and from school.)

1051 "Cleveland teachers support the November anti-war actions," Burning River News, 11 11 14 01 69 (Cleveland area teachers voice opposition to the war in Vietnam.)

1052 "Collective statement by the Connecticut 9, Political Prisoners," Black Panther, 05 02 06 01 70

1053 "The Coming confrontation, the Church's war investment," Christian Century, 87:1209-1211, October 14, 1970.

1054 "Coming crackdown on smut peddlers; with excerpts from President Nixon's message to Congress, May 2, 1969," U.S. News, 63:52-3, July 21, 1969.

1054a "Coming to terms," Time, 94:82, October 24, 1969. (Homosexuality, the law, and individual conscience.)

1054b "Committees formed in Alpine County to deal with gays," Advocate, 12 09 01 03 70 (A utopian community is being planned and committees set up to deal with the takeover of the county by homosexuals.)

1055 "Common sense: towards a revolutionary socialist

strategy," Old Mole, 07 18 18 01 69

1056 "The Commune comes to America," Life, 67: 16b-24, July 18, 1969.

1057 "Communists are right about some things," Christianity Today, 13:26-27, June 6, 1969. (Obscenity and the law.)

1058 "Community control of education," Guardian, Liberation Forum. 05 25 11 01 68

1059 "Companies bullshit in pollution hearings: public support needed," Grok, 06 27 09 01 70 (Pollution industrial complex and the environmental crisis.)

1060 "Concentration camp ready as war nears," Berkeley Barb, 06 02 01 04 67 (Critical analysis of U.S. foreign policy, and L. B. Johnson.)

1061 "Concerning the obscene; symposium," Wilson Library Bulletin, 42:894-929, October, 1968.

1062 "Confrontation at University of Miami," Daily Planet, 02 28 20 01 70 (Dissention over many administrative policies at Miami.)

1063 "A Conservation at the University Centers for Rational Alternatives," Alternative, 12 -- 09 11 70 (An interview with Todorovich, president of UCRA whose goals and objectives are presented.)

1064 "Conspiracy laid to Macnamara," Berkeley Barb, 05 26 01 01 67

1065 "Conspiracy trial in Kentucky," Liberation News Service. (Conspiracy charges resulting from alleged police brutality in Louisville's racial disorders last summer.)

1066 "The Continuing crisis," Alternative, 12 -- 02 02 70 (Report on the revolution from many interesting angles.)

1067 "Controversy over Lacy U.S. attorney appointment," Common Sense, 03 15 02 01 70 (Controversy about the famed "De Carlo Tapes")

1068 "C. R. A. P. is better than C. L. E. A. N.," Berkeley Barb, 10 21 04 03 66 ("Two groups against proposition 16, the clean proposition to stiffen California pornography and censorship laws.")

1068a "Crisis in juvenile courts," U. S. News, March 24, 1969, pp. 62-64. (New directions and proposals for handling the wave of juvenile crime.)

1069 "Crisis in southern schools--six governors speak out," U. S. News, LXVIII:38-44, February 16, 1970.

1070 "Cuban revolution," Other Scenes, 05 -- 05 01 69

1071 "D. A. Duggan: moral censor," Pittsburgh Point, 02 05 01 03 70 (The censorship and obscenity laws questioned.)

1072 "Dallas man challenges Texas sodomy law," Advocate, 09 -- 02 04 69

1073 "D. C. whites organize to aid ghetto in case of rebellion," Berkeley Barb, 09 01 05 01 67 (Committee organized for emergency support in Washington, D. C.)

1073a "DDT: some junk is free, and some we have to buy--CBW," Alternative, 02 -- 05 03 70

1074 "Dear reader," Pencil In Title Of Your Own Choice, 01 -- 01 01 69 (Editorial policy from the three schools presented: "Published when necessary and necessary when published." Three schools represented are Burrell, Kiski, and Valley, all in the Pittsburgh area.)

1075 "Dear Uncle Tim," Grok, 04 16 03 70 (Dr. Timothy Leary's stint in prison in California.)

1076 "Decency brawl," Distant Drummer, 04 24 12 04 69 (Youth rally for decency ends in tragedy at Baltimore as 40,000 attend.)

1077 "Decker Wright tango--while Reighard fiddles," Two-Cents Plain Dealer, 02 23 01 01 70 (A direct confrontation between two personalities at the campus radio-station UMSR at Millersville State College.)

1078 "Defamation by wire tap; release of transcript of recorded New Jersey mafia conservations," Nation, 210:66-7, January 26, 1970.

1079 "Dellinger's Washington speech," Liberation, 14:4-5, January, 1970.

1080 "Demonstrations challenge New York University policies," Advocate, 10 28 01 01 70 (Demonstrations by the Gay Students League of NYU protesting the university's anti-homosexual policies and discrimination.)

1081 "Denver sued," Chinook, 08 21 03 01 69 (Illegal arrests made in Denver, and a civil suit by ACLU defending people with long hair and unconventional dress.)

1082 "Department store catalogue ruled obscene," Distant Drummer, 10 11 10 04 69 (Interesting catalogue termed erotic art and obscene.)

1083 "Diary of abortion victims: hack operation in apartment," Distant Drummer, 11 07 01 04 69

1084 "Dick Gregory is a mellow person," Son of Jabberwork, 04 19 06 01 68

1085 "The Die is cast," Atlantis News, 05 16 01 01 69 (Includes the contract proposals for operation Atlantis 1A in the Carribbean. Ultimate goal for this stage is sovereignty.)

1086 "Dissent," Veterans Stars and Stripes, 2:2, Summer, 1969.

1087 "The Dow protest: a narrative," Connections, 11 01 02 01 67 (Demonstration in Madison against Dow Chemical Company.)

1088 "Down with your Levis," Fifth Estate, 09 01 02 02 67 (A "burn-in" sponsored by SLAM.)

1089 "Duggan disarmed," Pittsburgh Point, 01 -- 22 02 70 (The obscenity issue with the District Attorney in Pittsburgh, Pa.)

1090 "Duke unions hassle," North Carolin Anvil, 09 27 01 02 69 (Unions and union activities in North Carolina.)

1091 "Durham's high school troubles," North Carolin Anvil, 02 28 02 01 70

1092 "Earth belongs to the people," Pittsburgh Fair Witness, 11 23 04 01 70 (Population crisis and technology.)

1093 "East meets west," The Atlantis News, 03 07 01 02 69 (Rise and fall of the Preform movement (West) and the similiarities with the Libertarian movement (East).)

1094 "Ecology," Win, 08 -- 05 01 69

1095 "Ecology. A cause becomes a mass movement," Life, 68:22-25, January 30, 1970.

1096 "Ecology action is ...," Win, 08 -- 31 01 69

1097 "Ecology and justice for all," Northwest Passage, 04 06 04 01 70

1098 "Ecology and politics," Helix, 06 05 04 01 69

1099 "Ecology revolution," Win, 08 -- 06 01 69

1100 "Eldridge: the ultimatum; statement from Eldridge on the extradiction of Bobby Seale," Grok, 04 -- 14 01 70

1101 "Eldridge Cleavers captured: cartons of Cleaver masks in San Francisco," Los Angeles Free Press, 12 13 01 01 68

1102 "Environmental teach-in," Pittsburgh Point, 03 26 04 01 70

1103 "Equal justice--a joke in Detroit," Fifth Estate, 05 15 04 01 67 (The courts and the administration of justice in Detroit.)

1104 "Equal rights for women," Pittsburgh Point, 11 06 05 03 69 (What the "proposed amendment to the

Pennsylvania Constitution prohibiting discrimination on the basis of sex," means.)

1105 "Equal rights for women? Things may never be the same," U.S. News, 69:29-30, August 24, 1970.

1106 "Erik Erikson: the quest for identity," Newsweek, 76:84-89, December 21, 1970. (Speaks about the controversy on youth and authority, on sexual politics, on America's mastery of machines, on the future of psychoanalysis, on old age, death, and identity.)

1107 "Evidence and intimidation of Fascist crimes by U.S.A.," Black Panther, 02 21 01 01 70

1108 "Faculty apathy," Two-Cents Plain Dealer, 03 03 01 01 69

1109 "Farmer revolutionaries and traditional farm organizations," Trans-action, 5:5, June, 1968.

1110 "The Fate of the underground newspaper," Distant Drummer, 01 22 01 02 70

1111 "F.B.I. on the wire," Economist, 220:144, July 9, 1966.

1112 "The Female strikes back," Pittsburgh Point, 06 05 01 01 69 (Controversy over "The Female" and "Therese and Isabelle.")

1113 "Fighting the enemy: the cold war," G. I. Voice, 02 -- 01 01 69

1114 "Five censorship bills in California legislature," Library Journal, 93:1403, April 1, 1968.

1115 "Five-thousand people tell Milmouse Nixon to stop the war in Viet-Nam," San Diego Free Press, 08 20 02 01 69 (Massive demonstration at the summer White-House.)

1116 "The Foreign language thing," Two-Cents Plain Dealer, 02 09 01 02 70 (The foreign language requirement at Millersville State College.)

1117 "Fort Dix explodes again," Liberation News Service, 06 07 03 02 69 (Conditions of stockades in the military.)

1118 "Fort Hood 3," New Left Notes, 10 07 03 03 66 (Court martialed for their refusal to obey orders to go to Vietnam.)

1119 "Fort Jackson G. I's sue for rights," Veterans Stars and Stripes, 04 -- 01 04 69

1119a "Fort Jackson G. I's win victory," Dull Brass, 05 15 01 02 69

1120 "Fort Lewis G. I's 'fed-up'," Old Mole, 11 07 06 01 69 (Interesting "chain of command" at Fort Lewis, Tacoma, Washington.)

1120a "Fort Sheridan G. I. speaks out," Dull Brass, 05 15 01 01 69

1121 "Foundations in a heap of trouble," Guardian, 05 10 08 01 69 (Government proposals to regulate tax-exempt foundations controversy.)

1121a "Free enterpriser, without any strings," Business Week, 76-9, October 6, 1962.

1121b "Free high school makes a hit," Pittsburgh Point, 07 10 06 03 69 (A drastic departure from the traditional aspects of the high school curriculum.)

1122 "Free Press interviews Mrs. Field on Warren Report 'errors'," Los Angeles Free Press, 12 08 01 03 67 (Marjorie Field and the Warren Commission report.)

1123 "Free speech for G. I's," G. I. Voice, 05 -- 01 02 69

1124 "Free the Catonsville nine," First Issue, 09 27 34 01 68 ("Seven men and 2 women napalmed about 800 draft records in Catonsville Md., on May 17, 1968.")

1125 "Freedom of the G. I. Press," The Ally, 09 01 -- 01 69

General

1126 "GAA zaps Harper's Magazine," Advocate, 11 25 01 01 70 (A peaceful sit-in by the GAA at the offices of Harper's Magazine to protest an article written by Joseph Epstein.)

1127 "Garrison claims Oswald told FBI of conspiracy," Los Angeles Free Press, 01 12 02 04 68

1128 "Garrison says, 'Now our government is lying: Behind the Garrison speech'," Los Angeles Free Press, 11 17 02 04 67

1129 "Garrison vs. Nixon," Great Speckled Bird, 02 24 03 03 69 (Garrison introduces evidence that Kennedy was shot from more than one direction.)

1130 "A Gay nation in the Sierras," Advocate, 11 11 01 01 70 (Description of a gay community proposed for Alpine County in the high Sierras in California.)

1131 "Gays in Louisville choosing sides over liberation group," Advocate, 10 14 02 02 70 (Confrontation between two groups in the gay liberation movement.)

1132 "Get the CIA in from the cold," Ramparts, 5:3-4, July, 1966.

1133 "Ginsberg on March: demonstration on spectacle as example, as communication," Berkeley Barb, 11 19 01 03 65 (Conspicious psychology of the march. (parade) "Can be made into an exemplary spectacle on how to handle situations of anxiety and fear/threat.")

1134 "G. I.'s and black power," G. I. Voice, 06 -- 01 01 69

1135 "G. I's and the anti-war movement," G. I. Voice, 05 -- 01 01 69

1136 "G. I's demand rights: G. I. march set," Fifth Estate, 03 05 03 02 69

1137 "G. I's resist Viet war," Veterans Stars and Stripes, 05 01 -- 04 68

1138 "G. I's revolt; Fort Riley explodes ...," Washington Free Press, 08 -- 14 01 69

1139 "G. I's united," G. I. Voice, 05 -- 01 02 69

1140 "Golf course discrimination," Crisis, LXVII: 440-41, August-September, 1960.

1141 "Golly gee, California is a strange state," Ramparts, 5:12-33, October, 1966.

1142 "Goons gang gay guerrillas," Berkeley Barb, 11 07 06 01 69

1143 "Government planning heroin charges to close down Fort Dix Coffee house," Liberation News Service, 07 19 01 01 69 (Alleged harassment by the government officials.)

1144 "Governor says he'll get rid of every long-hair," Grok, 04 -- 16 02 70 (Long-hair controversy at Nashville, Tennessee.)

1145 "Grape Boycott plans pilgrimage," Pittsburgh Point, 04 23 04 01 70

1146 "Grapes give gas," Daily Planet, 10 24 11 03 69

1147 "Grass is a gas," Conscience, 08 -- 09 01 69

1148 "Green Beret mystery," The Ally, 09 -- 07 03 69

1149 "Green Beret scandal recalls new team," Washington Free Press, 09 -- 04 01 69

1150 "Groups W broadcasters getting it together ...," Grok, 05 -- 19 03 70

1151 "Groupie guidelines for the revolution," Two-Cents Plain Dealer, 12 15 03 01 69 (A description of what women can do to become revolutionary.)

1152 "Guevara: new martyr, or a symbol of communist failure," U.S. News, 63:20, October 23, 1967.

1153 "Gulf action gets ready for action," Pittsburgh Point, 04 23 01 03 70

General

1154 "Hamburger Hill: was it worth it?" The Ally, 06 -- 01 01 69

1155 "Hassle over narcotics control: drug bill compromise still upsets scientists," Science News, 97:339, April 4, 1970.

1156 "Hayakawa, he's our man ...," Pittsburgh Point, 10 09 01 02 69 (Dr. S. I. Hayakawa's subject on the crisis in education at the United Fund of Allegheny County luncheon in Pittsburgh, Pa.)

1157 "Heavy time in pig city," Fifth Estate, 10 16 03 01 69 (Article is by the Fifth Estate staff and Liberation News Service.)

1158 "Hells Angels rumor bugs the ghetto," Berkeley Barb, 11 19 01 02 65 ("Rumors of 'impending incidents' involving Hells Angels and residents of the Berkeley-Oakland border.")

1159 "Here we go again?" Two-Cents Plain Dealer, 02 09 01 03 70 (Controversy in the History department over personalities and politics at Millersville State College.)

1160 "High court frees high priest, opens way for new marijuana laws," Marijuana Review, 06 -- 03 01 69 (The "Leary Case" and its implications for marijuana laws.)

1161 "High noon for the hospitals," Pittsburgh Point, 11 27 01 01 69

1162 "High school long hairs," Kaleidoscope, 01 03 03 03 69 ("Suit filed in U.S. District Court by the ACLU on behalf of two boys expelled from high school in Madison, Wisconsin.")

1163 "High school students pick up the fight, put the ruling class uptight," Liberation News Service, 09 18 05 01 69

1164 "High school students split," Fifth Estate, 05 16 15 02 68 (High School students protest the Vietnam war with student strikes.)

1165 "The Hilton bust," Pittsburgh Point, 06 26 11 01 69 (Protest episode at the Hilton Hotel in Pittsburgh, Pa.)

1166 "Hippies move to ease tension in Ocean Beach," San Diego Free Press, 03 14 03 01 69 (Relations between O.B. Hippies and S.D. police tense and allegedly deteriorating.)

1167 "The History department," Two-Cents Plain Dealer, 12 15 04 01 69 (An editorial asking the department to state its short-term and long-term goals at Millersville State College.)

1168 "Hitler Lives," Ann Arbor Argus, 06 19 03 01 69

1169 "Ho Chi Minh's last will and testament," San Jose Red Eye, 09 26 08 03 69

1170 "Homosexual rights," Berkeley Barb, 09 12 04 03 69

1171 "Homosexuality isn't valid reason to deny job, court tells university," Advocate, 09 30 01 03 70 (The question of homosexual civil rights and employment.)

1172 "Homosexuality not so bad, Lutherans, Unitarians decide," Advocate, 08 05 01 04 70

1173 "How I got in, and why I came out of the cold," (as told to the editors.) Ramparts, 5:17-21, April, 1967. (The first part of a 3 part series dealing with the Central Intelligence Agency.)

1174 "How many G.I's really died?" Two-Cents Plain Dealer, 02 23 03 03 70 (A reprint from the Guardian on the so-called credibility gap.)

1175 "How radicals make money," Time, 95:52, June 22, 1970.

1176 "How SDS will stir up workers," Nation's Business, 57:74-79, July, 1969.

1177 "How the caucus sees the difference," Pittsburgh Point, 10 30 03 01 69 (Following is the text

General

of the Black Caucus's evaluations of mayorality candidates Tabor and Flaherty, in Pittsburgh, Pa.)

1178 "How the CIA turns foreign students into traitors," (As told to the editors.) Ramparts, 5:22-24, April, 1967. (The second of a three part series dealing with the Central Intelligence Agency.)

1179 "How to foil the SDS," Pittsburgh Point, 07 31 05 01 69 ("Reprinted (article) is a notice distributed by the Pittsburgh C of C to all of its members. The editors of the Point feel that this remarkable document deserves wider circulation.")

1180 "Huey on women's and gay liberation," Grok, 09 -- 10 02 70 (Speaking for and about all the oppressed groups.)

1181 "Huey P. Newton attacks Carmichael," Burning Spear, 09 21 15 01 70 (Newton accuses Carmichael of "being an agent for the CIA.")

1182 "Human be-ins," Fifth Estate, 05 15 02 02 67 (Bryam Lake Park, Linden, Michigan.)

1183 "Hundred demonstrate: free Angela Davis," Burning Spear, 10 30 03 01 70

1184 "Hunger week," Pittsburgh Point, 02 05 01 03 70

1185 "I'm all right," Pittsburgh Point, 03 05 04 02 70 (Controversy over the underground newspaper of the same title.)

1186 "In America, the car is the king," Burning Spear, 12 01 16 01 70 (Description of the automobile industry as the profit maker.)

1187 "Inauguration days," East Village Other, 01 31 03 01 70 (Protest at the Capital during the presidential inauguration.)

1188 "Indians demand tribe rights," Guardian, 06 06 04 01 70 (Indian activism. "Confrontations between Indians and the BIA over 'tribe rights'.")

1189 "Indians fight for rights," Liberation News Service,

01 09 25 01 69

1190 "Industrial-military complex," San Diego Free Press, 04 11 13 01 69 (Government contracts "defense" and retired military officers.)

1191 "In search of a radical identity," New Left Notes, 04 29 04 01 66 (Reasons are radical.)

1192 "Interview: Baldwin/Newton," Great Speckled Bird, 03 02 10 01 70

1193 "Interview with Angela Davis," Black Panther, 11 01 05 01 69

1194 "Interview with Bearhead--Tom Swaney," Spokane Natural--Chief Joseph, 05 09 02 01 69

1195 "Interview with conspiracy eight attorneys," Black Panther, 11 08 18 01 69

1196 "An Interview with Harold Mulvey, judge in the Bobby Seale case," Black Panther, 05 31 28 01 70

1197 "Introduction to the New Party; Robert Kunst, state coordinator speaks out in an effort to intercept an ABM," Daily Planet, 04 18 06 01 69

1198 "Is abortion a right?" Christian Century, 87:624-31, May 20, 1970.

1199 "It's time to vote," Two-Cents Plain Dealer, 12 01 01 03 70 (An article about the appointment of students to the faculty senate and the responsibilities involved.)

1200 "JFK's killers known; investigator confirms," Berkeley Barb, 04 07 01 02 67 ("The Evidence is conclusive that ... a very powerful domestic force planned the events which culminated in the death of President Kennedy.")

1201 "Joan Baez critique of hippies," Berkeley Barb, 09 22 05 04 67

1202 "John Sinclair: ten years for two cigarettes of killer weed?" Grok, 06 27 10 03 70

General

1203 "J.O.M.O.: an ideological statement," Burning Spear, 12 01 09 01 70 (History of the J.O.M.O.)

1204 "Just like Joan Baez," Pittsburgh Point, 09 04 01 01 69 (Joan Baez and her concert sponsored by the Pittsburgh Draft Resistance at Point State Park.)

1205 "Kent Ford bail hearing," Willamette Bridge, 07 07 04 01 69

1206 "Kesey calls for sanity," Rolling Stone, 06 11 13 04 70

1206a "The Kid they killed at Altamont," Berkeley Barb, 12 19 01 02 69

1207 "Kiski area's underground--the games are over, school pride, the censor, education (and) a question of tactics," Pencil In Title Of Your Own Choice, 03 -- 01 01 69

1208 "KTLA cancels show on RFK probe," Los Angeles Free Press, 07 10 01 01 70 (KTLA radio station in Los Angeles.)

1209 "Kunstler lets his (short) hair down in Chicago," Distant Drummer, 02 05 12 02 70

1210 "Labor: the year of confrontation," Time, 95:87-88, April 13, 1970.

1210a "L.A. gay lib. pickets theatre, bar, changing community exploited," Advocate, 08 19 03 03 70 (Confrontation of the GLF and changing community concepts in Los Angeles.)

1211 "Language and conflict on the left," Paper Tiger, -- -- 03 01 68 (Dissatisfaction with progress being made on "the left.")

1212 "La Raza students shut down Safeway," Black Panther, 09 20 05 01 69

1213 "Latest plans for May 24 peace march," Pittsburgh Point, 05 -- 01 03 69 (Description of the organization for the Peace March on May 24th in

Pittsburgh.)

1214 "Lawrence Drug trials," Reconstruction, 05 21 03 01 69 (Aspects of drug and drug culture.)

1215 "Laws for children on obscenity argued," Publishers' Weekly, 193:69, January 29, 1968.

1216 "Learning about the Vietnamese," Pittsburgh Point, 01 08 11 01 70

1217 "Leary sentenced to ten years for pot," Grok, 04 -- 16 02 70 (Timothy Leary's sentence in Houston.)

1218 "Left conference sees U.S. as complex," North Carolin Anvil, 09 27 07 01 69

1219 "Legal abortions: a pregnant question," Christianity Today, 14:43, November 21, 1969.

1220 "A Lesson in civics at Perry High School," Pittsburgh Point, 12 11 01 01 69

1221 "Liberal vs. radicals: is there a radical difference," Humanist, 30:7-13, July-Aug., 1970.

1222 "The Liberation of Kate Millett," Time, 96:18-19, August 31, 1970.

1223 "Liberating Wilmington," Distant Drummer, 01 23 08 01 69 (Demonstration at Wilmington, Delaware with three goals presented. Demonstration was against the occupation by the National Guard and Dupont.)

1224 "Librarians ask McConnell case probe," Advocate, 11 11 03 03 70 (Controversy over hiring James McConnell as librarian at the University of Minnesota. Controversy is with the University Board of Regents.)

1225 "List of recognized chapters and branches and NCCFS of the Black Panther Party," Black Panther, 06 20 22 01 70

1226 "Lives of the presidents," Two-Cents Plain Dealer, 02 23 03 02 70 (An article about William H.

Duncan, theologian.)

1227 "Local 1199 aims at another target," Pittsburgh Point, 12 11 10 02 69

1228 "Local 1199 hits Pittsburgh," Pittsburgh Point, 11 06 11 06 02 01 69 ("Local 1199, the union that mobilized hospital workers in Charleston, S.C., earlier, has come to Pittsburgh.")

1229 "Local SDS breaks with National office," Northwest Passage, 10 21 05 01 69

1230 "The Love experiment in Haight," Avatar, 06 09 12 01 67 (Confrontations at Haight-Ashbury in San Francisco.)

1231 "LSD not to blame in Linkletter death," Chinook, 11 06 03 02 69 (Included in this article are quotes from both the girl's brother and father.)

1232 "Lucky rapes grapes," Renaissance, 01 15 04 01 70

1233 "Mafia and the law; release of FBI transcripts of recorded conversations of the New Jersey mafia," Commonweal, 91:444, January 23, 1970. (Wiretapping activities by the FBI in New Jersey.)

1233a "Malcolm X," Rising Up Angry, 09 -- 06 01 69

1234 "Malcolm X on power, politics and organizing," New Left Notes, 11 18 03 01 66 ("Philosophy of Black Nationalism.")

1235 "The 'man' menaces the mobilization," Berkeley Barb, 10 13 03 01 67

1236 "Man versus the computer," Kaleidoscope, 01 03 15 01 69 (The Human vs. the computer. "It takes a man to fix a machine.")

1237 "Manson's declaration of innocence," Los Angeles Free Press, 11 27 01 01 70 (The transcript of Manson's testimony.)

1238 "Marcuse, Angela address new cadre," Berkeley Barb,

10 31 05 01 69

1239 "Marcuse lathers legion," San Diego Free Press, 12 13 02 04 68 (A speech at the American Legion Post, San Diego County, California.)

1240 "Marijuana: is it time for a change in our laws?" Newsweek, 76:20-21, September 7, 1970.

1241 "Marijuana laws," Two-Cents Plain Dealer, 03 19 04 01 69

1242 "Marine Corps 'Underground'," Berkeley Barb, 06 17 02 03 66 (Controversy over "Gargoyle" published in North Carolina.)

1243 "Marxist listen," Washington Free Press, 08 01 11 01 69

1244 "Mattachine of Pittsburgh," Grok, 09 -- 10 01 70 (Goals and objectives of the society are outlined for the Pittsburgh organization.)

1245 "Mattachine raps CBS on job discrimination," Advocate, 07 22 04 01 70 (The New York chapter raps on discrimination in hiring.)

1246 "Mayday in New Haven," East Village Other, 05 05 01 01 70

1247 "The Meaning of company A," G. I. Press Service, 09 18 106 01 69

1248 "Menominee Indians," Connections, 03 11 11 01 69 (Problems of the American Indians.)

1249 "A Message for white radicals," Reconstruction, 03 03 06 01 69

1250 "Mexicans here protest U. C. bias," Berkeley Barb, 01 13 05 02 67 (Chicano-Anglo confrontations.)

1251 "The Military-agricultural complex," G. I. Free Press, 09 18 110 01 69

1252 "Minnesota Indians speak out," Liberation News Service, 04 17 18 02 69 (AIM and its efforts to

General 123

combat police action to Indian youth in Minnesota.)

1253 "Modern women," Two-Cents Plain Dealer, 03 08 03 02 70 (Article deals with the multi-dimensional role of today's women.)

1254 "Moratorium makes good," Northwest Passage, 10 21 02 01 69

1255 "The Moratorium, the war and the empire," Ramparts, 8:6-8, December, 1969. (National anti-war sentiment.)

1256 "Morgan-Gwyther trial," Willamette Bridge, 07 07 05 01 69

1257 "Morton Sobell free, glad to see America in ferment," Distant Drummer, 01 23 14 02 69 (Political nature of the Sobell trial.)

1258 "The Movement and pollution," Two-Cents Plain Dealer, 02 23 03 02 70 (The Silent majority, air-pollution, and the environmental crisis.)

1259 "Muhammed Ali at WSU," Fifth Estate, 05 29 16 01 69 ("The solution to the race problem is separation.")

1260 "My Snapper Days, by guess who," Two-Cents Plain Dealer, 02 17 01 01 69 (Background information on the underground newspaper.)

1261 "My Snapper Days, continued...," Two-Cents Plain Dealer, 03 03 06 01 69

1262 "Nader on the 'new left'," New Left Notes, 04 29 05 02 66 ("He's the original Lone Ranger, and he doesn't even have Tonto.")

1263 "National Guard murders four Kent students," Guardian, 05 09 03 01 70

1264 "Natural interview with Dr. Spock," Spokane Natural --Chief Joseph, 05 09 12 01 69

1265 "Nature is part of our humanity; we pay a tribute to Henry Beston," Green Revolution, 04 -- 01 03

        67 (Beston's "Outermost House" first published in 1928 is compared to Thoreau's Walden. The new edition to "Outermost House" is 1966.)

1266   "Nazis dismayed by Panthers," Berkeley Barb, 05 26 01 03 67 (The East Bay American Nazis, and the Black Panthers.)

1267   "NCCF harrassment...," Grok, 09 -- 03 01 70

1268   "The Need to get out of the war in Vietnam: an intellectual appeal," Two-Cents Plain Dealer, 10 27 01 02 69

1269   "A New coalition," Pittsburgh Point, 12 11 01 03 69

1270   "New desegregation targets: the north--and the suburbs," U.S. News, 69:25-27, December 14, 1970.

1271   "New drug discovered," Behind the Shield, -- -- (Vol. 9) 69

1272   "The New feminism," Ladies' Home Journal, 87:64-71, August, 1970.

1273   "The 'New Left' in action," U.S. News, 66:35-37, May 19, 1969.

1274   "New look at wiretapping: pro and con discussion," Senior Scholastic, 96:10-11, February 9, 1970.

1275   "New peace motto: 'Dow Shalt not kill,'" Los Angeles Free Press, 02 02 14 02 68 (Protesting the Dow-Chemical Corporation and its role in chemicals for the war effort.)

1276   "New urgency on Vietnam," Liberation, 14:4, July, 1969.

1277   "New York abortion: the butchers are out of business," Distant Drummer, 06 18 07 01 70

1278   "New York Panther 21 trial makes false start," Black Panther, 12 06 05 01 69 (New York 21 convicted of bombing conspiracy in Manhattan.)

General 125

1279 "News from the Plainfield Joint Defense Committee," Black Panther, 09 06 09 01 69 (Bobby Lee Williams and the defense committee in Plainfield, New Jersey.)

1280 "News release: Point Park peace committee takes firm stand on war," Grok, 04 -- 14 01 70 ("Editor's Note: The following is a letter sent to the officers in charge at the Marine Recruiting Station in the Federal Bldg., 1000 Liberty Ave., (In Pittsburgh) March 10, 1970.")

1281 "The Night they raided Wickersham," Two-Cents Plain Dealer, 02 08 04 02 70 (Description of the police raid on Wickersham Hall at Millersville State College and the principals involved.)

1282 "Nixon and Cambodia," Northwest Passage, 05 18 04 03 70 (Nixon and the escalation of war in Cambodia.)

1283 "Nixon's ghetto plan," Son of Jabberwork, 11 08 06 02 68

1284 "Nixon's magical mystery tour," The Ally, 09 -- 07 01 69

1285 "Nixon's role and plans," Newsweek, 58:72, July 10, 1961.

1286 "No new jails for Phila's children," Distant Drummer, 08 21 03 01 69 (Description of detention facilities in Philadelphia, studied by the ACIU.)

1287 "Noisy minority set for Washington," Pittsburgh Point, 11 06 01 01 69

1288 "North West Quakers demand action on war," Spokane Natural, 05 09 05 02 69

1289 "Northern Ireland's violent summer," Life, 69:48 September 4, 1970.

1290 "NOW v. the press," Pittsburgh Point, 01 08 02 03 10 (Hearings charging the Pittsburgh Press with the "practice of listing employment ads under separate 'male' and 'female' headings as a violation of the city's Human Relations ordinance.")

1291 "The Oakland seven strike back," First Issue, 03 11 10 01 68

1292 "Obedience to the law is freedom," Chicago Kaleidoscope, 06 06 18 01 69 (Public reaction to Army stockades.)

1293 "The Obscenity trip," Berkeley Barb, 10 24 10 01 69

1294 "October 1966. Black Panther Party Platform and Program," Black Panther, 01 04 21 01 69 ("What we want, what we believe.")

1295 "The Old (?) Nixon," Pittsburgh Point, 08 07 02 02 69 (Some relevant dispatches from The New York Times from several years ago.)

1296 "The Omnibus Bill," Illustrated Paper, 02 -- 04 02 67 ("The Bill to determine the culture of the Indian people.")

1297 "On television and free speech," Damascus Free Press, 05 -- 04 01 69

1298 "On the Vietnam moratorium: Connie Matthews at San Jose State," Black Panther, 10 25 11 01 69

1299 "One-thousand gays riot in New York," Advocate, 09 30 01 01 70 (Gays confront police with contentions of harassment.)

1300 "Open campus: are students ready?" Nation's Schools, 86:17-20, July, 1970.

1301 "Our actions were deemed necessary," Grok, 09 -- 09 01 70 (The boom boom. The August 24 explosion of the Army mathematics research center at Madison, Wisconsin.)

1302 "Our platform," Two-Cents Plain Dealer, 02 17 01 01 69 (A description of the editorial policy for future issues.)

1303 "Our platform: a destatement," Two-Cents Plain Dealer, 10 02 01 01 69 (Essentially a re-statement of editorial policy.)

1304 "Owens on probation," Pittsburgh Point, 02 12 04 01 70

1305 "Panther statement," Washington Free Press, 07 01 06 01 69

1306 "Panthers conference," Northwest Passage, 08 05 08 01 69

1307 "Panthers in Pittsburgh," Pittsburgh Point, 01 22 01 02 70

1308 "The Path of Angela Davis," Life, 69:21-27, September 11, 1970.

1309 "A Patriot speaks up," Common Sense, 05 01 03 02 70 (The patriot is Robert De Pugh.)

1310 "Peace decal unpatriotic?" Grok, 04 -- 18 01 70 (Controversy over the flag decal depicting the peace sign.)

1310a "The (Peace) symbol ... its origin--its meaning," Library News Bulletin, Washington State Library, Olympia, Washington. 38, No. 1:31-32, Jan-Mar., 1971.

1310b "Peace symbols; the truth about those strange designs," American Opinion, June, 1970, pp. 41-56.

1311 "Peaceful week for the Black Coalition," Pittsburgh Point, 10 02 01 03 69 (A discussion in the "Black construction coalition's conflict with the trade unions and builders.")

1312 "Pentagon off limits? The road to dictatorship," Rough Draft, 10 -- 06 01 69

1313 "Peoples' park," Miami Free Press, 06 -- 06 01 69

1314 "Persecution: witness for the ...," East Village Other, 12 01 20 01 67 (Students confronted and interrogated on college campuses by the FBI during anti-war demonstrations October 5-21.)

1315 "Perry busted as he, 7 others start fast," Advocate,

07 22 02 01 70 ('Fast' is over homosexual law reform.)

1316 "Pete Seeger raps," Miami Free Press, 05 20 14 01 69

1317 "Philadelphia Quakers arrested," Distant Drummer, 06 12 18 04 69 (Quaker action group and others arrested in Washington, D.C. protesting the U.S. involvement in the Vietnam war.)

1318 "Picnic for the King from the Gulf Action Project," Pittsburgh Point, 04 16 01 03 70 (A picnic to be held April 18, by "The conspiracy to incite monarchy, a subsidiary division of the Gulf Action Project" in honor of Richard King Mellon.)

1319 "Pig beating escalates colonial repression," Burning Spear, 12 01 03 01 70 (Confrontation at the 'colony' in St. Petersburg, Florida.)

1320 "Pigas fells black cop at the Barb," Berkeley Barb, 02 20 04 01 70

1321 "Pigs bomb Des Moines Panther headquarters," Black Panther, 05 11 02 01 69 (Bombed April 27, 1969. Free breakfast program temporarily halted.)

1322 "Pink Panthers gay revolution toughening up," Berkeley Barb, 04 18 11 04 69 (Rights for the "Pink Panthers" emphasized.)

1323 "Pittsburgh companies in the war business," Pittsburgh Point, 10 09 04 02 69 (A line-up of defense contracts let to Pittsburgh companies.)

1324 "Pittsburgh contributes: rehabilitation of our Mother earth and her peoples; Army urges cops to use CS gas," Grok, 04 -- 11 01 70 ("Concerning 'street cleaner,' 'pepper fog' and a 'new super strength type CS ... non-lethal street cleaner' of almost unbelievable power.")

1325 "The Pittsburgh 5," Pittsburgh Fair Witness, 11 23 19 03 70 (Confrontation in the court room during a police riot on March 19, 1970. Police allegedly pulled long hair.)

1326 "Pittsburgh 5: People's suit vs. pigs enters Federal Court," Grok, 09 -- 19 01 70 (Pittsburgh 5 vs. police over picketing at a draft board member's house.)

1327 "Pittsburgh's own political trials," Pittsburgh Point, 02 12 04 02 70 (Repressive tactics claimed in Pittsburgh.)

1328 "Plans laid for reading room for activists," Berkeley Barb, 02 25 05 03 66 (A Reading room is designed "where people can become acquainted with the political literature of activism.")

1329 "A Plea for Democracy," Two-Cents Plain Dealer, 04 24 02 02 69 (A list of demands presented to the administration at Millersville State College by the editors of the Plain Dealer.)

1330 "Policing the third sex," Newsweek, 74:76, October 27, 1969.

1331 "Policy of our house," Grok, 02 -- 02 01 70 ("Published as an alternative to tradition." It functions "independently and without political persuasion ...")

1331a "Pornography panel; chairman says report 'a beginning'," Advocate, 10 28 01 03 70 (Current status on obscenity.)

1332 "Possible site formed," The Atlantis News, 03 21 01 01 69 (Description of East Cay in the Carribbean. The site for Atlantis 1A.)

1333 "Power at Cornell out of the barrel of a gun," Black Panther, 05 11 05 01 69

1334 "Power to the people," Old Mole, 08 01 03 01 69

1335 "Preacher out to stop Alpine takeover," Advocate, 11 25 10 03 70 (Confrontations between Fundamentalists and GLF in attempts to establish a gay government in Alpine County, California.)

1335a "Presidential panel says porn harmless; may ask legalization," Advocate, 09 02 01 01 70 (Describes the stormy existence of the committee with various dissenting groups.)

1336 "President's report on pot: Presidential Commission revokes 'killer drug' theory," Great Speckled Bird, 04 10 16 01 68 (Description of the 340 page report especially "Narcotics and Drug Abuse.")

1337 "Presidio stockade," Great Speckled Bird, 02 07 02 03 69 (Description of 27 G.I's in the midst of a court-martial proceeding in San Francisco.)

1338 "Press conference with Charles Garry and David Hilliard," Black Panther, 11 08 03 01 69

1339 "Press release politics," Great Speckled Bird, 05 12 07 02 69 (Meeting of the Atlanta Student Mobilization Committee to discuss anti-war, high school student rights, defense of Fort Jackson 8, and plans for a high school counter-commencement rally.)

1340 "Prison rebellions in New York," Burning Spear, 10 13 08 01 70 (Open insurrection in New York's prisons. Article written by Liberation News Service.)

1341 "Progress report on Pittsburgh revolution," The Peacemaker, 09 -- 02 01 69

1342 "Proposals for meaningful student faculty relations," Two-Cents Plain Dealer, 03 03 08 01 69

1343 "The Prosecution of Dean Conway," Two-Cents Plain Dealer, 05 10 03 01 69 (Women students and dormitory problems at Millersville State College.)

1344 "Psychologists get gay lib therapy," Advocate, 11 11 01 01 70 (Direct confrontation between Los Angeles GLF and the Behavioral Modification Conference at the Biltmore Hotel.)

1345 "Public employees finance DOW," Burning River News, 07 07 06 01 69

1346 "Publishing is not a crime, we are not the criminals!" Los Angeles Free Press, 07 24 03 01 70

(Interview with CBS.)

1347 "Quotations from chairman Walker," Water Tunnel, 03 10 08 01 69 (Eric Walker, President, Pennsylvania State University.)

1348 "Racial clashes O.K. with brass?" The Ally, 09 -- 06 01 69

1349 "Racism," Washington Free Press, 08 01 09 01 69

1350 "Rampage," Ramparts, 8:54-59, August, 1969. ("...under the direction of Dugald Stermer, with Robert Scheer, former F.B.I. agent Bill Turner (who drafted the final report) Harvey Cohen and private investigator Harold Lipset, Ramparts compiled this detailed chronology of a bloody rampage through the streets of Berkeley, on Thursday, May 15, by a 15 man squad of 'peace officers,' including the tragic facts surrounding the killing of James Rector."

1351 "Reagan cheers, 'look' attacks Alioto oinks," Black Panther, 09 13 05 01 69

1352 "Rebelling women--the reason," U.S. News, 68:35-37, April 13, 1970.

1353 "Rebellions break out in Ft. Riley and Ft. Jackson stockades," Liberation News Service, 06 28 14 01 69

1354 "Redwood country for sex," Berkeley Barb, 07 21 03 03 67 (The sexual revolution and changing attitudes towards sexual freedom.)

1355 "Regarding obscenity and the Supreme Court," Wilson Library Bulletin, 41:997, June, 1967.

1356 "Regarding the recent self-felicitation by the Burrell administration on the New Dress Code," Pencil In Title Of Your Own Choice, 03 -- 02 01 69 (Controversy over the dress code at Lower Burrell High School, Penna.)

1357 "Rent-a-pig," Hard Times, 09 22 03 01 69

(Hoover and the F.B.I.)

1358 "Repression," Grok, 02 -- 14 01 70 (Repressive tactics in Pittsburgh, Pa.)

1359 "Repression again: this time it's international," Grok, 04 -- 21 01 70 (Struggles on the international level in the sights and travel areas.)

1360 "Repression and the Chicago eight," Ramparts, 8:7-10, January, 1970.

1361 "Resist and rebel: resist until death, let them have what remains," Pittsburgh Point, 11 04 02 01 70 (William Kunstler and Rennie Davis speak at Pittsburgh's Carnegie Hall on Oct. 23 about the revolutionary movement in this country.)

1362 "Resistance meets repression," Peninsula Observer, 06 30 04 01 69

1363 "Rev. Perry sets fast for gay rights on Hollywood Blvd.," Advocate, 07 08 01 05 70 (The fast was on Hollywood Blvd., June 28 by the spokesman for the group. The contention is that the laws discriminate against the homosexual.)

1364 "Rev. Ralph Abernathy speaking at the University of Miami," Daily Planet, 02 28 13 01 70

1365 "Revolution no game," Berkeley Barb, 06 27 03 01 69 (Eldridge Cleaver and aspects of the revolution.)

1366 "The Revolutionary value of art," Two-Cents Plain Dealer, 03 08 03 01 70 ("Describes the theoretical revolution expounded by revolutionary artists like, "The Beatles," "The Guerrilla Theater," "Norman Mailer," "Pueblo Picasso," and 'Henry Miller." The theoretical revolution is described as "that of the arts, religion, and philosophy.")

1367 "Right on, Nick Johnson," Rolling Stone, 06 11 16 01 70

1368 "Right to be let alone," Economist, 226:28, January, 6, 1968. (Individual rights of privacy questioned.)

General

1369 "A riot against the law's delay," Newsweek, 76:20-25, August 24, 1970. (Reform proposals and the law.)

1370 "Riot narrowly averted--Cops bust, beat SNCC member," Dallas Notes, 07 02 03 01 69

1371 "The Rise of the Fourth Reich: Garrison points toward a high-level government conspiracy," Los Angeles Free Press, 12 22 03 01 67

1372 "The Rise of the underground Church," Kaleidoscope, 07 12 02 02 68 (Movement of "free Churches" within the Roman Catholic Church.)

1373 "Rising clamor for black separatism," U.S. News, 69:82, September 21, 1970.

1374 "Robert Morris: dress rite--dress code 1 2 3 4," Pittsburgh Fair Witness, 11 04 13 01 70 (The highly controversial dress code at Robert Morris College in Pittsburgh, Pa.)

1375 "Rothbard draws big crowd," The Atlantis News, 02 07 01 01 69 (Confrontation between "libertarians and the present government-industry structure.")

1376 "Rothschild bank syndrome: USA faces disastrous collision between world anarchy and world order envisioned by the Jews," Common Sense, 06 15 01 01 70

1377 "Rubin vs. Ochs; perhaps not untypical," Fifth Estate, 05 01 07 01 68 (Yippie movement.)

1378 "A Sad ovation for the old man," Los Angeles Free Press, 04 16 06 01 65 (Sinclair (Upton) speaking at Beverly Hills High School tells the student body about social reform of another era and another time.)

1379 "San Diego gets big dick," San Diego Free Press, 01 16 04 01 69 (Nixon in San Diego and big business.)

1380 "San Diego high school administration slowly yields as

student awareness increases," San Diego Free Press, 03 11 03 01 69 (Liberalization in dress codes and ethnic studies at San Diego High Schools.)

1381 "San Francisco GLF affirms Alpine support," Advocate, 12 09 03 04 70 (GLF approves and supports efforts to establish a utopian society.)

1382 "San Quentin prisoners plan February 15 work strike," Los Angeles Free Press, 02 02 01 01 68

1383 "The School and the courts," Alternative, 02 -- 04 01 70 (Self government of schools, segregation in education, and the involvement of the school in courts of law.)

1384 "School desegregation: the final breakthrough," U.S. News, 69:15-16, September 14, 1970.

1385 "Schools ban Bird," Great Speckled Bird, 11 11 05 01 68 (Great Speckled Bird banned in Walker and Shamrock High Schools, in DeKalb, Georgia.)

1386 "SDS--a step forward," Helix, 07 04 04 01 69

1387 "SDS battles police," Fifth Estate, 10 02 02 02 69 (SDS has direct confrontation with police in Detroit.)

1388 "The SDS convention: a layman's guide," Helix, 07 04 04 03 69

1389 "SDS five on trial," Los Angeles Free Press, 05 29 13 01 70

1390 "SDS in court," Pittsburgh Point, 10 02 01 01 69 (Confrontation with Weathermen and Weatherwomen in Pittsburgh, Pa.)

1391 "SDS ousts Progressive Labor," Willamette Bridge, 07 07 06 03 69 (A Reprint from the Guardian.)

1392 "SDS vs. media," Reconstruction, 05 21 02 03 69

1393 "Sex crimes haven't gone up; nothing rotten in Denmark," Advocate, 09 16 08 01 70 (Sex crimes remained low where the sale of erotica was legalized in 1969 in Denmark.)

1394 "Sexual privacy release," Berkeley Barb, 12 22 04 01 67 (Sexual freedom and the right of privacy.)

1395 "SF library opposed to Taylor talk," Berkeley Barb, 06 23 07 04 67

1396 "Shadyside repression thwarted," Grok, 08 -- 05 01 70

1397 "Sheep massacre," Los Angeles Free Press, 04 05 21 04 68 (Protest over dead sheep at Dugway Proving Grounds, Utah.)

1398 "She's not gov. issue: don't eat scab grapes," Fatigue Press, 02 -- 03 02 69

1399 "Showdown--G.I's refuse to fight," Ally, 09 -- 01 01 69

1400 "The Silent majority: are they also invisible?" Distant Drummer, 12 25 06 01 70

1401 "Silent majority speaks out--on Nixon, Agnew, war, students: a survey," U.S. News, 68:34-39, June 8, 1970.

1402 "SMU banes Notes: student groups protest," Dallas Notes, 11 -- 07 01 67 (Southern Methodist bans the underground newspaper with the question of academic freedom in the balance.)

1403 "Socarides warns of homosexual epidemic," Advocate, 07 08 03 01 70 (Socarides believes that homosexuality is a medical problem, and all homosexuals should therefore be considered medical patients.)

1404 "Soc. can be fun--if you don't get fired," Two-Cents Plain Dealer, 10 27 01 03 69 (Controversy over tenure in the sociology department at Millersville State College.)

1405 "The Soc. department," Two-Cents Plain Dealer, 02 23 04 01 70 (Concerning the introductory courses for majors and non-majors at Millersville State College.)

1406 "Sociologists are revolting," Berkeley Barb, 09 04 13 01 69 (Sociology Liberation Movement.)

1407 "Some psycho-sexual aspects of homosexuality," Campus Underground, 12 09 07 01 68

1408 "Sorry, Huey," Advocate, 10 14 18 01 70 (Addressed to Huey Newton regarding the group alliances with which this editor disagrees.)

1409 "Space and war," Pittsburgh Point, 07 24 03 03 69 (Prominent Pittsburgh contract recipients aiding the moon shot in the industrial-military-government-educational complex.)

1410 "Spazm organized drive to bridge male-female gap," Berkeley Barb, 02 28 13 04 69

1411 "Spiro Agnew explains himself," Life, 67:34-35, November 28, 1969.

1412 "Spiro turns against Kim," Dallas Notes, 11 05 11 01 09 (The speech in Harrisburg, Pa. by Agnew "predicting repression of protest leaders.")

1413 "Spiro's daughter psychedelic," (UPS/LA Free Press) Chinook, 09 18 03 02 69

1414 "Splinterism plagues birch ale in Berkeley," Berkeley Barb, 02 18 03 02 66 ("The local chapter of the John Birch Society is split into factions, some advocating a religious approach, while others favor political indoctrination.")

1415 "Spock talks in Philadelphia," Distant Drummer, 11 07 03 01 69

1416 "SSOC dissolves," Great Speckled Bird, 06 16 03 01 69

1417 "Stanford sit-in report," New Left Notes, 06 24 04 03 66 (Protest is over using university facilities for selective service deferment examination.)

General 137

1418 "The Steel city 26: SDS women vamp on Pittsburgh," Liberation News Service, 09 13 01 01 69 (Confrontation between factions of the SDS (Weatherwomen) and police at South Hills High School in Pittsburgh, Pa.)

1419 "Steven Allen to speak for CALM," Berkeley Barb, 03 18 03 03 66 ("A grisly business that must be ended by the people of America.")

1420 "Street people get together," Fifth Estate, 08 21 21 01 69 (Five revolutionary groups plan formation of a coalition from Ann Arbor, Michigan.)

1421 "Strike call freaks out Pennsylvania town," Liberation News Service, 11 13 03 01 68 (Lancaster establishment meets with alleged overkill reaction with election week strike in local high schools.)

1422 "Strike set at Penn," Distant Drummer, 02 20 09 02 69 (Attempt to strike at research stoppage nationwide. Activities reported at University of Pennsylvania, Philadelphia, Pa.)

1423 "Student antiwar coalition splits," Guardian, 06 22 06 02 68 (A major split in the SMC.)

1424 "The Student independent left has initiated indictment proceedings against the history department of Millersville State College," Two-Cents Plain Dealer, 02 23 01 03 70

1425 "Student independent left message to the State Legislature," Two-Cents Plain Dealer, 12 01 01 02 69 (A letter by the SIL to the Pa. Legislature advocating a four-point program regarding: funds, scholarships, setting up of community colleges, etc.)

1426 "A Student on the board of trustees? or, this could be the start of something big," Two-Cents Plain Dealer, 11 10 03 01 69 (An editorial advocating that faculty as well as students should have a vote on the Board of Trustees of colleges.)

1427 "Student Senate passes buck; petition sent to deans," Two-Cents Plain Dealer, 02 24 01 01 69 ("Excerpts from Student Senate meeting of February 20,

1969.")

1428 "Students for progressive action," Two-Cents Plain Dealer, 03 03 07 01 69 ("A reprint of remarks made by a spokesman for SPA at a dinner meeting called by Dr. Duncan on Feb. 27, 1969.")

1429 "Students for progressive action is dead," Two-Cents Plain Dealer, 05 10 02 01 69

1430 "The 'Study Our Colleges' game," Two-Cents Plain Dealer, 12 01 03 03 69 (Describes the committee recently organized to study colleges and their primary objectives at Millersville State College.)

1431 "The Supreme (?) Court," Common Sense, 06 01 04 01 70 (A new look at the U.S. Supreme Court.)

1432 "Taps for bugs?" Economist, 222:422, February 4, 1967. (The wiretapping and privacy bit again.)

1433 "Tattoo renaissance," Time, 96:58, December 21, 1970. ("Tattoos are merely another physical form of expression ... a way to say something intimately with your body.")

1434 "Temple students turn tables," Distant Drummer, 04 30 03 01 70

1435 "Tenants organize," Free You, 06 17 01 01 70 (Discrimination in housing.)

1436 "Tenure status of Dr. James W. Hughes," Two-Cents Plain Dealer, 11 10 04 01 69 (The complete text of President William H. Duncan--November 4, 1969.)

1437 "Test case on methadone," Los Angeles Free Press, 06 05 03 02 70

1438 "Texas five faces death penalty," First Issue, 01 29 18 01 68 (Five from Texas Southern University accused of the death of a policeman.)

1439 "Theobold predicts police state," Spokane Natural-- Chief Joseph, 05 09 12 02 69

1440 "There has been and always will be Black Panthers," Black Panther, 05 04 06 01 69

1441 "Therese and Isabelle trial over; the story continues," Pittsburgh Point, 12 12 01 01 68

1442 "They were here when," Advocate, 11 11 03 01 70 (History, organization and structure of One, Inc.)

1443 "Three-hundred pickets confront Hell's Angels," Berkeley Barb, 10 22 02 03 65

1444 "Timothy Leary," San Francisco Oracle, 09 -- 01 01 66

1445 "Tom Hayden on Chicago and America," Pittsburgh Point, 11 06 08 01 69 ("Editor's Note: ... the following statement by Tom Hayden, another defendant, was issued at a press conference last Thursday, Oct. 30, when Bobby Seale was still shackled and gagged in the courtroom. It was reported by Liberation News Service.")

1446 "The Trial of Lonnie McLucas and the New Haven 9," Black Panther, 07 18 07 01 70

1447 "The trouble with peace now," G. I. Voice, 02 -- 02 02 69

1448 "Truth about the Pueblo," Black Panther, 01 25 12 01 69

1449 "Tune in/turn out/be-in," Berkeley Barb, 01 13 01 04 67 (Human be-in at Golden Gate Park in San Francisco.)

1450 "Turning from confrontation," New Republic, 163:5-6, August 1, 1970.

1451 "Two L.A. girls attempt first legal gay marriage," Advocate, 07 08 01 02 70 ("The first marriage in the nation designed to legally bind two persons of the same sex was performed in L.A. June 12 by Rev. Troy D. Perry. A legal test is expected.")

1452 "UCLA journalism professor defends the Free Press," Los Angeles Free Press, 07 24 03 03 70

140   Confrontation, Conflict and Dissent

1453 "The Ultra-right and cold war liberalism," Studies
      On The Left, 3:3-8, Number 1, 1962. (Right, ul-
      tra right, radical right and middle. (?)

1454 "Underground paper in Ann Arbor," Fifth Estate, 10
      15 02 04 67 ("Looking Glass" arrives in Ann
      Arbor with sentiments both pro and con.)

1455 "The Underground press," Daily Planet, 08 04 18
      04 69

1456 "Underground press has tribal meeting," Fifth Estate,
      05 15 05 01 67 (UPS members meet in San
      Francisco "to express attitudes and aims of the
      majority of UPS papers.")

1457 "Underground, underground press," Grok, 02 -- 07
      01 70

1458 "University of Nebraska homo course ready," Advo-
      cate, 08 19 10 01 70 (A controversial course
      scheduled for the fall semester of 1970. Implica-
      tions for both students and profs. brought out.)

1459 "University of Nebraska shifts homophile course to
      psychologist," Advocate, 09 02 02 01 70 (Con-
      troversy ends over the graduate level homophile
      studies course. It has been shifted from the Eng-
      lish Dept. to the Psychology Dept.)

1460 "Unprivate lives (American electronic listening de-
      vices,") Economist, 214:998, March 6, 1965.

1460a "Unruh's son's friend's seeds?" Los Angeles Free
      Press, 03 01 02 02 68

1461 "Up from irrelevance," Studies On The Left, 5:3-14,
      Number 2, 1965. (About a "radical center" the
      radical movement and the implications for social
      change written by Tom Hayden, Norm Frichter, and
      Alan Cherise. Reply by James Weinstein and oth-
      ers.)

1462 "Uppity nigger indicts regents," San Diego Free Press,
      10 01 05 01 69 (Angela's speech at San Diego
      State.)

General 141

1463 "Values?" Two-Cents Plain Dealer, 03 19 04 01 69 (Educational and political values examined.)

1464 "Variable obscenity laws popular in one third the U.S.," Library Journal, 94:4192, November 15, 1969.

1465 "Veteran's look at the war," Two-Cents Plain Dealer, 10 02 05 02 69

1466 "Vice-President's daughter caught with marijuana: National news media kills story after White House pressure," Grok, 02 -- 12 01 70 (A reprint of an article which appeared in the Los Angeles Free Press on Sept. 5, 1969.)

1467 "Vicious: VDC reply to gazette series," Berkeley Barb, 11 05 01 03 65 (Confrontations between VDC and gazette series at Berkeley.)

1468 "Viet moratorium," Pittsburgh Point, 10 02 01 02 69 (Planning for moratorium activities for October 15th in Pittsburgh, Pa.)

1469 "Vietnam and riot control: proving grounds for CBR weapons," Fatigue Press, 06 -- 03 01 69

1470 "Vigilantes destroy N.Y. park to rout homosexuals," Advocate, 09 -- 26 01 69

1471 "War: America's Edsel," Two-Cents Plain Dealer, 12 15 01 01 69 (Modern warfare and Vietnam.)

1472 "A Warning from the 'weathermen'," Pittsburgh Point, 10 02 03 02 69 (Editor's Note: During the past month, the SDS group known as "weathermen" (and women) has achieved notoriety in Pittsburgh. The following article was written by several members of the group, which has now been named the "Steel City SDS.")

1473 "Warning to environmentalists," Northwest Passage, 03 23 17 01 70

1474 "Washington, November 15," North Carolin Anvil, 11 22 07 01 69

1475 "Water Tunnel," Distant Drummer, 02 20 03 03 69 (Rise and fall of the underground newspaper at Penn State University. Original title for the paper was Garfield Thomas Water Tunnel.)

1476 "We are going to make America better," Time, 96:6-7, July 6, 1970.

1477 "We don't need weathermen to tell which way the wind blows," Burning River News, 10 14 07 01 69

1478 "Weathermen hit rough weather," Pittsburgh Point, 09 18 06 01 69 (The SDS Weathermen and their problems with the Pittsburgh, Pa. courts.)

1479 "Weatherwomen," Pittsburgh Point, 10 09 02 03 69 (Description of the 26 women of the SDS arrested at South Hills High School in Pittsburgh, Pa.)

1480 "Welfare forces invade N.Y. capitol: Rockefeller nonplussed," Liberation News Service, 03 01 03 01 69 (About 2,500 welfare recipients protest welfare budget cut of 5% in Albany, N.Y.)

1481 "Welfare is a right ... not a privilege," Grok, 08 -- 12 01 70

1482 "We've been lucified," Los Angeles Free Press, 09 09 18 01 66 (Description of the LA Free Press. A reprint from Time Magazine, July 29, 1966.)

1483 "What happened to Robert De Pugh?" Common Sense, 05 01 03 01 70

1484 "What is underground?" Avatar, 06 09 06 02 66

1485 "What JOMO believes," Burning Spear, 10 13 02 01 70 (Article has fourteen points on what the Junta of Militant Organizations believes.)

1486 "What's going on inside America," U.S. News, 68:17-23, May 25, 1970. ("Survey of campus dissent, anti-war protests, strike disorders, crime, (and) pollution.") Known as chapter 2.

1487 "What's going on inside America," U.S. News, 68:27-28, June 1, 1970. (Known as chapter 3.)

1488 "What's in a word? Phuque won't do," Los Angeles Free Press, 03 19 03 01 65 (The "phuque rebellion" and John Thompson.)

1489 "Where are the Clark Kents of yesteryear? They are infiltrating the movement, and here is how to get rid of them," Ramparts, 9:38-42, December, 1970. (Alleged rumors of infiltration and undercover agents within the movement.)

1490 "Where are they now?" Newsweek, 76:8, August 3, 1970. (The Black Panthers and NAACP.)

1491 "White Panther party ten point platform--revised," Daily Planet, 10 08 22 03 69 (A platform for the needs of all the people.)

1492 "White Panther statement," Dallas Notes, 01 08 04 01 69

1493 "White repression and black response," Black Panther, 03 09 06 01 69 (Confrontation in Jackson, Mississippi.)

1494 "Who's listening?" Economist, 231:45-6, June 21, 1969. (Bugging.)

1495 "Who's who in the CIA," Los Angeles Free Press, (Organizational chart presents the structure of the American Intelligence Services.)

1496 "Why Huey?" Black Panther, 05 25 02 01 69

1497 "William Kunstler defends Bobby Lee Williams," Black Panther, 08 09 23 01 69 (Williams is accused of inciting a crowd to murder a policeman.)

1498 "Wins on both coasts: Pentagon protesters jubilant," Berkeley Barb, 10 27 03 04 67 (Pentagonism and peace marches.)

1499 "Withdrawal the hard way," G. I. Press Service, 09 18 102 01 69

1500 "Woman's lib. in Russia: the myth and the reality," U.S. News, 69:74-75, November 16, 1970.

1501 "Women arise," Life, 69:16B, September 4, 1970.

1502 "Women can quit group therapy and start work on the issues," North Carolin Anvil, 09 27 04 01 69

1503 "Women sit-in at football game," Los Angeles Free Press, 08 28 02 03 70 (A confrontation with LA police at the Rams-Raider football game in LA.)

1504 "Women up from under--in Pittsburgh--in Vietnam," Grok, 06 27 15 01 70

1505 "Women up from under all of us," Grok, 09 -- 05 01 70

1506 "The women who know their place," Newsweek, 76:16-18, September 7, 1970.

1507 "Women's lib's growning pain," Newsweek, 76:47, August 31, 1970.

1508 "A word of explanation," Pencil In Title Of Your Own Choice, 04 -- 01 01 69 ("If you find something in poor taste, stop reading!" Regarding statements which caused controversy in this and previous issues of the underground newspaper at Burrell High School.)

1509 "World in revolution," Hartford's Other Voice, 07 14 02 01 69

1510 "Writer defends 'dirty' words," Dallas Notes, 12 -- 04 01 67 ("Shock" words defended by John Ciardi.)

1511 "WSU library workers organize," Fifth Estate, 05 01 24 01 69

1512 "You can't eat a stadium. No boon for the north side," Grok, 08 -- 03 01 70 (Labor problems and confrontations over the new "Three Rivers Stadium" in Pittsburgh, Pa.)

1513 "Young Lords move in New York," Movement, 11 -- 08 01 69 (Young Lords organization and their "strength in numbers" movement.)

1514 "Young Lords seize Church in N.Y.," Burning Spear, 10 30 14 01 70 (Lords seize Peoples Church over death of their comrade.)

1515 "The Zap zap general," The G. I. Organizer, 07 05 04 01 69

PERIODICALS

1516 Aber, Joel. "Economics of women's liberation," The Militant, 11 14 04 01 69

1517 Abrams, Arnold. "My Lai two years later," Atlas, 19:13-15, April, 1970.

1518 Adamo, S. J. "Not fit to print? New York bishops pastoral letter," America, 123:568-70, December 26, 1970. (The abortion issue, its significance and the religious aspects.)

1519 Adhikary, Mukundah Das. "The New Science," San Francisco Oracle, 01 14 04 01 67 (Astrology and Evangeline Adams.)

1520 Africa Research Group. "A smuggled account from a guerrilla fighter. Southern Africa," Ramparts, 8:8, October, 1969. (Tactics of guerrilla warfare.)

1521 Agut, J. R. "Miami at war with hippies," Florida Free Press, 03 14 06 01 68 (Description of alleged police harassment in Dade County, Florida.)

1522 Ahlstrom, Sydney E. "The Radical turn in theology and ethics: why it occurred in the 1960's," Annals of the American Academy, 387:1-13, January, 1970. (Includes bibliography.)

1523 Aiken, Ellsworth N. "Moratorium!" Grok, 02 -- 04 01 70 (Thoughts about the November 13-15 peace march moratorium at Washington with illustrations.)

1524 Albert, Martin L. "Vietnam: the doctor's dilemma," Nation, 206:823-4, June 24, 1968.

1524a Albert, Stewart. "The Black flag," Berkeley Barb, 10 14 12 01 66

1525 _____. "Freeing Huey: here's how to do it," Berkeley Barb, 04 25 03 01 69

1526 _____. "...Piss in the voting booths," Fifth Estate, 10 31 07 01 68 ("American election itself is the candidate and millions of Americans are going to vote against it.")

1527 Alinder, Gary. "Gays dispel high school myths," Distant Drummer, 05 28 05 01 70

1528 Allan, William. "The Peace symbol," This Week--Supplement to the Pittsburgh Press, February 28, 1971, pp. 8-12. (Origin and history of the peace symbol.)

1528a Allen, A. Dale Jr. "What to do about sex discrimination," Labor Law Journal, September, 1970, pp. 563-576.

1529 Allen, James N. "A defense of activism," Conscience, 08 -- 14 01 69

1530 Allen, Jesse. "Newark community union," Studies On The Left, 4:80-84, Number 4, 1965. (Confrontation with landlords and living conditions in Newark.)

1531 Allen, Robert L. "Presidio G. I's defense puts Army on trial," Guardian, 04 26 05 01 69 (Famous "Presidio Mutiny Case" in California.)

1532 Althoff, Barbara. "Russell war crimes tribunal," Western Activist, 10 20 04 02 66 (History of the war crimes tribunal.)

1533 American Friends Service Committee. "American Friends view of Gulf Oil," Pittsburgh Point, 04 30 03 01 70

1534 Anderson, Allen J. "War crimes tribunal," New Left Notes, 12 16 01 01 66 (First session called to order by Lord Russell on November 13, 1966 in London.)

1535 Anderson, Jervis. "Panthers: Black men in extremis," Dissent, 17:120, March-April, 1970.

1536 Anderson, Michael. "Defend yourself," Berkeley Barb, 10 17 05 01 69

1537 Andrews, Tim. "Wallace in Omaha," Los Angeles Free Press, 04 05 10 01 68

1538 Angle, Roger. "Outrage in York, Pa.," Liberation News Service, 10 18 17 01 68 (Interracial conflict in York after a football game when City Hall became involved.)

1539 Angrist, Shirley S. "Role conception as a predictor of adult female roles," Sociology and Social Research, 50:448-459, July, 1966.

1540 Anonymous (New York State). "A Minister looks at wife-swapping," Modern Utopian, 05 08 05 01 64 (A Minister considers the biblical view and gives the question some religious significance. His definition of adultery is well worth reading. Another Minister's view from a southern state is printed on page 8 of the same issue.)

1541 Apostolides, Alex. "Gov. Ronnie and college board overkill Summerskill," Los Angeles Free Press, 12 22 06 01 67

1542 _____. "Meredith Quinn speaks," Los Angeles Free Press, 02 07 16 01 69 (Quinn is a spokesman for the plight of the Indians.)

1543 Applebaum, Jerry. "Chicano leader charges U.S. with genocide," Los Angeles Free Press, 09 19 02 03 69 (Chicano-Anglo confrontations on Broadway's induction center.)

1543a Arnstein, George E. "University as corporation: toward a new identity," College and University Business, 48:51-58, March, 1970.

1544 Aronowitz, Stanley. "New York City: after the rent strikes," Studies On The Left, 4:85-89, Number 4, 1965. (Strike at NYC forcing landlords to make essential repairs.)

1545 Aronson, James. "Beyond old and new left: the emergence of a third force," Liberation, 14:22-25, August-September, 1969.

1546 Aronson, Ronald. "The Movement and its critics," Studies On The Left, 6:3-19, Number 1, Jan.-Feb., 1966. (Discussions of various viewpoints and disagreements within the movement.)

1547 Arthur, Stephanie. "Nasty Margaret Mead," Daily Planet, 11 24 06 01 69 (Views of Margaret Mead on drug abuse, especially marijuana.)

1548 Ascheim, Skip. "Resistance: Boston style," Avatar, 10 27 04 01 67

1549 Ascoli, Max. "The Unpossessed: war opposed by intellectuals in the U.S.," Reporter, 37:15, December 28, 1967.

1550 Ashley, Bob. "Scuttling academic freedom," North Carolin Anvil, 12 20 06 01 69

1551 Assael, Henry. "Constructive role of interorganizational conflict," Administrative Science Quarterly, 14:573-582, December, 1969. (A description of conflicts within the automobile distribution system. Manufacturer-dealer relations are discussed.)

1552 Babcock, John. "D.A. clears police in Jimmie Rodgers' 'fall'," Los Angeles Free Press, 03 29 02 01 68

1553 Backstrom III, Carl. "Americans for freedom," Los Angeles Free Press, 07 24 14 01 70

1554 Bain, Helen. "We must be reasoning activists," Today's Education, 59:22-25, September, 1970.

1555 Bakan, David. "The Future of human relations," Vital Speeches of the Day, 36:219-223, January 15, 1970.

General 149

1556 Baldwin, James. "James Baldwin on Stokeley: from dreams of love to dreams of terror," Los Angeles Free Press, 02 23 01 01 68

1557 Ballard, Jim. "Panthers rap--at Friends' meeting...," Distant Drummer, 04 02 03 01 70

1558 Balser, Henry. "The Balsy Chicago report," First Issue, 03 19 13 01 68 (Discussion of the degree of racism in America and what this will eventually mean in the future.)

1558a Banner, David K. "Pollution: symptom of a value crisis," Training and Development Journal, December, 1970, pp. 16-19.

1559 Bannowsky, Flip. "The Great obscenity bust," Heterodoxical Voice, 06 -- 01 01 68 (Confrontation at the University of Delaware over distribution of what was allegedly called "dirty leaflets.")

1560 Barad, Huntley. "Radical Madison conservation group emerges," Chicago Kaleidoscope, 01 03 07 01 69 (CRAP'S major offensive "to get the crap out of the environment.")

1561 Barg, Peter. "Local justice," The Paper, 06 -- 03 01 66 (Administration of justice in the courts.)

1562 Barkley, Katherine, and Steve Weissman. "The Eco-establishment," Ramparts, 8:48-58, May, 1970. (Major environmental and ecological problems.)

1563 Barnette, Rodney. "Three L.A. Panthers murdered by pigs: pigs plotted murders of L.A. Panthers," Black Panther, 09 07 06 01 68

1564 Barraclough, Geoffrey. "The Storms of the 70's: alignments and confrontations," Nation, 210:6-8, January 12, 1970.

1565 Barry, Ernie. "Was the real JFK killed?" Berkeley Barb, 07 21 03 04 67

1566 Basing, Mary. "Bradley, Times fight Garrison," Los Angeles Free Press, 12 29 01 03 67 (The alleged plot against JFK.)

1567 Baxandall, Lee. "Camp and community," Studies On The Left, 5:97-98, Number 2, 1965.

1568 Behrend, Celeste. "Norval Reece on the McCarthy trail," Pittsburgh Point, 02 26 03 02 70

1569 _____, and Charles C. Robb. "It's happening at Taylor-Allderdice," Pittsburgh Point, 06 05 01 02 69 (Confrontations in the high schools of Pittsburgh, Pa.)

1570 Bellini, Carol. "Impressions from the public safety building," Pittsburgh Point, 08 28 02 03 69 (Description of those charged with inciting-to-riot. Repressive tactics reported.)

1571 Bensky, Larry. "Broken peace pipes over Alcatraz," Distant Drummer, 12 04 06 01 69 (Alcatraz was taken over at dawn on November 20. Indians feel that the island is more than suitable for a reservation.)

1572 _____. "Conspiracy: a new nation," Great Speckled Bird, 12 01 08 01 69 (Chicago 8.)

1573 Beppler, Bill. "My Snapper days--to conclusion," Two-Cents Plain Dealer, 03 19 03 01 69

1574 Bercut, Florence, "Mystical Atlantis," Indian Head, 11 17 05 01 67 (More controversy about Plato's story of Atlantis.)

1575 Berger, Dan. "Nixon's war," Distant Drummer, 04 09 10 01 70

1576 _____. "Why Cambodia?" Distant Drummer, 05 07 08 03 70

1577 Berland, Oscar. "Radical chains: the Marxian concept of Proletarian mission," Studies On The Left, 6:27-51, Number 5, Sept.-Oct., 1966. (On page 52 a reply is appended by Ronald Aronson.)

1578 Berman, Bruce A. "Confrontation at the justice department," Pittsburgh Press, 11 20 04 01 69

General 151

(Protest on behalf of the Chicago 8, now 7.)

1579 Bernard, Jessie. "The Status of women in modern patterns of culture," Annals of the American Academy, 375:3-14, January, 1968.

1580 Berrigan, Daniel. "Notes from the underground; or I was a fugitive from the F.B.I.," Commonweal, XCII:263-265, May 29, 1970.

1581 Berry, Marva. "Open letter to pig Mayor Lindsay," Black Panther, 04 06 13 03 70

1582 Bess, Donovan. "Muckraking: 1965--The Menace of the barbie dolls," Muckrakers Guide, Ramparts--Special Collector's edition, pp. 25-28. ("Both boys and girls are introduced to a precocious, joyless sexuality, to fantasies of seduction and to conspicuous consumption.")

1583 Bettelheim, Bruno. "Growing up female," Harper's Magazine, 225:120-128, October, 1962.

1584 Bingler, John H. Jr. "We need justice and disorder," Pittsburgh Point, 02 19 05 01 70

1585 Bitten, Ron. "Chicago--October 11," Old Mole, 08 15 14 01 69

1586 Black Construction Coalition. "Statement of the Black Construction Coalition, September 29, 1969," Pittsburgh Point, 10 02 05 01 69

1587 Black Panther Party. "Message to America...," Black Panther, 06 20 12 01 70

1588 Black, Pearl Charie. "The Meaning of Freedom Corner," Pittsburgh Point, 10 02 07 01 69 ("Located on the northeast side of Center Avenue and Crawford Street in the Lower Hill ... serves as an unofficial boundary line, separating the ghetto of the lower hill from the heart of the city's affluent business areas.")

1589 Black, Vonda. "What women's liberation really means," Free You, 06 17 07 01 70

1590 Blakkan, Renee. "Liberalized abortion law in New York," Guardian, 07 11 06 01 70 (Concerning the liberal abortion law in New York City which went into effect on July 1, 1970.)

1591 _____. "Nationwide demonstration by women," Guardian, 09 05 03 01 70 (August 26 strike for women's liberation.)

1592 _____. "New York women 'ogle' construction workers," Guardian, 06 20 03 02 70 (Construction workers in New York City and women clash over ideologies. Women advocate "among other liberating actions--biting the hand that feels you.")

1593 _____. "Thirty-thousand women march for rights in N.Y. demonstration," Guardian, 09 05 04 01 70 (Includes the "Third World Women's Alliance.")

1594 _____. "Three thousand protest against war at Ft. Dix," Guardian, 05 23 03 01 70 (Confrontation between the people and military-civilian policies at Ft. Dix.)

1595 _____. "Women's legislation in Congress," Guardian, 09 19 04 01 70 (Description of six women's rights bills and court cases in congress.)

1596 _____. Women's rights fight in congress," Guardian, 07 18 03 01 70

1597 Blank, Dennis. "John Sinclair: victim of repression," Grok, 06 27 11 01 70

1598 Blazer, Sam. "Amplifying the 'Strawberry Statement,'" Los Angeles Free Press, 07 24 33 02 70

1599 Bloom, Bernie. "Pittsburgh must breathe," Grok, 04 -- 15 01 70 (Location of sources where pollutants are rampant and the crisis in the environment.)

1600 Bloom, Marshall. "HUAC hawk urges underground probe," Los Angeles Free Press, 12 15 02 01 67

1601 _____. "HUAC confronts underground press,"

Dallas Notes, 12 -- 04 01 67 ("HUAC calls for an investigation of underground newspapers... the purpose of these newspapers (allegedly) will be to slander and libel everyone who opposes these traitors in their attempts to destroy the American government.")

1602 Bloustein, Edward J. "Man's work goes from sun to sun, but woman's work is never done," Psychology Today, 1:38-41, March, 1968.

1603 Boardman, Krist. "Reflections on the postal strike," Distant Drummer, 04 02 05 01 70

1604 Boggio, Jim. "Tricky Dickie's vs. trick," Counterpoint, 06 23 05 01 69

1605 Bookchin, Murray. "Toward an ecological solution," Ramparts, 8:7-10, May, 1970.

1606 Booth, Paul. "Students and workers," Ramparts, 8:19-20, September, 1969. (SDS and the working class.)

1607 Boyd, James. "From far right to far left--and further--with Karl Hess," New York Times Magazine, December 6, 1970, p. 48. (Political ideology.)

1608 Boyle, Kay. "No one can be all things to all people," Evergreen Review, 14:63, August, 1970. (By a writer who was denied an interview by prison officials and why.)

1609 Brecher, Jeremy. "Moratorium; where to ...?" Liberation, 14:7-14, December, 1969.

1610 Brewer, Drew. "Racism still there," Dallas Notes, 05 07 05 01 69 (Confrontations at Southern Methodist University.)

1611 Brien, A. "Intellectual love-feast," New Statesman, 76:108, July 26, 1968. (Obscenity and pornography laws.)

1612 Briggs, Peter. "Credibility gap," News From Nowhere, 11 -- 02 01 69 (Sins of omission or commission concerning the press at the moratorium at DeKalb Senior High School, in DeKalb, Illinois.)

1613 Brightman, Carol. "Vietnam: Hey: Folks, that war is escalating," Liberation News Service, 12 19 01 01 68

1614 _____. "Vietnam: The war escalates," Hard Core, 12 20 03 01 68 (The war as capitalism as seen by this writer.)

1615 Brockett, E. D. "Gulf's eye view of Gulf Oil," Pittsburgh Point, 04 30 02 01 70

1616 Brogan, Varley. "Who killed Bobby?" Los Angeles Free Press, 07 03 06 04 70

1617 Bronston, William, and Frantz Fanon. "New York's tombs of torture," Black Panther, 08 30 06 01 69 (Work and living conditions in New York's prisons.)

1618 Broslawsky, Farrel. "Hookers for Kennedy," Los Angeles Free Press, 03 29 03 03 68

1619 _____. "What's left of the left since LBJ left?" Los Angeles Free Press, 04 05 03 01 68

1620 Brown, Brendan. "The Crime of abortion," Vital Speeches, 36:549-553, July 1, 1970.

1621 Brown, Connie. "Cleveland: conference of the poor," Studies On The Left, 5:71-74, Number 2, 1965. (Community People's Conference formed from ERAP.)

1622 Brown, Harrison. "The Combustibility of humans," Saturday Review, 66:14-17, June 24, 1967.

1623 Brown, H. Rap. "Let Rap rap!" Black Panther, 03 16 07 01 68

1623a Brown, James Jr. "Black youth and big business," Electronic Age, 30:20-22, Winter, 1970-71. ("Graduates of black schools are too often overlooked by corporate recruiters, and the black with work skills must face segregation barriers imposed by many craft unions.")

1624 Brown, Leonard. "Save Deena Metzger," Los Angeles Free Press, 05 29 02 04 70

1625 Brown, P. K. "SMU...new library but no books," Dallas Notes, 04 16 05 01 69

1626 Brown, Robert McAfee. "Mayday for America: mobilizing the outraged," Commonweal, XCII:266-268, May 29, 1970. ("Miscalculation as applied to Nixon, the Senate, the Congress, and implications for students regarding the future.")

1627 _____. "Why I oppose our policy in Vietnam," Presbyterian Life, 21:14-17, January 15, 1968.

1628 Browning, Frank. "From rumble to revolution: The Young Lords," Ramparts, 9:19-25, October, 1970. ("Revolutionary organization of Puerto Rican youth in the U.S.")

1629 Brustman, Susan. "An evening with Lenny Bruce," Los Angeles Free Press, 03 26 03 01 65 (Description of an interview with Bruce covering such subjects as obscenity, law, sex, and busts.)

1630 Buckley, William F. Jr. "Catholics and abortion," National Review, 22:1366-7, December 15, 1970.

1631 Buckman, Peter. "Ireland's niggers," Ramparts, 8:19-22, July, 1969. (Includes an interview with Bernadette Devlin, youngest member of the House of Commons.)

1632 Burlage, Robb. "The New Left and the economics of health," Paper Tiger, 05 -- 13 01 68 (Crisis is reported in American health care. Includes item-incidents revealing acute problems between black and white in the health professions.)

1633 Burry, Jim. "Regents break UC rules, fire Angela Davis for her politics," Los Angeles Free Press, 09 26 01 01 69

1634 Burton, Steven J. "Garrison says Howard has cleared himself," Los Angeles Free Press, 03 01 25 01 68

1635 Burton, Steven J. "Gunshot just misses Kennedy death witness," <u>Los Angeles Free Press</u>, 11 10 03 04 67

1636 _____. "New evidence on Bradley," <u>Los Angeles Free Press</u>, 02 02 06 03 68 (Bradley, Garrison and the JFK investigation.)

1637 _____. "Third indictment for Garrison," <u>Los Angeles Free Press</u>, 03 08 05 01 68

1638 Butler, Willis P. "Cuba's revolutionary medicine," <u>Ramparts</u>, 7:6-14, May, 1969.

1639 Cadden, Vivian. "How women see themselves," <u>Redbook</u>, 129:46-47, May, 1967.

1640 Cahill, David. "Barb on strike," <u>The Spectator</u>, 07 29 07 01 69

1641 Callahan, Daniel. "Contraception and abortion: American Catholic responses," <u>Annals of the American Academy</u>, 387, January, 1970.

1642 Callaway, Howard. "Facist America?" <u>Water Tunnel</u>, 05 12 13 01 69

1643 Camarano, Chris. "A letter from Camp Venceremos," <u>Ramparts</u>, 9:6-14, August, 1970. (Life in a Cuban commune described by one who advocates optimistic enthusiasm.)

1644 Cannon, Ralph A. "Pornography, sex and the church," <u>Christian Century</u>, 80:576-9, May 1, 1963.

1645 Cannon, Terence, and Reese Erlich. "The Oakland seven," <u>Ramparts</u>, 7 34-37, April, 1969. (Written by two of the seven, this is their story of their indictment in helping to organize the "Stop the Draft Week demonstration at the Oakland Induction Center in October, 1967.")

1646 Cantor, Paul. "End the war now, Mr. Nixon, or the people will end your administration," <u>Berkeley Barb</u>, 10 31 04 01 69

1647 Capouya, Emile. "After the failure of nerve," <u>Studies</u>

On The Left, 3:3-13, Number 3, 1963. (Ideologies and the movement.)

1648 Carasso, Roger. "The Dilemma of the belated colossus," Lux Verite, 05 -- 06 01 68

1649 Carmichael, Stokely. "A Message from Stokely Carmichael," Burning Spear, 09 21 14 01 70 (A letter to the general conference concerning Congress of African Peoples.)

1650 _____. "Stokely teaches here," San Diego Free Press, 11 01 03 ·01 68 ("Excerpts from a speech given ... at a rally in Ocean View Park held Sat. October 26.")

1651 Carpenter, John. "Peter Fonda ... the easy rider," Los Angeles Free Press, 06 11 32 02 69

1652 Carroll, Al. "On illegitimate capitalist 'the game'," Black Panther, 06 20 07 01 70 (The complexes--Industrial-Military-Government-Educational complex.)

1653 Carter, Francis. "Over all, the sisters 'in Niantic State Farm for women' are treated with no regard for their health ...," Black Panther, 07 18 12 01 70

1654 Cervantes, Lucius. "Woman's changing role in society," Thought, 40:325-368, Autumn, 1965.

1655 Chamberlain. "Obstacles to change in the university," National Association of Student Personnel Administrators, 8:29-34, July, 1970.

1656 Chamberlain, Anne. "Commercialization of J.F.K.," Saturday Evening Post, 237:20-21, November 21, 1964.

1657 Chamberlain, Gary L. "Crime, confessions and the Supreme Court," America, 117:32-4, July 8, 1967.

1658 Chamberlain, Gary M. "Riot control," American City, 82:87-9, March, 1967.

1659 Chamberlain, John. "Is there a statute of limitations

on justice?" National Review, 19:1257-8, November 14, 1969.

1660 Chamberlain, John. "Rival to Cosa Nostra?" Harper, 231:118, December 9, 1965.

1661 _____. "Which way with LBJ," National Review, 15:525-7, December 17, 1964.

1662 Chamberlin, J. Gordon. "Ecumenical tangle," Christian Century, 85:75-7, January 17, 1968.

1663 Chambers, Alex A. "Negro in congress of the U.S.," Negro History Bulletin, 24:143, March, 1961.

1664 Chambers, Donald E. "Willingness to adopt atypical children," Child Welfare, 49:275-9, May, 1970.

1665 Chambers, Ernest W. "We have marched, we have cried, we have prayed, excerpt from testimony before President's riot commission," Ebony, 23:29-32, April, 1968.

1666 Chambers, Ernie. "Omaha, city of Fascism," Black Panther, 07 26 03 01 69 (Repressive tactics seen in Omaha.)

1667 Chandler, Christopher. "The Black Panther killings," New Republic, 162:21-24, January 10, 1970.

1668 Charyn, Marlene. "Fascism," Peninsula Observer, 07 28 07 01 69

1669 _____. "Feds hit Panthers on cue from Alioto?" Peninsula Observer, 06 30 10 02 69

1670 _____. "N.Y. Times tells stately lies," Peninsula Observer, 06 30 10 01 69 (Controversial reporting.

1671 Chason, Gary. "Sexual freedom league: the naked truth," The Rag, 08 17 01 01 66

1672 Che Guevara, Ernesto. "CIA finds a publisher," Ramparts, 7:58-60, November 30, 1968.

1673 _____. "Contemporary documents: Commandante Ernesto Che Guevara. From 'Notes for the study of the ideology of the Cuban Revolution,' Verde Olivo, Oct. 8, 1960."

Studies On The Left, 1:75-85, Number 3, 1960.

1674 _____. "Contemporary documents: From analysis of the Cuban situation, IN 'La Guerra de Guerillas,' published in early 1960," Studies On The Left, 1:79-84, Number 3, 1960.

1674a _____. "Memoirs of the revolutionary war, by Che Guevara," Ramparts, 6:27-36, January, 1968.

1675 Chenu, M. D., and Friedrich Heer. "Is the modern world atheist?" Cross Currents, Winter, 1961.

1676 Cherry, Jim. "NEA expels school superintendent," School and Society, 98:14-15, January, 1970.

1677 Chervenak, Chris. "An experiment in learning," Distant Drummer, 06 12 12 01 69 (A new concept of learning with "group interaction.")

1678 Chicago Journalism Review. "Let them eat cake mix," Liberation News Service, 04 17 14 02 69 (An article in the Chicago Tribune concerning the "inadequate welfare budget.")

1679 Chicago (Seed). "Panthers battle pigs in Chicago," Washington Free Press, 08 -- 11 01 69

1680 Chomsky, Noam. "Some tasks for the left," Liberation, 14:38-43, August-September, 1969.

1681 Choudhury, Malay Roy. "In defense of obscenity," Guerrilla, 01 -- 03 01 67 (Written in the first person in the form of poetry.)

1682 Christensen, Gayle. "Fascism and George Wallace," Campus Underground, 11 04 06 01 68 (Anti-Marxism, racism, anti-intellectualism, nationalism, etc.)

1683 Cisler, Lucinda. "Abortion reform: the new tokenism," Ramparts, 9:19-25, August, 1970.

1684 Clamage, Dena. "Women's liberation: the only path is revolution," Fifth Estate, 03 05 07 01 69

1685 Clark, John. "Suppression," Black Panther, 01 24

03 04 70

1686 Clarkson, Paul. "When people are powerful the schools are free," Peninsula Observer, 06 30 03 01 69

1687 Cleath, R. L. "Gays go radical," Christianity Today, 15:40-41, December 4, 1970.

1688 Cleaver, Eldridge. "An aside to Ronald Reagan," Black Panther, 06 21 10 01 69

1689 _____. "The black man's stake in Vietnam," Black Panther, 03 23 16 01 69

1690 _____. "The Black moochie, a novella," Ramparts, 8:21-27, October, 1969. (Part one of a two part series on Cleaver's experiences while growing up in Los Angeles. Second part appears in Ramparts, 8:8-15, November, 1969.)

1691 _____. "Cleaver from exile; from somewhere in the third world. Eldridge Cleaver sent this message through the underground," Washington Free Press, 08 -- 10 01 69

1692 _____. "Death of Bobby Hutton; excerpts from Eldridge Cleaver," Grok, 06 -- 07 02 70

1693 _____. "Eldridge Cleaver discusses revolution: an interview from exile," Black Panther, 11 11 10 01 69

1694 _____. "Eldridge Cleaver on women's liberation," Guardian, 08 02 05 01 69 (The article was written as a message to Erica Huggins.)

1695 _____. "First tape from Cleaver," Willamette Bridge, 07 18 21 01 69

1696 _____. "Happy birthday Huey," Black Panther, 02 28 03 02 70

1697 _____. "Huey's standard," Black Panther, 03 15 03 01 70

1698 _____. "Message to sister Erica Huggins," Black

General

Panther, 01 03 09 01 70

1699 _____. Method, time and revolution," Black Panther, 05 31 18 01 70

1700 _____. "My Father and Stokely Carmichael," Ramparts, 5:10-14, April, 1967.

1701 _____. "No. 2 affidavit of Eldridge Cleaver," Black Panther, 04 06 10 01 70

1702 _____. "On denial of passport," Black Panther, 12 20 09 01 69

1703 _____. "On Phil Hutchins," Black Panther, 06 20 09 01 70

1704 _____. "On Richard the pig-hearted Nixon," Black Panther, 05 19 02 01 70

1705 _____. "The Pentagon," Black Panther, 05 31 14 01 70

1706 _____. "Political struggle in America: 1968," Black Panther, 03 16 08 01 68

1707 _____. "Private prisoner exchange urged," Daily Planet, 11 24 04 02 69 (On the exchange of political prisoners in Vietnam.)

1708 _____. "Revolution and education," Black Panther, 06 28 12 01 69 (Concerns black studies, the schools and the environment. Transcriptions from tapes.)

1709 _____. "Revolution no game," Los Angeles Free Press, 06 11 03 01 69

1710 _____. "Solidarity of the peoples until victory or death," Black Panther, 10 25 12 01 69

1711 _____. "Somewhere in the third world," Black Panther, 07 12 12 01 69

1712 _____. "Sorties in mad Babylon," Ramparts, 5:16-26, August, 1966. (A selection of letters from Cleaver to his lawyer while serving his sentence in

Folsom prison in California.)

1713 Cleaver, Eldridge. "Statement to all reactionary journalists and pressmen of the U.S. of America," Black Panther, 11 08 02 01 69

1714 _____. "Three notes from exile," Ramparts, 8:29-30, September, 1970. ("A Note to my friends--An open letter to Stokely Carmichael--On meeting the needs of the people.")

1715 _____. "To my black brothers in Vietnam," Black Panther, 03 22 04 01 70

1716 _____. "We have found it here in Korea," Black Panther, 01 03 16 01 70

1717 Cleaver, Kathleen. "On Eldridge Cleaver," Ramparts, 7:4-11, June, 1969.

1718 Cleaver, Tom. "Angela Davis charged with murder," Guardian, 08 22 04 01 70

1719 _____. "G. I's get 14 years," Guardian, 02 22 04 01 69 ("Presidio 27")

1720 _____. "Huey Newton is freed on $50,000 bail," Guardian, 08 15 03 01 70 (Freed on August 5 by a California court.)

1721 _____. "Jury selection starts in Los Siete case," Guardian, 06 27 07 01 70

1722 Clecak, Peter. "Tom Hayden and the new left," Nation, 210:21-23, January 12, 1970.

1723 Clogger, T. J. "Big ear," Contemporary Review, 210:201-3, April, 1967. (Wiretapping legality.)

1724 Cloke, Kenneth. "How to get out of the Army: separation for homosexuality," Liberation News Service, 12 05 08 01 68 ("Army regulation 635-89")

1725 Clor, H. "Obscenity and public morality," Saturday Review, 52:80-1, May 10, 1969.

1726 Coats, Bob. "Black Beret organizer jailed in S. J.,"

Peninsula Observer, 07 14 05 01 69

1727   Coffin, Stephanie, and Perry Treadwell. "Peachtree creek is full of shit!" Great Speckled Bird, 02 23 02 03 70 (Pollution-industrial complex and the ecological environment.)

1728   Coffin, Tom. "The Radical right," Great Speckled Bird, 03 24 08 01 69

1729   _____. "Underground press rising," Great Speckled Bird, 06 28 04 03 69 ("A theory of journalism, definition of life-style, and extension of the opposition to the capitalistic press.")

1729a Cohen, E. E., and L. B. Mayhew. "The New work ethic," Electronic Age, 30:17-20, Winter, 1970-71. ("Young workers today are affected and influenced by the same factors as campus youth, and they are reacting in like fashion.")

1730   Cohen, Fred, Marc Weiss, and Jeff Blum. "SDS lesson: radicals must analyze U.S.," Peninsula Observer, 07 14 06 01 69

1731   Colaianni, James F. "Napalm: made in U.S.A.: a smalltown diary," Ramparts, 5:46-50, August, 1966.

1732   Cole, Rob. "Just call it Metropolitan Community Church U.S.A.," Advocate, 08 19 01 01 70 (The first of two articles dealing with the Church as it is now. Some Church doctrine is explained.)

1733   _____. "Military policies on gays make no sense," Advocate, 07 08 07 01 70 (Questions and answers concerning homosexuality before and after military service.)

1734   _____. "NACHO 'liberated' on final day," Advocate, 10 14 08 01 70 (The second of two articles on the 1970 NACHO convention.)

1735   Coles, Robert. "Still hungry in America," Great Speckled Bird, 06 30 12 01 69

1736   Collier, Peter. "A Daily for your mind," Ramparts, 7:44-50, June, 1969. (Some interesting sidelights of the CBS Television Network, and the Smothers Brothers television show.)

1737 Collier, Peter. "The Red man's burden: better red than dead," Ramparts, 8:26-38, February, 1970. (The Alcatraz story.)

1738 _____. "The Theft of a nation: apologies to the Cherokees," Ramparts, 9:35-45, September, 1970. (Confrontations of the Cherokees with established power structures in Oklahoma.)

1739 Collins, Don. "I wouldn't know one from a bale of hay: topic of the day in Alpine," Advocate, 11 25 02 01 70 (Efforts of the GLF to set up a gay government in Alpine County in California.)

1740 Conger, W. B. "Forced birth control--legal genocide?" Los Angeles Free Press, 10 16 04 01 70 (Human life principle and the government's role in overpopulation.)

1741 Connelly, Joel. "Nixon discovers the environment and related topics," Northwest Passage, 02 09 12 01 70

1742 _____. "Rhetoric pollution in Seattle," Northwest Passage, 05 18 16 01 70

1743 _____. "Two movements: YSA and SLF," Northwest Passage, 05 18 13 01 70

1744 _____, Frank Kathman, and Chris Condon. "David Brower; an interview," Northwest Passage, 02 23 06 01 70

1745 Conspiracy Staff Members. "The Conspiracy experience," Liberation, 04 -- 28 01 70

1746 Cooke, Michael. "Homosexual and capitalism: why don't they like us?" Liberation News Service, 08 28 12 01 69 (Originally published by the Committee for Homosexual Freedom.)

1747 Cooper, Richard T. "A town turns on its children," Nation, 211:517-519, November 23, 1970. (Kent State episode.)

1748 Corwin, Ronald G. "Patterns of organizational conflict," Administrative Science Quarterly, 14:507-519, December, 1969. (Relationships were derived from measures from 1500 questionnaires, 600 interviews in 28 public high schools.)

1749 Coryell, Schofield. "Irish crisis continues to mount," Guardian, 06 06 14 01 70 (Catholic and Protestant confrontations in Ireland.)

1750 Cottrell, Beekman W. "How curious can one get?" Pittsburgh Point, 04 09 08 01 70 (Conscience and choice regarding obscenity and the law.)

1751 Covert, John. "The Assassination of Fred Hampton," Grok, 06 -- 07 01 70

1752 _____. "More killings; more protests," Pittsburgh Point, 05 21 05 01 70 (Protests over killings at Kent State, Jackson State and six blacks in Augusta, Georgia.)

1753 _____. "Mrs. King coming for hospital strike," Pittsburgh Point, 03 12 01 01 70

1754 _____. "A New jury--the same old problem," Pittsburgh Point, 03 05 03 01 70

1755 _____. "New priorities day: celebrating life," Pittsburgh Point, 04 16 01 01 70 (Celebration of this day sponsored by the War Tax Resistance, the New Priorities Coalition, Gulf Action Project, and Tactical Police Force.)

1756 _____. "Norval Reece," Grok, 06 -- 08 01 70

1757 _____. "Peace restored in city court," Pittsburgh Point, 03 26 01 01 70 (A confrontation at court with police and anti-draft demonstrators in Pittsburgh.)

1758 _____. "Reece campaign bubbling at last," Pittsburgh Point, 05 14 01 03 70 (The Norval Reece campaign in Pittsburgh.)

1759 _____. "A School where kids come first," Pittsburgh Point, 03 19 01 02 70 ("Free school at

Warrendale, a State Correctional Institute for boys in Pennsylvania.")

1760 Covert, John. "The Sun was hot; the crowd was cool," Pittsburgh Point, 05 14 03 01 70 (100,000 demonstrate in Washington, D. C. against government action in Cambodia and Vietnam.)

1761 _____. "The Trial is over, but not the danger," Pittsburgh Point, 02 19 01 01 70 (Chicago Conspiracy Trial.)

1762 _____. "Tripping through the Mellon patch," Pittsburgh Point, 04 30 01 03 70 (Gulf Oil demonstration at the shareholders meeting, by Gulf Action Project.)

1763 _____. "A Week of pain and outrage," Pittsburgh Point, 05 07 02 01 70 (Protest over Nixon's Cambodia decision.)

1764 _____. "What's ailing the jury system," Pittsburgh Point, 02 26 01 03 70 ("Examination and hearings in criminal court into how grand jurors are selected.")

1765 Cox, Donald. "Last Hurrahs of Mayor Tate," Distant Drummer, 05 28 01 02 70

1766 Cray, Ed. "FBI ears demonstrate need for wiretap ban," Los Angeles Free Press, 01 07 03 04 66 ("An invasion of privacy.")

1767 Croan, Robert. "New York survives prurient interest," Pittsburgh Point, 06 26 10 01 69 (Description of "where it's at," and the significance of legal implications concerning "I Am Curious Yellow," "Oh Calcutta," and "Hair.")

1768 Cross, Christopher T. "Student involvement is must,' College and University Journal, 9:23-24, Spring, 1970. (Student participation in governance.)

1769 Crowley, Louise. "What's it all about--anarchy?" Other Scenes, 07 15 07 01 69

1770 Cruse, Harold. "Revolutionary nationalism and the

Afro-American," Studies On The Left, 2:12-25, Number 3, 1962. (Revolutionary nationalism and the status of the negro and his history in America.)

1771 Cullen, Mike. "Urban renewal? or negro removal?" Heterodoxical Voice, 04 -- 01 01 68 (Problems of ghetto housing.)

1772 Dahlgren, Kathy. "Mass industry, part I.," Old Mole, 08 15 10 01 69

1773 _____. "SCLC waters down Charleston strike," Old Mole, 07 04 03 01 69 (Hospital workers and their plight at Charleston, S.C.)

1774 Dana, Jame. "Getting ready for the big one," Pittsburgh Point, 07 17 02 02 69 (Emperor Haile Selassie I of Ethiopia and his visit to the Kennedy Space Center.)

1775 Darlington, Sandy. "Revolution's getting groovy: Oakland 7 acquitted," Ann Arbor Argus, 04 14 09 01 69

1776 Davenport, John. "The U.S., the law, and Chief Justice Burger," Fortune, 82:146-150, September,

1777 Davidson, Carl. "Behind the 'antiwar amendment'," Guardian, 06 06 07 01 70 (Hawks and Doves in the Senate on the Vietnam War.)

1778 _____. "Crime laws limit democratic rights," Guardian, 08 08 06 01 70 (Reaction to Nixon's approval of the D.C. crime bill.)

1779 _____. "Prisoners rebel in overcrowded New York City jail," Guardian, 18 22 06 01 70 (Confrontation between inmates at New York's Tombs Prison and prison officials.)

1780 Davis, Wayne H. "The Ecology of affluence," Northwest Passage, 02 23 05 01 70

1781 Davy, J., and A. Wilson. "Secret world war of the antennae," Atlas, 15:17-19, March, 1968. (Wiretapping.)

1782 Deakin, James. "Big brass bombs," Veterans Stars and Stripes Forever, 01 -- 01 01 68

1783 Decter, Midge. "The Liberated women," Commentary, 50:33-44, October, 1970.

1784 Deglau, Paul. "Disagreements with the new left," The Rag, 10 14 08 01 66

1785 Degler, Carl N. "Revolution without ideology: the changing place of women in America," Daedalus, 93:653-670, Spring, 1964.

1786 Dellinger, Dave. "Conversations with Ho," Liberation, 14:2-6, October, 1969.

1787 Demaio, Don. "Burak brings charges against Sprague," Distant Drummer, 05 22 03 01 69 (Shakeup in Philadelphia involving WXUR radio station.)

1788 _____. "Labor committee on trial," Distant Drummer, 10 23 05 01 69

1789 _____. "Mysterious phone calls intersperse Burak trial," Distant Drummer, 11 07 01 02 69

1790 _____. "The Rights of the unborn child," Distant Drummer, 06 18 07 01 70

1792 _____. "You were not wearing a pink gardenia: so how could I tell it was you, or, should a gentleman offer a typarillo to Jerry Rubin," Distant Drummer, 05 09 02 01 69

1792 Demchak, J. M. "Pittsburgh underground," Los Angeles Free Press, 09 13 42 01 68

1793 Denson, Ed. "What happened at the hippening," Berkeley Barb, 01 20 01 01 67 (Be-in at Haight-Ashbury.)

1794 De Rosa, Tony. "Gays aren't fruits," Los Angeles Free Press, 10 16 20 02 70 (Analysis of why homosexuals must be accepted as equal and human.)

1795 _____. "Gays in a shocking situation," Los Angeles

General

Free Press, 10 23 11 02 70 (Militant gays confrontation with Philip Feldman and Anticipatory Avoidance Learning--Electric Shock Treatment.)

1796 _____. "Some of your best friends are gay," Los Angeles Free Press, 06 19 09 03 70

1797 De Souza, Steve. "Sartorial prejudice," Distant Drummer, 11 02 03 01 69

1798 De Swede, John. "Earth people's park," East Village Other, 02 11 15 01 70

1799 Deutsch, M. "Conflicts: productive and destructive," Journal of Social Issues, 25:7-41, January, 1969.

1800 Deutscher, Isaac. "The Making of a revolutionary: from Isaac Deutscher's unfinished biography of Lenin," Introduction by David Horowitz. Ramparts, 9:38-47, August, 1970.

1801 _____, A. J. Muste, and Dave Dellinger. "Marxism and nonviolence," Liberation, 10-16, July, 1969.

1802 Devine, J. Travers. "Revolution--American style," Grass Roots Forum, 10 21 04 01 67

1803 Devine, Laurie. "The Color of justice," Pittsburgh Point, 07 31 01 02 69 (Description of a fundraising affair for the Pittsburgh 3 Defense Fund.)

1804 _____. "Strom Thurmond's ordeal at Pitt.," Pittsburgh Point, 05 29 03 01 69 (Strom Thurmond's attempted address at the Pitt Student Union.)

1805 Dewart, Leslie. "The Cuban crisis revisted," Studies On The Left, 5:15-40, Number 2, 1965. (Analysis of reasons why the Soviets placed strategic weapons in Cuba.)

1806 Diamond, Steve. "Columbia's new dean," Los Angeles Free Press, 08 30 13 01 68

1807 Dickinson, John K. "Ideology and prediction," Studies On The Left, 2:26-34, Number 3, 1962. (Essays on ideologies which predict intellectual and psychological processes.)

1808 Diehl, Digby. "The Gospel according to Peanuts," Los Angeles Free Press, 03 01 26 01 68

1809 _____. "Prof. Thompson defends Garrison," Los Angeles Free Press, 01 05 03 01 68

1810 Dietrich, Marion. "First woman into space," McCalls, 88:80, September, 1961.

1811 Dillman, Terry. "When college students grade the faculty," Class Student Guide, Fall, 1970, p. 25. (A reprint from Today's Education for February, 1970.)

1812 Dimitroff, George. "The Black Panther Party comes forth to combat the raging tide of fascism," Black Panther, 06 07 12 01 69

1813 Dixon, Marlene. "The Restless eagles: Women's Liberation, 1969," Motive, 29:18-23. Numbers 6 and 7, 1969.

1814 _____. "Why women's liberation?" Ramparts, 8:58-63, December, 1969.

1815 Doggett, David. "SDS severs ties with SSOC," Kudzu, 04 05 03 01 69

1816 Donald, David. "Radical historians on the move," New York Times Book Review, July 19, 1970, p. 1. (An account of the American Historical Associations' 84th annual convention in Washington, D.C., and the "Radical Caucus" element in the membership.)

1817 Donaldson, Stephen. "Bill of rights for homosexuals," Liberation News Service, 11 17 B1 02 68 (Twenty-six homosexual rights organizations meeting in Chicago.)

1818 Donner, Frank. "HUAC: the Dossier-Keepers," Studies On The Left, 1:7-25, Number 4, 1961. (Chronology of the activities of the HUAC and its relationship to the FBI and other agencies in government.)

1819 Dorsey, Ellie. "The 'sexist' society," First Issue, 02 -- 43 01 69

1820 Douglas, Angela. "Gays federal fast," Los Angeles Free Press, 07 10 05 01 70

1821 _____. "Gays march on Hollywood Blvd.," Los Angeles Free Press, 07 03 05 01 70

1822 _____. "Hatshepsut sure was a drag," Los Angeles Free Press, 10 30 64 02 70

1823 _____. "Transvestites and transexuals--teach-in," Los Angeles Free Press, 06 05 12 01 70

1824 Douglas, Judi. "Birth control," Black Panther, 02 07 07 01 70

1825 Douglas, Val. "The Youth make the revolution," Black Panther, 08 02 12 01 69

1826 Draper, Anne. "Grape boycott grows," Los Angeles Free Press, 08 16 06 04 68

1827 Draper, Hal. "In defense of the new radicals," New Politics, 4:5-28, Summer, 1965.

1828 _____. "On Marcuse: a critique of pure elitism," Independent Socialist, 03 -- 06 01 69 ("The Defense of Gracchus Babeuf before the High Court of Vendome. Edited and translated by J. A. Scott, with an essay by Herbert Marcuse. University of Massachusetts Press, 1967.")

1829 Dreifus, Claudia. "The Abortion--murder game," East Village Other, 04 07 06 01 70

1830 _____. "Assassination, U.S.A.: EVO interviews Mark Lane on America and the assassinations," East Village Other, 07 09 03 01 69 (Illustrations add to the text of this article.)

1831 _____. "Black Panther women face tough battles," East Village Other, 01 28 13 03 70

1831a Dreifus, Claudia. "Gay power comes to the Village Voice," East Village Other, 09 03 11 01 69

1832 _____. "High school confidential," East Village Other, 03 14 08 01 69 (Confrontation over suspension of Bronx high school student.)

1833 _____. "Mark Lane: assassinations yesterday, today and tomorrow," East Village Other, 07 16 05 01 69 (Interview with Mark Lane and his comments on assassinations.)

1834 _____. "A Radical's bitter diary," East Village Other, 12 24 10 01 69 (Radical ideology.)

1835 _____. "Round two: young MDS vs. the establishment," East Village Other, 08 06 02 03 69 (Young MD radicals vs. Blue Cross.)

1836 _____. "The Young doctors revolt: radicals in the profession," East Village Other, 07 30 03 01 69 (Confrontation at the National Convention of the American Medical Association.)

1837 Dreyer, Thorne. "Law and order meets the underground press," Liberation News Service, 11 27 28 02 68 ("Media of the revolution ... notable is the outrage and fear which it creates in those whose interests it opposes.")

1838 _____. "Law harasses underground papers," Guardian, 12 07 07 01 68

1839 _____. "Underground press meets the censors," Pittsburgh Point, 01 02 03 01 69 (Confrontations described between censors and the underground press written by Mr. Dreyer of the Liberation News Service.)

1840 Drukman, Elaine. "CBW: nightmare plan," The Ally, 06 -- 07 01 69

1841 Dryer, Ivan. "Mary Sirhan joins hunt for RFK assassin," Los Angeles Free Press, 06 26 01 05 70

1842 _____. "New evidence that Sirhan missed Bobby,"

Los Angeles Free Press, 06 12 01 04 70

1843 _____. "RFK probe rally due," Los Angeles Free Press, 07 17 02 03 70 (The Theodore Charach probe.)

1844 Drysdale, Dickey. "Pay the bond or go to jail," Pittsburgh Point, 06 04 02 01 70

1845 Duclow, Donald. "Herbert Marcuse and 'Happy Consciousness'," Liberation, 14:7-15, October, 1969.

1846 Duffett, John. "Tribunal finds U.S. guilty," Los Angeles Free Press, 12 29 03 01 67 (Russell International War Crimes Tribunal.)

1847 Duncan, Donald. "America's Devil's Island," Muckraker's Guide--Ramparts, Special Collector's edition, pp. 8-14. ("Preview: 1969--Inside the Army stockade at San Francisco's Presidio where 21 prisoners have tried to kill themselves.")

1848 _____. "Mace: the methods of madness," Ramparts, 6:62-63, June 29, 1968.

1849 _____. "Muckraking: 1966--'I quit'," Muckrakers Guide--Ramparts, Special Collector's edition, pp. 41-46. ("Memoirs of a special forces hero.... We can best immortalize our fallen members by striving for an enlightened future where Man has found another solution to his problems rather than resorting to the futility and stupidity of war.")

1850 _____. "The Prisoner," Ramparts, 8:51-56, September, 1969. (Sergeant George S. Smith's story of his imprisonment by the National Liberation Front in November, 1965, and the resultant effects on his life.)

1851 Duronio, Dick. "Dickie's peace," Grok, 05 -- 05 01 70 (Nixon, politics, government, and foreign affairs.)

1852 _____. "New death ray: CO_2 Laser," Grok, 05 -- 04 01 70

1853 _____, and Z. Eddie. "From Corfu Prison," Grok,

04 -- 12 01 70 (A letter from two brothers "who were arrested for smuggling hashish into Greece from Turkey." The prison is on the Aegean Sea on the Isle of Corfu.)

1854   Dutton, John M., and Richard E. Walton. "Interdepartmental conflict and cooperation: two contrasting studies," Human Organization, 25:207-220, 1966.

1855   Du Vall, Joyce. "Women's strike--1970," Los Angeles Free Press, 08 28 01 01 70 (August 26, 1970.)

1856   Eberle, Paul. "Arbogast and Margolis are alive and well in L.A.: Arbogast: Homosexuality is a pain in the ass," Los Angeles Free Press, 01 12 13 01 68

1857   _____. "Assassination prober's wife attacked," Los Angeles Free Press, 07 03 06 01 70 (Sirhan-Charach Case.)

1858   _____. "Bible-banger McIntire preaches hate at Southland rally to defend Bradley," Los Angeles Free Press, 01 12 01 01 68

1859   _____. "Blacks, lily whites greet Alabaman on campaign tour," Los Angeles Free Press, 11 10 01 01 67 (George Wallace campaign.)

1860   _____. "CBS stamps out reality, smothers Smothers Brothers comedy hours," Los Angeles Free Press, 04 11 06 01 69

1861   _____. "Cleaver raps with national press," Los Angeles Free Press, 09 27 07 01 68

1862   _____. "Cops bust 'The Beard' nightly," Los Angeles Free Press, 02 02 01 01 68 (Question of censorship involved.)

1863   _____. "Cuban raider 'Skip' Hall denies conspiracy charges," Los Angeles Free Press, 01 12 01 04 68

1864   _____. "FBI 'swinger' turns fink," Los Angeles

Free Press, 06 20 01 01 69

1865 _____. "Hays plan to liberate a county," Los Angeles Free Press, 10 23 10 01 70 (The takeover of Alpine County, Calif. by 500 gays.)

1866 _____. "Governor Edmund G. Brown meets the L.A. Free Press," Los Angeles Free Press, 10 30 48 01 70 ("Brown's views about contemporary affairs conducted in an interview.")

1867 _____. "Homosexuality is a pain in the ass," Los Angeles Free Press, 01 12 13 01 68 (Views of Arbogast vs. those of Margolis.)

1868 _____. "The Minutemen," East Village Other, 07 23 03 01 69 (Interview with Dean Morris on the Minutemen organization.)

1869 _____. "Mort Saul: America--love it or leave it," Los Angeles Free Press, 11 21 43 01 69

1870 _____. "Mort Saul speaks out on the future of America," Los Angeles Free Press, 01 19 03 01 68

1871 _____. "My brothers' keeper," Los Angeles Free Press, 03 29 03 01 68

1872 _____. "Our cameras are weapons ... our films are tools," Los Angeles Free Press, 11 22 14 01 68 (Definition of obscenity in question.)

1873 _____. "Peace and freedom nominated Jacobs," Los Angeles Free Press, 03 22 01 01 68 (Jacobs and the Peace and Freedom Party.)

1874 _____. "Ramparts editor: America at moment of crisis," Los Angeles Free Press, 12 22 09 01 67

1875 _____. "San quentin inmates reveal surrealistic nightmare: Legislative hearings held inside walls," Los Angeles Free Press, 02 28 07 01 69 (Convicts tell of complaints and grievances before legislative committee.)

1876 Eberle, Paul. "This people's war produces a people's communism," Los Angeles Free Press, 10 16 03 01 70 (An interview with Robert Scheer after his visit to North Vietnam.)

1877 _____. "Tribunal's captured U.S. footage shows atrocities," Los Angeles Free Press, 05 03 06 01 68 (Investigation into U.S. war atrocities.)

1878 _____. "Walter Hurst, Pandora Box defender, to seek bench as municipal judge," Los Angeles Free Press, 03 15 01 03 68

1879 _____. "Welfare game 'put heads in a spin'," Los Angeles Free Press, 05 23 24 01 69 (Payment program and how it works.)

1880 _____. "Witness to alleged Rodgers beating may fear for her life, newsmen claim," Los Angeles Free Press, 01 26 01 01 68

1881 _____, and Sue Marshall. "Chicanos rip off the Democratic Party," Los Angeles Free Press, 10 09 01 01 70 (Confrontations between Chicano activists and the Democratic Party in California.)

1882 Eby, Kermit. "The Teamsters and Hoffa," Studies On The Left, 2:68-73, Number 3, 1962.

1883 Edwards, Harry, and Jack Scott. "After the Olympics: buying off protest," Ramparts, 8:16-21, November, 1969. (Boycotts of the Mexico City Olympics.)

1884 Egelson, Nick. "Letter to the movement; re-creation, self-transformation and revolutionary consciousness," Liberation, 15:45-50, April, 1970.

1885 Ehrlich, Paul. "Eco-catastrophe!" Ramparts, 8:24-28, September, 1969. (Dr. Ehrlich "predicts what our world will be like in ten years if the present course of environmental destruction is allowed to continue.")

1886 _____. "The Population explosion, fact and fiction," Northwest Passage, 02 23 12 01 70

1887 Eisenscher, Michael. "North Koreans unimpressed with heroism of Pueblo," Distant Drummer, 10 23 16 01 69

1888 _____. "The Pueblo affair--told by its captors," Black Panther, 11 01 09 01 69 (Reprinted from People's World.)

1889 Elle, Lawrence. "Germ warfare at U. of P.," New Left Notes, 12 02 09 01 66 (Confrontation at the Univ. of Pennsylvania over germ warfare research for the Army.)

1889a Elliott, A. Wright. "The Alliance of business and youth," Electronic Age, 30:34-37, Winter, 1970-71. ("Increased communication with youth is a major prerequisite if businesses are to gain the perspective needed to foster workable approaches for the improvement of society.")

1890 Elliott, Ward. "Are we trying to stop the war machine by getting rid of the brakes," Alternative, 12 -- 05 01 70 (Current assault on ROTC.)

1891 Erikson, Erik. "Inner and outer space: reflections on womanhood," Daedalus, 93:582-606, Spring, 1964.

1892 Erlich, Paul R. "Pardon me, but your end of the boat is sinking," Los Angeles Free Press, 11 22 03 01 68 (Control of population.)

1893 Erlich, Reese. "Convention mayhem splits SDS forces," Los Angeles Free Press, 06 11 01 01 69

1894 Eshelman, William R. "Missouri quicksand: an indepth survey," Wilson Library Bulletin, 44:266-267, November, 1969. (Controversy over the dismissal of Joan Bodger, children's consultant for the State Library.)

1895 Espy, Robert Hamilton Edwin. "NCC chief proposes general ecumenical council," Christianity Today, 14:30, December 19, 1969.

1896 Evans, D. M. "Industrial disposal wells: solution or more pollution?" School Science and

Mathematics, 70:483-6, June, 1970.

1897 Evers, Joanne. "Sorcerer's strange class in witchery," Berkeley Barb, 06 30 02 02 67

1898 Fairfield, Dick. "The New dropout creating an alternative life style," Grok, 06 27 08 01 70 (A condensed version of a speech from Alternative dealing with communal life styles of living.)

1899 Farrel, Fred. "Our civilization in grip of death-wish it will persecute anyone who tries to save it: moment of truth," Common Sense, 05 01 01 01 70

1900 _____. "Race, reason and common sense: can we ever be a nation?" Common Sense, 06 01 01 01 70 (Race problems and civil rights.)

1901 _____. "Vietnam: what is it all about? After nine years of futility and 40,000 deaths ...," Common Sense, 01 15 01 01 70

1902 _____. "Why great capitalists support communism," Common Sense, 06 15 01 03 70

1903 Fay, John. "The Playboy culture: sexual liberation," Indian Head, 08 28 08 01 67 (Playboy and its implications for sexual freedom.)

1904 Federick, Don. "New abortion method," Los Angeles Free Press, 05 29 02 01 70

1905 Felsenstein, Lee. "King nearer to Stokely?" Berkeley Barb, 05 19 06 04 67 (Views of both King and Carmichael on contemporary social problems.)

1906 Ferrell, Tom. "If the silent majority could talk, what would it say?" Esquire, 73:146-151, May, 1970.

1907 Feuer, Alan. "We got the fever; we're hot ...," Fifth Estate, 06 03 01 01 70 (Detroit High School students "walkout in search of an education." Protests ran from the dress code to the lack of any black administrator, plus assignments of lockers.)

1908 Fine, David. "High school movement," Heterodoxical

Voice, 04 -- 02 03 68 (High School groups organize in Delaware.)

1909 Fine, Jessie. "Bless you Angela--Local girl makes good--will force UC Regents to eat humble shit," San Diego Free Press, 10 01 07 01 69 (Angela's story and the circumstances surrounding her dismissal from UC.)

1910 Fisher, Tom. "A Small town's race problem may be too hot to cool off," North Carolin Anvil, 07 26 01 02 69

1911 Fitch, Bob. "Nixon: with a little help for his friends," Ramparts, 8:58-64, March, 1970.

1912 Fitzgerald, Dennis. "Texaco thinks time is right," Chicago Kaleidoscope, 03 28 15 01 69 (Controversy over the raising of gasoline prices.)

1913 Flash, J. Jack. "Frisco moratorium," Berkeley Barb, 10 17 02 01 69

1914 Fletcher, H. L. "Intellectual freedom: bills in legislature dealing with obscenity and pornography in California," American Library Association Bulletin, 62:1354-7, December, 1964.

1915 Foote, Nelson N. "New roles for men and women," Marriage and Family Living, 23:325-329, November, 1961.

1916 Foreman, Clark H. "In defense of Robert F. Williams," Studies On The Left, 3:66-67, Number 1, 1962.

1917 Forman, Alex, and F. P. Salstrom. "Revolution, diggers styles," Distant Drummer, 10 03 04 01 69 (Another view of the movement.)

1918 Forman, James. "Black writers hail Frantz Fanon," Guardian, 11 23 21 01 68 (Description of Fanon's contribution to revolutionary socialism especially in Africa.)

1919 Forsberg, Clarence J. "Three reasons to stop the killing," Together, 14:48-49, July, 1970. (War atrocities in Vietnam.)

1920 Fox, Andrew. "How Wallace can/will be elected president: Notes on the Che Guevara of main street," Los Angeles Free Press, 10 18 03 01 68

1921 Frame, Scotty. "Fort Hood soldiers riot," Dallas Notes, 12 -- 03 01 67 (October 3, 1967--198 light infantry brigade riots at Fort Hood, Texas.)

1922 Francis, Leonard R. "Hard hats or political Ku Klux Klan," Black Panther, 07 18 05 05 70

1923 Franklin, Ted. "Exploitation at Woodstock," Pittsburgh Point, 08 24 10 01 69 (From the Liberation News Service the description of the Woodstock Festival exploitation.)

1924 Freed, Donald. "A Case of pre-dawn, no-knock Nazism," Los Angeles Free Press, 07 24 07 01 70 (No-Knock Crime Bill.)

1925 _____. "Huey Newton--the people must burn the pig constitution," Los Angeles Free Press, 09 11 03 01 70

1926 Freemond, Jules. "Capitalist hangout under siege," East Village Other, 12 01 04 01 67 (Peace movement demonstration at the New York Hilton.)

1927 Freistadt, Hans. "Modern Marxism and scientific knowledge: any common ground?" Studies On The Left, 1:62-74, Number 3, 1960. (Does Marxist philosophy and the formal content of science have anything in common?)

1928 Fruchter, Norm. "Mississippi: notes on SNCC," Studies On The Left, 4:74-80, Number 4, 1965.

1929 Furst, Randy. "Cops brutalize 'love generation'," Guardian, 07 27 03 01 68 (Confrontation with police at Hashburg riot.)

1930 _____. "Penn State: 'godforsaken hole'," Guardian, 11 16 09 01 68 (Concerning the detachments of individuals from the mainstream of

General 181

education.)

1931 Fusfeld, Daniel R. "The Basic economics of the urban and racial crisis," Michigan Academician, II Winter, 1970.

1932 Gall, Dennis. "Twelve on trial--a courtroom confrontation," Kaleidoscope, 05 23 03 01 69 (The trial of 12 of the Milwaukee 14.)

1933 Gallup, George. "The Public's attitude toward the public schools," Phi Delta Kappan, 22:99-112, October, 1970.

1934 Gamson, William A. "Rancorous conflict in community politics," American Sociological Review, 31:71-81, 1966.

1935 Gans, Herbert J. "Rational approach to radicalism," Studies On The Left, 6:37-53, Number 1, Jan.-Feb., 1966. (Replies to this article are by Staughton Lynd and James Weinstein.)

1936 Gardner, David. "Mister Rockefeller builds his dream house," Ramparts, 8:36-39, September, 1969. (Implications involved with the Rockefeller South Mall building complex. Highly illustrated with color models by Carl Howard.)

1937 Gardner, Fred. "Fort Ord," Great Speckled Bird, 06 02 19 01 69 (Demonstration protesting stockade conditions at Fort Ord.)

1938 _____. "Hassles over attempts to set up coffeehouse for G.I's at Fort Carson, Colorado," Liberation News Service, 08 02 09 01 69

1939 Garrett, James. "Black power and black education," Washington Free Press, 04 16 08 01 69

1940 Garry, Charles. "Speech by Charles Garry at benefit in his behalf--December 19, 1969," Black Panther, 12 27 05 01 69

1941 Garver, Paul. "Mellon proves charity pays," Grok, 06 27 10 01 70

1942   Gaughan, Joe. "Indians' plans reach beyond island center," Berkeley Barb, 01 02 04 01 70

1943   Geerdes, Clay. "Berkeley forecast: Haight revisited," Los Angeles Free Press, 06 20 03 01 69

1944   _____. "Hayakawa plus new power plus revolution =Freak," Los Angeles Free Press, 12 28 02 01 68

1945   _____. "Student-worker alliance: viable or naive --will it work?" Los Angeles Free Press, 08 01 07 01 69

1946   Gellen, Martin. "The Making of a pollution-industrial complex," Ramparts, 8:22-27, May, 1970.

1947   Genet, Jean. "Here and now for Bobby Seale," Black Panther, 05 31 26 01 70 (A reprint from Ramparts.)

1948   _____. "Bobby Seale, the Black Panthers and us white people," Black Panther, 03 28 07 01 70

1949   _____. "I must begin with an explanation of my presence in the U.S.," Black Panther, 05 09 06 01 70

1950   Genovese, Eugene D. "The Legacy of slavery and the roots of black nationalism," Studies On The Left, 6:3-26, Number 6, Nov.-Dec., 1966. (Black struggles for equality in America. Comments by Herbert Aptheker, C. Vann Woodward, and Frank Kofsky. A rejoinder by the author is appended.)

1951   Gentile, Charles. "King assassination quickens black polarization," Florida Free Press, 03 18 07 01 68 ("The assassination of M.L.K. on April 5, 1968 did more to polarize the black peoples than 500 Stokely Carmichaels, or 1,000 Rap Browns could ever do.")

1952   Gerber, A. "The Right to receive and possess pornography; an attorney foresees the end of legal restrictions," Wilson Library Bulletin, 44:641-644, February, 1970.

1953 Gershman, Carl. "The New left in the Nixon era," Pittsburgh Point, 01 02 01 01 69

1954 _____. "SDS, or the new thermidor," Pittsburgh Point, 05 05 05 01 69 (Confrontationism and the significance of SDS.)

1955 Gerth, Hans H. "C. Wright Mills, 1916-1962," Studies On The Left, 2:7-11, Number 3, 1962. (Autobiographical account of the controversial figure and his political ideology.)

1956 Gettys, Montgomery III. "Family fun, Franklin Institute exposed," Distant Drummer, 05 07 03 01 70

1957 Gibson, Barbara. "Women: masturbation," Great Speckled Bird, 12 22 06 01 69 (A reprint from Kaleidoscope--Women's Liberation Supplement.)

1958 Gibson, Kenneth Allen. "Black mayors," Newsweek, 76:16, August 3, 1970.

1959 Gilman, Richard. "There's a wave of pornography, obscenity, sexual expression," New York Times Magazine, September 8, 1968, pp. 36-37.

1960 Girling, J. L. S. "Crisis and conflict in Cambodia," Orbis, 14:349-365, Summer, 1970.

1961 Gitlin, Todd. "New left: old traps," Ramparts, 8:20, September, 1969.

1962 _____, and John Simon. "The Meaning of people's park," Liberation, 14:17-21, July, 1969.

1963 Glaberman, Martin. "Marxism, the working class and the trade unions," Studies On The Left, 4:65-70, Number 3, 1964. (Argumentative discussion of the role of the working class as an agency of social change. Included in the same issue is a reply by Aronowitz.)

1964 Gleason, Ralph. "Lenny Bruce," Miami Free Press, 07 02 17 01 69

1965 Glenn, Hortense M., and James Walters. "Feminine

stress in the twentieth century," Journal of Home Economics, 58:703-707, November, 1966.

1966 Glick, Brian, and Kathy Boudin. "Guide to the grand jury," Liberation, 14:56-58, August-September, 1969.

1967 Glusman, Paul. "Behind the Chicago conspiracy trial," Ramparts, 8:39-47, January, 1970.

1968 _____. "Eldridge on Weatherman; Seale on ice," Berkeley Tribe, 11 07 03 01 69

1969 _____. "The Government is entitled to a fair trial here," Black Panther, 11 29 05 01 69 (The People put the government on trial.)

1970 _____. "One, two, three ... Many SDS'S," Ramparts, 8:6-16, September, 1969. (Description of the activities and various factions of the SDS.)

1971 _____. "War of nerves defeats CIA--Dow on campus," Berkeley Barb, 11 10 07 04 67

1972 Gold, Elliot M. "New Left concentration camps--fact or fancy?" Los Angeles Free Press, 12 20 03 01 68

1973 Gold, Mike. "Chicago Conspiracy," Washington Free Press, 08 -- 07 01 69

1974 Gold, U. "Obscenity gap," National Review, 21:597, June 17, 1969.

1975 Goldberg, Art. "Oakland 7 conspiracy trial opens," Guardian, 01 18 04 01 69

1976 _____. "The Perils of the pill," Ramparts, 7:45-48, May, 1969.

1977 Goldberg, Marilyn. "New light on the exploitation of women," Liberation, 14:23-27, October, 1969.

1978 Goldberg, Philip. "Are women prejudiced against women?" Transaction, 5:28-30, April, 1968.

1979 Goldhaber, Nat. "The Streets belong to which people?

General 185

East Village Other, 08 06 07 01 69 ("In a community the streets belong to all the people.")

1980 Goldin, Gerald A. "Earth day happening," Distant Drummer, 04 23 01 01 70

1981 ———. "Panthers rap--at Penn," Distant Drummer, 04 02 03 03 70

1982 ———. "Politics of earth week," Distant Drummer, 04 23 03 01 70

1983 ———. "Supreme Court shackles, gags defense," Distant Drummer, 04 09 01 02 70

1984 Goldman, Lawrence. "W. J. Ghent and the left," Studies On The Left, 3:21-40, Number 3, 1963. (Somewhat autobiographical account of the controversial figure from Indiana.)

1985 Goodell, Charles E. "Duke, U.N.C. differ sharply on Oct. 15 moratorium," North Carolin Anvil, 10 04 01 02 69 (Views from the two schools are contrasted with the senator from North Carolina.)

1986 Goodman, Allan E. "South Vietnam: neither war nor peace," Asian Survey, 10:107-132, February, 1970.

1987 Goodman, Paul. "Reflections on the moon," Liberation, 14:60-62, August-September, 1969. (Questions about priorities and the industrial-military complex.)

1988 ———. "Three types of resistance," Los Angeles Free Press, 03 15 26 01 68

1989 Gore, D. "Skirmish with the censors," American Library Association Bulletin, 63:193-203, February, 1969. (Discussion: 63:553-6, May, 1969.)

1990 Gorer, Geoffrey. "Man has no 'killer' instinct," New York Times Magazine, November 27, 1966.

1991 Gould, Howard. "Miami's rainy day SDS," Daily Planet, 05 11 01 01 70

1992 Goulden, Joseph C. "Voices from the silent majority,"

Harper's, 240:67-68, April, 1970.

1993 Government Employees' Exchange. "CIA head raps," Washington Free Press, 05 16 09 01 69

1994 Graham, Fred P. "Black crime: the lawless image," Harper's, 241:64-65, September, 1970.

1995 Grannemann, Glenn N. "Strom Thurmond's ordeal at C.M.U.," Pittsburgh Point, 01 22 01 03 70 (Thurmond's speech at Carnegie-Mellon University in Pittsburgh.)

1996 Grannis, C. B. "Where do you draw the line? Withdrawal of facsimile Mother Goose for offensive language," Publishers Weekly, 195:73, April 14, 1969.

1997 Gray, David. "The Unmentioned issue--community control," Part I. Distant Drummer, 04 09 11 01 70

1998 _____. "The Unmentioned issue--community control," Part II. Distant Drummer, 05 07 05 01 70

1999 Green, Jack. "The Voice of the silent majority: civil rights, integration and Jews ...," Common Sense, 02 01 01 01 70

2000 Greene, Fred. "The Case for and against military withdrawal from Vietnam and Korea," Annals of the American Academy, 390:1-19, July, 1970.

2001 Greenhouse, Linda J. "After July 1, an abortion should be as simple to have as a tonsillectomy, but ...," New York Times Magazine, June 28, 1970, p. 7.

2002 _____. "Constitutional question: Is there a right to abortion?" New York Times Magazine, January 25, 1970, pp. 30-31. (Discussion February 22, 1970, p. 14.)

2003 Greenleaf, Richard. "Studies on the right," Studies On The Left, 3:57-59, Number 1, 1962. (A reply to the article by Cruse of 2:12-25, Number 3, 1962. Cruse's reply to this is carried in 3:60-65,

Number 1, 1962.)

2004 Greenspan, Ralph. "The Company thinks it's God," Pittsburgh Point, 01 15 04 01 70 (Discrimination in industry.)

2005 Greenwood, Frank. "Genocide definition fits America," Los Angeles Free Press, 07 12 06 01 68 (Alleged crime of genocide by Americans against Afro-Americans and the Red man.)

2006 _____. "Panther's must merge with the people," Los Angeles Free Press, 09 13 25 01 68

2007 _____. "U.S. founded by racists," Los Angeles Free Press, 05 10 17 02 68

2008 Greenwood, Tamu Debra. "High school students protest--cops--school--draft," Free Student, 11 22 01 01 67 (Repressive tactics in high school described.)

2008a Gregg, Richard, A. Jackson McCormack, and Douglas J. Pedersen. "The Rhetoric of black power: a street level interpretation," Quarterly Journal of Speech, 55:151-160, April, 1969. (The purpose of the article is to "provide some examples and interpretation of the rhetoric of black power based on observations made while conducting a class in oral communication in the Harrisburg, Pa. ghetto.")

2009 Groomer, Ray. "Doctor Spock raps in Boulder," Chinook, 10 09 03 02 69

2010 Groth, Ned. "Ecology: blips, blips, blips, blips, blips," Peninsula Observer, 06 30 16 01 69 (Pollution-industrial complex.)

2011 Grubbe, Peter. "Asian nightmare--a U.S. pullout," Atlas, 18:28-30, July, 1969.

2012 Grunwald, Henry. "Thoughts on a troubled El Dorado," Time, 95:18-21, June 22, 1970. (More problems at Kent State University.)

2013 Grusendorf, Arthur A. "American teen-agers' belief concerning causes of juvenile delinquency," Rocky

Mountain Social Science Journal, 6: October, 1969.

2014 Guerrero, Gene. "A Hip community," Great Speckled Bird, 02 09 02 01 70 ("Atlanta Borealis.")

2015 Guevara, Gay. "Gay Liberation Front mounting Alpine assault," Los Angeles Free Press, 11 27 13 03 70

2016 Gwin, Jim. "Close the schools and watch the community die," Great Speckled Bird, 04 21 08 01 69 (Resentment and protest in the black community in Scottdale High School, DeKalb County, Georgia.)

2017 _____. "Death of high school democracy," Great Speckled Bird, 04 14 07 02 69 (Administrative activities and student body suspensions at Columbia High School in DeKalb County, Georgia.)

2018 _____. "Equality for longhairs," Great Speckled Bird, 05 19 02 01 69 (Confrontation at the famous Waffle House in Atlanta for refusing to serve waffles to longhairs.)

2019 _____. "High school repression," Great Speckled Bird, 03 17 03 01 69

2020 _____. "New mobe and in high school,". Great Speckled Bird, 12 22 05 01 69 (High school mobilization in Clayton County and Atlanta School Districts.)

2021 Gwin, Pam, and Bob Malone. "Law 'n order," Great Speckled Bird, 06 30 02 01 69

2022 Haag, E. van den. "Is pornography a cause of crime?" Encounter, 29:52-6, December, 1967. (Reply by J. W. Lambert, 30:55-7, March, 1967.)

2023 Haber, Barbara, and Alan Haber. "With a little help from our friends," Paper Tiger, 10 -- 11 01 67 ("Radicals in the Professions Conference." Problems of the individual as he relates to the radical movement, and the alternatives open to him. Consists of two parts.)

General 189

2024 Hacker, Michael S. "Blue laws--blue balls," Daily Planet, 11 10 02 01 69 (An attorney protests the absurdity of the statutes which are still in force, in effect today in Florida.)

2025 _____. "On Capital Punishment," Miami Free Press, 07 18 03 01 69

2026 Hadden, Jeffrey K. "Clergy involvement in civil rights," Annals of the American Academy, 387, January, 1970.

2027 Halberstam, M. J. "Abortion: a startling proposal," Redbook, 134:78-79, April, 1970.

2028 Hall, Standish. "Civil rights ... for whom?" Common Sense, 02 01 03 02 70

2029 _____. "Failure of integration," Common Sense, 02 01 04 01 70

2030 Hallowell, John. "Gore Vidal on homosexuality: 'I'm given credit for having invented it'," Advocate, 11 11 16 01 70 (An exclusive interview conducted with a controversial writer.)

2031 Halprin, Burt. "Anti-Fascism conference--two views: Panther Conference--Conference a bummer," Northwest Passage, 08 05 08 01 69

2032 Halstead, Ron. "Dow Chemical target for napalm protest," Fifth Estate, 07 30 05 02 66

2033 Hamilton, Becky. "Repression: High school," Great Speckled Bird, 06 02 18 01 69 (Underground newspaper at Choctawthalchie High School, Fort Walton Beach, Florida, causes up-tightness by administration.)

2034 Hamilton, Mary. "Harlem 6 win retrial," Guardian, 12 07 03 02 68

2035 _____. "Liberation News service sprouts two heads," Los Angeles Free Press, 08 30 24 01 68 (Reprinted from the Guardian.)

2036 _____. "U.S. military is target for G. I. Week,"

Guardian, 10 19 04 01 68 (National mobilization committee helps organize G. I's. against the war.)

2037 Hamilton, Mary. "Welfare mothers face lean days," Guardian, 04 06 07 01 68

2038 Haroldson, Thomas. "The Nude-in, latest protest," Fifth Estate, 02 15 04 01 68 (Two San Francisco State College teenagers express in the nude their "total commitment to sexual freedom." Article explores possibilities for future nude-ins.)

2039 Harris, Bennie. "Exposing Fascist methods of investigation," Black Panther, 05 19 03 01 70

2040 Harris, Roger D. "Radical critique of a liberal," Kudzu, 11 12 08 01 68 (Analysis of strategies of confrontation with a speech at Millsaps College.)

2041 Haskell, Gordon K. "Civil liberties: to hell in a basket," Dissent, 17:116, March-April, 1970.

2042 Hayden, Casey (et al.). "Sex and Caste," Liberation Magazine, Part I. April, 1966; Part 2. December, 1966. (Women and the radical movement.)

2043 Hayden, Tom. "All for Vietnam," Ramparts, 9:26-27, September, 1970.

2044 _____. "Chicago--the alternative convention: address by Tom Hayden at Alternative Convention in Grant Park, Thursday August 29.," Los Angeles Free Press, 09 13 03 01 68

2045 _____. "Hayden: the Walker Report," Old Mole, 01 13 04 01 69 (From Liberation News Service, and edited by Vernon Grizzard who was one of the marshall coordinators for the National Mobilization Committee in Chicago.)

2046 Hayman, Ed. "Rough Draft--distribution at Ft. Eustis pleases editors, astonishes some G.I's.," Rough Draft, 10 -- 01 01 69

2047 Hayward, Claude. "No war toys sandcastle built on Venice Beach," Los Angeles Free Press, 07 13

01 03 65 (NWT "group dedicated to the removal of war 'make believe kill' toys from the market ...,")

2048 Head, Robert. "A Word on welfare," Nola Express, 01 27 04 01 68

2049 Heins, Marjorie. "Games children play," First Issue, 05 08 20 01 68 (Reprinted from the Rat. Describes brainwash games now on the market. "Toys, the long elaborate line of heirs to monopoly.")

2050 Henig, Peter. "Privacy yields to progress: the system experts study New Haven, Connecticut," New Left Notes, 06 19 01 01 67 (A two year study involves, "IBM's first attempt to program an entire city.")

2051 Hennessy, Tom. "Apollo, Agnew," Pittsburgh Point, 07 24 07 01 69 (Agnew going to Mars?)

2052 _____. "The Army eyes the Yough," Pittsburgh Forum, 11 20 01 01 70 (U.S. Army Corps of Engineers and their proposals for the Yough (river) in Pittsburgh.)

2053 _____. "Contemptible justice," Pittsburgh Point, 02 19 10 03 70

2054 _____. "Dirty movies," Pittsburgh Point, 08 28 08 01 69 (An imaginary dream of the authors attendance at a movie called "Gidget Is Curious, Part 5.")

2055 _____. "Operation ecology," Pittsburgh Point, 04 23 10 01 70

2056 _____. "Racial isolation," Pittsburgh Point, 06 12 11 01 69 ("An imaginary nightmare, in which the author was in charge of a citizen committee attempting to work with the Board of Education to resolve racial problems in Pittsburgh schools.")

2057 _____. "Ultimate weapons," Pittsburgh Point, 07 17 05 03 69 (An imaginary "sure-fire method of bringing North Vietnam to its knees.")

2058 Henri, (Brother). "Black struggle: revolution or liberation?" Burning Spear, 12 01 13 01 70 (Concerns revolution, white radicals, genocide and the black-liberation struggle.)

2059 Henry, Carol. "Domestic and international genocide," Black Panther, 04 25 15 03 70

2060 Herman, Edward S. "The Alice in Wonderland economics of the SDS Labor committee," Distant Drummer, 10 11 04 01 69

2061 ———. "More on SDS: Labor committee economics," Distant Drummer, 10 23 07 01 69

2062 Herrup, Paul. "New Democratic Coalition of Pennsylvania: (NDCP) Will it survive and grow?" Pittsburgh Point, 04 03 01 01 69 (Goals, objectives, etc. of the newly found organization.)

2063 Hersh, Seymour M. "Germ warfare: for Alma Mater, God and Country," Ramparts, 8:21-28, December, 1969. (Describes the biological warfare establishment in three parts. Part of the research for this article was subsidized by the Fund For Investigative Research.)

2064 ———. "On uncovering the great nerve gas cover-up," Ramparts, 7:13-18, June, 1969.

2065 ———. "Twenty-thousand guns under the sea," Ramparts, 8:41-44, September, 1969. (Interesting undersea aspects of the nation's military policy and what is involved with oceanographic undersea military bases in establishing underwater missile systems.)

2066 Hess, Karl. "An open letter to Barry Goldwater," Ramparts, 8:28-31, October, 1969.

2067 ———. "Who is Melvin Laird?" Ramparts, 8:27-31, August, 1969.

2068 Heusdenstamm, F. K. "An analysis of a high school underground paper," Educational Leadership,

General 193

28:20-22, October, 1970.

2069 Hewitt, Masai. "Seize the time--submit or fight," Black Panther, 12 13 03 02 69

2070 Hewitt, Ray. "Seize the time," Black Panther, 09 13 03 01 69

2071 Hightower, Charles. "Cops strike in Ocean-Hill-Brownsville," Liberation News Service, 10 09 15 01 68

2072 Hill, Amie. "You get a tattoo if you really dig your body," Rags, 12 -- 31 01 70 (More on tattooing and its significance for individuals who want more of self-expression.)

2073 Hill, Hugo. "Vietnam: Paris: View from Saigon," Abas, 02 -- 08 01 69

2074 _____. "Vietnam: Racist Red Cross," Distant Drummer, 10 03 08 01 69

2075 Hilliard, David. "If you want peace, you've got to fight for it," Black Panther, 01 03 04 01 70

2076 _____. "Lumpen-Proletarian discipline versus bourgeous reactionism," Black Panther, 08 09 11 01 69

2077 _____. "Pig--an international language," Black Panther, 12 27 09 01 69

2078 Himmelbauer, Sue. "War tax resistance," Pittsburgh Point, 03 12 05 02 70

2079 Hinckle, Warren. "Left wing Catholics," Ramparts, 6:15-26, November, 1967.

2080 _____, and Marianne Hinckle. "A History of the use of the unusual movement for women power in the U.S., 1961-1968," Ramparts, 6:23-31, February, 1968.

2081 _____, Robert Scheer, and Sol Stern. "The University on the make (or how MSU helped arm Madame Nhu) Muckrakers Guide, Ramparts--Special

Collector's edition, pp. 52-60. (Part of the introduction to this article was written by Stanley K. Sheinbaum, coordinator of the Vietnam project at Michigan State University. Material for the article originated in Mr. Scheer's pamphlet "How the U.S. Got Involved in Vietnam.")

2082 Hochschild, Adam. "Communism on Treasure Island: Cuba's isle of Pines," Liberation, 14:15-21, December, 1969.

2083 Hodel, Mike. "American Civil Liberties Union gives McCone Watts testimony," Los Angeles Free Press, 10 15 01 02 65 (McCone Commission on the Watts riots.)

2084 Hodel, Mike. "Governor Brown should read the McCone Commission Report," Los Angeles Free Press, 12 10 05 04 65 (The report costing $250,000 contains eighteen suggestions for improving race relations in L.A. Report has a sub-title: Violence in the City--An End or a Beginning.)

2085 Hodges, Donald Clark. "Socialists in search of an ethic," Studies On The Left, 3:14-33, Number 2, 1963. (Foundations of socialism and its interrelationships with other ideologies are presented, including a critique of Hook, Fromm, and Feuer.)

2086 Hoffman, Abbie. "How SDS spurned the yippies," Distant Drummer, 04 24 04 01 69 (Contentions between SDS and Yippies.)

2087 ———. "Revolution can be fun," Pittsburgh Point, 01 29 01 01 70 (Excerpts from a speech by Abbie at Pitt concerning the Chicago Conspiracy Trial.)

2088 ———. "The United States of special effects," Pittsburgh Point, 07 31 03 02 69 (Abbie's thoughts on "the man on the moon." Article is from the Liberation News Service.)

2089 Hoffman, Fred. "Cleaver not 'intimidated' by court decision," Los Angeles Free Press, 11 29 01 02 68

2090 _____. "Panther party calls for anti-fascist front in Oakland," Los Angeles Free Press, 06 11 01 01 69

2091 _____. "Stokeley teaches in Watts," Los Angeles Free Press, 08 30 08 01 68

2092 _____. "Yorty pinko dealings bared," Los Angeles Free Press, 12 28 01 04 68

2093 Hoffman, Joan. "Hypocrisy triumphs," Los Angeles Free Press, 10 25 01 02 68

2094 _____. "Interview with Mark Rudd," Los Angeles Free Press, 10 11 01 01 68

2095 _____. "Racism charged in Pasadena schools," Los Angeles Free Press, 12 20 05 01 68

2096 Hoffman, Michael J. "The Moral equivalent of war?" Distant Drummer, 10 23 01 08 69

2097 Holland, Vincent. "The New left," News From Nowhere, 09 -- -- 01 68

2098 Holtom, Gerald. "The Nuclear disarmament symbol," Win Peace And Freedom Through Non-Violent Action, 5, Number 17:27, October 1, 1969.

2099 Holtz, Betty. "Students did it," Pittsburgh Point, 03 12 07 03 70 (Students at Carlow College's intermediate school aids the Sioux under the Kennedy Foundation.)

2100 Honey, P. J. "Problem of democracy in Vietnam," World Today, 16:71-79, February, 1960.

2101 Horowitz, David. "Bertrand Russell: The final passion," Ramparts, 8:38-43, April, 1970. (Discussion of a meeting in Chelsea in 1964 of the Bertrand Russell Peace Foundation to discuss plans for setting up an International War Crimes Tribunal to investigate America's war in Vietnam.)

2102 _____. "Billion dollar brains: how wealth puts knowledge in its pocket," Ramparts, 7:36-44, May, 1969.

2103 Horowitz, David. "Hand-me-down Marxism and the new left," Ramparts, 8:16-19, September, 1969.

2104 _____. "Malvenido Rockefeller!" Ramparts, 8:20-25, February, 1970. (A description of Nelson A. Rockefeller's trip to Latin America where he was assigned to a fact-finding trip.)

2105 _____. "Revisionist tales of negotiations with the communists," Ramparts, 6:49-54, June 29, 1968. (Description of attempts to negotiate conflicts on a global scale--beginning with Yalta, Korea, Geneva, and Laos.)

2106 _____. "Rocky takes a trip," Ramparts, 8:60-61, August, 1969. (Rockefeller's controversial trip to Latin America on a presidential fact-finding tour which witnessed 10 deaths and one trip was cancelled.)

2107 _____. "Sinews of empire," Ramparts, 8:33-43, October, 1969. (The role of foundations in academia is described. The schools of international affairs, and their interrelationships with government is explained.)

2108 _____, and David Kolodney. "The Foundations (charity begins at home)" Ramparts, 7:38-48, April, 1969.

2109 Horowitz, Irving Louis. "The Unfinished writings of C. Wright Mills: the last phase," Studies On The Left, 3:3-23, Number 4, 1963.

2110 Houts, Peter S., and Doris R. Entwisle. "Academic achievement effort among females: achievement attitudes and sex-role orientation," Journal of Counseling Psychology, 15:284-286, May, 1968.

2111 Howard, Alan. "The Day we invaded Fort Dix," Daily Planet, 11 10 08 01 69 (Protest at Fort Dix to free the soldiers who had been thrown into the stockade for resisting the war in Vietnam.)

2112 Howe, Florence. "The Education of women," Liberation, 14:49-55, August-September, 1969.

2113 Howe, Irving. "Political terrorism: hysteria on the left," New York Times Magazine, April 12, 1970, p. 25. ("All I propose to do here is to look into the rationales developed by the far-out wings of the new left, the responses these get from half sympathetic students, and the likely repercussions of terrorism.")

2114 Howell, David L. "Near crisis in mercury pollution," Guardian, 08 15 06 01 70 (Mercury-Battery manufacturing pollution.)

2115 Hoy, Bill. "How Tiny Tim eats BLT sandwiches, drinks cokes, gets interviewed by D.D. and ignores bores," Distant Drummer, 02 05 28 01 69

2116 Humes, James C. "Dissent and involvement: the need for catalysts," Vital Speeches, 36:183-184, January 1, 1970.

2117 Hunsucker, Suzanne. "Who wants equality; women in Wyoming," Nation, 211:465-468, November 9, 1969.

2118 Hunt, Linda, Gary Hunt, and Nancy Scheper. "Nixon's guaranteed annual poverty: hunger in the welfare state," Ramparts, 8:64-70, December, 1969. ("This article is based on original research done by the Southern Rural Research Project.")

2119 Hunt, Tom. "Nixon's calls cease fire fallacy," Loopwhole, 10 24 03 03 69

2120 Hurwitt, Robert. "Ramparts 'hippie' article raises row," Berkeley Barb, 06 09 07 02 67

2121 Hyson, Brenda. "Building Fascism in America," Black Panther, 03 28 06 01 70

2122 Ingerson, David. "Cleveland militants take over A & P.," Burning River News, 07 21 04 01 69 (Boycott of the California grapes at A & P in Cleveland.)

2123 ———. "Politics of sacrifice," Burning River News, 06 23 03 01 69 (The effectiveness of the arrests in the "movement" and its significance.)

2124   Ireland, Waltraud. "The Rise and fall of the suffrage movement," Leviathan, 05 -- 04 01 70

2125   Irwin, T. "New abortion laws: how are they working?" Today's Health, 48:20-3, March, 1970.

2126   Israeli, Phineas. "Don't call us radical right, Bircher birches," Berkeley Barb, 01 03 11 01 69 (Interesting perceptive analysis of ideologies.)

2127   _____. "The Gay blues," Berkeley Tribe, 11 07 07 01 69

2128   Itkin, Michael Francis. "The Homosexual liberation movement; what direction," Berkeley Barb, 12 05 16 01 69

2129   Ivey, Allen E., and Westen H. Morrill. "Confrontation, communication and encounter: a conceptual framework for student development," Journal of the Association of Deans and Administration of Student Affairs, 7:226-234, April, 1970.

2130   Jackson, Don. "Cure for homosexuals?" Los Angeles Free Press, 06 26 16 01 70 (What cure?)

2131   _____. "Gay liberation movement invades Los Angeles," Berkeley Barb, 10 24 05 04 69

2132   _____. "Los Angeles gay establishment," Berkeley Barb, 11 28 15 04 69

2133   _____. "Rafferty and Dudley swim in cesspool," Berkeley Barb, 12 12 04 01 69

2134   Jackson, Ed. "Gays attack laws, police in three separate court actions," Advocate, 09 -- 01 01 69

2135   Jacobs, Bonye. "High school conference," Great Speckled Bird, 04 14 02 03 69 (Some 70 Southern High School students attend the Atlanta conference.)

2136   Jacobs, Paul. "How the CIA makes liars out of union leaders," Ramparts, 5:25-28, April, 1967.

2137   Jamal, Hakim A. "Black Panthers growl over brother

General

shooting," <u>Los Angeles Free Press</u>, 02 02 13 01 68

2138 _____. "Eartha Kitt wins hearts of black people," <u>Los Angeles Free Press</u>, 01 26 08 01 68 ("Eartha speaks for the people.")

2139 Janeway, Elizabeth. "A Skeptical report on the experts who tell women how to be women," <u>McCall's</u>, 93:95-96, June, 1966.

2140 Jarrell, Willoughby. "Reality in athletics and in academe," <u>Great Speckled Bird</u>, 02 24 05 01 69 ("Contends that men are scaring women out of athletics. Why a double standard?")

2141 Jassen, Jeff. "Slug-happy cops wreck havoc in the Haight," <u>Berkeley Barb</u>, 04 07 01 01 67 ("Look! Look! the lady has two--count 'em-- gallant escorts.")

2142 Jay, Karla. "Here comes the lavendar menace," <u>Los Angeles Free Press</u>, 08 14 55 01 70 (Women and their efforts to become liberated.)

2143 Jay, Martin. "Metapolitics of utopianism," <u>Dissent</u>, 17:342, July-August, 1970.

2144 Jencks, Christopher, and Milton Kotler. "A Government of the black, by the black, and for the black," <u>Ramparts</u>, 5:51-54, July, 1966. (Struggles in the civil rights movement and the underlying conflicts over political strategy, especially in Mississippi.)

2145 Jenkins, Don. "A Non-interview with Tom Hayden," <u>Reconstruction</u>, 03 03 09 01 69

2146 Jensen, Pennfield. "A Student manifesto on the environment," <u>Natural History</u>, 79:20-22, April, 1970.

2147 Jezer, Martin. "A Yippie history," <u>Florida Free Press</u>, 06 30 10 01 68 (Reprinted from <u>Liberation Magazine</u>.)

2148 _____. "Earth read-out. How many harvests have we left?" <u>East Village Other</u>, 02 04 11 04 70

2149 Johnson, George R. "Yab-yum controversy: beauty or obscenity?" 12 08 03 01 67 (Controversy over posters purchased by a police officer in Milwaukee, Wisconsin. Reprinted from the Sentinel.)

2150 Johnson, Grant, and Barbara Johnson. "A Visit with John Gwynne, abortionist," Los Angeles Free Press, 07 10 06 01 70

2151 Johnson, Roger. "Do we dare be silent? The chief characteristics of Fascism," Black Panther, 07 12 05 01 69

2152 Johnston, Art. "The Lesson of the battle of the people's park," Ann Arbor Argus, 06 19 04 01 69

2153 Johnstone, Billy. "Woodstock is beautiful," Grok, 06 -- 03 02 70

2154 Jones, F. "In the year of the pig," Pittsburgh Point, 09 25 07 01 69 (An "underground" movie night at the Pittsburgh Playhouse. Included was "In the Year of the Pig.")

2155 Jones, Frank B. "Huey and history," Black Panther, 09 07 02 01 68

2156 Jones, Lew. "Army brass harass anti-war G.I's," San Diego Free Press, 03 14 06 01 69

2157 Jones, Ruth M. "New mobe plans fall offensive," Pittsburgh Point, 07 07 05 01 69 ("A fall offensive against continuation of the Vietnam war to be directed by a new mobilization committee to end the war in Vietnam. This succeeds the National Mobilization Committee responsible for previous demonstrations.")

2158 Joseph, Tony. "Right on brothers!" Son of Jabberwork, 11 08 04 01 68 (Mexico Olympics.)

2159 Josephson, Eric, and Geoffrey Bauman. "The Persecution and suicide of SDS," Pittsburgh Point, 06 26 01 02 69 (Both authors attended the SDS National Convention as delegates from the Pittsburgh chapter.)

General 201

2160 Joyce, Frank H. "Crime and punishment of John Sinclair," Fifth Estate, 08 07 02 02 69 ("I sentence you to not less than nine and one-half and not more than ten years in the state penitentiary--Judge Robert J. Colombo.")

2161 _____. "Dr. Spock--a test for the movement," Fifth Estate, 01 15 07 01 69

2162 _____. "Who killed John Leroy?" Berkeley Barb, 08 25 05 04 67

2163 Judson, H. "Critic between," Encounter, 30:57-60, March, 1968. (Definition of obscenity.)

2164 Kane, Martin. "An Assessment of black is best," Sports Illustrated, 34:72-83, January 18, 1971.

2165 Kaner, Leslie. "A Women's lib. hitchhiking guide," Los Angeles Free Press, 10 16 13 01 70 (Suggestions for women who hitchhike alone.)

2166 Karlen, Peter. "The Political significance of the JFK assassination," San Diego Free Press, 03 14 12 01 69 (First of a three part article. Second part is in March 28, 1969, page 12. Third part is in April 11, 1969, page 8.)

2167 Karol, K. S. "Castro on the contradictions in Cuba," Ramparts, 9:43-48, December, 1970. (The Revolution in Cuba.)

2168 Katzman, Al. "Floating cities," Alchemist, 02 -- 03 01 69 (Crisis existing between large urban areas and man's ability to cope with the human problems of living in the technological society.)

2169 Kaufman, Arnold S. "Teach-ins: new force for the times," Nation, June 21, 1965, pp. 666-670.

2170 Kaufman, Don. "Nixon flips on drugs," Berkeley Barb, 07 16 09 01 69

2171 Kaufman, George. "Confrontation politics new radical weapon," Berkeley Barb, 02 18 02 01 66 ("Going over the heads of elected representatives to the American people.")

2172 Kaufman, George. "Tact 'n' tact both help the right," Berkeley Barb, 01 14 01 03 66 (Two organizations both with the acronym TACT--one political, the other governmental.)

2172a _____. "There is no Ho Chi Minh trail, Scheer tells crowd of 1,000," Berkeley Barb, 02 25 01 04 66 (Description of Scheer's visit to Southeast Asia.)

2173 Kaufman, Mike. "Fort Dix erupts," Fifth Estate, 10 16 06 03 69 (Fort Dix erupts with a march on the Army training depot.)

2174 Kemperman, Bob. "Anti-war march invades Key Biscayne," Daily Planet, 11 24 01 02 69

2175 _____. "BAMM," Daily Planet, 02 28 15 01 70

2176 Kennedy, Eugene C. "The Soma-environmental revolution, pornography, synergistic consciousness, sex with patients," New York Times Magazine, December 20, 1970, p. 52.

2177 Kentifield, Calvin. "Turning off the Tijuana Gross," Esquire, 73:8-16, May, 1970.

2178 Kepner, Jim. "Can't fire gay just because he's gay, court tells CSC," Advocate, 09 -- 04 01 69

2179 Keys, J. Bernard. "The Value of a college education: a conceptual model," Rocky Mountain Social Science Journal, 6: October, 1969. (Values in higher education.)

2180 Kilander, H. F. "Impact of offensive and obscene material on children and youth," School and Society, 97:326-30, Summer, 1969.

2181 Kindle, Charles. "Conspiracy against the Panthers?" Pittsburgh Point, 01 15 02 01 70 ("Some 28 Black Panthers killed by police raids.... Yet nothing is mentioned of the KKK, Cosa Nostra or Mafia, which rob and kill for money and racism.")

2182 _____. "What's wrong with the black coalition,"

Pittsburgh Point, 12 11 03 01 69

2183 Kissinger, Clark. "Chicago schools disrupted," Guardian, 10 19 09 01 68

2184 _____. "G.I. paper on the move," Guardian, 11 02 05 01 68 ("Vietnam G.I. Newspaper")

2185 _____. "SDS founder attacked," Fifth Estate, 05 15 08 01 69 (Confronted from many angles.)

2186 Klaber, Thomas. "Old Gory," Berkeley Barb, 09 05 03 01 69

2187 Klawitter, Sonja. "Day care centers and women's liberation," The Spectator, 07 29 12 01 69

2188 Kohn, Jaokoy. "I saw the best minds of my generation," East Village Other, 03 14 06 01 69 (Interview with Allen Ginsberg.)

2189 Kois, John. "The Fifteen strike," Chicago Kaleidoscope, 05 31 03 01 69

2190 Kopkind, Andrew. "Hard times: up the country," Ramparts, 9:8-9, December, 1970. (Communal living in Guilford, Vermont.)

2191 Kossoy, Victor E. "The Crow bar," Abas, 01 -- 06 01 69 (Interpersonal relationships involved in counterpoint resentment.)

2192 Kramer, Mark. "Hugh Hefner thinks young," Liberation News Service, 08 30 A-9 01 68 (Hefner confronts cops.)

2193 Kramer, Mike. "Counter-institution turns to counter insurgency," Liberation News Service, 04 10 21 01 69 (The cost of confrontation.)

2194 Krug, J. F. "Intellectual freedom," American Library Association Bulletin, 62:481-4, May, 1968.

2195 Kuh, R. H. "Obscenity, censorship and the nondoctrinaire liberal," Wilson Library Bulletin, 42:902-9, May, 1968.

2196 Kuminski, Gridley. "Words become numbers in Metzger's trial," Los Angeles Free Press, 07 17 19 02 70

2197 Kunkin, Art. "Do we really want to be underground: five years of the Free Press," Los Angeles Free Press, 06 27 10 01 69 (Article was written to celebrate five years of continuous weekly publication.)

2198 _____. "Free press editor nervously takes on Joe Pyne," Los Angeles Free Press, 09 03 10 01 65 (Confrontation between the editor of the FREEP and Joe Pyne.)

2199 _____. "How to tell if your phone is bugged," Los Angeles Free Press, 06 28 01 01 68

2200 _____. "Jury commits crime in convicting Freep. U.S. Constitution found guilty," Los Angeles Free Press, 07 17 01 01 70

2201 _____. "Local FBI agent answers Mark Lane," Los Angeles Free Press, 09 13 01 03 68 (Conflict of interests and ideas.)

2202 _____. "Photos reveal new evidence, Garrison says," Los Angeles Free Press, 12 22 01 03 67

2203 _____. "Teach-out organized following UCLA ban," Los Angeles Free Press, 10 22 01 04 65 (Controversy over the rejection of Lipton's "extension course in West-Coast avant-garde literature." Free University of California formed.)

2204 _____. "Was Salazar murdered?" Los Angeles Free Press, 09 04 01 02 70 (Confrontation between police and the Mexican-American anti-war protest in East Los Angeles which resulted in the death of Ruben Salazar.)

2205 Kurtz, Alan. "LBJ's cop-out," Pittsburgh Point, 01 01 11 01 70

2206 Lack, Lawrence. "House tightens welfare strings," Los Angeles Free Press, 09 01 05 03 67

("Get tough on welfare campaign.")

2207 _____. "The New left: too cool for Marx?" Los Angeles Free Press, 12 09 03 01 66

2208 Lacouture, Jean. "Charlie's long march," Ramparts, 5:12-14, July, 1966. (Chronicles the historical development of the Viet-Cong in its various stages.)

2209 _____. "How to talk to Mr. Ho," Ramparts, 6:42-46, October, 1966.

2210 Lai, Kristin. "Congress on racial equality fights over money," Los Angeles Free Press, 06 05 02 01 70

2211 Laibow, Rima E. "Napalm: made in U.S.A.," Fifth Estate, 01 01 12 01 67 ("Unfortunates are the children of Vietnam.")

2212 Lamb, Robert. "New Reform Party takes roots," Campus Underground, 12 09 09 01 68 (Speech given by the coordinator of the party in Cedar Rapids on November 24, 1968.)

2213 Lambotte, Robert. "Biafra exploitation," Los Angeles Free Press, 10 11 12 01 68

2214 Lammers, Cornelis J. "Strikes and mutinies: a comparative study of organizational conflicts between rulers and rules," Administrative Science Quarterly, 14:558-572, December, 1969. (Describes three types of protest movements--promotion of interests, secession, and seizure of 20 strikes and 20 mutinies were examined.)

2215 Lampe, Keith. "Earth read-out: People's Park ecology," Madison Kaleidoscope, II. 05 20 03 01 69 (About politics of ecology in America relating the People's Park issue to the broad questions of planetary survival.)

2216 _____. "Ecology and the movement," Win, 08 -- 33 01 69

2217 _____. "Not insecticide--genocide," San Diego Free Press, 06 27 06 01 69 (DDT and its effect on ecology.)

2218 Lampe, Keith. "Quake fault finders," Berkeley Barb, 03 28 07 01 69 (Protest by ecology activists against government planning for safety during earthquakes in the Bay Area.)

2219 Landau, Saul. "On arresting movies in San Francisco," Studies On The Left, 4:100-105, Number 4, 1965. (Confrontation in S.F. of the showing of Jean Genet's "Un Chant D'Amour.")

2220 Lane, Lois. "Leary love rap," Berkeley Barb, 12 26 03 01 69

2221 Lane, Mark. "Chicano moratorium ends in violence and death," Los Angeles Free Press, 09 04 01 01 70 (Confrontations between police and the Chicano Mexican community.)

2222 _____. "Garrison and the case of the cancelled banquet," Los Angeles Free Press, 04 05 06 01 68

2223 _____. "L.A. FBI men blast J. Edgar Hoover," Los Angeles Free Press, 08 02 01 04 68 (Shake-up in the FBI ranks in L.A.)

2224 _____. "Mark Lane interviews Huey Newton in jail," Los Angeles Free Press, 07 24 01 01 70

2225 _____. "Mark Lane: 'Killer on TV'," Los Angeles Free Press, 07 03 01 03 70

2226 Langston, Robert. "Politics of scum," Great Speckled Bird, 03 02 22 02 70 (Environmental crisis.)

2227 Lathrop, Peter (pseud.). "Teach-ins: new force or isolated phenomenon?" Studies On The Left, 5:41-52, Number 2, 1965. (Significance of "teach-ins" and their implications for the future.)

2228 Laurence, Leo E. "Church helps homos job hunt," Berkeley Barb, 10 20 07 01 67 (Task force organized in San Francisco to help gays who have been fired from jobs.)

2229 _____. "Gay fifteen get shaft," Berkeley Tribe, 11 07 07 04 69

2230 Law Commune in New York City. "The Law commune: insurgency in the courts," Liberation, 04 -- 14 01 70

2231 Lawrence, John. "WBSI: Researching the power structure and playing the heavy games," San Diego Free Press, 05 09 08 01 69 (WBSI of La Jolla, California.)

2232 Lazar, Robert J. "Jewish Communal life in Fargo, N. Dak.: the formative years," North Dakota History, 36, Fall, 1969.

2233 Leach, William Spencer. "The White left--serious or not?" Fifth Estate, 01 09 07 01 69 (Seriousness of whites in the revolutionary movement.)

2234 Lear, Len. "Discipline under Public Welfare," Distant Drummer, 12 18 05 01 69

2235 _____. "GE investigated," Distant Drummer, 08 21 05 01 69 (Human Relations Commission investigates GE.)

2236 Le Blanc, Paul. "Theory and practice," Pittsburgh Fair Witness, 11 04 05 01 70 (Effects of revolutionary struggle on society.)

2237 _____, and Joseph White. "The Splintering of SDS," Pittsburgh Point, 10 16 03 01 69 (Confrontations in the sectioning of the SDS. Excellent history of the genesis of the local RSU.)

2238 Lee, Charles. "Battle of the busts in S.F.," Advocate, 09 02 01 04 70 (Confrontations between the S.F. District Attorney's office and the gay community.)

2239 Lee, Shirley Thurston. "The Abortion underground," Los Angeles Free Press, 08 30 20 01 68 (A reprint from Modern Utopian.)

2240 Lee, Tom. "Back in school: high school students unite," Fifth Estate, 10 02 05 01 69 (Four inner-city schools shut down when a walkout occurred on Friday Sept. 19, in support of Ahmed Evans.)

2241 Lens, Sidney. "Notes on the Chicago trial," Liberation, 14:6, November, 1969.

2242 Lerner, Gerda. "New approaches to the study of women in American history," Journal of Social History, 3, Fall, 1969.

2243 Lester, Julius. "SNCC versus Panthers," Los Angeles Free Press, 09 06 05 01 68

2244 _____. "To hell with protest," Liberation News Service, 01 03 01 01 68 (The psychology of protest. A reprint from SNCC Newsletter.)

2245 Levenson, Bruce. "Allderdice: the gem is costume jewelry," Pittsburgh Point, 06 26 06 01 69 (Written by a graduate of Taylor-Allderdice High School in Pittsburgh.)

2246 Levenstein, Chuck. "The Democratic Convention and the New Left," Paper Tiger, 05 -- 04 01 68 ("Perspectives on the Democratic Convention.")

2247 Levin, B. "...mare's nest," Spectator, 204:131-2, January 29, 1960. (Electronic surveillance and thoughts on wiretapping.)

2248 Levinson, Cec. "Huey is my brother too," Black Panther, 01 25 01 07 69

2249 _____. "The Power of the Black Panther Party," Black Panther, 03 16 02 01 69

2250 Levitt, Dennis. "Conflicting statements surrounding the death of Jerry Lee Amie," Los Angeles Free Press, 07 24 10 01 70

2251 _____. "GM: mark of exploitation," Los Angeles Free Press, 10 08 04 02 70 (Concerns GM, minorities, and the polluted air we breathe.)

2252 _____. "Nixon's Security Act 1984," Los Angeles Free Press, 08 14 01 01 70 (Concerns the proposed series of 'anti-crime bills' including the Defense Facilities and Industrial Security Act of 1970.)

2253 _____. "No-knock: blueprint for a police state," Los Angeles Free Press, 07 31 04 02 70 (Controversy over the crime bill, especially the no-knock provision.)

2254 _____. "On the line with the UAW.," Los Angeles Free Press, 09 18 13 01 70 (The September 14 strike.)

2255 _____. "Pit river occupation force," Los Angeles Free Press, 10 23 04 01 70 (Struggle of the Indians to reclaim their ancestral land.)

2256 _____. "Regents fire Davis," Los Angeles Free Press, 06 26 12 01 70 (Angela)

2257 _____. "Right wingers attack demonstrators," Los Angeles Free Press, 06 12 01 01 70

2258 _____. "We are the keepers of this land," Los Angeles Free Press, 10 23 14 01 70 (Confrontations between Indians and government over land in the Cleghorn Mountains in California.)

2259 _____, and Linda Gage. "The Manifesto of the National Front for Liberation," Los Angeles Free Press, 12 25 05 01 70

2260 _____. "This week the NLF is ten years old. Happy birthday," Los Angeles Free Press, 12 18 03 01 70

2261 Lewis, Joseph. "Looking back on the laughable 60's," Pittsburgh Point, 01 15 05 03 70

2262 _____. "The War machine on parade," Pittsburgh Point, 11 13 07 01 69 ("One side speaks, the silent majority will have its say about Vietnam in the guise of Veteran's Day. Pictures illustrate the text.")

2263 Lewis, Raymond. "Malcolm ...," Black Panther, 05 19 11 01 70

2264 Liberation News Service. "Abbie Hoffman tells it like it is ... speaking of pigs," Los Angeles Free Press, 10 04 06 01 68

2265 _____. "Against the American grain: confrontation in Berkeley," Distant Drummer, 05 29 11 01 69

2266 _____. "Augusta 7," Grok, 06 -- 18 01 70

2267 _____. "Bobby Seale raps on the conspiracy trial, the New Haven Panther trial, and the New York Panther 21 trial," Black Panther, 03 07 08 01 70

2268 _____. "Condemned to die," The Militant, 11 14 08 03 69 (Carl Stokes and Ahmed Evans.)

2269 _____. "Conspiracy fights government spy tactics," Distant Drummer, 11 02 10 01 69 (Resistance to government.)

2270 _____. "Dave Dellinger goes to jail," Pittsburgh Point, 02 12 05 03 70

2271 _____. "Death penalty for underground editor," Distant Drummer, 10 11 09 04 69

2272 _____. "Fort Dix epilog," Distant Drummer, 11 07 10 01 69

2273 _____. "General Electric--electric octopus," Black Panther, 01 17 07 01 70

2274 _____. "High school named for Angela Davis," Burning Spear, 12 01 16 02 70 (Thomas Jefferson High School, Los Angeles, California.)

2275 _____. "Jean Genet: an interview," Grok, 05 -- 07 01 70

2276 _____. "Law commune," Great Speckled Bird, 09 01 20 01 69 (Alternative institution to established law firms is set up by 7 New York lawyers. Objectives are: Free legal defense for the movement, and to organize other lawyers in sympathy with the movement.)

General 211

2277 _____. "Nerve gas snafu: chemical warfare fifteen miles from New York," Washington Free Press, 08 -- 15 01 69

2278 _____. "Nixon's corporate welfare plan," Northwest Passage, 09 09 04 01 69

2279 _____. "Panther leader shackled, silenced at Chicago trial," Distant Drummer, 11 07 03 02 69

2280 _____. "SDS splits with Progressive Labor," Dallas Notes, 07 02 04 01 69

2281 _____. "Two counts of murder: Jock Yablonski--it's execution; Fred Hampton--it's justified," Pittsburgh Point, 01 29 01 02 70 (Two interesting and contrasting views.)

2282 _____. "United Front against Fascism," Fifth Estate, 07 10 06 03 69

2283 _____. "Why a United Front against Fascism?" Peninsula Observer, 07 28 03 01 69

2284 Lieberman, E. James. "Psychochemicals as weapons," Bulletin of Atomic Scientists, 18:11-14, January, 1962.

2285 Lipow, Arthur. "Assault on academic freedom at UC," Independent Socialist, 09 -- 08 01 68 (The decision of the U.S. Regents is to limit participation college courses at Berkeley.)

2286 Lipset, Hal. "The Case for bugging," Ramparts, 7:39-44, September 7, 1968. (Questions concerning the right of privacy.)

2287 Lipton, Lawrence. "The Dick-Daley revised history of CZechago," Los Angeles Free Press, 09 20 03 03 68

2288 _____. "Politics of ecstasy: Tim Leary, parapolitics plus ecstasy," Los Angeles Free Press, 06 11 30 01 69

2289 _____. "Yippies to visit hog capital," Los Angeles Free Press, 08 16 07 01 68

2290   Litwak, Eugene. "Models of bureaucracy which permit conflict," American Journal of Sociology, 67:177-184, 1961.

2291   Lizzie and John. "Free Shadyside," Grok, 06 27 22 03 70 (Alleged repressive tactics in Shadyside, Pittsburgh.)

2292   Loewenberg, Peter. "An interview with Richard Drinnon," Studies On The Left, 1:76-81, Number 4, 1961. (Interview with the assistant professor of history at U.C. (Berkeley) and his confrontations with the administration.)

2293   Loewenstein, Eddie. "Community sit-in at Drexel," Distant Drummer, 02 05 01 02 70

2294   Lofflin, John. "Message from Cambodia," Engage, 3:16-17, November 1, 1970.

2295   Lomax, Louis E. "Mississippi eyewitness," Muckrakers Guide, Ramparts--Special Collector's edition, pp. 20-24. (Lomax "wrote the following document after he and nine other researchers, negro and white had gone to Mississippi and learned the facts from eyewitnesses to the actual events that transpired.")

2296   Lombardi, John. "The Real free press," Distant Drummer, 06 26 03 01 69

2297   Long, L. "The Day a nation remembered: Germany erases Hitler's snub of Jesse Owens," Ebony, 15:77-82, April, 1960.

2298   Love, Adam. "A Utopian answer to mate-swapping," Modern Utopian, 05 08 03 01 64 (Controversy over the concept of mate-swapping and the utopian answer.)

2299   Lovin, Roger. "Crusin in the concrete commune," Los Angeles Free Press, 07 03 36 01 70

2300   _____. "The Infernal choke," Los Angeles Free Press, 07 17 14 01 70 (Ecological problems and the environment.)

General 213

2301 Lowenstein, Eddie. "Russian roulette with head start," Distant Drummer, 09 13 03 01 69 (Teaching and learning episodes with Head Start at Philadelphia Schools.)

2302 Luc Godard, Jean. "Bobby Seale's life," Black Panther, 04 25 04 01 70

2303 Lucas, Donald. "Homosexuality or neurosis," Campus Underground, 02 10 12 01 69 (The third of a series on the subject of homosexuality.)

2304 _____. "Is homosexuality a disease or illness?" Campus Underground, 01 27 06 01 69 (Part two in the series.)

2305 _____. "Psycho-sexual aspects of homosexuality," Campus Underground, 02 24 14 01 69 (The fourth and last in the series.)

2306 Lukas, J. Anthony. "The Second confrontation in Chicago," New York Times Magazine, March 29, 1970, pp. 10-11.

2307 Lyman, Mel. "To all who would know," Avatar, 07 21 13 01 66 ("The Hip movement is gilt ridden; it represents everything it condemns.")

2308 _____. "What is the underground?" Avatar, 07 07 07 01 67 (History, practical applications and ideals of the movement according to Lyman.)

2309 Lynd, Staughton. "Guerrilla history in Gary," Liberation, 14:17-20, October, 1969.

2310 _____. "Radicals and white racism," Liberation, 14:26-30, July, 1969.

2311 _____. "So you want a revolution?" News From Nowhere, 12 -- 08 01 68 (Edited speech by Lynd given at Northern Illinois University on Oct. 29, 1968.)

2312 _____. "Socialism, the forbidden word," Studies On The Left, 3:14-20, Number 3, 1963. (Of, for, by and about Socialism and the implications for political persuasion in the future.)

2313   Lynd, Staughton. "Waiting for righty: the lessons of the Oswald case," Studies On The Left, 4:135-141, Number 2, 1964. (Analysis of the Oswald Case and the Warren Commission Report.)

2314   Lyons, Carl. "Talmudic law rules USA; civil rights are not civil rights but social rights, and not amenable to legislation," Common Sense, 03 01 01 01 70

2315   McCaa, Robert, and William Sywak. "U.S. funds UCLA--with political strings attached," Los Angeles Free Press, 11 22 13 01 68

2316   McCabe, Charles. "What's wrong with California?" Berkeley Barb, 08 22 12 01 69 (Remarks ... before the Commonwealth Club of California by a S.F. Chronicle columnist, August 8, 1969.)

2317   McCleary, Alix. "Newton convicted," Los Angeles Free Press, 09 13 10 03 68

2318   McDonald, Donald. "The American dilemma: 1967. An interview with Gunnar Myrdal," Center Magazine, Center For The Study of Democratic Institutions, Vol. 1 No. 1, October-November, 1967, pp. 30-33.

2319   MacDougall, Alexander. "Free press now on trial," Los Angeles Free Press, 06 12 01 02 70

2320   _____. "No evidence of crime as F.P. trial ends 3rd week," Los Angeles Free Press, 06 26 01 03 70

2321   _____. "The Trials of selecting a jury," Los Angeles Free Press, 06 19 01 03 70

2322   _____. "Two counts dismissed in Free Press trial," Los Angeles Free Press, 07 03 01 01 70

2323   McDowell, Jim. "Five jailed for bugging Gen. Taylor," Berkeley Barb, 08 27 01 01 65 (Protestors confront Taylor in San Francisco by Berkeley's Vietnam committee.)

2324   McGrath, W. E. "How to pass a law! South Dakota

anti-obscenity bill," Library Journal, 93:1943, May 15, 1968.

2325 Machado, Manuel A. "Chicano studies: a Mexican-American dissents," University Bookman, 10:75-81, Summer, 1970. (Recent studies relating to injustices to the Mexican-American and his heritage.)

2326 McKelvey, Donald. "Some notes on participatory democracy," New Left Notes, 05 06 08 01 66 (Compares direct with representative ideologies interspersed with historical background.)

2327 McLaughlin, Joseph F. "Free education," Pittsburgh Point, 07 31 11 01 69 (Some thoughts about the free educational venture recently organized in Pittsburgh.)

2328 McLeod, Richard. "Dissent and reaction in Missouri," Wilson Library Bulletin, 44:269-276, November, 1969. ("The free speech conflict in Missouri. The case reflects the state of intellectual freedom in Missouri's State Library, it also provides a damning picture of the state university in Columbia where the issue was initially provoked by the administration.")

2329 McLuhan, Marshall. "Adopt a college," Chinook, 10 02 03 01 69 (Description of flaws in the present educational set-up, with some ideas for reform and change. A reprint from Pterodactyl.)

2330 Maguire, Micha. "God Reagan's law and order," Los Angeles Free Press, 06 05 13 01 70

2331 Main, Jeremy. "Only radical reform can save the courts," Fortune, 82:110-114, August, 1970.

2332 Majdalany, Gebran. "Reflections on racism, anti-semitism, and zionism," Liberation, 14:36-39, November, 1969.

2333 Malcolm, Andrew. "Drug abuse and social alienation," Today's Education, 59:29-31, September, 1970.

2334 Malcolm X. "Malcolm X talks to young people," Black Panther, 05 19 12 01 70 (Reprinted from the Young Socialist.)

2335 Malloy, Kathleen. "Reply to Gershman," Pittsburgh Point, 01 02 06 01 69 ("Editor's Note: the letter below is the latest of a correspondence that stemmed from an article by Carl Gershman, 'New Ideology In The New Left' published in the Point Sept. 5. Miss Malloy wrote on Oct. 24 to criticize 'serious misrepresentations' in Mr. Gershman's article. On Nov. 7 Mr. Gershman replied that 'Merely to claim an error without offering an alternative interpretation contributes nothing to a further elucidation of the subject. The following, then, is Miss Malloy's alternative.")

2336 Manson, Charles. "An Open letter to Tim Leary from Charles Manson. Revelation brings blood, love knows no sin," Los Angeles Free Press, 10 09 03 01 70

2337 Marcus, Raymond. "Blow-up! November 22, 1963; new facts about the Mary Moorman photo," Los Angeles Free Press, 11 24 02 01 67

2338 Marcuse, Herbert. "The End of utopia," Ramparts, 8:28-34, April, 1970.

2339 _____. "Marcuse on class conflict, black power, universities," Guardian, 11 16 08 02 68 (Interview conducted by Robert L. Allen. Third part is contained in the Guardian, November 23, 1968, p. 11.)

2340 _____. "Marcuse on radical perspectives," Liberation News Service, 12 12 01 01 68 (Complete text of speech given by Marcuse at the 20th Anniversary program of the Guardian.)

2341 _____. "Marcuse on the hippie revolution," Berkeley Barb, 08 04 09 01 67

2342 Margolin, Bruce M. "Gay penal code demanded," Los Angeles Free Press, 10 16 18 02 70 (The author strongly advocates a revision of the penal code affecting the gay person.)

2343 Margolis, Michael. "This Byrd won't fly," Pittsburgh

Point, 04 16 05 01 70 (Myths concerning Byrd Brown for congress.)

2344 Marighella, Carlos. "The Job of an urban guerrilla," Los Angeles Free Press, 11 06 11 02 70 (The "Minimanual" of urban guerrilla warfare.)

2345 Marine, Gene. "America the raped," Ramparts, 5:34-45, April, 1967. (Confrontations between the so-called "conservationists" and "Engineers" and the ever important ecology of America.)

2346 _____. "A Short history of the California water plan as it relates to the questions of ecology, waterlords and the creation of deserts," Ramparts, 8:36-41, May, 1970.

2347 Marshall, Field. "Prey for pigs," Black Panther, 10 04 05 01 69

2348 Marshall, Sue. "CIA in the LAPD???" Los Angeles Free Press, 07 10 03 01 70

2349 _____. "Genocide petition speed-up called for," Los Angeles Free Press, 10 23 13 02 70 (Multi-racial petition to be presented to the U.N. by minority groups.)

2350 _____. "Huey is at Finland station," Los Angeles Free Press, 06 19 05 01 70

2351 _____. "In praise of the Soledad Brothers: Morton Sobell speaks in absentia," Los Angeles Free Press, 10 16 09 01 70 (A speech which was to have been delivered by Sobell to the families of the Soledad Brothers.)

2352 Martello, Leo Louis. "New York primary a victory for gays," Advocate, 08 05 02 02 70 (Bella Abzug and the 17th Congressional District in New York.)

2352a Massaron, Paul. "Voice of the young worker: change or be changed!" Electronic Age, 30: Winter, 1970-71. ("The young worker's desire for individuality is in every way equal to that of his student counterpart.")

2353 Massett, L. "Abortion legislation: a fundamental challenge," Science News, 97:75-6, January 17, 1970.

2354 Mathe, Judy. "Abortion: blame us all," Distant Drummer, 05 21 03 01 70

2355 _____. "Stockade prisoners protest killing of 19 year old," Distant Drummer, 02 05 17 01 69

2356 Mathews, Stephnie. "Atrocious service cited at Southern bell hearing," Daily Planet, 11 24 19 01 69 (Protest Bell's request for 32 million.)

2357 Mauney, Ann. "NWRO pickets Sears," Great Speckled Bird, 04 21 14 01 69 (Confrontation between Sears and NWRO.)

2358 _____. "Welfare militants," Great Speckled Bird, 07 07 02 01 69

2359 Maxson, R. E. "Film students jack off to the tune of 'Cambodia'," Los Angeles Free Press, 05 29 05 01 70

2360 _____. "Peace ecology coalition," Los Angeles Free Press, 08 21 07 05 70 (Description of the coalition of Quaker supported groups in anti-war and ecology factions. Coalition was formed in July of 1970.)

2361 Mayers, Patrick. "Life at Taft High School--in land of milk and honey--turns really sour," Los Angeles Free Press, 10 03 02 02 69 (Students versus administration over dress codes, curriculum, suspensions, etc.)

2362 Melman, S. "American needs, and limits on resources: the priorities problem," Teachers College Record, 68:493-8, March, 1967.

2363 Mendicino, Ellen S. "What money can buy," Berkeley Barb, 02 07 08 01 69 (Abortion.)

2364 _____. "Where most men fail?" Berkeley Barb, 01 03 10 05 69 (In defense of women.)

2365 Meriwether, Louise M. "Doctor King's death unifies L.A. black community," Los Angeles Free Press, 04 12 03 01 68

2366 Metefsky, George. "Right on, culture freeks!" Miami Free Press, 10 08 19 01 69 (Repression, culture, White Panther Party, and the movement.)

2367 Meyer, Karl. "A Fund for mankind," Renaissance, 01 15 08 01 70

2368 Milinaire, Catherine. "Henna tattooes: the easy way out," Rags, 12 -- 33 02 70 (Description of Henna Tattooes.)

2369 Miller, Connie. "Vigil ... police riot," Grok, 04 -- 10 01 70 (Description of the "Draft Resistance Week," on March 19, and a resistance statement on March 20.)

2370 Miller, Henry. "Obscenity and the law of reflection," Kentucky Law Journal, 51: No. 4, 577-590, Summer, 1963.

2371 Miller, William G. "New Brunswick: Community Action Project," Studies On The Left, 5:74-79, Number 2, 1965. (Analysis of CAP in New Brunswick, New Jersey.)

2372 _____. "Can the debate on Vietnam continue to be rational?" Presbyterian Life, 20:28-30, June 1, 1967.

2373 Millett, Kate. "Sexual politics," New Republic, 163:26, August 1, 1970.

2374 Mills, Billy G. "Black protest at Olympics," Los Angeles Free Press, 11 01 16 01 68

2375 Mills, C. Wright. "On the New Left," Studies On The Left, 1:63-72, Number 4, 1961. ("In slightly different form this essay has appeared as a 'Letter To The New Left' in New Left Review, Number 5, in England, as well as in periodicals in several other countries.")

2376 Milstein, Tom. "A Perspective on the Panthers,"

Commentary, 50:35-43, September, 1970.

2377 Minh Vy, Nguyen. "Statement by Mr. Nguyen Minh Vy, on behalf of the delegation of the government of the democratic republic of Vietnam, at the 73rd plenary session of the Paris Conference on Vietnam, July 2, 1970," Black Panther, 07 18 17 01 70

2378 Minton, Robert, and Stephen Rice. "Using racism at San Quentin," Ramparts, 8:18-24, January, 1970.

2379 Mintz, Elliot. "We were freed by a great network of love," Los Angeles Free Press, 10 23 01 01 70 (Conversational interview with Dr. Timothy Leary, from Algiers since his escape from prison.)

2380 Miranda, Doug. "Lonnie faces death in the electric chair at the hands of the Connecticut fascists," Black Panther, 04 18 04 01 70

2381 Mitchell, Bill. "Coffee houses open across U.S. to fulfill social needs of young people," Old Market Press, 02 01 06 01 68 (History of coffee houses and especially the "Old Market Coffee House" Kentucky Avenue, Paducah, Kentucky.)

2382 Mitchell, John. "Wiretapping; constitutionality and efficiency," Vital Speeches, 37:34-7, November 1, 1970. (An address given October 5, 1970.)

2383 Mitchell, Juliet. "The Longest revolution," New Left Review, 40:November-December, 1966. (Women's Lib.)

2384a Moffett, Toby. "High-school students: somebody's stealing their future," Electronic Age, 30:7-9, Winter, 1970-71. ("Today's high school students do not look upon business as 'the enemy'." Instead, they view business as somewhat irrelevant.")

2385 Molotch, Harvey. "Oil in the velvet playground: Santa Barbara," Ramparts, 8:43-51, November, 1969.

2386 Molz, Kathleen. "Panel discussion on censorship and pornography," Wilson Library Bulletin, 42:926-9,

May, 1968.

2387 Moore, John E. "People of the community vs. the slumlords and the Fascist pigs of Winston-Salem," Black Panther, 03 28 02 01 70 (Discrimination and repressive tactics reported in Winston-Salem.)

2388 Moore, P. W. "Wiretaps: disclosed or leaked? Trial of the Chicago 8," Nation, 209, 432-4, October 27, 1969.

2389 Moreland, C. K. Jr. "Trach's politics of inspiration," Son of Jabberwork, 11 08 04 02 68 (Boycott of the Mexico City Olympics.)

2390 Morgan, Griscom. "Short term financing for intentional communities: Homer L. Morris Fund," Modern Utopian, 05 08 09 01 64 (History of the Homer L. Morris Fund.)

2391 Morgan, Jeanne. "Texas editor, former Dallas sheriff tell FP amazing new information about Kennedy assassination," Los Angeles Free Press, 03 01 01 01 68

2392 Morgan, Robin. "Women's Liberation," Pittsburgh Point, 07 31 04 01 69 (Women's Liberation Groups state their causes.)

2393 Morthland, John. "Nixon in public: he was mumbling at his feet," Rolling Stone, 06 11 10 02 70

2394 Morton, Peggy. "A Woman's work is never done," Leviathan, 05 -- 32 02 70

2395 Mosby, Donald Y. "Black G.I.'s find Viet bias," Veterans Stars and Stripes, 08 -- 01 01 68

2396 Moschzisker, F. Von. "Abortion comes out of the shadows; with an anonymous interview," Life, 68:20b-29, February 27, 1970.

2397 Moses, Bob. "Mississippi: 1961-1962," Liberation, 14:6-17, January, 1970.

2398 Moursund, Andy. "Vietnam victory march," North Carolin Anvil, 04 11 01 01 70

2399 Moynihan, Daniel P. "Policy vs. program in the 70's," Public Interest, 20:90-100, Summer, 1970.

2400 Mulherin, Cathy. "The People need their park," Peninsula Observer, 06 30 05 01 69

2401 _____, and Jim Mulherin. "People's Park: Living socialism is killed," Peninsula Observer, 05 26 20 01 69

2402 Murray, George. "For a revolutionary culture," Black Panther, 09 07 12 01 68

2403 Muse, Charlie. "Chicago jail," Great Speckled Bird, 08 18 18 01 69 (Physical conditions of jails in Cooke County, Chicago.)

2404 Muston, Ray. "Student participation becomes more formalized," College and University Business, 48:12-14, March, 1970.

2405 Nachman, Larry David. "The Marxist romantics: obituary for SDS," Nation, 209:558-561, November 24, 1969.

2406 Naison, Mark. "In defense of SDS," Liberation, 14:31-34, August-September, 1969.

2407 Narramore, Cly de M. "Ecology and the Christian," Psychology For Living, 12:3, July-August, 1970.

2408 Neary, John. "Pornography goes public," Life, 69:19-25, August 28, 1970.

2409 Neff, Renfreu. "The Theatre of oppression: Panther 21, New York City, in pig we trust," East Village Other, 05 05 12 01 70

2410 Neff, Richard. "Marihuana--a key issue," Distant Drummer, 05 02 03 01 70

2411 Newcomb, Fred T., and Roy Watson. "Expose Oswald photo as fake," Distant Drummer, 01 09 04 01 69 (Warren Commission exhibits 133A and 133B by experiments.)

2412 Newham, Blaine. "Wow, like let's really try to win,"

General 223

Sports Illustrated, 33:50-54, October 12, 1970.

2413 Newport, Robert S. Jr. "Allstate unfair," Los Angeles Free Press, 09 18 14 01 70 (Charges unfair practices in the insurance business.)

2414 Newton, Huey. "Huey from jail," Los Angeles Free Press, 03 22 05 01 68

2415 _____. "Message from the minister of defense Huey P. Newton on the peace movement," Black Panther, 09 27 10 01 69

2416 _____. "Prison, where is thy victory," Black Panther, 07 12 02 01 69

2417 Niceswanger, Bruce (Bruno). "The 'Positive' left," Campus Underground, 11 18 03 02 68 (Interpretations of the New Left.)

2418 Niemeyer, Gerhart. "The Homesickness of the new left," National Review, 22:779-783, July 28, 1970.

2419 Nixon, Richard M. "What's right with America," Case and Comment, 75:3-7, November-December, 1970. ("What is right about America enables us to correct those things that are wrong. Discussion of 'Poverty and Welfare,' 'Vietnam,' 'Peace Now,' 'The Economy,' 'Environment,' 'Black and White,' 'Governments Role,' 'Role of the People,' 'Respect for Law,' 'Message to Youth,' 'We Act for All Mankind,' (and) 'This Is A Beautiful Country'.")

2420 Nobbs, Russ. "Spokane freaked by story of 10,000 hippies to come," Spokane Natural, 05 09 01 01 69

2421 Nobile, Philip. "The Priest who stayed out in the cold," New York Times Magazine, June 28, 1970, p. 8.

2422 North, Robert Bruce. "A Proposal to boycott Pan American Airlines," Los Angeles Free Press, 06 05 16 01 70

2423 Novasky, U. S. "Government and Martin Luther King," Atlantic, 226:43-52, November, 1970.

2424 O'Brien, Basil. "Gay Liberation Front doesn't want your acceptance," Distant Drummer, 06 18 05 01 70

2425 O'Brien, Conor Cruise. "Contemporary forms of imperialism," Studies On The Left, 5:13-26, Number 2, 1965. (History and development of the term "imperialism" and its many uses. Comment on the article by Timothy F. Harding on p. 27 of the same issue as well as that of O'Brien on p. 39.)

2426 O'Brien, David J. "Eugene Genovese and the student left," Liberation, 14:29-33, October, 1969.

2427 O'Brien, Jim. "Connections editor unfit--says Boy Scout," Distant Drummer, 03 27 12 04 69 (Editor of Connections under fire by Wisconsin Senator.)

2428 Ofari, Earl. "The Legacy of Martin Luther King, Jr.: I have a dream," Liberation News Service, 04 05 18 01 69

2429 _____. "Whites in black liberation?" Los Angeles Free Press, 07 10 32 02 70

2430 Ogar, Richard A. "American Indians in trek to coast," Berkeley Barb, 09 15 02 01 67 ("An attempt to unify all nations in order to overcome all evil government politicians.")

2431 Oglesby, Carl. "A Program for liberals," Ramparts, 6:20, February, 1968.

2432 Oko, Tristine. "Angela Davis makes the top ten; can justice be served?" Los Angeles Free Press, 08 21 03 03 70

2433 O'Loughlin, Ray. "Second U.S. revolution," Burning River News, 07 21 03 01 69 (Description of Berkeley, the "focal point of the second American revolution.")

2434 Oppenheimer, Martin. "Alienation or participation: the sociology of participatory democracy," New Left Notes, 11 25 04 01 66

2435 Orvino, Jennie. "Dow attacked in Washington," Chicago Kaleidoscope, 03 28 05 01 69

2436 Osborn, Jim. "Chicano leaders charged with conspiracy," Los Angeles Free Press, 06 07 26 01 68 (Charged with conspiracy in the walkouts at five East Los Angeles High Schools.)

2437 Oslick, Alan. "Panther offices raided: local CD squad aids Hoover team," Distant Drummer, 10 03 01 02 69

2438 ———. "Rutgers University President charged with neglect of duty," Distant Drummer, 10 11 01 04 69

2439 ———. "Why have families?" Distant Drummer, 10 11 09 01 69

2440 Our Man In Prague (Hard Times). "Counter-revolution within the counter-revolution," Hard Times, 11 10 01 01 69

2441 Owens, Jesse. "My great Olympic prize," Reader's Digest, 67:132-35, October, 1960.

2442 Pacific Studies Center. "Black Monday's Sunday allies labor," Ramparts, 8:34-38, January, 1970.

2443 Pain, Lincoln. "Scabby grapes," Washington Free Press, 08 -- 05 01 69

2444 Paine, Tom. "Radical press: more hassle," Liberation News Service, 01 16 12 01 69 (Underground newspaper busted and hassled for alleged obscenity.)

2445 Parks, Gordon. "Black Panthers: the hard edge of confrontation. Interview (with) Eldridge Cleaver in Algiers. A visit with Papa Rage," Look, 68:18-26, February 6, 1970.

2446 Parmalee, Patty. "Marines confined to base," Guardian, 05 23 03 01 70 (The "People's Armed Forces Day" march on May 16.)

2447 ———, and Fran Furey. "Reagan's Sacramento

disneyland," Los Angeles Free Press, 10 30 01 01 70 (Confrontations in higher and public education in California and descriptions of dissatisfaction from both citizens and educators.)

2448 Patrick, James E. "The Decade of crisis for education," Vital Speeches, 36:502-505, June 1, 1970.

2449 Patterson, William L. "The Black athlete and democracy U.S.A.," Black Panther, 12 13 13 01 69

2450 _____. "Greetings to Huey P. Newton," Black Panther, 02 28 04 01 70

2451 _____. "Judicial terror poses as law and order," Black Panther, 11 15 03 01 69

2452 Paulson, Pat. "How I lost the Presidency," Spokane Natural, 05 09 04 01 69

2453 Paylor, Ann. "Males vs. females: a two-way problem," Advocate, 11 25 26 03 70 ("Hostility between the sexes in the gay community.")

2454 Peacock, Mary, and Lisa Phoenix. "You were thinking, maybe of getting your ass tattooed?" Rags, 12 -- 28 01 70 (Highly controversial aspects of the significance of tattooes and what they mean to individuals who are permanently marked. Interesting historical aspects as a symbol of expression, as well as attitudes around the country with some examples.)

2455 Peck, Abe. "Two thousand scream at Seale trial in Chicago," Los Angeles Free Press, 06 19 07 01 70

2456 Peck, Sidney M. "The Political consciousness of rank-and-file labor leaders," Studies On The Left, 1:43-51, Number 4, 1961. ("The politics of organized American workers is informed by class as well as job concerns.")

2457 Peddle, Iris. "A Word on our commune," San Diego Free Press, 09 03 05 04 69 (Goals and objectives of the "work democracy" principle of communal living in Ramona, California.)

2458   Peek, B. M. "SDS: it's too bad," Conscience, 08 -- 24 01 69

2459   Pell, Eve. "The Soledad brothers: how a prison picks its victims," Ramparts, 9:31, August, 1970.

2460   Pence, David. "The High school education," Behind the Shield, 10 03 01 01 69

2461   Pepper, William F. "The Children of Vietnam," Ramparts, 5:44-68, January, 1967. (Preface to this article is by Dr. Benjamin Spock.)

2462   Perkins, David. "Picknicking with the liberals," Screw, 08 01 06 01 69

2463   Perkins, Emily, and Jay Sargeant. "Ally with campus workers!" New Left Notes, 07 30 01 01 69

2464   Perry, Diane. "New FAT leader promises action," Pittsburgh Point, 06 26 01 02 69 (An interview with James Givner newly elected president of this group.)

2465   _____. "Operation dig hits the stadium," Pittsburgh Point, 07 24 01 01 69 (Confrontations between this organization (operation dig) and the unions to interrupt construction on the new Three Rivers Stadium.)

2466   Peterson, Dan. "Hip village--fact and fiction," Kaleidoscope, 03 15 05 01 68 (Description of communal life styles in the U.S.)

2467   Phantom Dealers, Inc. "Viva Sativa: an instructive guide to growing your own smoke," Distant Drummer, 04 02 09 01 70

2468   Philo, Nancy. "Baez speaks," Fifth Estate, 03 20 05 03 69

2469   Pilpel, H. F. "Three legal issues: literary law front, 1967," Publishers Weekly, 193:47-8, January 29, 1968.

2470   _____. "What is the rule for seizing obscene materials," Publishers Weekly, 193:22, January 1,

1968.

2471 _____, and K. P. Norwick. "Crux of obscenity; how to whom and where," Publishers Weekly, 194:36-7, July 29, 1968.

2472 _____. "Some obscenity battles yet to be fought in court," Publishers Weekly, 194:42-3, December 30, 1968.

2473 _____. "Supreme court approves variable obscenity," Publishers Weekly, 193:32, May 27, 1968.

2474 Podhoretz, Norman. "Revolutionary suicide," Commentary, 50:23, September, 1970.

2475 Pondy, Louis R. "Organizational conflict: concepts and models," Administrative Science Quarterly, 12:296-320, 1967.

2476 _____. "Varieties of organizational conflict," Administrative Science Quarterly, 14:499-505, December, 1969. (An introduction to "seven empirical studies of conflict within and between organizations.")

2477 Popkin, Richard. "Thanatology: a blossoming," San Diego Free Press, 06 13 10 01 69 (History of thanatology and its uses.)

2478 Powers, Jerry, and Sandi Stein. "Jim Morrison doors lead surrenders to Miami court," Daily Planet, 11 24 01 01 69

2479 Pratt, Annis. "Abortion march," Great Speckled Bird, 05 12 03 02 69 ("NOW and NARAL join forces to protest existing abortion laws in Georgia.)

2480 Primula, Ron. "Computers threaten right to privacy," Los Angeles Free Press, 01 17 05 02 69 (The right to privacy and the credit card controversy.)

2481 Pritchard, Ken. "Fidel to be Rubin's lawyer," Ann Arbor Argus, 05 08 02 01 69 (Announced by Jerry at Bowling Green State University, Ohio on April 19.)

2482 protean/RADISH. "Ho dies," Rough Draft, 10 --

General 229

04 01 69

2483 Quegg, Dave. "On the Milwaukee 14: acting out a life style," Campus Underground, 12 09 08 01 68 (Milwaukee 14 burns draft files with homemade napalm. A statement of the 14 is included in this article.)

2484 Quinley, Harold E. "The Protestant clergy and the war in Vietnam," Public Opinion Quarterly, 34:43-52, Spring, 1970.

2485 Quinn, Mary. "The Grape boycott and the TPF," Pittsburgh Point, 02 12 04 01 70

2486 ———. "Grape boycott goes on," Pittsburgh Point, 06 04 10 02 70

2487 Rabinowitz, Dorothy. "The Activist cleric," Commentary, 50:81-83, September, 1970.

2488 ———. "The Radicalized professor: a portrait," Commentary, 50:62-64, July, 1970.

2489 Rabinowitz, Victor. "An exchange on SNCC," Studies On The Left, 5:83-95, Number 2, 1965. (A reply to this article is made by Norm Fruchter.)

2490 Raleigh, Doug. "Alternative education," Los Angeles Free Press, 06 06 32 01 69

2491 Ransom, David. "Fascism," Peninsula Observer, 07 28 01 01 69

2492 ———. "Federal repression hits SDS national office," Peninsula Observer, 05 26 09 01 69

2493 Rapoport, Roger. "Catch 24,400 (or Plutonium is my favorite) element," Ramparts, 8:16-21, May, 1970. (Dow Chemical Company.)

2494 Raskin, Marcus G. "The Man who came in from the cold (war)," Ramparts, 6:32-34, February, 1968. (Contains a description of the appointment of Charles Hitch, as president of the University of California and his activities with the Rand Corporation.)

2495 Raup, Philip Jr. "An Activist party for the new left," Paper Tiger, 05 -- 09 01 67 (Description of the goals and objectives of the new left with some examples of communal living in the U.S.)

2496 Ray, Michele. "The Execution of Che by the CIA," Ramparts, 6:23-37, March, 1968.

2497 Recca, Ron. "Kill," Grok, 04 -- 06 03 70 (Nuclear weapons and biological warfare.)

2498 _____. "Recca's eccentric bibliography," Grok, 04 -- 07 01 70 (Interesting "teach-in" reading in preparation for the environmental crisis.)

2499 _____. "Recca's eco info; environmental teach-in...April 1-4," Grok, 04 -- 04 01 70 (A line-up by function and event of what Pittsburgh is doing for the environmental teach-in. The activities include an environmental workshop.)

2500 _____. "Spaceship earth...countdown to death," Grok, 04 -- 03 01 70 (Hand drawn illustrations depict what man has done to his own environment.)

2501 Regan, J. J. "Obscenity problem: time for a truce?" Catholic World, 207:70-71, May, 1968.

2502 Register, Richard. "Arcology," Los Angeles Free Press, 07 24 44 01 70 (Problems of ecology and environment.)

2503 Reinholz, Mary. "Credibility gap gaffed," Los Angeles Free Press, 06 12 03 01 70

2504 _____. "Girls--arm yourselves," Los Angeles Free Press, 07 17 10 01 70

2505 _____. "Women's liberation divided on tactics, theory," Los Angeles Free Press, 06 11 08 01 69

2505a Reiss, Albert J. Jr. "Social integration of queers and peers," Social Problems, 103-20, January, 1961.

General

2506   Rembar, Charles. "As long as it doesn't offend our own ideas," Wilson Library Bulletin, 42:896-901, May, 1968.

2507   _____. "End of obscenity; excerpt," Library Journal, 93:1868, May 1, 1968.

2508   _____. "End of obscenity," New Republic, 158:31-2, June, 1968. (Review.)

2509   Remsberg, Charles, and Bonnie Remsberg. "Here she comes, Miss nude America," Esquire, 73:160, May, 1970. (Miss nude America beauty pageant.)

2510   Resnick, Mayer R. "The History of Ronald Reagan's UC tuition manifesto," Los Angeles Free Press, 01 19 03 01 68

2511   Reston, James B. "Can Nixon trust the Army?" Los Angeles Free Press, 06 26 01 01 70

2512   Rice, Charles O. "The Radical Catholic," Catholic World, 211:156-160, July, 1970. (Article was first given in lecture form at NYU.)

2513   Richmond, Al. "Workers against the war," Ramparts, 9:28-32, September, 1970. (West coast labor activism against the Vietnam war.)

2514   Richmond, Claude. "Why are you killing those children?" Atlas, 19:46-47, September, 1970. (The Vietnam war.)

2515   Richter, Edward. "Peace activism in Vietnam," Studies On The Left, 6:54-63, Number 1, January-February, 1966. (Description of peace movements. Introduction by Carl Oglesby.)

2516   Rieker, Richard. "Duggan loses 'T & I'; ready for 'Curious'," Pittsburgh Point, 11 20 05 01 69 (The District Attorney objects to questionable movies in Pittsburgh.)

2517   _____. "NOW strikes at job discrimination," Pittsburgh Point, 09 18 05 01 69 (NOW files complaints of discrimination against three Pittsburgh organizations with violations of City Ordinance 3495.)

2518 Rieker, Richard. "Right-wing youth group organizing here," Pittsburgh Point, 09 25 01 01 69 (NYA is a coalition of American Youth who are dedicated to action for America against red anarchy.)

2519 _____. "Rival teachers back in school," Pittsburgh Point, 09 04 01 01 69 (Pittsburgh Federation of Teachers, and the Pittsburgh Teachers Education Association, versus the school board over wages.)

2520 _____. "Time to protest about dirty air," Pittsburgh Point, 09 11 01 03 69 (A proposal for standards is presented.)

2521 _____. "Women organize for rights at Pitt," Pittsburgh Point, 01 29 03 01 70

2522 Rieker, Robert. "D.A. Duggan foiled again," Pittsburgh Point, 05 01 01 01 69 (Controversy over the film "The Female" brings voices of protest again.)

2523 Riga, Peter. "The Catholic and obscenity," Catholic World, 205:340-345, September, 1967.

2524 Rios, Ann. "Soledad prisoners face murder trial in San Francisco," Guardian, 07 04 06 01 70

2525 Robb, Alison. "Something new in schools," Pittsburgh Point, 04 16 01 01 70 (The Free high school concept.)

2526 OMIT

2527 Robb, Charles C. "After the meeting, Gulf still lives," Pittsburgh Point, 04 30 01 01 70

2528 _____. "Attack of the Weatherwomen," Pittsburgh Point, 09 11 01 02 69 (Some 60 SDS women (a faction of the Weathermen) staged a guerrilla raid on South Hills High School in Pittsburgh. The raid later became known as the "no-bra" raid, and presented implications for Pittsburgh activists.)

2528a _____. "Confrontation in Pittsburgh," Nation, 209:272-274, September 22, 1969. (Black Construction Coalition.)

General

2529 _____. "Getting down to the nitty-gritty," Pittsburgh Point, 09 04 01 03 69 (BCC and the construction industry sit down in efforts to moderate differences.)

2530 _____. "A Good old-fashioned peace march," Pittsburgh Point, 05 29 01 02 69 (March for Peace and Justice to end the war in Vietnam with illustrated text.)

2531 _____. "Gulf and Mellon--big name polluters," Pittsburgh Point, 04 09 01 01 70 (Forum discusses "Direction For Action.")

2532 _____. "Half a million voices sang as one," Pittsburgh Point, 11 20 01 03 69 (The weekend in Washington, D.C. featured among others Dr. Spock, and Pete Seeger.)

2533 _____. "'I'm All Right' awaits the word," Pittsburgh Point, 03 05 01 03 70 (Controversial underground newspaper)

2534 _____. "It's a new ball game," Pittsburgh Point, 08 07 01 01 69 (Labor problems with the building trades in Pittsburgh.)

2535 _____. "Justice in city court," Pittsburgh Point, 09 04 02 01 69 (Description of how justice is administered in Pittsburgh.)

2536 _____. "Made in Pittsburgh--for Vietnam," Pittsburgh Point, 04 24 01 02 69 (Interesting article dealing with the defense department's procurement contracts to Pittsburgh's major members of the military-industrial-government complex.)

2537 _____. "Mark Rudd: revolutionary," Pittsburgh Point, 10 -- 09 02 69 (Mark Rudd's visit to Carnegie-Mellon University to "recruit a fighting force for Chicago and the revolution to follow.")

2538 _____. "Mayor Daley as liberal leader," Pittsburgh Point, 06 19 01 01 69 (Daley and his comments at the U.S. Conference of Mayors in Pittsburgh.)

2539 Robb, Charles C. "More hearings in city court," Pittsburgh Point, 09 18 04 01 69 (Hearings stem from the Black Coalition demonstration at Manchester Bridge in Pittsburgh.)

2540 _____. "Nixon, know theyself," Pittsburgh Point, 06 05 01 02 69

2541 _____. "A Noisy lunch at the Duquesne Club," Pittsburgh Point, 05 29 01 01 69 (Demonstrators arrested. The article includes the "Manifesto of the Duquesne Club Fourteen.")

2542 _____. "On the picket with Cesar Chavez," Pittsburgh Point, 11 06 01 02 69 (Struggle of grape workers for union recognition.)

2543 _____. "Pittsburgh companies aid the war machine," Pittsburgh Point, 01 01 05 01 70

2543a _____. "A Political act at Carnegie-Mellon," Pittsburgh Point, 09 25 04 01 69 (C-M students staged a demonstration "in support of the Black Construction Coalition's demand for more black memberships in craft unions." Blocked was the new construction site of the new computer science building on campus.)

2544 _____. "The Politicians meet the crisis," Pittsburgh Point, 09 18 02 01 69 (Description of political views regarding the Black Coalition between the two mayoral candidates in Pittsburgh.)

2545 _____. "Resistance in poetry," Pittsburgh Point, 05 01 01 02 69 (An evening entitled "Celebrate Resistance" sponsored by the Pittsburgh Draft Resistance and the Pitt students for peace.)

2546 _____. "Sorry, moon," Pittsburgh Point, 07 24 01 02 69 (Many still contest and protest the huge amounts of money spent on the space program.)

2547 _____. "Two black men in a white court," Pittsburgh Point, 12 11 01 03 69 (Author questions the administration of justice.)

2548 _____. "The War goes on: so does resistance," Pittsburgh Point, 04 03 01 03 69 (Description of the draft resistance in Pittsburgh, and the efforts of Msgr. Charles Owen Rice.)

2549 _____. "What's missing on the moon," Pittsburgh Point, 07 31 01 01 69 ("The whole thing seemed to be unreal, unhuman, not because it was so extraordinary, but because it was so totally technological, so untactile, so unsensual.")

2550 Robbed-Bird. "Indians 'reclaim' ancestral lands," Guardian, 06 27 06 01 70 (Indian Liberation Movement.)

2551 Robbins, John W. "Conservatism versus objectivism," Intercollegiate Review, 6: Winter, 1969-70.

2552 Robbins, Paul Jay. "Dig the Montgomery march," Los Angeles Free Press, 04 02 01 04 65

2553 Robert, Warren Penn. "Rafferty dinosaur runs again," Los Angeles Free Press, 05 29 18 01 70 (Rafferty and education in California.)

2554 Roberts, Dick. "What Nixon's speech revealed about American Democracy," The Militant, 11 14 04 01 69

2555 Robertson, Byron. "Hoffman you're a pig!" Black Panther, 11 22 04 01 69

2556 Robertson, Collette. "With women's liberation at U. of Chicago," Campus Underground, 02 24 07 01 69

2557 Robinson, Robbie. "Black high school students organize," Burning Spear, 12 01 14 01 70 (BSU coalition in Kentucky.)

2558 Rodd, Bill, and Joe Burke. "Byrd Brown makes his move," Pittsburgh Point, 03 12 01 02 70 (Brown and the NAACP in Pittsburgh.)

2559 Rodriguez, Carlos. "Dissenters in uniform: torture at Fort Dix," Berkeley Barb, 08 08 03 03 69 (Alleged torture reported in the stockades at Fort

Dix.)

2560 Roesel, Richard. "Arm bands for peace," Great Speckled Bird, 04 21 09 01 69 (Interesting background story about the wearing of black arm bands.)

2561 Rolfe, Lionel. "Big daddy Unruh," Los Angeles Free Press, 07 10 02 02 70 (Jesse Unruh.)

2562 _____. "In memorum, Pat McGee," Los Angeles Free Press, 06 19 16 02 70

2563 _____. "Reagan's Reinecke rebellion," Los Angeles Free Press, 07 10 09 02 70

2564 Romaine, Howard. "Parks belong to aldermen," Great Speckled Bird, 06 16 07 01 69 (People's Park.)

2565 Rose, William. "Which way for hippies in New Mexico?" Liberation News Service, 09 11 10 01 69 (Political confrontations and the hippies in New Mexico.)

2566 Rosen, Summer M. "The Case for a radical politics," Studies On The Left, 4:32-38, Number 3, 1964. (Radical politics.)

2567 Rosenberg, Mark. "Judge sheds a tear for Milwaukee Priest," Guardian, 06 14 08 01 69 (Eleven of the 14 sentenced for napalming selective service files.)

2568 Rosenblum, Art. "Astrological birth control 100% effective, Reds say," Distant Drummer, 07 02 04 01 70

2569 Rosenblum, Sue. "Fellowship farm," New Hard Times, 11 21 04 01 68 (Community of social change.)

2570 Rosenson, Mary. "Liberation for women only? Feminists vs. women's liberation," North Carolin Anvil, 06 06 06 01 70

2571 Rossi, Alice. "Women--terms of liberation," Dissent,

General 237

17:531, November-December, 1970.

2572 Rossof, Dave (et al.). "Report on Oakland United Front Conference," New Left Notes, 07 30 04 01 69

2573 Rothkrug, Barbara. "High school students attempt union," Liberation News Service, 11 17 04 02 68 (Conference held in New York to consider union for high schools.)

2574 _____. "Welfare rights: militancy in Manhattan," Liberation News Service, 04 17 01 01 69 (Protest and demonstration protesting N.Y. State's welfare budget.)

2575 _____. "Women resisters destroy hundreds of draft files," Liberation News Service, 07 05 20 01 69 ("To thwart the operation of the draft in Manhattan, N.Y.")

2576 Rothlind, Dale. "Air consumers, arise!" Willamette Bridge, 07 07 08 01 69 (Pollution-industrial complex.)

2577 Rountree, Martha. "Crusade for morality," Vital Speeches, 36:597-602, July 15, 1970.

2578 Rubin, Gayle. "Woman as nigger," Ann Arbor Argus, 03 28 07 01 69 (Explores the roles of both men and women in our modern society.)

2579 Rubin, Jerry. "What a day at white haul," East Village Other, 12 15 05 02 67 ("The purposes of mass action are many, but the primary one should be the deepening of a movement of individuals who can change America.")

2580 _____. "The Yippies are coming," Florida Free Press, 03 14 11 01 68 ("A Yippies is anyone who wants to be. A Yippies sounds like the name. Say it loud and you'll see what I mean. Yippie! Yippie!")

2581 Ruether, Rosemary. "The White left in the mother country," Commonweal, 93:143-145, November 6, 1970. ("The left, year by year, builds up its symbiosis with the right on lines that couldn't be better if they were written by the CIA.")

2582 Rustin, Bayard. "April 4," Pittsburgh Point, (Observation of the first anniversary of the slaying of Dr. Martin Luther King Jr.)

2583 Sadler, Lendon. "Grady Grope vs. Board of miseducation," Great Speckled Bird, 04 26 02 01 68 (Experiences with the school board in Atlanta over an underground newspaper, Grady Grope.)

2584 Salstrom, F. P. "And peace: a future in post-urban communal living," Los Angeles Free Press, 08 01 03 03 69 (Back-to-the-land communality program.)

2585 Sanders, Ed. "The Case of the Susan Atkins rip-off," Los Angeles Free Press, 07 24 01 03 70

2586 _____. "The Crisis of the brassiere," Los Angeles Free Press, 07 03 04 02 70 (The Charles Manson Trial.)

2587 _____. "Linda Kasabian in the citadel honk," Los Angeles Free Press, 08 14 01 03 70

2588 _____. "Manson assumes cruciform; judge nails him down," Los Angeles Free Press, 06 19 01 04 70

2589 _____. "Talk to Charles Manson--$1,000 a crack," Los Angeles Free Press, 06 05 03 01 70

2590 _____. "The World's oldest living jury," Los Angeles Free Press, 07 17 04 02 70

2591 Sanders, Ellen. "John and Yoko rap ... about America, about leadership, about revolution, about life," Los Angeles Free Press, 06 11 33 01 69

2592 Sartre, Jean-Paul. "Ideology and revolution," Studies On The Left, 1:7-16, 1960.

2593 _____. "If they ask you for the moon," First Issue, 11 11 03 01 68 ("Man's need is his fundamental right over all others ... if someone asked

2594 ———. "Intellectuals and revolution: interview with Jean-Paul Sartre," Ramparts, 9:52-55, December, 1970. (Political ideology and intellectualism. Interview conducted by J. C. Garot and translated by Bruce Rice.)

2595 ———. "On genocide," Ramparts, 6:36-42, February, 1968.

2596 ———. "Sartre's essay on genocide," Burning River News, 12 16 06 01 69 (Portions of this essay were delivered by Sartre at the International War Crimes Tribunal in 1967.)

2597 ———, and Bertrand Russell. "Jean-Paul Sartre and Bertrand Russell speak out on Mexico and its Olympics," Los Angeles Free Press, 11 01 02 03 68

2598 Satlow, I. D. "Consumer economics: will there be enough food?" Business Education World, 49:25, November, 1968.

2599 Sawyer, Lynwood. "Who are the brain police?" Daily Planet, 11 24 06 02 69 (Description of a raid made by police on a book and movie shop in Miami.)

2600 Saxton, Al. "Tim Carey vs. Joe Pyne return bout on Saturday," Los Angeles Free Press, 10 01 03 04 65 (The controversy is over Carey's The World's Greatest Sinner.)

2600a Schanche, Don A. "Burn the mother down," Saturday Evening Post, Number 23:31, November 16, 1968. (Cleaver and the BPP.)

2601 Schechter, Dan, Michael Ansara, and David Kolodney. "The CIA as an equal opportunity employer," Ramparts, 7:25-33, June, 1969.

2602 Schechtman, Michael. "Holiday commune a thing to groove," Berkeley Barb, 08 25 06 01 67

2603 Scheer, Robert. "Dialectics of confrontation: who ripped off the park," Ramparts, 8:42-53, August, 1969. (Crisis in Berkeley and the People's Park episode.)

2604 _____. "Muckraking: 1964--Hang down your head Tom Dooley," Muckrakers Guide, Ramparts--Special Collector's edition, pp. 15-19. ("It was at this juncture of history that the Vietnamese Catholics became a pawn of American Foreign Policy.")

2605 Schleier, Curt. "How was it done," New York Times Book Review, July 12, 1970, p. 5.

2606 Schneider, Mark. "Buffalo 9 on trial for assault," Guardian, 02 22 06 01 69 (Confrontation with police at a Church over two draft resisters who had taken sanctuary.)

2607 Schoenfeld, Eugene. "Are yippies hippies?" North Carolin Anvil, 07 27 07 01 68

2608 _____. "Principal turns on for 18 years," Dallas Notes, 12 -- 04 01 67 (Fired because she had smoked marijuana for the past 18 years.)

2609 School Of Living. Brookville, Ohio. "A List of intentional communities, formed or in process supplied by School of Living, Brookville, Ohio (plus additions known to printer--marked*)," Liberation News Service, 10 16 11 01 68 (Some sixty communities are listed nationwide.)

2609a Schrag, Peter. "America's other radicals," Harper, 241:35-46, August, 1970.

2610 Schreiber, James A. "Atom arms to Vietnam," Berkeley Barb, 05 19 01 05 67

2611 _____. "Panther ambush," Berkeley Barb, 05 05 03 04 67

2612 Schulder, Diane B. "What is a 'conspiracy'?" Pittsburgh Point, 08 07 06 01 69 ("Editor's Note: The author is a lawyer who assisted Dr. Spock's counsel at the trial and appeal; opinions expressed are her own. The article is from the Liberation

News Service.")

2613 Schultz, John. "An interview with Robert F. Williams," Studies On The Left, 2:51-62, Number 3, 1962. (An interview with the former President of the Monroe branch of the NAACP who challenged the non-resistance policy in North Carolina.)

2614 Schultz, Ray. "New Haven," East Village Other, 05 05 12 01 70

2615 Schurmann, Franz. "Ho Chi Minh: a eulogy," Ramparts, 8:52-60, November, 1969.

2616 _____. "Is Nixon winning?" Liberation, 14:13-16, February, 1970.

2617 _____. "The National Liberation Front asks the American left: where are you now that we really need you?" Ramparts, 8:14-22, August, 1969.

2618 _____. "What the NLF wants," Ramparts, 8:19-20, April, 1970.

2619 Schwartz, Herman. "Wiretapping and eavesdropping: pros and cons," Current History, 53:31-37, July, 1967.

2620 Schwartz, Jon, and Bill Callahan. "War makers, strike breakers, fight G.E.!" Liberation, 14:5-12, February, 1970. (General Electric Corporation.)

2621 Schwartz, Ray. "Welfare today," Los Angeles Free Press, 07 25 33 02 69

2622 Scott, Jack. "Jocks--1, War--0," Ramparts, 9:15-18, August, 1970. (Cal Jocks at Berkeley.)

2623 Scott, Peter Dale. "Air America: flying the U.S. into Laos," Ramparts, 8:39-54, February, 1970. (Early history of Air America.)

2624 Scott, Robert L., and Donald K. Smith. "The Rhetoric of confrontation," Quarterly Journal of Speech, 55:1-8, February, 1969.

2625 Seale, Bobby. "Bobby Seale speaks from jail,"

Pittsburgh Point, 11 06 09 01 69 ("Editor's Note: The following note was written by Bobby Seale in his Chicago jail cell, smuggled into the courtroom on Thursday, October 30, and given to Jerry Rubin who released it later that day.")

2626 Seale, Bobby. "Bobby speaks to Scandinavia," Black Panther, 10 25 10 01 69

2627 _____. "Chairman Bobby Seale talks about conspiracy of trial and the arresting of the patriots," Black Panther, 02 28 07 02 70

2628 _____. "Exploitation--on--wheels," Black Panther, 05 31 03 01 70 (Repressive tactics described.)

2629 _____. "Message to all progressive forces," Black Panther, 11 15 10 01 69

2630 _____. "Pig tricks against Chicago defendants," Black Panther, 10 11 04 02 69

2631 _____. "Seize the time: the next Panther victim," Ramparts, 8:18-29, June, 1970.

2632 _____. "What is there to talk about," Black Panther, 12 13 05 02 69 (The movement, current state of affairs, and the BPP.)

2633 Segers, Mary C. "The New civil rights: fem. lib!" Catholic World, 211:203-207, August, 1970.

2634 Seiler, J. A. "Diagnosing interdepartmental conflict," Harvard Business Review, 41:121-132, September-October, 1963.

2635 Seingrass, Bob. "G.I's in mutiny trial," Fifth Estate, 11 28 04 01 68 (Mutiny at Presidio and confrontations with Army brass.)

2636 Selkirk, Errol. "U.C. moratorium," Berkeley Barb, 11 21 03 01 69

2637 Severy, Bruce. "Grape union winning big victory," Guardian, 08 08 04 01 70

2638 Seward, Becky. "Review of Utica teach-in on war,"

General 243

New Patriot, 01 18 03 03 68 (Organized purpose was to end the war in Vietnam.)

2639 Shagnasty, Oliver. "Witch strikes," Spectator, 07 29 10 01 69 (Witchcraft.)

2640 Shakur, Afeni. "Fascist courts try New York Panther 21," Black Panther, 02 07 10 01 70

2641 ———. "The Prisons and jails are filled with political prisoners," Black Panther, 07 18 11 03 70

2642 Shapiro, S. "Big brother is watching your kids," American Library Association Bulletin, 62:1089-92, October, 1968. (Obscenity and the law.)

2643 Shayne, Bob. "What is a Lenny Bruce," Los Angeles Free Press, 08 16 34 01 68

2644 Shear, Jeff. "Old Main's old men," Water Tunnel, 03 10 18 02 69 (Pennsylvania State University.)

2645 Shecter, Leonard. "The Coming revolt of the athletes," Look, 54:43-47, July 28, 1970.

2646 Shero, Jeff. "Playboy's tinseled seductress," Rag, 10 10 04 01 66 (Playboy Magazine.)

2647 ———. "RAT reports on bomb plot," East Village Other, 11 19 03 01 69

2648 Shidler, Sam. "The New left isn't ready for me," Campus Underground, 12 09 03 03 68 (Written by one who feels alienated from everything.)

2649 Shuba, George. "Presidio mutiny case: partial victory," Liberation News Service, 03 22 01 01 69

2650 Shuett, Suzanne. "On women," San Diego Free Press, 11 15 10 01 68

2651 Siegel, Ed. "Spock-in-the-box," Guardian, 06 22 07 01 68

2652 Silber, Irwin. "Alternative media meeting emits a

confused message," Guardian, 06 27 08 02 70 (Role of communication technology.)

2653 Silber, Irwin. "Five thousand march against war at Fort Dix," Guardian, 10 18 03 01 69 (Marchers invade Fort Dix.)

2654 Simmons, Bob. "Yoga and the psychic mind," San Francisco Oracle, 06 -- 07 01 66

2655 Sinclair. "The Meaning of conspiracy laws," Fifth Estate, 11 28 03 04 68 (Ethics of governmental judicial procedures are compared with radical procedures in conspiracy laws.)

2656 Sinclair, Magdalene. "I just wanna testify," Dallas Notes, (UPS) 09 17 04 01 69 (Personal story written by John's wife and reprinted from Ann Arbor Argus. John is serving a 10 year term in Southern Michigan Prison.)

2657 Singer, Cris. "The Chicago conspiracy," Fifth Estate, 04 03 03 01 69

2658 Skir, L. "We're freakin on in! look at gay power," Mademoiselle, 71:150-1, September, 1970.

2659 Sklar, Martin J., and James Weinstein. "Socialism and the new left," Studies On The Left, 6:62-70, Number 2, March-April, 1966. (Comparative ideologies.)

2660 Slater, B. R. "Effect of noise on pupil performance," Journal of Educational Psychology, 59:239-43, August, 1968.

2661 Smith, Chip. "An Open letter to the executive committee of the faculty and the deans of the University of Pennsylvania School of Medicine," Distant Drummer, 10 03 03 01 69

2662 Smith, Jack A. "Where the revolution is at," Guardian, 06 22 01 02 68

2663 _____, and Tanya R. Smith. "Juche: North Korea leaps ahead," Guardian, 09 12 02 01 70 (A description of Korea today. The whole issue is

General

"entirely devoted to an in-depth study (report) on the Democratic People's Republic of Korea.")

2664 Smith, Jim. "Shop raided for 'obscenity'," Dallas Notes, 10 15 13 02 69 (Shop raided for possession of obscene materials at North Richland Hills in Fort Worth, Texas.)

2665 Smith, John. "The Anti-war movement inside the armed forces," Independent Socialist, 07 -- 04 01 68

2666 Smith, Marvin. "Synanon's thousandth member," Los Angeles Free Press, 04 12 07 01 68

2667 Smith, Michael. "Analysis of a victory: free speech for G.I's," Fifth Estate, 05 29 15 01 69

2668 Smith, Ralph Lee. "Law and order, 1970," Nation, 210:774-783, June 29, 1970.

2669 Smothers, Tom, and Dick Smothers. "TV censorship closes generation dialogue--Tom and Dick," Los Angeles Free Press, 05 02 30 01 69 ("Excerpts from remarks ... at the annual banquet of the American Society of Newspaper Editors, April 18, 1969.")

2670 Smukler, Michael, and Carol McEldowney. "Welfare rights action," Burning River News, 01 25 02 01 69 (Confrontation in Ohio's welfare department and implications for recipients of funds.)

2671 Smylie, James H. "American religious bodies, just war, and Vietnam," Journal of Church and State, 11: Autumn, 1969.

2672 _____. "Prudes, lewds and polysyllables," Commonweal, 89:671-3, February 28, 1969.

2673 Snyder, Gary. "Four changes--population--pollution--consumption--transformation," Northwest Passage, 03 09 (Page Insert) 70

2674 Sontag, Susan. "Some thoughts on the right way (for us) to love the Cuban revolution," Ramparts, 7:6-19, April, 1969.

2675 Sparrow, J. "Hullabaloo and ...," Spectator, 204:130, January 29, 1960.

2676 Spencer, Larry D. "The Threat and relevance of the ultra-right," Studies On The Left, 3:103-108, Number 3, 1963. (Description of ideologies of both left and right.)

2677 Spinard, Norman. "The American revolution 1970-- not a shot away," Los Angeles Free Press, 10 23 03 01 70 (Ideas about the present revolution as well as some thoughts about guerrilla warfare in the U.S.)

2678 _____. "You've come a long way baby," Los Angeles Free Press, 09 11 04 02 70 (The "response to women's liberation.")

2679 Spradley, James P. "Moral career of a bum; excerpt from You owe yourself a drunk," Trans-Action, 7:16-29, May, 1970.

2680 Stamberg, Margie. "Addict center: new left commune?" Guardian, 11 23 09 01 68 (Rehabilitation commune for drug addicts in New York and Connecticut.)

2681 _____. "CUNY offers pacification program," Guardian, 07 19 16 01 69 (A Master plan for open admissions to all high school graduates.)

2682 Star, J. "Faces of the boys in the band; a changing view of homosexuality," Look, 33:62-8, December 2, 1969.

2683 Stayton, Dick. "Torture at Treasure Island," Berkeley Barb, 08 08 04 01 69

2684 Steele, Bill. "G.I's fight Army brass," Fifth Estate, 01 23 09 01 69

2685 Steele, Lloyd. "The Homosexual imagination; boys in the band," Los Angeles Free Press, 05 29 43 03 70

2685a Stermer, Dugald (ed.). "The People's Park: a history in pictures," Ramparts, 8:35-40, August, 1969.

2686 _____. "Who owns the park?" Ramparts, 8:8-10, August, 1969. ("Includes the original position paper of the Park's People, by F. Bardacke.")

2687 Stern, Daniel J. "Defensive reactions to political anxiety: the American anti-communist liberal and the invasion of Cuba," Studies On The Left, 2:3-8, Number 2, 1961. (Psychological aspects of ideology as it relates to social change.)

2688 Stern, David H. "Council to ban hitchhiking," Los Angeles Free Press, 10 16 13 04 70 (An antihitchhiking ordinance is to be drawn up by the Los Angeles City Council in light of the percentages of rapes and robberies recorded in the city.)

2689 Stern, Max. "On being a great power," Los Angeles Free Press, 12 17 01 04 66 (Paul Goodman speaks on U.S. actions in Vietnam.)

2689a Stern, Sol. "The Defense intellectuals," Ramparts, 5:32-37, February, 1967. (Articles dealing with the "New Politics convention held in Chicago on August 29 to September 4, 1967.")

2690 _____. "A Short account of international student politics and the cold war, with particular reference to the NSA, CIA, etc.," Muckrakers Guide, Ramparts--Special Collector's edition, pp. 87-97.

2691 _____. "War catalog of the University of Pennsylvania," Ramparts, 5:32-40, August, 1966.

2692 Stickgold, Mark. "Panthers busted," Ann Arbor Argus, 06 19 11 01 69

2693 Stillman, Elinor. "Boycott Safeway: farm workers reap grapes of wrath," Peninsula Observer, 05 26 06 02 69

2694 Stone, Harvey. "G.I. coffee houses for peace," Fifth Estate, 08 01 08 01 68 ("Summer of support" project within G.I. ranks supporting the anti-war movement at Fort Jackson, and Fort Leonard Wood, among others.)

2695 Stone, Richard. "The Underground press succeeds by

intriguing rebels and squares," Wall Street Journal, March 4, 1968. (Also reprinted in the Los Angeles Free Press for March 8, 1968, p. 25.)

2696 Street, David, and John C. Leggett. "Economic deprivation and extremism," American Journal of Sociology, 67:53-57, 1961.

2697 Strong, Dennis M. "Life inside Presidio," Liberation News Service, 05 31 10 01 69 (Alleged brutality, written by one who refused to cooperate with military authorities.)

2698 Students For A Democratic Society--Press Release. "Sculpture censored," Los Angeles Free Press, 04 05 12 02 68

2699 _____. "SDS calls Pueblo incident desperate move," Fifth Estate, 02 15 12 01 68

2700 Such, Rod. "Blacks march through Georgia," Guardian, 05 30 03 01 70 (A peace march against repression in Atlanta, Georgia.)

2701 _____. "Los Angeles Chicanos in mass action," Guardian, 09 05 06 01 70 (National Chicano Moratorium in Los Angeles on August 29, 1970.)

2702 _____. "Millions protest against Cambodia invasion throughout U.S.," Guardian, 05 23 06 01 70 (Description of anti-war centers during May, 1970.)

2703 _____. "A New constitution?" Guardian, 09 19 01 01 70 (The September 4-7 conference of the plenary session of the "Revolutionary People's Constitutional Convention," held in Philadelphia.)

2704 _____. "Panthers call for constitutional convention," Guardian, 06 27 04 01 70

2705 _____. "Seven-day black uprising in Jersey town," Guardian, 07 18 04 01 70 (Asbury Park in New Jersey.)

2706 Suiter, John. "Black Panthers draw battle lines," Berkeley Barb, 08 08 10 01 69

2707 _____. "Indians rip off rok running the blockade," Berkeley Barb, 11 28 03 01 69 (Alcatraz.)

2708 _____. "Seale in S.F. county jail," Berkeley Barb, 11 14 03 01 69 (Interview with Bobby Seale.)

2709 Sullivan, Susan. "Women: redefinition--a pedestrian account," Great Speckled Bird, 02 09 09 02 70

2710 Sundberg, Jim. "Rightists are frustrated people," Spokane Natural--Chief Joseph, 05 09 13 01 69

2711 Supak, Jon. "The Hip radical: what's ahead?" Old Mole, 09 13 10 01 68

2712 Surowiec, Mike. "Alienated or alligned: a statement of S.S.I's position," Western Activist, 10 20 01 01 66 (S.S.I's policy on student rights, civil rights, and national affairs.)

2713 Sweeney, Michael. "From dustbowl to Saigon: the 'people's bank' builds an empire," Ramparts, 9:37, November, 1970. (History of the "Bank of America.")

2714 _____. "To burn the bank--peacefully," Los Angeles Free Press, 10 30 26 01 70 (Confrontations between bank burners and Bank of America officials.)

2715 Sylvester, Eugene A. "Dix prisoners rebel against lousy food," San Diego Free Press, 02 14 06 01 69 (Food riot at Fort Dix.)

2716 Taing, R.D. "Turn me on," Pittsburgh Fair Witness, 11 23 05 01 70 (Sexual freedom.)

2717 Taube, Skip. "Mother--country rising up angry," Black Panther, 10 18 05 01 69 (White Panther Party.)

2718 Taylor, Vonna. "The Wilmington 13," Heterodoxical Voice, 04 -- 03 02 69 (Controversy over setting bail for the 13 who were indicted for assaulting a federal law officer.)

2719 Tepperman, Jean. "Communal living--you have to start or you won't get it after the revolution," Old Mole, 10 24 14 01 69 (Communal living "vs. the outside world.")

2720 Thiher, Gary. "Malcolm X; wretched of the earth--black men speak out," Rag, 11 07 04 01 66 ("White Americans need not fear black power if they understand it.")

2720a Thomas, Gordon B. "The Challenge of change," Electronic Age, 30:32-34, Winter, 1970-71. ("Americans can work together for positive change through more constructive use of our nation's human resources, combined with the energy of our nation's youth.")

2721 Thomas, Niel. "Federal court voids part of state obscenity act," Pittsburgh Point, 11 06 05 01 69 (The editor's note and the addendum to this article is well worth reading.)

2722 Thomas, Norman. "Toward total disarmament," Dissent, 7:163-166, Spring, 1960.

2723 Thomas, Wendell. "Intentional communities make for peace," Modern Utopian, 05 08 26 01 64 ("A new culture based on peace is the only way to eliminate war." Article is a reprint from Fellowship, November, 1965.)

2724 Thompson, James D. "Organizational management of conflict," Administrative Science Quarterly, 4:389-409, 1960.

2725 Thornburg, Richard L. "The Continuing American revolution," Pittsburgh Point, 09 18 03 01 69 ("Excerpts from an address by the author," with the above title.)

2726 Thornley, Kerry, and Cara Thornley. "A Manual for the yin revolution," Chinook, 12 18 08 01 69 (Power, evil, betrayal, political games, and personality destruction.)

2727 Thrasher, Sue, and David Nolan. "SSOC defended," Great Speckled Bird, 06 30 07 01 69

General 251

2728 Tobin, R. L. "Sports as an integrator," Saturday Review, 50:32, January 21, 1967. (Racial integration through sports.)

2729 Tornquist, Elizabeth. "Abortion business in N.C.," North Carolin Anvil, 03 07 01 01 70

2730 _____. "Abortions," North Carolin Anvil, 03 14 01 03 70 (Part of a series.)

2731 _____. "Abortions," North Carolin Anvil, 03 21 01 01 70 (Last in the series.)

2732 _____. "Abortions and where to get them," North Carolin Anvil, 02 28 01 01 70

2733 _____. "Durham school board--a twitching of dead bodies," North Carolin Anvil, 08 30 02 01 69 (Crisis in education at Durham Public Schools in North Carolina.)

2734 _____. "N.C'S political prisoners," North Carolin Anvil, 01 24 01 01 69

2735 _____. "On destruction of natural resources," North Carolin Anvil, 05 09 10 01 70 (Environmental crisis and conservation.)

2736 _____. "Our Black Panther trial," North Carolin Anvil, 12 20 01 01 69

2737 _____. "Racial schizophrenia coming up everywhere," North Carolin Anvil, 04 04 04 01 70

2738 _____. "SCLC," North Carolin Anvil, 12 13 01 01 69

2739 Torrence, Michael. "The Murder of Donald Miller," Black Panther, 04 25 08 01 70

2740 Trounstine, Phil. "Tricky Dick's reinforced protective reaction strikes," Free You, 05 11 03 02 70

2741 Truskier, Andy. "Epilogue to People's Park," Chinook, 10 23 04 01 69 (Chronology of the People's Park confrontations at Berkeley.)

2742 Tucker, Nancy. "New York City has largest turnout, longest gay march," Advocate, 07 22 01 03 70 (Demonstration in the form of a parade demonstrating gay power and pride.)

2743 Turner, Jon. "Yale corporation and the Black Community," Black Panther, 05 02 04 04 70

2744 Turner, William W. "De Pugh and the Minutemen: wonderland of the mind," Ramparts, 8:10-12, June, 1970. (Clash in ideologies of right-wing factions and government agencies.)

2745 _____. "The Garrison Commission and the assassination of President Kennedy," Ramparts, 6:43-68, January, 1968.

2746 _____. "I was a burglar, wiretapper, bugger, and spy for the FBI," Muckrakers Guide, Ramparts--Special Collector's edition, pp. 47-51. (The author served as an FBI agent from 1951 to 1961.)

2747 _____. "JFK investigation goes on," Grinding Stone, 04 30 05 01 69 (Theories still hold that JFK was killed by a conspiracy.)

2748 _____. "The Minutemen," Ramparts, 5:69-76, January, 1967.

2749 _____. "Some disturbing parallels," Ramparts, 6:33-36, June 29, 1968. (Comparative study of striking parallels between the King and Kennedy assassinations, along with some criticisms of the Warren Commission Report.)

2750 Tyack, David B. "Growing up black: perspectives on the history of education in northern ghettos," History of Education Quarterly, 9: Summer, 1969.

2751 United Press Syndicate, and Liberation News Service. "Panther conference against Fascism," Spokane Natural, 08 01 05 03 69

2752 Unruh, Jesse M. "Legislative ethics and conflict of interest," Yearbook of the National Conference of State Legislative Leaders, Number 4, November, 1969, p. 36.

General

2753   Ury, C. M. "Bibliography on environmental problems," Phi Delta Kappan, 51:570-2, June, 1970.

2753a Van Gelder, Lindsy. "Emancipation proclamation: freeing the young working woman," Electronic Age, 30:22-25, Winter, 1970-71. ("Job discrimination against women begins under the christmas tree.")

2754   Vareia, M. E. "Chicanos confront Presbyterians," Dallas Notes, 06 04 04 01 69 (Chicanos confront Presbyterians at the Presbyterian National meeting at San Antonio, Texas, May 16-21, 1969.)

2755   Verb, Hal. "JFK death plotters tracked to California," Berkeley Barb, 09 22 03 01 67

2756   _____. "JFK killed in Cuba deal, expert charges," Berkeley Barb, 11 10 04 04 67

2757   _____. "Mafia plot to kill Garrison verified," Berkeley Barb, 12 29 07 02 67

2758   _____. "Proof: Ruby near when JFK was slain," Berkeley Barb, 10 14 01 01 66

2759   _____. "Three thousand protest Redwood City napalm plant as Morse speaks," Berkeley Barb, 06 03 02 03 66 (Wayne Morse speaks at the Redwood City napalm plant.)

2760   Vivas, Eliseo. "Herbert Marcuse: philosopher en titre of the new nihilists," Intercollegiate Review, 6: Winter, 1969-70.

2761   Waibel, Terry. "Black Panthers serving breakfast," Pittsburgh Point, 04 23 01 03 70

2762   _____. "The 'Flag Case' in city court," Pittsburgh Point, 03 12 01 03 70

2763   _____. "Public assistance--never on weekends," Pittsburgh Point, 02 26 02 02 70

2764   _____. "Tenants organize," Pittsburgh Point, 03 19 02 03 70

2765   Wallace, Jo Ann. "A Chance for black children to

learn," <u>Peninsula Observer</u>, 05 20 02 03 69 ("Sneak-out program" at East Palo Alto, and Mrs. Wilks's efforts at an equal educational opportunity for everyone.)

2766 Waller, Joseph. "On contradictions," <u>Burning Spear</u>, 09 21 10 01 70 (Contradictions of "White Power Structure" to a revolvement and the resulting implications for the Black Liberation struggle.)

2767 Walley, David, and Claudia Dreifus. "Playboy after the dark ages--Hugh Hefner and the women's revolution," <u>East Village Other</u>, 02 11 06 03 70

2768 Walton, Richard E., John M. Dutton, and Thomas P. Cafferty. "Organizational context and inter-departmental conflict," <u>Administrative Science Quarterly</u>, 14:522-542, December, 1969. (A study of 300 managers with inter-departmental liaison responsibilities.)

2769 Warner, Denis. "How Hanoi sees the war," <u>Reporter</u>, 37:17-20, August 10, 1967.

2770 _____. "South Vietnam exists," <u>Reporter</u>, 37:18-20, September 21, 1967.

2771 _____. "Vietnam: hard battles still to be fought," <u>Reporter</u>, 38:16-19, May 2, 1968.

2772 _____. "Vietnam: the need for loyal opposition," <u>Reporter</u>, 37:25, December 14, 1967.

2773 _____. "Vietnam's militant Buddhists," <u>Reporter</u>, 31:29-31, December, 1964.

2774 Warwick, Dick. "The Rise of Fascist America," <u>Conscience</u>, 08 -- 20 01 69

2775 Waskow, Arthur I. "Business, religion, and the left," <u>Liberation</u>, 14:46-48, August-September, 1969.

2776 _____. "The Religious upwelling of the New Left," <u>Liberation</u>, 14:36-37, July, 1969.

2777 Wasserman, Judy. "Administration gnaws at black civil liberties," <u>Peninsula Observer</u>, 07 28 09

01 69

2778 Waters, Mary Alice. "Key problems facing antiwar forces," The Militant, 11 14 07 02 69

2779 Watson, Dave. "The Real radicals in the high schools," Fifth Estate, 07 10 07 01 69

2780 Watson, John. "League of revolutionary black workers: an interview with John Watson ... Part I," Fifth Estate, 05 01 14 01 69 (Part II of this article appears in the May 15 issue p. 12.)

2781 Watts, Alan. "Wit's end: Alan Watts 'talks'," Grok, 05 -- 03 01 70

2782 Weatherby, Andre. "Confrontation with Kansas City Power and Light Company," Black Panther, 09 27 02 01 69

2783 Webb, Marilyn Salzman. "Abortion," Washington Free Press, 08 01 17 01 69

2784 _____. "America's comic culture," Grinding Stone, 04 30 07 01 69 (Examples of American life portrayed in comics and what they (comics) are supposed to tell us about ourselves. A reprint from the Guardian.)

2785 _____. "Another view of 'The Lion of Judah'," Pittsburgh Point, 08 07 07 01 69 ("Editor's Note: ...Following is an account of another aspect of Emperor Haile Selassie's recent visit to the U.S." The article is from the Liberation News Service.)

2786 _____. "DC9 tell why they hit DOW office," Guardian, 04 12 06 01 69

2787 Weinstein, Henry. "Breathing space: a talk with Mitch Goodman," Liberation, 14:31-35, July, 1969.

2788 Weinstein, James. 'Nach Goldwasser Uns?" Studies On The Left, 4:59-64, Number, 3, 1964. (Fascism and its possible connection with the Kennedy assassination. Staughton Lynd answers the same communication in the same issue.)

2789 Weinstein, James. "Weathermen (Revolutionary Youth Movement) A lot of thunder but a short reign," Socialist Revolution, 1: January-February, 1970.

2790 Weintraub, Roberta. "Women: fat of the land," Los Angeles Free Press, 06 05 01 03 70

2791 Weisberg, Barry. "April 22: a one day teach-in is like an all day sucker," Liberation, 15:38-41, April, 1970.

2792 _____. "The Politics of ecology," Liberation, 14:20-25, January, 1970.

2793 _____. "Politics of ecology," San Jose Red Eye, 02 12 08 01 70

2794 _____. "Raping Alaska. The Ecology of oil," Ramparts, 8:26-33, January, 1970.

2795 Weiskopf, Doug. "American Legion convention to be faced by radicals," Los Angeles Free Press, 06 05 13 04 70

2796 Weissman, Steve. "Businessmen against the war," Ramparts, 9:32-37, December, 1970. (Business executives move for Vietnam peace.)

2797 Weller, Don (illus.). "Support your local police state," Ramparts, 6:43-45, February, 1968. (A photographic collection of "non-lethal" weapons, copies from the advertisements of the companies who make them.)

2798 Welles, Earl. "Politics of disorientation," Berkeley Barb, 10 03 03 01 69 (Historical aspects of the Berkeley movement.)

2799 Wells, Lyn. "Sisters United: they haven't seen anything yet," Great Speckled Bird, 02 23 08 03 70

2800 Welsh, David. "Brothers of Passamaquoddia: the Royal screwing of the Passamaquoddia," Muckrakers Guide, Ramparts--Special Collector's edition, pp. 98-103. (Description of the Passamaquoddy Indians and their plight.)

2801 _____. "Building Lyndon Johnson," Muckrakers Guide, Ramparts--Special Collector's edition, pp. 104-114. (Building programs which provide the base construction for the war effort in Vietnam.)

2802 _____, and David Lifton. "The Case for three assassins," Ramparts, 5:77-100, January, 1967. (A special report investigating the assassination of President Kennedy. Includes a preface, index, and a recapitulation.)

2803 _____, and William Turner. "In the shadow of Dallas," Muckrakers Guide, Ramparts--Special Collector's edition, pp. 61-72. ("These are not the only ones to have died mysteriously possessing criminal knowledge about the killings of President Kennedy, officer J. D. Tippit or Lee Harvey Oswald. But this is the story of ten....")

2804 Wendt, Larry. "Food ecology," Renaissance, 01 15 05 01 70

2805 _____. "War is bullshit," San Jose Red Eye, 11 20 03 01 69

2806 Wesley, S. M. "The Creative visionary and the new revolution," Berkeley Barb, 08 22 08 01 69

2807 West, Charles C. "A Christian views Vietnam: conflict of moral responsibilities," Presbyterian Life, 20:5-8, December 15, 1967.

2808 West, Phyllis. "Student group grows after typo appears," Los Angeles Free Press, 10 29 01 03 65 ("Inflated in membership from 3,000 to 300,000 by a typographical error circulated nationally.")

2809 Wheeler, Gerald R. "The Welfare system; people eating bureaucracy--must exploit to survive," Los Angeles Free Press, 07 11 02 04 69

2810 Wheeler, Tim. "Jailing of Abernathy fails to break strike," Black Panther, 07 05 11 01 69 (Demands of hospital workers in Charleston, South Carolina.)

2811 Whitfield, M. "Let's boycott the Olympics," Ebony, 19:95-96, March, 1964.

2812 Wiener, Jon. "Woodstock revisited," Pittsburgh Point, 11 06 10 01 69 (Reflections about the Woodstock Festival.)

2813 Wiggins, J. R. "The Right and responsibilities of dissent," Freedom and Union, 23:10-15, 1968.

2814 Wilfong, Robert G. "Be-in," Mother of Voices, 12 01 05 01 67 ("Brigadier General Casimir Pulaski Memorial Ecumenical Be-in.")

2815 Wilkinson, Bob. "Capital confrontation," Connections, 09 19 11 01 67 ("Confrontation from protest to resistance.")

2816 Will, George F. "The Woman problem," Alternative, 12 -- 07 02 70

2817 Williams, Henri. "Historical synopsis of the black movement," Burning Spear, 10 13 10 01 70 (Chronicles historically the movement in Louisville with the structure of JOMO.)

2818 Williams, Ora. "No justice in Amerikkka," Black Panther, 12 27 10 01 69

2819 Williams, William Appleman. "Historiography and revolution; the case of Cuba. A commentary on a polemic by Theodore Draper," Studies On The Left, 3:78-102, Number 3, 1963. (Analysis and interpretation of the Cuban Revolution from both Williams and Draper. Lively arguments.)

2820 Willis, Ellen. "Women and the myth of consumerism," Ramparts, 8:14-16, June, 1970. (Consumermism and implications of it for revolutionary points of view.)

2821 Wilson, Darryl. "An American Indian speaks out," Los Angeles Free Press, 10 30 63 02 70

2822 Wilson, Jame. "Hurricane Garrison flattens New Orleans," Los Angeles Free Press, 10 20 15 01 67

2823 Wilson, John. "A Coalition of militants," Liberation News Service, 01 23 10 01 69 (Comments on the coalition of militants.)

2824 Wilson, Tizell. "The Olympic boycott," Son of Jabberwork, 11 08 04 03 68

2825 Wingell, Bill. "A Time for holding hands: great to be gay," Distant Drummer, 07 10 08 01 69 (Homosexuals hold 'equal rights' demonstration in Philadelphia.)

2826 _____. "With Rev. McIntire and the boys down at Independence Hall," Distant Drummer, 06 18 10 01 70

2827 Winick, Charles. "Drug addicts getting younger," PTA Magazine, 65:6-8, September, 1970.

2828 Winters, Stanley B. "Urban renewal and civil rights," Studies On The Left, 4:16-31, Number 3, 1964. (Problems of the inner-city.)

2829 Witkin, Jim. "The May day resistance rally," Distant Drummer, 05 08 05 03 69

2830 Wittes, Glorianne, and Simon Wittes. "A Study of interracial conflict," American Education, 6:7-10, June, 1970.

2831 Wittman, Carl. "A Gay manifesto," Los Angeles Free Press, 08 14 56 01 70

2832 Wolfe, Robert. "American imperialism and the peace movement," Studies On The Left, 6:28-43, Number 3, May-June, 1966. (Imperialism and its significance for peace movements.)

2833 _____. "Intellectuals and social change," Studies On The Left, 2:63-68, Number 3, 1962. (Essay in response to C. Wright Mills on the "end of ideology, utopianism, and Marxism.")

2834 Wolkind, George. "Tonkin Bay revisited," Heterodoxical Voice, 03 -- 05 01 68

2835 Wood, Myrna. "An interview between two women,"

Leviathan, 05 -- 10 01 70

2836 Woode, Allen. "How the Pentagon stopped worrying and learned to love peace marchers," Ramparts, 6:47-51, February, 1968.

2837 Woodhead, M. M. "Effect of noise on the distribution of attention," Journal of Applied Psychology, 50:296-9, August, 1966.

2838 Woodley, Richard. "Cappital punishment, or whompin hippies dogpatch style," Esquire, 74:161, November, 1970.

2839 Woods, Sharla. "Bussing doesn't mean education," Black Panther, 04 25 06 01 70

2840 Woodwell, George M. "Science and the gross national pollution," Ramparts, 8:51-54, May, 1970.

2841 Wrong, Dennis H. "Reflections on the end of ideology," Dissent, 7:286-291, Summer, 1960.

2842 Wulp, Dave. "Socialists register gains in Cleveland elections," The Militant, 11 14 08 01 69

2843 Yarmolinsky, Adam. "How the Pentagon works," Atlantic, 219:56-61, March, 1967.

2844 Yates, Bill, and Mike McKeating. "War industries prosper: 735 million in 1966 in Buffalo," Buffalo Insighter, 09 25 01 01 67 (Defense production in Buffalo in government contracts.)

2845 Yokell, Mike. "A Guide to radical Boston," Paper Tiger, 05 -- 20 01 68 (Organization of the PACEM being an outgrowth of the New England Vietnam Summer.)

2846 York, Frank A. "Revolutionary 4th in Berkeley," Pittsburgh Point, 07 10 01 02 69 (Revolutionary celebration by members of the radical hip community in Berkeley.)

2847 Young, Allen. "Castro, Cuban revolution recall struggle, victory," San Diego Free Press, 01 01 11 01 69

2848 _____. "Pete Seeger on the Clearwater," Pittsburgh Point, 09 11 03 01 69 (The "Clearwater" sloop along the Hudson is part of a "counter-institution" in its effort to clean up industrial waste pollutants all across the country. The crew is interracial. The article is from the Liberation News Service.)

2849 _____. "SDS takes new turn," Fifth Estate, 07 10 05 01 69

2850 _____. "Senate report on the new left," Liberation News Service, 11 09 03 02 68 ("Memorandum prepared for the Subcommittee to investigate the Administration of the International Security Act and other Internal Security Laws of the Committee on the Judiciary, U.S. Senate, Ninetieth Congress, Second Session.")

2851 _____. "The War for the hearts and minds of G.I.'s," Liberation News Service, 11 07 E 01 68 (Civilians arrive at the base for a teach-in and love-in with the soldiers and a demonstration against war.)

2852 Youngblood, Gene. "Beard brief but beautiful," Los Angeles Free Press, 02 02 14 03 68

2853 _____. "Movies: under and overground," Los Angeles Free Press, 03 29 28 02 68

2854 Zatlyn, Ted. "Nisqually: the last Indian War rages," Los Angeles Free Press, 07 12 21 01 68 (Dick Gregory confronts Washington State authorities over fishing rights for the Nisqually Indians.)

2855 Zeitlin, Maurice. "Inside Cuba: workers and revolution," Ramparts, 8:10-20, March, 1970.

2856 Zelinsky, W. "How much is enough? The implications of further population growth in the United States," Journal of General Education, 20:4673, April, 1968.

2857 Zetteler, Mike. "Goodman comments: underground press and psychedelic art," Kaleidoscope, 12 22 03 01 67 (Goodman comments on LSD, underground press, and art.)

2858 Zetteler, Mike. "Walls have ears: wire tap," Kaleidoscope, 12 22 05 01 67 (How easy it is for one to be bugged unknowingly and inexpensively.)

2859 Zinn, Howard. "Dow shalt not kill," First Issue, 02 -- 11 01 68 (Demonstrations against Dow Chemicals.)

2860 Zorra, Victor. "In Hanoi, the doves have beaten the hawks," Atlas, 19:15-20, June, 1970.

2861 Zyn. "Ginsberg at Gonzaga University," Spokane Natural, 05 09 05 02 69

II. FIREARMS, CONTROL AND REGULATION

BOOKS

2862 American Bar Association. Firearms and legislative regulation. Research contributions, number 6. Chicago: Illinois, 1967. (Legal Economic Publications.)

2863 Armacost, Michael H. The Politics of weapons intervention. N.Y.: Columbia University Press, 1969.

2864 Bakal, Carl. Right to bear arms. N.Y.: McGraw-Hill, 1966.

2865 Beman, Lamar T. ...Outlawing the pistol. N.Y.: H. W. Wilson Company, 1926. (Reference Shelf Series, Vol. 3 Number 10.)

2866 Krug, Alan S. Does firearms registration work? A statistical analysis of New York State and New York City crime data. Connecticut: National Shooting Sports Foundation, Inc., 1968.

2867 National Shooting Sports Foundation, Inc. The True facts on firearms legislation: three statistical studies. Connecticut: The Association, 1968.

2868 Remington Arms Company. Shooting Promotion Department Safe gun handling. Bridgeport: Connecticut, (n.d.).

2869 Roberts, D., and A. P. Bristow. An Introduction to modern police firearms. N.Y.: Free Press of Glencoe, 1969.

2870 Sandys-Winsch, G. Gun law. London: Shaw and Sons, 1969. (Paper)

2871 Wels, B. G. Fell's guide to guns and how to use them safely, legally, responsibly. N.Y.: Fell, 1969.

EDITORIALS

2872 "Ahead now on gun control," U.S. News, 65:8-9, July 15, 1968.

2873 "Anti-gun extremists are at it again," (by) R. Starnes. Field and Stream, 68:12, April, 1964.

2874 "Arms and the law," Sports Illustrated, 19:15, December 9, 1963.

2875 "Bullet-proof politics?" Economist, 227:31, June 15, 1968.

2876 "Businessmen recoil; urge tougher gun controls," Business Week, June 8, 1968, p. 42.

2877 "Crackdown on criminals using guns?" U.S. News, 65:7, September 30, 1968.

2878 "Crime bill passes, what it calls for," U.S. News, 64:6, June 17, 1968.

2879 "Death in the past--buy a gun in the U.S. from a mail-order company," Economist, 206:506-7, February 9, 1963.

2880 "Drop that gun!" Commonweal, 88:428-9, June 28, 1968.

2881 "Final terms of gun control law," U.S. News, 65:11, October 21, 1968.

2882 "Going armed; report of National Commission on the causes...," Nation, 209:621, December 8, 1969.

2883 "Gun control," Rising Up Angry, 07 -- 04 01 69

2884 "Gun control confusion: gun control act of 1968,"

Conservationist (Albany) 23:36, April, 1969.

2885 "Gun control: melodrama, farce and tragedy," Christian Century, 85:831-2, June 26, 1968.

2886 "Gun controls: aimless or on target? Pro and con discussion," Senior Scholastic, 93:19-20, September 13, 1968.

2887 "Gun controls, how they work in other countries," U.S. News, 64:38-39, June 24, 1968.

2888 "Gun foes hit home," Business Week, June 22, 1968 p. 33.

2889 "Gun for Christmas," Economist, 229:31, December 21, 1968.

2890 "Gun law enfeeblements," America, 121:553, December 6, 1969.

2891 "Gun (or two) in every home," Nation, 206:69, January 15, 1968.

2892 "Gunning for reform--in America," Economist, 228:33-4, July 13, 1968.

2893 "Guns: like buying cigarettes," Newsweek, 71:46, June 17, 1968.

2894 "Guns of July, 1968; shootings indicate need for control," Newsweek, 72:21-2, July 15, 1968.

2895 "More good than bad ...," Time, 91:18, June 28, 1968.

2896 "New shot at guns," Economist, 227:43, June 22, 1968.

2897 "One lesson of the tragedy," America, 118:787, June 22, 1968.

2898 "Overkill; judiciary committee votes to postpone further consideration of all gun legislation," Newsweek, 72:18, July 8, 1968.

2899 "Power: the fist ... and the gun," Rising Up Angry,

09 -- 04 01 69

2900 "Question of enacting proposed federal gun control legislation," Congressional Digest, 45:289-314, December, 1966.

2901 "Shot down; federal control on guns," Time, 92:19, August 2, 1968.

2902 "Should campus security police be armed?" Symposium College Management, 4:44-6, October, 1969.

2903 "Sorry gun law," Economist, 227:20, June 8, 1968.

2904 "What congress is doing to curb sales of guns and ammunition," U.S. News, 65:8, August 5, 1968.

PERIODICALS

2905 Ace, G. "Arms and the disturbed man," Saturday Review, 50:12, September 16, 1967. (Psychological aspects related to the possession of arms.)

2906 Bakal, Carl. "Gun control, now: Excerpts from 'Right To Bear Arms'," Reader's Digest, 93:83-7, August, 1968.

2907 Berkowitz, Leonard. "Impulse, aggression, and the gun," Psychology Today, 2:18-22, September, 1968.

2908 Christopher, M. "Guns, Congress and the networks," Nation, 207:115-16, August 19, 1968.

2909 Condit, Tom. "Gun control and the climate of violence," Independent Socialist, 08 -- 08 01 68 (Discussion of pros and cons of gun control with a footnote by Hal Draper.)

2910 Cupps, Stephen. "Evading gun control," New Republic, 160:16-18, May 3, 1969.

2911 Deedy, J. "News and views; gun control act of 1968 amendments," Commonweal, 89:664, February 28,

Firearms Control 267

1969.

2912 Dodd, T. J. "Mail order guns," Ladies' Home Journal, 82:74-75, March, 1965.

2913 Drew, E. B. "Gun law that didn't go off," Reporter, 31:33-35, October 8, November 5, 1964.

2914 Fierce, Robert. "Gun control," Damascus Free Press, 05 -- 04 01 69

2915 Fisher, Richard. "The Gun as an instrument of frustration," Distant Drummer, 01 22 03 01 70

2916 Hamilton, Mary. "Crime bill: the omnibus crushes rights," Guardian, 06 29 03 04 68

2917 _____. "Who'll control gun controllers?" Guardian, 06 29 03 01 68

2918 Harris, R. "Annals of legislation," New Yorker, 44:56-8, April 20, 1968.

2919 Hess, Karl. "Should you own a gun?" American Mercury, 84:54-60, April, 1957.

2920 Jacobs, R. C., and B. Spiegelberg. "Do nothing gun law," New Republic, 159:19-22, July 20, 1968.

2921 Kane, M. "Bang! Bang! you're dead; has the right to bear arms become outmoded," Sports Illustrated, 28:70-74, March 18, 1968.

2922 Kopkind, Andrew. "Average American boy," New Statesman, 72:220-1, August 12, 1966.

2923 Lerner, M. "Freedom of guns," New Statesman, 68:984-5, December 25, 1964.

2924 Lichtenberg, James. "I'd still rather have my daughter smoking marijuana," East Village Other, 11 19 06 01 69

2925 Logsdon, G. "What farmers say about gun laws," Farm Journal, 92:37, September, 1968.

2926 McCalls (Magazine) Editors. "What women can do to

end violence in America," <u>Gun Control, Pro and Con</u>, Special Collectors Copy, New Chronicle Publishing Company, 1968. (Unpaged)

2927 Manchester, W. "Let us turn in our guns: an act of conscience," <u>Good Housekeeping</u>, 167:85, November, 1968.

2928 _____. "Outdoor life and the death of a President...," <u>Outdoor Life</u>, 140:323, October, 1967.

2929 Matthews, Jim. "Gun control pro and con," Los Angeles, California: <u>New Chronicle Publishing Company</u>, 1968. (Unpaged)

2930 Meyer, F. S. "Right of the people to bear arms," <u>National Review</u>, 20:657, July 2, 1968.

2931 Morris, N., and G. Hawkins. "Controlling violence...," <u>Current</u>, 111:48-53, October, 1969.

2932 Nanes, Allan S. "Federal control of firearms: is it necessary?" <u>Current History</u>, 53:38-42, July, 1967.

2933 National Commission on the Causes and Prevention of Violence. "90 million firearms and rising rapidly." excerpts from statement by the National Commission on Causes and Prevention of Violence, July 28, 1969. <u>U.S. News</u>, 67:40-41, August 11, 1969.

2934 O'Connor, Jack. "Keeping up with the gun control act of 1968," <u>Outdoor Life</u>, 144:68-9, September, 1969.

2935 Orth, F. L. "Gun control legislation: a question of extent," <u>Forensic Quarterly</u>, 41:233-42, May, 1967.

2936 Page, W. "Black power smoke; replicas not affected by gun control act of 1968," <u>Field and Stream</u>, 74:64-6, December, 1969.

2937 _____. "New gun law does affect sportsmen," <u>Field and Stream</u>, 73:126-8, February, 1969.

2938 Ridgeway, J. "Kind of gun control we need," <u>New</u>

Republic, 158:10-11, June 22, 1968.

2939 Rigert, J. "Playing American roulette," Commonweal, 90:72-5, April 4, 1969.

2940 Rolph, C. H. "Guns and violence," New Statesman, 69:71-72, January 15, 1965.

2941 _____. "Who needs a gun?" New Statesman, 79:70, January 16, 1970.

2942 Roucek, Joseph S. "Role of the gun in the American way of life," Study of Current English, 23:Number 10, October, 1968.

2943 Sherrill, R. "High noon on Capitol Hill; each year Americans buy 3 million more guns," New York Times Magazine, June 23, 1968, pp. 7-9.

2944 Stanford Research Institute. "Firearms in civil disorders; excerpt from study by the Stanford Research Institute," Current, 103:40-3, January, 1969.

2945 Woodley, R. "Marksman whose target is gun control," Life, 65:102a-102b, September 27, 1968.

III. THE GAP IN GENERATIONS, AND THE DRUG DILEMMA

BOOKS

2946 Ackerman, Nathan W. Treating the troubled family. N.Y.: Basic Books, 1966.

2947 Aldridge, John W. In the country of the young. N.Y.: Harper's Magazine Press, 1970.

2948 Andrews, Harry J. The Book of grass ... anthology on Indian Hemp. N.Y.: Grove Press, 1967.

2949 Arnstein, Helene S. Getting along with your grown-up children. Philadelphia: Lippincott, 1970.

2950 Arrow, Kenneth J. Social choice and individual values. 2nd ed. N.Y.: Wiley, 1963.

2951 Bacon, Margaret, and Mary B. Jones. Teen-age drinking. N.Y.: Thomas Y. Crowell, 1968.

2952 Barber, Bernard. Drugs and society. N.Y.: Russell Sage Foundation, 1967.

2953 Becker, Howard S. Outsiders. N.Y.: Free Press, 1963.

2954 Benson, Dennis C. The Now generation. Richmond, Virginia: John Knox Press, 1969.

2955 Bernstein, Saul. Youth on the streets; work with alienated youth groups. N.Y.: Association Press, 1964.

2956 Birenbaum, William M. Overlive; power, poverty, and the university. N.Y.: Delta Press, 1969.

2957 Birmingham, John (ed.). Our time is now: notes from the high school underground. N.Y.: Praeger, 1970.

2958 Blaine, Graham B. Jr. Youth and the hazards of affluence: the high-school and college years. N.Y.: Harper and Row, 1967.

2959 Bloomquist, E. R. Marijuana. N.Y.: Glencoe Press, 1968.

2960 Brown, Joe David. The Hippies. N.Y.: Time-Life Books, 1967.

2961 Buchanan, James M., and Nicos E. Devletoglou. Academia in anarchy; an economic diagnosis. N.Y.: Basic Books, 1970.

2962 Buse, Renee. The Deadly silence. N.Y.: Doubleday, 1965.

2963 Cain, Arthur H. Young people and crime. N.Y.: John Day, 1968.

2964 _____. Young people and drinking. N.Y.: John Day, 1963.

2965 Cain, E. They'd rather be right: youth and conservatism. N.Y.: Macmillan, 1963.

2966 Caldwell, William V. LSD psychotherapy. N.Y.: Grove Press, 1968.

2967 Cantelon, John E. College education and the campus revolution. Philadelphia: Westminster, 1969.

2968 Carey, James T. The College drug scene. New Jersey: Prentice-Hall, 1968.

2969 Carlsen, G. R. Books and the teen-age reader. N.Y.: Harper and Row, 1967. (See especially relevant sections.)

2970 Cashman, John. The LSD story. Connecticut: Fawcett, 1966.

2971 Cassel, Russell N. Drug abuse education. Boston:

Christopher, 1970.

2972 Chen, Sidney. The Drug dilemma. N.Y.: McGraw-Hill, 1968.

2973 Cohen, Sidney. The Beyond within; the LSD story. N.Y.: Atheneum, 1964.

2974 _____. Drug dilemma. N.Y.: McGraw-Hill, 1968.

2975 Coles, Robert. Children of crisis: a study of courage and fear. Boston: Little, 1967.

2976 CBS Television Network. Generations apart. A study of the generation gap conducted for CBS News by Daniel Yankelovich, Inc. for use in the CBS News series CBS reports. "A Question of Values," "A Profile of Dissent," (and) The "Youth International," New York: CBS, 1969.

2977 Cox, Harvey. The Feast of fools. Cambridge, Mass.: Harvard University Press, 1970.

2978 David, Carroll. Room to grow; study of parent-child relationships. Toronto: University of Toronto Press, 1966.

2979 Deane, Philip, and Lola Deane. Is this trip necessary? New Jersey: Thomas Nelson Inc., 1970. (Youthful drug users and questions teens ask about drugs and drug abuse.)

2980 Dennis, Lawrence. College and the student. Washington, D.C.: American Council on Education, 1966.

2981 De Ropp, Robert S. Beyond the drug experience. N.Y.: Dell, 1968.

2982 _____. Drugs and the mind. N.Y.: Grove Press, 1961.

2983 _____. The Master game; beyond the drug experience. N.Y.: Delacorte Press, 1968. (A Seymour Lawrence Book.)

2984 Donovan, Frank R. Wild kids: how youth has shocked its elders then and now. Harrisburg, Pennsylvania: Stockpole, 1967.

2985 Douglas, William O. Points of rebellion. N.Y.: Random, 1970.

2986 Duvall, Evelyn. Today's teen-agers. N.Y.: Association, 1966.

2987 Ebin, D. The Drug experience. N.Y.: Orion, 1961.

2988 Eldridge, William B. Narcotics and the law; a critique of the American experiment in narcotic drug control. Chicago: University of Chicago Press, 1967.

2989 Elliott, E. E. Tomorrow come sunrise. N.Y.: Harper and Row, 1970.

2989a Endore, Guy. Synanon. N.Y.: Doubleday, 1968.

2990 Erikson, Erik (ed.). Challenge of youth. N.Y.: Doubleday, 1963. (Original title: Youth, Change and Challenge.)

2991 _____. Identity youth and crisis. N.Y.: W. W. Norton, 1968.

2992 _____. Youth: change and challenge. N.Y.: Basic Books, 1963.

2993 Feigelson, Naomi. The Underground revolution. N.Y.: Funk and Wagnalls, 1970.

2993a Felson, H. G. Letters to a teenage son. N.Y.: Dodd, Mead, 1961.

2994 Feuer, Lewis S. Conflict of generations; the character and significance of student movements. N.Y.: Basic Books, 1969.

2995 Fiddle, Seymour. Portraits from a shooting gallery: life styles from the drug addict world. N.Y.: Harper, 1967.

2996 Fletcher, Grace N. What's right with our young

people. Clifton, New Jersey: Whiteside, 1966.

2997 Freedman, Mervin. College experience. San Francisco, California: Jossey-Bass, 1967.

2998 Fromme, Allan. The Ability to love. N.Y.: Farrar, Straus and Giroux, 1965.

2999 Fuller, John G. The Day of St. Anthony's fire. N.Y.: Macmillan, 1968. (Also available in paper.)

3000 Gardner, John W. No easy victories. N.Y.: Harper and Row, 1969.

3001 _____. Self renewal; the individual and the innovative society. N.Y.: Harper and Row, 1964.

3002 Ginott, Haim. Between parent and child. N.Y.: Macmillan, 1965.

3003 _____. Between parent and teenager. N.Y.: Macmillan, 1969.

3004 Girvetz, Harry K. (ed.). Contemporary moral issues. California: Wadsworth Publishing Company, 1963.

3005 Goheen, Robert. The Human nature of a university. New Jersey: Princeton University Press, 1969.

3006 Goldman, Ronald. Angry adolescents. Beverly Hills, California: Sage Publications, 1969.

3007 Goldstein, Richard. One in seven; drugs on campus. N.Y.: Walker and Company, 1966.

3008 Goode, Erich. The Marijuana smokers. N.Y.: Basic Books, 1970.

3009 Goodman, Paul. Growing up absurd. N.Y.: Random House, 1960.

3010 Greene, S., and R. Hamilton. What bothers us about grownups: a report card on adults by children. Vermont: Stephen Greene Press, 1970.

3011 Greene, Thayer A. Modern man in search of manhood. N.Y.: Association Press, 1967.

3012 Gurr, Ted. Why men rebel. New Jersey: Princeton University Press, 1970.

3013 Handel, Gerald. Psychosocial interior of the family. Chicago: Aldine, 1967.

3014 _____. College confidential. N.Y.: Trident, 1969.

3015 Hansel, Robert R. Like Father, like son--like Hell! N.Y.: Seabury, 1969.

3016 Heath, Douglas H. Explorations of maturity: studies of mature and immature college men. N.Y.: Appleton, 1965.

3017 Heath, Douglas H. Growing up in college: liberal education and maturity. San Francisco, California: Jossey-Bass, 1968. (Higher Education Series.)

3018 Hentoff, Nat. A Doctor among the addicts. N.Y.: Rand McNally, 1968.

3019 Hess, Albert G. Chasing the dragon; a report on drug addiction in Hong Kong. N.Y.: Free Press, 1965.

3020 Hofmann, Hans F. Discovering freedom. Boston: Beacon, 1969.

3021 Hook, Sidney. Academic freedom and academic anarchy. N.Y.: Cowles, 1970.

3022 Hunter, Evan. Sons. N.Y.: Doubleday, 1969.

3023 Hyde, Margaret O. Mind drugs. N.Y.: McGraw-Hill, 1968.

3024 Ilg, F., and L. Ames. Parents ask. N.Y.: Harper, 1962.

3025 Jacob, Philip E. Changing values in college. N.Y.: Harper, 1957.

3026 Jeffee, Saul. Narcotics: an American plan. N.Y.: Eriksson, 1966.

3027 Jenkins, James J. (ed.). Studies in individual differences. N.Y.: Appleton-Century-Crofts, 1961.

3028 Jervey, Edward D. Three way street. N.Y.: Vintage Press, 1969.

3029 Katz, Joseph (et al.). No time for youth: growth and constraint in college students. San Francisco, California: Jossey-Bass, 1968. (Higher Education Series.)

3030 Kavanaugh, Robert. The Grim generation. N.Y.: Trident, 1970. (Generational conflicts in a variety of areas and some suggestions are given for a resolvement of issues.)

3031 Keniston, Kenneth. The Uncommitted: alienated youth in American society. N.Y.: Dell, 1967.

3032 _____. Young radicals: notes on committed youth. N.Y.: Harcourt, Brace and World, 1968.

3033 Kephart, W. The Family, society, and the individual. Boston: Houghton, 1966.

3034 Kirkpatrick, Clifford. The Family: as process and institution. N.Y.: Ronald, 1963.

3035 Klein, Alexander (ed.). Natural enemies: youth and the clash of generations. Philadelphia: Lippincott, 1970.

3036 Krech, David. Individual in society. N.Y.: McGraw-Hill, 1962.

3037 Krieg, M. B. Green medicine. Chicago: Rand McNally, 1964.

3038 Kron, Yver J. Mainline to nowhere: the making of a heroin addict. N.Y.: Pantheon, 1965.

3039 Land, Herman W. What can you do about drugs and your child? N.Y.: Hart Publishing Company, 1970.

3040 Larner, Jeremy, and Ralph Tefferteller (eds.). The Addict in the street. N.Y.: Grove Press, 1970.

3041 Laurie, Peter. Drugs: medical psychological and social facts. N.Y.: Penguin, 1967.

3042 Leary, Timothy. High Priest. N.Y.: New American Library, 1968.

3043 Lenski, Gerhard E. Power and privilege. N.Y.: McGraw-Hill, 1966.

3044 Levine, E. Youth in a soundless world. N.Y.: New York University Press, 1956.

3045 Levy, David M. Maternal overprotection. N.Y.: Norton, 1966.

3046 Lindesmith, Alfred R. The Addict and the law. Indiana: Indiana University Press, 1965.

3047 _____. Addiction and opiates. Chicago: Aldine, 1968.

3048 Lorand, Rhoda L. Love, sex, and the teenager. N.Y.: Macmillan, 1965.

3049 Louria, Donald B. The Drug scene. N.Y.: McGraw-Hill, 1968.

3050 Marshall, William, and Gilbert W. Taylor. The Art of ecstasy. California: Borden, 1967.

3051 Masters, R. E. L., and Jean Houston. The Varieties of psychedelic experience. N.Y.: Dell, 1966.

3052 Maurer, David W. Narcotics and narcotic addiction. 3rd ed. Illinois: C. C. Thomas, 1967.

3053 Mays, John Barron. Young pretenders: teenage culture in contemporary society. 2nd ed. N.Y.: Schocken, 1968.

3054 Mead, Margaret. Culture and commitment. N.Y.: Published For American Museum of Natural History, Natural History Press, 1970.

3055 Merki, Donald J. Drug abuse: teenage hangup. Dallas, Texas: Texas Alcohol Narcotics Education, 1970. (Pam.)

3056 Michael, Donald N. Next generation; the prospects ahead for the youth of today and tomorrow. N.Y.: Random, 1965.

3057 Moore, Allen J. Young adult generation; a perspective on the future. Tennessee: Abingdon, 1969.

3058 Moscow, Alvin. Merchants of heroin; an in-depth portrayal of business in the underworld. N.Y.: Dial, 1968.

3059 Mowry, Charles E. The Church and the new generation. Tennessee: Abingdon, 1969.

3060 Musgrove, Frank. Family, education, and society. London: Routledge and K. Paul, 1966.

3061 Nixon, R. E. The Art of growing. N.Y.: Random House, 1962.

3062 Nowlis, Helen Howard. Drugs on the college campus. Introduction by Kenneth Keniston. N.Y.: Doubleday, 1969.

3063 Nuthall, Jeff. Bomb-culture. N.Y.: Delacorte, 1969.

3064 O'Donnell, John A. (ed.). Narcotic addiction. N.Y.: Harper, 1966.

3065 Ogburn, W. F., and M. F. Nimkoff. Technology and the changing family. Boston: Houghton, 1955.

3066 Oursler, William C. Marijuana: the facts, the truth. N.Y.: Eriksson, 1968.

3067 Packard, Vance. The Sexual wilderness. N.Y.: McKay, 1968.

3068 Parsons, Talcott. Family, socialization and interaction process. N.Y.: Macmillan, 1955.

3069 Perlman, Samuel. Student versus parents; problems

and conflicts. Cambridge, Mass.: H. A. Doyle, 1969.

3070 Perry, Helen Swick. The Human be-in. N.Y.: Basic Books, 1970.

3071 Petersen, Mark E. Drugs, drinks, and morals. Utah: Deseret, 1970. (Also available in paper.)

3072 Pettitt, George. Prisoners of culture. N.Y.: Scribner, 1970. (A controversial subject with a new look at youth.)

3073 Powers, John J. Jr. The Greatest adventure of all. N.Y.: Pitzer Public Relations Department, 1970.

3074 Robertson, J. L. What generation gap? A dialogue on America. Washington, D.C.: Acropolis, 1970. (Includes the speech that was reprinted in the U.S. News by the Vice-Chairman of the Federal Reserve System.)

3075 Rogan, Donald L. Campus apocalypse; the student search today. N.Y.: Seabury, 1969.

3076 Romm, Ethel G. Open conspiracy: what America's angry generation is saying. Harrisburg: Stackpole, 1969.

3077 Rosenbaum, Robert A. (ed.). Growing up in America. N.Y.: Doubleday, 1970.

3078 Sanford, Nevitt. Self and society. N.Y.: Atherton, 1966.

3079 Schaap, Richard. Turned on. N.Y.: New American Library, 1967.

3080 Schoenfeld, Eugene. Dear Doctor Hip Procrates. N.Y.: Grove Press, 1968.

3081 Sherif, Muzafer, and Carolyn W. Sherif (eds.). Problems of youth: transition to adulthood in a changing world. Chicago: Aldine, 1970.

3082 Shoemaker, Sydney. Self-knowledge and self-identity. N.Y.: Cornell University Press, 1963.

3083 Smart, Reginald G. Lysergic acid diethylamide (LSD) in the treatment of alcoholism. Toronto: University of Toronto Press, 1967.

3084 Smith, David E. The New social drug: cultural, medical and legal perspectives on marijuana. New Jersey: Prentice-Hall, 1970.

3085 Smith, Sally L. Nobody said it's easy! A practical guide to feelings and relationships for young people and their parents. N.Y.: Macmillan, 1965.

3086 Snyder, Ross. Young people and their culture. N.Y.: Abingden, 1969.

3087 Solomon, D. The Marijuana papers. Indianapolis: Bobbs-Merrill, 1965.

3088 Spender, Stephen. The Year of the young rebels. N.Y.: Random, 1968. (A review of this volume may be found in NASPA, Vol. 7, No. 4, April, 1970, p. 241.)

3089 Spock, Benjamin. Problems of parents. Boston: Houghton, 1962.

3090 Stearn, Jess. The Seekers. N.Y.: Doubleday, 1969.

3091 Stevens, Anita, and Lucy Freeman. I hate my parents. N.Y.: Cowles, 1970. (Analysis of children's anger towards parents and what can be done to achieve harmony on both sides.)

3092 Strong, Dennis F. Generation gap. California: Wadsworth Publishing Company, 1969.

3093 Struchen, Jeannette. Thank God for the red, white and black. Philadelphia: Lippincott, 1970.

3094 Surface, William. The Poisoned ivy. N.Y.: Coward-McCann, 1968.

3095 Taylor, Norman. Narcotics: nature's dangerous gifts. N.Y.: Dell, 1970.

3096 Travers, Milton. Each other's victims. N.Y.: Scribner's, 1970.

3097 Trent, James W., and Leland L. Medsker. Beyond high school. California: Jossey-Bass, 1968.

3098 U.S. Task Force on Narcotics and Drug Abuse. Task force report: narcotics and drug abuse. Washington, D.C.: GPO., 1967.

3099 Van Kaam, Adrian. Art of existential counseling. Pennsylvania: Dimension Books, 1966.

3100 Vaz, Edmund W. Middle-class juvenile delinquency. N.Y.: Harper and Row, 1967.

3101 Vermes, H., and Jean Vermes. Helping youth avoid the four great dangers: smoking, drinking, V.D., and narcotic addiction. N.Y.: Association Press, 1966.

3102 Wakefield, Dan (ed.). The Addict. Greenwich, Conn.: Fawcett, 1966.

3103 Walton, George Col. The Wasted generation. N.Y.: Chilton Books, 1965.

3104 Washburne, C. Primitive drinking. Conn.: College and University Press, 1961.

3105 Way, Walter (ed.). The Drug scene: help or hang-up? New Jersey: Prentice-Hall, 1969.

3106 Wein, Bibi. The Runaway generation. N.Y.: McKay, 1970.

3107 Wheelis, Allen B. The Quest for identity. N.Y.: Norton, 1958.

3108 Wilkins, Leslie T. Social deviance. New Jersey: Prentice-Hall, 1965.

3109 Williams, Elizabeth S. Narcotics and drug abuse. Conn.: Academic Paperbacks, 1970. (Urban American Series.)

3110 Williams, John B. Narcotics and hallucinogenics. California: Glencoe Press, 1967.

3111 Wolf, Leonard. Voices from the love generation.

Boston: Little, 1968.

3112 Wolfe, Tom. The Electric Kool-aid acid test. N.Y.: Farrar, Straus, and Giroux, 1968. (Original Title: Acid Test.)

3113 Wyden, P., and Barbara Wyden. Growing up straight. N.Y.: Stein and Day, 1968.

3114 Yablonsky, Lewis. The Hippie trip. N.Y.: Pegasus, 1968.

3115 _____. Synanon; the tunnel back. N.Y.: Macmillan, 1965.

3116 Young, Warren, and Joseph Hixson. LSD on campus. N.Y.: Dell, 1966.

3117 Zuk, Gerald H., and Ivan Boszormenyi-Nagy (eds.). Family therapy and disturbed families. California: Science and Behavior Books, Inc., 1967.

EDITORIALS

3118 "Abuses of drugs, a growing menace--symposium," Unesco Courier, 21:4-29, May, 1968.

3119 "Alarming rise in dope traffic," U.S. News, 65:43-5, September 2, 1968.

3120 "Alcoholism compounded: addiction to tranquilizers and stimulants," Science News, 94:338-9, October 5, 1968.

3121 "Americans abroad," Time, 95:36, April 13, 1970.

3122 "Amphetamines and barbiturates: the up and down drugs; questions and answers," Today's Education, 58:42-44, March, 1969.

3123 "Before your kid tries drugs," New York Times Magazine, 124: November 17, 1968.

3124 "Big lies about mind-affecting drugs," Vogue, 151:88-9

April 15, 1968.

3125 "Boy in the gold suit; death of Walter Vandermeer, pusher of heroin," Newsweek, 74:39, December 29, 1969.

3126 "Bridging the generation gap: a conversation between Rep. Morris Udall and three interns," New Republic, 163:11-13, November 28, 1970.

3127 "Busting the boys," Newsweek, 76:32, August 17, 1970.

3128 "But mom, everybody smokes pot!" McCalls, 95:68-9, September, 1968.

3129 "Children of the drug age; high school students," Saturday Review, 51:60-3, September 21, 1968.

3130 "Clandestine distribution of heroin, its discovery and suppression," Journal of Political Economy, 76:78-90, January, 1968.

3131 "Clinical and psychological effects of marijuana in man," Science, 162:1234-42, December 13, 1968.

3132 "Close-up; Chuck Dederich, Mr. Synanon goes public," Life, 66:36-8, January 31, 1969.

3133 "Closing the 'Generation Gap'--Search for a national policy: interview with Nixon's adviser on youth." U.S. News, 68:56-59, February 16, 1970.

3134 "Conference on drug abuse (papers read before the annual conference of mental health representatives of state medical societies, sponsored by the American Medical Association, Chicago, Illinois, March 16, 1968.) American Medical Association Journal, 206:1263-84, November 4, 1968.

3135 "Consider this: the generation gap," Grinding Stone, 09 30 03 03 68 (Interesting definition of what constitutes the generation gap and conflicts of interests within it.)

3136 "Cruel chemical world of speed; methedrine," Look, 32:53-9, March 5, 1968.

3137 "Crutch that cripples: drug dependence--excerpts," Today's Health, 46:11-12, September 1968. (Also) 46:12-15, October, 1968.

3138 "Dangers of drug abuse," PTA Magazine, 62:8-11, May, 1968.

3139 "Dope about dope; publications of the student association for the study of hallucinogens," Saturday Review, 53:80, September 19, 1970.

3140 "Dope-O-Scope," Warren Forest Sun, 04 19 06 01 68

3141 "David Crosby," Warren Forest Sun, 04 19 03 01 68

3142 "Drug menace: how serious? Interview with John E. Ingersoll, director, Federal Bureau of Narcotics," U.S. News, 68:38-42, May 25, 1970.

3143 "The Drug scene: high schools are higher now," Newsweek, 75:66-69, February 16, 1970.

3144 "Drugs: a viewpoint," Two-Cents Plain Dealer, 12 15 02 01 69 (The viewpoint is on marijuana, mescaline, and LSD.)

3145 "Drugs and narcotics: illusions and realities," Senior Scholastic, 94:5-10, March 21, 1969.

3146 "Drugs and the educational antidote," Nation's Schools, 85:49-52, April, 1970.

3147 "Encounter: how kids turn off drugs," Look, 33:40-5, April 15, 1969.

3148 "Gang busters," Rising Up Angry, 07 -- 10 01 69

3149 "The Generation gap in other countries," U.S. News, 67:56, August 18, 1969.

3150 "Generation without a future," Ally, 06 -- 04 05 69

3151 "Generational gapiosis," Wilson Library Bulletin, 43:134-39, October, 1968.

3152 "Generational revolt," Kudzu, 09 18 02 01 68

3153 "God's secret agent A.O.S. 3," Warren Forest Sun, 04 19 02 01 68

3154 "Growing menace of drugs--Nixon's plan to fight it," U.S. News, 67:60-62, July 28, 1969.

3155 "Hallucinogens of plant origin," Science, 163:245-54, January 17, 1969.

3156 "Heads and seekers; drugs on campus, counter-cultures and American society," American Scholar, 38:97-112, Winter, 1968-69.

3157 "Hey candyman! The roundup," The Word, 01 16 01 02 68

3158 "If pot were legal," Time, 96:41, July 20, 1970.

3159 "John Mitchell on marijuana," Newsweek, 76:22, September 7, 1970.

3160 "Junior junkie," Time, 95:36, February 16, 1970.

3161 "Key decisions coming; methadone therapy for heroin addicts," Science News, 95:364-5, April 12, 1969.

3162 "Kid-killers: a night with the drugged children of America," National Review, 21:434-5, May 6, 1969.

3163 "Kids and heroin," Reader's Digest, 88-92, June, 1970.

3164 "Kids and heroin: the adolescent epidemic," Time, 95:16-20, March 16, 1970.

3165 "LBJ and drug traffic; narcotics message," New Republic, 158:11, February 17, 1968.

3166 "Life on two grams a day; heroin in the high schools," Life, 68:24-32, February 20, 1970.

3167 "Marijuana, no victim no crime," Water Tunnel, 03 31 04 01 69

3168 "Mental illness, alcoholism, and drug dependence,"

Annals of the American Academy, 378:22-33, July, 1968.

3169 "Moderation in drug use at Michigan," School and Society, 98:134-5, March, 1970.

3170 "Narcotics and drug abuse: the federal response," Science, 162:1254, December 13, 1968.

3171 "On campus: drugs vs. drinking," Mademoiselle, 70:230, March, 1970.

3172 "Oregon: generation gap," Newsweek, 75:29, June 8, 1970.

3173 "Peyote road," New York Times Magazine, March 9, 1969, p. 30.

3174 "The Pill poppers; observers see peril from growing misuse of mood-changing drugs," Wall Street Journal, 172:1, December 19, 1968.

3175 "Riding the sex wave," Newsweek, 75:108, April 20, 1970.

3176 "Second coming of Synanon," Saturday Evening Post, 242:32-4, February 8, 1969.

3177 "Strengthening drug education," School and Society, 98:400, November, 1970.

3178 "Students and drug abuse," Today's Education, 58:35-8, March, 1969.

3179 "Students, drugs and protest," Current, 104:5-19, February, 1969.

3180 "To parents: plain talk on marijuana," Business Week, March 21, 1970, p. 121.

3181 "Town in trouble: plague of drugs among kids in California; awareness house," Life, 66:48-54, March 21, 1969.

3182 "Training teachers to deal with drugs," Pennsylvania School Journal, 118:259-261, May, 1970.

3183 "Truth about pot," Popular Science, 192:76-9, May, 1968.

3184 "Vietcong's secret weapon: marijuana," Science Digest, 65:14-18, April, 1969.

3185 "What about marijuana," National Review, 21:268, March 25, 1969.

3186 "What are narcotic drugs? questions and answers," Today's Education, 58:48-50, March, 1969.

3187 "What is LSD? questions and answers," Today's Education, 58:45-7, March, 1969.

3188 "When the young teach and the old learn," Time, 96:35-40, August 17, 1970.

3189 "Why adolescents drink and use drugs; with study-discussion program," PTA Magazine, 63:2-5, March, 1969.

3190 "Why so many teenagers fall for marijuana, with group discussion program," Parents' Magazine, 44:22, March, 1969.

3191 "Why students turn to drugs," Reader's Digest, 92:173-4, April, 1968.

3192 "Young generation: Soviet worry," U.S. News, 67:54-56, August 18, 1969.

3193 "Young Lords," Rising Up Angry, 07 -- 14 01 69

3194 "Youngsters and drugs: making sense of what's happening," Better Homes and Gardens, 48: October, 1970, p. 34.

3195 "Your adolescent's health: drug abuse among teenagers," PTA Magazine, 63:25-6, February, 1969.

3196 "Youth buffs rapped by youth," Library Journal, 95:200, January 15, 1970.

3197 "Youth in its frustrated festivals," Life, 69:34-37, August 14, 1970.

3198 "Youth in rebellion--why?" U.S. News, 68:42-46, April 27, 1970.

3199 "Youth is most vital," Spectator, 07 15 09 01 69

PERIODICALS

3200 Adherley, W. C., and G. Gibson. "Lighter fluid sniffing," American Journal of Psychiatry, 120:1056, May, 1964.

3201 Adelson, J. "What generation gap," New York Times Magazine, January 18, 1970, pp. 10-11.

3201a Ambrose, Myles J. "Narcotics," Vital Speeches, 36:612-615, August 1, 1970.

3202 Angel, K. "No marijuana for adolescents," New York Times Magazine, January 25, 1970, p. 9.

3203 Astor, G. "How I faced my son's drug arrest," Look, 34:87-8, December 15, 1970.

3204 Barrins, P. C. "Drug abuse: newest and most dangerous challenge," Education Digest, 35:24-6, January, 1970.

3205 Bart, Bill. "To be of use," New Generation, 52:9-12, Summer, 1970.

3206 Bell, J. N. "Hotline for troubled teen-agers; Los Angeles," Reader's Digest, 97:41-6, November, 1970.

3207 _____., and A. J. Linkletter. "We must declare war on drugs," Good Housekeeping, 170:94-5, April, 1970.

3208 Bender, L. "Drug addiction in adolescence," Comprehensive Psychiatry, 4:181, June, 1963.

3209 Birch, Alison Wyrley. "A Community where drug addicts grow up," PTA Magazine, 65:2-5, November,

1970.

3210 Blum, Sam. "Marijuana clouds the generation gap," New York Times Magazine, August 23, 1970, pp. 28-29.

3211 Bourjaily, V. "Middle age meets the kid ghetto," New York Times Magazine, November 29, 1970, pp. 46-7.

3212 Bowman, R. M. "Decoy: blessing in disguise," America, 123:114-17, September 5, 1970. (Discussion, 123:189, 275, September 26, and October 17, 1970.)

3213 Broderick, Dorothy M. "Conspiracy against youth," Library Journal, 95:214-15, January 15, 1970.

3214 Buckley, William F. Jr. "One father's war on marijuana," National Review, 22:1072, October 6, 1970.

3215 Burroughs, William S. "Academy--23," Warren Forest Sun, 04 19 04 01 68

3216 Carliner, Mike. "Pot--psychological effects," Distant Drummer, 04 03 18 01 69

3217 Cross, Robert D. "Is the generation gap widening? Yes, it is," Part I. PTA Magazine, 65:22-24, September, 1970.

3218 Dana, Jame. "From outer to inner space," Pittsburgh Point, 07 31 06 01 69 (Physiological aspects of drug users.)

3219 Dana, Jay. "At RAP--they do it with mirrors," Pittsburgh Point, 02 05 10 02 70

3220 Dea, John. "The Generation gap is only the death throes of Fascism," San Diego Free Press, 06 11 07 01 69

3221 De Leo, Lois. "School work and marriage: breaking out of the routine," New Generation, 52:29-32, Summer, 1970.

3222 Didion, Joan. "A Generation not for barricades,"

Life, 68:26, June 5, 1970.

3223 Disney, D. C. "Can this marriage be saved?" Ladies' Home Journal, 87:12, December, 1970.

3224 Dohner, V. Alton. "Drugs are not the problem," Education Digest, 36:25-28, November, 1970. (Emphasizes the misconceptions of drug problems and how we can educate ourselves towards these problems.)

3225 Eachus, Denise. "Where I am this minute is my reality," New Generation, 52:37-40, Summer, 1970.

3226 Eberle, Paul. "Mr. Linkletter raps: an exclusive interview," Los Angeles Free Press, 07 17 05 01 70

3227 ———. "Silence between the generations," Los Angeles Free Press, 03 01 06 01 68

3228 Eddy, N. B., H. Halback, and H. Isbell. "Drug dependence: its significance and characteristics," Bulletin World Health Organization, 32:721-733, 1965.

3229 Elkind, D. "Exploitation and the generational conflict," Mental Hygiene, 54:490-7, October, 1970.

3230 Elliott, R. "Narcotics: a crucial area of secondary school responsibility; full credited courses needed," Education Digest, 36:44-7, September, 1970.

3231 Esser, A. H., and V. R. Hannon. "Is there a generation gap in science," Science, 170:1336, December 18, 1970.

3232 Feuer, Lewis S. "Conflict of generations," Saturday Review, 52:53-66, January 18, 1969.

3233 Ford, Richard J. "Hermann Hesse: prophet of the pot generation," Catholic World, 212:15-19, October, 1970.

3234 Friedenberg, E. Z. "Current patterns of generational conflict," Journal of Social Issues, 25:21-30, April, 1969.

3235 Gafton, S. "What you can do about the drug problem," Parent's Magazine, 45:72-5, November, 1970.

3236 Gartner, M. "Silent generation meets the class of 1970," Saturday Review, 53:52-3, August 15, 1970.

3237 Gelinas, M. V. "Classroom drug scene; training sessions for educators," American Education, 6:3-5, November, 1970.

3238 Ginsberg, Allen. "Speed is a no-no," Distant Drummer, 04 02 11 01 70

3239 Goodhue, T. "Report on the two cultures; Orange County, California," New Republic, 162:12-13, June 20, 1970.

3240 Goodwin, David. "I'm part of my own education," New Generation, 52:13-16, Summer, 1970.

3241 Gray, Ted W. "The Teenage parent: an educational and social crisis," Phi Delta Kappan, 52:113-114, October, 1970.

3242 Green, Donald. "New yardsticks for youth," New Generation, 52:46-49, Summer, 1970.

3243 Hacker, Andrew. "The Violent black minority," New York Times Magazine, May 10, 1970, p. 25.

3244 Halleck, Seymour. "The Generation gap: a problem of values," Think, 34:3-7, September-October, 1968.

3245 Hamilton, Charles. "The Silent black majority," New York Times Magazine, May 10, 1970, p. 25.

3246 Harris, E., D. Harris, and Charles Winick. "Drug addicts getting younger; with study discussion program," PTA Magazine, 65:6-8, September, 1970.

3247 Harrison, Charles H. "The Drug epidemic--What's a teacher to do?" Scholastic Teacher, 96:4-5, May 4, 1970.

3248 _____. "Should the drug education bandwagon be rerouted?" Scholastic Teacher, 95:18-19, October 5,

1970.

3249 Haughton, Rosemary. "Some words on the generation gap: signs of the times," Catholic World, 211:5-6, April, 1970. (Personal viewpoints.)

3250 Heard, Gerald. "Can this drug enlarge man's mind?" Psychedelic Review, 1:7-17, June, 1963.

3251 Hentoff, Nat. "A Generation without a future," Evergreen Review, 13:47, June, 1969. (Description of the "power-elite" and according to this writer the gulf between the generations may grow deeper and wider.)

3252 Hering, M. B. "Law and marjane," American Libraries, 1:896-9, October, 1970.

3253 Herrera, F. "Generation gap and international development; youth movement," Americas, 22:13-20, April, 1970.

3254 Horowitz, Irving Louis (ed.). "Anti-American generation," Trans-action, 6:3-80, September, 1969. (Collection of comments by: Riesman, Folk, Brown, and Scott among others.)

3255 Hyson, Brenda. "Death of a narcotic user," Black Panther, 02 28 15 01 70

3256 Jacobyner, H. "Glue sniffing," New York State Journal of Medicine, 63:2415, August, 1963.

3257 Keeler, M. H., and F. J. Kune. "The Use of hyascamine as hallucinogen and intoxicant," American Journal of Psychiatry, 124:852, December, 1967.

3258 Keniston, Kenneth. "Youth, change and violence," American Scholar, Spring, 1968.

3259 Komapka, Gisela. "Is the generation gap widening," PTA Magazine, 65:6-8, October, 1970. (Part II.)

3260 Kurtz, Alan. "Drone probe zombie public narcotic # 1," Grok, 05 -- 10 01 70

3261 Land, H. W. "How to talk with your teenager about

drugs; excerpt from 'What you can do about drugs and your child'," Reader's Digest, 97:69-72, August, 1970.

3262 Lawrence, T., and J. Velleman. "Drugs/teens=alcohol/parents," Science Digest, 68:46-8, October, 1970.

3263 Leary, Timothy, and Richard Alpert. "The Politics of consciousness expansion," Harvard Review, 1:33-37, Summer, 1963.

3264 Leimbacher, Ed. "The Crash of the Jefferson Airplane," Ramparts, 8:14-16, January, 1970.

3265 Liberation News Service. "Head of IBM on revolt of youth in U.S.," Distant Drummer, 07 02 11 01 70

3266 Lifton, Robert J. "The Young and the old: notes on a new history," Atlantic, 224:83-88, October, 1969. (Part II.)

3267 Linkletter, Art. "We must fight the epidemic of drug abuse," Reader's Digest, 96:56-60, February, 1970.

3267a Long, Everett. "The Politics of pot," Kudzu, 08 02 10 01 69

3268 Lowe, Jim. "However, if you happen to be black," New Generation, 52:41-45, Summer, 1970.

3269 Lukas, Anthony. "The Making of a yippie," Esquire, 72:126-134, November, 1969.

3270 MacDonald, D. "What kind of revolution," Current, 121:28-30, September, 1970.

3271 Machiz, Marc. "America's values: worn out," U.S. News, 67:28-31, July 7, 1969.

3272 Mathe, Judy. "New ARA facts on abortion," Distant Drummer, 12 11 03 01 69 (Abortion facts in Philadelphia.)

3273 Meade, Kit. "Generation gap serves bosses," New Left Notes, 07 30 05 03 69

3274 Means, Richard K. "Drug abuse," Journal of Health Physical Education and Recreation, 41:23-24, May, 1970.

3275 Montesano, Randy. "A Human way of learning," New Generation, 52:24-28, Summer, 1970.

3276 Moraes, D. "Walk on London's wild side," New York Times Magazine, September 13, 1970, p. 100.

3277 Moskowitz, Ronald. "Leaving the drug world behind," Education Digest, 35:5-7, May, 1970.

3278 Mothner, Ira. "How can you tell if your child is taking drugs," Look, 34:42-57, April 7, 1970.

3279 Muller, J. D. "Unpublicized hallucinogens," Journal of the American Medical Association, 202:198, November 13, 1967.

3280 Murphy, F. D. "Yardsticks for a new era," Saturday Review, 53:23-5, November 21, 1970.

3281 Payne, R. B. "Nutmeg intoxication," New England Journal Medical, 269:36, July 4, 1963.

3282 Peale, Norman Vincent. "Silent majority of youth," Pittsburgh Press--Family Magazine, Sunday, May 3, 1970, p. 2.

3283 Podhoretz, N. "Like fathers like sons," Commentary 50:21, August, 1970. (Reply with rejoinder, by A. Kazin, 50:28, November, 1970.)

3284 Recherdson, Elliot. "The Generation gap," Vital Speeches, 36:583-584, July 15, 1970.

3285 Resnik, H. S. "Drugs; the landscape of grass and snow," Saturday Review, 53:23-5, August 15, 1970.

3286 Rieker, Richard. "The Failure of laws and programs," Pittsburgh Point, 07 10 01 01 69 (Part III of a series on drugs.)

3287 _____. "The Issue is human misery," Pittsburgh Point, 07 17 01 02 69 (Part IV of the series on drugs.)

3288 _____. "Our children are turning on," Pittsburgh Point, 06 26 01 01 69 (First part of the series on drugs.)

3289 Rorvik, David M. "Do drugs lead to violence?" Look, 34:58-61, April 7, 1970.

3290 Rose, William. "Hippy-I O Kai AY," Distant Drummer, 09 25 09 01 69

3291 Rosenthel, Alan. "Readers, experts examine drug problems," Today's Health, 48:19-23, September, 1970.

3292 Roszak, Theodore. "The Making of a counter culture," (excerpts) Horizon, 12:20-21, Spring, 1970.

3293 Rubenstein, A. "Struggle between founders and sons," Encounter, 31:64-69, November, 1968.

3294 Saal, H. "Swinging is better than any dope," Newsweek, 76:124-5, October 19, 1970.

3295 Schoonbeck, J. "Why did Walter die? heroin victim, W. Vandermeer of Harlem," Time, 94:12, December 26, 1969.

3296 Schwalb, Myrna. "Closing the generation gap," Pittsburgh Point, 04 16 07 01 70 (Generation gap exhibited at Pitt's Frick Fine Arts building by three young artists.)

3297 Scorpio, Paul. "LSD and me," Distant Drummer, 02 05 10 03 70

3298 Semark, Jim. "You gotta be a walking bahisattva," Warren Forest Sun, 04 19 03 02 68

3299 Shayon, R. L. "To youth with love; white house conference on the drug problem," Saturday Review, 53:57, November 21, 1970.

3300 Shenker, Alan. "Marijuana causes immortality," Grok, 06 27 16 01 70

3301 Skolnick, Jerome. "Comment: the generation gap," Trans-action, 6:4-5, November, 1968.

3302 Snider, A. J. "Junkie personality," Science Digest, 68:62, December, 1970.

3303 Stern, Linda. "The Substitute world called school," New Generation, 52:4-8, Summer, 1970.

3304 Stokes, R., and W. Abruzzi. "Rock doctor tells about 985 freakouts," Life, 69:37, August 14, 1970.

3305 Sutton, Horace. "Drugs: ten years to doomsday?" Saturday Review, 53:18-22, November 14, 1970.

3306 Toole, K. Ross. "I'm tired of the tyranny of spoiled brats," Reader's Digest, 96:129-132, June, 1970.

3307 Tournquist, Elizabeth. "Dope people in Raleigh," North Carolin Anvil, 04 18 01 01 70

3308 Tunley, R. "Five who came back from drugs," Seventeen, 29:92-3, January, 1970.

3309 Wald, George. "A Generation in search of a future," Grinding Stone, 04 -- 30 09 69 (A speech about the draft, Vietnam War, and other controversial areas by a Nobel Prize winner given at M.I.T.)

3310 Walley, David. "History reassesses itself--the first ten years," East Village Other, 01 07 06 01 70

3311 Wills, Garry. "The Making of the yippie culture," Esquire, 72:135-138, November, 1969.

3311a Winick, Charles. "Drug addiction and crime," Current History, 52:349-353, June, 1967.

3312 Wolfe, Leonard. "The Making of a hippie," PTA Magazine, 63:6-9, January, 1969.

3313 Wolk, D. J. "Youth and drugs, guidelines for teachers," Education Digest, 35:41-4, December, 1969.

3314 Young, Allen. "S.D.S. on drugs," Abas, 05 -- 09 02 69

IV. POLICE-COMMUNITY RELATIONS

BOOKS

3315 Adams, Thomas. Law enforcement: an introduction to the police roles in the community. New Jersey: Prentice-Hall, 1968.

3316 Alex, Nicholas. Black in blue: a study of the negro policeman. N.Y.: Appleton, 1969. (Paper)

3317 Anderson, Clinton H. Beverley Hills is my beat. New Jersey: Prentice-Hall, 1960.

3318 Applegate, Rex. Crowd and riot control. Harrisburgh: Stackpole, 1964.

3319 Arm, Walter. The Policeman. N.Y.: Dutton, 1969.

3320 Asch, Sidney H. Police authority and the rights of the individual. N.Y.: Arco, 1967.

3321 Banton, Michael. The Policeman and the community. N.Y.: Basic Books, 1965.

3322 Bayley, David H., and Harold Mendelsohn. Minorities and the police: confrontation in America. N.Y.: Free Press, 1969. (An exploration of relations between the police and the community based on opinion surveys in Denver in 1966. Some suggestions are made for police reforms in general.)

3323 Becker, Harold K. Issues in police administration. New Jersey: Scarecrow Press, 1970.

3324 _____. Law enforcement; a selected bibliography, by Harold K. Becker, and George T. Felkenes. New Jersey: Scarecrow Press, 1968.

3325 Becker, Harold K., George F. Felkenes, and Paul M. Whisenand. New dimensions in criminal justice. New Jersey: Scarecrow Press, 1968.

3326 Berkley, George E. The Democratic policeman. Boston: Beacon Press, 1969.

3327 Black, Algernon D. The People and the police. N.Y.: McGraw-Hill, 1968.

3328 Blum, Richard H. Police selection. Illinois: C. C. Thomas, 1964.

3328a Blum, Sam. The Police. N.Y.: American Jewish Committee, 1967. (Pam.) (Explanation of the role of the police in keeping the peace. A reprint from Redbook.)

3329 Blumberg, Abraham S. (ed.). Law and order: the scales of justice. Chicago: Aldine, 1970.

3330 Boles, Edmond D. The Secret of public relations. California: Boles and Associates, 1961.

3331 Bordua, David. The Police: six sociological essays. N.Y.: John Wiley and Sons, 1967.

3332 Bouma, Donald H. Kids and cops. Michigan: Eerdmans, 1969.

3333 Boyle, Hugh. Delinquency and crime. Conn.: Academic Paperbacks, 1970. (Urban America Series.)

3334 Bristow, Allen P. Effective police manpower utilization. Illinois: C. C. Thomas, 1969.

3335 Brown, William P. The Police and community conflict. Presented at the 8th annual national institute on police and community relations. Michigan: Michigan State University, May, 1962.

3336 Callan, George D. Police methods for today and tomorrow. Newark, New Jersey: Duncan Press, 1929. (Historical perspective.)

3337 Campbell, Judith. Police horses. New Jersey: A. S. Barnes, 1968.

3338 Chapman, Samuel G. Police patrol readings. Illinois: C. C. Thomas, 1964.

3339 Chevigny, Paul. Police power: police abuses in New York City. N.Y.: Pantheon Books, 1969.

3340 Chicago Park District. The Police and minority groups; a manual prepared for use in the Chicago Park District Police Training School. Division of Police. Chicago: 1947.

3341 Clark, Kenneth B. Dark ghetto: dilemmas of social behavior. N.Y.: Harper and Row, 1965.

3342 Clift, Raymond E. A Guide to modern police thinking. Cincinnati, Ohio: W. H. Anderson, 1965.

3343 _____. Police and public safety. Cincinnati, Ohio: W. H. Anderson, 1963.

3343a Coates, Joseph F. Nonlethal weapons for use by U.S. law enforcement officers. Virginia: Institute For Defense Analysis, (S-271) 1967.

3344 Cramer, James. Uniforms of world's police. Illinois: C. C. Thomas, 1968.

3345 Cray, Ed. The Big blue line. N.Y.: Coward-McCann Inc., 1967.

3346 Cressey, Suterland. Principles of criminology. N.Y.: Lippincott, 1960.

3346a Crockett, Thompson. Police chemical agents manual. Washington, D.C.: International Association of Chiefs of Police, Professional Standards Division, 1969.

3347 Curry, J. E., and Glen D. King. Race tensions and the police. Illinois: C. C. Thomas, 1962.

3347a Dempsey, William J. Jr. Is it wrong to handcuff the police? N.Y.: American Jewish Committee, 1967. (Pam.) (Reprinted from Catholic World.)

3348 Dinitz, Simon. Critical issues in the study of crime. Boston: Little, 1968.

3349 Drabek, Thomas (ed.). Law and the lawless: a reader in criminology. N.Y.: Random House, 1968.

3350 Earle, Howard H. Police-community relations: crisis in our time. Illinois: C. C. Thomas, 1967.

3351 Edwards, George. The Police on the urban frontier; a guide to community understanding. Foreword by Ramsey Clark. N.Y.: Institute of Human Relations Press, American Jewish Committee, 1968. (Discusses procedures involved in promoting cooperation between police and the community. Includes a discussion guide, and is identified as Pamphlet Series No. 9.)

3352 Eldefonso, Edward. Law enforcement and youthful offender. N.Y.: Wiley, 1967.

3353 Epstein, Charlotte. Intergroup relations for police officers. Maryland: William and Wilkins, 1962.

3354 Evans, M. Stanton, and Margaret Moore. The Lawbreakers; America's number one domestic problem. N.Y.: Arlington House, 1968.

3354a Federal Bureau of Investigation. Prevention and control of mobs and riots. Washington, D.C.: G.P.O., 1968. ("Based on the Army's FM 19-15 Number 134," emphasizes the need for prevention of civil disorders.)

3355 Fraternal Order of Police. Fort Pitt Lodge # 1. Riot Fact Finding Committee. Report on Civil Disorders, April 7, 1968. Pittsburgh, Pa. (Loose-leaf)

3356 Frost, Thomas M. A Forward look in police education. With an introduction by Timothy J. O'Connor. Illinois: C. C. Thomas, 1960.

3357 Gardiner, J. Traffic and the police. Mass.: Harvard University Press, 1969.

3358 Gardner, Erle Stanley. Cops on campus and crime in the streets. N.Y.: Morrow, 1970.

Police-Community Relations 301

3359 Gelhorn, Walter. When Americans complain. Mass.: Harvard University Press, 1966.

3360 Germann, A. C. (et al.). Introduction to law enforcement. Illinois: C. C. Thomas, 1962.

3361 Glaser, Daniel. The Effectiveness of a prison and parole system. Indiana: Bobbs-Merrill, 1969.

3362 Governor's Commission on the Los Angeles Riot. Violence in the city--an end or a beginning? Los Angeles, California: Jeffries Banknote Co., December 2, 1965.

3363 Harris, Richard. The Fear of crime. Introduction by Nicolas de B. Katzenbach. N.Y.: Praeger, 1969.

3364 Holcomb, Richard L. The Police and the public. Illinois: C. C. Thomas, 1964.

3365 _____. Police patrol. Illinois: C. C. Thomas, 1964.

3366 Holman, Mary. The Police officer and the child. Illinois: C. C. Thomas, 1962.

3367 Inbau, Fred E. Criminal law for the police. N.Y.: Chilton Book Company, 1969.

3367a International Association of Chiefs of Police. Campus disorders. Police Yearbook, 1970 ... Miami: IACP, September 27-October 2, 1969. Washington, D.C., 1970. (Police reaction to campus disorders recorded in a special workshop publication.)

3367b _____. Research and Development Division. Police capabilities. Problems and needs in dealing with civil disorders. A report submitted to the President's advisory committee on civil disorders. Washington, 1967. ("Emphasizes good communications involved at all levels regarding crowd control.")

3368 International Police Association. International bibliography of selected police literature. 2nd ed. (enlarged) London: M. and W. Publications, 1968.

3369   Jackson, Sir Richard. Occupied with crime. N.Y.: Doubleday, 1968.

3369a   Junta of Militant Organizations, and The Southern Conference Educational Fund. Crackdown in Florida. Florida: JOMO, (n. d.) (Confrontations between police and blacks in St. Petersburg, Florida.)

3370   Kenney, John P. Police operations; policies and procedures. Illinois: C. C. Thomas, 1968.

3371   _____, and D. G. Pursuit. Police work with juveniles. 2nd ed. Illinois: C. C. Thomas, 1962.

3372   Kilbane, Marjorie, and Patricia Claire. Police, courts and the ghetto. Conn.: Academic Paperbacks, 1970. (Urban American Series.)

3373   King, Glen D. Race tensions and the police. Illinois: C. C. Thomas, 1962.

3374   Klein, Herbert T. The Police: damned if they do, and damned if they don't. N.Y.: Crown, 1968.

3374a   Kobetz, Richard, and Carl W. Hamm (eds.). Campus unrest: dialogue or destruction ... Washington, D.C.: International Association of Chiefs of Police, 1970. (Workshop held for State Police officials and campus security directors at the University of Nebraska in May of 1970.)

3375   Kreml, Franklin M. The Evidence handbook for police. Illinois: Northwestern University Press, 1943.

3376   La Fave, Wayne R. Arrest. Boston: Little, 1965.

3377   Leonard, V. A. The Police of the 20th century. Brooklyn, New York: Foundation Press, Inc., 1964.

3378   Logan, Andy. Against the evidence; the Becker-Rosenthal affair. N.Y.: McCall, 1970.

3379   McMillan, George. Racial violence and law enforcement. Atlanta, Georgia: Southern Regional Council, 1960.

Police-Community Relations

3380 Marlo, John A., and R. Gene Wright. The Police officer and criminal justice. N.Y.: McGraw-Hill, 1970.

3380a Momboisse, Raymond M. Industrial security for strikes, riots, and disasters. Illinois: C. C. Thomas, 1968.

3380b _____. Riots, revolts and insurrections. Illinois: C. C. Thomas, 1967. (Still valuable for guidelines in controlling riots and revolts, as well as control procedures in keeping "collected.")

3381 Moynahan, James M. Police searching procedures. Illinois: C. C. Thomas, 1963.

3382 Murphy, Walter F. Wiretapping on trial: a case study in the judicial process. N.Y.: Random House, 1965. (Paper)

3382a National League of Cities, and U.S. Conference of Mayors. Street crime and the safe streets act ... Washington, 1970. ("State Planning and dollar distribution priorities under the Omnibus Crime Control and Safe Streets Act of 1968.")

3382b National Urban Coalition. Law and disorder II: State planning and programing under Title I of the Omnibus Crime Control and Safe Streets Act of 1968. Washington, 1970.

3383 Newman, Edwin S. Police, the law and personal freedom. N.Y.: Oceana Publications, 1964.

3384 Niederhoffer, Arthur. Behind the shield: the police in urban society. N.Y.: Doubleday, 1967.

3385 Norrgard, David L. Regional law enforcement; a study of intergovernmental cooperation and coordination. Chicago: Public Administration Service, 1969.

3386 Overstreet, Harry A., and Bonaro Overstreet. The FBI in our open society. N.Y.: Norton, 1969.

3387 Pantaleoni, C. A., and James C. Bigler. California criminal law; a guide for policemen. New Jersey:

Prentice-Hall, 1970.

3388 The Police Chief. Police and the changing community. Washington, D. C.: International Association of Chiefs of Police, 1965.

3389 Radano, Gene. Walking the beat. Ohio: World, 1968.

3390 Reiss, Albert J. Jr. (ed.). Studies in crime and law enforcement in major metropolitan areas. U.S. President's Commission on Law Enforcement and Administration of Justice, Field Survey III. Washington, D. C.: G. P. O., 1967.

3391 Rosenthal, Robert A. Riots? Conn.: Academic Paperbacks, 1970. (Urban America Series.)

3392 Roucek, Joseph S. (ed.). Sociology of crime. N.Y.: Philosophical Library, 1961.

3393 Saunders, Charles B. Jr. Upgrading the American police: education and training for better law enforcement. Brooklyn, New York: Brookings, 1970. (About educational requirements and training programs, contrasted with demands which are placed on police, in order to function adequately in today's society.)

3394 Savitz, Leonard. Dilemmas in criminology. N.Y.: McGraw-Hill, 1967. (See especially chapter 5-- "Law Enforcement in the U.S.")

3395 Scheur, James H. To walk the streets safely: science and technology in our criminal justice system. N.Y.: Doubleday, 1969.

3396 Siegel, Arthur I. (et al.). Professional police-human relations training. Illinois: C. C. Thomas, 1963.

3397 Skolnick, Jerome. Justice without trial. N.Y.: Wiley, 1966.

3398 Smith, Bruce. Police systems in the U.S. N.Y.: Harper, 1960.

3398a Smith, R. Dean, and Richard W. Kobetz. Guidelines

for civil disorder and mobilization planning. Washington, D.C.: International Association of Chiefs of Police, 1968.

3399 Smith, Ralph Lee. The Tarnished badge. N.Y.: Crowell, 1965. (Police systems and corruption in major American cities.)

3400 Sowle, Claude R. (ed.). Police power and individual freedom: the quest for balance. Chicago: Aldine, 1970.

3401 Specter, Arlen. Police guide to search and seizure, interrogation, and confession. Philadelphia: Chilton, 1967.

3402 Stuckey, Gilbert B. Evidence for the law enforcement officer. N.Y.: McGraw-Hill, 1969.

3403 Sullivan, John L. Introduction to police science. N.Y.: McGraw-Hill, 1969.

3404 Svensson, Arne. Techniques of crime scene investigation. N.Y.: American Elsevier, 1965.

3405 Tappan, Paul W. Crime, justice and correction. N.Y.: McGraw-Hill, 1960. (See especially chapter 11--"The Police and Crime Detection.")

3406 Tierney, Kevin. Courtroom testimony; a policeman's guide. N.Y.: Funk and Wagnalls, 1970.

3407 Towler, Juby E. The Police role in racial conflicts. Illinois: C.C. Thomas, 1964.

3408 Tunley, Paul. Kids, crime and chaos. N.Y.: Dell, 1964.

3409 Turner, William W. The Police establishment. N.Y.: Putnam, 1968.

3410 Uhnak, Dorothy. Policewoman. N.Y.: Simon and Schuster, 1963.

3410a U.S. Army. Military Police School. Fort Gordon, Georgia. Riot control. (Special Text) Georgia: Fort Gordon, Georgia, 1964. (Designed for law enforcement personnel with techniques for prevention of civil disorders.)

3411 U. S. Government. President's Commission on Law Enforcement and Administration of Justice. The Challenge of crime in a free society. A report by the President's Commission on Law Enforcement and Administration of Justice. Washington, D. C.: G. P. O., 1967.

3412 _____. Task force report: the police, by the President's Commission on Law Enforcement and Administration of Justice. Washington, D. C.: G. P. O., 1967.

3413 Vallow, Herbert P. Police arrest and search. Illinois: C. C. Thomas, 1962.

3414 Vollmer, August. The Police and modern society. California: University of California Press, 1936. (Role of the police historically.)

3415 Walker, Daniel. Rights in conflict. National Commission on the causes and prevention of violence. N.Y.: Dutton, 1968.

3416 Walker, T. Mike. Voices from the bottom of the world: a policeman's journal. N.Y.: Grove Press, 1970.

3417 Weston, Paul B., and Kenneth M. Wells. Criminal investigation: basic perspectives. New Jersey: Prentice-Hall, 1970. (Criminal investigation function of police is fully explored.)

3418 Whittemore, L. H. COP! A closeup of violence and tragedy. N.Y.: Holt, Rinehart, and Winston, 1969.

3419 Williams, E. W. Modern law enforcement and police science. Illinois: C. C. Thomas, 1967.

3420 Wilson, James Q. Varieties of police behavior: the management of law and order in eight communities. Cambridge, Mass.: Harvard University Press, 1968. (Explores the variety of problems faced by police and administrators in formulating policy, to meet the changing needs in a changing society.)

3421 Wilson, Orlando W. Police administration. 2nd ed. N.Y.: McGraw-Hill, 1963.

3422 _____. Police planning. 2nd ed. Illinois: C. C. Thomas, 1962.

3423 Winslow, Robert W. Crime in a free society. Selections from the President's commission on law enforcement and administration of justice. California: Dickenson, 1968.

EDITORIALS

3424 "Action for better law enforcement," San Diego Free Press, 01 30 10 01 69 (ABLE in San Diego initiated to collect information on police action.)

3425 "Better world of the policeman," Nation's Business, 55:84-6, October, 1967.

3426 "Black police vs. white at Tasker project," Distant Drummer, 06 11 01 01 70

3427 "Bolder cop killers hitting more often," U.S. News, 69:26, September 14, 1970.

3428 "Bust," Willamette Bridge, 07 18 19 01 69

3429 "Community control of police," Black Panther, 04 25 09 01 70

3430 "Confrontation takes a different shape," Berkeley Barb, 04 15 01 05 66 ("A dissenting element of American society refused to cooperate with the power structure which makes and enforces the rules.")

3431 "Confrontation tactics: defense against live attacks, or--you too can out-think police," San Diego Free Press, 12 13 05 02 68 (Description of how to out-flank the police on certain occasions and circumstances. The article is illustrated.)

3432 "Continued harassment," Black Panther, 01 31 09 02 70

3433 "The Cops up against the wall," Look, 34:17-21, July 28, 1970.

3434 "Crackdown on Coventry," Burning River News, 06 23 01 01 69 (Alleged police harassment in Cleveland.)

3435 "Des Moines Panther bombing," Black Panther, 05 19 15 01 69 (BPP and police confrontations in Des Moines.)

3435a "The Guard vs. disorder," National Guardsman, 24:2, June, 1970.

3436 "Human rights day honors repression," Distant Drummer, 01 08 03 01 70

3437 "In case of unrequested dealings ...," Rising Up Angry, 07 -- 16 01 69

3438 "Killing cops, the new terror tactics," U.S. News, 69:11-13, August 31, 1970.

3439 "Kunstler vs. Quinlan," Pittsburgh Fair Witness, 11 04 02 01 70 (Kunstler and the Pittsburgh 5 have a day in court to investigate the police riot of March 19, 1970.)

3440 "Law enforcement," Time, 96:14, July 27, 1970.

3441 "Lawsuit details escapades of two cops," Distant Drummer, 05 21 03 01 70

3442 "League of Women Voters condemns police tactics," San Diego Free Press, 01 30 09 01 69

3443 "Lindsay says he'll investigate," Advocate, 11 25 08 01 70 (A look into complaints from gay organizations concerning police harassment in New York.)

3443a "Malpractice by police trigger to Watts riots," Los

Police-Community Relations 309

Angeles Free Press, 08 20 05 01 65

3444 "Masotti Report," Burning River News, 07 07 02 01 70 (The Glenville Incident, and the controversial Masotti report in Cleveland.)

3445 "Needed: men with male gonads," Rolling Stone, 06 11 14 01 70

3446 "Nineteen year old sister murdered by Fascist K.C. pigs," Black Panther, 08 23 21 01 69 (Confrontation at a roller rink in K.C. Mississippi.)

3447 "Northside pigs hassle black youth club," Grok, 09 -- 15 02 70

3448 "Operation empathy; project in Covina, California," Newsweek, 74:104, December 15, 1969.

3449 "Over 600 arrested in California," Guardian, 06 20 08 02 70 (Description of a street rebellion in Santa Barbara California, and in the community of Isla Vista.)

3450 "Panthers and pigs," Christianity Today, 14:25, January 16, 1970.

3451 "Police and panthers: growing paranoia," Time, 94:14-16, December 19, 1969.

3452 "Portland police revolt?" Willamette Bridge, 07 18 05 02 69

3453 "Piggies go to court," Reconstruction, Vol. 1, Issue 8, p. 3, 1969.

3454 "Pittsburgh justice," Pittsburgh Point, 06 26 01 03 69

3455 "Police clamp down on news of two patrolmen charged with rape," Distant Drummer, 10 23 01 01 69

3456 "Police: tales of three cities," Time, 95:16-17, June 22, 1970.

3457 "Police under attack but standing fast," U.S. News, 69:35, September 21, 1970.

3458 "Policing the third sex," Newsweek, 74:76, October 27, 1969.

3459 "Protestors sue court-riot cops, in the U.S. district court for the Western District of Pennsylvania ...," Grok, 06 27 06 01 70

3460 "Rap sheet on cops: in case of unrequested dealings ...," Rising Up Angry, 09 -- 18 01 69

3461 "Safety equipment puts police emphasis on personal service," College and University Business, 48:99, April, 1970.

3462 "Supporting the police," Distant Drummer, 04 30 04 01 70

3463 "Tampa blacks under racist attack," Burning Spear, 10 13 04 01 70

3464 "Too much fun for fun city," Pittsburgh Point, 06 19 01 02 69 (Confrontations between "Hippies and police at the Pittsburgh Hilton Hotel.")

3465 "The War against the police," U.S. News, 69:82-6, October 26, 1970.

3466 "When cops meet students ...," Connections, 02 05 04 01 69 (Description of a federally funded project to help police-community relations, through a "Confrontation Seminar" with clinical psychologists.)

3467 "Why streets are not safe," U.S. News, 68:15-21, March 16, 1970.

3468 "Young arm of law; lowering the minimum age," Senior Scholastic, 96:15-17, March 2, 1970.

PERIODICALS

3469 Angelucci, Steve. "Instant Karma in Stratford New Jersey," Distant Drummer, 07 02 01 01 70

3469a Applebaum, Jerry. "Venice community response prevents riot," Los Angeles Free Press, 07 11 01 02 69

3469b Armbrister, Trevor. "White cop in the black ghetto," Saturday Evening Post, Number 23, Vol. 27, November 16, 1968.

3470 Atlantic (Periodical Supplement). "The Police and the rest of us," Atlantic, 223:74-135, March, 1969. (Special supplement dealing "with the police function in America.")

3470a Basing, Mary. "Police expert explains ghetto rioting," Los Angeles Free Press, 11 10 23 01 67

3471 Berkley, G. "How the police work," New Republic, 161:15-18, August 2, 1969.

3472 Berry, F. (et al.). "Terror in a teapot; Berkeley park confrontations," Nation, 208:784-8, June 23, 1969.

3473 Bittner, Egan. "The Police on skid-row: a study of peace keeping," American Sociological Review, 32:699-715, October, 1967.

3474 Black, Donald, and Albert J. Reiss Jr. "Police control of juveniles," American Sociological Review, 35:63-76, February, 1970.

3475 Blake, Eugene C. "Should the code of ethics in public life be absolute or relative?" Annals of the American Academy, January, 1966.

3476 Blum, Sam. "Police," Redbook, 128:76-7, February, 1967.

3477 Boesel, D. (et al.). "White institutions and black rage," Trans-action, 6:24-31, March, 1969.

3478 Bordua, David J., and Albert J. Reiss Jr. "Command, control and charisma: reflections on police bureaucracy," American Journal of Sociology, 72:68-76, July, 1966.

3479 Braun, S. "Cop as social scientist: inspector Fink of ninth precinct," New York Times Magazine, August 24, 1969, pp. 46-7.

3480 Bridge, Williamette. "Police press--Portland Panthers," Helix, 06 26 07 01 69

3481 Brooks, T. R. "Necessary force, or police brutality?" New York Times Magazine, December 5, 1965, pp. 60-61.

3482 Brown, Michael E. "Condemnation and persecution of hippies. Reply with rejoinder (by) A. Dobrin," Trans-action, 7:71-2, January, 1970.

3483 Brown, Sherry L. "Community control of police could have prevented the Orlando Jones murder," Black Panther, 02 28 06 01 70

3483a Browning, Frank. "They shoot hippies, don't they?" Ramparts, 9:14-23, November, 1970. (Confrontations between police and the community at Berkeley. The article is introduced by Tom Hayden.)

3484 Butler, Ellis Parker. "Pigs is pigs," Northwest Passage, 07 22 11 01 69

3485 Carleton, William G. "Cultural roots of American law enforcement," Current History, 53:1-7, July, 1967.

3486 Carrington, Frank. "Speaking for the police," Journal of Criminal Law, Criminology and Police Science, 61:244-279, June, 1970.

3487 Caughlan, John. "Seattle pigs murder another brother," Black Panther, 05 31 04 02 70

3488 Clamage, Dena. "Jesus called the cops," Fifth Estate, 07 10 03 01 69

3489 Clark, Gerald. "The Day the Montreal police went on strike," Reader's Digest, 96:107-112, February, 1970.

3490 Cole, Rob. "Law enforcement ... or sadism?" Advocate, 12 09 02 01 70

Police-Community Relations 313

3491 Connery, Colin. "Cops crackdown on community control," Liberation News Service, 02 15 05 01 69 (Police confront the Tompkins Square Community Center at the Lower East Side in N.Y.)

3492 Covert, John. "Confrontation in city court," Pittsburgh Point, 03 19 01 02 70

3493 _____. "The Cops tell how their riot started," Pittsburgh Point, 04 23 01 01 70

3494 _____. "Eight hours in county jail," Pittsburgh Point, 03 26 01 02 70 ("Violating an injunction against mass picketing at Presbyterian University Hospital in support of efforts to unionize hospital workers.")

3495 _____. "Police mismatch: dogs against kids," Pittsburgh Point, 03 05 01 02 70 (Confrontation with police in East Liberty, Pittsburgh at a dance where several persons were bitten by K-9 dogs.)

3496 _____. "The Police show they don't forget," Pittsburgh Point, 05 21 01 03 70

3497 Cray, Ed. "Search and seizure law constitutional question," Los Angeles Free Press, 11 19 01 02 65

3498 Demaio, Don. "Of broken windows," Distant Drummer, 05 15 03 01 69 (Description of police practices in Philadelphia.)

3499 _____. "Polemic," Distant Drummer, 06 12 04 01 69 (Police-community relations in Philadelphia.)

3500 Drabek, Thomas, and J. Eugene Haas. "How police confront disaster," Trans-action, 6:33-38, May, 1969.

3501 Dreifus, Claudia. "Newsreal," East Village Other, 07 02 06 01 69 (Police vs. the underground press. Targets are Acid Flesh, Screw, Kiss, and Washington Free Press among others. The article is from Liberation News Service.)

3501a Drescher, Earl L. "Diary of a peace march," Police Chief, 37:16-24, March, 1970.

3502 Eberle, Paul. "Panther group harassed by Metro squad," Los Angeles Free Press, 07 11 01 01 69

3503 _____. "Unconstitutional anti-hippie law will be challenged by ACLU," Los Angeles Free Press, 09 13 01 01 68

3504 _____. "When the police run amok," Los Angeles Free Press, 10 02 01 01 70 (Intriguing article about inside the ranks of police officers.)

3505 England, Ralph W. Jr. "The Police in our changing cities," Current History, 59:273-277, November, 1970.

3506 Fairfield, Roy P. "Police state: can it happen here?" Humanist, 30:6, July-August, 1970.

3507 Farber, Jerry. "A Lot of people were smiling," Los Angeles Free Press, 08 27 03 03 65 (Jerry describes in sequential order the riot at Avalon and Imperial streets in L.A.)

3508 Fleming, Thomas J. "The Policeman's lot," American Heritage, 21:4-17, February, 1970.

3509 Fletcher, John. "Does local government want better law enforcement?" North Carolin Anvil, 09 27 02 01 69

3510 _____. "Professionalism and the police in a southern factory town," North Carolin Anvil, 08 30 07 01 69

3511 Friggens, Paul. "The World's most versatile police," Reader's Digest, 97:134-138, July, 1970.

3512 Geerdes, Clay. "Bay bulls but beaver buffs," Los Angeles Free Press, 08 22 30 01 69 (Police activities in the Bay Area.)

3513 Germann, A. C. "Community policing: an assessment," Journal of Criminal Law, Criminology and

Police Science, 60:89-96, March, 1969.

3514 Gilbert, Mitch. "Police brutality: Philly's time bomb," Distant Drummer, 12 11 01 04 69 ("Part one of a series which asks: How bad is the problem of police abuse in Philadelphia?")

3515 _____. "Police brutality: Philly's time bomb," Distant Drummer, 12 18 01 01 69 (Part II of the series investigating police-community relations in Philadelphia.)

3516 G. K. "Berkeley police practices questioned," Berkeley Barb, 01 05 05 05 68

3517 Goldberg, Art, and Gene Marine. "O'Brien: I want to kill a nigger," Ramparts, 8:10-18, July, 1969.

3518 Goodman, Bob. "Slam, brutality: hassled by police?" Great Speckled Bird, 09 22 04 01 69

3519 Grafton, Samuel. "What do we want from our policemen?" McCalls, 92:110-11, May, 1965.

3520 Gronau, Gerald. "Computerized cops," Los Angeles Free Press, 06 05 05 04 70

3521 Haines, Steve. "Killer cops at large," Berkeley Barb, 04 25 07 01 69

3522 Hall, Richard. "Dilemma of the black cop," Life, 69:60-63, September 18, 1970.

3523 Hallworth, G. L. "Are we handcuffing the police," America, 120:128-9, February 1, 1969.

3524 Hare, Nathan. "The Ambivalent public and crime," Crime and Delinquency, 9:145-51, April, 1963.

3525 Harney, Malachi L. "The U.S. Bureau of narcotics," Current History, 53:23-30, July, 1967.

3526 Harrington, J. J. "One way to handle crime," U.S. News, 67:62-5, December 22, 1969.

3527 Hennessy, Tom. "Mace the nation," Pittsburgh Point, 09 11 05 02 69 (A dialogue interview concerning a new full television program designed for policemen.)

3528 Hoffman, Fred. "The Police chief visits a love-in," Los Angeles Free Press, 12 05 05 01 68

3529 Hoffman, Joan. "Idea: community control of police," Los Angeles Free Press, 08 01 11 01 69 (Decentralization of police departments.)

3530 _____. "Troops invade Venice," Los Angeles Free Press, 08 23 10 01 68

3531 James, Howard. "The Police; enemies or friends?" PTA Magazine, 64:2-5, June, 1970.

3532 Jassen, Jeff. "Pre-dawn raid on Barb scribe," Berkeley Barb, 06 09 01 01 67

3533 Jenkins, Diahnne. "Pigs caught red handed using brute force against the people of New York," Black Panther, 05 20 06 01 70

3534 Johnson, Elmer H. "Interrelatedness of law enforcement programs: a fundamental dimension," Journal of Criminal Law, Criminology and Police Science, 60:509, December, 1969.

3535 Jurow, George L., and Stephen M. Raphael. "Police protection," Dallas Notes, 11 -- 09 01· 67 (Describes citizens expanded rights in dealing with policemen.)

3536 Kamisar, Yale. "When the cops were not handcuffed," New York Times Magazine, November 7, 1965, pp. 34-35.

3537 Kelley, J. B. "Law and order equals status quo?" America, 121:323-6, October 18, 1969.

3538 Key, Douglas. "Police raid gay-in," Los Angeles Free Press, 06 05 08 01 70

3539 Kimble, Joseph Paul. "Night thoughts of a police chief," Nation, 210:490-492, April 27, 1970.

3540 Kleberg, John. "Selection process of police officers

is first line of campus defense," College and University Business, 48:95-97, April, 1970.

3541 Knebel, Fletcher. "Police in crisis: white cop and black rebel," Look, 32:14-21, February 6, 1968.

3542 Kunkin, Art. "FP files press pass suit against city and county and Los Angeles police attack free press party in Elysian Park, Sunday," Los Angeles Free Press, 09 27 01 03 68

3543 Kupferberg, Tuli. "How to think about the police," Berkeley Barb, 12 08 09 02 67

3544 Lang, Frances. "State police," Ramparts, 9:12-13, December, 1970. (Confrontation between FBI and the Secret Service as to which is to become the dominant federal police.)

3545 Laurence, Leo E. "Gays hit New York cops," Berkeley Barb, 06 04 05 01 69 (Clash at Stonewall Inn in Greenwich Village.)

3546 Lear, Len. "New police manual offers clear guidelines for dealing with hippies and blacks," Distant Drummer, 04 24 18 01 69 (Proposed guidelines for police officers to use during demonstrations which haven't been adopted as yet.)

3547 _____. "Parents, police get nowhere," Distant Drummer, 08 21 08 04 69

3548 Leitsch, Dick. "Police raid on New York club sets off first gay riot," Advocate, 09 -- 03 03 69

3549 Levitt, Dennis. "Cuban exiles bomb socialist hall; new committee to force police to act," Los Angeles Free Press, 06 05 03 03 70

3550 Levy, B. "Cops in the ghetto: a problem of the police system," American Behavorial Scientist, 11:31-4, March, 1968.

3551 Liberation News Service. "Police go berserk in Isla Vista--1,000 arrested," Los Angeles Free Press, 06 19 01 01 70

3552   Lundy, Joseph R. "The Invisible police," Nation, 209:629-632, December 8, 1969.

3553   Malthy, Jan. "Top cop can't split blacks," Peninsula Observer, 07 28 05 01 69

3554   Marine, Gene. "The Persecution and assassination of the Black Panthers as performed by the Oakland Police under the direction of Chief Charles R. Gain, Mayor John Reading, et al," Ramparts, 6:37-46, June 29, 1968. (Consists of four acts, a prologue, several intermissions, and a denouncement regarding confrontations between the police and the Black Panthers, on Tuesday April 23, 1968 in Oakland City Hall, California.)

3555   Marshall, Sue. "Chicanos protest 'massacre'," Los Angeles Free Press, 07 17 08 01 70

3556   _____. "Police kill two innocent Chicanos," Los Angeles Free Press, 07 24 06 01 70

3557   Mathe, Judy. "The Police and the community--inhuman relations," Distant Drummer, 06 05 03 01 69

3558   Matheis, Karen. "Twelve students arrested: rights denied," Grinding Stone, 11 21 01 03 68 (Experience of one who was arrested.)

3559   Maxson, R. E. "Police conduct investigation of own 'excessive' force," Los Angeles Free Press, 08 21 05 01 70 (Description of efforts of the L.A. Police Dept. to solve its own internal problems.)

3560   Meany, George (ed.). "Crime in America," American Federalist, 77:6-13, February, 1970.

3561   Packer, Herbert L. "Law and order in the seventies," New Republic, 162:12-13, January 10, 1970.

3562   Pain, Lincoln. "Pig $huck," Washington Free Press, 08 -- 04 02 69

3563   Peter, Viviane. "Can a 19 year-old make a good policeman?" Pittsburgh Press--Parade Magazine, April 12, 1970, p. 6.

3564 Peterson, Virgil W. "Local and state law enforcement today," Current History, 53:8-14, July, 1967.

3565 Phelan, W. D. Jr. "Authoritarian prescription," Nation, 209:467-73, November 3, 1969.

3566 Pohl, Connie. "Guns in the classroom; solutions get cheaper," Madison Kaleidoscope, 07 04 12 01 69

3567 Powe, Wilbur. "The Parents of Everett Junior High School students demand: no more pigs brutalizing our youth," Black Panther, 04 -- 06 02 70

3568 Powell, John. "Campus security needs professionals with emphasis on people problems," College and University Business, 48:94-95, April, 1970.

3569 Pyes, Craig Randolph. "U.C. cop conspiracy," Berkeley Tribe, 11 07 10 01 69

3570 Reichley, A. James. "The Way to cool the police rebellion," Fortune, 78:109, December, 1968.

3571 Remos, Vince. "D.C. pigs cooler than Chicago's," Dallas Notes, 11 19 02 01 69 ("March of Death" concept.)

3572 Rieker, Richard. "The Police in Hazelwood," Pittsburgh Point, 06 12 05 01 69

3573 Robb, Charles C. "Tactical force does it again," Pittsburgh Point, 10 16 01 03 69

3574 Roberson, Marcis. "Open terror against black people by the pigs at Columbia Point project," Black Panther, 07 18 05 01 70

3575 Robinson, Donald W. "Police in the schools," Today's Education, 59:18-22, October, 1970. (Presents a variety of viewpoints about the role of police in the school system.)

3576 Rodd, Bill. "What happened to the Pittsburgh Police?" Pittsburgh Point, 08 28 02 01 69 ("Commentary on the behavior of Pittsburgh Police on 8-26-69, as compared to their behavior in the

April, 1968 disorders: being derived from public and other sources.")

3577 Sagalyn, Arnold. "Danger of police overreaction," Journal of Criminal Law, Criminology and Police Science, 60:517, December, 1969.

3578 Schreiber, James A. "Buggers bared cops bug kids," Berkeley Barb, 10 06 03 04 67

3579 Schultz, Ray. "The Night the cops got whipped," East Village Other, 03 03 13 01 70

3580 Serra, Normand. "A Study in police power procedure," Octopus, 08 -- 20 01 69

3580a Shafikh, James. "Police riot mars peace march," Los Angeles Free Press, 06 26 01 01 67

3581 Sikes, Melvin P. "A symposium on innovations in police techniques: recruit selection, community service and community relations," Journal of Criminal Law, Criminology and Police Science, 60:237-271, June, 1969.

3582 Silenus. "Hate busts follow love meet: police fury lashes blindly in Haight," Berkeley Barb, 01 20 01 03 67

3583 Such, Rod. "Honoring the 'Paper Tiger'," Guardian, 07 11 03 01 70

3584 ———. "Uprisings in 10 cities, cops kill 4," Guardian, 08 08 05 01 70 (Confrontations between police and community factions on a nationwide scale.)

3585 Tepperman, Jean. "FUST organizes on Commons," Old Mole, 06 06 03 01 69 (Anti-war activities on the Commons in Boston, Mass.)

3586 Terris, B. J. "Role of the police," Annals of the American Academy, 374:58-69, November, 1967.

3587 Tiffany, Lawrence P. "The Fourth amendment and police-citizen confrontations," Journal of Criminal Law, Criminology and Police Science, 60:442,

December, 1969.

3588 Tornquist, Elizabeth. "Harassment directed at quaker house," North Carolin Anvil, 06 06 03 01 70

3589 _____. "Highway patrol caught on horns of dilemma," North Carolin Anvil, 05 09 01 01 70

3590 _____. "KKK and the police," North Carolin Anvil, 03 28 01 01 70

3591 _____. "Police crush freedom house," North Carolin Anvil, 06 06 01 01 70

3592 Vinson, Fred M. Jr. "Federal law enforcement," Current History, 53:15-22, July, 1967.

3593 Vorenberg, J., and J. Q. Wilson. "Is the court handcuffing the cops?" New York Times Magazine, May 11, 1969, pp. 32-3.

3594 Wade, Timothy. "Sociopsychoeconomic interpretation of cops," Los Angeles Free Press, 05 10 06 01 68

3595 Waskow, Arthur I. "Toward community control of the police," Trans-action, 7:4-7, December, 1969.

3596 White, Joe. "Tune in your local police D.J.," Los Angeles Free Press, 06 05 05 01 70

3597 Whitney, Mary. "Greater freedom for women has increased the security problem," College and University Business, 48:97-98, April, 1970.

3598 Wilson, James Q. "The Police and their problems: a theory," Public Policy, 12:189-216, 1963.

3599 Young, Roland. "A Case study of pig harassment," Black Panther, 02 07 04 01 70

V. THE PREGNANT QUESTION--SEX EDUCATION

BOOKS

3600 American Friends Service Committee. Who shall live? Man's control over birth and death. N.Y.: Hill and Wang, 1970. (Also available in paper.)

3601 Arnstein, Helene S. Your growing child and sex. N.Y.: Bobbs-Merrill, 1967.

3602 Bacon Pamphlet Service. Teaching sex education--a guide for teachers. N.Y.: Bacon Pamphlet Service, (n.d.)

3603 Baruch, Dorothy (Walter). New ways in sex education; a guide for parents and teachers. N.Y.: McGraw-Hill, 1959.

3604 Bauer, W. Moving into manhood. N.Y.: Doubleday, 1963.

3605 _____. Way to womanhood. N.Y.: Doubleday, 1965.

3606 Bausch, N. J. A Boy's sex life. Notre Dame, Ind.: Fides, 1969.

3607 Beck, Lester F. Human growth. N.Y.: Harcourt, Brace and World, 1969.

3608 Behrman, S. J., Leslie Corsa Jr., and Ronald Freedman (eds.). Fertility and family planning; a world view. Michigan: University of Michigan Press, 1970. (Also available in paper.)

3609 Bell, R. Marriage and family interaction. Illinois: Dorsey, 1967.

Sex Education

3609a   Bell, Robert R. Premarital sex in a changing society. New Jersey: Prentice-Hall, 1966. (Includes notes and bibliography on marital, extramarital and postmarital sex.)

3610   Benell, Florence B. Educational approach to veneral disease control; a VD education guide for grades 7-12. Palo Alto, California: National Press, 1965.

3611   Bird, Joseph W., and Lois F. Bird. The Freedom of sexual love. N.Y.: Doubleday, 1967. (Paper)

3612   _____. Marriage is for grownups, by Joseph and Lois Bird. N.Y.: Doubleday, 1969.

3613   Blenkinsopp, Joseph. Sexuality and the Christian tradition. Daton, Ohio: Pflaum, 1969. (Paper)

3614   Bohannan, Paul. Love, sex, and being human. N.Y.: Doubleday, 1970. (Paper)

3615   Borowitz, Eugene B. Choosing a sex ethic. N.Y.: Schocken, 1969.

3616   Breasted, Mary. Oh! sex education. N.Y.: Praeger, 1970. (A look at both sides of sex education in public schools. Part of text originally appeared in the Village Voice.)

3617   Brenton, Myron. The American male. N.Y.: Coward-McCann, 1966.

3618   Broderick, Carefred B., and Jessie Bernard. The Individual, sex, and society. Baltimore: Johns Hopkins Press, 1969.

3619   Cain, Arthur H. Young people and sex. N.Y.: John Day, 1967.

3620   Calderone, Mary S. (et al.). Release from sexual tensions. N.Y.: Random House, 1968.

3621   Carr, Donald E. The Sexes. N.Y.: Doubleday, 1970.

3622   Cervantes, Lucius. And God made man and woman;

a factual discussion of sex differences. Chicago: Regnery, 1960. (Discussion of social and personal significance of sexual differences.)

3623 Chanter, A. G. Sex education in the primary school. N.Y.: St. Martin's Press, 1966.

3624 Child Study Association of America. Sex education and the new morality. A search for a more meaningful social ethic. N.Y.: Columbia University Press, 1968.

3625 _____. Sex education: recommended reading prepared by the book review committee. N.Y.: The Association, 1969. (Pam.)

3626 _____. What to tell your children about sex. N.Y.: Duell, Sloan and Pearce, 1964.

3627 _____. When children ask about sex, by the staff of the association: revised by Ada Daniels and Mary Hoover. N.Y.: The Association, 1969.

3628 Comfort, Alex. The Anxiety makers. N.Y.: Dell, 1970.

3629 Courtenay, M. Sexual discord in marriage. Philadelphia: Lippincott, 1968.

3630 Crow, Lester D., and Alice Crow. Sex education for the growing family. Boston: Christopher, 1970.

3631 Cunneen, Sally. Sex: female; religion: Catholic. N.Y.: Holt, Rinehart, and Winston, 1968.

3632 Davis, M. Sexual responsibility in marriage. N.Y.: Dial, 1963.

3633 De Lestapis, S. Family planning and modern problems. N.Y.: Herder and Herder, 1961.

3634 Demant, V. A. Christian sex ethics; an introduction. N.Y.: Harper, 1965. (Describes both the "personal and the communal aspects of sexual relationships." Originally lectures to undergraduate students.)

3635 Demarest, Robert J., and John H. Sciarra. Conception, birth and contraception; a visual presentation. N.Y.: McGraw-Hill, 1970.

3636 De Martino, Manfred F. The New female sexuality. N.Y.: Julian Press, 1969.

3637 De Vinck, Jose. The Virtue of sex. Indiana: Abbey Press, 1970. (Sexual love book for all faiths.)

3638 Duvall, Evelyn. Love and the facts of life. N.Y.: Association Press, 1965. (A revision of the 1956 edition with the addition of three new chapters.)

3639 _____. Why wait till marriage? N.Y.: Association Press, 1965.

3640 _____, and Sylvanus M. Duvall (eds.). Sex ways in fact and faith; bases for Christian family policy. N.Y.: Association Press, 1961.

3641 Ehrmann, Winston W. Premarital dating behavior; with an introduction by Margaret Mead. N.Y.: Holt, 1960.

3642 Eickhoff, Andrew R. A Christian view of sex and marriage. N.Y.: Macmillan, 1966. (Contains a section on Christian attitudes toward sex education.)

3643 Ellis, Albert. The Folklore of sex. N.Y.: Grove Press, 1970.

3643a _____, and Albert Abarbanel (eds.). Encyclopedia of sexual behavior. N.Y.: Hawthorne Books, Inc., 1961.

3644 Ellis, Havelock. Psychology of sex. N.Y.: Emerson Books, 1964.

3644a Farber, Bernard. Family: organization and interaction. San Francisco, California: Chandler Publishing, 1964.

3645 Frank, Lawrence Kelso. The Conduct of sex; biology and ethics of sex and parenthood in modern life. N.Y.: Morrow, 1961.

3646 Franzblau, Rose N., and Abraham N. Franzblau. A sane and happy life. N.Y.: Harcourt, Brace and World, 1963.

3647 Gagnon, John, and William Simon (eds.). The Sexual scene. Chicago: Aldine, 1970.

3648 Gibert, Henri. Love in marriage; the meaning and practice of sexual love in Christian marriage; with an introduction by George A. Kelly; translated from the French by Andre Humbert. N.Y.: Hawthorn, 1964.

3648a Ginsberg, Eli (ed.). The Nation's children. N.Y.: Columbia University Press, 1960. (Includes "The Changing Negro Family," by Lewis Hylan.)

3649 Glassberg, B. Y. Teen-age sex counselor. N.Y.: Barron's Educational Series, 1965.

3650 Gordon, Sol. Facts about sex. N.Y.: Day, 1970.

3651 Greenblatt, Augusta. Teen-age medicine: questions young people ask about their health. Foreword by Walter R. Anyan, Jr., M.D. N.Y.: Cowles, 1970.

3652 Greene, Gael. Sex and the college girl. N.Y.: Dial, 1964.

3653 Grodon, Albert I. Intermarriage, interfaith, interracial, interethnic. Boston: Beacon, 1964.

3654 Group For The Advancement of Psychiatry (Committee On The College Student). Sex and the college student; a developmental perspective on sexual issues on the campus. N.Y.: Atheneum, 1966.

3655 Gruenberg, Sidonie M. The Wonderful story of how you were born. New and revised edition. N.Y.: Doubleday, 1970.

3655a Grunwald, Henry. Sex in America. N.Y.: Bantam Books, 1964. (Paper)

3656 Guidance Associates (Harcourt, Brace and World). Family life and sex education: a new curriculum including--human sexuality: a modern approach--a unique series of sound filmstrips produced in consultation with a special committee of SIECUS. Sex Information and Education Council of the U.S. (Consists) of two parts. Catalog Number F104800.

3657 Guttmacher, Alan Frank. Understanding sex: a young person's guide. Foreword by Millicent McIntosh. N.Y.: Harper, 1970.

3658 Hatch, Claudia (ed.). What you should know about sex and sexuality. New Jersey: Scholastic Book Service, 1969.

3659 Hays, H. R. The Dangerous sex: the myth of feminine evil. N.Y.: Putnam, 1964.

3660 Hernton, Calvin C. Sex and racism in America. N.Y.: Grove Press, 1970.

3661 Hettlinger, Richard. Living with sex; the students dilemma. N.Y.: Seabury Press, 1967. (Growing Up With Sex, published in September, 1971.)

3662 Hilu, Virginia (ed.). Sex education and the schools. N.Y.: Harper and Row, 1967.

3663 Hofmann, Hans F. Sex incorporated; a positive view of the sexual revolution. Boston: Beacon, 1967. (Includes sections on homosexuality and premarital sex.)

3664 Hofstein, Sadie. The Human story. Facts on birth, growth, and reproduction. N.Y.: Lothrop, Lee and Shepard, 1970.

3665 Jenkin, Noel, and Karen Vroegh. Contemporary concepts of masculinity and femininity. Chicago, Illinois: Department of Mental Health--Institute for Juvenile Research, 1964.

3666 Johnson, Eric W. Love and sex in plain language. Philadelphia: Lippincott, 1965. (Revised edition, 1968.)

3667 _____. Sex: telling it straight. Philadelphia: Lippincott, 1970.

3668 Johnson, Warren R. Human sexual behavior and sex education. Philadelphia: Lea and Fibiger, 1968.

3669 Jones, K. L. Sex. N.Y.: Harper and Row, 1969.

3670 Kelly, Audrey. A Catholic parent's guide to sex education. N.Y.: Hawthorn, 1962.

3671 Kelly, George A. Your child and sex; a guide for Catholic parents. N.Y.: Random House, 1965.

3672 Kilander, Holger F. Sex education in the schools; a study of objectives, content, methods, materials, and evaluation. N.Y.: Macmillan, 1969. (Includes lesson plans for all levels.)

3673 Kirkendall, Lester A. Premarital intercourse and interpersonal relationships. N.Y.: Julian, 1961.

3674 _____, and Robert N. Whitehurst (eds.). Sexual revolution. N.Y.: Pegasus, 1970.

3675 Kling, S. Sexual behavior and the law. N.Y.: Geis, 1965.

3676 Krich, Aron M. (ed.). The Sexual revolution. Edited and introduced by Aron Krich. N.Y.: Dell, 1963.

3677 Landers, Ann. Ann Landers talks to teen-agers about sex. New Jersey: Prentice-Hall, 1963.

3678 Lehman, Edna S. Talking to children about sex. N.Y.: Harper and Row, 1970. (Individual dialogues for parents on how to communicate with children about sex.)

3679 Leist, Marielene. A Fresh look at sex education. N.Y.: World, 1970. (A guidebook to be used at various age levels in teaching children about human sexuality.)

3680 Leshan, Edna J. Sex and your teen-ager; a guide for parents. N.Y.: McKay, 1969.

3681 Linner, Birgitta. Sex and society in Sweden; in collaboration with Richard J. Litell; preface by Lester A. Kirkendall. N.Y.: Pantheon, 1967. (Evolution of the Swedish attitudes and solutions as well as materials used in some public schools.)

3682 Lipton, Lawrence. The Erotic revolution. California: Sherbourne, 1965.

3683 Lorand, Rhoda L. Love, sex and the teenager. N.Y.: Macmillan, 1965.

3684 Lowen, Alexander. Love and orgasm. N.Y.: Macmillan, 1966. (Relationship of sexual behavior with personality.)

3685 MacAvoy, J. Husband and wife. Indiana: Abbey Press, 1970. (Sexual guide for Catholic couples emphasizing spiritual love.)

3686 Maccoby, Eleanor E. The Development of sex differences. California: Stanford University Press, 1966.

3687 McCurdy, Harold Grier. The Personal world. N.Y.: Harcourt, Brace and World, 1961.

3688 Mace, David R. The Christian response to the sexual revolution. N.Y.: Abingdon, 1970. (The Role of sex in a Christian life.)

3689 _____. Youth considers marriage. N.Y.: Nelson, 1966. (Paper)

3690 McLaughlin, John. Love before marriage. N.Y.: World, 1970. (Defends traditional values. Reexamines the teachings on premarital chastity.)

3690a Martinson, Floyd M. Marriage and the American ideal. N.Y.: Dodd, 1960.

3691 Mazur, Ronald. Commonsense sex. Boston: Beacon, 1968.

3692 Menninger, Karl A. Love against hate. N.Y.: Harcourt, Brace and World, 1959.

3693 Moore, T. W. Sex, sex, sex. Philadelphia: United Church Press, (Pilgrim) 1969.

3694 Murphy, Charles, and Linda Day. Sex: a book for teenagers. N.Y.: Herder and Herder, 1970. (Self-analysis of the individual, his freedom and responsibility in light of confused standards of today.)

3695 NAIS Institute on Sex Education. Princeton, New Jersey. 1966. Sex education and the schools, edited by Virginia Hilu. N.Y.: Harper and Row, 1967. (Includes models of programs.)

3696 National Catholic Education Association. Sex education; a guide for parents and educators. Washington, D.C.: NCEA, 1969. (Pam.)

3697 National School Public Relations Association. Sex education in schools. (Education U.S.A. special report stock no. 411-12732) Washington, D.C.: NSPRA, 1969.

3698 Nelson, Jack (ed.). Teenagers and sex: revolution or reaction? New Jersey: Prentice-Hall, 1970.

3699 Odenwald, Robert P. The Disappearing sexes. N.Y.: Random House, 1965.

3700 Oraison, Marc. Being together: our relationships with other people. N.Y.: Doubleday, 1970.

3701 _____. The Human mystery of sexuality. N.Y.: Sheed and Ward, 1967. (Originally published in France.)

3702 Packard, Vance. Sexual wilderness; the contemporary upheaval in male and female relationships. N.Y.: McKay, 1968.

3703 Pexton, Myron R. The Expectant father. Boston: Christopher, 1970.

3704 Piers, Maria W. Growing up with children. Chicago: Quadrangle, 1966. (Paper) (Major problems of child rearing.)

3705 Pike, James A. Teen-agers and sex. New Jersey: Prentice-Hall, 1966. (Presents a program of sex instruction advocating that it begin early in life.

Sex Education

Some conflicting viewpoints explained.)

3706 Pittenger, Norman. Making sexuality human. Philadelphia: Pilgrim Press, 1970. (Discussion of the "sexual ethic" for our time.)

3707 Pomeroy, Wardell B. Boys and sex. N.Y.: Delacorte Press, 1968. (Designed to serve boys and their parents about sexual problems.)

3708 _____. Girls and sex. N.Y.: Delacorte, 1969. (Serves girls and their parents about sexual problems.)

3709 Puner, Helen. Not while you're a freshman; a chapter in the life of monologue. N.Y.: Coward-McCann, 1965. (Written in a conversational style the argument is for chastity.)

3710 Queen, Stuart A., Robert A. Habenstein, and John B. Adams. The Family in various cultures. Philadelphia: Lippincott, 1961.

3710a Rainwater, Lee. And the poor get children. Chicago: Quadrangle, 1960.

3711 Ramsey, Charles E. Problems of youth: a social problems perspective. California: Dickenson, 1967.

3712 Reiss, Ira Leonard. Premarital sexual standards in America: a sociological investigation of the relative social and cultural integration of American sexual standards. N.Y.: Free Press, 1961.

3713 Reuben, David. Everything you always wanted to know about sex and were afraid to ask. N.Y.: McKay, 1969.

3714 Richardson, Frank H. For young adults only: the doctor discusses your personal problems. N.Y.: Tupper and Love, 1961.

3715 Rubin, Isadore, and Lester A. Kirkendall (eds.). Sex in the adolescent years; new directions in guiding and teaching youth. N.Y.: Association Press, 1968.

3716 Ryan, John, and Mary Ryan. Love and sexuality: a Christian approach. N.Y.: Holt, Rinehardt, and Winston, 1967.

3717 Schoenfeld, Eugene. Dear Doctor Hip Pocrates; advice your family doctor never gave you. Preface by Joel Fort. N.Y.: Grove, 1969. (Letters from a column of advice in the Berkeley Barb.)

3718 Schulz, Esther D. Family life and sex education: curriculum and instruction. N.Y.: Harcourt, Brace and World, 1969.

3719 Schur, Edwin M. (ed.). The Family and the sexual revolution; selected readings. Indiana: Indiana University Press, 1965.

3720 SIECUS. Sexuality and man. Introduction by Mary S. Calderone. N.Y.: Scribner's, 1970.

3720a Smith, Ernest A. American youth culture. N.Y.: Free Press, 1962.

3721 Southard, Helen F. Sex before twenty. N.Y.: Dutton, 1967.

3722 St. John-Stevas, Norman. Law and morals. (Twentieth Century Encyclopedia of Catholicism, Section 16) N.Y.: Hawthorn, 1965. (Examination of morals, religion and law from a Catholic point of view. Other topics include suicide, and capital punishment.)

3723 _____. Life, death and the law; law and Christian morals in England and the U.S. Indiana: Indiana University Press, 1961. (Includes controversial material on contraception, artifical insemination, sterilization, homosexuality, suicide, and euthanasia.)

3724 Valente, Michael F. Sex: the radical view of a Catholic theologian. N.Y.: Bruce, 1970. (Provocative study of both Catholic and non-Catholic attitudes with theological references.)

3724a Vincent, Clark. Unmarried mothers. N.Y.: Free Press of Glencoe, 1961.

3725 Vinck, Jose de. The Virtue of sex. N.Y.: Hawthorn, 1966.

3726 Walsh, Mary McAna. Parent child and sex. Ohio: George A. Pflaum, 1970. (Paper)

3727 What Shall I Tell My Child? The World famous Scandinavian system of sex education; introduction by Theodore Reik. N.Y.: Crown, 1966.

3727a Whitman, Howard. The Sex age. N.Y.: Charter Books, 1962.

3728 Wood, Frederic C. Sex and the new morality. N.Y.: Association Press, 1968.

EDITORIALS

3729 "Beyond sex education," Christian Century, 86:1371, October 29, 1969.

3730 "Birchers down on sex," Dallas Notes, 01 22 03 02 69

3731 "Eight Grokies ask questions about sex ... about sex," Grok, 05 -- 09 02 70

3732 "Facts about sexual freedom," PTA Magazine, 62:2-6, April, 1968.

3733 "Family life and sex education," Mental Hygiene, 54:591-2, October, 1970.

3734 "Grant v. Lee," Time, 96:52-3, August 31, 1970.

3735 "Interfaith statement on sex education," Catholic School Journal, 68:43-5, December, 1968.

3736 "M.D. blames parents and schools for sex education gap," Today's Health, 48:13, January, 1970.

3737 "The Pill," Rising Up Angry, 09 -- 13 01 69

3738 "Promote free sex: open the conference rooms,"
Two-Cents Plain Dealer, 03 08 01 01 70

3739 "Sex education: symposium," North Carolin Anvil,
01 10 01 01 70

3740 "Sex education flare-ups would ban courses, materials; discussion," Library Journal, 94:4185, November 15, 1969.

3741 "Sex education hits the British airwaves," Atlas, 19:16, April, 1970.

3742 "Sex: how to read all about it," Newsweek, 76:38-39, August 24, 1970.

3743 "Sex education in school; debate splits town in Wisconsin," Life, 67:34-41, September 19, 1969.

3744 "Sex education moves forward: New Jersey joint pastoral letter," America, 121:483, November 22, 1969.

3745 "Sex education on the defensive," Nation's Schools, 84:19, August, 1969.

3746 "Sex in the classroom," Time, 94:50, July 25, 1969.

3747 "Should sex education be offered in grade school?" Good Housekeeping, 169:12, July, 1969.

3748 "Threat to freedom of teaching learning and reading: campaign against sex education," Publishers Weekly, 196:66, September 22, 1969.

3749 "Why the furor over sex education," U.S. News, 67:44-6, August 4, 1969.

PERIODICALS

3750 Beavan, K. A. "Sex education platters," Times Education Supplement, 2804:474, February 14, 1969.

3751 Bell, J. N. "Why the revolt against sex education," Good Housekeeping, 169:92-3, November, 1969.

3751a Bell, Robert R. "Some factors related to the sexual satisfaction of the college educated wife," Family Life Coordinator, 43-47, May, 1964.

3752 Benell, Florence B. "Frequency of misconceptions and reluctance to teach controversial topics related to sex among teachers," American Association of Health, Physical Education, and Recreation, 40:11-16, March, 1969.

3753 Bennett, V. D. C. (et al.). "Experimental course on sex education for teachers," Mental Hygiene, 53:625-31, October, 1969.

3754 Berne, E. "Sex in human loving," Life, 69:11, December 18, 1970.

3755 Bettelheim, Bruno. "Right and wrong way to teach sex," Ladies' Home Journal, 87:26-7, January, 1970.

3756 Bjork, R. M. "International perspective on various issues in sex education as an aspect of health education," Journal of School Health, 39:525-37, October, 1969.

3757 Bloom, J. L. "Sex education for handicapped adolescents," Journal of School Health, 39:363-7, June, 1969.

3758 Bottel, Helen. "Helping your teens to handle sex," Reader's Digest, 96:140-142, March, 1970.

3759 Breasted, M. "Oh! sex education!" Christianity Today, 15:33-4, December 18, 1970.

3760 Calderone, Mary S. "Sexuality and the college student," Journal of The American College Health, 17:189-193, February, 1969.

3761 Cohen, Joshua Franz. "They call it sex education," Distant Drummer, 09 18 03 04 69 (Controversy in the West Chester Area Schools, Philadelphia over the sex education program.)

3762 Cohen, R. M. "Teaching sex in school," New Republic, 160:11-12, June 28, 1969.

3763 Cross, Virginia. "Where do babies come from," The Paper, 08 -- 03 05 01 66

3764 Darden, J. S. "Progress report of the health guidance in sex education," Journal of School Health, 38:462-3, September, 1968.

3765 Don. "Fifty per cent VD rise predicted," Spokane Natural, 08 01 03 02 68

3766 Donaldson, J. L. "Innovative programs in sex education," Education Digest, 35:46-48, April, 1970. (This article is digested from the PTA Magazine, whose reference follows.)

3767 _____. "Innovative programs on sex education; with study discussion program," PTA Magazine, 64:26-8, 35-6, January, 1970.

3768 Dorr, R. "Current attacks on sex education," Illinois Education, 58:111-14, November, 1969.

3769 Dunbar, E. "Sex in school: Watkins Glen, New York, and Anaheim, California," Look, 33:15-17, September 9, 1969.

3770 Faber, N. G. "Sex for credit; University of Minnesota," Look, 33:39-40, April 1, 1969.

3771 Farnsworth, Dana L. "Sex mores and sex morals," PTA Magazine, 64:2-5, April, 1970.

3772 Fehrle, Carl C. "The Natural birth of sex education," Educational Leadership, 27:573-577, March, 1970.

3773 Ferm, D. W. "Latest scoop on Swedish sex," Christian Century, 87:45-8, January 14, 1970.

3774 Fleming, Thomas and Alice Fleming. "What kids still don't know about sex," Look, 54:59-60, July 28, 1970.

3775 Forman, I. "Sex and family living: Boston

University Training project for teachers," American Education, 5:11-13, October, 1969.

3776 Fort, J. "How to teach about drugs and sex," CTA Journal, 65:22-4, January, 1969.

3777 Friggens, Paul. "Shameful neglect of sex education," PTA Magazine, 61:4-7, May, 1967.

3778 Fulton, W. C. "Why is there a sex information and education council of the U.S.? Why a new separate organization," Journal of School Health, 35:232-3, May, 1965.

3779 Gallagher, James J. "Sex differences in expressive thought of gifted children in the classroom," Personnel and Guidance Journal, 45:248-253, November, 1966.

3780 Gilbert, Mitch. "Sex is all the rage," Distant Drummer, 05 28 06 02 70

3781 Goodheart, Barbara. "Sex in the schools: education or titillation," Today's Health, 48:28-30, February, 1970.

3782 Goodman, W. "Controversy over sex education," Redbook, 133:9, September, 1969.

3783 Gordon, S. "Anti-sex education crusaders; a new threat to the schools," Changing Education, 4:26-7, Fall, 1969.

3784 Guttmacher, Alan Frank. "Sex education in the school," Parents Magazine, 44:40, April, 1969.

3785 Gwin, Pam. "Christopher Columbus died of VD," Great Speckled Bird, 06 30 14 01 69

3786 Haag, E. Van Den. "Why sex education?" Current, 112:31-5, November, 1969.

3787 Hammond, Liz. "A Radical solution to single family living," Damascus Free Press, 05 -- 05 01 69

3788 Harris, E., D. Harris, and J. L. Donaldson. "Innovative programs in sex education with study-discussion program," PTA Magazine, 64:26-8, 35-6, January, 1970.

3789 Hartley, Ruth E. "Children's perceptions of sex preference in four culture groups," Journal of Marriage and the Family, 31:380-387, May, 1969.

3790 _____. "Current patterns in sex roles: children's perspectives," Journal of the National Association of Women Deans and Counselors, 25:3-13, October, 1961.

3791 Hawkins, B. A. "How one city teaches sex education and family life," PTA Magazine, 63:24-6, June, 1969.

3792 Heifetz, Henry. "The Anti-social act of writing," Studies On The Left, 4:3-20, Number 2, 1964. (Legal and respectable attitudes towards sex and the variations in the way it is handled in America.)

3793 Hendryson, Elizabeth. "The Case for sex education," PTA Magazine, 63:20-21, May, 1969.

3794 Higdon, R. M. "How mothers answer--where do babies come from?" Today's Health, 48:34-5, October, 1970.

3795 Hill, P. L. "Deviations from sexual norms," New Jersey Education Association Review, 39:417-19, March, 1966.

3796 Hoag, Van Den. "Why sex education," National Review, 21:956-8, September 23, 1969.

3797 Hoffman, Martin. "Homosexuality," Today's Education, 59:46, November, 1970.

3798 Hoffman, R. J. "Teachers view; should schools teach sex education?" Minnesota Journal of Education, 47:27, December, 1966.

3799 Holzman, S. "Will the schools survive the attack on sex education," Scholastic Teacher--Scholastic Teacher Secondary Teachers Supplement, October 6, 1969, pp. 10-12.

3800 Holzschlag, P. "Is Catch-22 male chauvinest?" Commonweal, 93:69-70, October 16, 1970. (Discussion.)

3801 Hope, David. "Sexual liberty movement to follow civil rights," Los Angeles Free Press, 04 09 04 02 65 ("Young people should be educated completely about their sexuality.")

3802 Hoyman, H. S. "Should we teach about birth control in high school sex education," Education Digest, 34:20-3, February, 1969.

3803 Huber, Joe. "Married students vs. married dropouts," Phi Delta Kappan, 52:115, October, 1970. ("How do our schools treat students who have married? This report of a survey of 827 schools in the North Central Area provides some revealing answers.")

3804 Huffman, J. "Sex education in public schools," Christianity Today, 13:5-8, September 26, 1969.

3805 Johnson, Miriam M. "Sex role learning in the nuclear family," Child Development, 34:319-333, June, 1963.

3806 Johnson, Warren R., and M. Schutt. "Sex education attitudes of school administrators and school board members," Journal of School Health, 36:64-8, February, 1966.

3807 Josselyn, Irene M. "The Sources of sexual identity," National Elementary Principal, 46:25-9, November, 1966.

3808 Kaenel, K. von, and E. Zitek. "Sex education in the sixth grade," Education Digest, 34:17-19, February, 1969.

3809 Karmel, Louis J. "Sex education no! sex information, yes!" Phi Delta Kappan, 52:95-6, October, 1970.

3810 Kilander, Holger F. "Impact of offensive and obscene material on children and youth," School and Society, 97:326-30, Summer, 1969.

3811   Kirk, Russell. "American moral crisis," National Review, 21:858, August 26, 1969.

3812   _____. "Silliness in sex education--Catholic schools," National Review, 21:1274, December 16, 1969.

3812a   Kirkendall, Lester A. "Circumstances associated with teenage boys' use of prostitution," Marriage and Family Living, May, 1960, pp. 145-149.

3813   _____, and D. Calderwood. "Family, the school and peer groups; sources of information about sex," Journal of School Health, 35:290-7, Summer, 1965.

3814   Le Masters, E. E. (et al.). "A Cool look at sex education," PTA Magazine, 65:2-6, December, 1970.

3815   Lee, L. K., and M. Smith. "Opinions about sex education by low income negro mothers," Journal of Home Economy, 61:359-62, May, 1969.

3816   Levenson, Sam. "Sense about sex," PTA Magazine, 65:5, October, 1970.

3817   Liberation News Service. "Sex can kill," Liberation News Service, 12 14 04 02 68 (Evidence for the study was supplied by 1,000 married couples. A monkey headed the research.)

3818   _____. "Topless bottomless greet playboy in Iowa," Chicago Kaleidoscope, 02 28 23 01 69 (Nude confrontation at Grinnell, Iowa, with Playboy's manager of college promotion.)

3819   Lingeman, Richard. "Selling sex," American Notebook. New York Times Book Review, March 1, 1970, p. 20.

3820   Link, W. R. "Teachers view of sex education," Independent School Bulletin, 29:43-4, December, 1969. (Discussion 29:10-11, May, 1970.)

3820a   Lowrie, Samuel H. "Early marriage: premarital pregnancy and associated factors," Journal of Marriage and the Family, February, 1965, pp. 48-56.

3821 Luckey, E. B. "Sex education a school responsibility?" Virginia Journal of Education, 61:11-14, January, 1968.

3822 _____. "Sex education: develop an attitude before you develop a program," American School Board Journal, 156:20-2, April, 1969.

3823 McGuigan, F. E. "Social revolution and sex education," Clearing House, 43:421-4, March, 1969.

3824 McHugh, J. T. "Sex education in the Catholic schools," Catholic School Journal, 68:19-23, March, 1968.

3825 McLaughlin, J. "Education in human sexuality: two Catholic programs," America, 121:494-7, November 22, 1969.

3826 Magdeline, Sister Anna. "Can we communicate values?" Catholic School Journal, 68:28-9, March, 1968.

3827 Nowack, Dorothy, and Margaret M. Conant. "Sex education K through 6," PTA Magazine, 65:6-9, November, 1970.

3828 Oberteuffer, D. "Some things we need, and some things we do not need in sex education," Journal of School Health, 40:54-65, February, 1970.

3828a Pilpel, H. F. "Sex vs. the law: a study in hypocrisy," Harpers, January, 1965, p. 36.

3828b Poffenberger, Thomas. "Individual choice in adolescent premarital sex behavior," Marriage and Family Living, November, 1960, p. 326.

3829 Poland, Jefferson. "Sex courses cinch for 'shadow college'," Berkeley Barb, 02 11 03 02 66 ("Shadow colleges" often try to fill the gap on sex education which others avoid.)

3829a Reiss, Ira Leonard. "Premarital sexual permissiveness among negroes and whites," American Sociological Review, October, 1964, pp. 688-689.

3829b Reiss, Ira Leonard. "Sexual codes in teen-age culture," Annals of the American Academy, November, 1961, p. 55.

3830 _____. "Teenage sexual codes," Annals of the American Academy, 238:53-63, November, 1961.

3831 Reuben, D. "Love and sex," McCalls, 98:26, December, 1970.

3832 Rosser, D. "Are you ready to defend sex education?" School Management, 13:82, October, 1969.

3833 Smallenberg, C., and H. Smallenberg. "Teen-agers and sex; with study discussion program," PTA Magazine, 60:4-7, October, 1965.

3834 Smith, M. "Some reservations about sex education," Parents Magazine, 44:66-7, November, 1969.

3835 Somerville, Don H. "Sex education," Grinding Stone, 11 -- 08 01 69 (A reprint from Helix tracing aspects of sex education as it is taught today.)

3836 Spock, Benjamin. "Sex education in the schools," Redbook, 132:40, January, 1969.

3837 Star, Jack. "The Presbyterian debate over sex," Look, 34:54, August 11, 1970.

3838 Steinmetz, U. G. "Total approach to sex education," Spectrum, 45:8-9, September, 1969.

3838a Stokes, Walter R. "Our changing sex ethics," Marriage and Family Living, August, 1962, pp. 269-271.

3839 Stone, Carla Sydney. "Students initiate new course at Pitt," Pittsburgh Point, 06 19 10 03 69 ("CAS-1, Human Sexuality ... students and the administration sat down and talked and listened to each other. For the first time a revolution has taken place--quietly.")

3840 Sutherland, Z. "Books for young people," Saturday Review, 52:56, October 18, 1969.

3840a Tebor, Irving R. "Male virgins: conflicts and group support in American culture," Family Life Coordinator, March, 1961.

3841 Thorne, Richard. "A Step toward sexual freedom in Berkeley," Berkeley Barb, 02 04 05 02 66

3842 Wake, F. R. "Are parents the best sex educators?" PTA Magazine, 60:8-10, November, 1966.

3843 Warren, Margaret. "Library sex education: a report from Dallas," Wilson Library Bulletin, 44:593-4, February, 1970.

3844 Weinstock, H. R. "Issues in sex education," Education Forum, 34:189-96, January, 1970.

3845 Westlake, H. G. (ed.). "Argument for sex education in the elementary schools," Illinois Education, 58:115-116, November, 1969.

3846 _____. "Sex education controversy," Illinois Education, 58:117-119, November, 1969.

3847 Wilcox, John. "Rubbers, locusts, yak dung," Other Scenes, 05 -- 26 01 69

3848 Wilkes, P. "Sex and the married couple; W. Master's V. Johnson's therapy," Atlantic, 226:82-4, December, 1970.

3849 Woolston, L. S. "Sex education in the schools," New York State Education, 53:6-8, June, 1966.

3850 Zazzaro, Joanne. "Sex education; a controversy becomes a crisis," Education Digest, 35:9-11, November, 1969.

3851 _____. "War on sex education," American School Board Journal, 157:7-11, September, 1969.

VI. STUDENT DISSENT

BOOKS

3852 Abeles, Elvin. The Student and the university; a background book on the campus revolt. N.Y.: Parents' Magazine Press, 1969. (Contains sections on student activism.)

3852a Adams, James F. (ed.). Understanding adolescence: current developments in adolescent psychology. Boston: Allyn and Bacon, 1968.

3853 Ailken, Jonathan, and Michael Beloff. Short walk on the campus. N.Y.: Atheneum, 1966.

3854 Ali, Tariz (ed.). New revolutionaries: a handbook of the international radical left. N.Y.: Morrow, 1969.

3854a Altbach, Philip G. Student politics and higher education in the U.S.: a select bibliography. Rev. ed. Mass.: Harvard Center For International Affairs, 1968. (Introduction by Seymour M. Lipset.)

3854b American Civil Liberties Union. Academic freedom, academic responsibility, academic due process in institutions of higher learning. N.Y.: ACLU, 1966.

3854c _____. Statement on ROTC and educational institutions. N.Y.: ACLU, 1970.

3855 American Council On Education. Campus disruption during 1968-1969. Washington, D.C.: Publication Division: ACE, 1969.

3856 _____. Faculty role in campus unrest. Washington, D.C.: Publication Division: ACE, 1969.

3857   Anderson, Walt. The Age of protest. California: Goodyear Publishing Company, 1969.

3858   Atlantic Monthly (Periodical). Troubled campus. N.Y.: Little, 1966.

3859   Avorn, J. L., and Andrew Crane. Up against the ivy wall: a history of the Columbia crisis. N.Y.: Atheneum, 1969.

3860   Axelrod, Joseph (et al.). Search for relevance: the campus in crisis. California: Jossey-Bass, 1969.

3861   Baker, Michael A. (et al.). Police on campus: the mass police action at Columbia University, Spring, 1968. N.Y.: New York Civil Liberties Union, 1969.

3861a Bander, Edward J. (ed.). Turmoil on the campus. N.Y.: H. W. Wilson Company, 1970.

3861b Barbour, Floyd B. (ed.). The Black power revolt: a collection of essays. Boston: Extending Horizon Books, 1968.

3862   Barlow, Bill, and Peter Shapiro. An End to silence: the San Francisco State student movement in the sixties. N.Y.: Pegasus, 1970.

3863   Barzun, Jacques. The American university, how it runs, where it is going. N.Y.: Harper, 1968.

3864   Bayer, Alan E., and Alexander W. Astin. Campus disruption during 1968-1969. Washington, D.C.: American Council on Education, 1969.

3865   _____, _____, and Robert F. Boruch. Social issues and protest activity: recent student trends. Washington, D.C.: American Council on Education, 1970.

3866   Becker, Howard S. (ed.). Campus power struggle. Chicago: Aldine, 1970. (Trans-action Books, No. 1.)

3867   Beinecke, William S. Conflict and human progress. The S and H Foundation, Inc., June 5, 1969. 16pp.

3868 Bell, Daniel, and Irving Kristol. Confrontation: the student rebellion and the universities. N.Y.: Basic Books, 1969. (Collection of essays analyzing student revolt in the U.S. during the 60's.)

3869 Bienen, Henry. Violence and social change: a review of current literature. Chicago: University of Chicago Press, 1969.

3870 Birenbaum, William M. Overlive; power, poverty, and the university. N.Y.: Delacorte Press, 1969. (Available in Delta Paperback.)

3871 Blair, James W. Student rights and responsibilities. Cincinnati, Ohio: Associated Student Governments, 1969.

3871a Bolton, Charles D., and Kenneth C. W. Kammeyer. The University student: a study of student behavior and values. New Haven, Conn.: College and University Press, 1967.

3872 Bourges, Herne. The French student revolt. N.Y.: Hill and Wang, 1968.

3873 Breines, Paul. Critical interruptions: New Left perspectives on Herbert Marcuse. N.Y.: Herder and Herder, 1970.

3874 Bressler, Marvin. Student politics before the advent of the new left. Paper presented at the 32nd annual meeting of the Southern Sociological Society, 1969.

3875 Brickman, William W., and Stanley Lehrer (eds.). Conflict and change on the campus: the response to student hyperactivism. N.Y.: School and Society Books, 1970. (Short readings with some forty authors covering student unrest.)

3875a Bryant, Barbara E. High school students look at their world: issues, government, school, family, future. Columbus, Ohio: R. H. Goettler and Associates, 1970. ("...an attitudinal study. The opinions expressed are those of high school students--not what others think about them, but what a statewide sample of 1097 students feel about contemporary issues and their schools.... High school students are proposing changes ...the attitudes presented here, both in their communalities and differences, will be of interest to parents, as well as school administrators and all who work with those of high school age." "This study was completed in cooperation with the Ohio Department of Education, Kent State University, and the Buckeye Association of School Administrators.")

3876 Buchanan, James M., and Nicos E. Devletoglou. Academia in anarchy: an economic diagnosis. N.Y.: Basic Books, 1970. (Dissent is here given an economic diagnosis--consumers, producers, and owners.)

3877 Butz, Otto (ed.). To make a difference; a student look at America, its values, its society, and its systems of education. N.Y.: Harper, 1967.

3878 Cain, Edward. They'd rather be right: youth and the conservative movement. N.Y.: Macmillan, 1963.

3879 Califano, Joseph A. Jr. The Student revolution: a global confrontation. N.Y.: Norton, 1970. (Surveys the campus scene with implications directed toward the roots of the problems.)

3879a California. Regents. University of California. Special Forbes Committee. Report on the University of California and recommendations. Submitted by Jerome C. Byrne. California: 1965.

3880 California. University Academic Senate. Senate Committee on Education. Education at Berkeley. Report of the Berkeley faculty senate. Berkeley, California: University of California Press, 1965.

3881 California. University of California. Berkeley. The Minority student on the campus: expectations and possibilities. Papers from the 12th annual college and university self-study institute, July 6-9, 1970. Sponsored by the Center for Research and Development in Higher Education. California: University of California, 1970.

3882 Cantelon, John E. College education and the campus revolution. Philadelphia: Westminster Press, 1969.

3883 Cantor, Norman F. The Age of protest: dissent and rebellion in the 20th century. N.Y.: Hawthorn, 1970.

3884 Center For The Study of Democratic Institutions. The Establishment and all that. Illustrated by Robert Osborn. California: Center Magazine, 1969.

3884a Chambers, Merritt M. Freedom and repression in higher education. Indiana: Bloomcraft Press, 1965.

3884b Clouse, R. R. Linder (et al.). Protest and politics. South Carolina: Attic Press, 1968.

3885 Cohen, Mitchell, and Dennis Hale. The New student left; an anthology. Boston: Beacon, 1966.

3886 _____. The New student left. Rev. ed. Boston: Beacon, 1967.

3887 Cohn-Bendit, Daniel. The French student revolt; the leaders speak. N.Y.: Hill and Wang, 1968.

3888 _____, and Gabriel Cohn-Bendit. Obsolete communism. The left wing alternative. N.Y.: McGraw-Hill, 1968.

3889 Columbia University. New York. Fact Finding Commission on Columbia Disturbances. Crisis at Columbia: report of the fact-finding commission appointed to investigate the disturbances at Columbia University in April and May, 1968. N.Y.: Vintage, 1968.

3890 Corson, William R. Promise or peril: the black college student in America. N.Y.: Norton, 1970. (Deals with statistics and interviews to support the implications derived from a serious study regarding the past and present dangers in American society.)

3891 Cox, Archibald. Crisis at Columbia: the Cox

Commission report. N.Y.: Vintage Books, 1968.

3892 Coyne, John R. Jr. The Kumquat statement: anarchy in the groves of academe. N.Y.: Cowles, 1969.

3893 Danforth Foundation, and the Ford Foundation. The School and the democratic environment (papers and other materials drawn from a conference sponsored by the Danforth Foundation and the Ford Foundation) N.Y.: Columbia, 1970. (Focuses on symptoms concerning school unrest.)

3894 Davidson, Carl. The New radicals in the multiversity: an analysis and strategy for the student movement. Chicago: Students For A Democratic Society, 1968.

3895 De Jouvenel, Bertrand. Academic youth and social revolution. Washington, D.C.: American Council On Education, 1969.

3896 De Vane, William. Higher education in twentieth century America. Mass.: Harvard University Press, 1965.

3897 Dietze, Gottfried. Youth, university, and democracy. Baltimore: Johns Hopkins Press, 1970. (Surveys the role of the university and its relationship to youth and society.)

3898 Divale, William T. I lived inside the campus revolution. N.Y.: Cowles, 1970. (Campus activism written by a one-time under-cover FBI agent.)

3899 Divoky, Diana (ed.). How old will you be in 1984? Expressions of student outrage from the high school free press. N.Y.: Avon, 1969. (Paper) (A portrait of dissenting youth through the underground journals.)

3900 Douglas, Bruce. Reflections on protest. Virginia: John Knox, 1968. (Paper)

3901 Douban, Elizabeth, and Joseph Adelson. The Adolescent experience. N.Y.: John Wiley, 1966.

3902 Draper, Hal. Berkeley: the new student revolt.

N.Y.: Evergreen, 1969.

3902a Dunlap, Riley. A Bibliography of empirical studies of student political activism. Oregon: University of Oregon--Department of Sociology, 1969. (Mimeographed)

3903 Edwards, Harry. Black students. N.Y.: Free Press, 1970.

3904 Ehrenreich, J., and B. Ehrenreich. Long march, short spring: the student uprising at home and abroad. N.Y.: Monthly Review Press, 1969.

3905 Emmerson, Donald K. (ed.). Students and politics in developing nations. N.Y.: Praeger, 1968.

3906 Erickson, Kenneth (et al.). Activism in the secondary schools: analysis and recommendations. Eugene: Bureau of Educational Research--College of Education. University of Oregon, 1969.

3907 Erikson, Kai T. Wayward Puritans. N.Y.: Wiley, 1967.

3908 Erlich, John, and Susan Erlich (eds.). Student power, participation and revolution. N.Y.: Association Press, 1970. (Also available in paper.) (Collection of essays and interviews concerning student rebellions.)

3909 Esslin, Martin. The Theater of the absurd. N.Y.: Doubleday, 1961.

3910 Etzioni, A. The Active society. N.Y.: Free Press, 1968.

3911 Eurich, Alvin (ed.). Campus 1980: the shape of the future in American higher education. N.Y.: Delacorte, 1968.

3912 Executive Systems, Inc. The Establishment meets students. Lawrenceville, Illinois: Executive System, Inc., 1970. (Talks and panel discussions on the ideology of campus conflicts.)

3913 Feldman, Kenneth A., and Theodore M. Newcomb.

The Impact of college on students. California: Jossey-Bass, 1969. (Higher education series consisting of two volumes.)

3914 Feuer, Lewis S. What is alienation? IN M. Stein and A. Vidich, (eds.) Sociology on trial. New Jersey: Prentice-Hall, 1963.

3915 Fields, A. Belden. Student politics in France: a history of L'Union Nationale des Etudiants de France. N.Y.: Basic Books, 1970.

3916 First, Wesley. University on the heights. N.Y.: Doubleday, 1969. (Essays concerning life at Columbia University.)

3917 Fish, Kenneth L. Conflict and dissent in the high school. N.Y.: Bruce, 1970. (Conflicts, strikes, violence and unrest in high schools.)

3918 Foley, James A., and Robert K. Foley. The College scene. N.Y.: Cowles, 1969.

3919 Footlick, Jerrold K. The College scene now. Princeton, New Jersey: Dow Jones, 1967. (Paper)

3920 Fortune Magazine (Editors). Youth in turmoil. N.Y.: Time Inc., 1969.

3921 Foster, Julian, and Durwood Long (eds.). Protest! Student activism in America. N.Y.: Morrow, 1970. (Description of political activism of youth. Case histories of confrontations are included.)

3922 Frankel, Charles. Education and the barricades. N.Y.: Norton, 1968.

3922a Frazier, Edward F. Black bourgeoisie. N.Y.: Free Press, 1967. (Sociological analysis.)

3923 Freedman, Mervin. The College experience. California: Jossey-Bass, 1967.

3924 Freedman, Morris. Chaos in our colleges. N.Y.: McKay, 1963.

3925 Friedlander, Albert H. (ed.). New styles in campus

ministry, "never trust a God over 30," N.Y.: McGraw-Hill, 1967.

3926 Gardner, John W. The Recovery of confidence. N.Y.: Norton, 1970.

3927 Gerzon, Mark. The Whole world is watching: a young man looks at youth's dissent. N.Y.: Viking, 1969.

3928 Glazer, Nathan. Remembering the answers: essays on the American student revolt. N.Y.: Basic Books, 1969.

3929 Goldsen, Rose K. (et al.). What college students think. Princeton, New Jersey: Van Nostrand, 1960.

3930 Gorovitz, Samuel (ed.). Freedom and order in the university. Cleveland, Ohio: Western Reserve, 1967.

3931 Gould, Samuel B. Today's academic condition. N.Y.: McGraw-Hill, 1970. (Contends that the university is alienated from society and not students. Examines critically the traditional aspects of the teaching-learning process.)

3932 Grant, Joanne. Confrontation on campus: the Columbia master plan. N.Y.: New American Library, 1970. (Paper) (Demonstrations in the spring of 1968.)

3933 Graubard, Stephen R., and Geno A. Ballotti (eds.). The Embattled university. N.Y.: Braziller, 1970. (essays from two issues of Daedalus. A distinguished list of contributors discuss: campus unrest, university governance, and youth culture.)

3934 Gregory, Susan. Hey, white girl! N.Y.: Norton, 1970. (Personal account of a white girl at her senior year in a "black-inner-city Chicago school.")

3935 Gustaitis, Rasa. Turning on. N.Y.: Macmillan, 1969.

3936 Hare, A. Paul, and Herbert H. Blumberg. Nonviolent

direct action: American cases: social-psychological analyses. Washington, D.C.: Corpus Publications, 1969.

3937 Hart, Richard L., and J. Galen Saylor (eds.). Student unrest: threat or promise? Washington, D.C.: Association For Supervision and Curriculum Development, 1970.

3937a Hazen Foundation. Committee On The Student in Higher Education. The Student in higher education. New Haven, Conn.: Hazen Foundation, 1968.

3938 Heirich, Max. The Beginning: Berkeley, 1964. N.Y.: Columbia University Press, 1970. (The Free Speech movement and the problems of campus upheavals.)

3939 Heist, Paul. The Dynamics of student discontent and protest. Berkeley, California: University of California. Center for the Study of Higher Education, 1967.

3940 _____. Intellect and commitment: the faces of discontent. Berkeley, California: University of California. Center for the Study of Higher Education, 1965.

3941 Hersey, John. Letter to the alumni. N.Y.: Knopf, 1970. (The Annual letter written to Pierson College Alumni.)

3941a Hodgkinson, Harold L. Institutions in transition: a study of change in higher education. Berkeley: Carnegie Commission On Higher Education, 1970. (First of a two-part series.)

3942 Hook, Sidney. Academic freedom and anarchy. N.Y.: Cowles, 1970.

3943 Horowitz, David. Student. N.Y.: Ballantine, 1969. (Paper)

3944 Jacobs, Paul, and Saul Landau. The New radicals. N.Y.: Vintage Books, 1966.

3945 Jaffe, Harold, and John Tytell. The American

experience. N.Y.: Harper and Row, 1970. (Collection of essays pertaining to conflicts of students, both on and off the campus.)

3946 Jencks, Christopher, and David Riesman. The Academic revolution. N.Y.: Doubleday, 1968.

3946a Joughin, Louis (ed.). Academic freedom and tenure: a handbook of the American Association of University Professors. Madison, Wisconsin: University of Wisconsin Press, 1967.

3947 Kahn, Roger M. Rank and file student activism: a contextual test or three hypotheses. Paper presented at the 64th annual meeting of the American Sociological Association, 1969.

3948 Kane, J. Voices of dissent: positive good or disruptive evil? New Jersey: Prentice-Hall, 1969. (Paper)

3949 Kaplan, Morton A. Dissent and the state in peace and war. N.Y.: New York University Press, 1970.

3950 Katope, Christopher G., and Paul Zalbrod (eds.). Beyond Berkeley: a source book in student values. N.Y.: World, 1966.

3951 Kelman, Steven. Push comes to shove: the escalation of student protest. Boston: Houghton, 1970. (Description of the Harvard disorders of 1969, and an evaluation of the causes.)

3952 Keniston, Kenneth. The Uncommitted: alienated youth in American society. N.Y.: Harcourt, Brace and World, 1965.

3953 _____. The Young radicals. N.Y.: Harcourt, Brace and World, 1968.

3954 Kennan, George F. Democracy and the student left. Boston: Little, 1968. (Also available in paper.)

3954a Kent State. Kent State University. Chapter of the American Association of University Professors. Special Committee of Inquiry Report. Kent State tragedy. Kent, Ohio. 1969. (Report of the SDS protest demonstration on April 16, 1967. Also known as the "Rudrum Report." Part 2 of this report is titled "Investigation of SDS--Kent State University," and published by G.P.O., 1969.)

3955 Kerpelman, Larry C. Student activism ideology and personality. Proceedings of the 76th annual convention of the American Psychological Association, 1968. pp. 377-8.

3956 Kerr, Clark. The Uses of the university. Cambridge, Mass.: Harvard University Press, 1963.

3956a Kline, Stephen J. Principles and procedures of campus government. Stanford, California: Council for the Academic Community, 1970.

3957 Kornbluth, Jesse. Notes from the new underground: an anthology. N.Y.: Viking Press, 1968.

3958 Kronovet, Esther, and Evelyn Shick (eds.). In pursuit of awareness: the college student in the modern world. N.Y.: Appleton, 1967.

3959 Kruytbosch, Carlos E., and Sheldon L. Messinger (eds.). State of the university: authority and change. California: Sage, 1970.

3960 Kvaraceus, William C. (et al.). Negro self concept: implications for schools and citizenship. N.Y.: McGraw-Hill, 1965.

3961 Lasch, Christopher. The Agony of the American left. N.Y.: Knopf, 1969.

3962 Lee, Calvin B. T. The Campus scene: 1900-1970. N.Y.: McKay, 1970. (Confrontations from early 1900 to the present.)

3962a _____. Whose goals for American higher education? Washington, D.C.: American Council On Education, 1968.

3963 Lineberry, William P. (ed.). Colleges at the crossroads. N.Y.: Wilson, 1966.

3964 Lipset, Seymour Martin (ed.). Student politics. N.Y.: Basic Books, 1967.

3965 _____, and Philip G. Altbach (eds.). Students in revolt. Boston: Houghton, 1969. (Volume 14 of the Daedalus Library.) (Nineteen contributors present articles dealing with a variety of viewpoints concerning worldwide student activism.)

3966 _____, and Sheld S. Walim. Berkeley student revolt: facts and interpretations. California: Anchor Books, 1965. (Paper)

3967 Lloyd-Jones, Esther, and Herman A. Estrin. The American student and his college. Boston: Houghton, 1967.

3968 Lorber, Richard, and Ernest Fladell. The Gap. N.Y.: McGraw-Hill, 1968.

3969 Lombardi, John. Student activism in junior colleges: an administrator's views. Washington, D.C.: American Association of Junior Colleges, 1969.

3970 Luce, Phillip Abbott. The New left. N.Y.: McKay, 1966.

3971 McEvoy, James, and Abraham Miller. Black power and student rebellion. California: Wadsworth, 1969.

3972 Mallery, David. Ferment on the campus: an encounter with the new college generation. N.Y.: Harper, 1966.

3973 Martin, David (ed.). Anarchy and culture: the problem of the contemporary university. N.Y.: Columbia University Press, 1969.

3973a Martin, Warren B. Alternative to irrelevance: a strategy for reform in higher education. Nashville: Abingdon Press, 1968.

3974 Menashe, Louis, and Ronald Radosh (eds.). Teach-ins, U.S.A.: reports, opinions, documents. N.Y.: Praeger, 1967.

3975 Metzger, Walter P., Sanford Kadish, and Arthur De Bardeleban. Dimensions of Academic Freedom. Illinois: University of Illinois Press, 1969.

3976 Michael, Donald N. The Next generation: the prospects ahead for the youth of today and tomorrow. N.Y.: Vintage, 1965.

3976a Michigan. Michigan State Senate. Michigan State Senate committee to investigate campus disorders and student unrest. Lansing, Michigan: 1970. (Mimeographed)

3977 Miller, Albert H. Problems of the minority student on the campus. Washington, D.C.: Association of American Colleges, January 15, 1969.

3978 Miller, Daniel R., and Guy E. Swanson. The Changing American parent. N.Y.: Wiley, 1958.

3979 Miller, Michael V., and Susan Gilmore. Revolution at Berkeley; the crisis in American education. N.Y.: Dell, 1969. (Introduction by Irving Howe.)

3980 Mills, Theodore. Group transformation: an analysis of a learning group. New Jersey: Prentice-Hall, 1964.

3981 Minter, W. John. The Individual and the system: personalizing higher education. Colo.: Western Interstate Commission for Higher Education, 1967.

3982 Mock, Kathleen R. The Potential activist and his perception of the university. Washington, D.C.: American Psychological Association, September 2, 1968.

3982a Momboisse, Raymond M. Control of student disorders. California: MSM Enterprises, 1968. (Presents measures and proposals dealing with student disturbances.)

3983 Moos, Malcolm, and Francis E. Rourke. The Campus and the state. Baltimore: Johns Hopkins Press, 1960. (Concerns the managerial controls governing state colleges and universities.)

3984 Morison, Robert S. (ed.). Contemporary university: USA. Boston, Houghton, 1966.

3985 Morison, Samuel Eliot, Frederick Merk, and Frank Freidel. Dissent in three American wars. Cambridge: Harvard University Press, 1970. (Records public opinion during three of the "little wars.")

3986 National Conference On Higher Education. Stress and campus response, edited by G. Kerry Smith. (Current Issues in Higher Education) San Francisco, California: Jossey-Bass, 1968.

3987 National School Public Relations Association. Education U.S.A.: high school student unrest. Washington, D.C.: National School Public Relations Association, 1969.

3988 National Society of Professors (Forum). Campus unrest: what to do until the riot squad comes. Washington, D.C.: NSP, November-December, 1970. ("Crisis of understanding.")

3989 Nelson, Jack, and Jack Bass. The Orangeburg massacre. Cleveland, Ohio: World, 1970. (Documents the killing of three black students at South Carolina State, when they demonstrated over efforts to integrate a bowling alley.)

3989a New York (State) Albany. Temporary Commission to Study the Causes of Campus Unrest. The Academy in turmoil. Albany, New York: 1970.

3990 Newfield, J.A. Prophetic minority. N.Y.: New American Library, 1967. (Paper)

3991 Nichols, David C. (ed.). Perspectives on campus tensions. Washington, D.C.: American Council on Education, 1970. (Describes various views on sources pertaining to conflict and discontent on campuses.)

3992 _____, and Olive Mills. The Campus and the racial crisis. Washington, D.C.: American Council on Education, 1970.

3993 Nieburg, H. L. Political violence: the behavioral process. N.Y.: St. Martin's Press, 1969.

3994 Nowlis, Helen H. Drugs on the college campus. N.Y.: Doubleday, 1969.

3995 O'Brien, James. A History of the New Left--1960-1968. Boston: New England Free Press, 1968.

3996 Oglesby, Carl. The New Left reader. N.Y.: Grove Press, 1969.

3996a Orrick, William H. Shut it down: a college in crisis--San Francisco State College, October 1968-April 1969. A report to the National Commission on the causes and prevention of violence. Washington, D.C.: G.P.O., 1969. (Chronological account of the troubles at San Francisco State.)

3997 Otten, C. Michael. University authority and the student. The Berkeley experience. California: University of California Press, 1970. (Concerns the governance of colleges and universities using Berkeley as a case study.)

3998 Perkins, James A. University in transition. New Jersey: Princeton University Press, 1966.

3999 Peterson, Richard E. Reform in higher education--goals of the right and of the left. Washington, D.C.: Association of American Colleges, January 15, 1969.

4000 _____. The Scope of organized student protest in 1964-1965. Princeton, New Jersey: Educational Testing Service, 1966. (Pam.)

4000a Public Interest. The Universities. A special issue of "The Public Interest." N.Y.: National Affairs, Incorporated, 1968. (Pam.)

4001 Rapoport, Roger, and Lawrence J. Kirshbaum. Is the library burning? N.Y.: Random House, 1969.

4002 Research Organizing Cooperative. Strike at Frisco State. San Francisco: R.O.C., 1969. (Pam.)

4003 Ridgeway, James. The Closed corporation: American Universities in crisis. N.Y.: Random House, 1969.

4004 Robinson, Lora H., and Janet D. Schoenfeld. Student participation in academic governance. Review 1. Washington, D.C.: Eric Clearinghouse on Higher Education. George Washington University, 1969.

4005 Rogan, Donald L. Campus apocalypse; the student search today. N.Y.: Seabury, 1969. (Essays concerning student disaffection written by a Chaplain.)

4006 Rokeach, Milton. The Open and closed mind. N.Y.: Basic Books, 1960. (Paper)

4007 Roszak, Theodore. Making of a counter culture. N.Y.: Doubleday, 1969.

4008 Sampson, Edward E., and Harold A. Korn (eds.). Student activism and protest. California: Jossey-Bass, 1970. (Nine contributors discuss activism on college campuses.)

4008a Sanford, Nevitt (ed.). The American college: a psychological and social interpretation of higher learning. N.Y.: Wiley, 1962.

4009 _____. Where colleges fail; a study of the student as a person. California: Jossey-Bass, 1967.

4010 Sasajima, Masu (et al.). Organized student protest and institutional climate. New Jersey: Educational Testing Service, March, 1967. Research Bulletin. (Pam.)

4011 Schwab, Joseph J. College curriculum and student protest. Chicago: University of Chicago Press, 1969.

4012 Scimecca, Joseph, and Roland Damiano. Crisis at St. John's: strike and revolution on the Catholic campus. N.Y.: Random House, 1967.

4012a Scott, M. B., and S. M. Lyman. Revolt of students. N.Y.: Merrill, 1970. (Paper)

Student Dissent 361

4013   Seale, Patrick, and Maureen McConville. Red flag/ black flag: French revolution. N.Y.: Putnam, 1968. (Description of student revolts at Paris during May and June of 1968, and the resultant bloodshed.)

4013a Segal, Patricia. Annotated bibliography on student rebellion and revolutionary movements. California: Claremont Graduate School, Claremont, California, 1970. (Mimeographed)

4014   Seidenbaum, Art. Confrontation on campus: student challenge in California. Ward Ritchie, 1969. (Also available in paper.) (Describes nine California campuses during student confrontations in the crucial period of 1968-9.)

4015   Seligman, Ben B. Economics of dissent. Chicago: Quadrangle, 1968.

4016   Servan, Schreiben J. J. The Spirit of May. N.Y.: McGraw-Hill, 1969.

4017   Shinto, William. The Drama of student revolt. Valley Forge, Pennsylvania: Judson Press, 1970. (Paper) (Descriptions of "various dramatic styles such as epic and tragic to analyze the roles taken by particular student groups including the 'silent majority'.")

4018   Smelser, N. J. Theory of collective behavior. N.Y.: Free Press, 1963.

4019   Stanton, Charles M. The Committed student; a new and rare breed. Paper presented at the 21st National Conference on higher education sponsored by the Association for Higher Education. Chicago: March 15, 1966.

4020   Stinchcombe, Arthur L. Rebellion in a high school. Chicago: Quadrangle, 1964. (Paper)

4020a Stone, Isidor F. The Killings at Kent State; how murder went unpunished. Introd. by Stephen Young. N.Y.: Random House, 1970.

4021   Strout, Cushing, and David I. Grossvogel. Divided

we stand: reflections on the crisis at Cornell. N.Y.: Doubleday, 1969.

4021a Students For A Democratic Society. Port Huron statement. N.Y.: League For Industrial Democracy, Student Department, 1964. (The 1962 reorganization convention of the SDS at Port Huron, Michigan.)

4022 Suchlicki, Jaime. University students and revolution in Cuba. Florida: University of Miami Press, 1969.

4023 Taubman, William. View from Lenin Hills. N.Y.: Coward-McCann, 1967.

4024 Taylor, Harold. Students without teachers: the crisis in the university. N.Y.: McGraw-Hill, 1969.

4025 Taylor, Robert N. This damned campus. Philadelphia: United Church Press, 1969. (Paper)

4026 Tussman, Joseph. Experiment at Berkeley. N.Y.: Oxford University Press, 1969.

4026a Urban Research Corporation. On strike ... shut it down! A report of the first national student strike in U.S. history. Chicago: Urban Research Corporation, 1970. (A description of the May student strikes, listed by states, with accounts of Kent and Jackson States.)

4026b U.S. Library of Congress. Legislative Reference Service. The New Left: Students for a Democratic Society by Richard S. Jones. Washington, D.C.: 1969. (Multilith) (Includes a supplement.)

4026c U.S. President. Commission on an All-Volunteer Armed Force. The Report of the President's commission on an all-volunteer armed force. Washington, D.C.: G.P.O., 1970. (Also published by Collier Books, and is alternately known as "The Gates Commission Report.")

4026d U.S. Senate. Committee On Government Operation. Permanent Subcommittee on Investigations. Staff study of campus riots and disorders, October

1967-May 1969. Washington, D.C.: G.P.O., 1969.

4027 Von Hoffman, Nicholas. The Multiversity: a personal report on what happens to today's students at American universities. N.Y.: Holt, 1966.

4028 Wallerstein, Immanuel M. University in turmoil; the politics of change. N.Y.: Atheneum, 1969.

4029 Waskow, Arthur I. Running riot; official disaster and creative disorder in American society. N.Y.: Herder and Herder, 1970.

4030 Weaver, Gary R., and James H. Weaver (eds.). The University and revolution. New Jersey: Prentice-Hall, 1970. (Paper)

4031 Westby, David L. The Alienation of generations and status politics: alternative explanations of student political activism. IN Roberta Sigel (ed.) Political Socialization. N.Y.: Random House, 1968.

4032 Westley, William. The Silent majority. California: Jossey-Bass, 1969.

4033 Williams, Sylvia Berry. Hassling. Boston: Little, 1970. (Describes built-up pressures between students and administration at Cubberley High School in Palo Alto, California.)

4033a Williamson, E.G., and John L. Cowan. The American student's freedom of expression; a research appraisal. Minneapolis: University of Minnesota Press, 1966.

4034 Wolff, Robert Paul. The Ideal of the university. Boston: Beacon, 1969.

4035 Wolin, Sheldon S., and John H. Schaar. The Berkeley rebellion and beyond: essays on politics and education in the technological society. N.Y.: Random House, 1970. (Paper)

4036 Young, Alfred F. Dissent: explorations in the history of American radicalism. De Kalb: Northern Illinois University Press, 1968.

4037 Zinn, Howard. SNCC: the new abolitionists. Boston: Beacon, 1969.

4038 Zorza, Richard. The Right to say we: the adventures of a young Englishman at Harvard and in the youth movement. N.Y.: Praeger, 1969. (An account of the meetings at Harvard stadium in support of the strike demands.)

4039 Zweig, Ferdynand. The Student in the age of anxiety. N.Y.: Free Press, 1964.

EDITORIALS

4040 "Academic calm of centuries broken by a rampage," Life, 66:24-35, April 25, 1969.

4041 "American youth: its outlook is changing the world," (A Special Issue) Fortune, 79: Number 1, January, 1969.

4042 "Another type of student activism--helping people," U.S. News, 67:32-34, October 27, 1969.

4043 "Answer to riots--the Rochester Plan," U.S. News, 67:58-61, August 4, 1969.

4044 "Answers to liberal questions on campus uprising," Guardian, 06 06 09 01 70 (The article circulated by the New University Conference. Typical 'liberals' problems are posed and replies are given.)

4045 "At war with war," Time, 95:6-11, May 18, 1970.

4046 "Behind the unrest in high schools," U.S. News, 66:12, June 2, 1969.

4047 "Berkeley's Bastille Day," Willamette Bridge, 07 18 06 01 69

4048 "Black students disrupt southern high schools," Liberation News Service, 01 25 04 02 69

Student Dissent 365

4049 "Blacks in south react to murders," Guardian, 05 30 07 01 70 (Organizing of the black militants in the south.)

4050 "Boycotts ... and more boycotts," High School Independent Press, 10 07 12 01 68 (Black students present their demands in Elizabeth and Linden, New Jersey High Schools.)

4051 "Busting the ban on SDS," Nola Express, 09 12 06 01 69

4052 "California: university on trial," Newsweek, 76:83-94, November 23, 1970.

4053 "Campus communique," Time, 95:44-45, April 20, 1970.

4054 "Campus crackdown: colleges strike back at violence," U.S. News, 69:16-20, September 7, 1970.

4055 "Campus crisis: report to Nixon on causes of student unrest," U.S. News, 69:28-29, August 3, 1970.

4056 "Campus meets legislature," Time, 95:47-48, June 8, 1970.

4057 "Campus politics," New Republic, 163:10, August 1, 1970.

4058 "Campus revolt: no end in sight," U.S. News, 68:82, April 13, 1970.

4059 "Campus revolts over?" U.S. News, 68:53-55, February 16, 1970.

4060 "Campus '69: the quiet year--so far," Life, 67:40-46, December 12, 1969.

4061 "Can we learn?" Connections, 03 11 14 01 69 (Struggle for demands at the University of Wisconsin.)

4062 "CCNY--shut down," East Village Other, 04 30 06 01 69 (More student dissent at City College of New York.)

4063 "Chaos on campus," New Republic, 159:14-15, January 6, 1968.

4064 "Chicago's sit-in," Economist, 42: February 15, 1969.

4065 "Columbia University: still at the crossroads," Science, 162:878-884, November, 1968.

4066 "Crisis at Columbus, Ohio," Black Panther, 03 16 10 01 69

4067 "CWRU lies exposed," Burning River News, 05 30 04 01 69 (Student demands at CWRU.)

4068 "Dissent," Life, 66:38-43, January 10, 1969.

4069 "Duke gassed," Kudzu, 03 18 05 03 69 (Blacks and others protest over tokenism and racism. Police gassed administration building at Duke University.)

4070 "Education," San Diego Free Press, 01 01 07 03 69

4071 "A Fist fight on a quiet campus," Liberation News Service, 11 07 12 02 68 (Confrontation at George Washington University at the SDS sponsored student strike rally.)

4072 "The Following is the complete text of President Walker's reply to the nine student demands," Water Tunnel, 03 10 03 01 69

4073 "Free high school classes open Monday," Pittsburgh Point, 06 26 06 03 69 (No classrooms and both teacher and student plan "what they want to study and how they want to go about it." Courses are taught by volunteers.)

4074 "Goals of (and obstacles to) first international education year--1970," Phi Delta Kappan, 51:250, January, 1970.

4075 "Guard fired in self-defense," U.S. News, 69:33-35, November 2, 1970.

4076 "Harvard and beyond; university under siege," Time,

93:47-50, April 18, 1969.

4077 "High school activists tell what they want," Nation's Schools, 83:30, December, 1968.

4078 "High school confidential," Washington Free Press, 09 -- 07 01 69

4079 "High school students unite," Fifth Estate, 10 17 04 03 68 (Student ferment at Mumford High School in Detroit.)

4080 "High schools--mass liberation: what they do, who they are, what they say," Old Mole, 10 24 08 01 69 (Description of high schools in Boston, and their organizational efforts.)

4081 "How do you view what's happening at Harvard?" Radcliffe Quarterly, June, 1969.

4082 "How San Diego cops solved the bussing question at Lincoln High School," San Diego Free Press, 04 25 01 06 69 (Twenty-two student demands presented to the administration at Lincoln High in San Diego.)

4083 "How to keep order without killing," Time, 95:25-26, May 25, 1970.

4084 "How to reduce campus disorder ... excerpts from statement by the National Commission on the causes and prevention of violence," U.S. News, 66:92-94, June 23, 1969.

4085 "How TWA, Bevo Francis, Che Guevara and the yippies conspired to cross state lines to commit campus riots," Abas, 05 -- 08 01 69

4086 "Impact of college unrest--Scranton Commission's view," U.S. News, 69:69, October 5, 1970.

4087 "In the aftermath of Kent State indictments," U.S. News, 69:32-3, November 2, 1970.

4088 "An intimate revolution in campus life," Life, 69:32-40, November 20, 1970.

4089 "Jackson State: 1,000 rounds in 7 seconds," Rolling Stone, 06 11 01 01 70

4090 "Jerry Farber talks at SDSC--knocks grading," San Diego Free Press, 11 30 02 01 68

4091 "Kent and Cambodia," Commonweal, 14:235-36, May, 1970.

4092 "Kent State," Grok, 06 -- 19 01 70

4093 "The Kent State case," Newsweek, 75:33-34, May 25, 1970.

4094 "Kent State: four deaths at noon," Life, 68:31, May 15, 1970.

4095 "Kent State: martyrdom that shook the country," Time, 95:12-13, May 18, 1970.

4096 "Lesson in free speech," Great Speckled Bird, 03 02 03 02 70

4097 "Listen to youths, Hickel mutes Nixon," U.S. News, 68:84, May 18, 1970.

4098 "Mood of America," U.S. News, 67:22-26, July 7, 1969.

4099 "More nude-ins for SF state," Berkeley Barb, 10 06 04 04 67

4100 "More on campus atrocity No. 2," Spectator, 04 22 23 01 69

4101 "Muckraking: 1968--Hail Columbia!" Muckrakers Guide, Ramparts--Special collector's edition, pp. 115-119.

4102 "Mutiny at a great university," Life, 64:36, May 10, 1968.

4103 "My God! They're killing us," Newsweek, 75:31-33, May 18, 1970.

4104 "The New student crusade: working in the system," Time, 95:19-20, May 25, 1970.

Student Dissent 369

4105 "New University Conference (NUC) program on war and militarization," Pittsburgh Point, 04 03 01 02 69 (Newly formed organization of both graduate and undergraduate students at the University of Pittsburgh.)

4106 "Newark Hi: fed up!" Heterodoxical Voice, 05 -- 04 03 69 (Description of student dissatisfactions at Newark High School.)

4107 "Nixon and Hayakawa hang from the same purse string," San Diego Free Press, 01 30 03 03 69 ("Who is trying to buy U.C. and State Colleges?")

4108 "Nixon's effort to solve problems of youth unrest," U.S. News, 67:74-78, November 17, 1969.

4109 "And Now Yale," Time, 95:59-60, May 4, 1970.

4110 "One school board's policy on student dissent," School Management, 13:43-44, August, 1969.

4111 "One week in Paris," Ramparts, 6:20-23, June 29, 1968.

4112 "Oppression at Delta State," Kudzu, 12 17 03 01 68 (Protest by students over dormitory living conditions.)

4113 "Outside agitators," Washington Free Press, 06 15 15 01 69

4114 "Peace on campuses--new survey," U.S. News, 69:66, November 16, 1970.

4115 "Penn students win demands," Campus Underground, 03 10 06 01 69 (Confrontation between students and the University Board of Trustees relating to university expansion into ghetto areas in Philadelphia.)

4116 "Police incite riots: strike continues at Berkeley," San Diego Free Press, 02 28 06 01 69

4117 "Policing the campus," Time, 95:44, May 25, 1970.

4118 "Politics and the university," Newsweek, 75:96-7, May 18, 1970.

4119 "Protest: make war, not peace," Time, 95:27, April 27, 1970.

4120 "Protest season on the campus," Time, 95:19-20, May 11, 1970.

4121 "The Radical center," Humanist, 30:5-7, May-June, 1970.

4122 "The Radicals move in," Newsweek, 75:33-34, April 27, 1970.

4123 "The Real crisis on the campus," U.S. News, 66:40-44, May 19, 1969. (An interview with Sidney Hook.)

4124 "The Real revolution on campus," U.S. News, 68:28-31, January 12, 1970.

4125 "The Rebellion of the campus," Newsweek, 75:28-30, May 18, 1970.

4126 "Recommendations on student activism in high schools," School and Society, 97:342-43, October, 1969.

4127 "Remember Kent," Pittsburgh Fair Witness, 11 23 03 01 70 (Investigation of the incidents on May 1-4, 1970.)

4128 "The Revolt of the student prince," Realites, 232:62-71, March, 1970.

4129 "R.O.T.C. war games on campus," News From Nowhere, 1:2, Summer, 1969.

4130 "Seaside bewitched," Willamette Bridge, 07 18 07 01 69

4131 "S.D.S.," News From Nowhere, 1:8, Summer, 1969.

4132 "SDS runs CIA off Duke campus," North Carolin Anvil, 02 14 03 01 70

Student Dissent 371

4133 "The Silent minority on campus," Grok, 09 -- 07 01 70 (About the governance of the campuses as compared with power and decision-making in the business world.)

4134 "Special report: student unrest in public schools," School Management, 12:50-98, November, 1968.

4135 "Spring riot season--coming on strong," U.S. News, 68:40, May 4, 1970.

4136 "State college," Distant Drummer, 03 06 03 01 69 (Confrontation at Penn State University.)

4137 "Statement by the New York High School Student Union," Liberation News Service, 04 10 15 01 69 (Demonstration to free the 21 Black Panthers at Long Island City High School.)

4138 "Strange hold," News From Nowhere, 11 -- 02 01 68 (Administration vs. students at Northern Illinois University.)

4139 "Strategies for coping with student disruption," School Management, 13:45-65, June, 1969.

4140 "The Strike begins," Connections, 02 05 01 01 69 (Demands presented by students at University of Wisconsin, Madison. Reprinted from San Francisco Express Times.)

4141 "Student activism steers away from SDS and toward educational reforms," Nation's Schools, 84:41, July, 1969.

4142 "A Student campaign to get peace elected," Life, 68:45-48, June 5, 1970.

4143 "Student leaders denounce state college Chancellor Dunke," San Diego Free Press, 01 16 03 01 69

4144 "Student power and the business of intellectuals," Ramparts, 6:24-25, June 29, 1968. (An interview with the controversial leader of the Nanterre group Daniel Cohn-Bendit. Also known as "Danny the Red.")

4145 "Student power at Hartford public," Hartford's Other Voice, 07 14 06 01 69

4146 "Student protest here and abroad," Newsweek, 71:40-48, May 6, 1968.

4147 "Student unrest in Michigan: one state's protest profile," College and University Business, 48:72-75, March, 1970.

4147a "Student unrest will spread to high schools many fear," Nation's Schools, 82:71, September, 1968.

4148 "Student violence: into a more dangerous era," U.S. News, 68:28-31, May 18, 1970.

4149 "Student violence widens range," U.S. News, 68:24-26, March 16, 1970.

4150 "Students fight back at Durfee High," Old Mole, 03 28 05 01 69 (Confrontation with administrators over dress code, academic tracking system, etc. at Durfee High School at Fall River, Mass.)

4151 "Students for a Democratic stomach ache," Miami Free Press, 06 06 05 02 69 (A 'sick-in' at Florida State University.)

4152 "Students in a ferment, chew out the nation," Life, 58:24-33, April 30, 1965.

4153 "Study of Columbia situation," School and Society, 96:389-390, November 9, 1968.

4154 "Teacher's role in campus revolt," U.S. News, 68:36-38, June 15, 1970.

4155 "Temple students turn tables," Distant Drummer, 04 30 03 01 70

4156 "Terrorism on the left," Newsweek, 75:26-28, March 23, 1970.

4157 "Troubled campus: an Atlantic Supplement," Atlantic, 216:107-160, November, 1965.

4158 "Trustee Power: Death Valley to Disneyland," San

Diego Free Press, 01 01 08 01 69 (Trustees, profiteers, and the educational system in California.)

4159 "UCSD tension grows: Marcuse re-hiring," San Diego Free Press, 01 01 09 02 69

4160 "Under a sigh of peace," Life, 67:33-35, October 24, 1969.

4161 "Universities in ferment," Newsweek, 75:66-68, June 15, 1970.

4162 "The Universities: rulers and rebels," Nation, 211:169, September 7, 1970.

4163 "UTA tense, rebel theme remains," Dallas Notes, 11 19 03 01 69

4164 "Voice of protest," Newsweek, 75:73, May 18, 1970.

4164a "What happens when students criticize," Nation's Schools, 84:59-60, September, 1969.

4164b "What high school activists are doing," Nation's Schools, 85:61-66, March, 1969.

4165 "What student activists are doing," Nation's Schools, 83:61-66, March, 1969.

4166 "What's behind Japan's high school radicals?" Atlas, 19:21, June, 1970.

4167 "What's wrong with the high schools," Newsweek, 75:65-66, February 16, 1970.

4168 "When if ever, do you call in the cops?" New York Times Magazine, May 4, 1969, pp. 34-5.

4169 "When the national guard is called," U.S. News, 68:32, May 18, 1970.

4170 "When the stones come on someone's going to be killed," Distant Drummer, 12 25 05 01 70

4171 "Who guards against the guard?" Newsweek, 75:33, May 18, 1970.

4172 "Who owns the park," Washington Free Press, 06 15 15 01 69

4173 "Will campus restlessness lead to improved education?" Phi Delta Kappan, 52:74-78, October, 1970.

4174 "Within police state you have pigs in library," Berkeley Barb, 01 24 08 01 69 (Police and students confront each other in the library at San Francisco State.)

4175 "Your education or your hair," Old Market Place, 03 15 04 01 68 (Individual hair styles on-the-line. A reprint from Liberation News Service.)

4176 "Youth unrest, what worldwide survey shows," U.S. News, 69:76-79, October 26, 1970.

PERIODICALS

4177 Abbott, C. Michael. "Demonstrations, dismissals, due process, and the high school: an overview," School Review, 77:128-43, June, 1969.

4178 Abram, Morris B. "Eleven days at Brandeis, as seen from the President's chair," New York Times Magazine, February 16, 1969, pp. 28-29.

4179 _____. "The Restless campus," College and University Journal, 8:34-39, Fall, 1969.

4180 Ackerly, Robert L. "Controlling student conduct," Education Digest, 35:12-15, April, 1970. (The article is condensed from The Reasonable Exercise of Authority, 7-19, published by the National Association of Secondary School Principals, 1969.)

4181 Akerlund, Knut. "Schools, strikes, and students: Swedish style," Phi Delta Kappan, 51:430-432, April, 1970.

4182 Allen, J. E. Jr. "Campus activism and unrest; adoption or (an) address, June 9, 1968," School and Society, 96:357-359, October 26, 1968.

4183 Allott, Gordon. "Campus unrest," Vital Speeches, 36:758-761, October 1, 1970.

4184 Andelson, Robert V. "Campus unrest," Vital Speeches, 36:619-621, August 1, 1970.

4185 Anderson, Barbara. "Ordeal at San Francisco State College," Library Journal, 95:1275-1280, April 1, 1970.

4186 Andrews, James R. "Confrontation at Columbia: a case study in coercive rhetoric," Quarterly Journal of Speech, 55:9-16, February, 1969.

4187 Anrig, Gregory R. "Trouble in the high schools," American Education, 5:2-4, October, 1969. (Also available in the American School Board Journal, 157:20-24, October, 1969.

4188 Anthony, Richard, and Philip W. Semas. "The Many voices of the New Left," New Republic, 160:12-16, June 29, 1968.

4189 Aptheker, Bettina. "Berkeley's meddlesome regents," Nation, 211:169-173, September 7, 1970.

4190 Ardery, Philip P. Jr. "Physiognomy of the radical left," National Review, 22:577, June 2, 1970.

4191 Aron, Raymond. "Student rebellion: vision of the future or echo from the past?" Political Science Quarterly, 84:289-310, June, 1969.

4192 Ashbaugh, Carl R. "High school students activism," Nation's Schools, 85:94-96, February, 1969.

4193 Ashley, Bob. "Durham High remains out-wardly calm," North Carolin Anvil, 12 20 07 01 69

4194 Atkins, Neil P. "What do they want," Educational Leadership, 27:441, February, 1970.

4195 Auerill, L. I. "Ecology of discontent," Christian Century, 86:835-838, June 18, 1969.

4196 Austin, C. G. "Student protests and the establishment," Journal of Higher Education, April, 1968, pp. 223-225.

4197 Avi, Zede. "What's in store for state," Berkeley Barb, 08 15 06 01 69 (Hayakawa and San Francisco State.)

4198 Avorn, J. L. "Columbia: to be a revolutionary or not to be?" Look, 34:13-14, May 13, 1969.

4199 Babbidge, H. D. Jr. "Student unrest and college athletics," Scholastic Coach, 38:5, October, 1968.

4200 Baker, David. "Pioneer students strike," Ann Arbor Argus, 04 14 03 03 69 (Protest over the "Free Press" policy of the administration at Ann Arbor's Pioneer High School.)

4201 Barlow, Bill. "Black ghetto at S. F. State," Berkeley Barb, 12 15 10 01 67

4202 Barton, Allen H. "The Columbia crisis: campus Vietnam and the ghetto," Public Opinion Quarterly, 32:333-351, Fall, 1968.

4203 Bay, Christian. "Comment: academic citizenship in a time of campus revolt," Trans-action, 6:4-7, January, 1969.

4204 _____. "Political and apolitical students: facts in search of theory," Journal of Social Issues, 23:76-91, July, 1967.

4204a Bayer, Alan E., and Alexander W. Astin. "Violence and disruption on the U. S. campus, 1968-1969," Educational Record, 50:337-350, Fall, 1969. (Campus unrest in some 382 institutions during 68-69 school year.)

4205 Beavan, K. A. "ROTC widely resented," Times (London) Education Supplement, 60, January 10, 1969.

4206 Beichman, Arnold. "Battle of Columbia," Encounter, 31:23-39, July, 1968.

4207 _____. "Will teachers be the new drop-out," New York Times Magazine, December 7, 1969.

4208 Bennett, John H. "High schools and the ban on the student press," New Left Notes, 01 06 03 01 67

4209 Berg, Kenneth R. "Tell it like it is," Proceedings of the 76th annual convention of the American Psychological Association, 1968, pp. 697-698.

4210 Berger, Pauline. "Student revolt at CCNY," Independent Socialist, 01 14 19 01 67 (CCNY-SDS rally and confrontation with the U.S. Army-Marine Corps over campus recruitment.)

4211 Bernreuter, Robert G. "The College student: he is thinking, talking, acting," Penn State Alumni News, July, 1966.

4212 Bettelheim, Bruno. "College student rebellion: explanations and answers," Phi Delta Kappan, 50:511-514, May, 1969.

4213 _____. "Student revolt; the hard core," (statement before the house special subcommittee on education, March 20, 1969) Vital Speeches, 35:405-410, April 15, 1969.

4213a Bickel, Alexander M. "The Tolerance of violence on the campus," New Republic, 162:15-17, June 13, 1970.

4214 Bishop, Gordon. "Linden, New Jersey, Friday evening February 7," Liberation News Service, 02 13 08 01 69 (Communication problems??)

4215 Blackburn, Dan. "Up against the marble wall," Nation, 210:719-721, June 15, 1970.

4216 Blank, Blanche D. "Running the campus," Nation, 210:690-692, June 8, 1970.

4217 Bloustein, Edward J. "New student and his role in American colleges," Liberal Education, 54:345-364, October, 1968.

4218 Bosc, S., and J. M. Bouguereau. "Exemplary student movement of Berlin," Black and Red, 01 -- 16 01 69 (Part I.)

4219 _____, _____. "Exemplary student movement of Berlin," Black and Red, 03 -- 54 01 69 (Part II.)

4220 Bottomore, T. B. "Students observed," University Quarterly, September, 1968, pp. 425-433.

4221 Bowen, H. R. "Student unrest in the United States," International Bureau of Education Bulletin, Fourth Quarter, 1968, pp. 236-240.

4222 Bradley, Gene E. "What businessmen need to know about the student left; how does it view violence and destruction; what does it owe communism; can its members be won to the corporate side," Harvard Business Review, 46:49-60, September-October, 1968.

4223 Brammer, Lawrence. "The Coming revolt of high school students," Bulletin of the National Association of Secondary School Principals, 52:13-21, September, 1968.

4224 Brann, J. W. "Continued at Columbia," Commonweal, 89:7-8, October 4, 1968.

4225 Brant, Pasha. "Are you willing to be a nigger again?" High School Independent Press, 11 18 A-6 01 68 (The "Ocean-Hill-Brownsville Project.")

4226 Braungart, Richard G. "Family status, socialization and student politics," Paper presented at the 64th annual meeting of the American Sociological Association, 1969.

4227 _____. "SDS and YAF: backgrounds of student political activists," Paper presented at the 61st annual meeting of the American Sociological Association, August 31, 1966.

4228 Brayman, Rick, and Mary Schonover. "Massacre at Kent State," Daily Planet, 05 25 01 01 70

4229 Brickman, W. W. "Anarchy vs. freedom in academia," School and Society, 96:346, October 26, 1968.

4230 Brienberg, Elizabeth. "More on FSM," Studies On The Left, 5:95-97, Number 2, 1965. (Questions concerning the governance of the U. of C. and its member campuses from the Regents on down.)

4231 Brock, William E. III. "Gut issues of campus unrest," College and University Journal, 8:45-48, Fall, 1969.

4232 Brooks, T. R. "Metamorphosis in SDS. The New Left is showing its age," New York Times Magazine, June 15, 1969, pp. 14-15.

4233 Brogan, D. W. "Student revolt," Encounter, 31:20-25, July, 1968.

4234 Browder, Leslie H. Jr. "What to do before students demonstrate," Nation's Schools, 85:86-87, April, 1970.

4235 Brustein, Robert. "Honest, intelligible radical politics," New Republic, 163:15-17, September 26, 1970.

4236 _____. "When the Panther came to Yale," New York Times Magazine, June 21, 1970, pp. 7-9.

4237 _____. "Whose university? The case for professionalism," New Republic, 162:16-18, April 26, 1969.

4238 Buchanan, James M. "Student revolts, academic liberalism, and constitutional attitudes," Social Research, 35:666-680, Winter, 1968.

4239 Buckley, Neil. "HUAC struggle at Penn State," Water Tunnel, 02 20 01 02 67 (President Eric Walker and the HUAC.)

4240 Bulkley, Joel. "Shortcomings in UNC disruption policy are illustrated again," North Carolin Anvil, 04 18 01 02 70

4241 Bunzel, John H. "Costs of the politicized college," Educational Record, 50:131-137, Spring, 1969.

4242 Burck, C. "Student activists: free-form revolutionaries," Fortune, 80:108-111, January, 1969.

4243 Burnham, S. "Twelve rebels of the student right," New York Times Magazine, March 9, 1969, pp. 32-33.

4244 Butler, William R. "The Campus and the student," Vital Speeches, 36:566-569, July 1, 1970.

4245 Carey, Richard W. "Student protest and the counselor," Personnel and Guidance Journal, 48:185-91, November, 1969.

4246 Casey, Thomas J. "Student unrest: roots and solutions," Liberal Education, 55:244-254, May, 1969.

4247 Cass, J. "Can the university survive the black challenge?" Saturday Review, 51:68-71, October 26, 1968.

4248 Cassata, Mary B. "Student unrest and the library," Wilson Library Bulletin, 45:78-85, September, 1970.

4249 Cassell. "Mississippi Valley State College boycott," Kudzu, 02 -- 03 01 69

4250 Chandler, Mike. "Peace cause on trial in students armband case," Dallas Notes, 12 03 03 01 69 (Description of a federal suit over the wearing of black armbands in Dallas Schools.)

4251 _____. "Suit filed against U.T.A's President," Dallas Notes, 12 03 09 01 69 (The "rebel theme" controversy at the University of Texas at Arlington.)

4252 Chapman, J. L. "Board of trustees and student behavior," School and Society, 96:363-364, October 26, 1968.

4253 Chappell, Bill. "Crime, some call it dissent," Vital Speeches, 36:423-425, May 1, 1970.

4254 Childs, Charles. "Guns come to Cornell," Life, 66:20-28, May 2, 1969.

4255 Clark, Marguerite. "Dangers of drug abuse," PTA Magazine, 62:8-11, May, 1968.

4256 Cohill, Judge Maurice B. Jr. "The Complex problem delinquency: struggle between young and old is continual and worrisome ...," This Week Magazine, Pittsburgh Press, Sunday April 20, 1969, p. 4.

4257 Conner, Frederick W. "Anarchist echoes in academia," Improving College and University Teaching, 17:157, Summer, 1969.

4258 Cottrell, Beekman W. "If ...," Pittsburgh Point, 06 26 09 01 69 (More controversy over the movie about the rebellion of youth.)

4259 Cox, Donald. "50,000 overkill at Independence Mall," Distant Drummer, 05 14 01 01 70

4260 Coyne, John R. Jr. "The End of the multiversity," National Review, 22:560-561, June 2, 1970.

4261 Cranston, M. "Are student rebels neo-communists?" Current, 104:19-25, February, 1969.

4262 Cronin, Peggy. "Call for student power at Wayne State," Fifth Estate, 05 15 03 01 67

4263 Cross, K. Patricia. "Some correlates of student protest," National Association of Student Personnel Administrators, 8:38-48, July, 1970.

4264 Cuozzi, Bob. "Sounds of the movement," Hartford's Other Voice, 07 14 07 01 69

4265 Daniels, John. "Eastern Michigan student action," Fifth Estate, 03 05 02 03 69 (Over 100 black students seized the administration building and chained themselves inside.)

4266 Davidson, Carl. "Neutralizing campus radicals," Guardian, 11 23 06 01 68 (College administrators developing counter-insurgency plans to handle student rebellions.)

4267 Davis, B. H. "From the general secretary; campus upheaval," American Association of University Professors Bulletin, 54:292-294, September, 1968.

4268 Davis, Roger. "Eastern erupts," Ann Arbor Argus, 03 13 03 01 69 (Upheaval at Eastern Michigan University.)

4268a De Cecco, John P. "High schools: decision making in a democracy," Electronic Age, 30:14-17, Winter, 1970-71. ("The Major source of conflict involves the students lack of choices both as students and as citizens.")

4269 Diamond, David. "Student and the teacher," American Record Guide, 34:1129-30, August, 1968.

4270 Diamond, Edwin. "Class of '69: the violent years," Newsweek, 73:68-73, June 23, 1969.

4271 Diamond, Steve (et al.). "The Columbia revolution," Los Angeles Free Press, 05 10 03 01 68

4272 Dick, Bernard F. "We/they: the new campus dialogue," National Review, 22:562-563, June 2, 1970.

4273 Dickie, Allan. "The New 'breed' on the university campus," Educational Forum, 33:27-29, November, 1968.

4274 Diekhoff, John S. "Campus unrest--review of the Scranton Commission report," PTA Magazine, 65:9-12, December, 1970.

4275 Divoky, Diane. "The Way it's going to be," Saturday Review, 52:83-84, February 15, 1969.

4276 Donovan, Bernard. "Jailbreak: New York high school shutting it down," Old Mole, 05 23 06 01 69

4277 Duberman, M. "On misunderstanding student rebels," Atlantic, 223:63-70, November, 1968.

4278 Duerr, Edwin C. "Police on the campus: crisis at SFSC," Educational Record, 50:126-130, Spring, 1969

4279 Dunbar, Ernest. "Trouble: the high school radicals," Look, 34:70-80, March 24, 1970.

4280 Eberle, Paul. "San Fernando Valley State--San Francisco State," Los Angeles Free Press, 12 13 12 01 68

4281 _____. "Valley State student uprising," Los Angeles Free Press, 11 08 03 04 68

4282 Eddy, E. D. "Scratching the surface: campus unrest in 1968, adaption of an address, June, 1968," School and Society, 97:16-18, January, 1969.

4283 Edgerton, Karl R. "UC Chancellor says 'Don't stop dissent'," Argo, 03 -- 09 02 69 ("The Universities purpose is to save people--not to throw them out.")

4284 Edwards, Clifford W. "Muhammad Ali on campus," Catholic World, 210:69-73, November, 1969.

4285 Eisen, Jonathan, and David Steinberg. "The Student revolt against liberalism," Annals of the American Academy, 382:83-84, March, 1969.

4286 Elam, S. M. "Does student power equal democracy's strength," Phi Delta Kappan, 50:1-2, September, 1968.

4287 Engo, Robert, and John Williams. "Blacks on campus," Nation, 209:537-40, November 17, 1969.

4288 Enrages of Harvard. "Guerrillas in the classroom: a review by those who done it," Liberation News Service, 03 27 15 01 69 ("An account of the Enrages themselves who have been sentenced to jail in their efforts to bring radical politics into the classroom.")

4289 Etheridge, Eugene W. "Student rights and the campus riots," College and University, 45:15-23, Fall, 1969.

4290 Etzioni, A. "Confessions of a professor caught in a revolution," New York Times Magazine, September 15, 1968, pp. 25-27.

4291   Euwema, Ben. "What's wrong with students," This Week Magazine, Pittsburgh Press, Sunday, June 8, 1969, p. 10.

4292   Evans, T. D. "How one college handled student unrest," Journal of College Placement, 95:96, April, 1969.

4292a   Fairlie, Henry. "How to keep a campus together," Interplay, 3:4-12, July, 1970.

4293   Farber, Jerry. "The Student as nigger," Distant Drummer, 01 08 11 01 70

4294   Fearon, Christopher P. "Campus protest and the administrator," Bulletin of the National Association of Secondary School Principals, 53:28-35, September, 1969.

4295   Fine, David. "Organizing in high schools, or hitting the system where it hurts," Heterodoxical Voice, 01 -- 10 01 69

4296   Fink, Newton W., and Benjamin Cullers. "Student unrest in the public schools," Clearing House, 44:4-15, March, 1970.

4297   Fischer, John. "Case for the rebellious students and their counterrevolution," Harper's, 237:9-12, August, 1968.

4298   Fish, Kenneth L. "Coping with student activism in secondary schools," Education Digest, 35:8-11, October, 1969.

4299   Flack, M. J. "Innovation and the university in crisis: three proposals," Educational Record, 34:349, Summer, 1968.

4300   Flacks, Richard. "The Liberated generation: roots of student protest," Journal of Social Issues, 23:52-75, July, 1967.

4300a   _____. "Social and cultural meanings of student revolt," Social Problems, 7:340-357, Winter, 1970.

4301   Fleming, K. "We'll blow up the world; a

nineteen-year-old U.S. terrorist tells his story," Newsweek, 76:49-50, October 12, 1970.

4302 Flexner, Hans. "Institutional response to change," Journal of Higher Education, 233-243, January, 1969.

4303 Fox, Josef W. "Quest for relevance," Campus Underground, 12 09 02 01 68 (Dr. Fox pleads for relevance in the curriculum in education.)

4304 _____. "Thoughts on campus rebellion," Campus Underground, 11 18 02 01 68 (Description of why no real revolution will take place on college campuses.)

4305 Friedland, William H., and Harry Edwards. "Confrontation at Cornell," Trans-action, 6:29-36, June, 1969.

4306 Frymier, Jack R. "Why students rebel," Educational Leadership, 27:346-350, January, 1970.

4307 Furlong, William Barry. "The Guardsmen's view of the tragedy at Kent State," New York Times Magazine, June 21, 1970, pp. 12-13.

4308 Gaddis, Mary, and Scott Brand. "The Student as commodity," News From Nowhere, 03 -- 10 01 69 (Protest demonstrated over student housing services at Northern Illinois University.)

4309 Galbraith, John Kenneth. "Berkeley in the age of innocence," Atlantic, 223:62-68, June, 1969.

4310 Gall, Dennis. "High school administrators hassled," Kaleidoscope, 01 17 03 01 69

4311 _____. "Homestead high school smothers student rights," Kaleidoscope, 02 14 02 02 69

4312 Garwood, John D. "Capitalism's greatest threat," Public Utilities Fortnightly, 83:25-31, February 13, 1969.

4313 Gideons, H. D. "Student activists and faculty irrelevance," American Association of Colleges for

Teacher Education. Yearbook, 180-189, 1968.

4314 Gitlin, Todd. "Revolution in the revolution," Los Angeles Free Press, 12 05 03 03 68

4315 G. K. "Day the campus shook," Berkeley Barb, 12 01 03 02 67

4316 Glassman, James K. "Students in France," Atlantic, 226:25-32, September, 1970.

4317 Glatthorn, Allan A. "From rebellion to reconstruction," Pencil In Title of Your Own Choice, 02 -- 01 01 69 ("A reprint from the April 1969 issue of the Pennsylvania School Journal.")

4318 Glazer, Nathan. "The Campus crucible, part I; student politics and the university," Atlantic, 224:43-53, July, 1969.

4319 _____. "Campus rights and responsibilities: a rule for lawyers," American Scholar, 39:445-462, Summer, 1970.

4320 _____. "Student politics in a democratic society," American Scholar, 36:202-17, September, 1967.

4321 _____. "Student power in Berkeley," University Quarterly, 404-424, September, 1968.

4322 Goldman, Louis. "Varieties of alienation and educational responses," The Record, 331-339, 1968.

4323 Good, T. L., and D. A. Bates. "Politics and youth; attitudes of young Americans," Clearing House, 43:396-400, March, 1969.

4324 Goodell, Charles E. "Bridging the gulf with dissenting youth," Current, 122:32-4, October, 1970.

4324a Goodheart, Eugene. "The Rhetoric of violence," Nation, 210:399-402, April 6, 1970.

4325 Goodman, Ace. "Top of my head," Saturday Review, 52:4, April 12, 1969.

4326 Goodman, Paul. "Black flag of anarchism," New

York Times Magazine, July 14, 1968, pp. 10-11.

4327 Gorton, Richard A. "Militant student activism in the high schools: analysis and recommendations," Phi Delta Kappan, 51:545-548, June, 1970.

4328 Gosselin, Bob. "Campus conspiracy," New Mexico A & M Conscience, 01 17 01 01 69

4329 Gottlieb, Art. "Fight to death," Berkeley Barb, 01 10 05 04 69 (The Teacher's strike at SF.)

4330 Gould, Howard. "UM finally gets it on; thank you Mr. President," Daily Planet, 05 25 01 01 70

4331 Graham, Dave. "Repression: How to fight it," High School Independent Press, 11 18 A-4 01 68 (History of the high school movement and the concerns of youth.)

4332 Grant, William. "Little student support for violence --Michigan's Fleming," The Chronicle of Higher Education, November 3, 1969, p. 5.

4333 Graubard, Stephen R. (ed.). "The Contemporary university: U.S.A.," Daedalus, 93:1027-1032, Fall, 1964.

4334 Green, Edith. "Campus issues in 1980," PTA Magazine, 62:18-20, April, 1968.

4335 Green, Ken. "Black at whitworth," Spokane Natural, 05 09 03 01 69

4336 Green, Randy. "Dorm beer busts," Spectator, 04 22 10 01 69

4337 Greene, W. "Militants who play with dynamite," New York Times Magazine, October 25, 1970, pp. 38-9.

4338 Griffin, B. B. "Harvard ablaze," America, 120:586-588, May 17, 1969.

4339 Griffith, W. "People's Park: 270' x 450' of confrontation," New York Times Magazine, June 29, 1969, pp. 5-7.

4340 Gudridge, Beatrice M. "Is student protest spreading to the high school?" Today's Education, 57:30-32, October, 1968.

4341 Haber, W. "Critique of student activism," School and Society, 97:138-140, March, 1969.

4342 Halleck, S. L. "Hypotheses of student unrest," Phi Delta Kappan, 50:2-9, September, 1968.

4343 Halperin, Irving. "San Francisco State College diary," Educational Record, 50:121-125, Spring, 1969.

4344 Hamburger, Hilary. "SF State college strike described by participant," San Diego Free Press, 01 01 08 04 69

4345 Harrington, John H. "L. A's student blowout," Phi Delta Kappan, 50:74-79, October, 1968.

4346 Harris, David. "The University's tragedy," Cauldron, 10 10 02 02 67 ("The real tragedy is that most students have bought the university built on their own degradation, lock, stock, and barrel.")

4347 Harris, Louis. "The Life poll: what people think about their high schools," Life, 67:24, May 16, 1969.

4348 Harris, S. "San Fernando's black revolt," Commonweal, 89:549-552, January, 1969.

4349 Harvey, William. "College students today: extremists or activists?" Phi Delta Kappan, 52:84-85, October, 1970.

4350 Hayakawa, S. I. "Gangsters cash in on student revolt: exclusive interview with S. I. Hayakawa," U. S. News, 668:38-41, February 24, 1969.

4351 Hayden, Tom. "Two, three, many Columbias," Ramparts, 6:40, June 15, 1968.

4352 Hays, Samuel P. "Right face, left face: the Columbia strike," Political Science Quarterly, 311-327, June, 1969.

4353 Heath, G. L. "Political extra-curricula at Upsala and California," School and Society, 97:223-227, April, 1969.

4354 Heimel, Cynthia. "Crepe paper revolutionaries," Distant Drummer, 04 17 02 01 69

4355 ———. "Temple action," Distant Drummer, 04 03 07 01 69

4356 Heitzer, Art. "San Francisco State students continue protest," Kaleidoscope, 01 17 06 01 69

4357 Henderson, Algo D. "Brick throwing at the colleges," National Association of Student Personnel Administrators, 8:17-28, July, 1970.

4357a Herman, Joseph. "Injunctive control of descriptive student demonstrations," Virginia Law Review, 56:215-238, Spring, 1970.

4358 Herwaldt, Fred. "Rapping with rebellious youth," Christian Reader, December 5, 1969, pp. 22-24.

4359 Hessen, Robert. "Campus or battleground? Columbia is a warning to all American Universities," Son of Jabberwork, 11 08 10 01 68

4360 Higby, Kirby. "The South campus caper," Berkeley Barb, 05 20 05 01 69

4361 Hilberry, C. "Civil disobedience at Oberlin," Educational Record, 133-138, Spring, 1968.

4362 Hill, E. "Revolution at the University of Connecticut," New York Times Magazine, February 23, 1969, pp. 28-29.

4363 Hitchcock, James. "The Romantic rebel on the campus," Yale Review, 57:31-37, Autumn, 1957.

4364 Hoag, Von den. "The Campus and the law," National Review, 47:1212-1213, December, 1969.

4365 Hoffman, Fred. "Local high schools in turmoil," Los Angeles Free Press, 12 20 01 01 68

4366 Hoffman, Fred. "San Francisco State: when worlds collide," Los Angeles Free Press, 12 28 01 01 68

4367 Hofstadter, Richard. "Columbia's ordeal," Phi Delta Kappan, 50:15-17, September, 1968.

4368 Hollister, Charles A. (et al.). "Rights of children," American School Board Journal, 156:8-16, June, 1969.

4369 Hook, Sidney. "Students, universities," Phi Delta Kappan, 51:195-198, December, 1969.

4370 _____. "Trojan horse in American higher education," Educational Record, 21-29, Winter, 1969.

4371 _____. "Who is responsible for campus violence," Saturday Review, 52:22-25, April 19, 1969.

4372 Hoover, John Edgar. "The SDS and the high schools," PTA Magazine, 64:2-5, January, 1970. (Part 2-- 64:8-9, February, 1970.)

4373 House Committee On Internal Security. "The Background of the tragedy at Kent State University," American Legion Magazine, 89:22-27, July, 1970.

4374 Howard, Alan. "High school round-up," Liberation News Service, 05 01 18 01 69 (High school offensive against the school system in Queens, New York.)

4375 Howe, Irving. "New course for the New Left," Saturday Review, 52:8-11, May 30, 1970.

4376 Hunt, Jane. "Principals report on student protest," American Education, 5:4-5, October, 1969.

4377 Hutchins, Francis G. "The Campus crucible: moralists against managers," Atlantic, 224:53-56, July, 1969. (Part II.) (See 4318 for Part I.)

4378 Hykes, Elizabeth. "Indiana University of Pennsylvania protests ROTC," Pittsburgh Point, 09 25 03 03 69 (IUP freshmen register opposition to the ROTC program with a march.)

4379   Israeli, Phineas. "Student masses win: UC battle," Berkeley Barb, 01 31 03 01 69 (Revolution at Berkeley and TWLF.)

4380   Jacobson, Jon. "Strike supporters ready for campus whenever it blows," Berkeley Barb, 01 03 05 03 69 (Confrontation between students and strikers at SF State, and the TWLF.)

4381   Jansen, D. G. "Characteristics associated with campus social-political action leadership," Journal of Counseling Psychology, 552-562, November, 1968.

4382   _____, and B. B. Winborn. "Perceptions of a university environment by social political action leaders," Personnel and Guidance Journal, 47:218-222, November, 1968.

4383   Janssen, Peter (ed.). "Universities under the gun," Newsweek, 73:26-30, May 5, 1969.

4384   Jessup, John K. "Yale proves dissent doesn't have to turn out that way," Life, 68:39-40, May 15, 1970.

4385   Johnson, Dale L. "On the ideology of the campus revolution," Studies On The Left, 1:73-75, Number 4, 1961. (Ideological similarities and differences between campus dissenters and the Cuban revolution.)

4386   Johnston, O. W. "Amnesty vs. order on college campuses," School and Society, 96:364-365, October 26, 1968.

4387   J. R. S. "The Great Water Tunnel obscenity trial: hanging a jury," Distant Drummer, 04 24 06 01 69 (Historical chronology of the underground paper Water Tunnel at Penn State University.)

4388   Kampf, Louis. "The Radical faculty," Humanist, 29:9-10, December, 1969.

4389   Katz, Joseph. "Student activism; its implications for education and career planning," Journal of College Placement, 32-35, December, 1968.

4390 Katz, Joseph, and Nevitt Sanford. "Causes of the student revolution," Saturday Review, 48:64-66, December 18, 1965.

4391 Kauffman, J. F. "Vietnam and the campus," Journal of College Placement, 111-112, October, 1968.

4392 Kaufman, Bob. "The Berkeley liberation program; who does it speak for? Who does it speak to?" Peninsula Observer, 07 14 12 01 69

4393 Kearn, Francis E. "Campus activism," Yale Review, 58:28-44, Autumn, 1968.

4394 Kelman, S. "Beyond new leftism," Commentary, 47:67-71, February, 1969.

4395 Keniston, Kenneth. "Report analysis: fact-finding commission on Columbia disturbances; Cox Commission," Harvard Educational Review, 373-39, Spring, 1969.

4396 _____. "Students, drugs and protest," Current, 5-19, February, 1969.

4397 _____. "Truth about today's college students," U.S. News, 60:42-7, May 30, 1966.

4397a _____. "What's bugging the students?" Educational Record, 51:116-129, Spring, 1970.

4398 _____. "You have to grow up in Scarsdale to know how bad things really are," New York Times Magazine, April 27, 1969, pp. 27-29.

4399 Kerpelman, Larry C. "Student political activism and ideology: comparative characteristics of activists and non-activists," Journal of Counseling Psychology, 8-13, January, 1969.

4400 Kerr, Clark. "A Cure for college strife: interview with Clark Kerr," U.S. News, 65:52-56, December 30, 1968.

4401 Ketels, Violet, and Renee Weber. "The Student revolt," Main Currents in Modern Thought, 123-129, 1968.

4402 Khoury, George. "Scenes," Hartford's Other Voice, 07 14 07 02 69

4403 Kinnison, W. A. "New power relationships on the campus; student and the non-academic employee," Journal of Higher Education, 39:309-315, June, 1968.

4404 Kirk, Grayson. "Message to alumni, parents and other friends at Columbia," School and Society, 377-383, October 26, 1968.

4405 _____. "Youth on the college campus," Vital Speeches, 32:248, February 1, 1966.

4406 Kirk, Russell. "The University and revolution: an insane conjunction," Intercollegiate Review, 6: Winter, 1969-70.

4407 Kirzner, Israel M. "The 'Power' problem on campus: an economist's view," Intercollegiate Review, 6: Spring, 1970.

4408 Kittredge, Jack. "Community and struggle at U. of Wisconsin," New Left Notes, 05 27 04 01 66

4409 Knowles, Warren P. "How to deal with campus chaos: interview with Wisconsin's Governor," U.S. News, 66:31-33, March 3, 1969.

4410 Knox, G. H. C. "Notes of a young radical; arts festival at Columbia University to benefit political prisoners," Saturday Review, 53:48-51, August 15, 1970.

4411 Kramer, Mark, and HSIPS. "It's happened to their youngsters too," High School Independent Press, 11 18 A-3 01 68 (Student confrontations with school officials at Massachusetts High Schools.)

4412 Krouse, Peggy. "Berkeley revisited: where social scientists fail," Phi Delta Kappan, 48:421, April, 1966.

4413 Kruybosch, C. E., and S. L. Messinger. "State of the university; authority and change," American Behavorial Scientist, 11:1-48, May, 1968.

4414   Kudela, Raphael M. "Facing student unrest," Clearing House, 44:547-552, May, 1970.

4415   Kukla, David A. "Protest in black and white: student radicals in high schools," Bulletin of the National Association of Secondary School Principals, 54:72-86, January, 1970.

4416   Kunen, James S. "Why colleges are revolting," News From Nowhere, 03 -- 02 01 69

4417   La Fong, Karl. "Jackson and Augusta massacre," Hartford's Other Voice, 05 26 02 01 70

4418   Lane, R. E. "Political education in the midst of life's struggles," Harvard Educational Review, 468-494, Summer, 1968.

4418a Lankes, George. "Campus violence and the law," Police Chief, 37:38-42, March, 1970.

4419   Laqueur, Walter. "Reflections on youth movements," Commentary, 47:33, June, 1969.

4420   Lasky, M. J. "Revolution diary," Encounter, 31:81-92, August, 1968.

4421   Lauter, Paul, and Florence Howe. "What happened to the free university," Saturday Review, 53:80-82, June 20, 1970.

4422   Lawrence, Buffy. "The Judge who couldn't laugh," Distant Drummer, 03 05 01 01 70

4423   Le Blanc, Paul. "SDS--past, present, future," Pittsburgh Point, 07 03 01 01 69

4424   Lee, Garber O. "Courts cite constitution to uphold 'Long Hair' rights," Nation's Schools, 85:86, February, 1970.

4425   Lee, Lawrence. "Let's halt the epidemic of addiction," Roto Magazine--Pittsburgh Press, 32-35, May 3, 1970.

4426   Lehrer, Stanley. "Higher education and the disenchanted students; excerpts from leaders, teachers, and learners in academe: partners in the educational process," School and Society, 97:427-31, November, 1969.

4427 Leonard, George B. "Beyond campus chaos," Look, 33:73-82, June 10, 1969.

4428 Levine, Herbert. "Common front at Buffalo," Nation, 210:520-522, May 4, 1970.

4429 Levitt, Dennis. "Isla Vista revolution--Round 3," Los Angeles Free Press, 06 12 02 03 70

4429a Liberation News Service, and E. G. Crichton. "People's Park," News From Nowhere, 1:6, Summer, 1969.

4430 Lipset, Seymour Martin. "Political thrust motivating campus turmoil," Saturday Review, 52:23-25, March, 1969.

4431 _____. "Rebellion on campus," American Education, 4:28-31, October, 1968.

4432 _____. "Student politics," Comparative Education Review, 10:No. 2, 1966.

4433 Litwak, L. J., and John H. Bunzel. "Battle for a college; why San Francisco State blew up," Look, 33:61-62, May 27, 1969.

4434 Lombardi, John. "A Lot of people were crying, and the guard walked away," Rolling Stone, 06 11 06 01 70

4435 Lowenhagen, Chuck. "Anatomy of a student demonstration," Bulletin of the National Association of Secondary School Principals, 53:81-86, December, 1969.

4436 Lowenstein, Eddie. "In-fighting at Acme," Distant Drummer, 11 21 06 01 69

4437 _____. "Where have all the protestors gone?" Distant Drummer, 01 29 03 01 70

4438 Lusky, Louis, and Mary H. Lusky. "Columbia 1968:

the wound unhealed," Political Science Quarterly, 84:169-288, June, 1969.

4439 Lutz, Rolland Roy Jr. "The 'New left' of restoration Germany," Journal of the History of Ideas, 31:235-252, April-June, 1970.

4440 Lynd, Staughton. "A Program for post-campus radicals," Liberation, 14:44-45, August-September, 1969.

4441 Lyons, Carl. "Court of last resort is people: return to private school threat to the establishment and the best antidote to the racial crisis: the school crisis," Common Sense, 04 01 01 01 70

4442 McAree, Christopher P. "Ecology of colleges and universities and the psychotherapy of students," Psychotherapy and Psychosomatics, 15:45, 1967.

4443 McClain, B. T. "In support of dissent," California Teachers Association Journal, January, 1969, p. 8.

4444 McCorquodale, Dave. "High schools blow up: black rebellion, white response," Heterodoxical Voice, 10 -- 10 01 69 (Rebellion in Delaware High Schools.)

4445 McDaniel, H. B., and Betty A. Truce. "Students should be taught the law," Today's Education, 58:23-24, April, 1969.

4446 McEvoy, J., and A. Miller. "On strike: shut it down, the crisis at San Francisco State College," Trans-action, 6:18-23, March, 1969.

4447 McGee, Senator, and Senator Cotton. "Should the U.S. continue to assist colleges where campus disorders exist," American Legion Magazine, 87:24-25, September, 1969.

4448 McGowan, William N. "About student unrest," Journal of Secondary Education, 43:255-59, October, 1968.

4449 MacGrew, John F. "Needed: a policy for riot control in schools and school districts," Journal of

Secondary Education, 43:291-93, November, 1968.

4450 McKay, B., K. Wilner, and A. Becker. "Some students speak: responses to the Columbia crisis," The Record, 57-65, October, 1968.

4451 McKenney, J. W. "Revolt of youth," California Teachers Association Journal, 4-7, January, 1969.

4452 MacLeish, A. "Revolt of a diminished man, excerpt from an address," Saturday Review, 52:16-19, June 7, 1969.

4453 McLeod, Richard. "Dissent and reaction in Missouri," Wilson Library Bulletin, 44:269-277, November, 1969.

4454 McLuhan, Marshall. "Where it's at, where it's going," Campus Call, 10:3-4, January, 1970. (McLuhan-isms on education.)

4455 McNett, I. "Campus unrest: confrontation increasingly means litigation," Science, 166:486-8, October 24, 1969.

4456 McPeak, Alice. "Kent, Kent, Kent, Kent," Burning River News, 04 26 01 01 69

4457 Maher, Michael. "War in Berkeley," Reconstruction, Vol. 1, Issue number 8, p. 4, 1969.

4458 Majoult, J. "Crisis in the university," International Bureau of Education Bulletin, 235-236, Fourth Quarter, 1968.

4459 Malone, D. H. "Testimony on student unrest before California legislature committee," American Association of University Professors Bulletin, 55:91-93, March, 1969.

4460 Marburger, Carl. "Trouble in high schools: New Jersey responds," Compact, 3:36-38, October, 1969.

4461 March of the News--Front Page of the Week. "Campus violence--no end in sight," U.S. News, 66:11-12, May 19, 1969.

4462 Marine, Gene, and Reese Erlich. "School's out," Ramparts, 19-25, December 14-28, 1968.

4463 Marshall, Sue. "VSC rips off student funds," Los Angeles Free Press, 08 14 07 02 70 (A confrontation between associated students of San Fernando Valley State College (Calif.) and the school administration over student funds.)

4464 Mathews, J. "Columbia sweats it out," New Republic, 159:8, October 5, 1968.

4465 Maxson, R. E. "Radical student government elected at Valley State," Los Angeles Free Press, 06 05 14 01 70

4466 May, Henry F. "Living with crisis: a view from Berkeley," The American Scholar, 38:588-605, Autumn, 1969.

4467 Mayhew, L. B. "Changing the balance of power," Saturday Review, 51:48-49, August 17, 1968.

4468 _____. "Consequences of student protest; summary of an address," School and Society, 96:388, November 9, 1968.

4469 Mead, Margaret. "Why students are angry," Redbook, 132:50, April, 1969.

4470 _____. "Women on campus," Campus Call, 10:7-9, January, 1970. (A plea for campuses to be less academic and more friendly to adult married women on campuses.)

4471 _____. "Youth revolt: the future is now," Saturday Review, 53:23-25, January 10, 1970.

4472 Menen, Aubrey. "Why French students riot," New York Times Magazine, April 26, 1970, p. 26.

4472a Meredith, Robert. "The New Left: an introductory bibliographical commentary," Radical Amerikan Studies, 1:3-8, May, 1970.

4473 Miles, Michael. "Whose university?" New Republic, April 12, 1969. Also in Current, Number 108,

June, 1969.

4474 Miller, T. K., and G. P. Pilkey. "College student personnel and academic freedom for students," Personnel and Guidance Journal, 46:954-960, June, 1968.

4475 Mills, Vicky. "Rebel theme ousted at U.T.A.," Dallas Notes, 11 05 03 01 69 (Militants protest at UTA ousting the confederate rebel theme.)

4476 Mitchell, John N. "Colleges must outlaw terror, excerpts from an address," U.S. News, 66:75, May 12, 1969.

4477 Mitzman, Arthur. "The Campus radical in 1960," Dissent, 7:142-148, Spring, 1960. (Student movements against segregation and bomb testing.)

4478 Morris, Peter. "The Meaning of the Berkeley war," New Society, 47-49, July 10, 1969.

4479 Morthland, John. "Why Toby Moffett stepped down," Rolling Stone, 06 11 12 03 70

4480 Moskowitz, Ronald. "Leaving the drug world behind," American Education, 6:3-6, January-February,

4481 Moss, Andrew. "Student movement prepares for revolutionary work," Peninsula Observer, 07 14 07 01 69

4482 Muller, Steven. "Restructuring the university," College and University Journal, 8:49-54, Fall, 1969.

4483 Nagler, Michael. "Berkeley: the demonstrations," Studies On The Left, 5:55-62, Number 1, 1965. (Chronology of the uprising at Berkeley, written by one from within, beginning with December 3, 1964.)

4484 Naramore, John A. "ROTC wounded!" Reconstruction, 05 21 04 01 69

4485 National Education Association. Research Division. "Teacher opinion poll: amount of student unrest," Today's Education, 58:87, September, 1969.

4486 National Education Association. Research Division. "What the courts are saying about students rights," NEA Research Bulletin, 47:86-89, October, 1969.

4487 Neff, C. B. "Administrative challenge of the new student activism," Journal of Higher Education, 69-76, February, 1968.

4488 Neff, Richard. "SDS Rizzo, the VFW and the plot to destroy nearly everything," Distant Drummer, 04 03 03 01 69

4489 Nelson, B. "Brandeis: how a liberal university reacts to a black take-over," Science, 169:1431-1434, March 28, 1969.

4490 Neumann, Harry. "The Permanent war of students and teachers," Journal of General Education, 21:271-279, January, 1970.

4491 New University Conference. "Degrading education," Spectator, 04 22 05 01 69

4492 Newcomb, Theodore. "University heal thyself," Political Science Quarterly, 351-356, June, 1969.

4493 Newman, Sally. "Modern methods schools," Pittsburgh Point, 08 14 06 01 69 (A description of the "English Modern Methods Schools." Team cooperation and effective communication is the key to the success of the system.)

4494 Niceswanger, Bruce (Bruno). "'That' kind of student," Campus Underground, 10 21 03 02 68 (The author explains the differences between 'this' kind of student and 'that' kind of student.)

4495 Nixon, Richard M. "Campus revolutionaries; the rights of students, an address," Vital Speeches, 36:546-548, July 1, 1969.

4496 Nobbs, Russ. "Authorities actions increase unrest," Spokane Natural, 05 09 01 02 69

4497 Noble, Jeanne L. "What are adolescents scared of," PTA Magazine, 63:6-8, October, 1968.

4498 Nottingham, Marvin A. "Conflict intervention in Palm Springs," Journal of Secondary Education, 44:147-49, April, 1969.

4499 Novak, Michael. "Students and the university: the vacuum," Christian Century, 87:413, April 8, 1970.

4500 Ohles, J. F. "Realities and student power," Record, 53-56, October, 1968.

4501 _____. "University and the unstudent," School and Society, 96:361-362, October 26, 1968.

4502 Oppenheimer, Martin. "The Student movement as a response to alienation," Journal of Human Relations, 1-16, 1968.

4503 Orbell, J. M. "Protest participation among southern negro college students," American Political Science Review, 61:446-456, June, 1967.

4504 Osborn, Jim. "Brown, black ghetto students strike East L.A. high schools," Los Angeles Free Press, 03 08 01 04 68

4505 _____. "High school walkouts: demonstrations sweep L.A. area, students protest sub-standard facilities, faulty curriculum," Los Angeles Free Press, 03 15 01 02 68

4506 Padgett, I. F. "New Breed in search of a new morality," Liberal Education, 435-442, October, 1968.

4507 Palmer, Charles. "College student unrest," Today's Education, 58:25-33, November, 1969.

4508 _____. "Where student power is headed," Campus Call, 10:5-6, January, 1970. (Analysis of the decade ahead by the President of the National Student Association.)

4509 Panush, Louis, and Edgar A. Kelley. "The High school principal: pro-active or reactive roles?" Phi Delta Kappan, 52:90-92, October, 1970.

4510 Parent, A. "The SDS and student unrest," Conscience,

08 -- 23 01 69

4511 Parente, W., and M. McCleery. "Campus radicalism and a relevant political science," Journal of Higher Education, 316-325, June, 1968.

4512 Parkinson, Tom. "Berkeley litany," Spectator, 07 15 09 01 69

4513 Payne, Raymond, Barbara Pittard, and C. Ray Wingrove. "Student reaction to campus demonstrations," Paper presented at the 32nd annual meeting of the Southern Sociological Society, 1969.

4514 Peters, C. F. "Activism: the message it holds for placement and recruitment," Journal of College Placement, 49-52, February, 1969.

4515 Peterson, Richard E. "The Student left in American higher education," Daedalus, 1:293-317, Winter, 1968.

4516 Petras, James. "Confrontation politics and intellectuals in retreat," Liberation News Service, 07 05 18 02 69 ("Students and the struggle against on-campus military and educational arms of imperialism.")

4517 Pietrofesa, John J., and William Van Hoose. "An Analysis: student dissent," Clearing House, 44:395-400, March, 1970.

4518 Pileggi, Nicholas. "Revolutionaries who have to be home by 7:30," Phi Delta Kappan, 50:561-69, June, 1969.

4519 Plimpton, Calvin H. "Communication to President Nixon made public May 2, 1969," New Republic, 163:7, May 17, 1969.

4520 Pohlmann, Bruce. "High school action," New Left Notes, 15 15 02 03 67 (SDS attempts at organization in Chicagoland.)

4521 Poole, John E. "Third world colleges, beware of ...," Black Panther, 03 09 07 01 69

4521a Powell, R. S. Jr. "Alienation of campus youth," Electronic Age, 30:4-6, Winter, 1970-71. ("Campus discontent arises from a sense of powerlessness and frustration and a feeling that society, and especially big business have neglected individual values.")

4522 _____. "Student power and the student role in institutional governance," Liberal Education, 55:24-31, March, 1969.

4523 Quann, C. J. "Student unrest. A double image," College and Universities, 44:256-262, Spring, 1969.

4524 Rader, Dotson. "More about Columbia," New Republic, 158:23-5, June 8, 1961.

4525 _____, and Craig Anderson. "Rebellion at Columbia; report from the barricades," New Republic, 158:9-11, May 11, 1968.

4526 Ratterman, P. H. "The New breed of students," Paper presented to discussion group 24 at the 21st National Conference on Higher Education, sponsored by the Association for Higher Education, Chicago, March 15, 1966.

4527 Reilly, William S. J. "Campus '69," Vital Speeches, 36:270-272, February 15, 1970.

4528 Reisman, D. "Changing campus and a changing society," School and Society, 97:215-222, April, 1969.

4529 Reiss, Ira Leonard. "The Sexual renaissance in America," Journal of Social Issues, 22:No. 2, April, 1966.

4530 Richer, Ed. "Campus liberation: another look at academic freedom," Los Angeles Free Press, 10 16 20 01 70

4531 _____. "The Student strike: collegiate revolt inevitable," Los Angeles Free Press, 05 29 20 01 70

4532 Rieker, Richard. "Time out on the campus," Pittsburgh Point, 10 16 07 03 69 (The Vietnam

Moratorium program at the University of Pittsburgh.)

4533 Ritchie, Miller. "Pea size colleges answer the campus rebellion," The Lion, 52:10-14, February, 1970.

4534 Roberts, Thomas B. "Campus explosion," College and University Journal, 9:35-36, Spring, 1970.

4535 _____. "Many student activists feel that middle-class society needlessly blocks personal growth," Today's Education, 59:22-3, January, 1970.

4536 Robinson, Chris. "But what do the students really want?" Guardian, 06 07 04 01 69 ("Should college students have a greater say in the running of colleges?")

4537 _____. (Comp.). "A Week in the life of ...the campus revolt," Guardian, 04 26 04 01 69 (Confrontations with police on the nation's major campuses.)

4538 Roche, John P. "Violence on the campus: police unpopular but necessary," Section 2--Pittsburgh Press, April 26, 1970.

4539 Rockefeller, John D. "In praise of young revolutionaries," Saturday Review, 51:18-20, December, 1968.

4540 Rogers, R. "Black guns on campus: Black Panthers and the U.S.," Nation, 208:558-560, May 5, 1969.

4541 Rowe, Robert N. "What place has college in a young man's life?" Phi Delta Kappan, 52:88-89, October, 1970.

4542 Rowland, Howard Ray. "The Campus ombudsman," Today's Education, 58:37-39, October, 1969.

4543 Rowls, Betty M. "Student unrest justified," College and University Journal, 8:40-44, Fall, 1969.

4544 Rubenstein, Ben, and Morton Levitt. "Rebellion and responsibility," Yale Review, 57:16-30, August, 1969.

4545 Rudd, Mark. "Victorious struggle," Nola Express, 07 18 11 01 69

4546 Ryan, J. J. "Student unrest: the educational reasons," Catholic World, 208:7-9, October, 1968.

4547 Ryan, W. G. (et al.). "Students search for freedom," Middle States Association of Colleges and Secondary Schools, Proceedings, 1967, pp. 80-92.

4548 Ryman, E. C. "Student revolt against society or against institutions?" International Bureau of Education Bulletin, Fourth Quarter, 247-250, 1968.

4549 Sampson, Edward E. (ed.). "Stirrings out of apathy: student activism and the decade of protest," Journal of Social Issues, 23: Number 3, July, 1967.

4550 _____. "Student activism and the decade of protest," Journal of Social Issues, 23:1-33, July, 1967.

4551 Sanford, David. "Kent State gag," New Republic, 163:14-17, November 7, 1970.

4552 _____. "Protest at Pennsylvania: a model for campus dissent?" New Republic, 160:19-21, March 15, 1969.

4553 Sapir, Marc, and Carrie Sapir. "Students shut counterinsurgency center," Peninsula Observer, 05 26 01 01 69

4554 Sayre, Nora. "Revolt for fun and profit," Esquire, 74:71-73, August, 1970.

4555 Schlesinger, Arthur M. Jr. "Existential politics and the cult of violence," Phi Delta Kappan, 50:9-15, September, 1968.

4556 Schrag, Peter. "After Kent State: the first hundred days," Saturday Review, 53:12-15, August 29, 1970.

4557 Schroth, B. A. "Violence and understanding: campus unrest and the Scranton Report," Catholic World, 212:119-22, December, 1970.

4558 Schultz, Roy. "Kick ass junction," East Village Other, 04 21 06 01 70

4559 Scott, Robert L. "Messages gauged on ivied walls," Quarterly Journal of Speech, 55:183-187, April, 1969.

4560 Seale, Bobby. "Revolutionary action on campus and community," Black Panther, 01 10 10 01 70

4561 Seeman, Melvin. "On the meaning of alienation," American Sociological Review, December, 1959, pp. 783-791.

4562 Selk, M. "Styles of handling student demonstrations," Bulletin of Atomic Scientists, 25:36-38, June, 1969.

4563 Selkirk, Errol. "The Blood runs cold," Berkeley Barb, 10 10 05 01 69 (The Black studies program at the University of California.)

4564 Semas, Philip W. "At Berkeley where it all began, activism has become a way of life," Chronicle of Higher Education, 4:1, January 24, 1970.

4565 _____. "Some students will take up guns: panel on campus unrest is told," Chronicle of Higher Education, 4:1, August 31, 1970.

4566 Shoben, Edward J. Jr. "Student unrest: some forms within chaos," Bulletin of the National Association of Secondary School Principals, 52:1-12, September, 1968.

4567 _____. "Students and civil disobedience," Journal of General Education, 218-226, October, 1968.

4568 _____. "Toward remedies for restlessness: issues in student unrest," Liberal Education, 221-230, May, 1968.

4569 _____, and P. R. Werdell. "SDS and SNCC: profiles of two student organizations," School and Society, 96:365-372, October 26, 1968.

4570 Shorris, Earl. "Doctor Hayakawa in thought and action," Ramparts, 8:39-42, November, 1969.

4571 Sisk, John P. "The Intolerable allegories of dissent," Catholic World, 210:55-58, November, 1969.

4572 Slater, R. Giuseppi. "The San Francisco State strike: eclipse," Distant Drummer, 03 13 10 01 69

4573 ———. "San Francisco State: struggle continues," Dallas Notes, 02 05 06 01 69

4574 Smith, Victoria. "Students live to fight another day: from the University of Connecticut," Liberation News Service, 11 13 01 01 68 (Students and the Dow Chemical Company at the University of Connecticut.)

4574a Snyder, L. J. "Campus conflict and strategies for student-administration bargaining," National Association of Women Deans and Counselors Journal, 106-111, Spring, 1968.

4575 Soares, Louise, and Anthony Soares. "Social learning and disruptive social behavior," Phi Delta Kappan, 52:82-83, October, 1970.

4576 Sorel, Jules. "Education for revolt," Independent Socialist, 01 -- 14 01 67 (The school and the "educational factory," and the role of the teacher in the radical movement.)

4577 Sparzo, F. J. "Facing the issues of student unrest," School and Society, 96:359-361, October 26, 1968.

4578 Spence, Larry D. "Berkeley: what it demonstrates," Studies On the Left, 4:63-68, Number 4, 1965.

4579 Spender, S. "What the rebellious students want," New York Times Magazine, March 30, 1969, pp. 56-57.

4580 Spiegel, John P. "Campus conflict and professorial egos," Trans-action, 6:41-50, October, 1969.

4581 ———. "Psychosocial factors in riots: old and new," American Journal of Psychiatry, 281-285, 1968.

4582 Sprouls, Joseph R. "Potentially constructive force,"

Bulletin of the National Association of Secondary School Principals, 53:23-27, September, 1969.

4583 Squires, Raymond. "Do students have civil rights?" PTA Magazine, 63:2-4, September, 1968.

4584 Starr, Paul. "Black Panthers and white radicals," Commonweal, 294-297, June 12, 1970.

4585 Stein, M. L., and Joseph V. Ricapito. "Student revolt: Italian style," Saturday Review, 53:69-71, February 21, 1970.

4586 Stern, G. "Myth and reality in the American college," American Association of University Professors Bulletin, 408-414, Winter, 1966.

4587 Stern, Peter S. "Stanford's community of consent," Nation, 211:174-177, September 7, 1970.

4588 Stern, Sol. "On Herbert Marcuse; the metaphysics of rebellion," Ramparts, 6:55-60, June 29, 1968.

4589 Strata, Liz S. "Jocks defend," Spokane Natural, 05 09 01 01 69

4590 Stupak, Ronald J. "The Student as enemy ... of the student," Phi Delta Kappan, 52:79-81, October, 1970.

4590a Susajima, Masu, Junius A. Davis, and Richard E. Peterson. "Organized student protest and institutional climate," American Educational Research Journal, 5:291-304, May, 1968.

4591 Swerdloff, Howard. "New York City high schools: students vs. administration," Liberation News Service, 04 26 14 01 69 (High schools prepare for D-Day.)

4592 Symonds, Gardinar. "The Campus and the corporation," Vital Speeches, 36:378-382, April 1, 1970.

4593 Tannenbaum, Abraham J. (ed.). "Alienated youth," Journal of Social Issues, 25: Number 2, April, 1969. (Includes an impressive list of contributors to this special issue.)

4594 Tatz, Mark. "U(niversity) of W(ashington) clash," Spokane Natural, 05 09 05 01 69

4595 Taylor, Harold. "The Student revolution," Phi Delta Kappan, 51:62-67, October, 1969.

4596 Tessler, Mark A., and Ronald D. Hedlund. "Students aren't crazies," New Republic, 163:17-18, September 12, 1970.

4597 Thelwell, Michael. "From San Francisco State and Cornell: two black radicals report on their campus struggles," Ramparts, 8:47-59, July, 1969. (Includes the article by Dr. Nathan Hare--acting chairman of the Black Studies Department at San Francisco State.)

4598 Thompson, S. "How student activists differ," Nation's Schools, 84:28, April, 1969.

4599 Thomson, Scott D. "Activism: a game for unloving critics," North Central Association Quarterly, 43:335-41, Spring, 1969.

4600 Thornburg, H. "Statistics of dissent," Arizona Teacher, 10, March, 1969.

4601 Tonsar, Stephen J. "Alienation and relevance," National Review, 21:636-638, July 1, 1969.

4602 _____. "Faculty responsibility for the mess in higher education," Intercollegiate Review, 6, Spring, 1970.

4603 _____. "The Mess in higher education," Vital Speeches, 36:250-253, February 1, 1970.

4604 Toole, K. Ross. "I am tired of the tyranny of spoiled brats," U.S. News, 68:76-78, April 13, 1970. (The minority on college campuses.)

4605 Tornquist, Elizabeth. "Dissent comes to Greenville finally," North Carolin Anvil, 01 03 01 01 70

4606 _____. "How not to handle disorder," North Carolin Anvil, 12 06 01 01 69

4607 Tornquist, Elizabeth. "NCCU disruption amounts to very little," North Carolin Anvil, 02 28 04 01 70

4608 _____. "Union battles at Duke becoming exercise in futility," North Carolin Anvil, 11 15 03 01 69

4609 Trager, Frank N. "ROTC on campus: challenge and response," American Legion Magazine, 87:18-46, December, 1969.

4610 Trent, James W., and Judith L. Croise. "Commitment and conformity in the American college," Journal of Social Issues, 23:34-51, July, 1967.

4611 Tribble, Ike. "Trust: a new approach to student unrest," Educational Leadership, 27:392-96, January, 1970.

4612 Trilling, Diana. "On the steps of law library," Commentary, 46:29-55, November, 1968.

4613 Trimberger, Ellen K. "Why a rebellion at Columbia was inevitable," Trans-action, 5:28-38, September, 1968.

4614 Tropman, J. E., and J. L. Ehrlich. "New political realities: academia and the cities," Journal of Higher Education, 301-308, June, 1968.

4615 Trout, G. D. Jr. (et al.). "Youth makes itself heard; changing context of youth participation," Education Digest, 34:24-27, October, 1968.

4616 Trou, W. C. "Great revolt in higher education," School and Society, 96:373-377, October 26, 1968.

4617 Trump, J. Lloyd, and Jane Hunt. "Nature and extent of student activism," Bulletin of the National Association of Secondary School Principals, 53:150-60, May, 1969.

4618 Urquhart, Mike. "State of emergency," Independent Socialist, 03 -- 02 01 69

4619 Vanocur, Sander. "The Public and higher education,"

College and University Journal, 8:59-63, Fall, 1969. (Current Biography for January 1963 carries a biography of Vanocur.)

4620 Vareia, M. E. "Chicano students stand up," Liberation News Service, 03 27 12 01 69 (Upheaval at West High School, Denver.)

4621 Vick, George R. "Confrontation in the university: academic freedom versus social commitment," Intercollegiate Review, 6: Spring, 1970.

4622 Walk, Karen. "Santa Barbara--Why it happened," Distant Drummer, 03 12 03 01 70

4623 Wallace, Jo Anne. "Free speech eliminated in Paly high schools," Peninsula Observer, 01 22 04 01 69

4624 Wallace, Rue, Warren Friedman, and Linda Friedman. "The Movement at work: the community college scene," Liberation, 14:34-37, October, 1969.

4625 Walsh, J. "Confrontation at Stanford: exit classified research," Science, 169:534-537, May 2, 1969.

4626 Warren, Dave. "How the Berkeley 3 won their acquittal," Militant, 11 14 10 01 69

4627 Wasserman, Mirian, and John Reimann. "Student rebels vs. school defender," Urban Review, 4:9-17, October, 1969.

4628 Watts, William A., and David Whittaker. "Profile of a non-conformist youth culture. A study of the Berkeley non-students," Sociology of Education, 178-200, Spring, 1968.

4629 _____, Steve Lynch, and David Whittaker. "Alienation and activism in today's college youth: socialization patterns and current family relationships," Journal of Counseling Psychology, 1-7, January, 1969.

4630 Ways, Max. "On the campus: a troubled reflection of the U.S.," Fortune, 72:130-135, September,

1965. (Consists of two parts.)

4631 Ways, Max. "University's position is secure but," College and University Journal, 8:55-58, Fall, 1969.

4632 Weaver, Donna. "Woman: one more exploited ...," Grinding Stone, 11 -- 07 02 69 (Oppression of women voiced by a student.)

4633 Weber, Paul J. "The Revolution on American campuses," Catholic World, 210:248-252, March, 1970.

4634 Wedge, Bryant. "The Case study of student political violence: Brazil, 1964, and Dominican Republic, 1965," World Politics, 21:183-206, January, 1969.

4635 Wesley, S. M. "Disantiestablishmentarianism: the radical middle, another alternative," Berkeley Barb, 10 03 07 01 69

4636 Westby, David L., and Richard G. Braungart. "Class and politics in the family backgrounds of student activists," American Sociological Review, 31:690-692, October, 1966.

4637 Widmer, Kingsley. "Why the colleges blew up: California State Colleges system," Nation, 208:237-241, February 24, 1969.

4638 Wilson, James Q., and Harold R. Wilde. "The Urban mood," Commentary, 48:52-61, October, 1969.

4639 Wilson, P. K. "Blacks confront SMU," Dallas Notes, 05 07 03 01 69 (Black demands at SMU "aimed at correcting the injustices of institutional racism.")

4640 Wirth, Thomas H. "900 busted in Miss.," Great Speckled Bird, 02 23 12 01 70

4641 Wolfe, Alan. "Hard times on campus," Nation, 210:623-627, May 25, 1970.

4642 Wolfson, Dave. "Killings at Kent," Pittsburgh Point, 05 07 04 01 70

4643 Woodring, Paul. "Campus stress," Saturday Review,

52:72, March 15, 1969.

4644 _____. "A View from the campus: the struggle for black identity," Saturday Review, 52:62, January 18, 1969.

4645 Wrenn, R. L. "Authority, controversy and today's student," Personnel and Guidance Journal, 46:949-953, June, 1968.

4646 Yokell, Mike. "The Student radical: after graduation what?" Paper Tiger, 12 -- 21 01 67 (Description of consistent themes of student movements.)

4647 Young, Allen. "Academia in rebellion," Chicago Kaleidoscope, 01 03 05 01 69 (Counter-guerrilla warfare on campuses on a nationwide scale.)

4648 _____. "America--Academia in rebellion," Liberation News Service, 12 14 01 01 68

4649 Young, Roland. "Murders at Kent State College," Black Panther, 05 19 05 01 70

4650 Zagoria, Donald S. "Mediation: a path to campus peace?" Monthly Labor Review, 92:9, January, 1969.

4651 Zaremba, Elaine. "Student voices," Wilson Library Bulletin, 45:54-61, September, 1970.

4652 Zogby, Jim. "Students and slum lords," Distant Drummer, 04 09 04 01 70

VII. ANTI-BALLISTIC MISSILE SYSTEMS

BOOKS

4653 Abel, Elie. The Missile crisis. Philadelphia: Lippincott, 1966.

4654 American Security Council. National Strategy Committee. The ABM and the changed strategic military balance. Washington, D.C.: Acropolis, 1970. (Thirty-one experts view the ABM from many angles.)

4655 _____. USSR vs. USA; the ABM and the changed strategic military balance; a study by a special American Security Council Committee of 31 experts, co-chaired by Willard F. Libby and others. 2nd ed. Washington, D.C.: Acropolis, 1969.

4656 Anti-ballistic Missile: Yes or No? (For: Donald G. Brennan and Leon S. McGovern. Against: Jerome B. Wiesner and George S. McGovern) Introduction by Hubert H. Humphrey. Epilogue by William O. Douglas. N.Y.: Hill and Wang, 1969.

4657 Arbrister, Trevor. A Matter of accountability. N.Y.: Coward-McCann, 1970.

4658 Baar, James. Spacecraft and missiles of the world. N.Y.: Harcourt, Brace and World, 1962.

4659 Bader, William B. The United States and the spread of nuclear weapons. N.Y.: Pegasus, 1970.

4660 Boskey, Bennett, and Mason Willrich (eds.). Nuclear proliferation: prospects for control. N.Y.: Dunellen, 1970. (Description of controversial aspects of the Treaty on the Non-Proliferation of Nuclear Weapons.)

Anti-Ballistic Missile Systems

4661 Burgess, Eric. Guided weapons. N.Y.: Macmillan, 1957.

4662 ———. Long-range ballistic missiles. N.Y.: Macmillan, 1960.

4663 Center For the Study of Democratic Institutions. Anti-ballistic missile. N.Y.: Hill and Wang, 1969. (Paper)

4664 Chayes, Abram, and Jerome B. Wiesner (eds.). ABM; an evaluation of the decision to deploy an antiballistic missile system. N.Y.: Harper and Row, 1969.

4664a Di Certo, J. J. Missile base beneath the sea. N.Y.: St. Martin's, 1967.

4665 Gatland, Kenneth W. Development of the guided missile. N.Y.: Philosophical Library, 1952.

4666 Holst, Johan I., and William Schneider Jr. (eds.). Why A.B.M? Policy issues in the missile defenses controversy. N.Y.: Pergamon, 1969.

4667 Jerger, Joseph J. Systems preliminary design. Princeton, New Jersey: Van Nostrand, 1960.

4668 Kennedy, Edward. ABM: an evaluation of the decision to deploy an anti-ballistic missile system. N.Y.: New American Library, 1970.

4669 Kintner, William R. (ed.). Safeguard: why the ABM makes sense. N.Y.: Hawthorn, 1969.

4670 Lapp, Ralph E. Arms beyond doubt: the tyranny of weapons technology. N.Y.: Cowles, 1970.

4671 Parson, Nels A. Guided missiles in war and peace. Cambridge: Harvard University Press, 1956.

4672 Republican Party. Public Relations Division. The Missile defense question: is LBJ right? Russia deploys anti-missile network, U.S. refuses to keep pace. A background report. Washington, D.C.: 1967.

4673 Russell, Bertrand. Common sense and nuclear warfare. N.Y.: Simon and Schuster, 1959.

4674 Schelling, Thomas C., and M. H. Halperin. Strategy and arms control. N.Y.: Twentieth Century Fund, 1961.

4675 Schurmann, Franz. Crisis effects from the arms race. IN Anti-Ballistic Missile: Yes or No? Center For The Study of Democratic Institutions. N.Y.: Hill and Wang, 1968, pp. 74-75.

4676 Schwiebert, Ernest G. A History of the U.S. air force ballistic missiles, with supplementary material by the editors of Air Force/Space Digest. N.Y.: Praeger, 1965.

4677 Scoville, Herbert, and Robert Osborn. Missile madness. Boston: Houghton, 1970.

4678 Stanley, D. T. (et al.). Men who govern. N.Y.: Brookings Institute, 1967. (Profiles of political executives.)

4679 Stockholm International Peace Research Institute. SIPRI. SIPRI yearbook of world armaments and disarmament, 1968-1969. N.Y.: Humanities Press, 1970.

4680 Teller, E., and A. L. Latter. Our nuclear future: facts, dangers, and opportunities. N.Y.: Criterion, 1958.

4681 Thayer, George. The War business: the international trade in armaments. N.Y.: Simon and Schuster, 1969.

4682 Thurmond, Strom. Speech by the Hon. J. Strom Thurmond, U.S. Senator--Republican, South Carolina. IN Anti-Ballistic Missile: Yes or No? Center For the Study of Democratic Institutions. N.Y.: Hill and Wang, 1968. pp. 132-137.

4683 Twining, N. F. Neither liberty nor safety. N.Y.: Holt, 1966.

4684 Tyrrell, C. Merton. Pentagon partners, the new

nobility. N.Y.: Grossman, 1970.

4685 Ullman, J. E. (ed.). Potential civilian markets for the military-electronics industry: strategies for conversion. N.Y.: Praeger, 1970.

4686 Wainhouse, D. W. (et al.). Arms control agreements. Baltimore: Johns Hopkins Press, 1969.

4687 Waskow, Arthur I. (ed.). Debate over thermonuclear strategy. N.Y.: Heath, 1965.

4688 Wheeler, Harvey. Technology versus democracy. IN Anti-Ballistic Missile: Yes or No? Center For the Study of Democratic Institutions. N.Y.: Hill and Wang, 1968, pp. 71-74.

4689 Wiesner, Jerome B. Balance of terror? IN Anti-Ballistic Missile: Yes or No? Center For the Study of Democratic Institutions. N.Y.: Hill and Wang, 1968, pp. 58-61.

4690 _____. Disagreement by the numbers. IN Anti-Ballistic Missile: Yes or No? Center For the Study of Democratic Institutions. N.Y.: Hill and Wang, 1968, pp. 49-53.

4691 _____, and Charles Abraham. ABM: A report prepared for Senator Edward M. Kennedy and the American public. N.Y.: Harper and Row, 1969.

4692 Wilkinson, F J. Edged weapons. N.Y.: Doubleday, 1970.

4693 Wilson, T. W. Jr. Great weapons heresy. Boston: Houghton, 1970.

4694 Yale, Wesley (et al.). Alternative to armageddon. New Jersey: Rutgers University Press, 1970.

4695 Yarmolinsky, Adam. Military establishment: its impacts on American society. N.Y.: Harper, 1971.

EDITORIALS

4696 "AB Missile system," Two-Cents Plain Dealer, 03 31 04 02 69 (Some views from a different perspective regarding the ABM from natural and social scientists from Millersville State College.)

4697 "A. B. M.," Abas, 06 03 06 01 69

4698 "ABM: a missed opportunity," America, 121:56-57, August 2, 1969.

4699 "ABM: a nuclear watershed," Time, 93:22-7, March 14, 1969.

4700 "ABM: an expensive deterrent," Science News, 95:301-302, March 29, 1969.

4701 "ABM and MIRV," Nation, 208:813, June 30, 1969.

4702 "ABM and national priorities," Saturday Review, 51:24, December, 1968.

4703 "ABM--damned if we do, more damned if we don't," Saturday Evening Post, 240:88, November 4, 1967.

4704 "ABM debate: discussion," Bulletin of Atomic Scientists, 24:31-34, March, 1968.

4705 "ABM debauch," Nation, 209:67-8, July 28, 1969.

4706 "ABM duel goes on; three congressional hearings," Newsweek, 73:30, April 7, 1969.

4707 "ABM--how good?" Science News, 93:279, March 23, 1968.

4708 "A+B+M=Lunacy," New Republic, 160:7-8, March 8, 1969.

4709 "ABM: not really settled," Time, 93:12-13, March 21, 1969.

4710 "ABM: scientists loyal opposition finds a forum," Science, 163:1309-11, March 21, 1969.

Anti-Ballistic Missile Systems

4711 "ABM through thick and thin," Time, 93:23-4, February 28, 1969.

4712 "ABM: who needs it?" New Republic, 160:7-9, April 5, 1969.

4713 "After the ABM vote," U.S. News, 67:6, August 13, 1969.

4714 "Another look at the ABM," National Review, 21:162-3, February 25, 1969.

4715 "Anti-Anti ABM," Time, 93:29-30, June 6, 1969.

4716 "Antiballistic missile decision," America, 120:350, March 29, 1969.

4717 "Antimissile protection for U.S. Pros and Cons," U.S. News, 66:30-1, March 10, 1969.

4718 "Arms: how much is enough?" Newsweek, 73:21, February 10, 1969.

4719 "Arms talks," New Republic, 160:9-10, February 8, 1969.

4720 "Bastille day in Mellon Square," Pittsburgh Point, 07 10 01 01 69 (Contains a letter written to Mrs. Finkelhor from Thomas M. Kerr, Pres. of the American Civil Liberties Union--Pittsburgh Branch, protesting Pittsburgh's corporate involvement in the Vietnam war, and demonstrators should have the right to assemble in Mellon Square.)

4721 "Coming to a head: ABM decision," Science News, 95:280, March 22, 1969.

4722 "Controlling the arms race; ABM debate," Current, 106:3-21, August 25, 1969.

4723 "Decision on ABM," Newsweek, 73:24-5, March 24, 1969.

4724 "Fateful pause for ABM," Business Week, 27, February 15, 1969.

4725 "For Canada's Trudeau: fallout from U.S. ABM,"

4726 "Far from deployed; ABM system," Science News, 96:127-8, August 16, 1969.

4727 "From sentinel to safeguard," Christian Century, 86:396-7, March 26, 1969.

4728 "Go, or no go? Sentinel missile systems," Senior Scholastic, 94:14-15, March 14, 1969.

4729 "Go, signal for more ABM's--new fight ahead in congress," U.S. News, 58:34-5, February 16, 1970.

4730 "Great ABM counterfeit," Commonweal, 90:499-500, August 22, 1969.

4731 "If you're puzzled about ABM," U.S. News, 67:60-1, August 25, 1969.

4732 "Middle ground? Nixon's ABM decision," Senior Scholastic, 94:23-4, March 28, 1969.

4733 "Missing card; opposition to ABM system," Time, 90:22-23, September 29, 1967.

4734 "Nazi disrupts peace rally," Dallas Notes, 05 07 09 01 69 (Paint thrown on speakers at the Safeguard Anti-Ballistic Missile System demonstration at Ferris Plaza, Dallas, Texas.)

4735 "New peril for U.S; latest in the ABM debate," U.S. News, 66:10, March 31, 1969.

4736 "New satellite ICBM detection system pressed," Aero Technology, 21:13, April 22, 1968.

4737 "Nixon's ABM decision: what it means, with text of statement," U.S. News, 66:38-9, March 24, 1969.

4738 "Oversell and overkill: protracted controversy over the safeguard ABM system," Newsweek, 74:18, July 7, 1969.

4739 "Overtalk? Safeguard ABM debate," Newsweek, 73:37-8, May 26, 1969.

4740 "Paper war; ABM dispute," Time, 93:18-19, May 16, 1969.

4741 "Political masterplan for the future," Atlas, 18:19-21, October, 1969.

4742 "Selling the ABM," Nation, 202:259-60, March 3, 1969.

4743 "This month's feature: the U.S. and anti-missile defense," Congressional Digest, 47:257-288, November, 1968.

4744 "Thirty-five thousand against ABM," Distant Drummer, 07 03 02 02 69 (ANNP gathers 35,000 signatures against the ABM.)

4745 "Time has come to act," U.S. News, 67:26-28, July 14, 1969.

4746 "To ABM or not to ABM," National Review, 21:266, March 25, 1969.

4747 "Trudeau's ABM doubts," U.S. News, 66:14, April 7, 1969.

4748 "The War machine," Pittsburgh Point, 07 10 03 03 69 (A line-up (in money) of industrial and corporation contracts let to Pittsburgh firms during the month of April.)

4749 "Why congress is confused about ABM," U.S. News, 66:86, May 26, 1969.

4750 "X-rays, missiles and anti-missiles," National Review, 19:557, May 30, 1967.

PERIODICALS

4751 Alsop, S. "ABM and the liberals," Newsweek, 74:84, August 11, 1969.

4752 Boffey, P. M. "ABM critical report by scientists

brings sharp Pentagon rebuttal," Science, 164:807-10, May 16, 1969.

4753 Bottome, E. M. "Mythology of the A.B.M.," Commonweal, 87:74-6, October 20, 1967.

4754 Brennan, Donald G. "Case for missile defense," Foreign Affairs, 47:433-48, April, 1969.

4755 Clark, Joseph S. (Sen.). "Sen. Clark: the immature and senseless ABM," Distant Drummer, 08 14 01 01 69

4756 Coffey, J. I. "Anti-ballistic missile debate," Foreign Affairs, 45:403-413, April, 1967.

4757 Cousins, Norman. "A.B.M. and national priorities," Saturday Review, 51:24, December 14, 1968.

4758 _____. "ABM: President Nixon's Vietnam?" Saturday Review, 52:22-3, March 8, 1969.

4759 Crawford, K. "ABM debate," Newsweek, 73:45, April 14, 1969.

4760 D'Arazien, Steve. "Blue water boondoggle," Nation, 211:498-500, November 16, 1970. (Under sea long-range missile system.)

4761 Garwin, Richard L., and Hans A. Bethe. "Anti-ballistic-missile systems," Scientific American, 218:21-31, March, 1968.

4762 Gomer, R. "A.B.M. decision," Atomic Science, 23:29, November, 1967.

4763 Goulden, Joseph C., and Marshall Singer. "Dial-a-bomb: AT&T and the ABM," Ramparts, 8:29-35, November, 1969.

4764 Hotz, R. "ABM debate," Aviation Week and Space Technology, 90:11, March 31, 1969.

4765 Inglis, D. R. "Anti-ballistic missile: a dangerous folly," Saturday Review, 51:26-7, September 7, 1968.

4766 _____. "Anti-missile drag-race," Saturday Review, 50:36, February 25, 1967.

4767 _____. "Nuclear threat, ABM systems, and proliferation," Bulletin of Atomic Scientists, 24:2-4, June, 1968.

4768 Jackson, H. M. "Russian leadership: the ABM address," Vital Speeches, 35:610-13, August 1, 1969.

4769 Javits, J. K. "Can President Nixon stop the arms race?" Saturday Review, 52:14-16, March 1, 1969.

4770 Jhirad, Sue, and Greg Sandow. "ABM," Old Mole, 02 21 05 03 69

4771 Kalkstein, M. "Anti-ABM; social dimensions of the missile crisis," Trans-action, 6:25-8, June, 1969.

4772 Kilmarx, Robert. "ABM and MIRV: in the context of salt," Vital Speeches, 36:602-604, July 15, 1970.

4773 Lall, B. G. "A.B.M. decision: 40 million for anti-ballistic missile establishmentarianism," Commonweal, 86:144-147, April 21, 1967.

4774 _____. "Congress debates the A.B.M.," Atomic Science, 23, 28-33, September, 1967.

4775 _____. "Gaps in the A.B.M. debate," Atomic Science, 23:45-46, April, 1967.

4776 Lapp, Ralph E. "Biography of the ABM," New York Times Magazine, 22-30, May 4, 1969.

4777 Larus, J. "Nuclear accidents and the ABM," Saturday Review, 52:10-13, May 31, 1969.

4778 Long, F. A. "Strategic balance and the A.B.M.," Bulletin of Atomic Scientists, 24:2-5, December, 1968.

4779 Lowenstein, Eddie. "City drive gains 4,000 signatures: the ABM issue," Distant Drummer, 06 19 04 01 69 (Concerted effort against the ABM in Philadelphia.)

4780   McGovern, George. "Case against the ABM.," Catholic World, 209:24-9, April, 1969.

4781   McGrory, M. "ABM: to resume or not to resume," America, 120:238, March 1, 1969.

4782   _____. "Nixon's first decision; go ahead with antiballistic missile system," America, 120:349, March 29, 1969.

4783   Meyer, F. S. "Anti-missile defense," National Review, 21:286, March 25, 1969.

4784   Moldauer, P. "ABM comes to town," Bulletin of Atomic Science, 25:4-6, January, 1969.

4785   Moss, N. "McNamara's A.B.M. policy: a failure of communications," Reporter, 36:34-6, February 23, 1967.

4786   Nelson, B. "A.B.M.: Senators request outside scientific advice in closed session," Science, 162:1374-75, December 20, 1968.

4787   Nixon, Richard M. "President Nixon modifies ballistic missile defense system," Department of State Bulletin, 60:273-5, March 31, 1969.

4788   Raser, John. "ABM and the MAD strategy," Ramparts, 8:36, November, 1969. (Description of the modern military game MAD and the environmental crisis.)

4789   Recca, Ron. "The Gammas 11 getcha," Grok, 04 -- 18 02 70 ("A sickening aspect of the antiballistic missile (ABM) defense program is that very simply this, 'defense' will kill you while 'protecting' you from enemy ('   ') weapons.")

4790   Robb, Charles C. "Bastille day in Mellon Square," Pittsburgh Point, 07 17 01 01 69

4791   Rosenberg, M. J. "Blind strategy of missile defense," Nation, 208:168-74, February 10, 1969.

4792   Rossi, Marna. "Peace flotilla heads downstream," Pittsburgh Point, 07 10 03 01 69 ("Part of a campaign designed to build an awareness of the importance of the anti-ballistic missile issue.")

4793 Rothstein, R. "A.B.M. proliferation and international stability," Foreign Affairs, 46:487-502, April, 1968.

4794 _____. "Nixon's ABM: very thin indeed," New Republic, 160:15-18, March 29, 1969.

4795 _____. "Reflections on the ABM decision," New Republic, 160:19-21, March 22, 1969.

4796 Rovere, Richard H. "Letter from Washington: sentinel anti-ballistic-missile system," New Yorker, 45:97-100, March 1, 1969.

4797 _____. "Letter from Washington: sentinel or safeguard ABM system," New Yorker, 45:112, March 22, 1969.

4798 Russett, B. M. "Complexities of ballistic missile defenses," Yale Review, 56:354-367, March, 1967.

4799 Soper, Will. "ABM risks atom war to aid the rich," Old Mole, 08 15 08 01 69

4800 Sternglass, E. J. "Death of all children; footnote to the A.B.M. controversy," Esquire, 72:1a-1d, September, 1969.

4801 Teller, E., and Jerome B. Wiesner. "ABM: the case for and against," U.S. News, 66:87-90, May 26, 1969.

4802 Towsend, J. R. "Rational horror," Pittsburgh Point, 06 04 04 03 69 ("Editor's Note: The following article refers to a speech in favor of the ABM given by Dr. Edward Teller at Carnegie-Mellon University on May 15, 1969. Dr. Towsend is a professor of Physics at the University of Pittsburgh.")

4803 Webb, Lee. "ABM and the liberals: if at first ...," Guardian, 08 16 07 01 69

4804 Wiesner, Jerome B. "The Case against an

antiballistic missile system," Look, 31:25-28, November 28, 1967.

4805 Wildavsky, Aaron. "The Politics of ABM," Commentary, 48:55-63, November, 1969.

4806 Wiley, J. P. "Activists take ABM fight to congress White House," Physics Today, 22:69, June, 1969.

4807 Winston, D. C. "One year delay in ABM possible," Aviation Week and Space Technology, 90:16-17, February 17, 1969.

4808 Yates, S. R. "Showdown on the ABM," Bulletin of Atomic Science, 25:29-32, March, 1969.

VIII. CIVIL DISOBEDIENCE, VIOLENCE AND NON-VIOLENCE

BOOKS

4809 Abraham, H. J. Freedom and the court: Civil rights and liberties in the U.S. N.Y.: Oxford University Press, 1971.

4810 Abrahamsen, David. Our violent society. N.Y.: Funk and Wagnalls, 1970.

4811 Agnew, Spiro T. Frankly speaking. N.Y.: Public Affairs Press, 1970. (Twelve addresses cover such topics as: street demonstrations, moratorium day observances, role of television and the press, and the obligations of education among others.)

4812 Allen, F. A. Borderland of criminal justice. Chicago: Chicago Press, 1964.

4813 American Civil Liberties Union. Day of protest, night of violence. A report of the American Civil Liberties Union of Southern California on the Century City Peace March. Los Angeles, California, 1967. (Pam.)

4813a American Jewish Committee. Survey of the report of the national advisory commission on civil disorders. N.Y.: AJC, 1969. (Pam.) (Co-published by 23 national organizations concerning the riots in American cities in 1967.)

4814 Amory, Cleveland. Who killed society? N.Y.: Harper, 1960.

4815 Amos, W. E., and C. F. Wellford. Delinquency prevention: theory and practice. New Jersey: Prentice-Hall, 1967.

4816 Arendt, Hannah. On violence. N.Y.: Harcourt, Brace and World, 1970.

4817 Arnold, Arnold. Violence and your child. Chicago: Regnery, 1970.

4818 Bedau, Hugo A. (ed.). Civil disobedience: theory and practice. N.Y.: Pegasus, 1969. ("The Politics of creative disorder.")

4819 Bell, Inge Powell. CORE and the strategy of nonviolence. N.Y.: Random House, 1968.

4820 Bernstein, Saul. Alternatives to violence; alienated youth and riots, race, and poverty. N.Y.: Association Press, 1967.

4821 _____. Youth on the streets. N.Y.: Association Press, 1964.

4822 Bettelheim, Bruno. The Informed heart. N.Y.: Free Press, 1960.

4823 Bienen, Henry. Violence and social change. Chicago: University of Chicago Press, 1969.

4824 Boehme, Lillian R. Carte Blanche for chaos. N.Y.: Arlington House, 1970. (An attack on the Kerner Report on Civil disorders in 1968. A description of the "statist" aspects of governmental intervention.)

4825 Bondurant, Joan V. (ed.). Nonviolence. N.Y.: Atherton, 1969.

4826 Bronowski, J. The Face of violence: essay. N.Y.: World, 1967.

4827 Brown, Richard Maxwell (ed.). American violence. New Jersey: Prentice-Hall, 1970.

4828 Buckman, Peter. The Limits of protest. Indianapolis: Bobbs-Merrill, 1970.

4829 Buss, A. H. The Psychology of aggression. N.Y.: John Wiley, 1961.

4830   Caffi, Andrea. A Critique of violence. N.Y.: Bobbs-Merrill, 1970.

4831   Cain, Arthur H. Young people and crime. N.Y.: Day, 1968.

4832   Campbell, Angus, and Howard Schurman. Racial attitudes in fifteen American cities. A report prepared for the National Advisory Commission on Civil disorder. Michigan: Institute For Social Research, 1969. (Interviews of attitudes of blacks and whites in 15 American cities. City vs. suburban differences.)

4833   Cantor, Norman F. The Age of protest: dissent and rebellion in the twentieth century. N.Y.: Hawthorn, 1970. (A century of protest in chronological order.)

4834   Canty, Donald. One year later: an assessment of the Nation's response to the crisis described by the National Advisory Commission on Civil Disorders. Urban America, Inc., and the Urban coalition. Forewords by John W. Gardner, and Terry Sanford. N.Y.: Praeger, 1969.

4835   Chametzky, Jules, and Sidney Kaplan (eds.). Black and white in American culture: an anthology from the Massachusetts Review. Massachusetts: University of Massachusetts Press, 1970.

4836   Cloward, R. A., and L. E. Ohlin. Delinquency and opportunity: a theory of delinquent gangs. N.Y.: Free Press, 1960.

4837   Coffi, Andrea. A Critique of violence. Indianapolis: Bobbs-Merrill, 1970.

4838   Cohn, E. N. The Great rights. N.Y.: Macmillan, 1963.

4839   Congressional Quarterly (Research Reports). Crime and justice in America. 2nd ed. Washington, D.C.: Congressional Quarterly Service, 1968. (Reviews aspects of crime in America and efforts made to reduce it.)

4840 Congressional Quarterly (Research Reports). Revolution in civil rights. 4th ed. Washington, D. C.: Congressional Quarterly Service, 1968.

4841 Connery, Robert. Urban riots: violence and social change. N. Y.: Vintage, 1969.

4842 Conrad, John. Crime and its correction. Berkeley, California: University of California Press, 1965.

4843 Daly, Charles. Urban violence. Chicago: University of Chicago Press, 1969.

4844 Davis, F. J. Society and the law. N. Y.: Free Press, 1962.

4845 De Alba, Joaquin. Violence in America: De Tocqueville's America revisited. Washington, D. C.: Acropolis, 1970.

4846 Demaris, Ovid. America the violent. N. Y.: Cowles, 1969.

4847 Deming, Barbara. Prison notes. Boston: Beacon Press, 1970. (Civil rights and nonviolent resistance.)

4848 Douglas, William O. Points of rebellion. N. Y.: Random House, 1970.

4849 Duncan, Donald. The New legions. N. Y.: Random House, 1967.

4850 Ellul, Jacques. Violence: reflections from a christian perspective. N. Y.: Seabury Press, 1969.

4851 Endleman, Shalom. Violence in the streets. Chicago: Quadrangle, 1969.

4852 Erikson, Erik. On the origins of militant non-violence. N. Y.: Norton, 1969.

4853 Falk, Richard A. Legal order in a violent world. New Jersey: Princeton University Press, 1970.

4854 Finn, James. A Conflict of loyalties. N. Y.: Pegasus, 1968.

4855 _____. Protest: pacifism and politics; some passionate views on war and nonviolence. N.Y.: Random House, 1968.

4856 Flaming, Karl H. The Ghetto riots: an out-growth of conflict with value and normative systems. Working paper. Milwaukee: University of Wisconsin Press, 1969.

4857 Fogelson, Robert, and Richard E. Rubenstein. Mass violence in America. N.Y.: Arno Press, 1969. (A selection of 43 volumes ranging from mass political conflict in pre-revolutionary days to the present.)

4858 Fortas, Abe. Concerning dissent and civil disobedience. N.Y.: New American Library, 1970. (Paper) (Lawful civil disobedience and non-violent dissent.)

4859 Freeman, Harry A. Civil disobedience. California: Center for the Study of Democratic Institutions, 1966.

4859a Gandhi, Mahatma. Non-violent resistance. (Satyagraha) N.Y.: Schocken, 1961.

4860 Geis, Gilbert. Man, crime and society. N.Y.: Random House, 1962.

4861 Gilbert, Ben W., and the Staff of the Washington Post. Ten blocks from the White House: anatomy of the Washington riots of 1968. N.Y.: Praeger, 1968. (A chronology of the April riots in Washington, D.C. in April of 1968.)

4862 Glaser, Daniel. Crime in the city. N.Y.: Harper and Row, 1970.

4863 Graham, Hugh Davis. Violence in America: historical and comparative perspectives; a report to the National Commission on the Causes and Prevention of violence. Washington, D.C.: Supt. of Documents, G.P.O., 1969.

4864 _____, and Ted Robert Gurr (eds.). The History of violence in America: historical comparative perspectives: a report submitted to the National Commission on the Causes and Prevention of Violence. N.Y.: Praeger, 1969.

4865 Gregg, Richard. Power of non-violence. Rev. ed. N.Y.: Schocken, 1966.

4866 Grimshaw, Allen D. (ed.). Racial violence in the United States. Chicago: Aldine, 1970.

4867 Grimshaw, Allen D. A Study of social violence: urban race riots in the U.S. Pennsylvania: University of Pennsylvania, 1954. (Unpublished Ph.D. dissertation.)

4868 Griswald, Erwin N. Dissent--1968 style. IN Reference Shelf Series, Vol. 40 Number 5, pp. 141-60. N.Y.: H. W. Wilson Company, 1968.

4869 Gurr, Ted Robert. Why men rebel. New Jersey: Princeton University Press, 1970.

4870 Hare, A. Paul (et al.). Nonviolent direct action. N.Y.: World, 1970.

4871 Harris, Richard. The Fear of crime. N.Y.: Praeger, 1969. (Account of what goes on in the name of the government. Introduction by Nicholas de B. Katzenbach.)

4872 _____. Justice: the crisis of law, order, and freedom in America. N.Y.: Dutton, 1969.

4873 Hayden, Tom. Rebellion in Newark: official violence and ghetto response. N.Y.: Vintage, 1967.

4874 Higham, Robin D. Bayonets in the streets: the use of troops in civil disturbances. Kansas: University of Kansas Press, 1969.

4875 Hill, Roy L. Rhetoric of racial revolt. Colorado: Golden Bell Press, 1964. (A collection of speeches made by negro civil rights leaders with analysis of styles and approaches.)

4876 Hofstadter, Richard, and Michael Wallace (eds.). American violence: a documentary history. N.Y.:

Knopf, 1970. (An anthology of violence arranged in eight categories with descriptions of how conflict and violence has changed American developments in the past, and gives insights into the future.)

4877 Horowitz, Irving Louis (ed.). The Anarchists. N.Y.: Dell, 1964.

4878 Horsburgh, H. J. N. Non-violence and aggression; a study of Gandhi's moral equivalent of war. N.Y.: Oxford University Press, 1968. (Gandhi's method of non-violent resistance--satyagraha.)

4879 Howe, Irving. The Radical imagination. N.Y.: New American Library, 1967.

4880 Jacobs, Paul. Prelude to riot: a view of urban America from the bottom. N.Y.: Vintage, 1968.

4881 Jones, H. Violence and reason: essays. N.Y.: Atheneum, 1965.

4882 Kaplan, Morton A. Dissent and the state in peace and war: an essay on the grounds of public morality. N.Y.: Dunellen, 1970. (Essays on American opinion and U.S. Foreign Policy. Some controversial alternatives are outlined.)

4883 Kennan, George F. Democracy and the student left. Boston: Little, 1968.

4884 King, Martin Luther, Jr. Strength to love. N.Y.: Harper and Row, 1963.

4885 _____. Stride toward freedom. N.Y.: Harper and Row, 1958.

4886 _____. Why we can't wait. N.Y.: Harper and Row, 1964.

4887 Lakey, George. Nonviolent action: how it works. Wallingford, Pennsylvania: Pendle Hill, 1969.

4888 Lange, David L. Violence and the media. National Commission on the Causes and Prevention of Violence. Washington, D.C.: Supt. of Documents,

G. P. O., 1969.

4889 Lens, Sidney. Radicalism in America. N.Y.: Apollo Editions, 1969.

4890 Lewin, Stephen (ed.). Crime and its prevention. N.Y.: H. W. Wilson Company, 1968.

4891 Lewis, Oscar. The Children of Sanchez. N.Y.: Random House, 1961.

4892 Lifton, Robert J. (ed.). The United States and Asian revolutions. Chicago: Aldine, 1970.

4893 Lincoln, E. Eric (ed.). Martin Luther King Jr.: A profile. N.Y.: Hill and Wang, 1969.

4894 Lincoln, James H. The Anatomy of a riot: a Detroit judge's report. N.Y.: McGraw-Hill, 1968.

4895 Loble, Lester H., and Max Wylie. Delinquency can be stopped. N.Y.: McGraw-Hill, 1967.

4896 Lynd, S. Nonviolence in America: documentary history. N.Y.: Bobbs-Merrill, 1966.

4897 McLennan, Barbara N. Crime in urban society. N.Y.: New York University Press, 1970.

4898 Madden, E. H. Civil disobedience and moral law in 19th century American philosophy. Washington: University of Washington Press, 1968.

4899 Mailer, Norman. The Armies of the night. Cleveland: World, 1968.

4900 Masotti, Louis H., and Jerome R. Corsi. Shoot-out in Cleveland: black militants and the police. N.Y.: Praeger, 1969.

4901 Methvin, Eugene R. The Riot makers. N.Y.: Arlington House, 1970.

4902 Miller, William R. Nonviolence: a christian interpretation. N.Y.: Schocken, 1966.

4903 Mitchell, J. Paul (ed.). Race riots in black and

white. New Jersey: Prentice-Hall, 1970. (Excerpts from a variety of sources on race riots.)

4904 Morris, Norval, and Gordon Hawkins. The Honest politician's guide to crime control. Chicago: University of Chicago Press, 1970.

4904a Muse, Benjamin. The American negro revolution from nonviolence to black power, 1963-1967. Indiana: Indiana University Press, 1968.

4905 National Commission on the Causes and Prevention of Violence. Violent crime, homicide, assault, rape, robbery. N.Y.: Braziller, 1970. (Intro.: "Toward a National Urban Policy," by Daniel P. Moynihan.)

4906 Nieburg, H. L. Political violence; the behavioral process. N.Y.: St. Martin's, 1969.

4907 Oppenheimer, Martin, and George Lakey. A Manual for direct action. Forword by Bayard Rustin. Chicago: Quadrangle, 1965. (Paper) (Description of a set of codified rules for participants in nonviolent movements.)

4908 Peck, James. Freedom ride. N.Y.: Simon and Schuster, 1961.

4909 Reckless, Walter E. The Crime problem. N.Y.: Appleton-Century-Crofts, 1967.

4910 Rose, Thomas (ed.). Violence in America; a historical and contemporary reader. N.Y.: Random House, 1969. (Nature and causes of violence.)

4911 Roszak, Theodore. The Dissenting academy. N.Y.: Random House, 1968.

4912 Rubenstein, Richard E. Rebels in Eden: mass political violence in the U.S. Boston: Little, 1969.

4913 Salerno, Ralph, and John S. Tompkins. The Crime confederation cosa nostra and allied operations in organized crime. N.Y.: Doubleday, 1969. (History of America's most successful industry and an analysis of the systems.)

4914 Sayler, R. H. (ed.). The Warren court. N.Y.: Chelsea House, 1969.

4915 Schlesinger, Arthur M. Jr. The Crisis of confidence: ideas, power and violence in America. Boston: Houghton, 1969.

4916 _____. Violence: America in the sixties. N.Y.: New American Library, 1970. (Paper)

4917 Schur, Edwin M. Our criminal society. New Jersey: Prentice-Hall, 1969.

4918 Scott, J. P. Aggression. Chicago: University of Chicago Press, 1958.

4919 Seale, Patrick, and Maureen McConville. Red flag, black flag: French revolution, 1968. N.Y.: Ballantine, 1968.

4920 Sharp, Gene. The politics of nonviolent action: an encyclopedia of method and action. Philadelphia: United Church Press, 1969.

4921 Short, James J., and Fred L. Slodtbeck. Group process and gang delinquency. Chicago: University of Chicago Press, 1965.

4922 Sibley, Mulford Q. (ed.). The Quiet battle: writings on the theory and practice of non-violent resistance. N.Y.: Doubleday, 1963.

4923 Skolnick, Jerome. The Politics of protest: a report of the National Commission on the Causes and Prevention of Violence. Task force on violent aspects of protest and confrontation. N.Y.: Simon and Schuster, 1969.

4924 Sorel, George. Reflections on violence. N.Y.: Peter Smith, 1971. (Reprint)

4925 Stevick, Daniel. Civil disobedience and the christian. N.Y.: Seabury, 1969.

4926 Supplemental Studies for the National Advisory Commission on Civil Disorders. N.Y.: Praeger, 1968. (Special studies in U.S. Economic and

Social Development (by) Praeger.)

4927 Talbot, Allan R. The Mayor's game: Richard Lee of New Haven and the politics of change. N.Y.: Praeger, 1970. (Paper) (Originally published in 1967 and reissued in paper. Includes sections on the social revolution, civil rights, and problems of the urban crisis.)

4928 Templin, Ralph T. Democracy and non-violence. Boston: Sargent Porter Inc., 1965.

4929 Toch, Hans H. Violent men: an inquiry into the psychology of violence. Chicago: Aldine, 1969.

4930 Tolstoy, Leo. Tolstoy's writings on civil disobedience and non-violence. N.Y.: Bergman Publishers, 1967.

4931 Trials of the resistance. Essays by Noam Chomsky (and others) with an introduction by Murray Kempton. N.Y.: Random House, 1970. (New York Review Book) (Trials of Civil Disobedience from 1967 to 1970.)

4932 Turner, William W. Invisible witness; the new technology of crime investigation. N.Y.: Bobbs-Merrill, 1968.

4933 Tussman, Joseph. Obligation and the body politic. N.Y.: Oxford University Press, 1960.

4934 Unnithan, T. K., and Yogendra Singh. Sociology of nonviolence and peace; some behavioral and attitudinal dimensions. Connecticut: Lawrence Verry, 1969.

4935 Velvel, Lawrence R. Undeclared war and civil disobedience: the American system in crisis. Foreword by Richard A. Falk. N.Y.: Dunellen, 1970.

4936 Veysey, Lawrence (ed.). Law and resistance: American attitudes toward authority. N.Y.: Harper and Row, 1970.

4937 Walker, Daniel. Rights in conflict: convention week in Chicago, August 25-29, 1968. N.Y.: Dutton,

1968.

4938 Walter, E. V. Terror and resistance: a study of political violence. N.Y.: Oxford University Press, 1969.

4939 Walzer, Michael. Obligations: essays on disobedience, war, and citizenship. Mass.: Harvard University Press, 1970.

4940 Weinberg, Arthur, and Lila Weinberg (eds.). Instead of violence; writings by the great advocates of peace and non-violence throughout history. N.Y.: Grossman, 1963.

4941 Wertham, Frederic. A Sign for Cain: an exploration of human violence. N.Y.: Macmillan, 1966.

4942 Westley, William. Violence and the police: a sociological study of law, custom, and morality. Mass.: MIT Press, 1970.

4943 Whittaker, Charles E., and Coffin William Sloan Jr. Law, order and civil disobedience. Washington: American Enterprise Institute for Public Research, 1967.

4944 Wright, Nathan. Ready to riot. N.Y.: Holt, Rinehart and Winston, 1968.

4945 Yablonsky, Lewis. The Violent gang. N.Y.: Macmillan, 1962.

EDITORIALS

4946 "American violence: terror and tragedy," PTA Magazine, 63:20-22, September, 1968.

4947 "As violence flares around the world," U.S. News, 48:93-7, May 16, 1960.

4948 "As violence spreads in high schools ...," U.S. News, 69:18-20, November 30, 1970.

Civil Disobedience 439

4949 "As violence spreads U.S. goes on guard," U.S. News, 69:15-16, November 2, 1970.

4950 "Attack on crime; and the haters," America, 112:412, March 27, 1965.

4951 "Attala and the Huns; killing of W. L. Moore," America, 108:658, May 11, 1963.

4952 "Billy Graham advises the wrong man; Martin Luther King," Christian Century, 80:606, May 8, 1963.

4953 "Bombs blast a message of hate," Life, 68:24-25, March 27, 1970.

4954 "Call for civil disobedience," New Left Notes, 12 09 07 02 66

4955 "Chicago: turning against the gangs," Time, 96:13, July 27, 1970.

4956 "Civil disobedience and where it leads--two sides," U.S. News, 67:27-28, December 22, 1969.

4957 "Communing in Meadville," Ramparts, 7 November 30, 1968, pp. 10-12. (How a hippie community was crushed in Meadville, Pennsylvania.)

4958 "Crime--control act for capital--a model for the nation?" U.S. News, 69:59, August 3, 1970.

4959 "Crime wave what can be done about it?" U.S. News, 61:46-51, August 1, 1966.

4960 "Crisis of violence; report of the President's Commission on Campus Unrest," Commonweal, 93:35-6, October 9, 1970.

4961 "Dissent and politics," Nation, 206:492, 1968.

4962 "The Dodge rebellion," Ramparts, 7:12, November 30, 1968. ("A group of black militants challenge Walter Reuther's UAW at a major plant.")

4963 "Dynamite is easy to buy-and to use," Life, 68:32, March 27, 1970.

4964 "Escalation of dissent; resist organization--statement of the Catholic intellectuals," Commonweal, 87:102-3, October 27, 1967.

4965 "Esquire: a special section on violence," Esquire, 68:39-66, July, 1967.

4966 "The Execution of Dr. King," Ramparts, 6:47, May, 1968.

4967 "Fighting crime in America," U.S. News, 67:46-53, August 18, 1969. (Interview with John N. Mitchell.)

4968 "Gandhi: the heritage of non-violence; symposium," UNESCO Courier, 22:4-32, 1969.

4969 "Home to roast; violence between white and black in America," Commonweal, 81:752, March 12, 1965.

4970 "How to stop rise in crime," U.S. News, 69:40-43, July 20, 1970. (Interview with Leon Jaworski.)

4971 "Humble parish Priest," Pittsburgh Point, 12 12 01 03 68 (A description of the documentary on the "labor priest" Msgr. Charles Owen Rice shown on television station WQED.)

4972 "In occupied Berkeley," Ally, 06 -- 04 02 60

4973 "Is it ever right to break the law? Pro and con discussion," Senior Scholastic, 84:12-13, March 6, 1964.

4974 "Is violence un-American?" Nation, 201:109, September 6, 1965.

4975 "Johnson statement on violence," New York Times Magazine, January 1, 1968, p. 7.

4976 "Law and higher law," America, 118:802, 1968.

4977 "Mister Bertrand Russell on civil disobedience," Argo, 03 -- 02 01 69

4978 "Natural law institute 1969: the student revolt: a symposium," Loyola Law Review, 15:219, 1968-1969.

4979 "Negro leaders on violence," Time, 86:17, August 20, 1965.

4980 "1984 supercar for 1968 superfuzz," Los Angeles Free Press, 12 15 01 02 67 (A reprint from Machine Design.)

4981 "The Oakland seven," Ramparts, 6:61, June 29, 1968. (A description of the Alameda County's Grand Jury indictment of STDW, October 16-20, 1968.)

4982 "Obeying unjust law, the Methodist view," U.S. News, 56:12, May 18, 1964.

4983 "On civil disobedience, 1967 symposium," New York Times Magazine, November 26, 1967, p. 9.

4984 "PEJ: how to control gangs," Distant Drummer, 09 04 06 01 69

4985 "Press exploitation of violence: death, violence, crime increase circulation," Los Angeles Underground, 03 -- 03 01 68 (A reprint from the L.A. Times for March 7, 8, and 9.)

4986 "Prisoners," Ann Arbor Argus, 06 19 03 03 69

4987 "Protest, a right and a responsibility--round table discussion from 1966 student burgesses at Williamsburg," Senior Scholastic, 88:10-13, May 6, 1966.

4988 "Public schools; new violence against teachers," Time, 94:49, November 14, 1969.

4989 "A Real bomber's chilling reasons," Life, 68:30-31, March 27, 1970.

4990 "Reflections on the right to dissent," America, 311, March 9, 1968.

4991 "The report on civil disorders," PTA Magazine, 62:17, April, 1968.

4991a "Riot control and the use of federal troops," Harvard Law Review, 81:638-652, 1968.

4992 "The Role of violence," Spectator, 07 15 07 01 69

4993 "Rolling to the 'Baez Opening' in our rollicking new rolls," Berkeley Barb, 12 24 01 03 65 (Joan's opening for the "Institute For The Study of Nonviolence," held at Carmel, California.)

4994 "Student power: a symposium," Humanist, 29:11-16, 1969.

4995 "Symposium--the draft, the war and public protest--civil disobedience and its alternatives," George Washington Law Review, 37:433-563, 1969.

4996 "Thoughts of the young radicals: series of personal statements," New Republic, 18:13-15, December 18, 1965.

4997 "To live outside the law you must be honest," Rising Up Angry, 09 -- 10 01 69

4998 "Urban riots: violence and social change," Academy of Political Science Proceedings, 29:1-190, 1968.

4999 "Violence commission report ignored," Kudzu, 04 05 04 01 69

5000 "Violence in America," Time, 90:18-19, July 28, 1967.

5001 "Violence in the factories," Newsweek, 75:66-67, June 29, 1970.

5002 "Violence not surprising," Science News, 90:68, July 30, 1966.

5003 "Violence will end only with political change," Great Speckled Bird, 01 31 02 01 69 ("We move toward an armed society which, while not clearly totalitarian could no longer be said to rest upon the consent of the governed.")

5004 "Violent protest: a debased language," Time, 95:15, May 18, 1970.

5005 "Youth and social action," Journal of Social Issues, October, 1964.

PERIODICALS

5006 Agnew, Spiro T. (et al.). "Agnew's talk with five students; text of television debate," U.S. News, 69:86-8, October 12, 1970.

5007 Alioto, Joseph. "Alioto on violence," Peninsula Observer, 07 28 16 01 69

5008 Allen, Robert L. "Black America reacts to King death," Guardian, 04 13 01 01 68

5009 Allen, Vernon. "Toward understanding riots: some perspectives," Journal of Social Issues, 26:1-18, Winter, 1970.

5010 Beach, John A. "Law versus conscience--the paradox of civil disobedience," New York State Bar Journal, 40:161-188, 1968.

5011 Beaney, William M. "U.S. courts and criminal justice," Current History, 53:69, August, 1967.

5012 Bedau, Hugo A. "Civil disobedience and personal responsibility for injustice," Monist, 54:517-535, October, 1970.

5013 _____. "The Issue of capital punishment," Current History, 53:82-87, August, 1967.

5014 _____. "On civil disobedience," Journal of Philosophy, 58:653-665, October 12, 1961.

5015 Bennett, John C. "Modes of dissent in a democracy U.S.: the politics of dissent," Social Action, 35:3-48, 1969.

5016 Bettelheim, Bruno. "Speaking out; children should learn about violence," Saturday Evening Post, 240:10, March 11, 1967.

5017   Blakey, George Robert. "Crisis in crime control," *America*, 113:238-240, September 4, 1965.

5018   ———. "Organized crime in the U.S.," *Current History*, 52:327-333, June, 1967.

5019   Bondurant, Joan V. "Reflections on non-violence," *Nation*, 206:592-6, May, 1968.

5020   Boorstein, Daniel J. "Dissent, dissension and the news," *Reference Shelf Series*, Volume 40, Number 5: pp. 199-213. N.Y.: H. W. Wilson Company, 1968.

5021   Boskin, J., and R. A. Rosenstone (eds.). "Protest in the sixties: symposium," *American Academy of Political and Social Science (Annals)*, 382:1-144, 1969.

5022   Botwin, C. "Violence and the city child," *New York Times Magazine*, January 11, 1970, p. 73.

5023   Bowen, William. "Crime in the cities," *Fortune*, 72:140-5, December, 1965.

5024   Bowles, C. "What negroes can learn from Gandhi," *Saturday Evening Post*, 230:19-21, March 1, 1958.

5025   Brahms, David M. "They step to a different drummer: a critical analysis of the current Department of Defense position vis-a-vis in-service conscientious objectors," *Military Law Review*, 47:1-34, 1970.

5026   Briand, P. L. "America the violent; address, July 8, 1970," *Vital Speeches*, 36:674-9, September 1, 1970.

5027   Brittain, V. "Dissent by demonstration," *Nation*, 188:252-4, March 21, 1959.

5028   Brittin, Charles. "Massive climax to a week of civil rights protest in Los Angeles," *Los Angeles Free Press*, 03 19 01 02 65 (L.A. demonstrates against Alabama atrocities. The demand is for government action against racist violence and intimidation in the south.)

Civil Disobedience 445

5029 Brown, Robert McAfee. "Because of Vietnam; in conscience I must break the law--civil disobedience," Look, 31:48, October 31, 1967.

5030 Brown, S. M. Jr. "Civil disobedience," Journal of Philosophy, 58:669-681, October 26, 1961.

5031 Buckley, William F. Jr. "Call to color blindness," National Review, 14:488, June, 1963. (Reply (by) M. Whalen, 15:120, August 13, 1963.)

5032 Cain, Edward R. "Conscientious objection in France, Britain, and the U.S.," Comparative Politics, 2:275-307, 1970.

5033 Callahan, Daniel. "Resistance and technology: theory of the new left versus technological man," Commonweal, 87:377-81, December 22, 1967.

5034 Calvert, Peter A. R. "Revolution: the politics of violence," Political Studies, 15:1-11, 1967.

5035 Cannon, Terry. "Law and order in Amerika," Washington Free Press, 07 01 08 01 69

5036 Caplan, Nathan. "The new ghetto man: a review of recent empirical studies," Journal of Social Issues, 26:59, Winter, 1970.

5037 Chamberlain, G. M. "Riot control," American City, 82:87-9, February, 1967.

5038 Charyn, Marlene. "Panthers lose in court; o.k. to urge violence," Peninsula Observer, 06 30 11 03 69

5039 Ciardi, John. "Cases of conscience," Saturday Review, 46:10-11, February 2, 1963.

5040 Cleaver, Eldrige. "An address given by Eldridge Cleaver at a rally in his honor given a few days before he was scheduled to return to jail," Ramparts, December 14-28, 1968, pp. 6-10.

5041 _____. "The Land question," Ramparts, 6:51-53, May, 1968.

5042   Cleaver, Eldrige. "Requiem for nonviolence," Ramparts, 6:48-49, May, 1968.

5043   Cleghorn, R. "Epilogue in Albany; were the mass marches worthwhile?" New Republic, 149:15-18, July 20, 1963.

5044   Cohen, Carl. "Conscientious objection," Ethics, 78:269-79, 1968.

5045   _____. "Essence and ethics of civil disobedience," Nation, 198:257-62, March 16, 1964.

5046   _____. "Fruits of protest," Nation, 202:357-64, March 28, 1966.

5047   _____. "Defending civil disobedience," Monist, 54:469-487, October, 1970.

5048   Cohen, M. "Civil disobedience in a constitutional democracy," Massachusetts Review, 10:211-26,

5049   Commager, Henry S. "Problem of dissent," Saturday Review, 48:21-23, 1965.

5050   Conant, R. W. "Rioting, insurrection and civil disobedience," American Scholar, 37:420-33, 1968.

5051   Conrad, John P. "Prisons and prison reform," Current History, 53:88-93, August, 1967.

5052   Cousins, Norman. "Casual approach to violence," Saturday Review, 40:20-1, August 31, 1957.

5053   _____. "Desensitization of twentieth century man," Saturday Review, 42:32, May 16, 1959.

5054   Cowan, Paul. "What makes Al Lowenstein run?" Ramparts, 7:46-51, September 7, 1968.

5055   Crespigny, A. de. "Nature and methods of non-violent coercion," Political Studies, 12:256-65, 1964.

5056   Dasgupta, Sugata. "Symposium (on) the draft, the war, and public protest--civil disobedience and its alternatives," Indian Journal of Social Work, 29:113-21, July, 1968.

5057 Dellinger, Dave. "The Future on non-violence," Studies On The Left, 4:90-96, Number 4, 1965. (Attitudes and theories concerning non-violent resistance.)

5058 _____. "Memoir of Czechago," Liberation, 04 -- 04 01 70

5059 Deutscher, Isaac. "Marxism and nonviolence," Liberation, 07 -- 10 01 69

5060 Dorsen, Norman, and David Rudovsky. "Some thoughts on dissent; personal liberty and war," American Bar Association Journal, 54:752-58, 1968.

5061 Drinnon, Richard. "The War on violence," Wilson Library Bulletin, 45:68-77, September, 1970.

5062 Duncan, Donald. "And blessed by the fruit ...," Ramparts, 5:30-31, May, 1967.

5063 Dye, Thomas R. "Inequality and civil rights in the states," Journal of Politics, 31, November, 1969.

5064 Eberle, Paul. "We are 18 months from open revolt in this country," Los Angeles Free Press, 12 15 03 01 67

5065 Egan, Edmund J. "Pacifism: the dynamics of dissent," Worldview, 10:8-11, 1967.

5066 Endres, M. E. "Civil disobedience and modern democracy," Thought, 43:499-506, 1968.

5067 England, Ralph W. Jr. "The Independent offender," Current History, 52:334-340, June, 1967.

5068 Fager, Charles E. "Demonstrate, yes, but not futilely," Christian Century, 85:259-62, February 28, 1968.

5069 Farber, Jerry. "Non-violence defense made in courtroom," Los Angeles Free Press, 10 29 03 01 65 (A defendant speaks out in the courtroom.)

5070 Feiffer, Jules. "Good morning! My name is Jules Feiffer--address," Ramparts, 6:37, May, 1968.

(Address given at San Jose State, March 11, 1968.)

5071 Fey, H. E. "Stride toward freedom: the Montgomery story, by Martin Luther King, Jr.," Christian Century, 75:1070-1, September 24, 1958. (A review.)

5072 Fischer, John. "Case for the rebellious students and their counterrevolution," Harper's, 237:9-12, 1968.

5073 _____. "Substitutes for violence," Harper's, 232:16, January, 1966.

5074 _____. "What young men need: a substitute for violence," Reader's Digest, 88:82-5, March, 1966.

5075 Fitzmorris, Paul E. "The Right to dissent--an American heritage," New York State Bar Journal, 41:467-75, 1969.

5076 Fogelson, Robert. "Violence and grievances: reflections on the 1960 riots," Journal of Social Issues, 261:141-164, Winter, 1970.

5077 Fortas, Abe. "Concerning dissent and civil disobedience," National Review, 20:911-12, September 10, 1968.

5078 Forward, John R., and Jay R. Williams. "Internal-external control and black militancy," Journal of Social Issues, 26:75-92, Winter, 1970.

5079 Frankel, Charles. "Is it ever right to break the law?" New York Times Magazine, January 12, 1964, p. 17.

5080 Gardner, John W. "Responsible versus irresponsible dissent," Science, 164:379, April 25, 1969.

5081 Geier, W. A. "Creative disruptions: race relations lecture at Vanderbilt University," Christian Century, 80:344, March 13, 1963.

5082 Geis, Gilbert. "Violence in American society," Current History, 52:354-8, June, 1967.

5083 Geismar, Maxwell. "Mark Twain on U.S.

imperialism, racism and other enduring characteristics of the republic," Ramparts, 6:65-71, May, 1968.

5084 Geschwender, James A. "Civil rights protest and riots: a disappearing distinction," Social Science Quarterly, 49:474-484, 1968.

5085 Gewirth, Alan. "Civil disobedience, law, and morality: an examination of justice Fortas' doctrine," Monist, 54:536-555, October, 1970.

5086 Giermanski, J. R. "Student civil liberties," Commonweal, 87:494-96, January 26, 1968.

5087 Gilbert, Mitch. "Act one of violence," Distant Drummer, 06 15 14 01 68

5088 Glaser, Daniel. "Crime and its control in the U.S.," Forensic Quarterly, 41:355-65, August, 1967.

5089 ———. "National goals and indicators for the reduction of crime and delinquency," Annals of the American Academy, 364:86-95, March, 1966.

5090 Glazer, Nathan. "Civil disobedience on campus: its methods, meaning and morality," College and University Business, 40:47-52, 1966.

5091 Gleason, Ralph, and Paul Krassner. "Obituaries on Lenny Bruce," Ramparts, 5:35-38, October, 1966.

5092 Goodman, Paul. "Students, professionals, and the resistance," First Issue, 03 19 16 01 68

5093 Gossett, William T. "The Politics of dissent; a lawyer speaks for a new confrontation," Michigan Quarterly Review, 8:263-67, 1969.

5094 Green, Ken. "Portland strike violent," Spokane Natural, 08 01 10 01 69

5095 Griffiths, B. "Ideal of non-violence," Commonweal, 67:327-30, December 27, 1957.

5096 Hamill, Pete. "Report from Olympic village," Ramparts, 7: November 30, 1968, pp. 22-27.

5097 Herberg, W. "Alienation, dissent, and the intellectual," National Review, 20:738-39, July 30, 1968.

5098 Herbers, John. "Critical test for the nonviolent way," New York Times Magazine, July 5, 1964, p. 5.

5099 Hobart, C. W. "Freedom, a neglected area for social research," Ethics, 75:153-65, 1965.

5100 Hoffman, Fred. "It doesn't matter who fired first," Los Angeles Free Press, 08 16 01 01 68

5101 _____. "Six-thousand attend peace march," Los Angeles Free Press, 11 01 03 01 68

5102 Hofstadter, Richard. "The Future of American violence," Harper's, 240:47-53, April, 1970.

5103 Hook, Sidney. "Neither blind obedience nor uncivil disobedience," New York Times Magazine, 52: June 5, 1966, p. 3.

5104 _____. "Social protest and civil obedience," Humanist, 27:157-59, 1967.

5105 Howard, D. "Humanism and terror," Commonweal, 93:225-6, November 27, 1970.

5106 Hughes, Graham. "Civil disobedience and the political question doctrine," New York University Law Review, 43:1-19, 1968.

5107 Igletzin, Lynne B. "Violence and American democracy," Journal of Social Issues, 26:165-186, Winter, 1970.

5108 Iwamoto, D. "Student violence and rebellion; how big a problem?" National Education Association Journal, 54:10-13, December, 1965.

5109 Jack, H. A. "Mahatma Gandhi: ten years after," Saturday Review, 41:24, January 25, 1958.

5110 Jacobs, Paul. "Prelude to riot--a view of urban America from the bottom," Los Angeles Free Press, 01 12 14 01 68

5111 Jassen, Jeff. "Violence flares on street of love," Berkeley Barb, 06 02 01 03 67 (Haight Street.)

5112 Johnson, P. "Are we a nation of hoods?" Reader's Digest, 89:127-9, December, 1966.

5113 Kamisar, Yale. "The Citizen on trial," Current History, 53:76-81, August, 1967.

5114 Katzman, Don. "The New Left as American as apple pie," East Village Other, 02 07 03 01 69 (Violence, concept of private property, and other alternatives for survival.)

5115 Kaufman, Arnold S. "Future for dissents; radical education and convention politics," Commonweal, 89:314-17, November 29, 1968.

5116 Keating, Kenneth B. "The Nature of responsible dissent: an analysis of the responsibilities of dissenters and the duties of the ruling majority," New York State Bar Journal, 41:52-58, 1967.

5117 King, Lawrence T. "Pickets in the valley," Commonweal, 73:64-7, October 14, 1960.

5118 King, Martin Luther Jr. "Declaration of independence from the war in Vietnam," Ramparts, 5:33-37, May, 1967.

5119 _____. "Nonviolence and racial justice," Christian Century, 74:165-7, February 6, 1957.

5120 _____. "Pilgrimage to non-violence," Christian Century, 77:439-41, April 13, 1960.

5120a Kirby, John B. "Violence and the conflict of American values," Rocky Mountain Social Science Journal, 6: October, 1969.

5121 Knopf, Terry Ann. "Race, riots, reporters," Commonweal, 93:336-340, July, 1970.

5122 Kopkind, Andrew. "White on black: the riot commission and the rhetoric of reform," Hard Times, 09 15 01 01 69

5123 Krutch, J. W. "If you don't mind my saying so," American Scholar, 37:15-18, 1967.

5124 _____. "What does violence say about man?" Saturday Review, 48:18-19, March 27, 1965.

5125 Kurtz, Paul. "Misuses of civil disobedience," Dissent, January-February, 1970.

5126 Ladd, John. "Morality and the ideal of rationality in formal organizations," Monist, 54:488-516, October, 1970.

5127 Lang, Berel. "Civil disobedience and nonviolence: a distinction with a difference," Ethics, 80:156-159, January, 1970.

5128 Lawrence, D. "Fallacy of civil disobedience," Reader's Digest, 87:111-112, October, 1965.

5129 Lebowitz, M. "Making the violent scene," Nation, 204:57-9, January 9, 1967.

5130 LeGrande, J. L. "Nonviolent civil disobedience and police enforcement policy," Journal of Criminal Law, Criminology and Police Science, 58:393-409, 1967.

5131 Leivy, Guenter. "Superior orders, nuclear warfare and the dictates of conscience: the dilemma of military obedience in the atomic age," American Political Science Review, 55:3-23, 1961.

5132 Liebman, Morris I. "Civil disobedience; address, August 11, 1964," Vital Speeches, 30:766-8, October 1, 1964.

5133 _____. "Civil disobedience: a threat to our law society," American Bar Association Journal, 51:645-47, 1965.

5134 Lipton, Lawrence. "Billyclubs blitz nonconvention," Los Angeles Free Press, 08 30 01 01 68

5135 _____. "Six days in August: the old order; a chronicle of disorder, violence and decay: The new order; a chronicle of the emerging life style.

Saturday August 24," Los Angeles Free Press, 09 06 03 01 68

5136 Lockshin, Arnold. "The Movement and suppression," Paper Tiger, 11 -- 06 01 67 (Suppression by governmental attacks as it relates to movement activities.)

5137 Lynn, Conrad J. "We must disobey! Civil disobedience: an analysis and rationale, significant cases involving negro rights are compared with cases that concern draft card burning, refusal of induction and other issues relating to the prosecution of the war in Vietnam," New York University Law Review, 43:648-720, October, 1968.

5138 Mabee, C. "Sit-ins and marches," Nation, 195:197-9, October 6, 1967.

5139 MacCallum, G. C. Jr. "Negative and positive freedom," Philosophical Review, 76:312-34, 1967.

5140 Macfarlane, L. J. "Justifying political disobedience," Ethics, 79:24-55, 1968.

5141 McGuire, Diarmuid. "The Violence of property," Free You, 05 11 08 01 70

5142 McNamara, R. J. "Ethics of violent dissent," Academy of Political Science Proceedings, 29:140-45, 1968.

5143 McWilliams, Wilson Carey. "Civil disobedience and contemporary constitutionalism: the American case," Comparative Politics, 1:211-27, 1969.

5144 Marine, Gene. "Getting Eldridge Cleaver," Ramparts, 6:49-50, May, 1968.

5145 Marshall, Burke. "The Protest movement and the law," Virginia Law Review, 51:785-803, 1965.

5146 Martin, Rex. "Civil disobedience," Ethics, 80:123-137, January, 1970.

5147 Marx, Gary T. "Civil disorder and the agents of social control," Journal of Social Issues, 26:19-57,

Winter, 1970.

5148 Mataxis, Theodore C. "This far, no further: how U.S. Army handles dissenters in uniform," Military Review, 50:74-82, 1970.

5149 Mead, Margaret. "Unwitting partners to youthful violence," Redbook, 125:24, May, 1965.

5150 Mecartney, John. "Civil disobedience and anarchy," Social Science, 42:205-212, 1967.

5151 Miller, William R. "Nonviolence in the racial crisis," Christian Century, 81:927-30, July 22, 1964. (Discussion, 81:1179, September 23, 1964.)

5152 Nanes, Allan S. "The Federal role in criminal investigation procedures," Current History, 53:107-110, August, 1967.

5153 Neary, John. "The Two girls from no 18," Life, 68:27-29, March 27, 1970.

5154 Neugeboren, J. "Disobedience now! The Stanford statement," Commonweal, 86:367-9, June 16, 1967. (Discussion, 86:443-5, July 14, 1967.)

5155 Neuhauer, D. E. "Some conditions of democracy," American Political Science Review, 61:1002-1009, 1967.

5156 Nixon, Richard M. "Responsible university leadership; violence and dissent," Vital Speeches, 36:738-40, October 1, 1970.

5157 Nolan, David. "Patrolmen acquitted of Orangeburg massacre," Liberation News Service, 06 05 09 01 69

5158 Novak, M. "Holding firm to the truth: Satyagraha," New Republic, 158:23-24, June 22, 1968.

5159 Ohmart, Howard. "The Community and the juvenile," Current History, 53:94-101, August, 1967.

5160 Paton, A. "Church, state and race," Christian Century, 75:278-80, March 5, 1958.

5161 Paulsen, Monrad. "The Role of juvenile courts," Current History, 53:70-75, August, 1967.

5162 Pemberton, John de J. Jr. "War protester," Current History, 55:23-27, July, 1968.

5163 Ploscawe, Morris. "New approach to the control of organized crime," Annals of the American Academy, 347:74-81, May, 1963.

5164 Plumb, J. H. "When does a riot become a revolution," Horizon, 10:46-47, 1968.

5165 Pocklington, Thomas. "Protest, resistance and political obligation," Canadian Journal of Political Science, 3:1-17, 1970.

5166 Porter, Herb. "Attorney analyzes causes of Watts demonstrations," Los Angeles Free Press, 08 20 04 03 65

5167 Poussaint, A. F. "Why blacks kill blacks; psychiatrist on ghetto violence," Ebony, 25:143-6, October, 1970.

5168 Powell, Lewis F. "Civil disobedience; prelude to revolution," New York State Bar Journal, 40:161-88, 1968.

5169 Prosch, H. "Limits to the moral claim in civil disobedience," Ethics, 75:103-11, 1965.

5170 ———. "Towards an ethics of civil disobedience," Ethics, 77:176-92, 1967.

5171 Puner, Nicholas. "Civil disobedience: an analysis and rationale," New York University Law Review, 43:720, 1968.

5171a Redlich, Norman, and Kenneth R. Feinberg. "Individual conscience and the selective conscientious objector: the right not to kill," New York University Law Review, 44:875-900, 1969.

5172 Regamey, P. "Mystique of non-violent action," Thought, 41:381-89, 1966.

5173 Reinholz, Mary. "Violence breeds counter-violence: Marcuse," Los Angeles Free Press, 05 23 07 01 69 ("Student violence is a direct reaction to the institutionalized violence perpetrated by this society.")

5174 Robison, Sophia N. "Juvenile delinquency," Current History, 52:341-348, June, 1967.

5175 Rogin, M. "Politics of outrage; notes on the student left," Commonweal, 84:99-102, 1966.

5176 Rostow, E. V. "Consent of the governed," Virginia Quarterly Review, 44:513-30, 1968.

5177 Rubin, Jerry. "The Academy award of protest," Fifth Estate, 04 03 03 01 69 (Indictment of crossing state lines to create civil disturbances. Jerry hopes he is worthy of the indictment along with the Beatles, Elvis Presley, Marilyn Monroe and Joe Nameth among others.)

5178 Ruby, Jack. "A Letter from jail by Jack Ruby," Ramparts, 5:18-21, February, 1967.

5179 Rusch, Richard B. "Crime and computers: computer technology is extending the reach of the law's long arm across the nation," Electronic Age, 29:32-34, Summer, 1970. (Application of computers to correcting crimes of violence.)

5180 Russell, Bertrand. "On American violence," Ramparts, 8:55-58, March, 1970.

5181 _____. "Civil disobedience," New Statesman, 61:245-6, February, 1961.

5182 Ryan, Sheila. "Obedience to the law ...," Spokane Natural, 05 09 03 01 69

5183 _____. "Violence: who do you believe," Chicago Kaleidoscope, 02 28 15 01 69 (Interim report on violence submitted to LBJ on January 9, 1969. Contradictions between this report and the Skolnick Report are described.)

5184 Sale, J. Kirk. "Ted Gold: education for violence,"

Nation, 210:423-429, April 13, 1970.

5185 Sartre, Jean-Paul. "A Psychoanalytic dialogue with a commentary," Ramparts, 8:43-49, October, 1969. (An abridged transcript of a "psychoanalytic dialogue with a reversal of roles between patient and analyst." Sartre's interpretation is superb.)

5186 Scheer, Robert. "Lord Russell," Ramparts, 5:16-23, May, 1967.

5187 _____. "On establishment law and people's disorder," Ramparts, 7:4, July, 1969.

5188 Schreiber, F. R., and M. Herman. "Psychiatrists analyze the Los Angeles riots," Science Digest, 58:18-22, November, 1965.

5189 Schwartz, E. K. "Family in an age of violence," New York Times Magazine, January 22, 1961, p. 47.

5190 Scott, J. P. "Anatomy of violence," Nation, 200:662-6, June 21, 1965.

5191 Scott, Jack. "The White Olympics," Ramparts, 6:54-61, May, 1968.

5192 Sears, David O., and John B. McConshay. "Racial socialization, comparison levels, and the Watts riots," Journal of Social Issues, 26:121-140, Winter, 1970.

5193 Shahn, B. "In defense of chaos," Ramparts, 6:12-13, December 14, 1968.

5194 Sheerin, J. B. "Clean conscience or Black Muslims?" Catholic World, 197:212-15, July, 1963.

5195 Sherk, J. H. "Position of the conscientious objector," Current History, 55:18-22, July, 1968.

5196 Sherrill, R. G. "Patriotism of protest," Nation, 13:463-66, December 13, 1965.

5197 Sibley, Mulford Q. "Anonymity, dissent, and individual integrity in America, with questions and answers," <u>American Academy of Political and Social Science</u>, 378:45-57, 1968.

5198 Sibley, Mulford Q. "Conscience, law, and the obligation to obey," <u>Monist</u>, 54:556-586, October, 1970.

5199 Simon, P. "Montgomery looks forward; institute on non-violence and social change," <u>Christian Century</u>, 75:104, January 22, 1958.

5200 Sisk, John P. "Intolerable allegories of dissent," <u>Catholic World</u>, 210:55-58, November, 1969.

5201 Skolnick, Jerome. "Excerpts from the politics of protest," <u>Dallas Notes</u>, 02 19 07 01 69

5202 Skolnickoff, E. B. "Public challenge of government action," <u>Science</u>, 164:499, 1969.

5203 Smith, H. W. "Call for courage in handling unrest; excerpt from address," <u>U.S. News</u>, 61:14, August 8, 1966.

5204 Stanley, M. "Turn to violence: a sociological view of insurgency," <u>International Journal of Comparative Sociology</u>, 8:232-44, 1967.

5205 Stern, Sol. "Trouble in an all American city," <u>New York Times Magazine</u>, July 10, 1966.

5206 Stocker, Michael. "Moral duties, institutions and natural facts," <u>Monist</u>, 54:602-624, October, 1970.

5207 Thigpen, R. B., and L. A. Downing. "Power, participation and the politics of disruption," <u>Christian Century</u>, 86:973-75, July 22, 1969.

5208 Thompson, S. M. "Authority of law," <u>Ethics</u>, 75:16-24, 1964.

5209 Tolstoy, Leo. "Advice to a draftee," <u>Atlantic Monthly</u>, 221:56-57, 1968.

5210 Tomlinson, T. M. "Ideological foundations for negro action: a comparative analysis of militant and non-militant views of the Los Angeles riot," <u>Journal of Social Issues</u>, 26:93-119, Winter, 1970.

5211   Tornquist, Elizabeth. "Causes of Stanford violence ignored," North Carolin Anvil, 11 08 05 01 69

5212   Tumin, Melvin M. "Violence and democracy," Dissent, 17:321, July-August, 1970.

5213   Turner, William W. "Assassinations," Ramparts, 7:6-12, September 7, 1968.

5214   Tyler, Gus. "The Criminal and the community," Current History, 53:102-106, August, 1967.

5215   Van Dusen, Lewis H. Jr. "Civil disobedience: destroyer of democracy," American Bar Association Journal, 55:123-26, 1969.

5216   Vander-Zanden, J. W. "Non-violent resistance movement against segregation," American Journal of Sociology, 68: March, 1963.

5217   Ver Eecke, Wilfried. "Law, morality and society: reflections on violence," Ethics, 80:140-145, January, 1970.

5218   Von Nostitz, S. "Dictatorship and resistance: the problem of how to resist," Western Political Quarterly, 20:161-72, 1967.

5219   Walker Commission Report. "Confrontation at the Conrad Hilton," Trans-action, 6:37-49, January, 1969. ("A key section from the Walker Commission Report, 'Rights in Conflict'.")

5220   Walters, Pat. "Why the negro children march," New York Times Magazine, March 21, 1965.

5221   Walzer, Michael. "Obligation to disobey," Ethics, 77:163-75, 1967.

5222   _____. "Politics of non-violent resistance," Dissent, 7:369-376, Autumn, 1960.

5223   Waskow, Arthur I. "Nonviolence and creative disorder," Christian Century, 82:1253-5, October 13, 1965.

5224   Weingartner, Rudolph H. "Justifying civil

disobedience," Columbia University Forum, 9:38-44, 1966.

5225 Whittaker, Charles E. "Dangers of mass disobedience," Reader's Digest, 87:121-4, December, 1965.

5226 Widmer, Kingsley. "Living-room confrontation: the rage against violence," Nation, 211:45-48, July 20, 1970.

5227 Wieck, David. "Dissidence," Monist, 54:587-601, October, 1970.

5228 Woetzel, Robert K. "Crime: an overview," Current History, 52:321-326, June, 1967.

5229 Woetzel, Robert K. "Crime and violence in American life," Current History, 55:230-233, October, 1968.

5230 Wolfe, D. "Concerning dissent and civil disobedience," Science, 161:9, 1968.

5231 Wolfgang, M. E. "Patterns of violence, symposium," American Academy of Political and Social Science, 364:1-157, March, 1966.

5232 Wyzanski, C. E. Jr. "On civil disobedience," Atlantic Monthly, 221:58-60, 1968.

5233 Zatlyn, Ted. "Watts ... A death in the family," Los Angeles Free Press, 08 16 01 03 68

5234 Zinn, Howard. "Force of nonviolence," Nation, 194:227-33, March 17, 1962.

IX. MILITARY SERVICE--COMPULSORY AND VOLUNTARY

BOOKS

5235 American Friends Service Committee. Peace Education Division. The Draft? N.Y.: Hill and Wang, 1968.

5236 Baxter, Archibald. We will not cease. Christchurch, New Zealand: Caxton Press, 1968.

5237 Bender, Ruie A. Soldiers of compassion. Scottdale, Pennsylvania: Herald Press, 1969.

5238 Blackwood, Alan. Face to face with your draft board; a guide to personal appearances. Berkeley, California: World Without War Council of Northern California, 1969.

5239 Carper, Jean. Bitter greetings; the scandal of the military draft. N.Y.: Grossman, 1967.

5240 Chapman, Bruce K. Our unfair and obsolete draft, and what we can do about it. N.Y.: Pocket Books, 1968.

5241 _____. The Wrong man in uniform. N.Y.: Trident Press, 1967.

5242 Cohen, E. E., and L. Kapp (eds.). Manpower policies for youth. N.Y.: Columbia University Press, 1966.

5243 Congressional Quarterly (Research Reports). U.S. draft policy and its impact. Washington, D.C. Congressional Quarterly, 1968.

5244 Davis, James W., and Kenneth Dolbeare. Little groups of neighbors: the selective service system.

Chicago: Markham, 1968. (Series in Public Policy Analysis.)

5245 Finn, James. A Conflict of loyalties: the case for selective conscientious objection. N.Y.: Pegasus, 1969.

5246 Gaylin, Williard. In the service of their country: war resisters in prison. N.Y.: Viking, 1970. (Contains some 26 case studies of imprisoned war resisters, and some explanations concerning alternatives to war service.)

5247 Gerhardt, James M. The Draft and public policy: issues in military manpower procurement, 1945-1970. Ohio: Ohio State University Press, 1970. (Description of inequalities existing in the selective service system.)

5248 Gleaves, S. Z., and L. T. Wertenbaker. You and the armed forces. N.Y.: Simon and Schuster, 1961.

5249 Glick, Edward Bernard. Peaceful conflict. Harrisburg, Pennsylvania: Stackpole Press, 1967.

5250 Griffiths, J. The Draft law: a college outline for the selective service act and regulations. Connecticut: Yale University Press, 1968.

5251 Haenni, A. L. Draftees or volunteers. N.Y.: Vantage, 1969.

5252 Harwood, Michael. Student's guide to military service. 4th ed. N.Y.: Meredith Press, 1968.

5253 Horton, Frank. How to end the draft. Washington, D.C.: National Press, 1967.

5254 How the draft can be ended. Washington, D.C.: National Press, 1967.

5255 Jacobs, Clyde E. The Selective service act: a case study of the governmental process. N.Y.: Dodd, 1968.

5256 Kellog, Walter G. The Conscientious objector. N.Y.: Da Capo Press, 1970. (Reprint)

Military Service 463

5257 Liston, Robert. The Draft. N.Y.: McGraw-Hill, 1969.

5258 Little, Roger W. (ed.). Selective service and American society. N.Y.: Russell Sage Foundation, 1969.

5259 Lynd, Alice. We won't go; personal accounts of war objectors. Boston: Beacon, 1968.

5260 Lynn, Conrad J. How to stay out of the Army. N.Y.: Grove Press, 1968.

5261 McCague, James. Second rebellion: the story of the New York City Draft riots. N.Y.: Dial, 1968.

5262 MacClain, Thomas B., David Zarefsky, and Garry Mathieson. Manpower for national security. Illinois: National Textbook Company, 1969.

5263 MacCloskey, Monro. You and the draft. California: Rosen Press, 1965.

5264 McNeill, William H. The Draft in the light of history. In: The Draft; a handbook of facts and alternatives, edited by Sol Tax. Chicago: University of Chicago, 1967.

5265 Marmion, Harry A. Selective service in America; conflict and compromise. N.Y.: Wiley, 1968.

5266 Miller, James C. III (ed.). Why the draft? The case for a volunteer Army. N.Y.: Penguin, 1968. (Paper)

5267 Moskos, Charles C. Jr. The American enlisted man. N.Y.: Russell Sage Foundation, 1970. ("Rank and file account of the thinking of the enlisted man...")

5268 National Advisory Commission On Selective Service. In pursuit of equity: who serves when not all serve? The Marshall Commission Report. Washington, D.C.: G.P.O., 1967.

5269 Reedy, George E. Who will do our fighting for us? N.Y.: World, 1969. (Proposes a draft by lottery for all eligible 19 year olds.)

5270 Reeves, Thomas C., and Karl Hess. The End of the draft: the feasibility of freedom. Intro. by Kenneth Boulding. Preface by Senator George McGovern. N.Y.: Random House, 1970. (Controversial account of why the U.S. should repeat the draft laws, and why freedom should be given priority over security.)

5271 Riley, T. The Draft. N.Y.: Vantage, 1969.

5272 Rothenberg, Leslie. The Draft and you. N.Y.: Anchor, 1969.

5273 Sanders, Jacquin. Draft and the Vietnam War. N.Y.: Walker and Co., 1966.

5274 Selective Service Law Reporter. Washington, D.C.: Public Law Education Institute, 1968.

5275 Shapiro, Andrew O., and John M. Stuker. Mastering the draft. N.Y.: Little, 1970. (For both registrant and parent on solving the many intricate problems of the Selective Service System.)

5275a Sherrill, R. Military justice is to justice as military music is to music. N.Y.: Harper, 1970.

5276 Sibley, Mulford Q., and Philip E. Jacob. Conscription of conscience ... Johnson Reprint, 1952.

5277 Stafford, Robert. How to end the draft. California: National Press Inc., 1967.

5278 Stevens, Franklin. If this be treason: your sons tell their own stories of why they won't fight for their country. N.Y.: McKay, 1970. (Stories about inequities in the SSS.)

5279 Tatum, Arlo, and Joseph S. Tuchinsky. Guide to the draft. Boston: Beacon, 1970. (Explores alternatives for the man faced by the draft. Includes forms used by Selective Service Counselors.)

5280 Tax, Sol (ed.). Draft, a handbook of facts and alternatives. Chicago: University of Chicago Press,

1967.

5280a Trytten, M. H. Student deferment in selective service: a vital factor in National Security. Minnesota: University of Minnesota Press, 1970.

5281 Upton, E. The Military policy of the U.S. Connecticut: Greenwood Press, 1969.

5282 U.S. Superintendent of Documents. It's your choice; how to chose the military service program that will serve you best. A guide to the opportunities open to volunteers for military service. U.S. Supt. of Documents. Washington, D.C.: G.P.O., 1968.

5283 U.S. Superintendent of Documents. Report of the task force on the structure of the selective service system. October 16, 1967. Washington, D.C.: G.P.O., 1967.

5284 Walton, George H. Let's end the draft mess. N.Y.: McKay, 1967.

5285 _____. Wasted generation. Philadelphia: Chilton, 1965.

5286 Wamsley, Gary L. Selective service and a changing America; a study of organizational-environmental relationships. N.Y.: Merrill, 1969.

5287 Zahn, Gordon Charles. War, conscience and dissent. N.Y.: Hawthorn, 1967.

5288 Zimmer, Timothy W. L. Letters of a C.O. from prison. Valley Forge, Pennsylvania: Judson Press, 1969.

EDITORIALS

5289 "ABC's of draft by lottery," U.S. News, 67:33-35, December 1, 1969.

5290 "Another says 'no'," Pittsburgh Point, 06 05 02 01 69 (Thomas Burgess's objections to being drafted.)

5291 "Beating the draft, 1970 style," Time, 96:67, November 16, 1970.

5292 "Busting the draft or the shit hits the fan," San Jose Red Eye, 09 26 04 01 69

5293 "By the numbers; reform bill passed," Newsweek, 74:30, December 1, 1969.

5294 "By the numbers: Richard Nixon's lottery plan," Newsweek, 73:38, May 26, 1969.

5295 "CCPA joins with CNVA vs. draft," Berkeley Barb, 02 25 01 05 66 (Two strong organizations join forces to protest SSS.)

5296 "Changes and grad students; plan to draft nineteen-year-olds," Science News, 96:264, September 27, 1969.

5297 "Coming changes in the draft; effects of the lottery," U.S. News, 67:37-39, December 1, 1969.

5298 "Draft board rip-offs," Distant Drummer, 05 28 02 03 70

5299 "Draft bonanza with few takers," U.S. News, 69:32, December 21, 1970.

5300 "Draft-by-lottery: moving up," U.S. News, 67:9, October 27, 1969.

5301 "Draft called forced labor," Berkeley Barb, 06 02 03 01 67

5302 "Draft card burning makes a communion," Pittsburgh Point, 04 09 05 02 70

5303 "Draft outlook for '70 and '71--interview with Curtis W. Tarr, Director, Selective Service," U.S. News, 69:46-51, July 6, 1970.

5304 "Draft protesters imprisoned," Distant Drummer, 04 09 03 02 70

Military Service   467

5305   "Draft vs. social justice," Nation, 209:461, March 3,
        1969.

5306   "Drafting by lot," National Review, 21:1254, December 16, 1969.

5307   "End to draft as punishment," U.S. News, 68:9, February 2, 1970.

5308   "Familiar scene in Federal Court," Pittsburgh Point,
        06 05 01 01 69 (The trial of a draft resister
        who said to the judge, "I don't take the law lightly
        ... but when I am put in a position where I
        might have to kill someone, I must disobey the
        law.")

5309   "Feeling the draft," Economist, 230:46, February 15,
        1969.

5310   "How deserters are caught and how not to," Washington Free Press, 09 13 -- 01 69

5311   "January draft: number one to thirty," U.S. News,
        67:5, December 29, 1969.

5312   "Leonard Boudin: Dr. Spock's attorney," East Village
        Other, 07 23 05 01 69 (Interview with the attorney for Dr. Spock.)

5313   "Lottery draft; how it's working," U.S. News, 68:8,
        January 19, 1970.

5314   "Luck of the draw," Time, 94:26, December 12, 1969.

5315   "Massachusetts v. Viet Nam," Time, 96:77, November 23, 1970.

5316   "New questions about the draft--the official answers,"
        U.S. News, 69:70-71, November 16, 1970. (Description of rules regarding the chances of youths
        being inducted.)

5317   "Numbers game," Newsweek, 74:37-8, December 15,
        1969.

5318   "Outlook now on draft changes," U.S. News, 67:12,
        November 10, 1969.

5319 "Pittsburgh draft resistance," Grok, 02 -- 10 03 70

5320 "Registrars play God with students," Campus Underground, 03 10 04 01 69

5321 "Rx for draft dodging; physicians engaged in draft counseling," Newsweek, 76:42-3, August 3, 1970.

5322 "Sanctuary offered draft resisters," Berkeley Barb, 11 24 10 01 67

5323 "S. D. resistance greets General Hershey," San Diego Free Press, 02 14 03 05 69

5324 "Selective service and higher education," School and Society, 96:186-8, March 16, 1968.

5325 "Statement on selective service and the junior college," School and Society, 96:155-6, March 2, 1968.

5326 "Teacher hits N.Y. files," Distant Drummer, 09 04 12 01 69 (A member of the 'New York Eight' who helped to destroy draft files.)

5327 "A Victory for draft resisters," Pittsburgh Point, 11 13 02 02 69 (Celebration by Pittsburgh draft resisters.)

5328 "You may have been drafted illegally," Ally, 09 -- 01 01 69

5329 "A Youth's reason for spurning the draft--a judge's answer," U.S. News, 68:27-28, June 8, 1970.

5330 "What the draft lottery does," U.S. News, 67:7, December 8, 1969.

5331 "Women's day at the draft board," Win, 08 -- 03 01 69

PERIODICALS

5332 Adams, I. "Youth without a country," Atlas, 13:47-48, January, 1967. ("Americans in Canada to avoid the draft.")

5333 Alsop, Stewart. "Dreadful systems," Newsweek, 76:80, August 31, 1970.

5334 ———. "Need to hate; dodgers in Canada," Newsweek, 76:80, July 27, 1970.

5335 American Council On Education. Commission on Federal Relations. "Selective service and student deferment," School and Society, 95:428-30, November 11, 1967.

5336 Beavan, K. A. "Opposition grows to Vietnam war; resignations and demonstrations," Times Education Supplement, 2744:1413, December 22, 1967.

5337 Boston Law Commune. "Draft lottery fraud," Old Mole, 12 17 02 03 69

5338 Brewington, Jack. "Resistance demonstration," San Jose Red Eye, 11 20 07 01 69

5339 Brock, William E. III, and Samuel S. Stratton. "Should the U.S. switch to a volunteer army? Yes, by William E. Brock III; No, by Samuel B. Stratton," American Legion Magazine, 84:12-13, April, 1968.

5340 Brokek, Ted. "Pick a number ... any number; on the art of lottery-dodging," Great Speckled Bird, 12 08 11 69

5341 Brooke, Edward W. "Military manpower: no easy answer. Views of Senators Brooke and Muskie on the all-volunteer army," Class Student Guide, Fall, 1970, p. 19.

5342 Brown, S. "From 1-A to 4-F and all points in between; draft counseling," New York Times Magazine, November 29, 1970, pp. 34-5.

5343   Chambers, Bette. "Draft to end," Spokane Natural--Chief Joseph, 05 09 09 01 69

5344   Clark, B. "Question is what kind of army?" Harper's, 239:80, September, 1969.

5345   Clatanoff, William B. Jr. "The Role of the armed forces," Current History, 55:13-18, July, 1968.

5346   Coffman, J. "CO and the draft," Library Journal, 94:2059-65, May 15, 1969.

5347   Cohen, C. "Conscientious objection," Ethics, 78:269-279, July, 1968.

5348   Cooney, John, and Dana Spitzer. "Hell, no, we won't go! deserters and draft dodgers in Canada and Sweden," Trans-action, 6:53-62, September, 1969.

5349   Cullinan, Terrance. "National service program abroad," Current History, 55:97-102, August, 1968.

5350   Davis, Harry R. "Christian neglect of political values: the case of selective objection," Christian Century, 86:1510-1514, November 26, 1969.

5351   Decker, Mike. "Washington protestors rush troop lines, burn draft cards," Los Angeles Free Press, 10 27 01 01 67

5352   Donovan, J. B. "Conscription; with a choice--proposals of a new national youth service for all young men and women," America, 120:726-7, June 28; Reply by T. E. Quigley 121:51, August 2, 1969.

5353   Dreifus, Claudia. "An opportunity to end the draft," East Village Other, 03 19 03 01 69 (Nine Senators including Senator Mark Hatfield introduce a bill to end the draft and replace it with a volunteer army.)

5354   Duncan, Donald. "Sanctuary--flight from freedom," Ramparts, 5:30-33, April, 1967. (The draft-dodger syndrome and the migration to Canada.)

5355   Eaton, J. W. "National service and forced labor,"

Journal of Conflict Resolution, 12:129-134, March, 1968.

5356 Eberly, Donald. "National needs and national service," Current History, 55:65-71, August, 1968.

5357 Ellingsworth, H. W. "Masked communicator: a plea for relevance; satire," Speech Teacher, 18:154-7, March, 1969.

5358 Figg, Donald. "What Uncle Sam doesn't know about Donald Figg won't hurt him," Ramparts, 5:12-14, August, 1966.

5359 Finkin, M. W. "Hershey letter," American Association of University Professors Bulletin, 53:412-13, December, 1967.

5360 Finneran, Mary. "The Draft dilemma," Together, 16:12-16, February, 1970.

5361 Fountain, L. "I am a draft counselor," McCalls, 98:73, October, 1970.

5362 Fox, Howard A. "Gays getting shafted, then drafted," Los Angeles Free Press, 08 14 59 02 70

5363 Fraenkl, H. "No guns," New Statesman, 66:695-6, November 15, 1963.

5364 Gage, Linda. "Father Berrigan arrested," Los Angeles Free Press, 08 14 02 05 70

5365 Gillie, D. "Men of conviction," Spectator, 203:204, August 5, 1960.

5366 GI Press. "Conscientious objectors unite at Fort Jackson," Rough Draft, 10 -- 03 06 69

5367 Gleazer, E. J. "Selective service problem," Junior College Journal, 38:3, February, 1968.

5368 Glick, Ted. "And it's a free country?" Two-Cents Plain Dealer, 10 02 01 02 69 (Conscription, Selective Service Systems, Vietnam escalation. Article was submitted by Mr. Glick, Lancaster draft resister.)

5369 Goldberger, P., and Curtis W. Tarr. "From cool campus to hot seat," Senior Scholastic, 97:16-17, November 2, 1970.

5370 Gregory, Keith. "Open letter to a draft board," Northwest Passage, 09 09 14 01 69

5371 Hall, Edward. "National service and the American tradition," Current History, 55:72-77, August, 1968.

5372 Harris, Mark. "A confrontation with the SSS," New Left Notes, 03 27 07 01 67

5373 Hays, Samuel. "Military training in the U.S. today," Current History, 55:7-12, July, 1968.

5374 Hershey, Lewis B. "The Operation of the selective service system," Current History, 55:1-6, July, 1968.

5375 Hollingsworth, M. "Americans and Vietnam, those who escape," New Statesman, 74:838, December 15, 1967.

5376 Jezer, Martin. "Draft stoppers discover New York is no Oakland," Los Angeles Free Press, 12 15 16 02 67

5377 Kennedy, Edward. "Random selection: an alternative to selective service," Current History, 55:93-96, August, 1968.

5378 King, T. R., and D. R. Taylor. "National high school debate subject; how can the U.S. best maintain manpower for an effective defense system," School Activities, 40:6-12, October, 1968.

5379 Kopkind, Andrew. "Are we in the middle of a revolution," New York Times Magazine, November 10, 1968, pp. 54-55.

5380 _____. "Five martyrs of Boston," New Statesman, 75:31-32, January 12, 1968.

5381 Langer, E. "Oakland seven; organizers of stop the draft week," Atlantic, 224:76-82, October, 1969.

5382 Lee, Ulysses. "The Draft and the negro," Current History, 55:28-33, July, 1968.

5383 Levitt, Dennis. "FBI busts Minnesota 8," Los Angeles Free Press, 07 17 02 02 70

5384 Liberation News Service. "New York women burn draft files," Fifth Estate, 07 10 17 03 69

5385 Lippincott, W. T. "Our catastrophic draft policy," Journal of Chemical Education, 45:353, June, 1968.

5386 Looney, D. L. "How to help your son face the draft," Better Homes and Gardens, 48:30, November, 1970.

5387 Lovelett, Bruce. "New draft rule may be regressive," Guardian, 06 27 05 01 70

5387a Margolin, Bruce M. "Inside the new draft laws," Los Angeles Free Press, 07 10 08 01 70

5388 Mead, Margaret. "The Case for compulsory national service," Current History, 55:84-85, August, 1968.

5389 Mitrisin, John. "The Pros and cons of a voluntary army," Current History, 55:86-92, August, 1968.

5390 Oi, Walter Y. "Can we afford the draft?" Current History, 55:34-39, July, 1968.

5391 Pearlman, Robert. "Two worlds of draft resistance," Paper Tiger, 12 -- 02 01 67

5392 Pemberton, John de J. Jr. "The War protester," Current History, 55:23-27, July, 1968.

5393 Peterson, Frank. "Resistance and the April action," Distant Drummer, 04 10 10 01 69 (Philadelphia resistance attempts to shut down draft boards.)

5394 Poppy, John. "The Draft: hazardous to your health," Look, 33:32-34, August 12, 1969.

5395 Robb, Charles C. "Westinghouse H.S. hears alternatives," Pittsburgh Point, 04 24 01 02 69

5396 Rumper, Herman. "In-service objectors have discharge rights," San Diego Free Press, 12 13 05 01 68

5397 Salstrom, F. P. "The Implications of draft file destruction," Distant Drummer, 01 08 09 02 70

5398 Sayre, Nora. "Fighting the draft," New Statesman, 75:373, March 22, 1968.

5399 Schwartz, Don. "The Pre-induction physical or 'How I got a free meal from my Uncle Sam,'" Burning River News, 05 09 04 01 69

5400 Scull, Jerolyn R. "Mounties back draft avoiders," Los Angeles Free Press, 11 17 01 03 67

5401 Sharp, L., and R. Krasnesor. "College students and military service: the experience of an earlier cohort," Sociology of Education, 41:390-400, Fall, 1968.

5402 Sherk, J. H. "The Position of the conscientious objector," Current History, 55:18-22, 1968.

5403 Smith, Gar. "Cardburning Boston style in church," Berkeley Barb, 10 27 07 01 67

5403a Steinberg, Jeff. "Buffalo resistance meets FBI harassment," Buffalo Insighter, 11 20 01 01 67

5404 Stickgold, Mark. "Thank you, you have just convicted Jesus Christ," Ann Arbor Argus, 06 19 02 01 69 (Description of the court trial of the Milwaukee 14 for draft card burning.)

5405 Swomley, J. M. Jr. "Why the draft should go," Nation, 209:108-110, August 11, 1969.

5406 Tax, Sol. "Society, the individual and national service," Current History, 55:78-83, August, 1968.

5407 Tobis, David. "Future U. S. domination may rely on volunteer army," Guardian, 12 06 06 01 69 (Lottery and military conscription.)

5408 Tomlinson, K. Y. "ROTC under attack," Reader's

Military Service

Digest, 95:231-4, November, 1969.

5409 Tyre, Marlene. "Inhuman treatment charged by families of Fort Hood three," Fifth Estate, 10 16 08 01 66

5410 Westmoreland, W. C. "Towards a volunteer army; address, October 30, 1970," Vital Speeches, 37:98-100, December 1, 1970.

5411 Wingell, Bill. "Draft board attackers come forward in Philadelphia," Guardian, 06 13 04 01 70

5412 Wolfle, Dael. "Selective service and college enrollment," Science, 167:129, January 9, 1970.

5413 Wood, James E. "Conscientious objection and the state," Journal of Church and State, 11: Autumn, 1969.

5414 Worstell, David. "Criminal call in Federal Court," Pittsburgh Point, 01 15 01 01 70

5415 _____. "Prisoners of war," Pittsburgh Point, 02 05 01 01 70

5416 _____. "Yessir? Know your rights--your alternatives to the military," Pittsburgh Point. 04 24 02 02 69

X. LIST OF ALTERNATIVE TABLOIDS

ABAS
(Ceased publishing in 1970)

ADVOCATE
Box 74695
Los Angeles, Calif. 90004

ALCHEMIST
Manhatten, Kansas

ALLY
Box 9276
Berkeley, Calif. 94709

ALTERNATIVE
Box 275
Naperville, Ill. 60504

ANN ARBOR ARGUS
708 Arch Street
Ann Arbor, Michigan 48104

ARGO
Box 12629 UCSB
Santa Barbara, Cal. 93107

ATLANTIS NEWS
RD-5 Box 22A
Saugerties, N. Y. 12477

AVATAR
145 Columbia Street
Cambridge, Mass. 02139

BEHIND THE SHIELD
5517 Marconi Street
Madison, Wisc. 53705

BERKELEY BARB
Box 5017
Berkeley, Calif. 95715

BERKELEY TRIBE
P. O. Box 9043
Berkeley, Calif. 94709

BLACK AND RED
Box 793
Kalamazoo, Mich. 49005

BLACK PANTHER
3106 Shattuck Avenue
Berkeley, Calif. 94705

BUDDIST ORACLE
14016 Orinoco Avenue
East Cleveland, Ohio 44112

BUFFALO CHIPS
Box 1122
Omaha, Nebraska 68101

BUFFALO INSIGHTER
Buffalo, New York

BURNING RIVER NEWS
(Formerly BIG US)
13037 Euclid Avenue
East Cleveland, O. 44112

BURNING SPEAR
1504 16th St. So.
St. Petersburg, Fla. 33733

CAMPUS UNDERGROUND
401 1/2 Main Street

Cedar Falls, Iowa 50613

CANELE
Ann Arbor, Michigan

CAULDRON
Ann Arbor, Michigan

CAULDRON
Hartford, Connecticut

CHICAGO KALEIDOSCOPE
Box 881
Madison, Wis. 53701

CHINOOK
1458 Pennsylvania Street
Denver, Colorado 80203

COMMON SENSE
Christian Educational Association
530 Chestnut Street
Union, New Jersey 07083

CONNECTIONS (now ceased)
Madison, Wisconsin

CONSCIENCE

COUNTERPOINT
Box 396
Stevens Point
Wisconsin 54481

DAILY PLANET
3514 S. Dixie Hwy
Coconut Grove
Florida 33133

DALLAS NOTES (Now OUTLAW TIMES)
Box 7140
Dallas, Texas 75209

DAMASCUS FREE PRESS
24524 Fosson Street
Damascus, Md. 20750

DISTANT DRUMMER
1736 Pine Street
Philadelphia, Pa. 19103

DULL BRASS
9 S. Clinton Street Room 225
Chicago, Ill. 60606

EAST VILLAGE OTHER
105 Second Avenue
New York, N.Y. 10009

FATIGUE PRESS
Box 1265
Killeen, Texas 76541

FIFTH ESTATE
4403 2nd Street
Detroit, Michigan 48201

FIRING LINE
4401 North Broadway
Chicago, Ill. 60640

FIRST ISSUE
308 Stewart Avenue
Ithaca, New York

FLORIDA FREE PRESS
516 44th St. West Palm Beach
Florida 33407

FREE PAGAN PRESS
Kansas City, Kansas

FREE PRESS OF SPRINGFIELD
Springfield, Massachusetts

FREE STUDENT
Los Angeles, California

FREE YOU
117 University Avenue
Palo Alto, California 94301

GI ORGANIZER
Box 704 Killeen,
Texas 76541

GI PRESS SERVICE
857 Broadway Room 307
New York, N.Y. 10003

GI VOICE
Box 825 Stuyvesant Station
New York, N.Y. 10009

GRAFITI
Philadelphia, Pennsylvania

GRANPA
520 East 12th Street
New York, N.Y. 10009

GRASS ROOTS (FORUM)
617 E. Valley Blvd.
San Gabriel, Calif. 91776

GREAT SPECKLED BIRD
187 14th Street N.E.
Atlanta, Georgia 30309

GREECE TODAY
P.O. Box 48052
Chicago, Illinois 60648

GREEN REVOLUTION
Lanes End
Homestead, Ohio 45309

GRINDING STONE
Box 785 Terre Haute
Indiana 47807

GROK
P.O. Box 7165 Oakland
Station
Pittsburg, Pa. 15213

GUARDIAN
32 W. 22nd Street
New York, N.Y. 10010

GUERRILLA
1107 W. Warren
Detroit, Michigan 48201

HAIGHT-ASHBURY TRIBUNE
1748 Haight Street
San Francisco, Calif. 94117

HARAMBEE
7228 South Broadway
Los Angeles, California

HARD CORE
780 West End Avenue
New York, N.Y. 10025

HARD TIMES
1065 31st Street N.W.
Washington, D.C.

HARTFORD'S OTHER VOICE
P.O. Box 936
Hartford, Conn. 06109

HELIX
3128 Harvard Street East
Seattle, Washington 98102

HETERODOXICAL VOICE
Box 24
Newark, Delaware

HIGH SCHOOL FREE PRESS
604 E. 11th Street
New York, N.Y. 10009

HIGH SCHOOL IND. PRESS
160 Claremont Avenue
New York, N.Y. 10027

HUMANITAS
308 Westwood Plaza #138
Los Angeles, Calif. 90024

Alternative Tabloids

ILLUSTRATED PAPER
Box 707
Mendocino, Calif. 95460

I'M ALL RIGHT
6002 Alder Street
Pittsburgh, Pa. 15206

INDEPENDENT SOCIALIST
Berkeley, California

INDIAN HEAD

INNER CITY VOICE
8661 Grand River
Detroit, Michigan 48204

JABBERWORK (THE WALL STREET)
235 First Street
San Jose, California

KALEIDOSCOPE
P. O. Box 90526
Milwaukee, Wisc. 53202

KUDZU
Box 22502 Jackson
Mississippi 39205

LEVIATHAN
249 Mullen Avenue
San Francisco, Calif. 94110

LIBERATION
339 Lafayette Street
New York, N.Y. 10012

LIBERATION NEWS SERVICE
160 Claremont Avenue
New York, N.Y. 10027

LOOP-WHOLE
64 East Lake
Chicago, Illinois

LOS ANGELES FREE PRESS
6013 Hollywood Blvd.
Los Angeles, Calif. 90028

LOS ANGELES UNDERGROUND
Los Angeles, California

LUX VERITE
Box 234 W. Lafayette
Indiana 47906

MADISON KALEIDOSCOPE
P. O. Box 881
Madison, Wisconsin 53701

MARIJUANA REVIEW
Lemar International Box 71 Norton Hall
SUNY at Buffalo, Buffalo, New York 14214

MAVERICK
Box 792
San Francisco, Calif. 94103

MAX
P. O. Box 2470
New York, N.Y. 10017

MIAMI FREE PRESS
3305 Grand Avenue
Cocnut Grove, Fla. 33133

MILE HIGH UNDERGROUND
Box 18029 Capital Hill Station
Denver, Colo. 80218

MILITANT
14 Charles Lane
New York, N.Y. 10014

MODERN UTOPIAN
Tufts University
P. O. Box 44 Boston, Massachusetts 02153

MOTHER OF VOICES
Box 429
Amherst, Mass. 01102

MOVEMENT
330 Grove Street
San Francisco, Calif. 94102

NEW HARD TIMES
Box 3272
Clayton, Mo. 63105

NEW LEFT NOTES
1103 E. 63rd Street
Chicago, Ill. 60637

NEW MEXICO A & M CONSCIENCE
Box 3BS
Las Cruce, N. M. 88001

NEW PATRIOT
308 Stewart Avenue
Ithaca, N. Y. 14850

NEWS FROM NOWHERE
Box 501
DeKalb, Ill. 60115

NOLA EXPRESS
Box 2342
New Orleans, La. 70116

NORTH CAROLIN ANVIL
Box 1148
Durham, N. C. 90046

NORTH WEST PASSAGE
2616 W. Maplewood Ave.
Bellingham, Wash. 98225

OLD MARKET PRESS
Box 521
Paducah, Kentucky 42001

OLD MOLE (MOLE MEDIA CENTER)
2 Brookline Center
Cambridge, Mass. 02139

OPEN DOOR
1021 East Wright
Milwaukee, Wis. 53212

ORACLE OF SAN FRANCISCO
460 Magnolia Avenue
Larkspur, Calif. 94939

ORACLE OF SOUTHERN CALIFORNIA
840 North Fairfax Avenue
Los Angeles, Calif. 90046

OTHER SCENES
Box 8 Village Station
New York, N. Y. 10014

PAPER TIGER
39 E. Springfield Street
Boston, Mass. 02118

PEACE AND FREEDOM NEWS
Peace Action Center
2525 Maryland Avenue
Baltimore, Maryland 21218

PEACEMAKER
10208 Sylvan Avenue
Cincinnati, Ohio 45241

PENCIL IN TITLE OF YOUR OWN CHOICE
Students of Lower Burrell, Kiski, and Valley High Schools--Pittsburgh, Pa.

PENINSULA OBSERVER
180 University Avenue
Palo Alto, Calif. 94709

Alternative Tabloids

PEOPLE'S WORLD
81 Clementina St.
San Francisco, Cal. 94105

PITTSBURGH FAIR WITNESS
Box 7165
Pittsburgh, Pa. 15213

PITTSBURGH POINT
Box 7345
Pittsburgh, Pa. 15213

RAG
609 W. 23rd Avenue
Austin, Texas 78705

RAGS
Rosy Cheeks Publications Inc.
30 E. 20th Street
New York, N.Y. 10003

RAMPARTS
2054 University Avenue
Berkeley, Calif. 94704

RENAISSANCE
San Jose Red Eye Media
48 So. Fourth Street
San Jose, Calif. 95113

RISING UP ANGRY
Box 3746 Mdse. Mart
Chicago, Illinois 60654

ROLLING STONE
746 Brannan Street
San Francisco, Cal. 94103

ROUGH DRAFT
Box 1205
Norfolk, Virginia 23501

SAN DIEGO FREE PRESS
751 Turquoise Street
San Diego, Calif. 92109

SAN JOSE RED EYE
4820 Fourth Street
San Jose, Calif. 95113

SON OF JABBERWORK
235 1st Street
San Jose, California

SPECTATOR
Box 1216 Bloomington,
Indiana 47401

SPOKANE NATURAL (Now known as PROVINCIAL PRESS)
Box 1276 Spokane,
Washington 99201

STUDIES ON THE LEFT
P. O. Box 2121
Madison, Wisconsin

UNION DEMOCRACY IN ACTION
New York, N.Y.

VANGUARD
203 Clayton Street
San Francisco, Cal. 94117

VETERANS STARS AND STRIPES FOR PEACE
Box 4598
Chicago, Illinois 60680

WARREN-FOREST SUN
499 W. Forest
Detroit, Michigan 48201

WASHINGTON FREE PRESS
3 Thomas Circle
Washington, D.C. 20005

WATER TUNNEL
State College Free Press
Box 136 State College
Pennsylvania 16801

WESTERN ACTIVIST
　Kalamazoo, Michigan

WILLIAMETTE BRIDGE
　S. W. 6th Street
　Portland, Oregon 97204

WIN
　P. O. Box 574
　Rifton, N. Y. 12471

INDEX

Abarbanel, Albert, 3643a
Abbott, C. Michael, 4177
Abel, Elie, 4653
Abeles, Elvin, 3852
Aber, Joel, 1516
Abernathy, Marbra G., 1
Abernathy, Ralph, 1364, 2700, 2810, 4049
ABORTION
   See also BIRTH CONTROL; FERTILITY, HUMAN; and POPULATION, CONTROL OF
   22, 25, 61, 160, 257, 400, 402, 407, 498, 547, 655, 723, 825, 950, 951, 952, 953, 954, 955, 956, 957, 958, 968, 1025, 1083, 1198, 1219, 1277, 1518, 1590, 1620, 1630, 1641, 1683, 1790, 1829, 1904, 2001, 2002, 2027, 2125, 2150, 2239, 2353, 2354, 2363, 2396, 2479, 2729, 2730, 2731, 2732, 2783, 3272, 3600, 3681, 3719
Abraham, Charles, 4689
Abraham, H.J., 1a, 4809
Abraham, Roger D., 2
Abrahamsen, David, 4810
Abram, Morris B., 168a, 4178, 4179
Abrams, Arnold, 1517
Abruzzi, W., 3304
Abse, Dannie, 3
Abt, John, 1183
Abzug, Bella, 2352
ACADEMIC FREEDOM (students and faculty) 13, 455, 458, 459, 654, 759, 985, 1030, 1063, 1402, 1550, 2285, 2292, 3021, 3854c, 3942, 3946a, 3975, 4021, 4229, 4474, 4530, 4547, 4621
Academy For Educational Development, 298

Ace, G., 2905
Acid-Test, 3112
Ackerley, W.C., 3200
Ackerly, Robert L., 4180
Ackerman, Nathan W., 4, 5, 2946
Ackland, Len, 134
ACTIVISM--POLITICAL AND EDUCATIONAL
   See also items listed in the section, "Student Dissent"
   1328, 1529, 1554, 2515, 3852b, 3864, 3875, 3898, 3907, 3955, 3965, 3982, 4008, 4031, 4042, 4077, 4126, 4165, 4182, 4242, 4298, 4327, 4389, 4393, 4399, 4487, 4514, 4535, 4549, 4550, 4564, 4598, 4599, 4617, 4629, 4636
Adamo, S.J., 1518
Adams, A. John, 6
Adams, Charles, 168
Adams, Evangeline, 1519
Adams, I., 5332
Adams, James F., 3852a
Adams, James L., 7
Adams, John B., 3710
Adams, Thomas, 3315
Adams, W.A., 903
Adelson, J., 3201
Adelson, Joseph, 3901
Adhikary, Mukandah Das, 1519
Adler, Renata, 8, 4324a
AFFLUENCE, 1780
Africa Research Group, 1520
African Research Group, 9
AFRO-AMERICAN (culture and literature) 447, 861, 1770, 1939, 2003, 2183, 4563, 4597
AGGRESSIVENESS (psychology) 594, 2907, 4829, 4878, 4918
Agnew, Kim, 1412, 1413, 1466

Agnew, Spiro T., 893, 1401, 1411, 1412, 1413, 1466, 2051, 4811, 5006
Agut, J. R., 1521
Ahlstrom, Sydney E., 1522
Aiken, Ellsworth N., 1523
Aiken, L., 10
Aiken, Michael, 11
Ailken, Jonathan, 3853
Air America, Activities Of, 2623
Akerlund, Knut, 4181
Akron, Ohio, 4165
Albany, Georgia, 253
Albany Movement, Georgia, 253
Albany, New York, 1480
Albert, Martin L., 1524
Albert, Stewart, 1524, 1525, 1526
Alcatraz, 1571, 1737, 1942, 2707
ALCOHOLISM (teen-age) 2951, 2964, 3071, 3083, 3101, 3104, 3120, 3171
Aldridge, John W., 2947
Alex, Nicholas, 3316
Ali, Muhammed, 1259, 4284
Ali, Tariq, 12, 3854
Alianza, 684
ALIENATION (in schools, from business and society, and from industry) 11, 27, 86, 1889a, 1930, 2333, 2434, 2648, 2712, 2955, 3031, 3952, 4031, 4322, 4502, 4521a, 4561, 4593, 4601, 4629, 4820, 5097
ALIENATION (in voting) 575
Alinder, Gary, 1527
Alioto, Joseph, 5007
Alioto, Mussolini, 1351, 1669
Allan, William, 1528
Allen, A. Dale, Jr., 1528a
Allen, F. A., 4812
Allen, James N., 1529
Allen, J. E. Jr., 4182
Allen, Jesse, 1530
Allen, Jonathan, 13
Allen, Robert L., 1531, 2339, 5008
Allen, Steve, 1419
Allen, Vernon, 5009
Alliance For Progress, 514

Allott, Gordon, 4183
Allport, Gordon, 585
Allstate Insurance Company, 2413
Alpert, Richard, 3263
Alpine County, California, 991, 1054b, 1130, 1335, 1381, 1739, 1865, 2015
Alsop, S., 4751
Alsop, Stewart, 14, 5333, 5334
Altbach, Philip G., 3854a, 3965
Alternative Convention, Grant Park, Chicago
See Democratic National Party Convention, Chicago, 1968
Althoff, Barbara, 1532
Altizer, Thomas J. J., 15, 16
Altshuler, Alan A., 17
Aluminum Corporation of America, 963
Ambrose, Myles J., 3201a
American Association of Junior Colleges, 3969
American Bar Association, 2862
American Businessmen's Club, 2413
American Civil Liberties Union 18, 1044, 2083, 3503, 3854b, 3854c
California, Southern, 1394, 4813; Denver, Colorado, 1081; Madison, Wisconsin, 1162; Philadelphia, Pennsylvania, 959, 1286; Pittsburgh, Pennsylvania, 4720
American Council On Education, 57, 3855, 3856, 3864, 3865, 3895, 3991, 3992, 4269, 5335
American Dream, The, 113
American Friends Service Committee, 19, 20, 21, 22, 1533, 2040, 2390, 3600, 5235
American Historical Association, 1816
American Jewish Committee, 22a, 4813a
American Legion Convention, 2795

Index 485

American Legion Post (San Diego County) 1239
American Library Association, 1224, 1395
American Medical Association, 968, 1835, 1836, 3134
American Psychological Association, 2176, 3955, 3982
American Red Cross
See Red Cross
American Security Council Committee. National Strategy Committee, 4654, 4655
American Society Of Newspaper Editors, 2669
American Sociological Association, 693, 1170, 3947, 4226, 4227
American Telephone And Telegraph Company, 4763
Ames, L., 3024
Ames, Louise Bates, 5
Amie, Jerry Lee, 2250
Amory, Cleveland, 4814
Amos, W. E., 4815
Amundson, Robert, 23
Ananda Community Life, 537
ANARCHISM (educational and political) 271, 403a, 809, 931, 1376, 3942, 3973, 4229, 4257, 4304, 4326, 4877, 5150
Andelson, Robert V., 4184
Anderson, Allen J., 1534
Anderson, Barbara, 4185
Anderson, Clinton H., 3317
Anderson, Jervis, 1535
Anderson, Michael, 1536
Anderson, Walt, 3857
Andrews, Harry J., 2948
Andrews, James R., 4186
Andrews, Tim, 1537
Angel Island, California, 2707
Angel, K., 3202
Angelucci, Steve, 3469
Angle, Roger, 1538
Angrist, Shirley S., 1539
Ann Arbor, Michigan, 4165
Anonymous (New York State) 1540
Anrig, Gregory R., 4187
Ansara, Michael, 2601
Anthony, Earl, 24
Anthony, Richard, 4188
ANTI-BALLISTIC MISSILE ..., 4656
ANTI-SEMITISM, 41, 204, 238, 245, 349, 438, 643, 714, 839, 890, 2332
Anticipatory Avoidance Learning (Electric Shock Treatment) 1795
Anyan, Walter R. Jr., 3651
Apostolides, Alex, 1541, 1542
Applebaum, Jerry, 1543, 2200, 3469a
Applegate, Rex, 3318
Appleman, Philip, 25
Aptheker, Bettina, 4189
Aptheker, Herbert, 26, 27, 28, 29, 1950
Arbogast, Bob, 1856, 1867
Arbrister, Trevor, 4657
Archer, Jules, 30
Archer, Sandra, 95a
Archibald, Peter, 479
Ardery, Philip P. Jr., 4190
Arendt, Hannah, 4816
Argus Tribe, 1168
Armacost, Michael H., 2863
ARM BANDS 2560
ARM BANDS (history and significance) 4250, 4411
ARM BANDS (U.S. Supreme Court case) Des Moines, Iowa, 2560
Arm, Walter, 3319
Armbrister, Trevor, 31, 3469b
ARMS CONTROL
See also DISARMAMENT
48, 72, 144, 266, 283, 319, 338, 514, 555, 881a, 902, 2722, 2864, 4659, 4660, 4718, 4719, 4722, 4769
Armstrong, John A., 32
Arnold, Arnold, 4817
Arnstein, George E., 1543a
Arnstein, Helene S., 2949, 3601
Aron, Raymond, 4191
Aronowitz, Stanley, 1544, 1963
Aronson, James, 1545
Aronson, Ronald, 1546, 1577
Arrow, Kenneth J., 2950
Arthur, Stephanie, 1547

Asbury Park, New Jersey, 2705
Asch, Sidney H., 3320
Ascheim, Skip, 1548
Ascoli, Max, 1549
Ash, William, 33
Ashbaugh, Carl R., 4192
Ashley, Bob, 1550, 4193
Ashley, Paul P., 34
Ashmore, Harry S., 35, 36
ASIA, SOUTHEAST 20, 35, 90, 94, 216, 221, 382, 535, 605, 613, 708, 756, 782, 824, 1958, 1986, 2011, 2168a
Assael, Henry, 1551
ASSASSINATION
See also MURDER
288, 348, 496, 608a, 691, 769, 1830, 1833, 1857, 2166, 2202, 2391, 2745, 2749, 2802, 5213
Association For Supervision And Curriculum Development, 3937
Association For The Study Of Abortion, 407
Association Of American Colleges, 3977, 3999
Association Of Self-Supporting Institutions, Madison College, Madison, Tennessee, 2609
Astin, Alexander W., 3864, 3865, 4204a
Astor, G., 3203
ASTROLOGY 1519
Atcheson, Richard, 37
ATHEISM 104, 543, 570, 642, 1675
ATHLETICS 285, 699, 705, 812, 1883, 2140, 2158, 2412, 2449, 2645, 2728, 4199
Atkins, Neil P., 4194
Atkins, Susan, 2585
ATLANTA BOREALIS 2014
Atlanta, Georgia, 253, 2018, 2700
Atlantic Monthly (Periodical) 3858
Atlantic (Periodical Supplement) 3470

Atlantis Development Corporation, 1085, 1332
Atlantis 1A (Carribbean) 1031, 1085, 1093, 1332, 1574
ATROCITIES AND WAR CRIMES--VIETNAM 403, 550, 785, 793, 1877, 1919, 2101
AUDIOBUSES (classrooms on wheels) 1050
Auerill, L. I., 4195
Augusta, Georgia, 4049, 4417
Augusta 7, 2266
Aukofer, Frank A., 38
Aumann, F., 39
Austin, C. G., 4196
AUTOMOBILE (industry) 1186
Avorn, J. L., 3859, 4198
Axelrod, Joseph, 3860
Ayres, Clarence E., 817a

Baar, James, 4658
Babbidge, H. D. Jr., 4199
Babbitt, Irving, 419
Babcock, John, 1552
Babouvist Company, 1828
Backstrom III, Carl, 1553
Bacon, Margaret, 2951
Bacon Pamphlet Service, 3602
Bader, William B., 4659
Baez, Joan, 1064, 1201, 1204, 2468, 4993
Bagguley, John, 936
Baier, Kurt, 40
BAIL SYSTEM (bond) 369
Bain, Helen, 1554
Bakal, Carl, 2864, 2906
Bakan, David, 1555
Baker, David, 4200
Baker, Michael A., 3861
Baldwin, James, 41, 42, 43, 44, 1192, 1556
Ballard, Jim, 1557
Ballotti, Geno A., 3933
Balser, Henry, 1558
Baltimore, Maryland, 1076, 4165
Bander, Edward J., 3861a
BANK OF AMERICA Santa Barbara, California, 2713, 3449, 2714
Banner, David K., 1558a

Bannowsky, Flip, 1559
Banton, Michael, 3321
Barad, Huntley, 1560
Barber, Bernard, 2952
Barbour, Floyd B., 45, 3861b
Barbour, I., 46
Barbour, Russell B., 47
Bardacke, F., 2686
Barg, Peter, 1561
Barker, Charles A., 48
Barker, Lucius Jefferson, 49, 50
Barker, Twiley Wendell, 49, 50
Barkley, Katherine, 1562
Barlow, Bill, 3862, 4201
Barndt, Joseph R., 51
Barnet, Richard J., 52, 53
Barnette, Rodney, 1563
Baron, Harold, 525
Barr, Stringfellow, 173
Barraclough, Geoffrey, 1564
Barrins, P. C., 3204
Barry, Ernie, 1565
Bart, Bill, 3205
Barton, Allen H., 4202
Baruch, Dorothy (Walter) 3603
Baruch, Robert F., 57
Baruch, Ruth, 54
Barzun, Jacques, 3863
Bashlow, R., 5380
Basing, Mary, 1566, 3470a
Bass, Jack, 3989
BASTARD BULLET: A SEARCH FOR LEGITIMACY FOR COMMISSION EXHIBIT "399." 2337
Bates, D. A., 4323
Bauer, W., 3604, 3605
Baughman, Emmett E., 55
Bauman, Geoffrey, 2159
Baumgartner, J. Stanley, 56
Bausch, W. J., 3606
Baxandall, Lee, 1567
Baxter, Archibald, 5236
BAY AREA EDUCATIONAL PROJECT 693
Bay, Christian, 4203, 4204, 4549
Bayer, Alan, 57
Bayer, Alan E., 3864, 3865, 4204a
Bayley, David H., 3322
Beach, John A., 5010
Beal, Christopher, 58

Beals, Carleton, 59
Beaney, William M., 5011
BEATLES, THE 5177
Beatman, F., 4
Beavan, K. A., 3750, 4205, 5336
Beck, Lester F., 3607
Becker, A., 4450
Becker, Harold K., 3323, 3324, 3325
Becker, Howard S., 2953, 3866
Becker-Rosenthal Affair, 3378
Beckwith, Steve, 1344
Bedau, Hugo A., 60, 4818, 5012, 5013, 5014
Behrend, Celeste, 1568, 1569
Behrman, S. J., 61, 3608
Beichman, Arnold, 4206, 4207
Beinecke, William S., 3867
BE-INS 721a, 1182, 1449, 1793, 2193, 2814, 3070
Belfrage, Sally, 62
Bell, Daniel, 63, 1647, 3868
Bell, Inge Powell, 4819
Bell, J. N., 3206, 3207, 3751
Bell, Jack, 64
Bell, R., 3609
Bell, Robert R., 3609a, 3751a
Belli, Melvin M., 65
Bellini, Carol, 1570
Beloff, Michael, 3853
Beman, Lamar T., 2865
Bender, L., 3208
Bender, Urie A., 5237
Bendiner, Robert, 66
Benell, Florence B., 3610, 3752
Benello, C. George, 67
Benne, Kenneth D., 68
Bennett, John C., 5015
Bennett, Lerone Jr., 69, 70, 71
Bennett, V. D. C., 3753
Benoit, Emile, 72
Bensky, Larry, 1571, 1572
Benson, Dennis C., 2954
Benston, Margaret, 73
Beppler, Bill, 1573
Berberding, William P., 74
Bercut, Florence, 1574
Berg, Ivar, 75
Berg, Kenneth R., 4209
Berger, Dan, 1575, 1576

Berger, Morroe, 76
Berger, Pauline, 4210
Berger, Peter L., 77
Bergler, Edmund, 78
Berkeley, California, 660, 987, 1158, 1350, 2433, 2603, 2846, 3472, 3481, 3516, 3578, 3841, 3879a, 3880, 3902, 3938, 3950, 3966, 3979, 3997, 4026, 4035, 4047, 4052, 4116, 4189, 4230, 4412, 4457, 4578, 4972
BERKELEY MOVEMENT, HISTORY OF, 2798, 3879a, 3902, 3938, 3950, 3966, 3979, 4035, 4230, 4483
Berkeley 3, 4626
Berkley, George E., 3326, 3471
Berkowitz, Leonard, 2907
Berland, Oscar, 1577
Berman, Bruce A., 1578
Bernard, Jessie, 79, 1579, 3618
Berne, E., 3754
Bernreuter, Robert G., 4211
Bernstein, Saul, 2955, 4820, 4821
Berrigan, Daniel, 80, 81, 1580, 5364, 5411
Berrigan, Philip, 82, 83, 696
Berry, F., 3472
Berry, Marva, 1581
Berson, Lenora E., 84
BERTRAND RUSSELL CENTER FOR SOCIAL RESEARCH. LONDON
See Russell, Bertrand
BERTRAND RUSSELL PEACE FOUNDATION 2101
Berube, M. R., 85
Bess, Donavan, 1582
Beston, Henry, 1265
Bethe, Hans A., 4761
Bettelheim, Bruno, 5, 1583, 3755, 4212, 4213, 4822, 5016
Beverly Hills, California, 3317
Beys Afroysim Case, 2028
Bhodan Center, Oakhurst, California, 2609

BIBLE READING IN THE PUBLIC SCHOOLS
See also RELIGION IN THE PUBLIC SCHOOLS
495
Bickel, Alexander M., 4213a
Bienen, Henry, 3869, 4823
Bigler, James C., 3387
Big Stone Colony, Graceville, Minnesota, 2609
Bingler, John H. Jr., 1584
Binzen, Peter, 86
BIOLOGICAL WARFARE
See also CHEMICAL WARFARE; PSYCHOLOGICAL WARFARE; WARFARE
21, 192, 212, 445, 607, 1397, 1840, 2063, 2064, 2360, 2497
Birch, Alison Wyrley, 3209
Bird, Caroline, 87, 87a
Bird, Joseph W., 3611, 3612
Bird, Lois, F., 3611, 3612
Birenbaum, William M., 2956, 3870
Birmingham, John, 2957
Birmingham, William, 1372
BIRTH CONTROL
See also ABORTION; BIRTH CONTROL MOVEMENT, HISTORY; FERTILITY, HUMAN; POPULATION, CONTROL OF
22, 25, 61, 160, 286, 522, 816, 889, 1740, 1824, 1976, 2568, 3719, 3722, 3724, 3802
BIRTH CONTROL MOVEMENT, HISTORY 513, 816
Bishop, Gordon, 4214
Bitten, Ron, 1585
Bittner, Egon, 3473
Bjork, R. M., 3756
Black, Algernon D., 3327
BLACK BERETS 1420, 1726
Black Construction Coalition 989, 1000, 1001, 1002, 1311, 1586, 2182, 2526, 2528a, 2529, 2539, 2543a, 2544
Black, Donald, 3474
Black, Eugene R., 90
Black, Hugo L., 154

BLACK LIBERATION MOVEMENT 321, 323, 388, 679, 680, 706, 813, 891b, 896, 904, 910, 2058, 2429, 2766
BLACK MANIFESTO
See also BLACK PANTHER PARTY-OFFICIAL MANIFESTO 321, 804
BLACK MONDAY 1001, 1002
BLACK MOOCHIE, THE 1690
BLACK MUSLIMS 585, 591, 5194
BLACK NATIONALISM
See NATIONALISM (black)
BLACK PANTHER PARTY 54, 91, 791, 1026, 1107, 1294, 1321, 1446, 1587, 1608, 1812, 1922, 2006, 2069, 2070, 2075, 2076, 2090, 2137, 2249, 2347, 2376, 2474, 2600a, 2631, 2703, 2751, 3435
BLACK PANTHER PARTY--CHAPTERS AND BRANCHES Boston, Massachusetts, 1019; Des Moines, Iowa, 1321, 3435; Oakland, California, 3554; Portland, Oregon, 3480
For A List Of Recognized Chapters See: 1225
BLACK PANTHER PARTY--OFFICIAL MANIFESTO
See also BLACK MANIFESTO 321, 815
BLACK PANTHERS 24, 54, 91, 174, 639, 812a, 814, 815, 893, 1003, 1004, 1005, 1006, 1007, 1016, 1266, 1305, 1306, 1307, 1440, 1490, 1535, 1557, 1563, 1667, 1669, 1679, 1685, 1708, 1710, 1948, 1981, 2031, 2181, 2243, 2376, 2402, 2437, 2445, 2474, 2611, 2692, 2704, 2736, 2761, 3450, 3451, 3502, 4137, 4540, 5038
Black, Pearl Charie, 1588
BLACK POLITICANS
See NEGRO--POLITICS AND POLITICANS
BLACK POWER SALUTE 285, 1009, 1014, 1883, 2158, 2374, 2824
BLACK SEPARATISM 321, 577, 1259, 1373
BLACK SILENT MAJORITY
See SILENT MAJORITY (black)
BLACK 6 CONSPIRACY CASE, LOUISVILLE, KENTUCKY 2817
BLACK STUDIES PROGRAM
See AFRO-AMERICAN (culture and literature)
Black, Vonda, 1589
Blackburn, Dan, 4215
Blackschleger, Herb, 92
Blackwood, Alan, 5238
Blaine, Graham B. Jr., 2958
Blair, James W., 3871
Blake, Eugene C., 3475
Blakey, George Robert, 5017, 5018
Blakkan, Renee, 1590, 1591, 1592, 1593, 1594, 1595, 1596
Blank, Blanche D., 4216
Blank, Dennis, 1597
Blank, Owen, 525
Blaustein, Albert P., 93
Blazer, Sam, 1598
Blenkinsopp, Joseph, 3613
BLONDE COBRA 2219
Bloodworth, Dennis, 94
Bloom, Bernie, 1599
Bloom, J. L., 3757
Bloom, Jack, 4626
Bloom, Marshall, 1600, 1601
Bloomquist, E. R., 2959
Bloomstein, Morris J., 95
Bloustein, Edward J., 1602, 4217
Bloy, Myron B. Jr., 96a
BLUE CROSS 1835
Blum, A., 96
Blum, Jeff, 1730
Blum, Richard H., 3328
Blum, San, 3210, 3328a, 3476
Blumberg, Abraham S., 97, 3329
Blumberg, Herbert H., 3936
Bly, Robert, 2545

Boardman, Krist, 1603
Bodger, Joan, 1894
Boehme, Lillian R., 4824
Boesel, D., 3477
Boffey, P. M., 4752
Boggio, Jim, 1604
Boggs, James, 98
Bohannan, Paul, 3614
Boles, Edmond D., 3330
BOLLING VS. SHARPE 948
Bolton, Charles D., 3871a
Bonachea, Rolando E., 99
Bond, Julian, 321, 3912
Bondurant, Joan V., 100, 4825, 5019
Bonhoeffer, Dietrich, 101
Bookchin, Murray
  See Herber, Lewis
Booksellers For Peace, 1018
Boorstein, Daniel J., 102, 5020
Booth, Paul, 1606
Bordua, David, 3331
Bordua, David J., 3478
Borne, Etienne, 104
Borowitz, Eugene B., 3615
Boruch, Robert F., 3856
Bosc, S., 4218, 4219
Bosch, Juan, 105
Boskey, Bennett, 4660
Boskin, J., 5021
Boston 5, 2651
Boston Law Commune, 5337
Boston, Massachusetts, 1548, 3585, 5379, 5403
Boszormengi-Nagy, Ivan, 3117
Bottel, Helen, 3758
Bottome, E. M., 4753
Bottomore, T. B., 106, 4220
Botwin, C., 5022
Boudin, Kathy, 1966
Boudin, Leonard, 5312
Bouguereau, J. M., 4218, 4219
Boulder, Colorado, 2009
Boulding, Elise, 503
Boulding, Kenneth E., 72, 107, 108, 456, 532a, 3991, 5270
Bouma, Donald H., 109, 3332
Bourges, Herne, 3872
Bourjaily, V., 3211
Bowen, H. R., 4221
Bowen, Michael, 2120

Bowen, William, 5023
Bowles, C., 5024
Bowles, Chester, 110
Bowling Green State University, Bowling Green, Ohio, 2481
Bowman, R. M., 3212
BOYCOTTS
  Barbie Dolls, 1582; Grapes, 343, 960, 1020, 1035, 1109, 1145, 1146, 1232, 1398, 1826, 2122, 2443, 2485, 2486, 2542, 2693; Kansas City Power And Light Company, 2782; Levi-Straus, Atlanta, Georgia, 1088; Mexico-City Olympics, 1883; Oakland Public Schools, Oakland, California, 1021; Pan-American Airlines, 2422; Safeway Stores, 1022, 1212, 2693; Sears, 2357; Standard Oil, Richmond, California, 995, 1023
Boyd, James, 1607
Boyd, Malcolm, 111, 112, 113
Boyd, William, 3912
Boyle, Hugh, 3333
Boyle, Kay, 1608
Bracey, John H. Jr., 114
Braden, William, 115
Bradley, Eugene, 1858
Bradley, Eugene Edgar, 1566
Bradley, Gene E., 4222
Bradley, Milton, 2049
Brahms, David M., 5025
BRAIN POLICE
  See POLICE, BRAIN
Brammer, Lawrence, 4223
Brand, Scott, 4308
Brandeis, Louis D., 118
Brandeis University, Waltham, Massachusetts, 4178, 4489
Brandt, Floyd S., 116
Brann, J. W., 4224
Brant, Pasha, 4225
Braun, S., 3479
Braungart, Richard G., 4226, 4227, 4636
Brayman, Rick, 4228

Index

Brazier, Arthur M., 117
Breasted, Mary, 3616, 3759
Brecher, Jeremy, 1609
Breckenridge, Adam C., 118
Breines, Paul, 119, 3873
Breitman, George, 120
Brennan, Donald G., 4656, 4661, 4754
Brennan, Garnet, 2608
Brenton, Myron, 121, 3617
Breslin, Jimmy, 633
Bressler, Marvin, 3874
Brewer, Drew, 1610
Brewington, Jack, 5338
Brewster, Kingman, 3941, 5340
Briand, P. L., 5026
Brickman, W. W., 4229
Brickman, William W., 3875
Bridge Mountain Community, Ben Lomond, California, 2609
Bridge, Williamette, 3480
Brien, A., 1611
Brienberg, Elizabeth, 4230
Brigadier General Casimir Pulaski Memorial Ecumenical Be-In, 2814
Briggs, Peter, 1612
Brightman, Carol, 1613, 1614
Brink, William, 122, 123
Brisbane, Robert Hughes, 124
Bristow, A. P., 2869
Bristow, Allen P., 3334
Brittain, V., 5027
Brittin, Charles, 5028
BROADCASTING, FREEDOM OF 215
Brock, William E. III, 4231, 5339
Brockett, E. D., 1615
Brodek, Ted, 5340
Broderick, Carlfred B., 3618
Broderick, Dorothy M., 3213
Broderick, Francis L., 125
Brodey, W., 152
Brodsky, Stanley L., 125a
Brody, David, 126
Brogan, D. W., 127, 4233
Brogan, Varley, 1616
Bronowski, J., 4826
Bronston, William, 1617
Bronx, New York, 1832
Brooke, Edward W., 5341

Brookes, Edgar Harry, 128
Brooks, T. R., 3481, 4232
Broom, Leonard, 129
Broomfield, J. H., 129a
Broslawsky, Farrel, 1618, 1619
Browder, Leslie H. Jr., 4234
Brower, David, 1744
Brown, Brendan, 1620
Brown, Byrd, 1752, 2343, 2558
Brown, Connie, 1621
Brown, Donald R., 130, 4549
Brown, Edmund G., 1866
Brown, Frederic, 131
Brown, H. Rap, 45, 1623, 1951, 2657, 5114
Brown, Harrison, 1622
Brown, James Jr., 1623a
Brown, Joe David, 2960
Brown, Judith, 132
Brown, Leonard, 1624
Brown, Michael E., 3254, 3482
Brown, P. K., 1625
Brown, Pat, 2084
Brown, Richard Maxwell, 4827
Brown, Robert McAfee, 133, 1626, 1627, 5029
Brown, S., 5342
Brown, S. M. Jr., 5030
Brown, Sam, 134
Brown, Sam Jr., 3912
Brown, Sherry L., 3483
Brown, Turner Jr., 135
BROWN VS. BOARD OF EDUCATION OF TOPEKA, KANSAS 948
Brown, William P., 3335
Browning, Frank, 1628, 3481
Broyles, J. A., 136
Bruce "Gypsy" Peterson, 1121a
Bruce, Lenny, 202, 1629, 1964, 2643, 5091
Brustein, Robert, 4235, 4236, 4237
Brustman, Susan, 1629
Bryan, John, 2093
Bryant, Barbara E., 3875a
Bryant, Ruth, 2817
Bryn Gweled, Bucks County, Southampton, Pennsylvania, 2609
Brzezinski, Zbigniew, 137
Bube, Richard H., 137a
Buber, Martin, 138

Buchanan, James M., 139, 2961, 3876, 4238
Bucher, Lloyd M., 31, 1448, 1888
Buckley, Neil, 4239
Buckley, William F., Jr., 140, 141, 142, 143, 1553, 1630, 3214, 5031
Buckman, Peter, 1631, 4828
Buffalo, New York, 2606, 2844, 5403a
Buffalo 9, 2606
BUGGING
  See WIRETAPPING
Bulkley, Joel, 4240
Bull, Hedley, 144
Bullock, Paul, 145
Bunzel, John H., 4241, 4433
Burak, Marvin, 1787, 1789
Burchett, Wilfred G., 146, 147, 148
Burck, C., 4242
BUREAU OF INDIAN AFFAIRS 1188, 1189, 1296
Burger, Warren, 93, 1776
Burgess, Eric, 4661, 4662
Burgess, Thomas, 5290
Burke, Joan Martin, 6
Burke, Joe, 2558
Burlage, Robb, 1632
Burnham, Margaret, 1183
Burnham, S., 4243
BURN-INS 1088
Burns, R. D., 319
Burns, Robert, 2133
Burroughs, William S., 3215
Burry, Jim, 1633
Burt, John J., 3814
Burton, Austin, 984
Burton, Steven J., 1634, 1635, 1636, 1637
Buse, Renee, 2962
Buss, A. H., 4829
BUSSING LAWS, SCHOOL
  See EDUCATION, CRISIS OF INTEGRATION, SCHOOL
BUST BOOK, THE 581
Butler, Ed., 149
Butler, Ellis Parker, 3484
Butler, William R., 4244
Butler, Willis P., 1638
Buttinger, Joseph, 150, 151
Butz, Otto, 3877

Cable, George W., 153
Cadden, Vivian, 1639
Cafferty, Thomas P., 2768
Caffi, Andrea, 4830
Cahill, David, 1640
Cahn, Edmond N., 154, 155, 156
Cahn, Lenore L., 154
Cain, Arthur H., 157, 2963, 2964, 3619, 4831
Cain, E., 2965
Cain, Edward, 3878
Cain, Edward R., 5032
Calder, Nigel, 158
Calderone, Mary S., 3620, 3720, 3760
Calderwood, Ann, 159
Calderwood, D., 3813
Caldwell, William V., 2966
Califano, Joseph A. Jr., 3879
CALIFORNIA GRAPE STRIKE (la causa)
  See BOYCOTTS (grapes)
CALIFORNIA. REGENTS. UNIVERSITY OF CALIFORNIA 3879a
CALIFORNIA REVOLUTION 622
California State College, Long Beach, California, 1028
CALIFORNIA (state) DESCRIPTION OF 1141
CALIFORNIA TRAINING FACILITY AT SOLEDAD
  See SOLEDAD PRISON, CALIFORNIA
California. University of California, Berkeley
  See University of California, Berkeley
CAL JOCKS, BERKELEY, CALIFORNIA 2622
Callahan, Bill, 2620
Callahan, Daniel, 160, 1641, 5033
Callan, George D., 3336
Callaway, Howard, 1642
Calley, William Laws, Jr., 446
Calvert, Peter A. R., 5034
Camarano, Chris, 1643
CAMBODIA 708, 1282, 1576, 1626, 1760, 1763, 1960,

2294, 2359, 2702, 4044, 4091
Camejo, Peter, 4626
CAMP (definition of) 1567
Campbell, Angus, 4832
Campbell, Judith, 3337
Camp Hill Village, Copake, New York, 2609
Camp Pendleton, California, 2446
CAMP VENCEREMOS
See VENCEREMOS
Camus, Albert, 161
Canning, Jeremiah W., 162
Cannon, Ralph A., 1644
Cannon, Terence, 1645, 5035
Cantelon, John E., 2967, 3882
Canterbury House, University of Michigan, Ann Arbor, Michigan, 95a
Cantor, Norman F., 3883, 4833
Cantor, Paul, 1646
Canty, Donald, 4834
Capaldi, Nicholas, 163
CAPITALISTS AND FINANCIERS --U.S. 601
CAPITAL PUNISHMENT 60, 154, 201, 495a, 1419, 2025, 2271, 2838, 3722, 5013
Caplan, Nathan, 5036
Capouya, Emile, 1647
Carasso, Roger, 1648
Carey, James T., 2968
Carey, Richard W., 4245
Carey, Tim, 2600
Carleton, William G., 3485
Carlin, Jerome E., 164
Carliner, Mike, 3216
Carlos, John, 1009, 2158, 2389
Carlow College, Pittsburgh, Pennsylvania, 2099
Carlsen, G. R., 2969
Carmel, California, 4993
Carmichael, Stokely, 165, 246, 810, 813, 1032, 1181, 1556, 1649, 1650, 1700, 1714, 1905, 1951, 2091
Carnegie Commission On Higher Education, 3941a
Carnegie Foundation, 1121
Carnegie-Mellon University, Pittsburgh, Pennsylvania, 1995, 2525, 2526, 2537, 4802
Carpenter, Edmund, 166
Carpenter, John, 1651, 3542
Carper, Jean, 5239
Carr, Donald E., 3621
Carrington, Frank, 3486
Carroll, Al, 1652
Carson, Josephene, 167
Carter, Francis, 1653
Carter, Robert L., 168
Casady, Si, 2689a
Case, Clifford P., 168a
Case Western Reserve University, Cleveland, Ohio, 4067
Casey, Thomas J., 4246
Cashman, John, 2970
Cass, J., 4247
Cassara, Beverly Benner, 169
Cassata, Mary B., 4248
Cassel, Russell N., 2971
Cassell, 4249
Castro, Fidel, 170, 171, 469, 516, 593, 647, 664, 1643, 2167, 2481, 2592, 2593, 2819, 2847
CATHOLIC CHURCH IN THE U.S. 697, 703
CATHOLIC ENCYCLICAL-HUMANAE VITAE 616
Catholic Worker Farm, Tivoli, New York, 2609
CATHOLICISM, LIBERAL 234
Catonsville 9, 81, 1124
Caughlan, John, 3487
Cayton, Horace R., 172
C.B.S. (News) 6
Cedar Rapids, Iowa, 2212
Celo Community, Burnsville, North Carolina, 2609
Center For Research And Development In Higher Education, University of California, Berkeley, 3881
Center For The Study Of Democratic Institutions, 173, 3884, 4663, 4859
CENTER (magazine)
See CENTER FOR THE STUDY OF DEMOCRATIC INSTITUTIONS

CENTRAL INTELLIGENCE
    AGENCY 9, 149, 348,
    523, 623, 976, 1042,
    1043, 1132, 1173, 1178,
    1489, 1495, 1580, 1806,
    1971, 1993, 2136, 2348,
    2496, 2601, 2690, 2822,
    4132
Century City Peace March, 4813
Cervantes, Lucius, 1654, 3622
Chamberlain, 1655
Chamberlain, Anne, 1656
Chamberlain, G. M., 5037
Chamberlain, Gary L., 1657
Chamberlain, Gary M., 1658
Chamberlain, John, 1659, 1660, 1661
Chamberlin, J. Gordon, 1662
Chambers, Alex A., 1663
Chambers, Bette, 5343
Chambers, Bradford, 174, 175, 176
Chambers, Donald E., 1664
Chambers, Ernest W., 1665
Chambers, Ernie, 1666
Chambers, Merritt B., 3884a
Chametsky, J., 177
Chametzky, Jules, 4835
Chandler, Christopher, 1667
Chandler, Mike, 4250, 4251
Chaney, James, 2295
Chanter, A. G., 3623
Chapman, Bruce K., 5240, 5241
Chapman, J. L., 4252
Chapman, Samuel G., 3338
Chappell, Bill, 4253
Charach, Theodore, 1616
Charach, Theodore (Probe) 1843
Charles, Ron, 3481
Charleston, South Carolina, 2810
Charlie Company, 446
Charyn, Marlene, 1668, 1669, 1670, 5038
Chason, Gary, 1671
Chasteen, Edgar, 1740
Chavez, Ceasar, 1035, 1826, 2542, 2637
Chayes, Abram, 4664, 4755
Cheadle, Vernon I., 4283
Che Guevara, Ernesto, 99, 178, 179, 180, 181, 420, 484, 630, 1152, 1672, 1673, 1674, 1674a, 2496, 2847, 4085

CHEMICAL WARFARE
    See also BIOLOGICAL WARFARE; COUNTERINSURGENCY (weapons); GUERRILLA WARFARE; PSYCHOLOGICAL WARFARE; WARFARE
    21, 131, 192, 212, 445,
    607, 1039, 1397, 1840,
    1848, 1852, 2064, 2217,
    2277, 2360
Chen, Sidney, 2972
Chenu, M. D., 1675
Cherise, Alan, 1461
Cherokee Indians (Oklahoma) 1738
Cherry, Jim, 1676
Chervenak, Chris, 1677
Chevigny, Paul, 3339
Chicago Commission On Race Relations, 182
Chicago Conspiracy 10, 209a
Chicago Conspiracy Trial, 209a,
    295, 430, 600, 1195,
    1572, 1761, 1967, 1973,
    2041, 2087, 2241, 2267,
    2279, 2306, 2384, 2455,
    2555, 2625, 2627, 2630,
    2657
Chicago 8, 193, 1195, 1360, 1572, 1578, 2388
Chicago 15, 2189
Chicago, Illinois, 182, 252,
    340, 362, 799, 812a,
    898, 1558, 1572, 1578,
    1585, 1967, 1973, 2044,
    2189, 2287, 2289, 2306,
    3571, 4064, 4520, 4955,
    5058
Chicago Journalism Review, 1678
Chicago Park District, 3340
Chicago (seed) 1679
Chicago's Black Caucus, 2689a
Chicano-Anglo (confrontations)
    1040, 1250, 1543, 1721,
    1881, 2221, 2325, 2436,
    2701, 2754, 3555, 3556,
    4620, 4891
CHILDREN AND SEX
    See Items Listed In The
    Section "The Pregnant
    Question - Sex Education.
CHILDREN--EDUCATION AND

MANAGEMENT
  See also Items Listed In The
    Section "The Gap In Genera-
    tions, And The Drug Dilem-
    ma." "The Pregnant Ques-
    tion - Sex Education."
    5, 571, 685, 686, 1286,
    2978, 3002, 3003, 3024
Children of Light Commune,
  Gila Bend, Arizona,
  2609
CHILDREN, RIGHTS OF, 4368
CHILDREN'S LIBERATION
  MOVEMENT, 4368
Child Study Association of Amer-
  ica, 3624, 3625, 3626,
  3627
Childs, Charles, 4254
Chisholm, Shirley, 1596
Chomsky, Noam, 184, 185,
  186, 273, 1680, 4931
Choudhury, Malay Roy, 1681
Christensen, Gayle, 1682
Christenson, Reo M., 187
CHRISTIAN ATTITUDES AND
  SEX EDUCATION
  See Items listed In the Sec-
    tion "The Pregnant Question
    - Sex Education," e.g.,
    3642, 3648, 3670
Christian Conservative Com-
  munity, Louisville, Illi-
  nois, 2609
Christian Democratic Legal
  Union, San Francisco,
  California, 1536
CHRISTIANITY AND SCIENCE,
  COMPARATIVE
  See also RELIGION AND
    SCIENCE
  46, 137a
Christiansen, Peter Hans, 2349
Christopher, M., 2908
CHRISTOPHER WEST (parade)
  1315
CHURCH AND STATE IN THE
  U.S. 671, 728, 860,
  934
CHURCHES--GOVERNMENTAL
  PROCESSES IN 7, 95a,
  556, 561a, 587a, 696,
  1053, 1732
Ciardi, John, 1510, 5039

Cisler, Lucinda, 1683
City College of New York, 4062,
  4210
CITY GOVERNMENT--DECEN-
  TRALIZATION 533
City University of New York,
  2681
CIVIL LIBERTIES--U.S. 1, 18,
  49, 50, 154, 265, 532,
  692a, 2041, 2777, 4809,
  5086
Civil Rights Act of 1964, 7,
  154, 441, 692a, 1928
Civil Rights Act of 1968, 2657
CIVIL RIGHTS COMMISSION
  See COMMISSION ON CIVIL
    RIGHTS, 1957-1965
CIVIL RIGHTS, HOMOSEXUAL
  See GAY LIBERATION FRONT
CIVIL RIGHTS--NORTHERN
  IRELAND 426
CIVIL RIGHTS, U.S. 6, 49, 62,
  71, 76, 93, 125, 135,
  154, 155, 165, 168,
  175, 229, 244, 253,
  280, 326, 329, 335,
  347, 371, 393, 394,
  395, 413, 441, 511,
  519, 520, 521, 532,
  586, 596, 609, 610,
  620, 674, 680, 692a,
  731, 771, 826a, 785a,
  834, 845, 891, 904,
  919, 1045, 1046, 1047,
  1928, 1999, 2026, 2028,
  2144, 2172, 2295, 2314,
  2397, 2489, 2552, 2720,
  2828, 3444, 4809, 4840,
  4847, 4875, 5028, 5063,
  5069, 5084
Claire, Patricia, 3372
Clamage, Dena, 1684, 3488
Clark, B., 5344
Clark, Gerald, 3489
Clark, Grenville, 456
Clark, John, 1685
Clark, Joseph S. (Sen.) 4755
Clark, Judy, 2556
Clark, Kenneth B., 188, 3341
Clark, Marguerite, 4255
Clark, Ramsey, 189, 209a,
  295, 422, 587b, 617,
  3351, 3893

Clark Report, 5265
Clarke, John Henrik, 190, 191
Clarke, Robin, 192
Clarkson, Paul, 1686
CLASSROOMS ON WHEELS
  (audio-buses)
  See AUDIOBUSES (CLASS-
  ROOMS ON WHEELS)
Clatanoff, William B. Jr.,
  5345
Clavir, Judy, 193
Clay, Cassius
  See Ali, Muhammed
Clayton, Al, 205
Clearwater Sloop, Hudson River,
  New York, 2848
Cleath, R. L., 1687
Cleaver, Eldridge, 174, 194,
  783, 791, 911, 1100,
  1101, 1365, 1688, 1689,
  1690, 1691, 1692, 1693,
  1694, 1695, 1696, 1697,
  1698, 1699, 1700, 1701,
  1702, 1703, 1704, 1705,
  1706, 1707, 1708, 1709,
  1710, 1711, 1712, 1713,
  1714, 1715, 1716, 1717,
  1861, 1876, 1968, 2089,
  2285, 2445, 2600a, 2636,
  2689a, 4626, 5040, 5042,
  5144
Cleaver, Kathleen, 1717
Cleaver, Tom, 1718, 1719,
  1720, 1721
Clecak, Peter, 1722
Cleghorn Mountains, California,
  2258
Cleghorn, R., 195a, 5043
CLERGY AND LAYMEN CON-
  CERNED ABOUT VIET-
  NAM 196
Cleveland, Ohio, 1051, 1621,
  2122, 3434, 3444, 3893,
  4900
Clift, Raymond E., 3342, 3343
Clogger, T. J., 1723
Cloke, Kenneth, 1724
Clor, H., 197, 1725
Clouse, R. R. Linder, 3884b
Cloward, R. A., 4836
Clutchette, John, 2459
Coalition of Militants, 2823

Coalition of Power Centers,
  804
COALITIONS
  See Black Construction
  Coalition; Coalition Of
  Militants; Coalition Of Power
  Centers; National Youth Alli-
  ance Coalition; New Demo-
  cratic Coalition Of Pennsyl-
  vania; Peace Ecology Coali-
  tion; Pittsburgh Coalition;
  Student Anti-War Coalition;
  White Coalition For Justice
  Without Repression
Coates, Joseph F., 3343a
Coats, Bob, 1726
Cobbs, Price M., 398
Coblentz, Stanton A., 198
COFFEE HOUSES
  Here are entered coffee
  houses in general. G.I. cof-
  fee houses are entered under
  COFFEE HOUSES, (G.I.)
  See also specific names of
  coffee houses, e.g., OLD
  MARKET COFFEE HOUSE,
  KENTUCKY AVENUE,
  PADUCAH, KENTUCKY,
  2381.
COFFEE HOUSES, (G.I.)
  Here are entered G.I. coffee
  houses for peace at Army
  towns and installations where
  the military has allegedly
  confronted the G.I's, and
  organizations with legal tac-
  tics, conspiracy charges etc.
    Fort Carson, Colorado;
    Fort Dix, New Jersey;
    Fort Hood, California;
    Fort Hood, Killeen,
    Texas; Fort Jackson,
    South Carolina; Fort
    Leonard Wood, Waynes-
    ville, Mo.; Fort Lewis,
    Tacoma, Washington
COFFEE SHOP PROJECTS
  (movements) G.I. 2665,
  2694
Coffey, J. I., 4756
Coffi, Andrea, 4837
Coffin, Stephanie, 1727

Coffin, Tom, 1728, 1729
Coffman, J., 5346
Cohen, Bernard B., 199
Cohen, Bernard C., 200
Cohen, Bernard Lande, 201
Cohen, C., 5347
Cohen, Carl, 5044, 5045, 5046, 5047
Cohen, E. E., 1729a, 5242
Cohen, Fred, 1730
Cohen, Harvey, 1350
Cohen, John, 202
Cohen, Joshua Franc, 3761
Cohen, M., 5048
Cohen, Mitchell, 203, 3885, 3886
Cohen, R. M., 3762
Cohen, Sidney, 2973, 2974
Cohill, Judge Maurice B. Jr., 4256
Cohn, E. N., 4838
Cohn, Norman, 204
Cohn-Bendit, Daniel, 3887, 3888, 4144
Cohn-Bendit, Gabriel, 3888
Colaianni, James F., 1731
Cole, James K., 1459
Cole, John, 2225
Cole, Rob, 1732, 1733, 1734, 3490
Coleman, James S., 887a
Coleman Report, 489a, 887a
Coles, Robert 205, 1735, 2975
COLLECTIVE SETTLEMENTS
 See COMMUNAL LIFE STYLE; COMMUNAL LIVING, U. S.
COLLEGES AND UNIVERSITIES
 --CRISIS OF 298, 434, 614, 765, 911, 985, 1543a, 1655, 1768, 3930, 3933, 4003, 4299, 4357, 4458
COLLEGES AND UNIVERSITIES
 --GOVERNANCE OF 614, 911, 985, 1199, 1426, 1430, 1543a, 1768, 2404, 2956, 3933, 3956a, 3983, 3997, 4003, 4004, 4133, 4473, 4522, 4536
Collier, Peter, 1736, 1737, 1738
Collins, Don, 1739
Colombo, Judge Robert J., 2160
COLONY, THE 1319
COLUMBIA BROADCASTING SYSTEM 206, 1012, 1346, 1860, 2976
COLUMBIA BROADCASTING SYSTEM (news) 847, 1245, 1736
COLUMBIA POINT PROJECT 3574
Columbia University. New York 1806, 3859, 3861a, 3889, 3891, 3916, 3932, 4065, 4101, 4102, 4153, 4186, 4198, 4202, 4206, 4224, 4271, 4351, 4352, 4359, 4367, 4395, 4404, 4410, 4416, 4438, 4450, 4464, 4524, 4525, 4613, 4901
Comfort, Alex, 3628
Comfort, Mark, 2611
COMICS (culture) 2784
Commager, Henry S., 110, 5049
COMMISSION ON CAMPUS UNREST
 See PRESIDENT'S COMMISSION ON CAMPUS UNREST
COMMISSION ON CIVIL DISORDERS
 See NATIONAL ADVISORY COMMISSION ON CIVIL DISORDERS
COMMISSION ON CIVIL RIGHTS 1957-1965, 275
COMMISSION ON LAW ENFORCEMENT AND ADMINISTRATION OF JUSTICE
 See PRESIDENT'S COMMISSION ON LAW ENFORCEMENT AND ADMINISTRATION OF JUSTICE
COMMISSION ON OBSCENITY AND PORNOGRAPHY 1331a, 1393
COMMISSION ON THE CAUSES AND PREVENTION OF VIOLENCE
 See NATIONAL COMMISSION ON THE CAUSES AND PREVENTION OF VIOLENCE

COMMISSION ON THE STATUS
  OF WOMEN
  See PRESIDENT'S COMMISION
  ON THE STATUS OF WOMEN
Committee For Homosexual
  Freedom, 1746
Committee Of Returned Volunteers, 206b
Commoner, Barry, 207
COMMONWEALTH OF PENNSYLVANIA VS. CITY OF
  PHILADELPHIA VS. THE
  BOARD OF DIRECTORS
  OF CITY TRUST OF
  PHILADELPHIA 948
COMMUNAL LIFE STYLE
  See also COMMUNAL LIVING,
  U.S.
  See also specific names of
  communes e.g., Communes
  of Ramona, California; Holiday Commune, Santa Cruz,
  California
    37, 111, 209, 432, 537,
    684a, 1056, 1433, 1643,
    1898, 2190, 2299, 2412,
    2457, 2466, 2584, 2609,
    2719, 2723, 4957
COMMUNAL LIVING, U.S.
  See also COMMUNAL LIFE
  STYLE
  For an alphabetical list of
  intentional communities see
  SCHOOL OF LIVING, BROOKVILLE, OHIO.
    37, 111, 432, 537, 684a,
    1056, 1898, 2190, 2232,
    2299, 2390, 2412, 2457,
    2495, 2584, 2609, 2680,
    2719, 4957
COMMUNES, LAW 2230, 2276
Communes Of Ramona, California, 2457
COMMUNISM
  See also MARXISM
    27, 140, 220, 579, 694,
    883, 1876, 1902, 2105,
    2609a
COMMUNISM, ANTI 19, 141,
  713
COMMUNISM, THEORY OF 149
COMMUNITIES, COOPERATIVE
  See COMMUNAL LIFE STYLE;

COMMUNAL LIVING, U.S.
COMMUNITY, BIRTH OF AND
  DEFINITION 1046, 1567
Community People's Conference,
  Cleveland, Ohio, 1621
Community Service, Inc. Yellow Springs, Ohio, 2609
COMMUNIVERSITIES, THEORIES
  3931
Conant, James, 3894
Conant, James B., 207a
Conant, Margaret M., 3827
Conant, R. W., 5050
Condit, Tom, 2909
Condon, Chris, 1744
Cone, James H., 208
CONFLICT, GENERATIONAL
  See Items Listed In The Section "The Gap In Generations
  And The Drug Dilemma."
CONFLICT, INTERDEPARTMENTAL 1854, 2634
CONFLICT, INTERORGANIZATIONAL 795, 1551
CONFLICT, INTERORGANIZATIONAL--PUBLIC
  SCHOOLS 222
CONFLICT, INTERRACIAL
  See also RIOTS
    69, 182, 236, 240, 311,
    327, 329, 349, 350, 429,
    443, 506, 518, 562, 577,
    645, 656, 666, 750, 755,
    827, 833, 907, 935, 970,
    1349, 1538, 1558, 2339,
    2737, 2830
CONFLICT, INTERRACIAL AND
  THE POLICE 3347, 3373,
  3379, 3407
CONFLICT OF INTERESTS 129a,
  255a, 389a, 486, 561a,
  1564, 1874, 1934, 2752,
  3135
CONFLICT, ORGANIZATIONAL
  503, 1748, 2214, 2290,
  2475, 2476, 2724, 2768
CONFLICT RESOLUTION 72,
  107
CONFLICT, THEORY OF 100,
  198, 239, 1799
CONFLICTS, POLICE AND
  COMMUNITY
  See Items Listed In The

Section, "Police-Community Relationships." e.g., 3335
CONFLICTS, POLITICAL
See also CONFLICTS, SOCIAL
129a, 199, 239, 487, 576
CONFLICTS, RELIGIOUS
See THEOLOGY, CONFLICTS
CONFLICTS, SOCIAL
See also CONFLICTS, POLITICAL
199, 223, 224, 239, 331, 487, 576
CONFRONTATION POLITICS
187, 314, 487, 817a, 1934, 2171, 2565, 4516
CONFRONTATION, THEORIES OF 69, 272, 317, 349, 640a, 693a, 817a, 1450, 1564, 2129, 2624
CONFRONTATION, WORLD 317, 638
Conger, W. B., 1740
CONGOLEAN MAULERS 1420
Congress Of African Peoples, 1649
Congressional Quarterly (Research Reports) 4839, 4840, 5243
CONJUGAL VISITING, PRISONERS
See PRISONERS--SEXUAL BEHAVIOR
Conkin, Paul K., 209
Connecticut 9, 1052
Connelly, Joel, 1741, 1742, 1743, 1744
Conner, Frederick W., 4257
Connery, Colin, 3491
Connery, Robert, 4841
Conrad, John, 4842
Conrad, John P., 5051
CONSCIENTIOUS OBJECTION
5025, 5032, 5044, 5171a, 5195, 5245, 5256, 5264, 5278, 5279, 5347, 5350, 5366, 5396, 5402, 5413
CONSERVATION (of natural resources) 2362, 2735
CONSERVATISM 64, 77, 423a, 660, 2551, 2965, 3878
Conspiracy Staff Members, 1745

CONSPIRACY, THEORY OF
See also Names Of Individual Conspiracies, e.g., Catonsville 9; Chicago Conspiracy Trial; Chicago 8; Fort Hood 3; Louisville "Black Six" Kentucky; Milwaukee 14; New Haven 9; New York Panther 21; Oakland 7; Texas 5
81, 1438, 1572, 1745, 1975, 2034, 2612, 2655
CONSTITUTIONAL LAW--U.S.
See U.S. CONSTITUTIONAL LAW
CONSUMER PROTECTION 676, 2673, 2820
CONSUMERISM THEORY OF
See CONSUMER PROTECTION
CONSUMPTION, CONSPICIOUS 1582
CONTEMPT POWER--LEGAL AND POLITICAL ISSUES INVOLVED IN 209a
CONTEMPT POWER OF CONGRESS 368
Contempt: Transcript Of The Contempt Citations, Sentences, And Responses Of The Chicago Conspiracy, 10, 209a
Coogan, Timothy Patrick, 211
Cooke, Michael, 1746
Cookson, John, 212
Coombs, P., 213
Cooney, John, 3254, 5348
Coons, A., 214
Coons, John E., 215
Cooper, Chester L., 216
COOPER--CHURCH (amendment) 1777
Cooper, John Charles, 217, 218
Cooper, Richard T., 1747
Cooperative Humanist Society, Johnson, Madison, Wisconsin, 2609
Copps, John A., 219
Cordier, Andrew W., 1806
CORFU PRISON (Isle Of Corfu) 1853
Cornell, R., 220
Cornell University, Ithaca, New York, 1333, 4021, 4254,

4305, 4597
CORRUPTION (in politics) 380
Corsa, Leslie Jr., 3608
Corsi, Jerome R., 4900
Corson, William R., 221, 3890
Cortes, James, 2817
Corwin, Ronald G., 222, 1748
Coryell, Schofield, 1749
Cosby, Pete, 2817
Coser, Lewis A., 223, 224
Coser, R., 225
Cottam, Richard W., 226
Cotton, Senator, 4447
Cottrell, Beekman W., 1750, 4258
CO_2 Laser, 1852
Coulken, John M., 5
Coult, Alan, 1293
Council On Economic Priorities, 227
COUNTERINSURGENCY (weapons)
See also BIOLOGICAL WARFARE; CHEMICAL WARFARE; GUERRILLA WARFARE; WARFARE
21, 345, 734
Courtenay, M., 3629
Cousins, Norman, 4757, 4758, 5052, 5053
Coventry Road, Cleveland, Ohio, 3434
Covert, John, 1751, 1752, 1753, 1754, 1755, 1756, 1757, 1758, 1759, 1760, 1761, 1762, 1763, 1764, 3492, 3493, 3494, 3495, 3496
Covina, California, 3448
Cowan, John L., 4033a
Cowan, Paul, 228, 5054
Cox, Archibald, 229, 3891
COX COMMISSION REPORT
3891, 4395
Cox, Donald, 1765, 4259
Cox, Harvey, 2977
Coyle, David C., 230
Coyne, John R. Jr., 3892, 4260
Craig, Roger D., 1635
Crain, Robert L., 231
Craise, Judith L., 4549
Cramer, James, 3344
Crane, Andrew, 3859
Cranston, M., 4261

Crawford, K., 4759
Cray, Ed, 1766, 3345, 3497
CREDIBILITY GAP 200, 545, 1174, 1612, 2503, 2834, 3455
Crespigny, A. de, 5055
Cressey, Donald R., 232
Cressey, Suterland, 3346
Crick, Bernard, 233
CRIME AND CRIMINALS--SEX 274
CRIME BILL (District Of Columbia)
See also NO KNOCK CRIME BILL (District Of Columbia) 1778
CRIME--FAIR TRIAL--PUBLICITY--FREE PRESS 337
CRIME, JUVENILE
See also JUVENILE DELINQUENCY--CAUSES; JUVENILE DELINQUENCY--U.S.
322, 916, 1068a, 2963
CRIME, ORGANIZED 232, 3378, 3560, 4913, 5017, 5088, 5163
CRIME, URBAN 617, 3560, 4917, 5088, 5214
CRIMINAL INVESTIGATION
See Items Listed In The Section "Police-Community Relationships." e.g., 3417, and "Civil Disobedience," e.g., 4932
CRIMINAL LAW
See LAW--REFORM
CRIMINOLOGY AND THE POLICE 3346, 3348, 3349, 3392, 3394, 3411, 3412, 3486, 3513, 3534, 3577, 3581, 3587
CRISIS CONFLICT AND PROSPERITY
See PROSPERITY AND CRISIS CONFLICT
Croan, Robert, 1767
Crockett, Thompson, 3346a
Croise, Judith L., 4610
Crompton, Louis, 1459
Cronin, Peggy, 4262
Crosby, David, 3141
Cross, Christopher T., 1768
Cross, K. Patricia, 4263

Cross, Robert D., 234, 3217
Cross, Virginia, 3763
Crow, Alice, 3630
Crow, Lester D., 3630
Crowley, Louise, 1769
Cruse, Harold, 235, 236, 1770, 2003
CUBA--POLITICS AND GOVERNMENT 299a, 560, 789, 832, 947
CUBAN MISSILE CRISIS, October 22, 1962, 707, 1805
CUBAN REVOLUTION 259, 268, 469, 493, 505, 588, 606, 664, 858, 941, 947, 972, 1013, 1070, 1638, 1673, 1674, 1674a, 1770, 2082, 2167, 2592, 2674, 2687, 2819, 2847, 2855, 4385
Cullen, Mike, 1771
Cullers, Benjamin, 4296
Cullinan, Terrance, 5349
CULTURE FREAKS 2366
Cunneen, Sally, 3631
Cuozzi, Bob, 4264
Cupps, Stephen, 2910
Currie, Gillette B., 237
Curry, J. E., 3347

Daane, James, 238
Dahlgren, Kathy, 1772, 1773
Dahrendorf, Ralf, 239
Daley, Richard, 807, 2287, 2538
Dallas, Texas, 4250, 4734
Daly, Charles, 4843
D'Amato, D. A., 58
Damiano, Roland, 4012
Dana, Jane, 1774, 3218
Dana, Jay, 3219
Danforth Foundation, 3893
Daniels, John, 4265
Daniels, Roger, 240
Danny The Red
   See Cohn-Bendit, Daniel
Danserau, Pierre, 241
D'Arazien, Steve, 4760
Darden, J. S., 3764
Darlington, Sandy, 1775
Dasgupta, Sugata, 5056
Dash, Samuel, 242

Dassman, Raymond E., 243
David, Jay, 244
Davidson, Carl, 1777, 1778, 1779, 3894, 4266
Davies, Alan, 245
Davis, Angela, 973, 1066, 1183, 1193, 1238, 1308, 1462, 1633, 1718, 1909, 2256, 2274, 2432
Davis, B. H., 4267
Davis, Carroll, 2978
Davis, David Brion, 246
Davis, F. J., 4844
Davis, Harry R., 5350
Davis, James W., 5244
Davis, Junius A., 4590a
Davis, M., 3632
Davis, Rennie, 193, 1361, 2044
Davis, Roger, 4268
Davis, Wayne H., 1780
Davis, Zelda, 2363
Davy, J., 1781
Day, Linda, 3694
Daytop Village (Rehabilitation Commune) 2680
Dea, John, 3220
Deakin, James, 1782
De Alba, Joaquin, 4845
Dean, Thomas, 742
Deane, Lola, 2979
Deane, Philip, 2979
De Antonio, Emile, 2154
De Bardeleben, Arthur, 3975
DE CARLO TAPES 1067
De Castro, Josue, 247
De Cecco, John P., 4268a
Decker, Mike, 5351
De Coy, Robert H., 248
Decter, Midge, 1783
Dederich, Chuck, 3132
Deedy, J., 2911
DEFENSE CONTRACTS
   See INDUSTRIAL-MILITARY-GOVERNMENT-EDUCATIONAL COMPLEX
DEFENSE FACILITIES AND INDUSTRIAL SECURITY ACT OF 1970
   See INDUSTRIAL SECURITY ACT OF 1970
DEFOLIATION 607
Deglau, Paul, 1784
Degler, Carl N., 1785

Degler, Stanley E., 249
De Jouvenel, Bertrand, 3895
De Koster, Lester, 249a
Delaware, University of, 1559
De Leo, Lois, 3221
De Lestapis, S., 3633
De Levita, David J., 250
Dellinger, Dave, 1079, 1786, 1801, 2270, 5057, 5058
Deloria, Vine Jr., 251
Delta State College, Cleveland, Mississippi, 4112
Demaio, Don, 1787, 1788, 1789, 1790, 1791, 3498, 3499
Demant, V. A., 3634
Demarest, Robert J., 3635
Demaris, Ovid, 252, 4846
De Martino, Manfred F., 3636
Demchak, J. M., 1792
Deming, Barbara, 253, 4847
DEMOCRACY 156, 2100, 2116, 2449, 2554, 3954, 4883, 4928, 5212, 5215
DEMOCRACY, PARTICIPATORY 67, 2326, 2434
Democratic National Party Convention, Chicago, 1968, 628, 807, 2044, 2246, 4937
Democratic People's Republic Of Korea, 2663
Dempsey, William J. Jr., 3347a
Dennis, Lawrence E., 254, 2980
Denson, Ed, 1793
Dentler, Robert A., 255
De Pugh, Robert, 1309, 1483, 2744
De Reuck, Anthony V., 255a
De Rham, Edith
  See Rham, Edith De
De Ropp, Robert S., 2981, 2982, 2983
De Rosa, Tony, 1344, 1794, 1795, 1796
DESEGREGATION, SCHOOL 722a, 857
Des Moines, Iowa, 2560, 3435
De Souza, Steve, 1797
De Swede, John, 1798
Detroit, Michigan, 349, 562, 833, 1103, 1387, 1388

DETROIT--RACE RELATIONS 562, 833
Deutsch, M., 1799
Deutscher, Irwin, 256
Deutscher, Isaac, 1800, 1801, 5059
De Vane, William, 3896
Devereux, G., 257
De Vinck, Jose, 3637
Devine, J. Travers, 1802
Devine, Laurie, 1803, 1804
Devletoglou, Nicos E., 139, 2961
Devlin, Bernadette, 258, 1631
Dewart, Leslie, 259, 1805
Dewey, John, 260
DIALECTICAL MATERIALISM
  See MARXISM
Diamond, David, 4269
Diamond, Edwin, 4270
Diamond, Steve, 1806, 4271
Di Certo, J. J., 4664a
Dick, Bernard F., 4272
Dickie, Allan, 4273
Dickinson, John K., 1807
Dicks, Ronald, 1832
Didion, Joan, 3222
Diehl, Digby, 1808, 1809
Diekhoff, John S., 4274
Dien Bien Phu, 302
Dierenfield, R. B., 260a
Dietrich, Marion, 1810
Dietze, Gottfried, 3897
Dillman, Terry, 1811
Dimitroff, George, 1812
Dinitz, Simon, 3348
DISARMAMENT
  See also ARMS CONTROL 48, 72, 144, 212, 266, 319, 338, 514, 902, 4659
Disch, Robert, 810
DISCRIMINATION
  Homosexual, 1171, 1245, 1363, 1794, 2134, 2178, 2228; In Advertising, 1290; In Business, 264, 735, 736, 1606, 1623a, 2753a; In Education, 235, 4639; In Government Service, 536; In Housing, 436, 805, 806, 879, 1015, 1435, 1530, 1544,

1771, 2387, 2764; In Industry, 311, 890, 2004, 2753a; In Jury Selection, 1754, 1764, 2321; In Military Service, 1134, 1715, 2395, 5409; In New York State, 450; In Sports, 1140, 2140, 2297, 2441; In The Health Professions, 1632; In Voting, 507, 855; Non-Professional Hospital Workers, 1753, 1773, 2810, 3494; On The Basis Of Color, 129, 235, 443, 534, 546, 643, 751, 805, 806, 838, 903; On The Basis Of Long Hair, 1044, 1081, 1144, 1162, 2018, 4175, 4424; On The Basis Of National Origin, 735, 736, 775, 776; On The Basis Of Sex, 1528a, 2117, 2517, 2753a, 4632; For General Articles On Discrimination See: 36, 43, 45, 51, 841a

Disney, D. C., 3223
Dissent (Magazine) 467
DISTRICT OF COLUMBIA COURT REFORM AND CRIMINAL PROCEDURE ACT OF 1970
    See NO-KNOCK CRIME BILL (District Of Columbia)
District Of Columbia 9, 2786
Divale, William T., 1909, 3898
Divoky, Diane, 260b, 3899, 4275
Dixon, Marlene, 261, 262, 1813, 1814, 2556
Dobrin, A., 3482
Dodd, Senator Thomas, 2917
Dodd, T. J., 2912
Doggett, David, 1815
Dohen, Dorothy, 263
Dohner, V. Alton, 3224
Dolbeare, Kenneth, 5244
Don, 3765
Donald, David, 1816
Donaldson, J. L., 3766, 3767, 3788
Donaldson, Stephen, 1817

Donner, Frank, 1818
Donovan, Bernard, 4276
Donovan, Frank R., 2984
Donovan, J. B., 5352
Donovan, Michael, 700
Doriot, George F., 264
Dorr, R., 3768
Dorsen, Norman, 265, 5060
Dorsey, Ellie, 1819
Dougherty, James E., 266
Douglas, Angela, 1820, 1821, 1822, 1823
Douglas, Bruce, 3900
Douglas, Emily Taft, 266a
Douglas, Jack, 266b
Douglas, Judi, 1824
Douglas, Val, 1825
Douglas, William O., 2985, 4848
Douvan, Elizabeth, 3901
DOW CHEMICAL COMPANY 1087, 1275, 1345, 1971, 2032, 2435, 2493, 2786, 2859, 4574
Downing, L. A., 5207
Drabek, Thomas, 3349, 3500
Drafts, C. Gene, 1008
Draper, Anne, 1826
Draper, Bruce, 3818
Draper, Hal, 1827, 1828, 2909, 3902
Draper, Theodore, 267, 268, 269, 2819
Dreifus, Claudia, 1829, 1830, 1831, 1831a, 1832, 1833, 1834, 1835, 1836, 2767, 3501, 5353
Drescher, Earl L., 3501a
DRESS CODES--HIGH SCHOOL 1356, 1907, 2361
Drew, E. B., 2913
Drexel Institute, Philadelphia, Pennsylvania, 2293
Dreyer, Thorne, 1837, 1838, 1839
Drinan, Robert F., 270
Drinnon, Richard, 271, 2292, 5061
Drop City, Trinidad, Colorado, 2609
DRUG ADDICTION AND CRIME
    See DRUGS AND DRUG CULTURE

See also Items Listed In The Section: "The Gap In Generations And The Drug Dilemma."

DRUGS AND DRUG CULTURE 37, 423, 927, 1147, 1155, 1214, 1240, 1241, 1271, 1437, 1547, 2170, 2333, 2410, 2467, 2827, 2952, 2968, 2971, 2972, 2974, 2979, 2981, 2982, 2984, 2987, 2988, 2995, 3007, 3018, 3026, 3038, 3039, 3040, 3046, 3047, 3049, 3051, 3052, 3055, 3058, 3062, 3064, 3071, 3095, 3098, 3101, 3102, 3105, 3109, 3110, 3118, 3119, 3121, 3122, 3123, 3124, 3125, 3126, 3127, 3128, 3129, 3130, 3136, 3137, 3138, 3139, 3140, 3142, 3143, 3144, 3145, 3146, 3147, 3148, 3154, 3155, 3156, 3157, 3160, 3161, 3162, 3163, 3164, 3166, 3167, 3168, 3169, 3170, 3171, 3174, 3177, 3178, 3179, 3180, 3181, 3183, 3186, 3189, 3191, 3194, 3195, 3202, 3203, 3204, 3206, 3207, 3208, 3209, 3216, 3218, 3223, 3224, 3228, 3230, 3235, 3237, 3238, 3239, 3246, 3247, 3248, 3250, 3252, 3253, 3255, 3257, 3261, 3262, 3267, 3274, 3276, 3277, 3278, 3279, 3281, 3285, 3286, 3287, 3288, 3289, 3291, 3294, 3295, 3299, 3302, 3304, 3305, 3308, 3313, 3314, 3994

DRUGS AND DRUG CULTURE-- PRICES AND SALE 423, 1073a, 1202, 2926

DRUGS (in military service) 975

Druingo, Fleeta, 2459
Drukman, Elaine, 1840
Dryer, Ivan, 1841, 1842, 1843
Drysdale, Dickey, 1844
Duberman, M., 4277

Duchene, Francois, 272
Duclow, Donald, 1845
Duerr, Edwin C., 4278
Duffett, John, 273, 1846
Duffy, Clinton T., 274
Duggan (District Attorney) Pittsburgh, Pennsylvania, 1071, 1089, 2522
Dugway Proving Ground, Utah, 1397
Duke University, Durham, North Carolina, 1985, 4069, 4132, 4608
Dulles, F., 275
Dumke, Glenn, 911, 4143
Dunbar, E., 3769
Dunbar, Ernest, 4279
Dunbar, Roxanne, 869
Duncan, Don, 1235
Duncan, Donald, 1847, 1848, 1849, 1850, 4849, 5062, 5354
Duncan, William H., 1226, 1436
Duncanson, Dennis J., 276
Dunlap, Riley, 3902a
Duquesne Club 14 (Pittsburgh, Pennsylvania) 2541
Durham, North Carolina, 1090
Duronio, Dick, 1851, 1852, 1853
Duscha, Julius, 277
Dutton, John M., 1854, 2768
Duvall, Evelyn, 2986, 3638, 3639, 3640
Du Vall, Joyce, 1855
Dye, Thomas R., 5063

Eaby, Christian, 1421
Eachus, Denise, 3225
Eames, Elizabeth R., 278
Earisman, Delbert L., 279
Earle, Howard H., 3350
East Bay American Nazis, 1266
Eastern Michigan University, Ypsilanti, Michigan, 4265, 4268
Eaton, J. W., 5355
EAVESDROPPING
See WIRETAPPING
Eban, Abba, 456
Eberle, Paul, 1856, 1857, 1858,

1859, 1860, 1861, 1862,
1863, 1864, 1865, 1866,
1867, 1868, 1869, 1870,
1871, 1872, 1873, 1874,
1875, 1876, 1877, 1878,
1879, 1880, 1881, 3226,
3227, 3502, 3503, 3504,
4280, 4281, 5064
Eberly, Donald, 5356
Ebin, D., 2987
Ebony, 280
Eby, Kermit, 1882
ECOLOGY
See also ENVIRONMENTAL CRISIS; POLLUTION--INDUSTRIAL COMPLEX
241, 243, 435, 440, 559,
720, 744, 766, 787,
833a, 882, 1094, 1095,
1096, 1097, 1098, 1099,
1258, 1324, 1473, 1560,
1562, 1599, 1605, 1727,
1741, 1798, 1885, 1980,
1982, 2010, 2052, 2055,
2146, 2148, 2215, 2216,
2217, 2226, 2300, 2345,
2346, 2360, 2407, 2500,
2502, 2735, 2792, 2793,
2794, 2804, 2848
Ecology Action, University of California, Berkeley, 2218
ECUMENICAL (revolution) 133, 1662
Eddie, Z., 1853
Eddy, E. D., 4282
Eddy, Elizabeth M., 281
Eddy, N. B., 3228
Eden West, Ben Lomand, California, 2609
Edgerton, Karl R., 4283
EDUCATION, COMMUNITY CONTROL
See also SCHOOLS, CENTRALIZATION
17, 66, 85, 306, 574,
722a, 782a, 873, 884,
1058, 1997, 1998, 4295
EDUCATION, CRISIS OF 5, 55,
66, 68, 213, 214, 255,
281, 306, 342, 359,
376, 397, 401, 419,
434, 442, 489a, 497,
510, 511, 517, 528,
538, 540, 556a, 569,
584a, 614, 638a, 661,
728, 741, 761, 802,
803, 828, 886, 925a,
932, 949, 970, 1021,
1038, 1058, 1069, 1091,
1156, 1343, 1383, 1686,
1930, 1933, 2056, 2071,
2329, 2448, 2490, 2644,
2681, 2765, 2839, 3852,
3863, 3908, 3912, 3933,
3937a, 3979, 4024, 4035,
4082, 4288, 4441
EDUCATION, ELEMENTARY
55, 819, 2765
EDUCATION, FREE 2327,
2490, 4421
EDUCATION, HIGH SCHOOL--FREE 1121b, 2525
EDUCATION, HIGHER 57, 139,
214, 298, 419, 434,
527, 584a, 614, 661,
702a, 921, 932, 1029,
1063, 1108, 1300, 1342,
2179, 2447, 2956, 3029,
3852, 3863, 3881, 3884a,
3896, 3911, 3913, 3931,
3933, 3937a, 3939, 3940,
3959, 3973a, 3981, 3999,
4019, 4024, 4288, 4303,
4370, 4406, 4426, 4515,
4602, 4603, 4616, 4618,
4619, 4621, 5324
EDUCATION, HISTORY--NORTHERN GHETTOS 2750
EDUCATION, MEDICAL 3, 2661
EDUCATION--PUBLIC AND HIGH SCHOOL
Appalachia, 803; Birmingham High School, Birmingham, Michigan, 990, 994; Boston Public Schools, 802; Chicago Public Schools, 803; Colorado Public Schools, 1050; Durham High School, Durham, North Carolina, 1091, 2733; Hartford, Connecticut, 4145; Jefferson County, Colorado, 803; Los

Angeles Public Schools, 4365; Mississippi Public Schools, 1038; New York City Public Schools, 41, 85, 4276; Ocean Hill-Brownsville School District, New York, 2071, 4225, 4295; Philadelphia Public Schools, 86, 761, 1050, 3761; Philadelphia Public Schools (Head Start) 2301; Pittsburgh Public Schools, 2056; San Diego High School, 1380; Scarsdale Public Schools, Scarsdale, New York, 4398; Topeka, Kansas, 803; General Articles On Public And High School Education may be found in: 2460, and 3987
EDUCATION, RELIGIOUS
See also BIBLE READING IN THE PUBLIC SCHOOLS; RELIGION IN THE PUBLIC SCHOOLS
700
EDUCATION RESEARCH--POLITICAL PROCESS
139, 2315
EDUCATION, SECONDARY
66, 207a, 334, 819, 925a, 3893
EDUCATION, SEGREGATION
See SEGREGATION IN EDUCATION
EDUCATION, URBAN 255, 281, 306, 442, 528
Edwards, Clifford W., 4284
Edwards, D. L., 282
Edwards, David W., 283
Edwards, George, 3351
Edwards, Harry, 284, 285, 1009, 1883, 3903, 4305
Egal, Arnie, 1328
Egan, Edmund J., 5065
Egelson, Nick, 1884
Eggleston, Norman E., 125a
Ehrenreich, B., 3904
Ehrenreich, J., 3904
Ehrilich, Paul, 286, 1885, 1886
Ehrlich, J. L., 4614
Ehrmann, Winston W., 3641

Eickhoff, Andrew R., 3642
Eisen, Jonathan, 4285
Eisenberg, D., 287
EISENHOWER COMMISSION, 762
Eisenhower, Milton, 4905
Eisenscher, Michael, 1887, 1888
Eismann, Bernard, 489
Elam, S. M., 4286
El Barrio, New York, 1514
Eldefonso, Edward, 3352
Eldridge, William B., 2988
Electric Shock Treatment
See Anticipatory Avoidance Learning (Electric Shock Treatment)
ELECTRONIC EAVESDROPPING
See WIRETAPPING
ELECTRONIC SURVEILLANCE
See WIRETAPPING
ELEMENTARY AND SECONDARY EDUCATION ACT OF 1965, 860
Elinson, Howard, 679
Elkind, D., 3229
Elle, Lawrence, 1889
Ellingsworth, H. W., 5357
Elliott, A. Wright, 1889a
Elliott, E. E., 2989
Elliott, R., 3230
Elliott, Ward, 1890
Ellis, Albert, 288, 3643, 3643a, 3801
Ellis, Havelock, 3644
Ellis, William W., 289
Ellul, Jacques, 4850
Emaus House, New York City, N.Y., 2609
Emmerson, Donald K., 3905
Empey, Lamar T., 289a
Endleman, Shalom, 4851
Endore, Guy, 2989a
Endres, M. E., 5066
England, Ralph W. Jr., 3505, 5067
ENGLISH MODERN METHODS SCHOOLS, 4493
Engo, Robert, 4287
ENRAGES OF HARVARD 4288
Entwisle, Doris R., 2110
ENVIRONMENTAL CRISIS
See also ECOLOGY;

POLLUTION--INDUSTRIAL
COMPLEX
    241, 243, 435, 439,
    440, 559, 744, 787,
    833a, 882, 1059, 1094,
    1095, 1096, 1097, 1098,
    1099, 1102, 1258, 1324,
    1473, 1560, 1599, 1605,
    1727, 1741, 1885, 1980,
    1982, 2010, 2146, 2148,
    2215, 2226, 2300, 2345,
    2498, 2499, 2500, 2531,
    -2735, 2753, 2848
Epps, Archie, 290
Epstein, Benjamin R., 291, 292
Epstein, Charlotte, 3353
Epstein, Cynthia F., 293
Epstein, Edward Jay, 294
Epstein, Jason, 295
Epstein, Joseph, 1126
EQUALITY FOR LONGHAIRS
    2018, 2825
EQUALITY OF OPPORTUNITY
    168, 175, 176, 312,
    436, 449a, 506, 507,
    536, 701, 935, 944,
    1104, 1105, 1950, 2117,
    2210, 2352a, 2601, 2825,
    4819, 5063
Erickson, Kenneth, 3906
Erikson, Erik, 1106, 1891,
    2990, 2991, 2992, 3933,
    4852
Erikson, Kai T., 3907
Erikson, Kenneth, 3907
Erlich, John, 3908
Erlich, Paul R., 1892
Erlich, Reese, 1645, 1893, 4462
Ernesto Che Guevara
    See Che Guevara, Ernesto
Ernst, Morris L., 296
EROTIC ART
    See also OBSCENITY (law);
    PORNOGRAPHY
    471, 1082
EROTICA--SALES, DENMARK
    1393
ESCALATION (of war) 808,
    1282, 1576, 1613, 1614,
    1626, 1648, 1760, 1763,
    1960, 2359, 2702, 2834,
    4091, 4954
Eshelman, William R., 1894
Espy, Robert Hamilton Edwin, 1895
Essenes Of Kosman, Palisades, Colorado, 2609
Esser, A. H., 3231
Essien-Udom, E. U., 297
Esslin, Martin, 3909
Estes, Nolan, 4250
Estrin, Herman A., 3967
Eszterhas, Joe, 297a
Etheridge, Eugene W., 4289
ETHICS, LEGISLATIVE, 2752
Etzioni, A., 3910, 4290
Eurich, Alvin, 3911
Eurich, Alvin C., 298
Euwema, Ben, 4291
Evans, Ahmed, 2240, 2268
Evans, D. M., 1896
Evans, M., 299
Evans, M. Stanton, 3354
Evans, T. D., 4292
Evergreen Review, 778
Evers, Joanne, 1897
Exchange, San Francisco, 2609
Executive Systems, Inc., 3912
EXPERIMENTATION WITH HUMANS
    See MEDICAL EXPERIMENTATION, HUMAN
EXTREMISM 11, 22a, 30, 168a,
    195a, 587, 704, 1561,
    2696

Faber, N. G., 3770
FACULTY--STUDENT MOVEMENT, BERKELEY, CALIFORNIA 4230
FACULTY-STUDENT RELATIONSHIPS
    See Items Listed In The Section "Student Dissent." e.g., 4313
Fagan, Richard R., 299a
Fager, Charles E., 300, 301, 5068
Fairfield, Dick, 1898
Fairfield, Roy P., 3506
Fairlie, Henry, 4292a
Falk, Richard A., 4853, 4935
Fall, Bernard B., 302, 303,

304, 305, 524
FAMILY PLANNING
See Items Listed In The Section "The Pregnant Question -Sex Education." e.g., 3633
FAMILY (social change) 4, 152, 225, 374, 512, 572, 599a, 924, 2439, 2946, 3013, 3033, 3034, 3065, 3068, 3117, 3710, 3805, 5189
Fanon, Frantz, 1617, 1918, 2581
Fantini, Mario, 306
Farber, Bernard, 3644a
Farber, Jerry, 3507, 4090, 4293, 5069
Farber, Seymour M., 307, 308
Fargo, North Dakota, 2232
Farmer, James, 125
Farnsworth, Dana L., 3771
Farrel, Fred, 1899, 1900, 1901, 1902
FASCISM
See also IDEOLOGY, THEORY OF
12, 287, 992, 1107, 1267, 1642, 1666, 1668, 1682, 1812, 2031, 2039, 2121, 2151, 2282, 2283, 2491, 2751, 2774, 2788, 3220
Fay, John, 1903
Fearon, Christopher P., 4294
FEDERAL AIR QUALITY ACT OF 1967, 427a
FEDERAL BUREAU OF INVESTIGATION 881, 1111, 1127, 1233, 1314, 1489, 1580, 1766, 1818, 1864, 2201, 2746, 3354a, 3386, 3544, 5383
Federick, Don, 1904
Fehrle, Carl C., 3772
Feiffer, Jules, 2192
Feigelson, Naomi, 309, 2993
Feinberg, Gerald, 310
Feinberg, Kenneth R., 2501, 5171a
Feldman, Adam, 2038, 4099
Feldman, Herman, 311
Feldman, Kenneth A., 3913
Feldman, Philip M., 1344, 1795

Feldman, Sam, 1452
Fellowship Farm, Pottstown, Pennsylvania, 2569
Felsen, H. G., 2993a
Felsenstein, Lee, 1905
Female, The (film) 2522
Ferber, Michael, 5312
Ferm, D. W., 3773
Ferman, Louis, 11, 312
Ferrell, Tom, 1906
FERTILITY, HUMAN
See also ABORTION; BIRTH CONTROL; POPULATION, CONTROL OF
22, 25, 61, 286, 392, 599a, 3600, 3608
Feuer, Alan, 1907
Feuer, Lewis S., 2085, 2994, 3232, 3914
Fey, H. E., 5071
Fiddle, Seymour, 2995
Field, Marjorie, 1122
Fields, A. Belden, 3915
Fierce, R., 2914
Figes, Eva, 313
Figg, Donald, 5358
Finch, Robert H., 3893
Fine, David, 1908
Fine, Jessie, 1909
Fink, Newton W., 4296
Finkin, M. W., 5359
Finn, James, 314, 315, 4854, 4855, 5245
Finneran, Mary, 5360
Firestone, Shulamith, 316
First, Wesley, 3916
Fischer, John, 4297, 5072, 5073, 5074
Fish, Kenneth L., 3917, 4298
Fishel, Wesley R., 317
Fisher, Paul, 318
Fisher, Richard, 2915
Fisher, Tom, 1910
Fisher, W. R., 319
Fishman, Katherine D., 319a
Fitch, Bob, 1911
Fitzgerald, Dennis, 1912
Fitzmorris, Paul E., 5075
Flack, M. J., 4299
Flacks, Richard, 2185, 4299a, 4300, 4549
FLAGS--U.S. (display procedures) 1316, 2762

Flaming Creatures, 2219
Flaming, Karl H., 4856
Flash, J. Jack, 1913
Fleming, Alice, 3774
Fleming, K., 4301
Fleming, Robben, 4332
Fleming, Thomas, 3774
Fleming, Thomas J., 3508
Fletcher, Grace N., 2996
Fletcher, H. L., 1914
Fletcher, John, 3509, 3510
Flexner, Abraham, 419
Flexner, Eleanor, 320
Flexner, Hans, 4302
Florida Memorial College, Miami, Florida, 4049
Florida State University, Tallahassee, Florida, 4151
Florida Statutes, 2024
Flynn, Elizabeth Gurley, 18
Fogelson, Robert, 4857, 5076
Foley, James A., 3718
Foley, Robert K., 3718
Folk, Hugh, 3254
FOLSOM PRISON, CALIFORNIA 1712
Fonda, Peter, 1651
Foner, Philip S., 321
FOOD SHORTAGE REPORT
See FOOD SUPPLY--U.S.
FOOD SUPPLY--U.S. 103, 205, 247, 712, 816a, 1184, 1735, 2598, 2804
Foote, Nelson N., 1915
Footlick, Jerrold K., 3919
Forbes Committee, University of California, 3879a
Ford Foundation, 1121, 3893
Ford, Kent, 1205
Ford, Richard J., 3233
Ford, William Wallace, 4734
FOREIGN INVESTMENTS, U.S.
See U.S. FOREIGN INVESTMENTS
FOREIGN POLICY
See ARMS CONTROL; IDEOLOGY, THEORY OF
Foreman, Clark H., 1916
Forer, Lois G., 322
Forest River Community, Fordville, North Dakota, 2609
Forman, Alex, 1917

Forman, I., 3775
Forman, James, 323, 1918
Forsberg, Clarence J., 1919
Forster, Arnold, 291, 292
Fort Carson, Colorado (Coffee House) 1938
Fort Dix, New Jersey 1117, 1143, 1292, 1594, 2111, 2173, 2272, 2559, 2653, 2694, 2715, 2851
Fort Eustis, Virginia, 2046
Fort Hood, California, 2694
Fort Hood, Texas, 500, 979, 1118, 1921, 2694, 5409
Fort Hood 3, 1118
Fort, J., 3776
Fort Jackson 8, 1339
Fort Jackson, South Carolina, 1119, 1119a, 1136, 1353, 2036, 2156, 2667, 2694, 5366
Fort, Joel, 3717
Fort Leavenworth, Kansas, 2036
Fort Leonard Wood, Missouri, 980, 2694
Fort Lewis, Oregon, 980, 2694
Fort Ord, California, 1937
Fort Riley, East Kansas, 1138, 1353
Fort Sheridan, Chicago, Illinois, 1120a
Fort Worth, Texas, 2664
Fortas, Abe, 2028, 4858, 5077, 5085
Fortune Magazine (Editors) 3920
Forward, John R., 5078
Foster, Julian, 3921
FOUNDATIONS
See also Individual Names Of Foundations, e.g., Carnegie Foundation; Kennedy Foundation; Triton Foundation; Religion In Education Foundation 753, 1121, 2102, 2107, 2108, 3867
Fountain, L., 5361
Fox, Andrew, 1920
Fox, Howard A., 5362
Fox, Josef W., 4303, 4304
Fraenkl, H., 5363
Frame, Scotty, 1921
Francis, Bevo, 4085

Francis, Leonard R., 1922
Frank, John P., 324
Frank, Lawrence Kelso, 3645
Frankel, Charles, 3922, 5079
Franklin Institute, Philadelphia, Pennsylvania, 1956
Franklin, John Hope, 325, 326
Franklin, Ted, 1923
Franzblau, Abraham N., 3646
Franzblau, Rose N., 3646
Fraternal Order Of Police. Fort Pitt Lodge # 1, 3355
Frazier, Edward F., 327, 328, 3922a
Free (pseud.)
See Hoffman, Abbie
FREE HIGH SCHOOL, 1121b, 4073
FREE PRESS, HIGH SCHOOL
See UNDERGROUND (newspapers) HIGH SCHOOL
FREE PRESS MOVEMENT-- HIGH SCHOOL
See HIGH SCHOOL--UNDERGROUND
Free University Of California, 2203
Freed, Donald, 1924, 1925
Freed, Leonard, 329
Freedman, Mervin, 2997, 3923
Freedman, Morris, 3924
Freedman, Ronald, 3608
FREEDOM, ACADEMIC
See ACADEMIC FREEDOM
FREEDOM CORNER, PITTSBURGH, PENNSYLVANIA 1588
FREEDOM, INTELLECTUAL
See INTELLECTUAL FREEDOM
FREEDOM OF SPEECH
See SPEECH, FREEDOM OF
FREEDOM RIDERS 330, 717
FREEDOM RIDERS SPEAK FOR THEMSELVES 330
FREEDOM, SEXUAL 721a, 1354, 1393, 1394, 1671, 1903, 2038, 2716, 3611, 3732, 3792, 3801, 3841, 4529
Freeland Community, Redwood City, California, 2609
Freeman, Harry A., 4859

Freeman, Howard E., 331
Freeman, Lucy, 3091
Freemond, Jules, 1926
Freidel, Frank, 3985
Freistadt, Hans, 1927
Frey, John, 1608, 1720
Fried, Morton, 332
Friedan, Betty, 333, 869, 1855
Friedenberg, Edgar A., 4593
Friedenberg, E. Z., 3234
Friedland, William H., 4305
Friedlander, Albert H., 3925
Friedman, Leon, 335, 335a
Friedman, Linda, 4624
Friedman, Murray, 336
Friedman, Warren, 4624
Friendly, Alfred, 337
FRIENDS, SOCIETY OF 1288, 1317, 1557, 2360
Friggens, Paul, 3511, 3777
Fromm, Erich, 5, 338, 339, 686, 1647, 2085
Fromme, Allan, 2998
Frost, Thomas M., 3356
Fruchter, Norm, 1461, 1928, 2489
Fry, John R., 340
Frymier, Jack R., 4306
Fulbright, J. W., 341
Full, Harold, 342
Fullbright, J. William, 915
Fuller, John G., 2999
Fulton, W. C., 3778
FUNDAMENTALISTS 1335
Furey, Fran, 2447
Furlong, William Barry, 4307
Furniss, W. Todd, 584a
Furst, Randy, 1929, 1930
Fusco, Paul, 343
Fusfeld, Daniel R., 1931

Gaddis, Mary, 4308
Gafton, S., 3235
Gage, Linda, 2259, 2260, 5364
Gagnon, John, 3647
Gain, Charles R., 3554
Galbraith, John Kenneth, 344, 4309
Gall, Dennis, 1932, 4310, 4311
Gallagher, James J., 3779
Galloway, Russell, 561a
Gallup, George, 1933

Galula, David, 345
Gamson, William A., 1934
Gandhi, Mahatma, 100, 4859a, 4878, 4968, 5024, 5109
GANGS
See JUVENILE DELINQUENCY--CAUSES; JUVENILE DELINQUENCY--U.S.
Gans, Herbert J., 1935
Gardiner, J., 3357
Gardner, David, 1936
Gardner, Erle Stanley, 3358
Gardner, Fred, 346, 1937, 1938
Gardner, John W., 3000, 3001, 3926, 4834, 5080
Garfield, Thomas (Water Tunnel) 1475, 4387
Garfinkel, Herbert, 347
Garot, J. C., 2594
Garrett, James, 1939
Garrison, Jim, 348, 1127, 1128, 1129, 1371, 1566, 1634, 1636, 1637, 1809, 1858, 2202, 2222, 2745, 2747, 2755, 2756, 2757, 2822
Garry, Charles, 321, 1338, 1940
Gartner, M., 3236
Garver, Paul, 1941, 4964
Garwin, Richard L., 4761
Garwood, John D., 4312
Gary, Indiana, 2309
GATES COMMISSION REPORT 4026c
Gathering Of The Tribes, 1449
Gatland, Kenneth W., 4665
Gaughan, Joe, 1942
Gault Case (1967) 322
GAY GUERRILLAS
See GUERRILLAS, GAY
GAY-INS 3538, 3545, 3548
GAY LIBERATION FRONT
Berkeley, California, 991; Los Angeles, California, 1210a, 1344, 1739, 1820, 1821, 1865, 2015, 2131, 2132; Louisville, Kentucky, 1131; New York, 1299, 1810, 2742, 3548; San Francisco, California, 1142, 1381, 2228, 2238; For General Articles See: 1180, 1322, 1794, 2127, 2128, 2134, 2229, 2424, 2658, 2831
Gaylin, Williard, 5246
GAY STUDENTS LEAGUE 1080
Geerdes, Clay, 1943, 1944, 1945, 3512
Geier, W. A., 5081
Geis, Gilbert, 4800, 5082
Geismar, Maxwell, 496, 5083
Gelhorn, Walter, 3359
Gelinas, M. V., 3237
Gellen, Martin, 1946
Geltman, Max, 349
General Electric Corporation, 2004, 2235, 2273, 2620
General Motors Corporation, 710, 1186, 2251, 2254
GENERATIONAL GAP AND SCIENCE
See SCIENCE AND THE GENERATIONAL GAP
GENERATION IN SEARCH OF A FUTURE 13
Genet, Jean, 480, 1947, 1948, 1949, 2219, 2275
GENETIC CONTROL--POPULATION
See POPULATION, CONTROL OF
GENOCIDE 204, 403, 788, 1543, 1740, 1889, 2005, 2058, 2059, 2217, 2349, 2595, 2596, 5403a
Genovese, Eugene D., 1950, 2426
Gentile, Charles, 1951
George F. Cake Corporation, 3481
George Washington University, Washington, D.C., 4071
George, Wesley, 350
Gerassi, John, 181
Gerber, A., 351, 1952
Gerberding, William P., 352
Gerhardt, James M., 5247
GERM WARFARE
See BIOLOGICAL WARFARE; CHEMICAL WARFARE; PSYCHOLOGICAL WARFARE; WARFARE

Germann, A. C., 3360, 3513
Gershman, Carl, 1953, 1954, 2335
Gerth, Hans H., 1955, 2679
Gerzon, Mark, 3927
Geschwender, James A., 5084
Gettleman, Marvin E., 353
Gettys, Montgomery III 1956
Gewirth, Alan, 5085
Ghent, W. J., 1984
Giannini, Amadeo Peter, 2713
Gibert, Henri, 3648
Gibson, Barbara, 1957
Gibson, Elsie, 354
Gibson, G., 3200
Gibson, Kenneth Allen, 1958
Gideonse, H. D., 4313
Giermanski, J. R., 5086
Gilbert, Ben W., And The Staff Of The Washington Post, 4861
Gilbert, Mitch, 3514, 3515, 3780, 5087
Giles, James, 853
Giles, John, 853
Giles-Johnson Case, 853
Gillie, D., 5365
Gillman, Joseph M., 355
Gilman, Richard, 1959
Gilmore, Donald H., 356
Gilmore, Susan, 3979
Ginger, Ann Fagan, 357
Ginott, Haim, 3002, 3003
Ginsberg, Allen, 619, 967, 1133, 2188, 2861, 3238
Ginsberg, Eli, 3648a
Ginsberg, M., 357a
Ginzberg, Eli, 358, 359, 360
G. I. PRESS, 5366
G. I. PRESS SERVICE 1958
Girling, J. L. S., 1960
Girvetz, Harry K., 3004
Gish, Arthur G., 361
Gitlin, Todd, 362, 1961, 1962, 4314
Gittell, M., 85
Gittell, Marilyn, 306
Gittler, Joseph B., 363
Givner, James, 2464
G. K. 3516, 4315
Glaberman, Martin, 1963
Glaser, Daniel, 3361, 4862, 5088, 5089

Glassberg, B. Y., 3649
Glassman, James K., 4316
Glatthorn, Allan A., 4317
Glazer, Nathan, 74, 3928, 4318, 4319, 4320, 4321, 5090
Gleason, Ralph, 1964, 5091
Gleaves, S. Z., 5248
Gleazer, E. J., 5367
Glenn, Hortense M., 1965
Glenville Incident, Cleveland, Ohio, 3444
Glick, Brian, 1966
Glick, Edward Bernard, 364, 5249
Glick, Ted, 5368
Glide Foundation, 2228
Glock, Charles Y., 365
Glusman, Paul, 1967, 1968, 1969, 1970, 1971, 4626
GOD IS DEAD CONTROVERSY, 410
God's Children Motorcycle Club, Ann Arbor, Michigan, 1420
Goheen, Robert F., 3005
Gold, Elliot, M., 1972
Gold, Harry, 366
Gold, Martin, 4593
Gold, Mike, 1973
Gold, Ted, 5184
Gold, U., 1974
Goldberg, Art, 1488, 1975, 1976, 3517
Goldberg, Arthur J., 369
Goldberg, Harvey, 367
Goldberg, Marilyn, 1977
Goldberg, Philip, 1978
Goldberger, P., 5369
Goldfarb, Ronald, 368, 369
Goldhaber, Nat, 1979
Goldin, Gerald A., 1980, 1981, 1982, 1983
Goldman, Emma, 271
Goldman, Lawrence, 1984
Goldman, Louis, 4322
Goldman, Peter, 370
Goldman, Ronald, 3006
Goldsen, Rose K., 3929
Goldstein, Richard, 3007
Goldston, Robert, 371
Goldwater, Barry, 64, 2066
Goldwin, Robert A., 372

Gollwitzer, Helmut, 373
Gomer, R., 4762
Gonzalez, Rodolfo, 111
Good, T. L., 4323
Goode, Erich, 3008
Goode, W., 374
Goodell, Charles E., 1985, 3912, 4324
Goodheart, Barbara, 3781
Goodheart, Eugene, 4324a
Goodhue, T., 3239
Goodlett, Carlton B., 2689a
Goodman, Ace, 4325
Goodman, Allan E., 1986
Goodman, Andrew, 2295
Goodman, Bob, 3518
Goodman, Mitchell, 375, 2787
Goodman, Paul, 5, 376, 377, 378, 379, 532a, 1647, 1987, 1988, 2689, 3009, 4326, 5092
Goodman, W., 3782
Goodman, Walter, 380
Goodwin, David, 3240
Goodwin, Richard N., 381
Gordon, Bernard K., 382
Gordon, Laura K., 735
Gordon, S., 3783
Gordon, Sol, 3650
Gore, D., 1989
Gorer, Geoffrey, 1990
Gorovitz, Samuel, 3930
Gorton, Richard A., 4327
Gosselin, Bob, 4328
Gossett, Thomas F., 383
Gossett, William T., 5093
Gottlieb, Art, 4329
Gottlieb, David, 384, 4593
Gottlin, Todd, 2689a
Gottschalk, H., 385
Goulart, Ron, 386
Gould Farm, Great Barrington, Massachusetts, 2609
Gould, Howard, 1991, 4330
Gould, Lawrence, 4593
Gould, Samuel B., 3931
Goulden, Joseph C., 387, 1992, 4763
Government Employees' Exchange, 1993
GOVERNMENT, RESISTANCE TO 161, 184, 186, 1027, 1548, 1755, 1760, 1969, 1988, 2078, 2111, 2123, 2269, 2369, 2430, 2548, 2829, 4818, 5092, 5399, 5403a
Governor's Commission On The Los Angeles Riot, 3362
Grafton, Samuel, 3519
Graham, Billy, 3583, 4952
Graham, Dave, 4331
Graham, Fred P., 1994
Graham, Hugh Davis, 4863, 4864
Grannemann, Glenn N., 1995
Grannis, C. B., 1996
Grant, Joanne, 388, 3932
Grant, William, 4332
Graubard, Stephen R., 3933, 4333
Gray, David, 1997, 1998
Gray, Francine du Plessix, 389
Gray, Ted W., 3241
Greeley, Andrew M., 389a
GREEN BERETS 1148, 1149, 2036
Green, Donald, 3242
Green, Edith, 4334
Green, Jack, 1999
Green, Ken, 4335, 5094
Green, Randy, 4336
Green, T. N., 390
Greenblatt, Augusta, 3651
Greene, Felix, 391
Greene, Fred, 2000
Greene, Gael, 3652
Greene, S., 3010
Greene, Thayer A., 3011
Greene, W., 4337
Greenhouse, Linda J., 2001, 2002
Greenleaf, Richard, 2003
Greenspan, Ralph, 2004
Green Valley School, Orange City, Florida, 2609
Greenville, South Carolina, 546, 964, 4605
Greenwich Village, New York, 1080, 3114, 3545
Greenwood, Frank, 2005, 2006, 2007
Greenwood, Mississippi, 62
Greenwood, Tamu Debra, 2008
Greep, Roy O., 392
Gregg, Richard, 2008a, 4865

Gregory, Dick, 393, 394, 395, 396, 1084, 2854, 5064
Gregory, Keith, 5370
Gregory, Susan, 397, 3934
Grier, William H., 398
Griffin, B. B., 4338
Griffin, Georgia, 2700
Griffin, John, 399
Griffith, W., 4339
Griffiths, B., 5095
Griffiths, J., 5250
Griffiths, Martha, 1596
Grimshaw, Allen D., 4866, 4867
Grinder, Robert, 4593
Grinnell, Iowa, 3818
Grisez, Germain G., 400
Griswald, Erwin N., 4868
GRISWOLD VS. CONNECTICUT 1965, 985
Grizzard, Vernon, 2045
Grodon, Albert I., 3653
Gronau, Gerald, 3520
Groomer, Ray, 2009
Gross, Beatrice, 401
Gross, Ronald, 401
Grossman, Jerome, 2689a
Grossvogel, David I., 4021
Groth, Ned, 2010
Group For The Advancement Of Psychiatry, 402
Group For The Advancement Of Psychiatry (Committee On The College Student) 3654
(GROUP) LEARNING EXPERIENCES, PHILADELPHIA, PENNSYLVANIA
  See LEARNING EXPERIENCES (GROUP) PHILADELPHIA, PENNSYLVANIA
Grove Press, 778, 2816
Grubbe, Peter, 2011
Gruenberg, Sidonie M., 3655
Grunwald, Henry, 2012, 3655a
Grusendorf, Arthur A., 2013
Guardian Newsweekly, 403
Gudridge, Beatrice M., 4340
Guerin, Daniel, 2014
Guerrero, Gene, 2014
GUERRILLA, URBAN 2309, 2344, 4620

GUERRILLA WARFARE
  See also COUNTERINSURGENCY (weapons); BIOLOGICAL WARFARE; CHEMICAL WARFARE; PSYCHOLOGICAL WARFARE; WARFARE
  21, 146, 180, 390, 505, 606, 702, 727, 734, 857a, 862, 1520, 1926, 2309, 2344, 2677
GUERRILLA WARFARE--ON CAMPUSES 4647
GUERRILLAS, GAY 1142
Guevara, Ernesto Che
  See Che Guevara, Ernesto
Guevara, Gay, 2015
GUIDANCE ASSOCIATES (Harcourt, Brace And World) 3656
GUIDED MISSILES 4671
Guilford, Vermont, 2190
GULF OF TONKIN (episode) 387
Gulf Oil Research Corporation, 206b, 1153, 1318, 1533, 1615, 1762, 2527, 2531
Gullo, John, 288
GUN AND FIREARMS--CONTROL AND REGULATION
  See Items Listed In The Section "Firearms, Control And Regulation."
GUN CONTROL ACT OF 1968, 2884, 2911, 2936
Gunnar, Myrdal, 456
Gurin, Patricia, 506
Gurr, Ted, 3012
Gurr, Ted Robert, 4864, 4869
Gurtov, Melvin, 404
Gurvich, William, 2822
Gustaitis, Rasa, 3935
Guttmacher, Alan Frank, 1740, 3657, 3784
Gwin, Jim, 2016, 2017, 2018, 2019, 2020
Gwin, Pam, 2021, 3785
Gwynne, John, 2150
Gwyther, David, 1256

Haag, E. Van Den, 2022, 3786
Haas, J. Eugene, 3500
Habenstein, Robert A., 3710
Haber, Alan, 2023
Haber, Barbara, 2023
Haber, W., 4341
Hacker, Andrew, 405, 3243
Hacker, Helen, 87a
Hacker, Michael S., 2024, 2025
Hadden, Jeffrey K., 2026
Haenni, A. L., 5251
Haight-Ashbury, San Francisco, California, 721a, 1230, 1449, 1793, 1929, 1943, 2141, 3114, 3582
Haight Street, 5111
Haines, Steve, 3521
Halbach, H., 3228
Halberstam, David, 405a, 406, 2027
Hale, Dennis, 203, 3885, 3886
Hall, Edward, 5371
Hall, Loran Eugene, 1863
Hall, Richard, 3522
Hall, Shirley W., 773
Hall, Standish, 2028, 2029
Hall, Wesley, 968
Halleck, Seymour, 3244
Halleck, S. L., 4342
Hallowell, John, 2030
Hallworth, G. L., 3523
Halperin, Irving, 4343
Halperin, M. H., 4674
Halprin, Burt, 2031
Halsell, Grace, 408
Halstead, Ron, 2032
Hamalian, Leo, 409
Hamburger, Hilary, 4344
Hamill, Pete, 5096
Hamilton, Becky, 2033
Hamilton, Charles, 3245
Hamilton, Charles V., 165 813
Hamilton, Kenneth M., 410
Hamilton, Mary, 2034, 2035, 2036, 2037, 2916, 2917
Hamilton, R., 3010
Hamilton, William, 16
Hamm, Carl W., 3374a
Hammond, Liz, 3787
Hampden-Turner, Charles, 411
Hampton, Fred, 965, 1751, 2281

Handel, Gerald, 3013
Handel, Lawrence, 3014
Handlin, Oscar, 412, 413
Hanh, Thich Nhat, 414
Hannon, V. R., 3231
Hansel, Robert R., 3015
Harbutt, Charles, 576
Harding, Timothy F., 2425
Hare, A. Paul, 3936, 4870
Hare, Nathan, 415, 3524, 4597
Harlem, New York (City) 188, 190, 349, 661, 688, 854, 3295, 5057
Harlem 6, 688, 2034
Harney, Father James, 2567
Harney, Malachi L., 3525
Haroldson, Thomas, 2038
Harper's Magazine, 1126
Harrington, J. J., 3526
Harrington, John H., 4345
Harrington, Michael, 173, 416, 417
Harris, Bennie, 2039
Harris, D., 3246, 3788
Harris, David, 4346
Harris, E., 418, 3246, 3788
Harris, Fred R., 398
Harris, Louis, 122, 123, 4344
Harris, Mark, 5372
Harris, Michael R., 419
Harris, R., 2918
Harris, Richard, 420, 421, 422, 423, 3363, 4871, 4872
Harris, Roger D., 2040
Harris, S., 4348
Harrisburg, Pennsylvania, 392a, 1412, 2008a
Harrison, Charles H., 3247, 3248
Harrison, Patti, 1503
Hart, Richard L., 3937
Hartley, Ruth E., 3789, 3790
Harvard University, 3896, 3927, 3951, 4038, 4076, 4081, 4338
Harvard Yard, 4038
Harvest Of American Racism, 5122
Harvey, Frank, 424
Harvey, William, 4349
Harwood, Michael, 5252
Haskell, Gordon K., 2041

Hassler, Alfred, 425
Hastings, Max, 426, 427
Hatch, Claudia, 3658
Hatch, Winslow, 584a
Hatfield, Mark, 5353
Haughton, Rosemary, 3249
Havinghurst, Clark C., 427a
Hawkins, B. A., 3791
Hawkins, G., 2931
Hawkins, Gordon, 4904
Hawkins, Sam, 2817
Hayakawa, S. I., 1156, 1944, 4107, 4197, 4350, 4356, 4380, 4570
Hayden, Bouie, 1752
Hayden, Casey, 2042
Hayden, Tom, 428, 429, 430, 1445, 1461, 1722, 2043, 2044, 2045, 2145, 2759, 3912, 4351, 4873
Hayman, Ed, 2046
Hays, H. R., 3659
Hays, Samuel, 5373
Hays, Samuel P., 4352
Hayward, Claude, 2047
Hazen Foundation, 3937a
Head, Robert, 2048
Headley, J. C., 431
Heard, Gerald, 3250
Heath, Douglas H., 3016, 3017
Heathcote School Of Living, Freeland, Maryland, 2609
Hedgepeth, William, 432
Hedlund, Ronald D., 4596
Heer, David M., 433
Heer, Friedrich, 1675
Hefferlin, J. B., 434
Hefner, Hugh, 111, 2192, 2767
Heifetz, Henry, 3792
Heifrich, Harold Jr., 435
Heilbroner, Robert L., 1647
Heimel, Cynthia, 4354, 4355
Heins, Marjorie, 2049
Heirich, Max, 3938
Heist, Paul, 3939, 3940
Heitzer, Art, 4356
HELL'S ANGELS 868, 1133, 1158, 1443
Helper, Rose, 436
Henderson, Algo D., 4357
Hendin, Herbert, 437
Hendryson, Elizabeth, 3793
Henig, Peter, 2050

Hennessy, Tom, 2051, 2052, 2053, 2054, 2055, 2056, 2057, 3527
Henri, (Brother) 2058
Henry, Carol, 2059
Hentoff, N., 438
Hentoff, Nat, 3018, 3251
Herber, Lewis, 439, 1605
Herberg, W., 5097
Herbers, John, 5098
Hering, M. B., 3252
Herman, Edward S., 2060, 2061
Herman, Joseph, 4357a
Herman, M., 5188
Herndon, James, 442
Hernton, Calvin C., 443, 444, 3660
Herrera, F., 3253
Herrup, Paul, 2062
Hersey, John, 3941
Hersh, Seymour M., 445, 446, 2063, 2064, 2065
Hershey, Lewis B., 5323, 5359, 5374
Herskovitz, Melville J., 447
Herwaldt, Fred, 4358
Herzog, Arthur, 448
Hess, Albert G., 3019
Hess, Karl, 1607, 2066, 2067, 2919, 5270
Hesse, Herman, 3233
Hessen, Robert, 4359
Hettlinger, Richard, 3661
Heussenstamm, F. K., 2068
Hewitt, Masai, 2069
Hewitt, Ray, 2070
Hickel, Walter J., 4097
Hickory Hill, Tappan, New York, 2609
Hicks, John H., 449
Hiestand, Dale L., 449a
Higbee, J., 450
Higby, Kirby, 4360
Higdon, R. M., 3794
Higgins, Marguerite, 451
Higham, Robin D., 4874
HIGH SCHOOL, FREE
    See FREE HIGH SCHOOL
High School Independent Press Service, 3899
HIGH SCHOOL MOVEMENT
    See HIGH SCHOOL--

UNDERGROUND
HIGH SCHOOL--UNDERGROUND
Abington Senior High
School, Abington, Pennsylvania, 4317; Abraham
Lincoln High School,
Southeast, San Diego,
California, 4082; Andrew
Jackson High School,
Queens, New York, 4374;
Argo Community High
School, Chicago, Illinois,
2183; Atlanta High School
District, Atlanta, Georgia, 2020; Austin High
School, Chicago, Illinois,
2183; Battin High School,
Elizabeth, New Jersey,
4050; Berwyn High School,
Chicago, Illinois, 4520;
Beverly Hills High School,
Beverly Hills, California,
1378; Brien McMahon
High School, Bridgeport,
Connecticut, 4175; Burrell Senior High School,
Lower Burrell, Pennsylvania, 994, 1030, 1074,
1356, 1508; Canarsie
High School, New York
City, New York, 4374;
Carver Senior High School,
New Orleans, Louisiana,
4374; Case Technical
High School, Detroit,
Michigan, 1164; Chamblee
High School, DeKalb,
Georgia, 2019; Chicago
High Schools, 2183; Choctawthalchie High School,
Fort Walton Beach, Florida, 2033; Clayton County
High School, Clayton
County, Georgia, 2020;
Clinton High School, Bronx,
New York, 4591; Columbia
High School, DeKalb
County, Georgia, 1385,
2017; Cook School Bussing
Program, Cook, Chicago,
2183; Cubberley High
School, Palo Alto, California, 4033; DeKalb
County School System,
Georgia, 1385;
DeKalb Senior High
School, DeKalb, Illinois,
1612; De La Warr High
School, Delaware, 4444;
Denby High School, Detroit, Michigan, 1164;
Detroit High Schools,
Detroit, Michigan, 978;
Durham High School,
Durham, North Carolina,
1091, 2733; Durfee High
School, Fall River, Massachusetts, 4150; East
Boston High School, Boston, Massachusetts,
4080; East Los Angeles
High School, Los Angeles, California, 2436,
4504; Erasmus High
School, Brooklyn, New
York, 4276, 4591; Fenger
High School, Chicago, Illinois, 2183; Fortier
High School, New Orleans, Louisiana, 4048;
Grady High School, Atlanta, Georgia, 2583;
Harrison High School,
Harrison, Chicago, Illinois, 2183; Homestead
High School, Milwaukee,
Wisconsin, 4311; Joliet
Central High School,
Linden, New Jersey,
4050, 4214; Kiski Area
Senior High School, Kiski, Pennsylvania, 994,
1074, 1207; Lakeshore
High School, Milwaukee,
Wisconsin, 4310; Lincoln
High School, New York
City, 4374; Long Island
City High School, New
York, 4137; Louisville
High School, Louisville,
Kentucky, 2557; McCaskey
High School, Lancaster,
Pennsylvania, 1421; Manheim Township High
School, Lancaster, Pennsylvania, 1421; Mar Vista

High School, San Diego, California, 1040; Marshall High School, Los Angeles, California, 2008; Morgan Park High School, Chicago, Illinois, 2183; Mount Greylock Regional High School, Williamstown, Massachusetts, 4411; Mumford High School, Detroit, Michigan, 1907, 4079; Newark High School, Newark, New Jersey, 4106; Newburgh Free Academy, New York City, 4374; Northern High School, Detroit, Michigan, 1907; Ocean Hill-Brownsville School District, 4295; Orr High School, Chicago, Illinois, 2183; Palo Alto School District, Palo Alto, California, 4623; Pasadena School System, Pasadena, California, 2095; Perry High School, Pittsburgh, Pennsylvania, 1220; Pioneer High School, Ann Arbor, Michigan, 4200; Proviso East High School, Maywood, Chicago, Illinois, 2183; Richmond Hills High School, Queens, New York, 1163; Riverside City High School, Chicago, Illinois, 4208; San Diego High School, San Diego, California, 1380; Scottdale High School, DeKalb County, Georgia, 2016; Shamrock High School, DeKalb, Georgia, 1385; South Hills High School, Pittsburgh, Pennsylvania, 1418, 1479, 2528; Springfield Garden High School, New York City, 4591; Taft High School, Bronx, New York, 1832; Taylor-Alderdice High School, Pittsburgh, Pennsylvania, 1569, 2245; Thomas Jefferson High School, Elizabeth, New Jersey, 4050; Thomas Jefferson High School, Los Angeles, California, 2274; Valley Senior High School, New Kensington, Pennsylvania, 994, 1074; Van Buren High School, Queens, New York, 4591; Walker High School, Chicago, Illinois, 2183; Walker High School, DeKalb, Georgia, 1385; West High School, Denver, Colorado, 4620; Westinghouse High School, Pittsburg, Pennsylvania, 5395; William H. Taft High School, West San Fernando Valley, California, 2361; Williams Bay High School, Madison, Wisconsin, 1162; Wilmington High School, Wilmington, Delaware, 4444; Zion Benton Township High School, Chicago; General Articles, 260b, 754, 825a, 1339, 1813, 1907, 1908, 2135, 2240, 2573, 2779, 2957, 3129, 3899, 3917, 4020, 4046, 4078, 4126, 4134, 4147a, 4164b, 4167, 4177, 4187, 4192, 4223, 4268a, 4276, 4277, 4279, 4296, 4327, 4331, 4340, 4347, 4372, 4415, 4435, 4460, 4498, 4505, 4948

Hightower, Charles, 2071
Hilberry, C., 4361
Hill, Annie, 2072
Hill, E., 4362
Hill, Hugo, 2073, 2074
Hill, P. L., 3795
Hill, Ron, 2071
Hill, Roy L., 4875
Hilliard, David, 1338, 2075, 2076, 2077, 2636
Hilu, Virginia, 3662

Himmelbauer, Sue, 2078
Hinckle, Marianne, 2080
Hinckle, Warren, 2079, 2080, 2081, 2120
Hine, Robert V., 452
HIPPIES--U.S. 279, 309, 619, 721a, 894, 1044, 1081, 1166, 1201, 1230, 1521, 1729a, 1793, 2120, 2141, 2193, 2307, 2341, 2420, 2466, 2565, 2607, 2711, 2814, 2838, 2846, 2857, 2960, 3111, 3114, 3312, 3464, 3481, 3482, 3503, 3546, 4268a, 4957
Hirsch, Morris, 1467
Hitch, Charles, 2494
Hitchcock, James, 4363
HITCHHIKING--GUIDES FOR WOMEN 2165
HITCHHIKING, ORDINANCE BAN--LOS ANGELES, CALIFORNIA 2688
Hixson, Joseph, 3116
Hoag, Van Den, 3796, 4364
Hobart, C. W., 5099
Ho-Chi-Minh, 303, 542, 1169, 1786, 2168a, 2209, 2482, 2615
Hochschild, Adam, 2082
Hodel, Mike, 2083, 2084
Hodges, Donald Clark, 2085
Hodgkinson, Harold L., 3941a
Hoffa, Jimmy, 482, 1882
Hoffman, Abbie, 193, 453, 454, 1926, 2086, 2087, 2088, 2264, 2279
Hoffman, Fred, 2089, 2090, 2091, 2092, 3528, 4365, 4366, 5100, 5101
Hoffman, Joan, 2093, 2094, 2095, 3529, 3530
Hoffman, Judge, 209a
Hoffman, Julius, 967, 1968, 2555
Hoffman, Martin, 3797
Hoffman, Michael J., 2096
Hoffman, R. J., 3798
Hoffman, Stanley, 3933
Hofmann, Hans F., 3020, 3663
Hofstadter, Richard, 246, 455, 4367, 4876, 5102
Hofstein, Sadie, 3664

Holcomb, Richard L., 3364, 3365
Holiday Commune, Santa Cruz, California, 2602
Holland, Vincent, 2097
Hollander, Nanci, 362
Hollingsworth, M., 5375
Hollins, Elizabeth J., 456
Hollister, Charles A., 4368
Hollywood, California, 1821
Holman, Mary, 3366
Holst, Johan I., 4666
Holt, John, 5
Holtom, Gerald, 2098
Holtz, Betty, 2099
Holzman, S., 3799
Holzschlag, P., 3800
Homer L Morris Fund, 2390
HOMOPHILE COURSES--STUDY AND TEACHING 1458, 1459
HOMOPHILE MOVEMENT
See also HOMOSEXUALITY
78, 1028, 1458, 1734, 1817, 2742
HOMOSEXUALITY
See also HOMOPHILE MOVEMENT
78, 1028, 1054a, 1054b, 1080, 1126, 1130, 1170, 1171, 1172, 1244, 1299, 1315, 1322, 1330, 1335, 1344, 1381, 1403, 1407, 1458, 1470, 1527, 1687, 1739, 1746, 1794, 1795, 1796, 1822, 1856, 1867, 1983, 2015, 2030, 2130, 2134, 2178, 2303, 2304, 2305, 2342, 2352, 2658, 2682, 2685, 2716, 2742, 2825, 2831, 3521, 3545, 3663, 3722, 3723, 3724, 3792, 3797, 5362
HOMOSEXUALITY (in military service) 724, 1733, 5362
Honey, P. J., 457, 2100
Hook, Sidney, 458, 459, 2085, 3021, 3942, 4123, 4369, 4370, 4371, 5103, 5104
Hooker, Evelyn, 1442, 1458
HOOKER REPORT 1442, 1458
Hoopes, Townsend, 460
Hoover, John Edgar, 881, 1357,

2181, 2223, 4372
Hoover, Mary B., 460a
Hope, David, 3801
Hopp, Ralph, 1224
Hopper, Columbua B., 461
Horowitz, David, 462, 463,
　　1800, 2101, 2102, 2103,
　　2104, 2105, 2106, 2107,
　　2108, 3943
Horowitz, Donald, 1067
Horowitz, Irving Louis, 464,
　　2109, 3254, 4877
Horsburgh, H. J. N., 4878
Horton, Frank, 5253
Horwitz, George D., 343
Hosmer, Stephen T., 465
HOSPITALS, PITTSBURGH,
　　PENNSYLVANIA 1161
Hotz, R., 4764
HOUSE COMMITTEE ON IN-
　　TERNAL SECURITY
　　4373
HOUSE COMMITTEE ON UN-
　　AMERICAN ACTIVITIES
　　140, 246, 428, 1600,
　　1601, 1818, 4239
HOUSE UN-AMERICAN ACTI-
　　VITIES COMMITTEE
　　See HOUSE COMMITTEE ON
　　UN-AMERICAN ACTIVITIES
Houston, Jean, 3051
Houts, Peter S., 2110
Howard, Alan, 2111, 4374
Howard, D., 5105
Howard, Jan, 164
Howard, Lawrence J. Jr.,
　　1634
Howard University, Washington,
　　D. C., 290
Howard, William E., 4658
Howe, Florence, 2112, 4421
Howe, Irving, 466, 467, 468,
　　2113, 3979, 4375, 4879
Howell, David L., 698, 2114
HOW TO END THE DRAFT
　　5254
Hoy, Bill, 2115
Hoyman, H. S., 3802
Huber, Joe, 3803
Huberman, Leo, 469, 859
Hudson, Kenneth, 470
Huffman, J., 3804
Huggins, Erica, 1694, 1698

Hughes, Douglas A., 471
Hughes, Everett, C., 87a
Hughes, Graham, 471a, 5106
Hughes, Larry, 472
Huie, William Bradford, 473
Hull, Roger H., 474
HUMAN EXPERIMENTATION,
　　MEDICAL
　　See MEDICAL EXPERIMENT-
　　ATION, HUMAN
HUMAN RELATIONS
　　See INTERPERSONAL RELA-
　　TIONS
HUMAN VALUES
　　See VALUES, HUMAN
HUMANITIES, TEACHING--
　　AMERICAN COLLEGES
　　AND UNIVERSITIES,
　　780
Humes, James C., 2116
Humphrey, Hubert H., 474a,
　　813, 1012, 4656
Hunsucker, Suzanne, 2117
Hunt, Gary, 2118
Hunt, Jane, 4376, 4617
Hunt, Linda, 2118
Hunt, Morton, 475
Hunt, Tom, 2119
Hunter, Evan, 3022
Hunter, Meredith, 1206a
Hurst, Jack, 2666
Hurst, Walter, 1878
Hurwitt, Robert, 2120
Hutchins, Francis G., 4377
Hutchins, Phil, 1703
Hutchins, Robert M., 173, 419
Hutterian Brothers, Expanola,
　　Washington, 2609
HUTTERITES 209
Hutton, Bobby, 1692
Hyde, Margaret O., 3023
Hykes, Elizabeth, 4378
Hylan, Lewis, 3648a
Hyson, Brenda, 2121, 3255

IDENTITY--INTERACTION OF
　　CULTURE AND PER-
　　SONALITY 250, 297,
　　1106, 1191, 1898, 3078,
　　3082, 3107, 4644
IDEOLOGICAL WARFARE
　　See PROPAGANDA

Index 521

IDEOLOGY, END OF 909,
  2833, 2841, 4385
IDEOLOGY, POLITICAL 74,
  77, 675, 1607, 1706,
  1955, 2594, 2687
IDEOLOGY, THEORY OF
  See also ACTIVISM, IDEOL-
  OGY; CONSERVATISM;
  FASCISM; IMPERIALISM;
  LIBERALISM; MARXISM;
  NEW LEFT; NIHILISM;
  PROLETARIAN MISSION,
  CONCEPT OF; RADICAL
  LEFT; RADICAL MIDDLE
  (CENTER); RADICALISM,
  IDEOLOGY; SOCIALISM
    12, 33, 63, 67, 77, 102,
    105, 110, 114, 127,
    128, 142, 143, 178,
    249a, 287, 299, 338,
    367, 372, 409, 417,
    423a, 463, 467, 483,
    529, 557, 583, 624,
    625, 626, 636, 637,
    709, 770, 797, 1029,
    1055, 1203, 1453, 1807,
    1918, 1955, 2076, 2085,
    2109, 2126, 2151, 2312,
    2326, 2375, 2551, 2592,
    2659, 2687, 2841, 4324a,
    4399
Iglitzin, Lynne B., 5107
Ilg, F., 3024
IMPERIALISM
  See also IDEOLOGY, THEORY
  OF
    12, 105, 624, 625, 650,
    797, 818, 877, 1650,
    2425, 2832, 4516, 5083
Inbau, Fred E., 3367
INDIAN AFFAIRS
  See BUREAU OF INDIAN
  AFFAIRS
Indiana State University, Terre
  Haute, Indiana, 3558,
  3921
Indiana State University of Penn-
  sylvania, Indiana,
  Pennsylvania, 4378
INDIAN LIBERATION MOVE-
  MENT 251, 311, 848,
  1188, 1248, 1542, 1571,
  1737, 2255, 2430, 2550,
  2821
INDIANS, AMERICAN
  See also Specific Names Of
  Indian Tribes, e.g., SIOUX
  INDIANS
    251, 848, 893, 905,
    984, 991, 1188, 1189,
    1194, 1248, 1252, 1296,
    1542, 1571, 1737, 1942,
    2255, 2258, 2430, 2550,
    2707, 2800, 2821, 2854
INDUSTRIAL-MILITARY-GOV-
  ERNMENT-EDUCATION-
  AL COMPLEX
  See also UNIVERSITY PARTI-
  CIPATION IN MILITARY EF-
  FORTS
    21, 56, 72, 108, 158,
    227, 277, 341, 344,
    348, 364, 486, 488,
    530, 553, 554, 555,
    565, 566, 650a, 611,
    684b, 709, 718, 732,
    733, 765, 772, 797a,
    881a, 1043, 1190, 1312,
    1323, 1375, 1409, 1422,
    1652, 1731, 1772, 1945,
    1987, 2032, 2262, 2367,
    2417, 2536, 2543, 2546,
    2549, 2610, 2691, 2699,
    2759, 2801, 2832, 2844,
    4530, 4670, 4763, 5092,
    5270
INDUSTRIAL SECURITY, ACT
  OF 1970, 2252
Ingersoll, John E., 3142
Ingerson, David, 2122, 2123
Inglis, D. R., 4765, 4766,
  4767
INSTITUTE FOR DEFENSE
  ANALYSIS 3343a
INSTITUTE FOR THE STUDY
  OF LIBIDINOUS SALI-
  VATION (San Diego,
  California) 1239
INSTITUTE FOR THE STUDY
  OF NON-VIOLENCE
  (Carmel, California)
  4993
INTEGRATION
  In Business, 264; In
  Sports, 699, 2728; Racial,
  1270, 1928, 2428

INTEGRATION, SCHOOL 109, 154, 349, 722a, 782a, 857, 2839, 4082
INTELLECTUAL FREEDOM 1510, 2194, 2328
INTENTIONAL COMMUNITIES
See COMMUNAL LIVING, U.S.; COMMUNAL LIFE STYLE
INTERFERENCE, COMPETITIVE 226
INTERNATIONAL ASSOCIATION OF CHIEFS OF POLICE 3346a, 3367a, 3367b
International Brotherhood Of Teamsters, Chauffeurs, Warehousemen and Helpers Union, 1882
INTERNATIONAL BUSINESS MACHINES 2050
INTERNATIONAL POLICE ASSOCIATION 3368
INTERNATIONAL WAR CRIMES TRIBUNAL
See also RUSSELL INTERNATIONAL WAR CRIMES TRIBUNAL
273, 476, 788, 1534, 2596
INTERPERSONAL RELATIONS
See also MALE-FEMALE RELATIONSHIPS
771, 1290, 1555, 2191, 3673
INTERRACIAL CONFLICT
See CONFLICT, INTERRACIAL
Investigator's Information Service, 477
IRELAND 211, 1631
IRELAND, NORTHERN--CIVIL RIGHTS
See CIVIL RIGHTS--NORTHERN IRELAND
IRELAND, NORTHERN--HISTORY 210
Ireland, Waltraud, 2124
IRISH-CATHOLIC RELIGIOUS QUESTION 258, 863, 1289, 1749
IRISH REPUBLICAN ARMY 210
Irwin, T., 2125
Isaacs, Harold R., 478

Isard, Walter, 479
Ishell, H., 3228
Isla Vista, California, 3449, 3551, 4429
Israeli, Phineas, 2126, 2127, 4379
Itkin, Michael Francis, 2128
Ivey, Allen E., 2129
Iwamoto, D., 5108

Jack, H. A., 5109
Jackson, Don, 1130, 2130, 2131, 2132, 2133
Jackson, Ed, 2134
Jackson, George, 480, 2459
Jackson, H. M., 4768
Jackson, Jonathan, 1718, 2432
Jackson, Mississippi, 1493, 4417
Jackson, Sir Richard, 3369
Jackson State College, Jackson, Mississippi, 1752, 3988, 4026a, 4049, 4089, 4094, 4417
Jackson State College Massacre, Jackson, Mississippi, 4049
Jacob, Philip E., 3025, 5276
Jacobs, Bonye, 2135
Jacobs, Clyde E., 5255
Jacobs, Harold, 481
Jacobs, Paul, 482, 483, 1873, 2136, 3944, 4880, 5110
Jacobs, R. C., 2920
Jacobson, Jon, 4380
Jacobyner, H., 3256
Jaffe, Harold, 3945
Jamal, Hakim A., 2137, 2138
James, Daniel, 484
James, H., 485
James, Howard, 3531
James S. Copley Memorial, 1239
Janeway, Eliot, 486
Janeway, Elizabeth, 2139
Janowitz, Morris, 487, 488
Jansen, D. G., 4381, 4382
Janson, Donald, 489
Janssen, Peter, 4383
Jarrell, Willoughby, 2140
Jassen, Jeff, 2141, 3532, 5111
Javits, J. K., 4769

Jaworski, Leon, 4970
Jay, Karla, 2142
Jay, Martin, 2143
Jeffee, Saul, 3026
Jencks, Christopher, 489a, 2144, 3946
Jenkin, Noel, 3665
Jenkins, Diahnne, 3533
Jenkins, Don, 2145
Jenkins, James J., 3027
Jensen, Pennfield, 2146
Jerger, Joseph J., 4667
Jervey, Edward D., 3028
Jessup, John K., 4384
Jessup, Josephine L., 490
Jezer, Martin, 2147, 2148, 5376
Jhirad, Sue, 4770
Joesten, Joachim, 491
John Birch Society 136, 249a, 292, 800, 996, 997, 1414, 2126, 2172, 3730, 4158
Johnson, Barbara, 2150
Johnson, Charles S., 492
Johnson, Dale L., 4385
Johnson, Elmer H., 3534
Johnson, Eric W., 3666, 3667
Johnson, George R., 2149
Johnson, Grant, 2150
Johnson, Haynes, 493
Johnson, J. R., 494
Johnson, Joseph E., 853
Johnson, Lyndon B., 1060, 1128, 1377, 1619, 2205, 2801, 2916, 3165, 4672, 4975
Johnson, Miriam M., 3805
Johnson, Nick, 1367
Johnson, P., 5112
Johnson, Richard M., 495
Johnson, Roger, 2151
Johnson, Warren R., 3668, 3806
Johnston, Art, 2152
Johnston, Norman, 495a
Johnston, O. W., 4386
Johnstone, Billy, 2153
J. O. M. O. (Ideological Statement) 1203
Jones, Beverly, 132
Jones, F., 2154
Jones, Frank B., 2155
Jones, H., 4881
Jones, K. L., 3669
Jones, Lee, 576
Jones, Lew, 2156
Jones, Marion, 54
Jones, Mary Brash, 2951
Jones, Orlando, 3483
Jones, Penn Jr., 496
Jones, Pirkle, 54
Jones, Richard S., 4026b
Jones, Ruth M., 2157
Joseph, Stephen M., 497
Joseph, Tony, 2158
Josephson, Eric, 2159
Josselyn, Irene M., 3807
Joughin, Louis, 3946a
Joyce, Frank H., 2160, 2161, 2162
Joyce, Mary R., 498
Joyce, Robert E., 498
Joyce, W., 499
J. R. S., 4387
JUDICIAL SYSTEM
 See LAW--REFORM
Judson, H., 2163
Junker, B. H., 903
Junta Of Militant Organizations, 1485, 3369a
Junta Of Militant Organizations And The Southern Conference Educational Fund
 See J. O. M. O. (Ideological Statement)
Jurow, George L., 3535
Just War, 746
Just, Ward S., 500, 501
JUSTICE, ADMINISTRATION OF 1a, 92, 95, 97, 154, 164, 189, 322, 324, 337, 357, 357a, 368, 369, 422, 471a, 508, 600, 737, 762, 853, 912, 988, 1103, 1124, 1561, 1578, 1644, 1659, 1761, 1764, 1803, 1966, 1969, 2021, 2053, 2331, 2432, 2451, 2535, 2547, 2640, 2668, 2818, 3325, 3329, 3348, 3380, 3395, 3397, 4812, 4872, 5011, 5012, 5119
JUSTICE, CRIMINAL
 See JUSTICE,

ADMINISTRATION OF
JUVENILE DELINQUENCY--
CAUSES
See also CRIME, JUVENILE;
JUVENILE DELINQUENCY
--U. S.
    322, 1068a, 2013, 2963,
    3100, 3332, 3333, 3474,
    4256, 4815, 4836, 4895,
    4955, 5174
JUVENILE DELINQUENCY--U. S.
See also CRIME, JUVENILE;
JUVENILE DELINQUENCY--
CAUSES
    289a, 322, 587b, 1068a,
    2013, 2963, 3100, 3332,
    3333, 3408, 3474, 4256,
    4815, 4921, 4945, 4955,
    4984
JUSTICE, MILITARY
See MILITARY JUSTICE
(or military injustice)

Kadish, Sanford, 3975
Kaenel, K. Von, 3808
Kahin, George, 502
Kahn, Herman, 532a
Kahn, Robert L., 503, 736
Kahn, Roger M., 3947
Kalkstein, M., 4771
Kalven, Harry, 209a
Kamisar, Yale, 3536, 5113
Kammeyer, Kenneth C. W.,
    3871a
Kamony, Franklin E., 2825
Kampf, Louis, 4388
Kane, J., 3948
Kane, M., 2921
Kane, Martin, 2164
Kaner, Leslie, 2165
Kansas City, Missouri, 3446
Kaplan, Morton A., 3949, 4882
Kaplan, S., 177
Kaplan, Sidney, 4835
Kapp, L., 5242
Kardiner, Abram, 504
Karl, Frederick R., 409
Karlen, Peter, 2166
Karmel, Louis J., 3809
Karol, K. S., 505, 2167
Kasabian, Linda, 2587
Kathman, Frank, 1744

Katope, Christopher G., 3950
Katz, Irwin, 506
Katz, Joseph, 3029, 4389, 4390
Katzenbach, Nicholas de B.,
    421, 1336, 3363, 4871
Katzman, Al, 2168
Katzman, Don, 5144
Kauffman, J. F., 4391
Kaufman, Arnold S., 2169,
    5115
Kaufman, Bob, 4392
Kaufman, Don, 2170
Kaufman, George, 2171, 2172,
    2172a
Kaufman, Joseph K., 4269
Kaufman, Mike, 2173
Kavanaugh, Robert, 3030
Kazin, A., 3283
Kearn, Francis E., 4393
Keating, Charles H. Jr., 1331a
Keating, Kenneth B., 5116
Keech, William R., 507
Keeler, M. H., 3257
Keeler, W. W., 1738
Keeton, Robert E., 508
Kefauver, Estes, 423, 509
Kelley, Edgar A., 4509
Kelley, J. B., 3537
Kellog, Walter G., 5256
Kelly, Audrey, 3670
Kelly, George A., 3648, 3671
Kelman, S., 4394
Kelman, Steven, 3951
Kemelman, Harry, 510
Kemperman, Bob, 2174, 2175
Kempton, Murray, 4931
Kendall, Robert, 511
Keniston, Kenneth, 3031, 3032,
    3063, 3258, 3952, 3953,
    4395, 4396, 4397, 4397a,
    4398, 4549
Kenkel, W., 512
Kennan, George F., 456, 3954,
    4883
Kennedy, David M., 513
Kennedy, Edward, 205, 4668,
    4691, 5377
Kennedy, Eugene C., 2176
Kennedy Foundation, 2099
Kennedy, John F., 348, 496,
    526, 580, 608a, 675,
    691, 769, 1127, 1128,
    1129, 1200, 1371, 1656,

1565, 1566, 1634, 1635,
1830, 1833, 2166, 2202,
2337, 2391, 2745, 2747,
2755, 2757, 2758, 2788,
2802, 2803, 2822
Kennedy, Robert F., 168a, 406,
514, 526, 608a, 726,
1208, 1618, 1637, 1842,
1843, 1857, 1871, 1928
Kennedy, Ted, 515
Kenner, Martin, 516
Kenney, John P., 3370, 3371
KENSINGTON, U.S.A., 336
Kent State University, Kent,
Ohio, 297a, 1263, 1486,
1747, 1752, 2012, 2702,
3435a, 3954a, 3988,
4026a, 4075, 4087, 4091,
4092, 4093, 4094, 4095,
4103, 4127, 4228, 4307,
4373, 4434, 4456, 4551,
4556, 4642, 4649
For A Chronology Of Events
At Kent State Beginning November 11-20, 1968, See
1486.
Kentifield, Calvin, 2177
Kephart, W., 3033
Kepner, Jim, 1028, 2178
Keppel, Francis, 517
Keppler, Ernest C., 2427
Kerista Mercurial, Silver
Spring, Maryland, 2609
KERNER COMMISSION REPORT
4824, 5003, 5122
Kerpelman, Larry C., 3955,
4399
Kerr, Clark, 3894, 3921, 3933,
3956, 4400, 4483, 4578
Kesey, Ken, 927, 1206
Ketels, Violet, 4401
Key Biscayne, Florida, 2174
Key, Douglas, 3538
Keys, J. Bernard, 2179
Khoury, George, 4402
KIBBUTZ
See UTOPIANISM
Kight, Morris, 1335, 1344
Kilander, Holger F., 2180,
3672, 3810
Kilbane, Marjorie, 3372
Kilhefner, Don, 1130, 1344
Killian, Lewis M., 518

Kilmarx, Robert, 4772
Kimble, Joseph Paul, 3539
Kindle, Charles, 2181, 2182
King, Coretta, 1753
King, Donald B., 519
King, Glen D., 3347, 3373
King, Martin Luther Jr., 42,
44, 125, 473, 520, 526,
589, 608a, 813, 893,
922, 1905, 1951, 2365,
2423, 2428, 2552, 2582,
4884, 4885, 4886, 4893,
4952, 4966, 5008, 5071,
5118, 5119, 5120, 5378
King, T. R., 5378
Kinnison, W. A., 4403
Kintner, William R., 4669
Kippley, John F., 522
Kirby, John B., 5120a
Kirk, Grayson, 4271, 4404,
4405
Kirk, Russell, 911, 3811, 3812,
4406
Kirkendall, Lester A., 3673,
3674, 3715, 3812a, 3813
Kirkpatrick, Clifford, 3034
Kirkpatrick, Lyman B., Jr.,
523
Kirshbaum, Lawrence J., 4001
Kirzner, Israel M., 4407
Kissinger, Clark, 2183, 2184,
2185, 2689a
Kitana, Harry H. L., 240
Kittredge, Jack, 4408
Klaber, Thomas, 2186
Klawitter, Sonja, 2187
Kleberg, John, 3540
Klein, Alexander, 3035
Klein, Herbert T., 3374
Kline, Stephen J., 3956a
Kling, S., 3675
Klonsky, Mike, 2135
Knapp, Stuart, 584a
Knebel, Fletcher, 3541
Knoebl, Kuno, 524
Knopf, Terry Ann, 5121
Knops, Mark, 1301
KNOWLEDGE, THEORY OF
278
Knowles, Louis L., 525
Knowles, Warren P., 4409
Knox, G. H. C., 4410
Kobetz, Richard W., 3374a,

3398a
Koch, Thilo, 526
Koerner, James D., 527
Kohl, Herbert R., 528
Kohler, Bob, 1299
Kohn, Jaokoy, 2188
Koinonia Farm, Americus, Georgia, 2390, 2609
Kois, John, 2189
Kolakowski, Leszak, 529
Kolko, Gabriel, 530, 531
Kolodney, David, 2108, 2601
Konopka, Gisela, 3259
Konvitz, M., 532
Koontz, Elizabeth, 759
Kopkind, Andrew, 2190, 2922, 5122, 5379, 5380
KOREA 1716, 2000
Korn, Harold A., 4008
Kornbluth, Jesse, 3957
Kossoy, Victor E., 2191
Kostelanetz, Richard, 532a
Kotler, Milton, 533, 2144
Kovel, Joel, 534
Kramer, Mark, 2192, 4411
Kramer, Mike, 2193
Kraslow, David, 535
Krasnesor, R., 5401
Krassner, Paul, 5091
Krause, Allison, 1263
Krech, David, 3036
Kreml, Franklin M., 3375
Krenwinkle Trial, 2589
Krich, Aron M., 3676
Krieg, M. B., 3037
Krislov, Samuel, 536
Kristol, Irving, 74, 3868
Kriyanda (Guru) 537
Kroll, Arthur M., 538
Kron, Yver J., 3038
Kronovet, Esther, 3958
Krouse, Peggy, 4412
Krug, Alan S., 2866
Krug, J. F., 2194
Krutch, J. W., 5123, 5124
Kruybosch, C. E., 4413
Kruytbosch, Carlos E., 3959
Kudela, Raphael M., 4414
Kuh, Richard H., 539, 2195
Kukla, David A., 4415
KU KLUX KLAN 3590
Kuminski, Gridley, 2196
Kune, F. J., 3257

Kunen, James S., 540, 4416
Kunkin, Art, 2197, 2198, 2199, 2200, 2201, 2202, 2203, 2204, 3542
Kunnes, Richard, 1836
Kunst, Robert, 1197
Kunstler, Arthur, 295
Kunstler, William M., 193, 983, 1195, 1209, 1326, 1361, 1497, 3439
Kupferberg, Tuli, 3543, 5380
Kurland, Philip B., 541
Kurtz, Alan, 2205, 3260
Kurtz, Norman R., 331
Kurtz, Paul, 5125
Kuyu, Kimitki, 2817
Kvaraceus, William C., 3960

LABOR-MANAGEMENT PROBLEMS 116, 126, 172, 1210, 2534
LABOR (problems) 126, 172, 549, 562, 1210, 1512, 1788, 2442, 2456, 2513, 2529, 2534
LABOR UNIONS 172, 482, 920, 1210, 2529, 2534
Lack, Lawrence, 2206, 2207
Lacouture, Jean, 542, 2208, 2209
Lacroix, Jean Paul, 543
Lacy, Frederick B., 1067
Lacy, Leslie Alexander, 544
Ladd, Bruce, 545
Ladd, Everett C., 546
Ladd, John, 5126
Lader, L., 547
La Fave, Wayne R., 3376
Laffin, John, 548
La Fong, Karl, 4417
Lai, Kristin, 2210
Laibow, Rima E., 2211
Laidler, Harry Wellington, 549
Laird, Melvin, 2067
Lakey, George, 4887, 4907
Lall, B. G., 4773, 4774, 4775
Lamb, Robert, 2212
Lambotte, Robert, 2213
Lammers, Cornelis J., 2214
Lamont, Corliss, 18
Lampe, Keith, 2215, 2216, 2217, 2218

Land, Herman W., 3039, 3261
Landau, Saul, 483, 2219, 3944
Landers, Ann, 3677
Lane, Lois, 2220
Lane, Mark, 550, 551, 1200, 1830, 1833, 2201, 2221, 2222, 2223, 2224, 2225
Lane, R. E., 4418
Lang, Berel, 5127
Lang, Daniel, 552
Lang, Frances, 3544
Lange, David L., 4888
Langer, E., 5381
Langston, Robert, 2226
Lankes, George, 4418a
LAOS 2623
Lapp, Ralph E., 553, 554, 555, 4670, 4776
Laqueur, Walter, 4419
La Raza, 684, 1212
Larner, Jeremy, 3040
Larson, Bruce, 556
Larson, Richard, 556a
Larus, J., 4777
Lasch, Christopher, 557, 558, 3961
Lasky, M. J., 4420
Lathrop, Peter (pseud.) 2227
Latter, A. L., 4680
Laurence, Leo E., 2228, 2229, 3545
Laurie, Peter, 3041
Lauter, Paul, 4421
LAVENDAR MENACE 2142
Law Commune In New York City, 2230, 2276
LAW COMMUNES
See COMMUNES, LAW
LAW, CONFLICT
See also LAW REFORM
39, 65, 88, 95, 97, 189, 201, 237, 351, 357a, 422, 485, 1776, 2024
LAW ENFORCEMENT
See Items Listed In The Section "Police-Community Relationships" e.g., 3469b
LAW--REFORM
See also LAW, CONFLICT
39, 65, 88, 92, 95, 97, 189, 201, 237, 322, 324, 351, 357, 357a, 422, 485, 508, 587b, 600, 689, 737, 856, 912, 1369, 1776, 1778, 2024, 2134, 2230, 2331, 2342, 2451, 3469b
Lawrence, Buffy, 4422
Lawrence, D., 5128
Lawrence, John, 2231
Lawrence, T., 3262
Laycock, George, 559
Lazar, Robert J., 2232
Lazo, Mario, 560
Leach, William Spencer, 2233
League Of Women Voters Of The U.S. 561, 3442
Lear, Len, 2234, 2235, 3546, 3547
LEARNING EXPERIENCES (GROUP) PHILADELPHIA, PENNSYLVANIA 1677
LEARNING, THEORY OF 3980
Leary Case, The (Marijuana) 1160
Leary, Howard, 3443
Leary, Timothy, 1075, 1160, 1217, 1444, 2220, 2288, 2336, 2379, 3042, 3263
Le Blanc, Paul, 2236, 2237, 4423
Lebowitz, M., 5129
Lee, Calvin B. T., 3962, 3962a
Lee, Charles, 2238
Lee, Garber O., 4424
Lee, L. K., 3815
Lee, Lawrence, 4425
Lee, Richard, 4927
Lee, Robert, 561a
Lee, Shirley Thurston, 2239
Lee, Tom, 2240
Lee, Ulysses, 5382
Lefcourt, Gerald, 2276
LEFT AND RIGHT (political science)
See RIGHT AND LEFT (political science)
LEFT WING, IDEOLOGY
See also IDEOLOGY, THEORY OF
809, 2079, 3888
Legal Aid Society, Philadelphia, Pennsylvania, 959

LEGAL AND POLITICAL ISSUES
    INVOLVED IN CONTEMPT
    POWER
    See CONTEMPT POWER--
    LEGAL AND POLITICAL
    ISSUES INVOLVED IN
LEGAL REFORM
    See LAW--REFORM; LAW,
    CONFLICT
LEGAL RIGHTS 856
Leggett, John C., 562, 2696
Le Grande, J. L., 5130
Lehman, Edna S., 3678
Lehman, J. F. Jr., 266
Lehrer, Stanley, 3875, 4426
Leiden, Carl, 563
Leimbacher, Ed, 3264
Leinwand, Gerald, 564
Leist, Marielene, 3679
Leitsch, Dick, 3548
Leivy, Guenter, 5131
Le Masters, E. E., 3814
Le May, Curtis E., 565
Lenin, Nikolai, 1800
Lens, Sidney, 566, 567, 2241, 4889
Lenski, Gerhard E., 3040
Leonard, George B., 568, 569, 4427
Leonard, V. A., 3377
Lepp, Ignace, 570
Lerner, Gerda, 2242
Lerner, Max, 2192, 2923
Leroy, John, 2162
Leshan, Eda J., 571, 3680
Leslie, G., 572
Lester, Julius, 573, 2243, 2244
Levenson, Bruce, 2245
Levenson, Sam, 3816
Levenstein, Chuck, 2246
Levin, B., 2247
Levin, Henry M., 574
Levin, Murray B., 575
Levine, E., 3044
Levine, Herbert, 4428
Levinson, Cec, 2248, 2249
Levitas, Mitchel, 576
Levitt, Dennis, 2250, 2251, 2252, 2253, 2254, 2255, 2256, 2257, 2258, 2259, 2260, 3549, 4429, 5383
Levitt, Morton, 4544

Levy, B., 3550
Levy, Charles L., 577, 2261
Levy, David M., 3045
Levy, Harold, 893
Levy, Howard, 2036, 4931
Lewin, Stephen, 4890
Lewis, Howard R., 578
Lewis, John, 502, 579
Lewis, Joseph, 2261, 2262
Lewis, N. N., 431
Lewis, Oscar, 4891
Lewis, Raymond, 2263
Lewis, Richard Warren, 580
Lewis, Robert, 3814
Libby, Willard F., 4655
LIBERALISM, IDEOLOGY
    See also IDEOLOGY, THE-
    ORY OF
    12, 110, 143, 228, 299,
    353, 933, 1221, 1453,
    2431, 2462, 4285
Liberation (Magazine) 2311
LIBERATION NEWS SERVICE
    Entered here are syndicated
    articles from the alternative
    tabloids wherever and
    whenever they could be found
    with the imprint LNS.
    581, 678, 987, 997,
    1120, 1157, 1183, 1257,
    1418, 1445, 1513, 1526,
    1571, 1601, 1775, 1836,
    1839, 1923, 1937, 2004,
    2035, 2045, 2088, 2264,
    2265, 2266, 4429a, 5376,
    5384, 2267, 2268, 2269,
    2270, 2272, 2273, 2274,
    2275, 2276, 2277, 2278,
    2279, 2280, 2281, 2282,
    2283, 2403, 2427, 2609,
    2694, 2747, 2751, 2754,
    2785, 2847, 2848, 3265,
    3501, 3551, 3817, 3818,
    4175, 4271
LIBERATION PUBLISHING
    HOUSE 582
LIBERTARIAN MOVEMENT
    1093
LIBERTARIANISM, RADICAL
    876
Liberty House, Jackson, Mis-
    sissippi, 2609
Lichtenberg, James, 2924

Lichtheim, George, 583
Lieberman, E. James, 2284
Lieberman, Harold, 1924
Liebman, Morris I., 5132, 5133
Life Science International, San Diego, California, 2609
Lifton, David, 2802
Lifton, Robert J., 584, 3266, 4893
Ligon, J. Frank, 584a
Lillian, Lewis M., 584b
Lincoln, C. Eric, 4893
Lincoln, Charles E., 585, 586
Lincoln, James H., 4894
Lindesmith, Alfred R., 3046, 3047
Lindsay, (Mayor) John, 1581, 2651, 3443
Lineberry, William P., 3963
Lingeman, Richard, 3819
Link, W. R., 3820
Linkletter, Art, 1231, 3207, 3226, 3267
Linner, Birgitta, 3681
Lipow, Arthur, 2285
Lippincott, W. T., 5385
Lipset, Hal, 2286
Lipset, Harold, 1350
Lipset, Seymour Martin, 586a, 587, 3964, 3965, 3966, 4430, 4431, 4432
Lipsyte, Robert, 394
Lipton, Lawrence, 2203, 2287, 2288, 2289, 3682, 5134, 5135
Liston, Robert, 5257
Litell, Richard J., 3681
Littell, Franklin H., 587a
Little Rock 9, 2041
Little, Roger W., 5258
Littleton, Colorado, 1188
Litwak, Eugene, 2290
Litwak, L. J., 4433
Lizzie and John (pseud.) 2291
Llano Colony, 209
Lloyd-Jones, Esther, 3967
Loary, Stewart M., 535
Lobenthal, Joseph S., 587b
Loble, Lester H., 4895
Local 1199 (Union) 1227, 1228
Lockhart, Dean William B., 1331a

Lockshin, Arnold, 5136
Lockwood, Lee, 588
Loewenberg, Peter, 2292
Loewenstein, Eddie, 2293
Lofflin, John, 2294
Logan, Andy, 3378
Logsdon, G., 2925
Lohman, Joseph, 3470a
Lokos, Lionel, 589
Lomax, Louis E., 590, 591, 2295
Lombardi, John, 2296, 3969, 4434
Long, Durwood, 3921
Long, Everett, 3267a
Long, F. A., 4778
Long, L., 2297
Longyear, Barry, 3267b
Loomis, Mildred J., 592
Looney, D. L., 5386
Lopez-Tresquet, R., 593
Lorand, Rhoda L., 3048, 3683
Lorber, Richard, 3968
Lorenz, Konrad, 594
Loretto Heights College, Denver, Colorado. Research Center On Woman See Research Center On Woman. Loretto Heights College, Denver, Colorado
Los Angeles, California, 1389, 1451, 2084, 2204, 2223, 2688, 2701, 3362, 3507, 3542, 3559, 5028, 5188, 5210
LOS ANGELES FREE PRESS CORP. 2200, 3542
LOS SIETE CASE See SIETE CASE
Lothstein, Arthur, 595
LOTTERY (DRAFT) See Items Listed In The Section "Military Service--Compulsory And Voluntary" e.g., 5289, 5294
Louis, Debbie, 596
Louisville Black Six, Kentucky, 1065
Louisville, Kentucky, 1131, 2817
Louria, Donald B., 3049
Love, Adam, 2298
LOVE-INS 1929, 2036, 2851,

3111, 3528, 3582
Lovelett, Bruce, 5387
LOVE STREET
  See HAIGHT STREET
Lovin, Roger, 2299, 2300
Lowe, Jim, 3268
Lowen, Alexander, 3684
Lowenhagen, Chuck, 4435
Lowenstein, Al, 5054
Lowenstein, Eddie, 2301, 4436, 4437, 4779
Lowrie, Samuel H., 3820a
LSD (Lysergic Acid Diethylamide) 1231, 2966, 2970, 2973, 3083, 3114, 3116, 3144, 3187, 3297
Lubasz, Heinz, 930
Lubeck, Steven G., 289a
Lubell, Samuel, 597
Lucas, Donald, 2303, 2304, 2305
Luc Godard, Jean, 2302
Luce, John, 598
Luce, Phillip Abbott, 599, 3970
Luckey, E. B., 3821, 3822
Luckin, Ed, 991
Luftig, Robert, 979
LUFTIG VS. MCNAMARA 979
Lui, William T., 599a
Lukas, J. Anthony, 600, 2306, 3269
Lundberg, Ferdinand, 601
Lundy, Joseph R., 3552
Lusky, Louis, 4438
Lusky, Mary H., 4438
Lutz, Rolland Ray Jr., 4439
Lyman, Mel, 2307, 2308
Lyman, S. M., 4012a
Lynch, Roberta, 1757
Lynch, Steve, 4629
Lynd, Alice, 5259
Lynd, S., 4896
Lynd, Staughton, 1935, 2309, 2310, 2311, 2312, 2313, 2531, 2788, 4440
Lynn, Conrad J., 602, 5137, 5260
Lyons, Carl, 2314, 4441

Mabee, C., 5138
McAfee, Kathy, 603
McAlister, John T., Jr., 604, 605
McAree, Christopher P., 4442
Macaulay, Neill, 606
MacAvoy, J., 3685
McCaa, Robert, 2315
McCabe, Charles, 2316
McCague, James, 5261
McCalls, (Magazine) 2926
MacCallum, G. C. Jr., 5139
McCarthy, Eugene, 675
McCarthy, Richard, 607
McClain, B. T., 4443
McClain, James, 1718
MacClain, Thomas B., 5262
McClave, Stevens, 1142
McCleary, Alix, 2317
McCleery, M., 4511
McClellan, Grant S., 608
MacCloskey, Monro, 5263
McClure, Michael, 1862, 2852
Maccoby, Eleanor E., 3686
McConahay, John B., 5192
McCone Commission Report, 2083, 2084
McConnell, Brian, 608a
McConnell, James M., 1171, 1224
McConville, Maureen, 4013, 4919
McCord, John H., 609
McCord, William, 610
McCormack, A. Jackson, 2008a
McCormick, Arthur, 610a
McCormick, Rory, 611
McCorquodale, Dave, 4444
McCurdy, Harold Grier, 3687
McDaniel, H. B., 4445
MacDonald, D., 3270
McDonald, Donald, 2318
MacDougall, Alexander, 2319, 2320, 2321, 2322
McDowell, Jim, 2323
Mace, David R., 3688, 3689
McEldowney, Carol, 2670
McEvoy, J., 4446
McEvoy, James, 3971
Macfarlane, L. J., 5140
McGee, Pat, 2562
McGee, Senator, 4447
McGinniss, Joe, 612
McGovern, George, 425, 4656, 4780, 5270
McGovern-Hatfield (Amendment)

1018, 1777
McGovern, Leon S., 4656
McGowan, William N., 4448
McGrady, M., 613
McGrath, Earl J., 614
McGrath, W. E., 2324
McGraw, James R., 396
MacGrew, John F., 4449
McGrory, M., 4781, 4782
McGuigan, F. E., 3823
McGuire, Diarmuid, 5141
Machado, Manuel A., 2325
McHugh, J. T., 3824
McIntire, Carl, 1335, 1858, 2826
McIntosh, Millicent, 3657
Mack, Raymond W., 615
McKay, B., 4450
McKeating, Mike, 2844
McKelvey, Donald, 2326
McKenney, J. W., 4451
Mackey, J. P., 616
Mackiz, Marc, 3271
McLaughlin, John, 3690, 3825
McLaughlin, Joseph F., 2327
MacLeish, A., 4452
McLeish, John, 616a
McLennan, Barbara N., 617, 4897
McLeod, Richard, 2328, 4453
McLucas, Lonnie, 1446, 2380
McLuhan, Marshall, 166, 532a, 2329, 4454
McMillan, George, 3379
McMillen, Wheeler, 618
McNamara, R. J., 5142
McNamara, Robert S., 565, 979, 1064, 4785
McNeill, Don, 619
McNeill, William H., 5264
McNett, I., 4455
McPeak, Alice, 4456
McPherson, James M., 620
McQuilkin, Frank, 621
McWilliams, Carey, 203
McWilliams, Wilson Carey, 622, 5143
Macy's Department Store, San Francisco, 2238
Madame Nhu, 2081
Madden, E. H., 4898
Mader, Julius, 623
Madison, Wisconsin, 1015, 1087, 1301, 1560, 4165
Magannis, Patricia, 723
Magdeline, Sister Anna, 3826
Magdoff, Harry, 624, 625, 859
Magee, Bryan, 626
Magic Mountain (Spartacist) Seattle, Washington, 2609
Magot, Richard, 306
Maguire, Micha, 2330
Maher, John Jr., 2689a
Maher, Michael, 4457
Mailer-Breslin Campaign (New York City) 633
Mailer, Norman, 627, 628, 633, 4899
Main, Jeremy, 2331
Majdalany, Gebran, 2332
Majoult, J., 4458
Malcolm, Andrew, 2333
Malcolm X, 42, 44, 120, 191, 290, 591, 629, 810, 1233a, 1234, 1712, 2263, 2334, 2720
MALE-FEMALE RELATIONSHIPS 316, 470, 568, 653, 663, 835, 849, 850, 1410, 1915, 2364, 2453, 2578, 2716, 3659, 3665, 3684
Mallery, David, 3972
Mallin, Jay, 630
Malloy, Kathleen, 2335
Malone, Bob, 2021
Malone, D. H., 4459
Malthy, Jan, 3553
Manchester, W., 2927, 2928
Mann, Kenneth W., 631
Manning, Robert, 632
Manso, Peter, 633
Manson, Charles, 1237, 2336, 2588, 2589, 2590
Manson Trial, 1237, 2586, 2588
Mao-Tse-Tung, 634, 757
Marburger, Carl, 4460
MARCH OF DEATH 3571
March Of The News. Front Page Of The Week, 4461
Marcus, Raymond, 2337
Marcuse, Herbert, 119, 635, 636, 742, 754, 930, 1238, 1239, 1828, 1845,

2338, 2339, 2340, 2341,
2760, 2820, 3873, 4159,
4588, 5173
Marek, Franz, 638
Margolin, Bruce M., 2342
Margolis, Jack, 1856, 1867
Margolis, Joseph B., 638a
Margolis, Michael, 2343
Marighella, Carlos, 2344
MARIJUANA
See also Items Listed In The Section "The Gap In Generations, And The Drug Dilemma."
37, 835a, 1160, 1240, 1241, 1466, 1547, 2410, 2608, 2924, 2948, 2959, 3008, 3066, 3084, 3087, 3131, 3144, 3159, 3165, 3180, 3184, 3185, 3190, 3210, 3214, 3300
Marin, Peter, 173
Marin City, California, 5322
Marine Corps Gazette, 390
Marine, Gene, 639, 2345, 2346, 3517, 3554, 4462, 5144
Markleeville, California, 1054b, 1739
Marlo, John A., 3380
Marmion, Harry A., 5265
MARRIAGE, MIXED
See MISCEGENATION
Marshall, Burke, 5145
Marshall Commission Report, 5265, 5268
Marshall, David, 2531
Marshall, Field, 2347
Marshall, Gen. S. L. A., 640
Marshall, Sue, 1881, 2348, 2349, 2350, 2351, 3555, 3556, 4463
Marshall, William, 3050
Martello, Leo Louis, 2352
Martin, David, 3973
Martin, George, 640a
Martin, Rex, 5146
Martin, Robert, 2133
Martin, Warren B., 3973a
Martinet, Gilles, 641
Martinson, Floyd M., 3690a
Marty, Martin, 642

Marx, Gary T., 643, 5147
Marx, Karl, 579, 923
MARXISM
See also IDEOLOGY, THEORY OF
12, 27, 33, 463, 494, 529, 579, 638, 641, 665, 742, 779, 883, 923, 1243, 1546, 1577, 1673, 1674, 1801, 1807, 1927, 1963, 2085, 2103, 2207, 2833, 5059
MARXISM-LENINISM 12
Mason, Alpheus T., 644
Masotti, Louis H., 645, 4900
MASOTTI REPORT, CLEVELAND, OHIO 3444, 4900
Massachusetts Institute Of Technology, 13, 3309
Massachusetts Racial Imbalance Law, 802
Massaron, Paul, 2352a
Massett, L., 2353
Masters, R. E. L., 3051
Mataxis, Theodore C., 5148
MATERIALISM, DIALECTICAL 1927
MATE-SWAPPING 1540, 2297
Mathe, Judy, 2354, 2355, 3272, 3557
Mathers, Karen, 3558
Mathews, J., 4464
Mathews, Stephnie, 2356
Mathieson, Garry, 5262
Matson, Floyd W., 646
Mattachine Society, 1244, 1245, 1442, 2305
Matthews, Connie, 1298
Matthews, Herbert L., 647
Matthews, Jim, 2929
Mauney, Ann, 2357, 2358
Maurer, David H., 3052
Maxson, R. E., 2359, 2360, 3559, 4465
May, Henry F., 4466
Mayer, Martin, 648
Mayers, Patrick, 2361
Mayhew, L. B., 1729a, 4467, 4468
Mays, John Barron, 3053
May Valley Coop. Renton, Washington, 2609
Mazur, Ronald, 3691

Index

Meacham, Stewart, 2040
Mead, Margaret, 1547, 3054, 3641, 4469, 4470, 4471, 5149, 5388
Meade, Kit, 3273
Meadville, Pennsylvania, 4957
Means, Richard K., 3274
Meany, George, 3560
Mecartney, John, 5150
MEDICAL EXPERIMENTATION, HUMAN 3, 655
MEDICAL LIBERATION FRONT 1835, 1836
Medina Report, 337
Medsker, Leland L., 3097
Meethan, A. Roger, 649
Meier, August, 114, 125
Meiklejohn, Alexander, 419
Meiman, Seymour, 650
Melbourne Village, Melbourne, Florida, 2609
Mellon, Richard "King" 1318, 1762, 1941
Melman, S., 2362
Melman, Seymour, 650a
Menashe, Louis, 651, 3974
Mendelsohn, Harold, 3322
Mendicino, Ellen S., 2363, 2364
Menen, Aubrey, 4472
Menninger, Karl A., 3692
MENOMINEE INDIANS, WISCONSIN 1248
MERCURY-BATTERY MANUFACTURING (pollution) 2114
Meredith, Robert, 4472a
MERITOCRACY 944
Meriwether, Louise M., 2365
Merk, Frederick, 3985
Merki, Donald J., 3055
Mermelstein, David, 353
Merriam, Eve, 652
Messinger, S. L., 4413
Messinger, Sheldon L, 164, 3959
Metefsky, George, 2366
Methvin, Eugene R., 4901
Metropolitan Community Church, Long Beach, California, 1028, 1041, 1732
Metzger, Deena, 1624, 2196
Metzger, Walter P., 654, 3975

Meyer, F. S., 2930, 4783
Meyer, Karl, 2367
Meyers, Donald W., 655
Miami, Florida, 1062, 1521, 2176, 2478, 2599
Miami, University Of, 1364
Michael, Donald N., 3056, 3976
Michaels, George M., 950
Michigan. Michigan State Senate. (Committee To Investigate Campus Disorders) 3976a
Michigan State University, East Lansing, Michigan, 2081
Middleton, Bruce, 2071
MIGRANT WORKERS
See also MINORITIES; MINORITY GROUPS
826, 1109
Miles, Michael, 4473
Milinaire, Catherine, 2368
Milio, Nancy, 656
MILITARY-AGRICULTURAL COMPLEX 1251
MILITARY EFFORTS AND UNIVERSITY PARTICIPATION
See UNIVERSITY PARTICIPATION IN MILITARY EFFORTS
MILITARY-INDUSTRIAL COMPLEX
See INDUSTRIAL-MILITARY-GOVERNMENT-EDUCATIONAL COMPLEX
MILITARY JUSTICE (or military injustice) 125a, 346, 500, 979, 980, 1024, 1039, 1086, 1117, 1119, 1119a, 1120, 1120a, 1121a, 1123, 1124, 1125, 1135, 1136, 1139, 1152, 1247, 1337, 1348, 1353, 1399, 1447, 1465, 1499, 1515, 1531, 1594, 1719, 1733, 1782, 1921, 2156, 2173, 2272, 2395, 2446, 2649, 2653, 2665, 2667, 2684, 2694, 2697, 2715, 2851, 5148, 5310, 5382, 5409
MILITARY STOCKADES
See STOCKADES, MILITARY

Miller, A., 4446
Miller, Abie, 657
Miller, Abraham, 3971
Miller, Al, 4071
Miller, Albert H., 3977
Miller, Arthur R., 658
Miller, Connie, 2369
Miller, Daniel R., 3978
Miller, Donald, 2739
Miller, Henry, 2370
Miller, James C. III, 5266
Miller, Jeffrey, 1263, 2702
Miller, Kelly, 659
Miller, Michael V., 660, 3979
Miller, T. K., 4474
Miller, Walter B., 3254
Miller, Warren, 661
Miller, William, 662
Miller, William G., 2371
Miller, William Lee, 2372
Miller, William R., 4902, 5151
Millersville State College, Millersville, Pennsylvania, 981, 986, 1048, 1077, 1108, 1116, 1159, 1167, 1199, 1226, 1281, 1329, 1342, 1343, 1404, 1405, 1424, 1425, 1426, 1427, 1428, 1436, 1573, 4696
Millett, Kate, 663, 1222, 2373
Mills, Billy G., 2374
Mills, C. Wright, 464, 664, 665, 1647, 1955, 2109, 2375, 2687
Mills, Olive, 3992
Mills, Theodore, 3980
Mills, Vicky, 4475
Millsaps College, Jackson, Mississippi, 2040
Milstein, Tom, 2376
Milwaukee 14, 1932, 2483, 2567, 5404
Milwaukee, Wisconsin, 38, 2483, 4165
Minh Vy, Nguyen, 2377
Minneapolis, Minnesota, 1171
Minnesota 8, 5383
Minnesota Library Association, 1224
Minnesota, University Of (St. Paul) 1171, 1224

MINORITIES
    AND THE POLICE, 3322, 3340; EMPLOYMENT, 885; INDIANS, 251; ON CAMPUS, 3881, 3977, 4133, 4604; MIGRANT WORKERS, 2284
MINORITY GROUPS 251, 325, 363, 383, 389a, 449a, 690, 738, 771, 775, 776, 826, 885, 887a, 1287, 1999, 2083, 2172, 2236, 2251, 2284, 2349, 3243, 3340, 3881, 3977, 4133
Minter, W. John, 3981
Minton, Robert, 2378
Mintz, Elliot, 2379
MINUTEMEN (organization) 1868, 2744, 2748
Miranda, Doug, 2380
MISCEGENATION 443, 906, 3653
MISSILE SYSTEMS (underwater) See UNDERSEA MILITARY BASES--UNDERWATER MISSILE SYSTEMS
Mississippi State Penitentiary, Parchman, Mississippi, 461
Mississippi Valley State College, Mississippi, 4249, 4640
Miss Nude America Beauty Pageant, 2509
Missouri State University, Columbia, Missouri, 2328
Mitchell, Bill, 2381
Mitchell, George S., 172
Mitchell, J. Paul, 666, 4903
Mitchell, John, 422, 1580, 2382, 3159, 4967
Mitchell, John N., 4476, 4967
Mitchell, Juliet, 667, 2383
Mitford, Jessica, 668
Mitrisin, John, 5389
Mitzman, Arthur, 4477
Moberg, David, 2384
Mock, Kathleen, R., 3982
Moffett, Toby, 2384a, 4479
Moldauer, P., 4784
Molnar, Thomas, 669
Molotch, Harvey, 2385

Molz, K., 2386
Momboisse, Raymond M., 670, 3380a, 3380b, 3982a
Monihan, Daniel Patrick, 743
MONIHAN REPORT 743
MONOPOLIES--U.S. 509
Monroe, North Carolina, 602, 2613
Montagu, Ashley, 5, 670a
Montesano, Randy, 3275
Montgomery, Alabama, 2552, 5071, 5199
Montgomery County, Maryland, 4165
Moody, Howard, 95a
Moore, Allen J., 3057
Moore, Barrington Jr., 930
Moore, John E., 2387
Moore, P. W., 2388
Moore, T. W., 3693
Moore, W. L., 4951
Moorman, Mary, 2337
Moos, Malcolm, 3983
Moraes, D., 3276
Moreland, C. K. Jr., 2389
Morgan, Griscom, 2390
Morgan-Gwyther Trial, 1256
Morgan, Jeanne, 2391
Morgan, Kip, 1256
Morgan, Richard E., 671
Morgan, Robin, 672, 673, 2392
Morgan, Ruth P., 674
Morgenthau, Hans J., 675
Morison, Robert S., 3984
Morison, Samuel Eliot, 3985
Morrill, Westen H., 2129
Morris, Dean, 1868
Morris, N., 2931
Morris, Norval, 4904
Morris, Peter, 4478
Morrison, Jim, 2478
MORRISON VS. STATE BOARD OF EDUCATION, MINNEAPOLIS, MINNESOTA 1171
Morse, Wayne, 2759
Morthland, John, 2393, 4479
Morton, Peggy, 2394
Mosby, Donald Y., 2395
Moscow, Alvin, 3058
Mosczisker, F. Von, 2396
Moses, Bob, 2397
Moskos, Charles C. Jr., 5267

Moskowitz, Ronald, 3277, 4480
Moss, Andrew, 4481
Moss, N., 4785
Mothner, Ira, 3278
Moursund, Andy, 2398
MOVIES--PICTURES IN EDUCATION 796
Mowbray, A. Q., 676
Mowry, Charles E., 3059
Moynahan, James M., 3381
Moynihan, Daniel P., 2399, 4905
Muhammed Ali
    See Ali, Muhammed
Mulherin, Cathy, 2400, 2401
Mulherin, Jim, 2401
Muller, J. D., 3279
Muller, Steven, 4482
Mulvey, Harold, 1196
Mumford, Lewis, 677, 1647
Mungo, Raymond, 678
Munoz, Rosalio, 1543
MURDER
    See also ABORTION; ASSASSINATION
    288, 1263, 1563, 1718, 1829, 2204, 2281, 2524, 2739, 4649
Murphy, Charles, 3694
Murphy, F. D., 3280
Murphy, Raymond J., 679
Murphy, Walter F., 3382
Murray, George, 2402
Muse, Benjamin, 680, 4904a
Muse, Charlie, 2403
Musgrove, Frank, 3060
Muskie, Edmund S., 5341
Muste, A. J., 1801
Muston, Ray, 2404
Myerson, Jack, 1758
Myerson, Michael, 681
My Lai, 1517
My Lai 4, 446
Myrdal, Gunnar, 188, 682, 683, 2318

Nabokov, Peter, 684
Nabors, Jim, 1238
Nachman, Larry David, 2405
Nader, Ralph, 1262
Nagler, Michael, 4483

NAIS INSTITUTE ON SEX
    EDUCATION 3695
Naison, Mark, 2406
Nameth, Joe, 5177
Nanes, Allan S., 2932, 5152
Nanteere Group
    See Cohn-Bendit, Daniel
NAPALM 1731, 2032, 2211,
    2483, 2759
Naramore, John A., 4484
NARCOTICS
    See DRUGS AND DRUG CUL-
    TURE
Narramore, Clyde M., 2407
Narrow Ridge, Newaygo, Michi-
    gan, 2609
Nashville, Tennessee, 1144
NATIONAL ADVISORY COM-
    MISSION ON CIVIL DIS-
    ORDERS 3367b, 4813a,
    4832, 4834, 5183
NATIONAL ADVISORY COM-
    MISSION ON SELECTIVE
    SERVICE 5268
NATIONAL ASSOCIATION FOR
    THE ADVANCEMENT
    OF COLORED PEOPLE
    1490, 1623a, 2558, 2613
NATIONAL CATHOLIC EDUCA-
    TION ASSOCIATION 3696
National Commission On The
    Causes And Prevention
    Of Violence, 428, 2878,
    2882, 2933, 3415, 3996a,
    4084, 4863, 4864, 4888,
    4905, 4923
National Committee To Combat
    Fascism, 1267
National Conference On Higher
    Education, 3986, 4526
National Education Association,
    1676
National Education Association
    (Research Division) 4485,
    4486
NATIONALISM (black) 114, 269,
    297, 752a, 1234, 1524,
    1950, 2474
NATIONALISM, IDEOLOGY
    See also IDEOLOGY, THE-
    ORY OF
    114, 269, 1770
NATIONAL LIBERATION
    FRONT--DOCUMENTS
    531
NATIONAL LIBERATION
    FRONT (history) 531,
    1850, 2259, 2260, 2618
NATIONAL LIBERATION
    FRONT (manifesto) 531,
    2259, 2617
NATIONAL LIBERATION FRONT
    OF SOUTH VIETNAM
    724, 1850
NATIONAL ORGANIZATION
    FOR WOMEN 1855
National School Public Relations
    Association, 3697, 3987
NATIONAL SECURITY STATE
    772
National Shooting Sports Founda-
    tion, Inc., 2867
National Society Of Professors
    (forum) 3988
National Student Association,
    2690, 4508
NATIONAL URBAN COALITION
    3382a, 3382b
Nearing, Helen, 684a
Nearing, Scott, 684a
Neary, John, 2408, 5153
Nebraska, University Of, Lin-
    coln, Nebraska
    See University Of Nebraska,
    Lincoln, Nebraska
Neff, C. B., 4487
Neff, Renfreu, 2409
Neff, Richard, 2410, 4488
NEGRO--DEFINITION AND
    RELIGIOUS ASPECTS
    248
NEGROES--CIVIL RIGHTS,
    HUMOR 396
NEGROES--EDUCATION (sec-
    ondary) CHICAGO 397
NEGROES, HISTORY 26, 42,
    71, 98, 124, 125, 153,
    244, 301, 326, 371, 388,
    395, 398, 447, 518, 521,
    534, 546, 610, 629, 731,
    751, 806, 813, 851
NEGROES--SOUTHERN STATES
    399, 504, 546
NEGROES, U.S. 2, 26, 28, 29,
    36, 41, 43, 44, 45, 51,
    69, 70, 71, 93, 98, 122,

123, 124, 125, 129, 165, 176, 188, 208, 235, 236, 244, 255, 289, 300, 301, 312, 326, 329, 336, 347, 359, 360, 370, 371, 388, 394, 395, 398, 437, 447, 478, 504, 506, 518, 519, 520, 521, 544, 562, 564, 573, 577, 585, 586, 590, 610, 620, 621, 629, 658, 659, 660, 679, 680, 682, 705, 706, 731, 743, 751, 774, 804, 805, 806, 813, 820, 845, 851, 852, 879, 880, 896, 901, 910, 939, 940, 971, 999, 1032, 1524, 1558, 1770, 1916, 1939, 2003, 2144, 2428, 2474, 2489, 2720, 2743, 4904a
NEGRO FAMILY 743
NEGRO POLICEMEN
  See Items Listed In The Section "Police-Community Relationships" e.g., 3316, 3522
NEGRO--POLITICS AND POLITICIANS 621, 682, 851, 852, 901, 2144
NEGRO WIT AND HUMOR 396
Neiburg, H. L., 684b
Neill, Alexander S., 685, 686
Neimark, Paul G., 705
Nelson, B., 4489, 4786
Nelson, Jack, 3698, 3989
Nelson, Truman, 687, 688
Neubauer, D. E., 5155
Neugeboren, J., 5154
Neuhaus, Richard John, 77
Neumann, Harry, 4490
Neville, Judge Philip, 1171
New Brunswick, New Jersey, 2371
New Buffalo Community, Taos, New Mexico, 2609
Newark, New Jersey, 349, 429, 833, 1530, 4106, 4873
Newby, Idus A., 689
Newcomb, Fred T., 2411
Newcomb, Theodore, 4492
Newcomb, Theodore M., 3913

NEW DEMOCRATIC COALITION OF PENNSYLVANIA 2062
New England CNVA, Voluntown, Connecticut, 2609
NEW ENGLAND VIETNAM SUMMER
  See PEACE ACTION COUNCIL OF EASTERN MASSACHUSETTS
Newfield, Jack, 690
Newfield, J. A., 3990
Newham, Blaine, 2412
New Harmony Homestead, Pennington, Minnesota, 2609
New Haven 9, 1446, 2267, 2614
New Haven, Connecticut, 1246, 4927
New Horizons, Torrington, Connecticut, 2609
NEW LEFT
  See also RADICAL LEFT; MARXISM-LENINISM
  12, 119, 203, 315, 352, 361, 409, 466, 483, 529, 532a, 557, 567, 595, 599, 635, 678, 681, 690, 739, 817, 839, 865, 931, 993, 1029, 1211, 1218, 1262, 1273, 1545, 1546, 1680, 1722, 1784, 1827, 1926, 1953, 1961, 1963, 1972, 2023, 2097, 2103, 2109, 2113, 2207, 2246, 2311, 2312, 2326, 2339, 2340, 2375, 2417, 2418, 2426, 2495, 2581, 2605, 2617, 2648, 2659, 2662, 2679, 2775, 2776, 2850, 3873, 3874, 3892, 3894, 3898, 3928, 3954, 3970, 3995, 3996, 4188, 4222, 4233, 4324a, 4375, 4394, 4439, 4515, 4883, 4901, 5033, 5173, 5175
NEW LEFT (history) 3995
Newman, Albert H., 691
Newman, Bernard, 692
Newman, Edwin S., 692a, 3383
Newman, Sally, 4493
New Politics Convention, Chi-

cago, September 4, 1967, 2689a
Newport, Robert S. Jr., 2413
NEW REFORM PARTY 2212
Newton, Huey, 174, 815, 965, 966, 1180, 1181, 1192, 1408, 1496, 1525, 1608, 1696, 1697, 1720, 1925, 2155, 2224, 2248, 2317, 2350, 2414, 2415, 2416, 2450
NEW UNIVERSITY CONFERENCE 4044, 4491
New York (City) 633, 1544, 1593, 2574, 4165
New York 8, 1593, 2574
New York (Lower East Side) 619, 3491
New York Panther 21 (Trial) 1278, 2267, 2409, 2640, 4137
New York (State) Albany. Temporary Commission To Study The Causes Of Campus Unrest, 3989a
New York Teacher's Strike, 1968, 648
New York Times (Newspaper) 1295, 1670
New York University, New York, 1080
Niantic State Farm, 1653
Niceswanger, Bruce (Bruno) 2417, 4494
Nichols, David C., 3991, 3992
Nichols, Paul, 1414
Nicholson, Joan, 5326
Nicolaus, Martin, 693
Nieburg, H. L., 3993, 4906
Niederhoffer, Arthur, 3384
Niemeyer, Gerhart, 2418
NIHILISM
See also IDEOLOGY, THEORY OF
12, 2760, 4304
Nimkoff, M. F., 3065
NISQUALLY INDIAN TRIBE, WASHINGTON (State) 2854
Nixon, R. E., 3061
Nixon, Richard M., 134, 612, 675, 1042, 1054, 1115, 1282, 1283, 1284, 1285, 1295, 1379, 1401, 1450, 1476, 1575, 1604, 1626, 1646, 1704, 1741, 1851, 1911, 1953, 2118, 2119, 2170, 2186, 2252, 2278, 2287, 2377, 2393, 2419, 2511, 2540, 2554, 2616, 2740, 3133, 3154, 4097, 4107, 4108, 4495, 4519, 4732, 4737, 4758, 4769, 4782, 4787, 5156, 5294
Nobbs, Russ, 2420, 4496
Nobile, Philip, 2421
Noble, Jeanne L., 4497
Nock, Albert Jay, 419
NO KNOCK CRIME BILL (District Of Columbia) 1778, 1924, 2253
Nolan, David, 5157
NON-VIOLENT RESISTANCE, THEORY OF
See also Items Listed In The Section "Civil Disobedience, Violence And Non-Violence" 5057
Nordhoff, Charles, 694
Norrgard, David L., 3385
North American Conference Of Homophile Organizations, 1734, 1817
North, Robert Bruce, 2422
Northern Illinois University, DeKalb, Illinois, 4138, 4308
Norwick, K. P., 2471, 2472, 2473
Notes For The Study Of The Ideology Of The Cuban Revolution, 1673
Nottingham, Marvin A., 212, 4498
Novak, M., 5158
Novak, Michael, 4499
Novasky, U. S., 2423
Nowack, Dorothy, 3827
Nowlis, Helen H., 3062, 3994
NUCLEAR WEAPONS
See WEAPONS (nuclear)
NUDE-INS 2038, 2509, 4099
Nuthall, Jeff, 3063

Oakland, California, 2572, 3554, 4981
Oakland Induction Center, Oakland, California, 1645
Oakland 7 (Oakland Induction Center, California) 1291, 1645, 1775, 1975, 4981, 5381
Oberlin College, Oberlin, Ohio, 4088, 4361
Oberteuffer, D., 3828
O'Brien, Basil, 2424
O'Brien, Conor Cruise, 2425
O'Brien, David J., 2426
O'Brien, James, 3995
O'Brien, Jim, 2427
OBSCENITY (law)
See also EROTIC ART; PORNOGRAPHY
197, 296, 335a, 356, 539, 608, 747, 758, 892, 982, 1034, 1054, 1057, 1061, 1071, 1082, 1089, 1112, 1114, 1215, 1293, 1331a, 1355, 1393, 1441, 1464, 1508, 1559, 1611, 1681, 1725, 1750, 1767, 1860, 1862, 1872, 1914, 1959, 1974, 1989, 1996, 2022, 2054, 2093, 2149, 2163, 2177, 2180, 2195, 2219, 2324, 2370, 2386, 2444, 2469, 2470, 2471, 2472, 2473, 2501, 2506, 2507, 2508, 2516, 2522, 2523, 2599, 2642, 2664, 2669, 2672, 2721, 2852, 2853, 3810
Ocean Hill-Brownsville Demonstration School District
See also Ocean Hill-Brownsville School District
85, 4225
Ocean Hill-Brownsville School District
See also Ocean Hill-Brownsville Demonstration School
85, 2071, 4295
Ochs, Phil, 1377
O'Connor, Jack, 2934
O'Connor, James, 695
O'Connor, John, 696, 697
O'Connor, Timothy J., 3356

Odenwald, Robert P., 3699
O'Donnell, John A., 3064
O'Douglas, William, 4656
Ofari, Earl, 2428, 2429
Ogar, Richard A., 2430
Ogburn, W. F., 3065
OGLE-IN 1592
Oglesby, Carl, 698, 2431, 2515, 3996, 4071
Ohio State University, Columbus, Ohio, 4066
Ohles, J. F., 4500, 4501
Ohlin, L. E., 4836
Ohmart, Howard, 5159
Oi, Walter Y., 5390
Ojile, Fred, 2483
Oko, Tristine, 2432
Older, Charles H., 1237
Old Market Coffee House, Kentucky Avenue, Paducah, Kentucky, 2381
Oliver, Ralph (Chip) 2412
O'Loughlin, Ray, 2433
Olsen, Jack, 699
Olson, James, 556a
OLYMPICS, MEXICO CITY
1009, 1883, 2158, 2374, 2389, 2597, 2811, 5096, 5191
Omaha, Nebraska, 1666
OMNIBUS CRIME BILL OF 1968, 421, 1296, 2199, 2916, 3382a, 3382b, 4871
Oneida Indian Tribe, New York State, 984
O'Neill, Robert, 700
O'Neill, Robert M., 700a
O'Neill, William L., 701
ONE, INC., 1442
One World Family Of The Messiah's World Crusade, 2412
OPERATION ATLANTIS I
See ATLANTIS IA (Caribbean)
Operation Empathy (Project) Covina, California, 3448
Oppenheimer, Martin, 702, 2434, 4502, 4907
Oraison, Marc, 3700, 3701
Orangeburg Massacre. South Carolina State College,

Orangeburg, South Carolina, 3989, 5157
Orange County, California, 3239
Orbell, J. M., 4503
Orben, Bob, 393
Order Of Aaron, Salt Lake City, Utah, 2609
Order Of St. Michael, Crown Point, Maryland, 2609
OREOS 415
ORGANIZED CRIME
See CRIME, ORGANIZED
ORLANDO VS. LAIRD 4935
Orrick, William H., 702a, 3996a
Orth, F. L., 2935
Orvino, Jennie, 2435
Osborn, Jim, 2436, 4504, 4505
Osborn, Robert, 4677
Osborne, John, 74
Osborne, William A., 703
Oslick, Alan, 2437, 2438, 2439
Oswald, Lee Harvey, 491, 691, 790, 1127, 1128, 2313, 2411, 2803
Oswald, Marie, 3814
Otten, C. Michael, 3997
Our Man In Prague (Hard Times) 2440
Ousler, William C., 3066
Overstreet, Bonaro, 3386
Overstreet, Harry A., 703a, 704, 3386
Owens, Jessie, 705, 2297, 2441
Owens, William A., 706, 1304
Owle, Jim, 1126
Owyhee Indian Reservation, Nevada, 1189

Pachter, Henry M., 707
Pacific Northwest Conference On Higher Education, 584a
PACIFIC STUDIES CENTER 708, 709, 710, 2442
PACIFISM 315, 926, 4855, 5065
Packard Motor Company, 11
Packard, Vance, 711, 3067, 3702

Packer, Herbert L., 3561
Paddock, Paul, 712
Paddock, William, 712
Padgett, I. F., 4506
Page, W., 2936, 2937
Pain, Lincoln, 2443, 3562
Paine, Tom, 2444
Palmer, Charles, 3912, 4507, 4508
Palm Springs, Florida, 4498
Pantaleoni, C. A., 3387
Panther 21 (New York)
See New York Panther 21 (Trial)
Panush, Louis, 4509
Parathion Poisoning, 2637
Parent, A., 4510
PARENT-CHILD RELATIONSHIPS
See also CHILDREN--EDUCATION AND MANAGEMENT; Also Items Listed In The Section "The Gap In Generations" and "The Pregnant Question-Sex Education" 3002, 3003, 3006, 3010, 3024, 3069, 3085, 3089, 3091, 3241, 3645, 3678, 3680, 3726, 3978
PARENT-CHILD-TEACHER RELATIONSHIPS
See also Items Listed In The Section "The Pregnant Question-Sex Education" 3603
Parente, W., 4511
Parenti, Michael, 713
Parkes, James, 714
Parkinson, Tom, 4512
Parks, David, 715
Parks, Gordon, 2445
Parmalee, Patty, 2446, 2447
Parson, Nels A., 4671
Parsons College, Iowa, 527
Parsons, Talcott, 3068
PARTICIPATORY DEMOCRACY
See DEMOCRACY, PARTICIPATORY (Also sometimes spelled "paticipatory")
PASSAMAQUODDY INDIANS, 2800
Paton, A., 5160
Patrick, James E., 2448

Patterson, William L., 1440, 2449, 2450, 2451
Paulsen, Monrad, 5161
Paulson, Pat, 2452
Paylor, Ann, 2453
Payne, Raymond, 4513
Payne, R. B., 3281
Peace Action Council Of Eastern Massachusetts, 2845
PEACE (addresses) 456
PEACE MARCHES 253, 347, 627, 1213, 1275, 1280, 1474, 1498, 1523, 1585, 1609, 1926, 1985, 2174, 2398, 2415, 2446, 2530, 2532, 2552, 2700, 2836, 3501a, 3580a, 4813, 5100, 5138
PEACE (symbol) 1310, 1528
PEACE (symbol) ORIGIN AND HISTORY 1310a, 1310b, 2098
Peacock, Mary, 2454
Peale, Norman Vincent, 3282
PEANUTS (comic strip) 1808
Pearlman, Robert, 5391
Peccli, A., 716
Peck, Abe, 2455
Peck, James, 717, 4908
Peck, Merton J., 718
Peck, Sidney M., 2456
Peckham, Morse, 719
Peddle, Iris, 2457
Pedersen, Douglas J., 2008a
Peek, B. M., 2458
Pell, Eve, 2459
Pemberton, John de J. Jr., 5162, 5392
Pence, David, 2460
Pennsylvania State University, University Park, Pennsylvania, 1475, 1930, 2644, 4072, 4136, 4211, 4239, 4387
Penny, Rob, 1008
PENTAGONISM 105, 341, 627, 650, 772, 881a, 1312, 1498, 1705, 2836, 2843, 4752
People Of The Living God, New Orleans, Louisiana, 2609
PEOPLE'S BANK
See BANK OF AMERICA
People's Community Conference, Cleveland, Ohio
See Community People's Conference, Cleveland, Ohio
PEOPLE'S PARK
1798, 1962, 2152, 2215, 2400, 2401, 2564, 2685a, 2706, 4172, 4339, 4429a; Berkeley, California, 987, 992, 2603, 2686, 2741, 3472; Miami, Florida, 1313; New York (Cooper Square) 1979; New York (St. Marks Place) 1979
For A Chronology Of People's Park Confrontations At Berkeley, See 2741.
Peoples' Press, 720, 721
Pepper, William F., 2461
Perkins, David, 2462
Perkins, Emily, 2463
Perkins, Faye, 3446
Perkins, James A., 1333, 3998
Perlman, Samuel, 3069
Perry, Diane, 2464, 2465
Perry, Georgia, 2700
Perry, Helen Swick, 721a, 3070
Perry,' Troy D., 1041, 1315, 1363, 1451, 1820, 2132
PESTICIDES 431, 440, 607, 618
Peter, Viviane, 3563
Peters, C. F., 4514
Peterson, Dan, 2466
Peterson, Frank, 5393
Peterson, Mark E., 3071
Peterson, Richard E., 3999, 4000, 4515, 4590a
Peterson, Virgil W., 3564
Petras, James, 516, 4516
Pettee, George Sawyer, 722
Pettigrew, Thomas, 722a
Pettis, Jerry, 3912
Pettitt, George, 3072
Pexton, Myron R., 3703
Phantom Dealers, Inc., 2467
Phelan, Laura Clarke, 723
Phelan, W. D. Jr., 3565
Philadelphia Bulletin (newspa-

per) 86
Philadelphia, Pennsylvania,
1415, 1787, 1791, 1925,
1956, 2703, 2825, 3272,
3498, 3499, 3514, 3515,
3546, 3547, 4744, 4779,
4984, 5393, 5411
PHILADELPHIA--RACE RELA-
TIONS 84
Phillips, Joseph Dexter, 797a
Phillips Petroleum, 1738
Philo, Nancy, 2468
Phoenix, Lisa, 2454
Phuque Defense Fund, 1488
Phuque Rebellion, 1488
Piers, Maria W., 3704
Pierson College, Connecticut,
3941
Pietrofesa, John J., 4517
Pike, Douglas, 724, 725
Pike, James A., 3705
Pileggi, Nicholas, 4518
Pilkey, G. P., 4474
Pilpel, H. F., 2469, 2470,
2471, 2472, 2473, 3838a
PINK PANTHERS 1322
PIT RIVER INDIAN TRIBE,
CALIFORNIA 2255, 2821
Pittard, Barbara, 4513
Pittenger, Norman, 3706
PITTSBURGH COALITION,
1269, 2528a
Pittsburgh 5, 1325, 1326, 3439
Pittsburgh, Pennsylvania, 960,
961, 974, 989, 1008,
1161, 1165, 1177, 1204,
1228, 1287, 1323, 1325,
1326, 1327, 1341, 1361,
1396, 1418, 1468, 1512,
1584, 1586, 1588, 1599,
1763, 1792, 1803, 1995,
2052, 2087, 2182, 2291,
2327, 2464, 2465, 2517,
2518, 2519, 2525, 2528a,
2534, 2535, 2536, 2539,
2541, 2543, 2548, 3439,
3447, 3454, 3464, 3492,
3493, 3494, 3495, 3572,
3573, 3576, 4720, 4790,
5308
Pittsburgh 3, 1803
Plainfield Joint Defense Com-
mittee, Plainfield, New
Jersey, 1279
Plainfield, New Jersey, 1497
Playboy (magazine) 1903, 2646,
3818
PLESSY VS. FERGUSON 948
Plimpton, Calvin H., 4519
Plimpton, Francis T. P., 640a
Plimpton, George, 726
Ploscawe, Morris, 5163
Plumb, J. H., 5164
Pocklington, Thomas, 5165
Podhoretz, Norman, 2474,
3283
Poffenberger, Thomas, 3828b
Pohl, Connie, 3566
Pohlmann, Bruce, 4520
Poindexter, David, 1183
Point Park Junior College,
Pittsburgh, Pennsylvania,
1280
Poland, Jefferson, 3829
POLICE, BRAIN 2599
POLICE, BRUTALITY
See Items Listed In The Sec-
tion "Police-Community Re-
lationships"
POLICE CHIEF, THE 3388
POLICE EDUCATION
See Items Listed In The Sec-
tion "Police-Community Re-
lationships" e.g., 3356
POLICE--REFORM AND THE
LAW
See Items Listed In The Sec-
tion "Police-Community Re-
lationships" e.g., 3322
POLICEWOMEN 3410
POLITICAL IDEOLOGY
See IDEOLOGY, POLITICAL;
IDEOLOGY, THEORY OF
POLITICS AND POLITICIANS--
NEGRO
See NEGRO--POLITICS AND
POLITICIANS
POLLUTION, AIR 427a, 439,
578, 649, 1258, 1896,
2251, 2520
POLLUTION--INDUSTRIAL
COMPLEX
See also ECOLOGY; EN-
VIRONMENTAL CRISIS;
POLLUTION, SMOG
243, 435, 559, 649,

833a, 834, 1059, 1258,
1324, 1473, 1558a, 1562,
1599, 1605, 1727, 1741,
1742, 1896, 1946, 1980,
1982, 2010, 2146, 2345,
2520, 2576, 2673, 2787,
2840, 2848
POLLUTION, MERCURY
  See MERCURY--BATTERY
  MANUFACTURING (pollution)
POLLUTION, NOISE 2660, 2837
POLLUTION, OIL 249, 2385,
  2794
POLLUTION, SMOG 243, 925
POLLUTION, WATER 439, 561
Pomeray, Wardell B., 3707,
  3708
Pomeroy, William J., 727
Pondy, Louis R., 2475, 2476
Pool, Joe, 1600
Poole, John E., 4521
Poor People's Washington Campaign, 300
POOR--U.S.
  See POVERTY--U.S.
Popkin, Richard, 2477
Poppy, John, 5394
POPULATION, CONTROL OF
  See also ABORTION; BIRTH
  CONTROL; FERTILITY,
  HUMAN
    22, 25, 61, 103, 286,
    392, 433, 599a, 610a,
    745, 867, 943, 1092,
    1622, 1886, 1892, 2213,
    2673, 2856, 3600, 3719
PORNOGRAPHY
  See also EROTIC ART;
  OBSCENITY (law)
    351, 356, 379, 471,
    539, 719, 975a, 1054,
    1068, 1082, 1335a, 1393,
    1559, 1611, 1644, 1914,
    1959, 2022, 2386, 2408,
    2470
Porter, Herb, 5166
Port Huron, Michigan, 4021a
Portland, Oregon, 3452, 3480,
  5094
POSTAL STRIKE
  See STRIKES AND LOCKOUTS--POSTAL
Poussaint, A. F., 5167

POVERTY--U.S.
  See also U.S.--SOCIAL
  PROBLEMS--1960
    416
Powe, Wilbur, 3567
Powell, Adam Clayton, 912
Powell, John, 3568
Powell, Lewis F., 5168
Powell, R. S. Jr., 4521a, 4522
Powell, Theodore, 728
Powelton Neighbors, Philadelphia, Pennsylvania, 2609
Powers, Jerry, 2478
Powers, John J. Jr., 3073
Powledge, Fred, 729, 729a
Pratt, Annis, 2479
PREFORM MOVEMENT 1093
PREJUDICE
  See also DISCRIMINATION;
  RACE QUESTION--U.S.
    36, 41, 45, 51, 62, 69,
    240, 311, 319a, 365,
    443, 587, 643, 703a,
    752b, 841b, 843, 850a,
    1797, 1978, 2007
Presbyterian National Committee (Meeting) San Antonio, Texas, 2754
PRESIDENT'S COMMISSION ON
  CAMPUS UNREST 3988,
  4114, 4960
PRESIDENT'S COMMISSION ON
  LAW ENFORCEMENT
  AND ADMINISTRATION
  OF JUSTICE 1336, 3390,
  3411, 3412, 3423
PRESIDENT'S COMMISSION ON
  THE STATUS OF WOMEN 206a
PRESIDENT'S COMMITTEE ON
  OBSCENITY AND PORNOGRAPHY 1335a
Presidio Army Base Stockade,
  San Francisco, California, 346, 980, 1337,
  1531, 1719, 2635, 2649,
  2697
Presidio Mutiny Case, 346,
  1531, 2649
Presidio 21, 1847, 2649
Presidio 27, 1719
Presley, Elvis, 5177
Preston, Richard A., 730

Prewitt, Kenneth, 525
Primula, Ron, 2480
PRISONERS (political)
See also Individual Names
Of Prisons, e.g., FOLSOM
AND SOLEDAD PRISONS,
CALIFORNIA
82, 548, 1033, 1052,
1075, 1707, 1720, 2524,
2641, 2734, 4410, 4986,
5415
PRISONERS--SEXUAL BEHAVIOR 461
PRISON RIOTS, (New York)
1340
PRISONS--WORK AND LIVING
CONDITIONS
See also Individual Names
Of Prisons, e.g., FOLSOM
PRISON; PRESIDIO; SAN
QUENTIN; SOLEDAD
125a, 1340, 1382, 1617,
1779, 1875, 2403, 2720a,
3361, 5051
Pritchard, Ken, 2481
PRIVACY, RIGHT OF 34, 118,
121, 242, 477, 658,
711, 917, 1368, 1394,
2050, 2199, 2286, 2480,
2858, 3401, 3497
Proctor, Samuel D., 731
PROLETARIAN MISSION, CONCEPT OF 1577, 2076
Prometheus Project, 310
PROPAGANDA 341, 499
Prosch, H., 5169, 5170
PROSPERITY AND CRISIS
CONFLICT 355, 1874
Protean/RADISH 2482
Proxmire, Senator William,
732, 733
PSYCHEDELIC LIFE 927, 928,
929, 1413, 1929, 2857,
3051
PSYCHOCHEMICAL WEAPONS
See WEAPONS (psychochemical)
PSYCHOLOGICAL WARFARE
See also BIOLOGICAL
WARFARE; CHEMICAL
WARFARE; WARFARE
418

PUBLIC ASSISTANCE
See PUBLIC WELFARE
PUBLIC INTEREST 4000a
PUBLIC WELFARE 1480, 1481,
1678, 1879, 2037, 2048,
2206, 2234, 2278, 2358,
2574, 2621, 2670, 2763,
2809
PUEBLO (ship) USS PUEBLO
31, 1448, 1887, 1888,
2699, 2834
Puerto Rican Youth In The
U.S., 1628
PUMP-HOUSE GANG 929
Puner, Helen, 3709
Puner, Nicholas, 5171
Pursuit, D. G., 3371
Pustay, John S., 734
Pyes, Craig Randolph, 3569
Pynes, Joe, 2198, 2600

QUAKERS
See FRIENDS, SOCIETY OF
Quann, C. J., 4523
Queen, Stuart A., 3710
Quegg, Dave, 2483
Questers, Los Banos, California, 2609
QUEST FOR COMMUNITY (dialogue) 68
Quigley, T. E., 5352
Quinlan, Francis, 3439
Quinley, Harold E., 2484
Quinn, Mary, 2485, 2486
Quinn, Meredith, 1542
Quinn, Robert P., 735, 736
Quinney, Richard, 737

Raab, Earl, 587, 738
Rabinowitz, Dorothy, 2487, 2488
Rabinowitz, Victor, 2489
RACE AND RELIGION--U.S. 47,
589, 703, 755, 773, 830,
840
RACE QUESTION--U.S.
See also CONFLICT, INTERRACIAL; DISCRIMINATION;
NEGROES, U.S.; PREJUDICE
36, 41, 43, 45, 51, 62,
69, 70, 83, 98, 113,
122, 123, 124, 125, 129,

153, 168, 177, 229, 255, 280, 289, 301, 311, 318, 325, 326, 327, 328, 335, 336, 349, 350, 370, 383, 388, 392a, 398, 429, 436, 437, 443, 444, 474a, 506, 525, 544, 564, 573, 577, 585, 590, 591, 645, 656, 659, 680a, 682, 703, 729, 738, 750, 774, 785a, 804, 805, 810, 827, 833, 843, 845, 848, 852, 861, 877, 879, 880, 886, 896, 910, 935, 938, 939, 940, 945, 962, 970, 999, 1049, 1259, 1349, 1558, 1900, 1910, 1931, 2008a, 2058, 2332, 2397, 2428, 2720, 2737, 4070, 4082, 4866, 4904a, 4969, 5121

Rackley, Alex, 1007, 1446
Radano, Gene, 3389
Rader, Dotson, 739, 4524, 4525
RADICAL FEMINISM OF NEW YORK 740
RADICALISM, IDEOLOGY
See also IDEOLOGY, THEORY OF
12, 67, 77, 102, 106, 352, 367, 389, 411, 428, 467, 468, 483, 557, 558, 567, 626, 660, 681, 739, 750, 760, 817, 878, 923, 942, 1017, 1175, 1221, 1249, 1730, 1827, 1834, 1935, 2058, 2310, 2311, 2566, 2609a, 2659, 2711, 3944, 4036, 4122, 4440, 4646, 4889
RADICAL LEFT
See also RADICALISM, IDEOLOGY
12, 22a, 74, 119, 203, 315, 352, 367, 372, 417, 466, 558, 567, 595, 681, 878, 1029, 1607, 2605, 3854, 4190

RADICAL MIDDLE (center) 8, 12, 372, 1453, 1461, 1607, 4324a, 4635
RADICAL POLITICS 372, 800, 1607, 2566, 4235, 4288, 4938, 5115
RADICAL PRESS
See UNDERGROUND (newspapers)
RADICAL RIGHT 22a, 149, 291, 372, 489, 532a, 558, 567, 752, 800, 1453, 1607, 1728, 2003, 2421, 2609a, 2710, 2813 1607, 2605, 3854, 4190
RADICALS--HIGH SCHOOL
See HIGH SCHOOL-UNDERGROUND
Radicals In The Professions Conference, New York, 2023
RADICAL THEOLOGY
See THEOLOGY, RADICAL
Radosh, Ronald, 651, 3974
Rafferty, Max, 5, 741, 2133, 2553, 2622, 4230
Raines, John C., 742
Rainwater, Lee, 743, 3710a
Raleigh, Doug, 2490
Raleigh, North Carolina, 3307
Ramparts (Magazine) 744, 1350
Ramsey, Charles E., 3711
Ramsey, Paul, 745, 746
Randall, Richard S., 747
Rand Corporation, 465, 2494
Randolph, A. Philip, 69
Ransom, David, 2491, 2492
Raphael, Stephen M., 3535
Rapoport, Roger, 2493, 4001
Raser, John, 4788
Raskin, Marcus G., 748, 2494, 2690
Ratterman, P. H., 4526
Raup, Philip Jr., 2495
Ray, James Earl, 473
Ray, Michele, 749, 2496
Reading, John, 3554
Reagan, Ronald, 992, 1351, 1541, 2316, 2330, 2447, 2510, 2563, 4158
Reardon Report, 337
Reba Place Fellowship, Evanston, Illinois, 2609

Recca, Ron (Mod Scientist) 2497, 2498, 2499, 2500, 4789
Recherdson, Elliot, 3284
Reckless, Walter E., 4909
Record, Wilson, 750
Rector, James, 1350, 2741
RED CROSS, 2074
Redding, J. Saunders, 751
Redekop, John H., 752
Redkey, Edwin S., 752a
Redlich, Norman, 154, 2501, 5171a
RED POWER MOVEMENT 984, 848
Reece, Norval, 1568, 1756, 1758
Reed, Manfred, 2817
Reed, Richard Y., 752b
Reedy, George E., 5269
Reeves, Thomas C., 753, 5270
Regamey, P., 5172
Regan, J. J., 2501
Register, Richard, 2502
Reich, Charles A., 754
Reichart, Sandford, 4593
Reichley, A. James, 3570
Reik, Theodore, 3727
Reilly, William S. J., 4527
Reimann, John, 4627
Reimers, David M., 755
Reinecke, Edwin R., 2563
Reinholz, Mary, 2503, 2504, 2505, 5173
Reischauer, Edwin O., 756
Reisman, D., 4528
Reiss, Albert J. Jr., 2505a, 3390, 3474, 3478
Reiss, Ira Leonard, 3712, 3829a, 3829b, 3830, 4529
Rejai, Mostafa, 757
RELIGION AND RACE--U.S.
See RACE AND RELIGION --U.S.
RELIGION AND SCIENCE
See also CHRISTIANITY AND SCIENCE, COMPARATIVE
46, 137a
Religion In Education Foundation, 162

RELIGION IN THE PUBLIC SCHOOLS
See also BIBLE READING IN THE PUBLIC SCHOOLS; EDUCATION, RELIGIOUS
260a, 495, 700, 860, 934
RELIGIOUS CONFLICTS
See THEOLOGY, CONFLICTS
RELIGIOUS EDUCATION
See EDUCATION, RELIGIOUS
Rembar, Charles, 335a, 758, 2506, 2507, 2508
Remington Arms Company, 2868
Remos, Vince, 3571
Remsberg, Bonnie, 2509
Remsberg, Charles, 2509
Renfield, Richard, 759
REPRESSIVE TACTICS 548, 877, 1065, 1073, 1168, 1252, 1314, 1327, 1334, 1358, 1359, 1360, 1362, 1396, 1412, 1493, 1570, 1597, 1626, 1666, 1685, 1844, 1899, 2077, 2123, 2141, 2244, 2266, 2347, 2366, 2387, 2409, 2572, 2628, 2700, 2705, 2778, 3585, 4288, 4876, 5136
REPRESSIVE TACTICS--HIGH SCHOOL
See also HIGH SCHOOL--UNDERGROUND; See also Individual Names Of High Schools Under This Heading
2008, 2017, 2019, 2020, 2033, 2095, 2361, 4214, 4311, 4331
REPRESSIVE TACTICS (in the military) 1143, 1399, 2653
Republican Party Convention, 1968, 628
Republican Party. Public Relations Division, 4672
Research Center On Woman. Loretto Heights College, Denver, Colorado, 653, 849
Research Organizing Cooperative, 4002
Resek, Carl, 760

Reserve Officers Training
   Corps, 1890
Resnick, Jerry, 2200
Resnick, Mayer R., 2510
Resnik, H. S., 3285
Resnik, Henry S., 761
Reston, James B., 762, 2511
Reuben, David, 3713, 3831
Reuther, Walter, 4962
Revolutionary People's Con-
   stitutional Convention,
   Philadelphia, Pennsyl-
   vania, 1925, 2703
Revolutionary Socialist Union,
   2237
REVOLUTION, THEORY OF--
   ORIGINATING AND
   SUSTAINING CAUSES
   See also HIGH SCHOOL--
   UNDERGROUND; And Indi-
   vidual Names Of High
   Schools Under This Heading;
   REPRESSIVE TACTICS--
   HIGH SCHOOL; SOCIAL
   CHANGE
      53, 123, 157, 233, 276,
      279, 303, 361, 370,
      375, 378, 453, 469,
      493, 563, 573, 586a,
      604, 638, 669, 670,
      687, 722, 783, 784,
      836, 895, 977, 1361,
      1365, 1366, 1420, 1509,
      1673, 1691, 1693, 1695,
      1699, 1701, 1708, 1709,
      1743, 1770, 1802, 1825,
      1884, 1917, 2175, 2402,
      2433, 2440, 2579, 2591,
      2594, 2605, 2677, 2725,
      2780, 2806, 4518
Rexroth, Kenneth, 763
Rham, Edith De, 764
Rhodes, Gerald, 1008
Rice, Charles O., 2512, 2548,
   4971
Rice, Stephen, 2378
Richardson, Frank H., 3714
Richer, Ed., 4530, 4531
Richmond, Al, 2513
Richmond, Claude, 2514
Richter, Edward, 2515
Ridgeway, J., 2938, 4003
Ridgeway, James, 765, 766

Riegel, Robert E., 767, 768
Riker, Richard, 2516, 2517,
   2518, 2519, 2520,
   2521, 2522, 3286,
   3287, 3288, 3572,
   4532
Riesman, David, 1647, 3254,
   3946
Riga, Peter, 2523
Rigert, J., 2939
RIGHT AND LEFT (political
   science) 195a, 468, 557,
   567, 2676
Rights In Conflict, 5219
RIGHTS, LEGAL
   See LEGAL RIGHTS
RIGHT WING, IDEOLOGY 195a,
   800, 876, 2172, 2257,
   2518, 2744
Riley, T., 5271
Rios, Ann, 2524
RIOTS
   See also CONFLICT, INTER-
   RACIAL; Also names of in-
   dividual places where riots
   have taken place, including
   those in the military, e.g.,
   Chicago, Illinois; Detroit,
   Michigan; Harlem, New
   York City; Milwaukee, Wis-
   consin; Newark, New Jersey;
   Watts, California
      38, 84, 145, 182, 284,
      429, 666, 688, 799,
      833, 898, 907, 908,
      1325, 1370, 1538, 1570,
      1921, 2083, 2705, 2715,
      3362, 3391, 3459, 3470a,
      3493, 3507, 4043, 4811,
      4813a, 4820, 4841, 4856,
      4867, 4874, 4880, 4894,
      4901, 4903, 4944, 4998,
      5009, 5050, 5076, 5121,
      5164, 5210
Ritchie, Miller, 4533
Rizzo, Frank, 959
Robb, Alison, 2525
Robb, Charles C., 1569, 2527,
   2528, 2528a, 2529, 2530,
   2531, 2532, 2533, 2534,
   2535, 2536, 2537, 2538,
   2539, 2540, 2541, 2542,
   2543, 2543a, 2544, 2545,

2546, 2547, 2548, 2549,
 3573, 4790, 5395
Robbed-Bird, 2550
Robbins, John W., 2551
Robbins, Paul Jay, 2552
Roberson, Ed, 1008
Roberson, Marcis, 3574
Robert Morris Junior College,
 Pittsburgh, Pennsylvania,
 1374
Robert, Warren Penn, 2553
Roberts, Charles, 769
Roberts, D., 2869
Roberts, Dick, 2554
Roberts, Michael D., 297a
Roberts, Myron, 770
Roberts, Thomas B., 4534,
 4535
Robertson, Byron, 2555
Robertson, Collette, 2556
Robertson, J. L., 3074
Robinson, Chris, 4536, 4537
Robinson, Donald W., 3575
Robinson, Lora H., 4004
Robinson, Robbie, 2557
Robison, Sophia N., 5174
Robson, William A., 233
Rochdale Association, New
 Haven, Connecticut,
 2609
Roche, John P., 771, 4538
Rochester, New York, 4043
Rockefeller Foundation, 1121
Rockefeller, John D., 4539
Rockefeller, Nelson, 1936,
 2104, 2106
Rodberg, Leonard S., 772
Rodd, Bill, 2558, 3576
Rodgers, Jimmy, 1552, 1880
Rodriguez, Carlos, 2559
Rodwell, Craig, 2825
Roesel, Richard, 2560
Rogan, Donald L., 3075, 4005
Rogers, R., 4540
Rogin, M., 5175
Rokeach, Milton, 4006
Roldan, Julio, 1514
Rolfe, Lionel, 2561, 2562,
 2563
Rolph, C. H., 2940, 2941
Romaine, Howard, 2564
Romm, Ethel G., 3076
Romo, Ricardo, 1881

Root, Robert, 773
Rorvik, David M., 3289
Rose, Arnold M., 774, 775
Rose, Caroline B., 775
Rose, Thomas, 4910
Rose, William, 2565, 3290
Rosen, Sumner M., 2566
Rosenbaum, Robert A., 3077
Rosenberg, M. J., 4791
Rosenberg, Mark, 2567
Rosenblum, Art, 2568
Rosenblum, Sue, 2569
Rosenson, Mary, 2570
Rosenstone, R. A., 5021
Rosenthal, Alan, 3291
Rosenthal, Robert A., 3391
Ross, Ishbel, 777
Rosser, D., 3832
Rosset, Barney, 778, 2816
Rossi, Alice, 869, 2571
Rossi, Marna, 4792
Rossiter, Clinton L., 779
Rossof, Dave, 2572
Rostow, E. V., 5176
Roszak, Theodore, 780, 781,
 3292, 4007, 4911
Rothbard, Murray, 1375
Rothenberg, Leslie, 5272
Rothkrug, Barbara, 2573, 2574,
 2575
Rothlind, Dale, 2576
Rothschild, U. P., 1376
Rothstein, R., 4793, 4794,
 4795
Roucek, Joseph S., 2942, 3392
Roundtree, Martha, 2577
Rourke, Francis E., 3983
Roussopoulos, Dimitri, 67
Rovere, Richard H., 782,
 4796, 4797
Rowe, Robert N., 4541
Rowland, Howard Ray, 4542
Rowls, Betty M., 4543
ROYAL CANADIAN MOUNTED
 POLICE 5400
Rubenstein, A., 3293
Rubenstein, Annette T., 782a
Rubenstein, Ben, 4544
Rubenstein, Richard E., 4857,
 4912
Rubin, Gayle, 2578
Rubin, Isadore, 3715
Rubin, Jerry, 783, 784, 1377,

1467, 1791, 2171, 2481,
2579, 2580, 2625, 5177
Ruby, Jack, 1128, 2758, 5178
Rudd, Mark, 911, 2537, 3932, 4545
Rudovsky, David, 5060
Rudrum Report
See also Kent State University, Kent, Ohio
3954a
Rudwick, Elliott, 114
Ruether, Rosemary, 2581
Rules Of Engagement, 3435a
Rumper, Herman, 5396
Rusch, Richard B., 5179
Russell, Bertrand, 10, 273, 278, 385, 462, 785, 1532, 1534, 2085, 2101, 2597, 4673, 4977, 5180, 5181, 5186
Russell, Carlos E., 2689a
RUSSELL INTERNATIONAL WAR CRIMES TRIBUNAL
See also INTERNATIONAL WAR CRIMES TRIBUNAL
273, 476, 788, 1532, 1846, 1877, 2101
Russelt, B. M., 4798
Rustin, Bayard, 125, 785a, 2582, 4907
Rutgers University, New Brunswick, New Jersey, 2438
Ryan, J. J., 4546
Ryan, John, 3716
Ryan, Mary, 3716
Ryan, Sheila, 5182, 5183
Ryan, W. G., 4547
Ryman, E. C., 4548

Saal, H., 3294
Sadler, Lendon, 2583
SAFEGUARD ANTIBALLISTIC MISSILE SYSTEM 4664, 4669, 4670, 4727, 4734, 4797
SAFE STREETS ACT OF 1968
See OMNIBUS CRIME BILL OF 1968
Sagalyn, Arnold, 3577
Said, Abdul A., 786
St. Francis Acres, Hampton, New Jersey, 2609

St. John-Stevas, Norman, 3722, 3723
St. John's University, Jamaica, New York, 4012
St. Mary Of The Woods College, Indiana, 4632
Salazar, Ruben, 2204
Sale, J. Kirk, 5184
Salerno, Ralph, 4913
Salinger, Pierre, 769
Salstrom, F. P., 1917, 2584, 5397
Sampson, Edward E., 4008, 4549, 4550
San Antonio, Texas, 2754
San Clemente, California, 1115
Sanders, Ed, 2585, 2586, 2587, 2588, 2589, 2590
Sanders, Ellen, 2591
Sanders, Jacquin, 5273
San Diego, California, 1040, 1166, 1379, 1650, 3424, 3442, 4082, 4090
San Diego State College, San Diego, California, 1462, 4090, 4143
Sandow, Greg, 4770
Sandys-Winsch, G., 2870
San Fernando Valley State College, Northridge, California, 4014, 4280, 4281, 4348, 4463, 4465
Sanford, David, 4551, 4552
Sanford, Nevitt, 3077, 4008a, 4009, 4390
Sanford, North Carolina, 5211
Sanford, Terry, 4834
San Francisco, California, 1536, 1913, 2323, 2524
San Francisco State College, San Francisco, California, 702a, 2038, 3862, 3921, 3996a, 4002, 4014, 4099, 4107, 4174, 4185, 4197, 4201, 4278, 4280, 4329, 4343, 4344, 4356, 4366, 4380, 4433, 4446, 4572, 4573, 4597
San Francisco Theological Seminary, 5322
Sanger, Margaret, 266a, 513
San Jose State College, San Jose, California, 5070

San Luis Obispo, California, 2379
San Quentin, California, 1382, 1875, 2378
Santa Barbara, California, 2385, 3449
Santmire, H. Paul, 787
Sapir, Carrie, 4553
Sapir, Marc, 4553
Sargeant, Jay, 2463
Sartre, Jean-Paul, 788, 789, 810, 2592, 2593, 2594, 2595, 2596, 2597, 5185
Sasajima, Masu, 4010
Satlow, I. D., 2598
Satz, David M. Jr., 1067
Saul, Mort, 1869, 1870
Saunders, Charles B. Jr., 3393
Sauvage, Leo, 790
Savitz, Leonard, 3394
Sawyer, Lynwood, 2599
Saxton, Al, 2600
Sayler, R. H., 4914
Saylor, J. Galen, 3937
Sayre, Nora, 3554, 5398
SCANDINAVIAN SYSTEM OF SEX EDUCATION, 3727
Schaap, Richard, 3079
Schaar, John H., 4035
Schanche, Don A., 791, 2600a
Schechter, Dan, 2601
Schechtman, Michael, 2602
Scheer, Robert, 194, 792, 947, 1874, 1876, 2081, 2171, 2168a, 2603, 2604, 5186, 5187
Schell, Jonathan, 793, 794
Schelling, Thomas C., 795, 4674
SCHEMPP AND ENGEL CASES, 260a
Scheper, Nancy, 2118
Scherer, Frederick M., 718
Scheuer, Sandy, 1263
Scheur, James H., 3395
Schillaci, Anthony, 796
Schiller, Herbert I., 797, 797a
Schiller, Lawrence, 580
Schleier, Curt, 2605
Schlesinger, Arthur M. Jr., 798, 4555, 4915, 4916

Schmitt, Karl M., 563
Schneider, Mark, 2606
Schneider, William Jr., 4666
Schneir, Walter, 799
Schoenberger, Robert A., 800
Schoenbrun, David, 801
Schoenfeld, Eugene, 2607, 2608, 3080, 3717
Schoenfeld, Janet D., 4004
Schonover, Mary, 4228
School Of Living. Brookville, Ohio, 592, 2609
SCHOOLS, CENTRALIZATION 17, 85, 306, 574
SCHOOLS (ghetto) 306, 497, 528, 2765
SCHOOLS, SELF GOVERNMENT See also EDUCATION, COMMUNITY CONTROL; EDUCATION, SECONDARY 66, 1383
Schoonbeck, J., 3295
Schrag, Peter, 802, 803, 2609a, 4556
Schreiber, F. R., 5188
Schreiber, James A., 2610, 2611, 3578
Schroeder, William, 1263
Schroth, R. A., 4557
Schuchter, Arnold, 804, 805
Schulder, Diane B., 2612
Schultz, John, 807, 2613
Schultz, Ray, 2614, 3579, 4558
Schulz, David A., 806
Schulz, Esther D., 3718
Schuman, Howard, 4832
Schur, Edwin M., 3719, 4917
Schurmann, Franz, 808, 2615, 2616, 2617, 2618, 4675
Schuster, Eunice M., 809
Schutt, M., 3806
Schwab, Joseph J., 4011
Schwalb, Myrna, 3296
Schwartz, Alan V., 296
Schwartz, Barry N., 810
Schwartz, Don, 5399
Schwartz, E. K., 5189
Schwartz, Herman, 2619
Schwartz, Jon, 2620
Schwartz, Ray, 2621
Schwartz, Richard F., 242
Schwerner, Michael, 2295
Schwiebert, Ernest G., 4676

Sciarra, John H., 3635
SCIENCE AND THE GENERA-
  TIONAL GAP, 3231
SCIENTIFIC-MILITARY-INDUS-
  TRIAL COMPLEX 210,
  684b
Scimecca, Joseph, 4012
Scorpio, Paul, 3297
Scott, Anne F., 811
Scott, Hugh, 4744
Scott, J. P., 4918, 5190
Scott, Jack, 812, 1883, 2622,
  5191
Scott, Joseph W., 3254
Scott, M. B., 4012a
Scott, Maurice Jr., 812a
Scott, Peter Dale, 2623
Scott, Robert L., 813, 2624,
  4559
Scoville, Herbert, 4677
Scranton Commission Report,
  1066, 4086, 4274, 4557
Scranton, William, 3988, 4274
Scull, Jerolyn R., 5400
Seale, Bobby, 174, 193, 814,
  815, 1016, 1036, 1037,
  1100, 1196, 1445, 1947,
  1948, 1968, 2267, 2279,
  2302, 2455, 2625, 2626,
  2627, 2628, 2629, 2630,
  2631, 2632, 2708, 4560
Seale, Patrick, 4013, 4919
Seaman, Barbara, 816
SEARCH AND SEIZURE LAW
  See Items Listed In The
  Section "Police-Community
  Relationships" e.g., 3401,
  3497; PRIVACY, RIGHT OF
Sears, David O., 5192
Seattle, Washington, 3487, 4165
SECRET SERVICE POLICE,
  3544
Seeger, Pete, 782, 1316, 2532,
  2848
Seeman, Melvin, 4561
Segal, Judith A., 816a
Segal, Patricia, 4013a
Segal, Ronald, 817
Segers, Mary C., 2633
SEGREGATION 492, 689, 729a,
  5216
SEGREGATION IN EDUCATION
  231, 782a, 921, 948,
  964, 1383, 1384, 2016,
  4477
Seidenbaum, Art, 4014
Seiler, J. A., 2634
Seiley, John, 3912
Seingrass, Bob, 2635
Seitz, J. C., 542
Selassie I, Haile (Emperor)
  1774, 2785
SELECTIVE SERVICE ACTS
  AND REGULATIONS
  See Items Listed In The Sec-
  tion "Military Service--
  Compulsory And Voluntary"
  e.g., 5250
Selective Service Law Reporter,
  5274
SELECTIVE SERVICE SYSTEM
  See Items Listed In The Sec-
  tion "Military Service--
  Compulsory And Voluntary"
  e.g., 5374
SELF-MUTILATION
  See TATTOES AND TATTOO-
  ING (including henna)
Seligman, Ben B., 4015
Selk, M., 4562
Selkirk, Errol, 2636, 4563
Sellers, Cleveland, 3989
Semark, Jim, 3298
Semas, Philip W., 4188, 4564,
  4565
SEPARATION OF CHURCH AND
  STATE
  See BIBLE READING IN THE
  PUBLIC SCHOOLS; EDUCA-
  TION, RELIGIOUS; RELI-
  GION IN THE PUBLIC
  SCHOOLS
SEPARATISM, BLACK
  See BLACK SEPARATISM
Serra, Normand, 3580
Servan-Schreiben, J. J., 818,
  4016
Sevareid, Eric, 113
Severy, Bruce, 2637
Sewal, Charles, 1374
Seward, Becky, 2638
SEX AND RELIGION
  See Items Listed In The Sec-
  tion "The Pregnant Question
  --Sex Education" e.g., 3631,
  3637, 3837

SEX EDUCATION, SEX IN-
    STRUCTION IN PUBLIC
    AND PRIVATE SCHOOLS
  See Items Listed In The
    Section "The Pregnant Ques-
    tion--Sex Education" e.g.,
    3616, 3620
Sex Information And Education
    Council Of The U.S.,
    3778
SEX, PREMARITAL
  See Items Listed In The
    Section "The Pregnant Ques-
    tion--Sex Education" e.g.,
    3609a, 3639, 3663, 3681
Sexton, Patricia Cayo, 819
SEXUAL FREEDOM
  See FREEDOM, SEXUAL
SEXUAL RESPONSIBILITY AND
    MARRIAGE
  See Items Listed In The
    Section "The Pregnant Ques-
    tion--Sex Education" e.g.,
    3632
SEXUAL REVOLUTION
  See Items Listed In The
    Section "The Pregnant Ques-
    tion--Sex Education";
    FREEDOM, SEXUAL
Shade, William G., 820
Shadyside, Pittsburgh, Pennsyl-
    vania, 1396
Shaffer, Helen B., 821
Shafikh, James, 3580a
Shagnasty, Oliver, 2639
Shahn, B., 5193
Shakur, Afeni, 2640, 2641
Shapiro, Andrew O., 5275
Shapiro, Peter, 3862
Shapiro, S., 2642
Shaplen, Robert, 822, 823,
    824
Sharp, Gene, 4920
Sharp, L., 5401
Shaull, Richard, 698
Shaw, Clay, 1129, 2166, 2747
Shaw Marth, Ashley Falls,
    Massachusetts, 2609
Shaw, Russell, 825
Shayne, Bob, 2643
Shayon, R. L., 3299
Shea Bill, Massachusetts, 915,
    4935

Shear, Jeff, 2644
Shearer, Derek, 772
Shecter, Leonard, 2645
Shedd, Mark, 761
Sheen, Fulton J., 3583
Sheerin, J. B., 5194
Sheer, Robert, 1350
Sheinbaum, Stanley K., 2081
Shenker, Alan, 3300
Sheppard, Harold L., 11
Sherif, Carolyn W., 3081
Sherif, Muzafer, 3081
Sherk, J. H., 5195, 5402
Sherman, S., 4
Shero, Jeff, 2646, 2647
Sherrill, R., 2943
Sherrill, R. G., 5196
Shidler, Sam, 2648
Shiloh Community, Sherman,
    New York, 2609
Shinto, William, 4017
Shirk, Evelyn, 3958
Shoben, Edward J. Jr., 4566,
    4567, 4568, 4569
Shoemaker, Sydney, 3082
Shorris, Earl, 4570
Short, James J., 4921
Shotwell, Louisa R., 826
Shuba, George, 2649
Shuett, Suzanne, 2650
Sibley, Mulford Q., 4922, 5197,
    5198, 5276
SIECUS 3656, 3720
Siegel, Arthur I., 3396
Siegel, Ed, 2651
Siegelman, Ellen, 365
Sierra Mountains, California,
    1130
SIETE CASE 1721
Sigel, Roberta, 4031
Sikes, Melvin P., 3581
Silber, Irwin, 2652, 2653
Silberman, Charles E., 826a,
    827, 828
SILENT MAJORITY 918, 971,
    1258, 1400, 1401, 1906,
    1992, 1999, 2262, 3282,
    4032
Silenus, 3582
Simmons, Bob, 2654
Simon, John, 1962
Simon, P., 5199
Simon, Randy, 1374

Simon, William, 3647
Sinclair, 2655
Sinclair, John, 1202, 1491, 1492, 1597, 2160, 2656
Sinclair, Magdalene, 2656
Sinclair, Upton, 1378
Singer, Cris, 2657
Singer, Marshall, 4763
Singh, Yogendra, 4934
SIOUX INDIANS 251, 1542, 2099
Sirhan-Charach Case, 1857
Sirhan, Mary, 1841
Sirhan, Sirhan, 1841, 1842, 1843
Sisk, John P., 4571, 5200
SIT-INS 907, 1126, 1417, 1503, 2293, 4064, 5138
Skir, L., 2658
Sklar, Martin J., 2659
Skolnick, Jerome, 3301, 3397, 4923, 5201
Skolnick Report, 5183, 5201
Skolnikoff, E. B., 5202
Sky View Acres, Pomona, New York, 2609
Slater, B. R., 2660
Slater, Don, 5362
Slater, Philip E., 829
Slater, R. Giuseppi, 4572, 4573
SLAVERY, LEGACY OF 1950
Sleeper, Charles F., 830
Sloan, William Coffin Jr., 4943
Slodtheck, Fred L., 4921
Smallenberg, C., 3833
Smallenberg, H., 3833
Smart, Reginald G., 3083
Smelser, N. J., 4018
Smith, Bruce, 3398
Smith, Chip, 2661
Smith, David E., 3084
Smith, Donald K., 2624
Smith, Duane E., 74, 352
Smith, Ernest A., 3720a
Smith, Gar, 5403
Smith, George S., 1850
Smith, G. Kerry, 3986
Smith, H. W., 5203
Smith, Jack A., 2662, 2663
Smith, Jim, 2664
Smith, John, 2665

Smith, M., 3815, 3834
Smith, Marvin, 2666
Smith, Michael, 2667
Smith, Page, 831
Smith, R. Dean, 3398a
Smith, Ralph Lee, 2668, 3399
Smith, Rebecca, 3814
Smith, Robert F., 832
Smith, Sally L., 3085
Smith, Tanya R., 2663
Smith, Tommie, 1009, 2158, 2389
Smith, Victoria, 4574
Smith, William Gardner, 833
Smothers Brothers (Television Show) 1316, 1736, 1860
Smothers, Dick, 2669
Smothers, Tom, 2669
Smukler, Michael, 2670
Smylie, James H., 2671, 2672
Snider, A. J., 3302
SNIFFING
    Glue, 3256; Lighter Fluid, 3200
Snyder, Gary, 833a, 2673
Snyder, L. J., 4574a
Snyder, Ross, 3086
Soares, Anthony, 4575
Soares, Louise, 4575
Sobel, Lester A., 834
Sobell, Morton, 1257, 2351
Socarides, Charles, 1403
SOCIAL CHANGE
    See also REVOLUTION, THEORY OF--ORIGINATING AND SUSTAINING CAUSES
    40, 366, 412, 607a, 615, 829, 836, 866, 1461, 1963, 2569, 2673, 3001, 4323, 4841, 4998
SOCIAL DISCRIMINATION
    See ANTI-SEMITISM
SOCIALISM
    See also IDEOLOGY, THEORY OF
    12, 583, 638, 695, 1055, 1918, 2085, 2312, 2659
SOCIALISM (Cuba) 695
Socialist Workers Party 4626
SOCIAL PROBLEMS-1960--U.S.
    See U.S. SOCIAL PROBLEMS-1960-

Society For Humane Abortions, 2363
Society For Preservation Of Early American Standards, Oxford, New York, 2609
SOCIETY OF BROTHERS Evergreen Community, Norfolk, Connecticut; New Meadow Run Community, Farmington, Pennsylvania; Woodcrest Community, Rifton, New York
For A General Article On The Society Of Brothers See 2609
Society Of Families, Frewsburg, New York, 2609
SOCIETY OF FRIENDS 5276
SOCIOLOGY LIBERATION MOVEMENT 1406
SODOMY (laws) 1072
SODOMY (trials) 1072
Sofia Perovskaya And Andrei Zelyabov Memorial, 1410
Solanas, Valerie, 835
SOLEDAD BROTHERS 1718, 2351, 2432, 2459, 2524
SOLEDAD PRISON, CALIFORNIA, 480, 2459, 2524
Solomon, D., 3087
Somerville, Don H., 3835
Sommer, John, 598
Sons Of Levi, Mansfield, Missouri, 2609
Sontag, Susan, 2674
Soper, Will, 4799
SORCERY 1897
Sorel, George, 4924
Sorel, Jules, 4576
Sorokin, Pitirim A., 836
Southard, Helen F., 3721
Southard, Samuel, 837
South Carolina State College, Orangeburg, South Carolina, 3989, 5157
SOUTHEAST ASIA
See ASIA, SOUTHEAST
Southern Bell Telephone, 2356
Southern Christian Leadership Conference, 2738, 4049
Southern Methodist University, Dallas, Texas, 1402, 1610, 1625, 4639
Southern Rural Research Project, 2118
Southern Student Organizing Committee, 1416, 2727
SOUTH VIETNAM 206, 582
Sovern, Michael I., 838
SOVIET UNION 32
Sowle, Claude R., 3400
Sparrow, J., 2675
Sparzo, F. J., 4577
Spater, Bill, 2698
Specter, Arlen, 3401
SPEECH, FREEDOM OF 163, 700a, 985, 1488, 4623
Spence, Larry D., 2676, 4578
Spender, S., 4579
Spender, Stephen, 3088
Sperber, Manes, 839
Spiegel, John P., 4580, 4581
Spiegelberg, B., 2920
Spike, Robert W., 840
Spinrad, Norman, 2677, 2678
Spiro, Melford E., 841
Spitzer, Dana, 3254, 5348
Spitzer, John, 193
Spock, Benjamin, 668, 841a, 841b, 842, 1264, 1415, 2009, 2161, 2461, 2532, 2651, 3089, 3836, 5312
SPORTS
See ATHLETICS
Sprague, Richard A., 1787
Sprouls, Joseph R., 4582
Squires, Raymond, 4583
Stack, Evan, 2679
Stafford, Robert, 5277
Stalvey, Lois Mark, 843
Stamberg, Margie, 2680, 2681
STANDING ROCK SIOUX, INDIANS 251
Stanford Statement, 5154
Stanford Research Institute, 2944
Stanford University, Palo Alto, California, 1417, 4014, 4587, 4625, 5154
Stanley, D. T., 4678
Stanley, M., 5204

STANLEY VS. GEORGIA 975a
Stanton, Charles M., 4019
Stapleton, Syd, 2842
Stapp, Andy, 844
Star, J., 2682
Star, Jack, 3837
Starnes, R., 2873
Starr, Paul, 4584
STATE RIGHTS 644
Stayton, Dick, 2683
Stearn, Jess, 3090
Steeger, Henry, 845
Steel-City 26, (Pittsburgh) 1418, 1472, 1479
Steele, Bill, 2684
Steele, Lloyd, 2685
Stein, David L., 846
Stein, Jean, 726
Stein, M. L., 4585
Stein, Maurice R., 930
Stein, Sandi, 2478
Steinberg, David, 4285
Steiner, Gary A., 847
Steiner, Stan, 848
Steinmetz, U. G., 3838
Steinnmann, Anne, 849
Sterling, Wallace, 1417
Stermer, Dugald, 1350, 2685a, 2686
Stern, Daniel J., 2687
Stern, David H., 2688
Stern, G., 4586
Stern, Karl, 850
Stern, Linda, 3303
Stern, Max, 2689
Stern, Peter S., 4587
Stern, Sol, 2689a, 2690, 2691, 4588, 5205
Sternglass, E. J., 4800
Stevens, Anita, 3091
Stevens, Franklin, 5278
Stevens, Warren K., 1031, 1093, 1332
Stevenson, Ian, 850a
Stevick, Daniel, 4925
Stewart, Evelyn S., 857
Stickgold, Mark, 2692, 5404
Stillman, Elinor, 2693
Stinchcombe, Arthur L., 4020
STOCKADES, MILITARY
Camp Pendleton, California, 2446; Fort Dix, New Jersey, 1117, 1292, 1594, 2111, 2559; Fort Hood, Texas, 500, 979, 1921; Fort Jackson, South Carolina, 1119, 1353; Fort Leonard Wood, Missouri, 980; Fort Lewis, Oregon, 980; Fort Lewis, Tacoma, Washington, 1120; Fort Ord, California, 1937; Fort Riley, Kansas, 1353; Presidio Army Base Stockade, San Francisco, California, 346, 980, 1337, 1531, 1847, 2635, 2649, 2697
Stocker, Michael, 5206
Stockholm International Peace Research Institute, 4679
Stokes, Carl, 2268, 2842
Stokes, R., 3304
Stokes, Walter R., 3838a
Stone, Carla Sydney, 3839
Stone, Chuck, 851
Stone, Harvey, 2694
Stone, Isidor F., 4020a
Stone, Richard, 2695
Stone, W. Clement, 4107
Storing, Herbert J., 852
St. Petersburg, Florida, 1319
Strata, Liz S., 4589
Stratford, New Jersey (Camden) 3469
Stratton, Samuel S., 5339
Strauss, Frances, 853
Strawberry Statement, 1598
Street, David, 2696
Striker, John M., 5275
STRIKES 1544
STRIKES AND LOCKOUTS--POSTAL 1603
Stringfellow, William, 854
Strip (Military) Base Shops G.I., 2665
Strong, Dennis F., 3092
Strong, Dennis M., 2697
Strong, Donald S., 855
Strouse, Jean, 856
Strout, Cushing, 4021
Struchen, Jeannette, 3093
Stuckey, Gilbert B., 3402
STUDENT ANTIWAR COALITION 1423

STUDENT FACULTY RELA-
TIONSHIPS
See Items Listed In The
Section "Student Dissent"
e.g., 4313, 4388
STUDENTS FOR A DEMO-
CRATIC SOCIETY
Chicago, Illinois, 1157,
3894, 4520; Cornell Uni-
versity, New York,
1333; Detroit, Michigan,
1387, 1388; Los Ange-
les, California, 1389;
Miami, Florida, 1991;
Port Huron, Michigan,
4021a; Pittsburgh, Penn-
sylvania, 1390, 1418,
1472, 1478, 1479, 2237,
2528; 1176, 1179, 1229,
1386, 1391, 1392, 1606,
1730, 1815, 1893, 1945,
1954, 1970, 2060, 2061,
2086, 2159, 2185, 2280,
2405, 2406, 2458, 2463,
2492, 2662, 2698, 2699,
2808, 2849, 3314, 3954a,
4051, 4090, 4131, 4132,
4141, 4265, 4372, 4411,
4423, 4488, 4510, 4954
Students For Progressive Action, 1428, 1429
Stupak, Ronald J., 4590
SUBVERSIVE ACTIVITIES
See HOUSE COMMITTEE
ON UN-AMERICAN ACTI-
VITIES
Such, Rod, 2700, 2701, 2702,
2703, 2704, 2705, 3583,
3584
Suchlicki, Jaime, 4022
SUICIDE, COMPARATIVE
3722, 3723
Suiter, John, 2706, 2707, 2708
Sullivan, John L., 3403
Sullivan, Neil V., 857
Sullivan, Susan, 2709
Summerskill, John, 1541, 3516
Sundberg, Jim, 2710
Sunnygoode Street Commune,
Ann Arbor, Michigan,
1420
Supak, Jon, 2711

SUPPLEMENTAL STUDIES FOR
THE NATIONAL ADVI-
SORY COMMISSION ON
CIVIL DISORDERS 4926
Surface, William, 3094
Surowiec, Mike, 2712
Susajima, Masu, 4590a
Sutherland, Elizabeth, 858
Sutherland, Z., 3840
Sutton, Horace, 3305
Svensson, Arne, 3404
Swaney, Tom, 1194
Swanger, Harry, 3439
Swanson, Guy E., 3978
Sweeney, Michael, 2713, 2714
Sweezy, Paul M., 469, 859
Swerfloff, Howard, 4591
Swimm, Dudley, 2133
Swomley, J. M. Jr., 860,
5405
Sylvester, Eugene A., 2715
Symonds, Gardinar, 4592
Synanon Foundation, Santa Moni-
ca, California, 2609
Synanon, Tomales Bay Ranch,
Santa Monica, Califor-
nia, 2666
Sywak, William, 2315
Szwed, John F., 861

Tabor, Joyce M., 735, 736
Tabor, Robert, 862
Taing, R. D., 2716
Talbot, Allan R., 4927
Tampa, Florida, 3463
Tanguy Homesteads, West
Chester, Pennsylvania,
2609
Tannenbaum, Abraham J.,
4593
Tappan, Paul W., 3405
Target, G. W., 863
Tarr, Curtis W., 5303, 5369
Tasker Project, 3426
Tate, James H., 1765
Tate, Willis M., 1610, 4639
TATTOES AND TATTOOING
(including henna) 1433,
2072, 2368, 2454
Tatum, Arlo, 5279
Tatz, Mark, 4594

Taube, Skip, 2717
Taubman, William, 4023
Tax, Sol, 5280, 5406
Taylor, D. R., 5378
Taylor, Gen. Telford, 864
Taylor, Gilbert W., 3050
Taylor, Harold, 4024, 4595
Taylor, Maxwell, 1395, 2323
Taylor, Norman, 3095
Taylor, Robert N., 4025
Taylor, Vonna, 2718
TEACHER STRIKES
See also Individual Names Of Places Where Teacher Strikes Have Taken Place, e.g., New York Teacher's Strike, 1968, 648
884
TEACHER UNIONS 96, 949, 2519
TEACHING 759, 884, 1554
TEACHING AND SEX EDUCATION
See Items Listed In The Section "The Pregnant Question-Sex Education"
TEACHING, COLLEGE AND UNIVERSITY--EVALUATION OF 888a, 1811
TEACHING, EVALUATION OF, HIGH SCHOOL 1030
TEACH-INS (theory of) 651, 1102, 1823, 2169, 2227, 2498, 2499, 2531, 2638, 2791, 2851, 3974
TEAMSTERS UNION
See International Brotherhood Of Teamsters, Chauffeurs, Warehousemen And Helpers Union
Tebor, Irving R., 3840a
TECHNETRONICS 137, 781
TECHNOLOGY 40, 115, 166, 310, 318, 339, 377, 488, 657, 677, 781, 872, 1092, 1236, 1392, 2652
TECHNOLOGY--IMPACT ON SOCIETY 266b, 377, 488, 553, 554, 555, 615, 631, 650a, 657, 677, 716, 781, 797, 872, 1106, 1236, 1392,
1625, 1780, 2050, 2480, 2549, 2652, 2720a, 3065, 3931, 5033
Tefferteller, Ralph, 3040
TELEVISION BROADCASTING, 847, 1297, 2669
Teller, E., 4680, 4801, 4802
Temple University, Philadelphia, Pennsylvania, 1434, 4155, 4354, 4355
Templin, Ralph T., 4928
Teodori, Massimo, 865
Tepperman, Jean, 2719, 3585
Terkel, Studs, 866
Terris, B. J., 3586
Tessler, Mark A., 4596
Texaco, Inc., 1912
Texas 5, 1438
THANATOLOGY 2477
Thayer, George, 4681
Thelwell, Michael, 4597
Theobold, Robert, 1439
THEOLOGY, CONFLICTS 133, 138, 208, 258, 260, 410, 556, 671, 697, 703, 742, 2487
THEOLOGY, RADICAL 15, 16, 95a, 101, 104, 138, 161, 218, 260, 282, 361, 373, 389, 570, 642, 696, 742, 888, 899, 1053, 1522, 2512
Therese And Isabelle (Movie) 1112, 1441, 2516
Thigpen, R. B., 5207
Thiher, Gary, 2720
THIRD WORLD 1691, 1711, 1714
THIRD WORLD WOMEN'S ALLIANCE 1593
Thomas, Gordon B., 2720a
Thomas, Niel, 2721
Thomas, Norman, 2722
Thomas, Wendell, 2723
Thomlinson, Ralph, 867
Thompson, Elizabeth J., 256
Thompson, Hunter S., 868
Thompson, James D., 2724
Thompson, John, 1488
Thompson, Josiah, 1809
Thompson, Mary Lou, 869
Thompson, Robert, 870
Thompson, S., 4598

Thompson, S. M., 5208
Thompson, Scott D., 4599
Thoreau, Henry David, 449, 1265
Thornburg, H., 4600
Thornburgh, Richard L., 2725
Thorne, Richard, 3841
Thornley, Cara, 2726
Thornley, Kerry, 1637, 2726
Thrasher, Sue, 2727
Thurmond, Strom, 1995, 4682
Tierney, Kevin, 3406
Tiffany, Lawrence P., 3587
Tijerina, Reies, 684
Tim, Tiny, 2115
TIMAEUS
See ATLANTIS
Tinker, Jerry M., 871
Tinker, John, 2560
Tinker, Mary Beth, 2560
Tippit, J. D., 2803
Tobin, R. L., 2728
Tobis, David, 5407
Toch, Hans H., 4929
Todorovich, M. M., 1063
Toffler, Alvin, 872
Tolstoy Farm, Davenport, Washington, 2609
Tolstoy, Leo, 4930, 5209
Tombs Prison (New York City) 1779
Tomlinson, K. Y., 5408
Tomlinson, T. M., 5210
Tompkins, John S., 4913
Tonsar, Stephen J., 4601, 4602, 4603
Toole, K. Ross, 3306, 4604
Toombs, New York, 1514
Tornquist, Elizabeth, 2729, 2730, 2731, 2732, 2733, 2734, 2735, 2736, 2737, 2738, 3307, 3588, 3589, 3590, 3591, 4605, 4606, 4607, 4608, 5211
Torrence, Michael, 2739
Totten, W. Fred, 873
Towle, Kathryn, 4483
Towler, Juby E., 3407
Towsend, J. R., 4802
Tract For Our Times--Editors, Liberation Magazine, 2311
Trager, Frank N., 874, 4609

TRANSEXUAL 1822, 1823
TRANSVESTITES 1823
Travers, Milton, 3096
Treadwell, Perry, 1727
Treasure Island, San Francisco, California, 2683
TREATY ON THE NON-PROLIFERATION OF NUCLEAR WEAPONS, 4660
Trent, James W., 3097, 4610
Trial Of The U 2, The 875
Trials Of The Resistance, 4931
Tribble, Ike, 4611
Trilling, Diana, 4612
Trimberger, Ellen K., 4613
Triton Foundation, Cambridge, Massachusetts, 2168
Triton Study, Cambridge Massachusetts, 2168
Triunes Incorporated, Oakland, California, 2609
Tronzo, Albert, 1481
Tropman, J. E., 4614
Trounstine, Phil, 2740
Trout, G. D. Jr., 4615
Trow, Martin, 3933
Trow, W. C., 4616
Truce, Betty A., 4445
Truman, Dean, 3932
Trump, J. Lloyd, 4617
Truskier, Andy, 2741
Trytten, M. H., 5280a
Tschetter Colony, Olivet, South Dakota, 2609
Tuccille, Jerome, 876
Tuchinsky, Joseph S., 5279
Tucker, Frank H., 877
Tucker, Nancy, 2742
Tucker, Robert W., 878
Tucker, Sterling, 879, 880
Tumin, Melvin M., 5212
Tunley, Paul, 3408
Tunley, R., 3308
Turner, Jon, 2743
Turner, William W., 881, 1350, 2201, 2744, 2745, 2746, 2747, 2748, 2749, 2803, 3409, 4932, 5213
Tussman, Joseph, 4026, 4933
Tuttle, Lyle, 1433
Twining, N. F., 4683
Tyack, David B., 2750
Tydings, Joseph, 2917

Tyler, Gus, 5214
Tyler, Robin, 1503
Tyre, Marlene, 5409
Tyrrell, C. Merton, 881a, 4684
Tytell, John, 3945

Udall, Stewart L., 882
Uhnak, Dorothy, 3410
Ulam, Adam B., 883
Ullman, J. E., 4685
UN-AMERICAN ACTIVITIES
    See HOUSE COMMITTEE ON UN-AMERICAN ACTIVITIES
Un Chant D'Amour, 2219
UNDERGROUND (church) 112, 1372
UNDERGROUND-HIGH SCHOOL
    See HIGH SCHOOL--UNDERGROUND
UNDERGROUND MOVEMENT
    309, 1484, 1546, 1580, 1629, 1713, 1792, 1802, 2307, 2308, 2695, 2993, 4264
UNDERGROUND (newspapers)
    998, 1110, 1260, 1261, 1302, 1303, 1320, 1331, 1402, 1452, 1454, 1455, 1456, 1457, 1475, 1482, 1573, 1600, 1640, 1713, 1729, 1792, 1837, 1838, 2197, 2200, 2271, 2296, 2320, 2322, 2427, 2444, 2647, 2695, 2857, 3501
UNDERGROUND (newspapers) HIGH SCHOOL 89, 825a, 990, 994, 1074, 1185, 1207, 1385, 1612, 2033, 2068, 2319, 2533, 2583, 4200, 4208
UNDERGROUND (newspapers) IN THE MILITARY
    1125, 1242, 2046, 2184
UNDERGROUND PRESS
    See UNDERGROUND (newspapers)
UNDERSEA MILITARY BASES--UNDERWATER MISSILE SYSTEMS 2065, 4760
Ungs, Thomas D., 693a

UNIONS AND UNION ACTIVITIES
    See also LABOR UNIONS;
    For Unions Connected With Teaching See: TEACHER UNIONS
    172, 900, 920, 1090, 1227, 1228, 1311, 2465, 2637
UNITED AUTO WORKERS 2251, 2254, 4962
United Farmworkers Organizing Committee, 1232, 1826
United Front Against Fascism, 2572
United Press Syndicate, 1456, 2751
Unity Village, Lees Summit, Missouri, 2609
UNIVERSITIES AND COLLEGES --GOVERNANCE OF
    See COLLEGES AND UNIVERSITIES--GOVERNANCE OF
University Of Buffalo, New York, 4428
University Of California. Academic Senate. Senate Committee On Education, Berkeley, 3880, 4283
University Of California, Berkeley, 2285, 2292, 2636, 3879a, 3881, 4014, 4052, 4107, 4116, 4320, 4309, 4315, 4321, 4379, 4392, 4412, 4457, 4466, 4478, 4483, 4512, 4353, 4564, 4578, 4628
University Of California, Los Angeles, 2315, 4014, 4107
University Of California, San Diego, 4159
University Of Chicago, Chicago, Illinois, 2556
University Of Connecticut, Storrs, Connecticut, 4362, 4574
University Of Michigan, Ann Arbor, Michigan, 4330
University Of Nebraska, Lincoln, Nebraska, 1458, 1459, 3374a

University Of North Carolina, Chapel Hill, North Carolina, 1985, 4240
University Of Oregon, Eugene, Oregon, 3907
University Of Pennsylvania, Philadelphia, Pennsylvania, 4115, 4552
University Of Pittsburgh, Pittsburgh, Pennsylvania, 2545, 3839, 4532
University Of Texas, Arlington, Texas, 4163, 4251, 4475
University Of Washington, Seattle, Washington, 4594
University Of Wisconsin, Madison, Wisconsin, 2427, 3921, 4061, 4140, 4408
UNIVERSITY PARADIGM
See INDUSTRIAL-MILITARY-GOVERNMENT-EDUCATIONAL COMPLEX
UNIVERSITY PARTICIPATION IN MILITARY EFFORTS
See also INDUSTRIAL-MILITARY-GOVERNMENT-EDUCATIONAL COMPLEX
650a, 684a, 1062, 1316, 1889, 1971, 2315, 2691, 4105, 4129, 4477, 4574
Unnithan, T. K., 4934
Unruh, Jesse M., 1460a, 2561, 2752
Upsala College, East Orange, New Jersey, 4353
Upton, E., 5281
Urban Research Corporation, 4026a
URBAN RIOTS
See RIOTS
Urofsky, Melvin, 884
Urquhart, Mike, 4618
Ury, C. M., 2753
Ushindi, Tamu, 2351
U. S. Army (Attempts At Unionization) 844
U. S. Army (Corps Of Engineers) 2052
U. S. Army (Military Police School) 3410a

U. S. Bureau Of Narcotics, 3523
U. S. Civil Service Commission, 885
U. S. Commission On Civil Rights, 886
U. S. Constitutional Law, 532
U. S. Department Of Labor. Wage And Labor Standards Administration, 887
U. S. Library Of Congress. Legislative Reference Service, 4026b
U. S. MONOPOLIES
See MONOPOLIES--U. S.
U. S. Office Of Education, 887a
U. S. President's Commission On An All-Volunteer Armed Force, 4026c
U. S. President's Commission On Law Enforcement And Administration Of Justice
See President's Commission On Law Enforcement And Administration Of Justice
U. S. Senate. Committee On Government Operation. Permanent Subcommittee On Investigations, 4026d
U. S. SOCIAL PROBLEMS-1960-8, 83, 97, 106, 111, 141, 173, 217, 230, 256, 272, 331, 366, 380, 405, 412, 416, 427, 515, 576, 597, 635, 646, 683, 729, 775, 866, 879, 880, 897, 908, 940, 1486, 1487, 1905, 1994, 2012, 2261, 2399, 2419, 2577, 3004, 3341, 3354, 3430
USS PUEBLO
See PUEBLO (ship) USS PUEBLO
U. S. Superintendent Of Documents, 5282, 5283
U. S. SUPREME COURT 495, 948, 1431
U. S. Task Force On Narcotics And Drug Abuse, 3098

U. S. VS. JULIUS AND ETHEL
ROSENBERG (Play)
1257
Utica, New York, 2638
UTOPIANISM 209, 379, 452,
763, 841, 895, 899a,
1029, 1031, 1054b, 1085,
2143, 2338, 2375, 2569,
2666, 2833, 2841
U-2 AFFAIR 875

Vahanian, Gabriel, 888
Valdes, Nelson P., 99
Vale, Yellow Springs, Ohio,
2609
Valente, Michael F., 3724
Vallow, Herbert P., 3413
VALUES, EDUCATIONAL 40,
162, 662, 1463, 2116,
2179, 2950, 3025, 3244,
3826, 3871a, 3950
VALUES, HUMAN 217, 223,
310, 339, 380, 460a,
837, 2720a, 2950, 3025,
3244, 3826
VALUES, POLITICAL
See also IDEOLOGY, THE-
ORY OF
128, 662, 1463, 2116,
3271, 5117, 5350
VALUES, SOCIAL 111, 223,
380, 460a, 837, 1463,
2950, 3271, 3950
Vanardo, Jerry, 4329
Van Cleve, Henry, 1235
Van Den Berghe, Pierce L.,
888a
Vanderbilt University, Nash-
ville, Tennessee, 5081
Vandermeer, Walter, 3125,
3295
Van Der Ryn, Sim, 3254
Vander-Zanden, J. W, 5216
Van Dusen, Lewish H. Jr.,
5215
Van Duyne Case, 337
Van Gelder, Lindsy, 2753a
Van Hoose, William, 4517
Van Kaam, Adrian, 3099
Vanocur, Sander, 4619
Vareia, M. E., 2754, 4620
Vaughan, Paul, 889

Vawter, Patricia, 4099
Vaz, Edmund W., 3100
Vecker, Karl, 1616
Velleman, J., 3262
Velvel, Lawrence R., 4935
Venceremos, 181, 1643
Venice, California, 3469a, 3530
Verb, Hal, 2755, 2756, 2757,
2758, 2759
Ver Eecke, Wilfried, 5217
Vermes, H., 3101
Vermes, Jean, 3101
Vetter, Craig, 890
Veysey, Laurence, 891, 4936
Vick, George R., 4621
Vidal, Gore, 2030
VIET-CONG 465, 724, 725,
749, 2208, 3184
VIETNAM--POLITICS AND
GOVERNMENT 425, 632,
725, 792, 864, 914,
1216
VIETNAM WAR 20, 35, 52, 53,
58, 80, 94, 134, 146,
147, 148, 150, 151,
184, 185, 186, 196,
206, 216, 221, 267,
270, 273, 276, 277,
302, 304, 305, 315,
317, 381, 387, 391,
403, 404, 405, 414,
424, 448, 451, 457,
460, 465, 472, 474,
479, 501, 502, 514,
524, 535, 550, 552,
598, 604, 605, 607,
613, 627, 632, 640,
692, 696, 698, 715,
721, 725, 748, 749,
756, 782, 785, 792,
793, 794, 798, 801,
808, 822, 823, 824,
842, 844, 859, 870,
874, 897, 914, 915,
918, 936, 946, 1012,
1024, 1051, 1113, 1115,
1135, 1137, 1154, 1174,
1216, 1254, 1255, 1268,
1276, 1280, 1285, 1288,
1298, 1317, 1399, 1401,
1447, 1450, 1465, 1468,
1469, 1471, 1517, 1549,
1575, 1613, 1614, 1627,

1646, 1648, 1689, 1707,
1715, 1849, 1877, 1901,
1913, 1919, 1960, 1986,
2000, 2011, 2040, 2043,
2047, 2057, 2073, 2074,
2096, 2100, 2111, 2157,
2174, 2211, 2262, 2294,
2372, 2377, 2395, 2461,
2484, 2513, 2514, 2515,
2604, 2610, 2638, 2671,
2689, 2769, 2770, 2771,
2772, 2773, 2796, 2805,
2807, 2815, 2860, 3309,
4202, 4391, 4720, 4758,
5029, 5118, 5137, 5273
VIETNAM WAR, LEGALITY OF
4935, 5029, 5118, 5137,
5273, 5336, 5375
Vigman, Fred K., 891a
Vincent, Clark, 3724a
Vinck, Jose de, 3725
Vinson, Fred M. Jr., 3592
Vivian, C. T., 891b
Vizzard, Jack, 892
VOCATIONAL TRAINING--
QUALIFICATIONS 75
Vollmer, August, 3414, 3481
Von Hoffman, Nicholas, 893,
894, 4027
Von Nostitz, S., 5218
Vorenberg, J., 3593
VOTING, NEGRO--IMPACT
OF 507
VOTING RIGHTS ACT OF 1965,
692a

Wade, Timothy, 3594
Wagner, Stanley P., 895
Wagstaff, Thomas, 896
Waibel, Terry, 2761, 2762,
2763, 2764
Wainhouse, D. W., 4686
Wake, F. R., 3842
Wakefield, Dan, 897, 3102
Wald, George, 13, 3309
Walderwoods Conference Center,
Hartland, Michigan,
1411
WALDON HOUSE, WASHING-
TON, D.C., 2609
Walim, Sheldon S., 3966
Walk, Karen, 4622

Walker Commission Report
See also National Commis-
sion On The Causes And
Prevention Of Violence;
Rights In Conflict
2045, 5003, 5219
Walker, Daniel, 898, 3415,
4937
Walker, Eric, 1347, 3894,
4072, 4136, 4239, 4387
Walker, John, 899
Walker, T. Mike, 3416
Wallace, George, 1537, 1682,
1859, 1920
Wallace, Jo Ann, 2765, 4623
Wallace, Michael, 4876
Wallace, Rue, 4624
Waller, Joseph, 2766, 2817
Wallerstein, Immanuel M.,
4028
Walley, David, 2767, 3310
Walsh, Chad, 899a
Walsh, J., 4625
Walsh, Mary McAna, 3726
Walsh, Robert E., 900
Walter, E. V., 930, 4938
Walters, James, 1965
Walters, Pat, 5220
Walton, George Col., 3103
Walton, George H., 5284, 5285
Walton, Hanes, 901
Walton, Richard E., 1854, 2768
Walzer, Michael, 4939, 5221,
5222
Wamsley, Gary L., 5286
WAR AND RELIGION 746
WAR ATROCITIES AND
CRIMES--VIETNAM
See ATROCITIES AND WAR
CRIMES--VIETNAM
Warburg, James P., 902
WARFARE
See also BIOLOGICAL WAR-
FARE; CHEMICAL WAR-
FARE; GUERRILLA WAR-
FARE; PSYCHOLOGICAL
WARFARE
192, 212, 332, 418,
445, 505, 606, 702,
727, 730, 734, 746,
871, 1471
Warner, Denis, 2769, 2770,
2771, 2772, 2773

Warner, W. Lloyd, 903
WARREN COMMISSION REPORT
    294, 496, 541, 551,
    580, 769, 790, 913,
    1122, 1200, 1371, 1809,
    2166, 2313, 2411, 2749,
    2756, 2822, 4914
Warren, Dave, 4626
Warren, Margaret, 3843
WARREN REPORT
    See WARREN COMMISSION
    REPORT
Warren, Robert Penn, 904
Warren, Samuel D., 118
Warrendale State Correctional
    Institute--Allegheny
    County, Pennsylvania,
    1759
Warwick, Dick, 2774
Washburn, Wilcomb E., 905
Washburne, C., 3104
Washington, D.C., 300, 1187,
    1498, 1523, 1760, 3571,
    3583, 4861, 5351
Washington, Joseph R. Jr.,
    906
Washington Post (Newspaper)
    893, 4861
WASHOE INDIANS, ALPINE
    CO., CALIFORNIA 991
Waskow, Arthur I., 907, 908,
    2775, 2776, 3595, 4029,
    4687, 5223
Wasserman, Judy, 2777
Wasserman, Miriam, 4627
Water Tunnel
    See Garfield Thomas (Water
    Tunnel)
Waters, Mary Alice, 2778
Watson, Dave, 2779
Watson, Goodwin, 5
Watson, John, 2780
Watson, Roy, 2411
Watson, Thomas J., 3265
Watts, Alan, 2781
Watts, California, 145, 833,
    1712, 2083, 2091, 3443a,
    5166, 5192, 5233
WATTS FESTIVAL 5100
Watts, William A., 4593, 4628,
    4629
Waxman, C. I., 909
Way, Walter, 3105

Wayne State University, Detroit,
    Michigan, 1259, 1511,
    4262
Ways, Max, 4630, 4631
WEAPONS
    See also ARMS CONTROL;
    COUNTERINSURGENCY
    WEAPONS; DISARMAMENT;
    INDUSTRIAL-MILITARY-
    GOVERNMENTAL EDUCA-
    TIONAL COMPLEX
    21, 56, 158, 488, 553,
    555, 718, 772, 881a,
    1469, 2497, 2863, 4661
WEAPONS (non-lethal) 2797,
    3343a
WEAPONS (nuclear) 4659, 4664,
    5131
WEAPONS (psychochemical)
    2284
Weatherby, Andre, 2782
Weatherby, William J., 910
WEATHERMEN 481, 1157,
    1390, 1472, 1477, 1478,
    1968, 2528, 2789
WEATHERWOMEN 1390, 1418,
    1472, 1479, 2528
Weaver, Donna, 4632
Weaver, Gary R., 911, 4030
Weaver, James H., 911, 4030
Webb, Lee, 4803
Webb, Marilyn Salzman, 2783,
    2784, 2785, 2786
Weber, Paul J., 4633
Weber, Renee, 4401
Wedge, Bryant, 4634
Weeks, Kent M., 912
Wein, Bibi, 3106
Weinberg, Arthur, 4940
Weinberg, Jack, 2798
Weingartner, Rudolph H., 5224
Weinglass, Leonard, 1195
Weinstein, Henry, 2787
Weinstein, James, 1461, 1935,
    2659, 2788, 2789
Weinstock, H. R., 3844
Weintraub, David, 2798
Weintraub, Roberta, 2790
Weisberg, Barry, 2791, 2792,
    2793, 2794
Weisberg, Harold, 913, 2756
Weiskopf, Doug, 2795
Weiss, Marc, 1730

Weiss, Peter, 914, 2689a
Weiss, Ted, 2689a
Weissman, Steve, 1562, 2796
Welch, Joseph, 246
Welch, Robert, 996, 997, 3730
WELFARE
  See PUBLIC WELFARE
Weller, Don, 2797
Welles, Earl, 2798
Wellford, C. F., 4815
Wells, John M., 915
Wells, Kenneth M., 3417
Wells, Lyn, 2799
Wells, Wesley Robert, 1033
Wels, B. G., 2871
Welsh, David, 2800, 2801, 2802, 2803
Wendt, Larry, 2804, 2805
Werdell, P. R., 4569
Werner, Herman O., 730
Wertenbaker, L. T., 5248
Wertham, Frederic, 4941
Wesley, S. M., 2806, 4635
West, Charles L., 2807
West, D. J., 916
West, Phyllis, 2808
Westby, David L., 4031, 4636
Western Behavioral Science Institute, La Jolla, California, 2231
Western Michigan University, 2712
Western Shoshone Nation Of Indians, Nevada, 1189
Westin, Alan F., 917
Westinghouse Broadcasting Company, 1150
Westlake, H. G., 3845, 3846
Westley, William, 4032, 4942
Westmoreland, W. C., 5410
Weston, Paul B., 3417
West Side Organization, Chicago, Illinois, 289
Whalen, M., 5031
What Shall I Tell My Child? 3727
Wheeler, Gerald R., 2809
Wheeler, Harvey, 4688
Wheeler, Tim, 2810
Wheelis, Allen B., 3107
White, Joe, 3596
White, Joseph, 2237

WHITE LEFT
  See also WHITE PANTHER PARTY
  2233
Whitehurst, Robert N., 3674
WHITE PANTHER PARTY (party platform) 1491, 1492, 2233, 2366, 2717
WHITE PANTHER PARTY
  See also WHITE LEFT
  1420
White, Ralph K., 918
White Rock Colony, Rosholt, South Dakota, 2609
Whitfield, M., 2811
Whitherspoon, Joseph P., 919
Whitman, Howard, 3727a
Whitney, Mary, 3597
Whittaker, Charles E., 4943, 5225
Whittaker, David, 4593, 4628, 4629
Whittemore, L. H., 3418
Whittington, Gale, 2131
Wicker, Tom, 810
Widick, B. J., 920
Widmer, Kingsley, 4637, 5226
Wieck, David, 5227
Wiener, Jon, 2812
Wiesner, Jerome B., 456, 4656, 4664, 4689, 4690, 4691, 4755, 4801, 4804
WIFE-SWAPPING
  See MATE SWAPPING
Wiggins, J. R., 2813
Wilcox, John, 3847
Wildavsky, Aaron, 4805
Wilde, Harold R., 4638
Wiley, J. P., 4806
Wilfong, Robert G., 2814
Wilhelm, Maria, 915
Wilkes, P., 3848
Wilkins, Leslie T., 3108
Wilkins, Roy, 125
Wilkinson, F. J., 4692
Wilkinson, Bob, 2815
Wilks, Gertrude, 2765
Will, George F., 2816
Williams, Bobby Lee, 1279, 1497
Williams, D. C., 4752
Williams, E. G., 4033

Williams, E. W., 3419
Williams, Elizabeth S., 3109
Williams, Henri, 2817
Williams, Hosea, 2700
Williams, Jay R., 5078
Williams, John, 4287
Williams, John A., 922
Williams, John B., 3110
Williams, Ora, 2818
Williams, Paul, 619
Williams, Robert F., 1490, 1916, 2613
Williams, Sylvia Berry, 4033
Williams, William Appleman, 923, 2819
Williamsburg, Virginia, 4987
Williamson, E. G., 4033a
Willis, Ellen, 2820
Willrich, Mason, 4660
Wills, Garry, 3311
Wilmington, Delaware, 1223, 2718
Wilmington 13, 2718
Wilner, K., 4450
Wilson, A., 1781
Wilson, August, 1008
Wilson, Darryl, 2821
Wilson, James Q., 3420, 3593, 3598, 4638
Wilson, Jane, 2822
Wilson, John, 2823
Wilson, Orlando W., 3421, 3422
Wilson, P. K., 4639
Wilson, Roger H. L., 307, 308
Wilson, Tizell, 2824
Wilson, T. W. Jr., 4693
Winborn, B. B., 4382
Wingell, Bill, 2825, 2826, 5411
Wingrove, C. Ray, 4513
Winick, Charles, 2827, 3246
Winnick, Charles, 3311a
Winslow, Robert W., 3423
Winston, D. C., 4807
Winston-Salem, North Carolina, 546, 2387
Winter, Gibson, 924
Winters, Stanley B., 2827
WIRETAPPING
   See also PRIVACY, RIGHT OF
      242, 421, 477, 1010, 1011, 1078, 1111, 1233, 1274, 1368, 1432, 1460, 1494, 1723, 1766, 1781, 2199, 2247, 2286, 2382, 2388, 2423, 2619, 2675, 2746, 2858, 2916, 3367, 3382, 4871
Wirth, Thomas H., 4640
Wise, Sydney F., 730
Wise, William, 925
WITCHCRAFT 1897, 2639
Witkin, Jim, 2829
Wittes, Glorianne, 2830
Wittes, Simon, 925a, 2830
Wittman, Carl, 2831
Wittner, Lawrence S., 926
Woetzel, Robert K., 5228, 5229
Wolf, Leonard, 3111
Wolfe, Alan, 4641
Wolfe, D., 5230
Wolfe, Leonard, 3312
Wolfe, Robert, 993, 2832, 2833
Wolfe, Tom, 927, 928, 929, 3112
Wolff, Kurt H., 930
Wolff, Robert P., 931, 932, 933
Wolff, Robert Paul, 4034
Wolfgang, M. E., 5231
Wolfle, Dael, 5412
Wolfson, Dave, 4642
Wolin, Sheldon S., 4035
Wolk, D. J., 3313
Wolkind, George, 2834
Wolterstorff, Nicholas, 934
WOMAN--SOCIAL AND MORAL QUESTION
   See also WOMEN'S LIBERATION MOVEMENT; WOMEN'S RIGHTS
      23, 167, 263, 307, 308, 333, 475, 490, 584, 652, 701, 764, 767, 768, 777, 821, 831, 891a, 1253, 1272, 1352, 1501, 1502, 1539, 1579, 1583, 1602, 1639, 1654, 1819, 1957, 1965, 2139, 2790, 3636
WOMEN
      Academic, 79, 254, 358, 2110, 2112, 2140; American, 169; As Ministers,

354; Black Panther, 1831;
Catholic, 263; Class And
Caste, 87a, 2042; Exploitation Of, 1977; Hitchhiking, 2165; In Athletics,
1503, 2140; In Government, 183, 887; In Politics, 811; In The South
(Negro) 167; On Campuses, 4470; Professional Careers Of, 293,
358; Radical, 316, 673,
740, 1151, 1352, 1592,
1684, 2575; Soviet, 130,
1500; Status Of, 206a,
254, 1579, 1654

WOMEN'S ALLIANCE
See THIRD WORLD WOMEN'S
ALLIANCE

WOMEN'S LIBERATION MOVEMENT
See also WOMEN'S RIGHTS
23, 73, 87, 132, 159,
206a, 261, 262, 313,
358, 603, 663, 667,
672, 673, 701, 740,
869, 1151, 1180, 1272,
1410, 1501, 1503, 1504,
1505, 1506, 1507, 1516,
1589, 1591, 1592, 1593,
1595, 1596, 1654, 1683,
1684, 1694, 1783, 1785,
1813, 1814, 1855, 1891,
1977, 1978, 2042, 2124,
2142, 2187, 2364, 2373,
2383, 2392, 2394, 2504,
2505, 2521, 2556, 2570,
2571, 2578, 2612, 2633,
2650, 2678, 2709, 2767,
2799, 2816, 2835

WOMEN'S LIBERATION MOVEMENT (Russia) 1500

WOMEN'S RIGHTS
See also WOMAN--SOCIAL
AND MORAL QUESTION;
WOMEN'S LIBERATION
MOVEMENT
23, 73, 87, 132, 159,
169, 206a, 293, 307,
308, 320, 475, 584,
603, 652, 764, 768,
821, 831, 869, 937,
1253, 1352, 1502, 1591,
1593, 1595, 1596, 1639,
1783, 1785, 1977, 2080,
2117, 2139, 2242, 2521,
2571

Wood, Forrest G., 935
Wood, Frederick C., 3728
Wood, James E., 5413
Wood, Michael, 2690
Wood, Myrna, 603, 2835
Woode, Allen, 2836
Woodhead, M. M., 2837
Woodland Hills Community, Independence, Missouri,
2609
Woodlawn Organization, 117
Woodley, Richard, 2838, 2945
Woodring, Paul, 4643, 4644
Woods, Sharla, 2839
WOODSTOCK FESTIVAL
See WOODSTOCK NATION
WOODSTOCK NATION 454,
1923, 2153, 2812
Woodward, C. Vann, 1950
Woodwell, George M., 2840
Woolf, Cecil, 936
Woolston, L. S., 3849
Woolstonecraft, Mary, 937
Word Of God Community, San
Fidel, New Mexico,
2609
World's Greatest Sinner, 2600
WORSHIP 95a
Worstell, David, 5414, 5415,
5416
Wrenn, R. L., 4645
Wright, Nathan, 938, 939, 940,
4944
Wright, R. Gene, 3380
Wrong, Dennis H., 2841
Wulp, Dave, 2842
WXUR (Radio Station) Philadelphia, Pennsylvania, 1787
Wyden, Barbara, 3113
Wyden, P., 3113
Wylie, Max, 4895
Wyzanski, C. E. Jr., 5232

Yablonski, Jock, 2281
Yablonsky, Lewis, 3114, 3115,
4945
Yab-Yum (Controversy)
See also OBSCENITY (law)

2149
Yagol, Sally, 2556
Yale University, New Haven, Connecticut, 4109, 4236, 4384
Yale, Wesley, 4694
Yancy, William L., 743
Yarmolinsky, Adam, 2843, 4695
Yates, Bill, 2844
Yates, S. R., 4808
Yglesias, Jose, 941
Yin Revolution, 2726
Yippie Festival Of Life, 2289
YIPPIES--U.S. 309, 846, 1377, 1526, 2086, 2147, 2289, 2580, 2607, 3269, 3311, 4085, 4268a
YOGA 2654
Yokell, Mike, 2845, 4646
York, Frank A., 2846
York, Herbert, 456
York, Pennsylvania, 1538
Yorty, Sam, 2092, 3227
Young, Alfred E., 942
Young, Alfred F., 4036
Young, Allen, 2847, 2848, 2849, 2850, 2851, 3314, 4647, 4648
YOUNG LORDS
See Puerto Rican Youth In The U.S. Young Lords Organization
Young Lords Organization, 1513, 1514, 3193
Young, Louise, 943
Young, Michael, 944
Young, Roland, 3599, 4649
Young, Stephen, 4020a
Young, Warren, 3116
Young, Whitney, 945
Youngberg, Alvin, 1475, 4387
Youngblood, Gene, 2852, 2853
Younge, Sammy Jr., 323
YOUTH AS CONSUMERS--U.S. 386
Youth International Party, 453
Youth Rally For Decency, 1076
YOUTH SOCIETIES 384

Zagoria, Donald S., 946, 4650
Zahn, Gordon Charles, 5287
Zalbrod, Paul, 3950
Zangrando, Robert L., 93
Zarefsky, David, 5262
Zaremba, Elaine, 4651
Zatlyn, Ted, 2854, 5233
Zazzaro, J., 3850, 3851
Zeitlin, Maurice, 947, 2689a, 2855
Zelinsky, W., 2856
ZEN 2726
Zetteler, Mike, 2857, 2858
Ziegler, Benjamin Munn, 948
Zimmer, Timothy W. L., 5288
Zimmerman, Michael, 842
Zinn, Howard, 2859, 4037, 5234, 5403
ZIONISM 2332
Zitek, E., 3808
Zitron, Celia, 949
Zogby, Jim, 4652
Zorra, Victor, 2860
Zorza, Richard, 4038
Zuk, Gerald H., 3117
Zweig, Ferdynand, 4039
Zyn 2861